W9-CDF-971

THE DYNAMICS OF FASHION

THE DYNAMICS OF FASHION

SECOND EDITION

Elaine Stone, Professor Emeritus

Fashion Institute of Technology, New York

Fairchild Publications, Inc.

New York

Executive Editor: Olga T. Kontzias
Assistant Acquisitions Editor: Carolyn Purcell
Editor: Sylvia Weber
Associate Production Editor: Elizabeth Marotta
Art Director: Adam B. Bohannon
Director of Production: Priscilla Taguer
Editorial Assistant: Suzette Lam
Copy Editor: Jennifer Plum, Words & Numbers
Cover and Interior Design: Adam B. Bohannon

Library of Congress Catalog Card Number: 2003102030

ISBN: 1-56367-280-4

GST R 133004424

Printed in the United States of America

Contents

Extended Contents

UNIT TWO

The Primary Level—The Materials of Fashion 91

UNIT FIVE

The Retail Level: The Markets for Fashion 339

Preface

Fashion is fast and forward, challenging and changing, and constantly in motion. This new edition of *The Dynamics of Fashion* is presented to students and instructors so that they can be on the cutting edge of what is happening in the business known as FASHION. This updated text will prepare students to learn and understand the innovation and challenge of careers in the global world of today's fashion business.

This second edition of *The Dynamics of Fashion* broadens, updates, and brings new perspectives of the fashion business to students' attention. It continues with the broadened scope of fashion and adds the newest and most up-to-date facts and figures used by professionals to keep the industry a vital and challenging career path.

All chapters have been substantially updated with new and current theories added. Recurring themes have been broadened and the change in the future direction of fashion globalization, retail competition, theories of customer service, and career paths have been expanded. Technology and its impact on the movement of fashion, and the threat of confrontations among nations are discussed in the context of the fashion business.

Organization of the Text

This edition of *The Dynamics of Fashion* uses the successful classroom-tested organization of the previous editions. It is structured in the following sequential learning order:

Unit One The Changing World of Fashion

The first unit examines how and why fashion evolves and changes. It explains the principles around which fashion revolves and the role that economic, sociological, and psychological elements play in the cyclical nature of fashion. It also covers the business scope of the industry including recent growth and expansion.

Unit Two The Primary Level: The Materials of Fashion

The growers and producers of the raw material of fashion, fibers, fabrics, trimming, leather, and fur are covered in this unit. New and fast moving advances in these industries coupled with an increasing variety of fashion goods using these materials are explained.

Unit Three The Secondary Level: The Producers of Apparel

The third unit begins with a new chapter on product development. Then, industry trends in apparel are highlighted in separate chapters on women's, men's, and children's apparel. Also, each market segment is compared and contrasted on the factors that are common to all. Product development, Quick Response, licensing, private label, specification buying, offshore production, and the use of factors are explained with examples that allow the student to put the terms and concepts for them in a "real world" context.

Unit Four The Secondary Level: The Other Fashion Producers

Today, the producers of innerwear, accessories, cosmetics, and fragrances, and home fashions no longer exist just to coordinate with apparel. These industries have become innovators and fashion trendsetters. This unit explains how each industry functions and covers current and future practices and trends.

Unit Five The Retail Level: The Markets for Fashion

This unit focuses on the elements of fashion marketing and reveals how markets operate to help manufacturers sell their products, and how retailers satisfy the needs of their target customer. It details both domestic and foreign markets and global sourcing. Different types of retailers are explained and current trends and emerging retail strategies for the 21st century are detailed.

Unit Six The Auxiliary Level: The Supporting Services
The myriad fashion services that work with all levels of the fashion industry are discussed. The unit explains their inter-connecting role in the fashion business from design to consumer. Magazines, newspapers, broadcast and TV media fashion consultants as well as trade associations are explained, along with the Internet.

Text Features

The Dynamics of Fashion provides hundreds of new examples and illustrations, and has many exciting special features that make the people, principles, practices, and techniques of the fashion business come alive in the minds of students. We believe that these features will help students to learn about the fashion business in an enjoyable manner. All these features are appropriate for class discussion, library research projects, and group projects.

Fashion Focus
A popular feature, the "Fashion Focus," highlights interesting people, places, and/or products that impact on the subject matter. This feature is found in every chapter and makes the chapter material more relevant to the student. Some examples are:

Ralph Lauren: True Blood from a Blue Blood

New Horizons—Fabrics that Travel Well for Adventure

Urban Brands Gain Spotlight

A Lifetime Achievement—The Women's Jewelry Association

A Look at Beauty—A Look at Jung

Allen Questrom: An All American Retailing Star

Then and Now
Then and Now is a feature that encourages the student to look to the past, present, and future of subjects that have a lasting imprint on fashion. Many are presented in exciting pictorial format. Some examples are:

How Women Have "Worn" Power through the 20th Century

TV Women

The Looks of Leather—20th Century to 21st Century

The Names That Have Stood the Test of Time

50 Years of Store Design

Toys are—Big Business Kids

Famous Designers
New to this edition is a compilation of famous designers, including noteworthy elements of their designs.

Glossary
The glossary has been updated and enlarged and now contains over 390 industry terms. A knowledge and understanding of the "language" of fashion gives students a firm footing upon which they can "step-out" into the industry and know they are speaking the right language.

Summary and Review
Each of the 19 chapters in the text concludes with four kinds of student-oriented activities designed to enrich and reinforce the instructional material. A Summary gives a quick reminder of key concepts. A "Trade Talk" section explains fashion and merchandising terms introduced for the first time in that chapter. The student will recognize these terms when they appear in subsequent chapters. These terms are also defined in the Glossary.

"For Review" asks questions about the key concepts of each chapter. These questions provoke thought, encourage classroom discussion, and develop recall of the material presented in the text.

"For Discussion" asks the student to explain the significance of a major concept and to support the explanation with specific illustrations. This activity affords the student an opportunity to apply theory to actual situations and to draw on his or her own background an experiences.

End of Unit Activities
The dynamics of fashion are practical in many types of businesses—some small, some large; some in large urban metropolitan areas; some in small suburban areas. The Exploring Careers activity performs the important role of helping students gain a greater awareness of available fashion-related careers. With background knowledge obtained from the text and the end-of-chapter activities, students will be able to select specific industries in which they have a personal interest, as well as the kinds of work-

ing environments and geographic locations in which they are most comfortable. A career journal is an ongoing project and serves as the terminal project using the assignments at the end of each unit. New to this edition is a compilation of famous designers from the 1960s through today.

Instructor's Manual

An instructor's manual is available and includes a number of options for organizing the course and contains general suggestions for teaching the course. It also contains supplementary assignments for each unit. The key to the text includes answers to all end-of-chapter exercises.

A useful feature is a text bank containing material for the individual units, and a final examination. The tests are composed of 100 objective questions each and are ready to duplicate.

A new addition to the instructor's manual is a glossary of over 100 supplementary terms.

Acknowledgments

The author is grateful to the many educators and business people who have given her encouragement, information, and helpful suggestions. Among these are my teaching colleagues at the Fashion Institute of Technology, who have supported the writing of *The Dynamics of Fashion* and the very helpful staff of professionals in the FIT library.

I am also indebted to the industry experts and professionals, both domestic and foreign, who gave of their time and expertise to insure the timeliness and accuracy of the information in this book.

Comments from readers selected by the publisher for the first edition were also very helpful. They included: Julie Bennett, Columbia College; Phyllis J. Brackelsberg, Iowa State University; Betsy C. Breseman, The Ohio State University; Janet P. Ciccarelli; Herkimer County Community College; Ellen Goldstein, Fashion Institute of Technology; Michele Granger, Southwest Missouri State University; Amy J. Harden, Ball State University; Shelley S. Harp, Texas Tech University; Debra McDowell, Southwest Missouri State University; Teresa Robinson, Middle Tennessee State University.

My appreciation and gratitude to the staff at Fairchild Publications. Thank you to Elizabeth Marotta for her help with the photo research and production of the second edition. Thanks to Nicholas Potinaksis, Amy Zarkos, and Suzzette Lam, who collaborated on the Powerpoint® presentation. I am also grateful to my former editor, Mary McGarry, for her invaluable support and encouragement. My extended thanks to Sylvia Weber for her photo research help with the first edition. Finally, to Olga Kontzias I say a heartfelt "Thank you."

I regret that space does not permit me to personally list and thank my friends in all segments of the fashion business who supplied, throughout the development of this edition, their encouragement as well as significant amounts of current and trend trade information. As always, I welcome instructors' and students' comments. They can be sent to me through Fairchild Publications or to my e-mail address: elaine_stone@fitnyc.edu.

This book is dedicated to Minnie M. Stone who served as a mentor, friend, and critic throughout my career. Best of all, she was a terrific mother.

NOT ONLY CLOTHES, BUT SHEETS, PILLOW-CASES, BLANKETS...

UNIT ONE

The Changing World of Fashion

FASHION—the very word conjures up excitement and interest in all of us, no matter what we plan to do for the rest of our lives. Fashion is the ultimate F word! It is faddish, familiar, fantasy, form, fatal, feasible, festive, finite, fit, fresh, and fun. Fashion is the most dynamic of American businesses. It thrives on change, and change is the engine that fuels it.

People long for excitement and variety in their lives and look to the fashion business to show them "what's new." Fashion does this through the merchandising of products that range from apparel to furniture, accessories to food, appliances to fragrance.

Ever since Adam and Eve wore fig leaves in the Garden of Eden, fashion has had the power to fascinate and excite. This power has been used by the trendsetters of history from Cleopatra to Josephine to Jackie O to Madonna to Gwyneth and Britney. Today, past eras conjure up images not only of the philosophy and social mores of the times, but also, in large part, the fashions of the times.

Wall Street and the global business community have joined the exciting world of fashion. Designers, manufacturers, and retailers have enjoyed impressive growth in their stock prices. Press coverage has crossed over from the purely "passion for fashion" reporting in consumer fashion and trade publications to become "hard news" in the *Wall Street Journal*, the *New York Times*, *Newsweek*, global television, and the Internet.

The fashion business is often paradoxical in its elements. It is both an art and a science and at the same time both personal and incredibly public. It is a business where opposites attract and, in turn, excite these opposites to reach out and engage the buying public.

Fashion can be viewed as an art because so much creativity is required to make its products. Unlike most other businesses where conformity is the norm, fashion nurtures innovation and creativity in those who work in the industry.

Fashion has always been considered a science as well. Modern fashion manufacturing was born during the industrial revolution and has matured in the age of technology. Without machines, clothing could never be mass-produced. Technology has revolutionized the way fashion is made. Almost all stages of clothing production from design to delivery rely to some extent on technology.

Fashion, always a highly personal business, is in the process of becoming even more so. Clothing design has always been about one person's—the designer's—ideas. Today, though, one cannot examine the personal element in fashion without also talking about the customer. Mass customization has taken root in the fashion industry, and may well transform the business.

Where the makers of fashion once got their ideas entirely from their own world of style, they now borrow freely from the external world. New fashion ideas now come from the world around us: the streets, innovative teenagers, a new play, a celebrity with his or her unique look.

But however personal fashion is on one level, the making of clothes is still very much a public business. In general, the fashion business must cater to a mass market, and these days, even to one with rapidly rising expectations. Thanks to modern communications, new ideas and trends now sweep across the country and the world and are adopted in a matter of days.

When we speak of fashion as a public business, we are also referring to the external forces that affect the business. Shifts in the economy, sociological influences, and demographic changes all contribute to change in fashion and therefore affect the fashion business.

All these contradictory elements work to keep the fashion business dynamic and ever-changing.

In this unit, you will examine how and why fashion evolves and changes. You will begin to develop a basic vocabulary and a working knowledge of:

- The principles around which the fashion world revolves—in Chapter 1.
- The environmental forces—the role that economic, demographic, sociological, and psychological elements play in the fashion business—in Chapter 2.
- The cyclical forces—how fashions change and how an understanding of this constant cycle of change can be used to predict and analyze current and future fashion—in Chapter 3.
- The business forces—the scope of the industry, its recent growth and expansion, and various new forms of ownership—along with the design forces—the role played by designers, manufacturers, and retailers in creating fashion—in Chapter 4.

The world of fashion operates in a far different way today than it did years ago. It moves faster and reaches more people. And perhaps most important, it is more businesslike. To understand the changes that have occurred and will occur in the future of the fashion industry, you must first understand the dynamics that underlie the fashion business.

CHAPTER 1

The Nature of Fashion

WHAT'S IN IT FOR YOU?

Everything you always wanted to know about the terminology, components, cycles, and principles of fashion.

Key Concepts:

- Marketing and merchandising in the fashion business
- The stages of the fashion cycle
- The intangibles of fashion

In 1850, in his book *Fashion: The Power That Influences the World*, George P. Fox said:

> *Fashion is and has been and will be, through all ages, the outward form through which the mind speaks to the universe. Fashion in all languages designs to make, shape, model, adapt, embellish, and adorn.*[1]

In 2000, Colin McDowell, Chairman of the Costume Society of Great Britain, argues that fashion is "the art form which albeit minor, reacts speedily and completely than any other to the social, political and cultural nuances of our time."[2]

Fashion involves our outward, visible lives. It involves the clothes we wear, the dances we dance, the cars we drive, and the way we cut our hair. Fashion also influences architecture, forms of worship, and lifestyles. It has an impact on every stage of life from the womb to the tomb.

People started covering their bodies with clothes to keep warm and be modest, but adornment—decoration—was already an important part of dressing. Pressure from peer groups and changes in lifestyle influence the type of adornment considered acceptable in a particular time or for a particular group. Basically, of course, the reasons people have for wearing clothes have not changed. Today, people still wear clothes to keep warm or cool and for the sake of modesty, but what we select for those purposes is very much influenced by a desire to adorn ourselves.

Because people are social animals, clothing is very much a social statement. By looking at the way a person dresses, you can often make good guesses about his or her social and business standing, sex-role identification, political orientation, ethnicity, lifestyle, and aesthetic priorities. Clothing is a forceful and highly visible medium of communication that carries with it information about who a person is, who a person is not, and who a person would like to be.

The Importance of Fashion

During recent years, the general interest in fashion has increased enormously. Fashion is one of the greatest economic forces in present-day life. To a great extent, it determines what people will buy. Change in fashion is the motivating factor for replacing clothes, cosmetics, furniture, housewares, and automobiles. Fashion causes changes in consumer goods and at the same time makes people want the new products, since the thought of being unfashionable is a fate worse than death to many people!

Fashion can be politically correct or politically incorrect. Different political ideologies are reflected in how people fashion their lifestyles. Culturally, fashion impacts our architecture, music, and museums. In the spring of 2001, an exhibition at the Museum of Modern Art in New York City took the term "dress for success" to a new meaning. The exhibition featured items such as a handbag that doubles as a mini file cabinet, a scarf and jacket equipped with a compact computer screen, and cocoons designed to give the wearer a little more privacy in the office. The show examined the balance between a person's work life and personal life, as well as the integral role designers can play in creating solutions for a time-starved, overworked society.[3]

Webster defines fashion as "prevailing custom, usage, or style,"[4] and in this sense it covers a wide range of human activity. The term is used in this book in a narrower sense: **fashion** here means the style or styles of clothing and accessories worn at a particular time by a particular group of people. Fashion in cosmetics and fragrances and in home furnishings is also covered.

The Fashion Business

Fashion today is big business; millions of people are employed in fashion-related activities. The **fashion industries** are those engaged in manufacturing the materials and finished products used in the production of apparel and accessories for men, women, and children. Throughout this book any reference to "fashion industries" means the manufacturing businesses unless others are specifically mentioned. The broader term **fashion business** includes all the industries and services connected with fashion: design, manufacturing, distribution, marketing, retailing, advertising, communications, publishing, and consulting; in other words, any business concerned with fashion goods or services.

Marketing

Today, marketing has become a major influence in the fashion business. What does marketing mean? Most people think of marketing only as promotion and selling. However, promotion and selling are only two aspects of marketing. The process of **marketing** includes diverse activities that identify consumer needs, develop good products, and price, distribute, and promote them effectively so that they will sell easily. "The aim of marketing is . . . to know and understand the customer so well that the product or service hits him [or her] and sells itself."[5]

Fashion Marketing and Merchandising

The fashion business has been rather slow in adopting the marketing techniques that have been so successful in the growth of consumer goods such as automobiles, packaged foods, and health and beauty aids. For many years fashion producers were concerned only with what was economical and easy for them to produce. They would spend considerable time and money trying to convince the consumer that what they had produced was what the consumer wanted. The producer had little or no interest in the wants and needs of the consumer.

Recently, however, the total process of marketing has been adopted by the fashion business and is being applied to the products and services of the fashion industries. The result is called **fashion marketing**: that is, the marketing of apparel, accessories, and other fashion-related products to the ultimate consumer.

We are also concerned with **fashion merchandising,** which refers to the *planning* required to have the right fashion-oriented merchandise at the right time, in the right place, in the right quantities, at the right prices, and with the right sales promotion for a specified target customer.

Misconceptions about Fashion

As the power of fashion to influence our lives grows, three misconceptions about it continue to be widely held. The first and most common misconception is that designers and retailers dictate what the fashion will be and then force it upon helpless consumers. It has been said that the industry is composed of "obsolescence ogres." In reality, consumers themselves decide what the fashion will be by influencing new designs and by accepting or rejecting the styles that are offered. Consumers are, in truth, "variety vultures."

The second misconception is that fashion acts as an influence on women only. Today, men and children are as influenced by and responsive to fashion as women. Fashion is the force that causes women to raise or lower their skirt lengths from minis to maxis, straighten or frizz their hair, and change from casual sportswear to dressy clothes. Fashion is also the force that influences men to grow or shave off their mustaches and beards, choose wide or narrow ties and lapels, and change from casual jeans into three-piece suits. And fashion is the force that makes children demand specific products and styles.

The third misconception is that fashion is a mysterious and unpredictable force. Actually, its direction can be determined and its changes predicted with remarkable accuracy by those who study and understand the fundamentals of fashion. Fashion was once considered an art form controlled by designers who dictated its content. But fashion has now evolved into a science that can be measured and evaluated.

FIGURE 1.1
From wild to wacky: Designer John Galliano sends this radical look down the runway—not to sell to the public, but to get "press buzz." Courtesy, Fairchild Publications, Inc.

The Terminology of Fashion

What is the difference between fashion, style, and design? Just what do high fashion, mass fashion, taste, classic, and fad mean? To avoid confusion when discussing fashion, we must first understand the meanings of these terms. The definitions that follow are based on the work of Dr. Paul H. Nystrom, one of the pioneers in fashion merchandising.[6]

Style

The first step in understanding fashion is to distinguish between "fashion" and "style," words that most people use interchangeably although there is an immense difference in their meanings. In general terms, a style is a characteristic or distinctive artistic expression or presentation. Styles exist in architecture, sculpture, painting, politics, and music, as well as in popular heroes, games, hobbies, pets, flirtations, and weddings.

In apparel, **style** is the characteristic or distinctive appearance of a garment—the combination of features that makes it unique and different from other garments. For example, T-shirts are as different from camp shirts as they are from peasant blouses. Riding jackets are as different from safari jackets as they are from blazer jackets.

Although styles come and go in terms of acceptance, a specific style always remains a style, whether it is currently in fashion or not. Some people adopt a style that becomes indelibly associated with them and wear it regardless of whether it is currently fashionable. Carmen Miranda's platform shoes, Katherine Hepburn's pleated trousers, the Duchess of Windsor's jewelry, Marilyn Monroe's white halter dress, Michael Jackson's glove, Mary J. Blige's sunglasses, and Jennifer Lopez's signature hip-huggers and low-waisted pants are all examples of personal style.

Some styles are named for the period of history in which they originated—Grecian, Roman,

Renaissance, Empire, Gibson Girl era (early 1900s), flapper era (1920s). When such styles return to fashion, their basic elements remain the same. Minor details are altered to reflect the taste or needs of the era in which they reappear. For example, the flapper style of the 1920s was short, pleated, and body skimming. That style can be bought today, but with changes for current fashion acceptance.

Fashion

On the other hand, a **fashion** is a style that is accepted and used by the majority of a group at any one time, no matter how small that group. A fashion is always based on some particular style. But not every style is a fashion. A fashion is a fact of social psychology. A style is usually a creation from an artist or a designer. A fashion is a result of social emulation and acceptance. A style may be old or new, beautiful or ugly, good or bad. A style is still a style even if it never receives the slightest acceptance or even approval. A style does not become a fashion until it gains some popular acceptance. And it remains a fashion only as long as it is accepted. Miniskirts, square-toed shoes, mustaches, and theatrical daytime makeup have all been fashions. And no doubt each will again be accepted by a majority of a group of people with similar interests or characteristics—for example, college students, young career men and women, retired men and women.

Fashions appeal to many different groups and can be categorized according to the group to which they appeal. **High fashion** refers to a new style accepted by a limited number of fashion leaders who want to be the first to adopt changes and innovation in fashion. High-fashion styles are generally introduced and sold in small quantities and at relatively high prices. These styles may be limited because they are too sophisticated or extreme to appeal to the needs of the general public, or they are priced well beyond the reach of most people. However, if the style can appeal to a broader audience, it is generally copied, mass-produced, and sold at lower prices. The fashion leaders or innovators who first accepted it then move on to something new.

To contrast with high fashion, **mass fashion** or **volume fashion**, consists of styles that are widely accepted. These fashions are usually produced and sold in large quantities at moderate to low prices, and appeal to the greatest majority of fashion-conscious consumers (see Figure 1.2). Mass fashion accounts for the majority of sales in the fashion business. Mass fashion is the "bread and butter" of the fashion banquet!

Design

There can be many variations of detail within a specific style. A **design** is a particular or individual interpretation, version, or treatment of a style. A style may be expressed in a great many designs, all different, yet all related because they are in the same style. A sweatshirt, for example, is a distinctive style, but within that style, variations may include different types of necklines, pockets, and sleeves. Another example is a satchel handbag which may be interpreted with different closures, locks, or handles. These minor variations are the different interpretations that change the design of a style.

In the fashion industries, manufacturers and retailers assign a number to each individual design produced. This is the **style number**. The style number of a product identifies it for manufacturing, ordering, and selling purposes. In this instance, the term "style number" is used

FIGURE 1.2
The fabulous peasant blouse interprets a high fashion original into an affordable fashion statement for mass market consumers.
Courtesy, Fairchild Publications, Inc.

rather than "design number," even though a design is being identified.

Taste

In fashion, **taste** refers to prevailing opinion of what is and what is not attractive and appropriate for a given occasion. Good taste in fashion, therefore, means sensitivity not only to what is artistically pleasing but also to what is appropriate for a specific situation. A style, such as an evening gown, may be beautiful. But if it is worn to a morning wedding, for example, it may not be considered in good taste.

Many styles are beautiful, but because they are not in fashion, good taste prevents their use. On the other hand, a present-day fashion may be inartistic or even ugly, but its common acceptance means that it is in good taste.

Nystrom described the relationship between good taste and fashion this way: "Good taste essentially is making the most artistic use of current fashion . . . bridging the gap between good art and common usage."[7]

Even during the height of acceptance of a particular fashion, it is considered in good taste only if it is worn by people on whom it looks appropriate. For example, miniskirts, tight pants, bikinis, and halter tops are considered in good taste only for slim people in good physical shape.

Timing, too, plays a part in what is considered good or bad taste. British costume authority James Laver saw the relationship between taste and fashion in terms of its acceptance level. A style, he said, is thought to be:[8]

"indecent"	10 years before its time
"shameless"	5 years before its time
"outré"	1 year before its time
"smart"	in its time
"dowdy"	1 year after its time
"hideous"	10 years after its time
"ridiculous"	20 years after its time

While the time an individual fashion takes to complete this course may vary, the course is always a cyclical one. A new style is often considered daring and in dubious taste. It is gradually accepted, then widely accepted, and finally gradually discarded.

For many decades, Laver's cycle has been accepted as the movement of most fashions. However, in the past few decades some fashions have deviated from this pattern. The fashion cycles have become shorter and have repeated themselves within a shorter space of time. For the student of fashion this presents an interesting challenge. What factors determine which fashions will follow the accepted cycles and which fashions will not? To understand the movement of fashion, it is important to understand that fashions are always in harmony with the times in which they appear. During the upheaval and unrest of the late 1960s, miniskirts made their appearance everywhere, from campus to office. Through the late 1980s and into the 2000s, the miniskirt served as a reminder that when fashion rules, actual rulers get nervous. The Prime Minister of Russia and Idi Amin in Uganda banned miniskirts as signs of Western influence, and Congo's President, Laurent Kabila, made banning of miniskirts his first act when he overthrew the dictatorship of Mobutu in 1997. In 2000, Swaziland identified the miniskirt as a reason for the spread of AIDS, and miniskirts were banned from schools.[9]

A Classic

Some styles or designs continue to be considered in good taste over a long period of time. They are exceptions to the usual movement of styles through the fashion life cycle. A **classic** is a style or design that satisfies a basic need and remains in general fashion acceptance for an extended period of time (see Figure 1.3a and b).

Depending upon the fashion statement one wishes to make, a person may have only a few classics or may have a wardrobe of mostly classics. A classic is characterized by simplicity of design which keeps it from being easily dated. The Chanel suit is an outstanding example of a classic. The simple lines of the Chanel suit have made it acceptable for many decades, and although it reappears now and then as a fashion, many women always have a Chanel suit in their wardrobes. Other examples of classics are blue denim jeans, blazer jackets, cardigan or turtleneck sweaters, and button-down oxford shirts. Among accessories, the pump-style shoe, the loafer, the one-button glove, the pearl necklace, and the clutch handbag are also classics. For young children, overalls and one-piece pajamas have become classics.

A Fad

A fashion that suddenly sweeps into popularity, affecting a limited part of the total population, and then quickly disappears is called a **fad** (see Figure 1.3c). It comes into existence by the in-

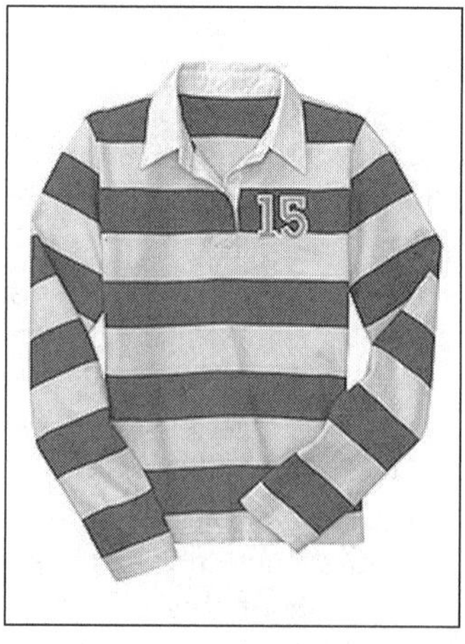

A B C

FIGURE 1.3

(a) Old Navy's striped Rugby illustrates updating a classic, while (b) this white, basic twill dress shirt remains a simple classic fashion. (c) Pucci's multicolored cotton and elastic shirt is an example of a popular fad.
Courtesy, Fairchild Publications, Inc.

troduction of some feature or detail, usually exaggerated, that excites the interest of the customer. The fad starts by being quickly accepted and then quickly imitated by others. Fads often begin in lower-price ranges, are relatively easy to copy, and therefore flood the market in a very short time. Because of this kind of market saturation, the public tires of fads quickly and they end abruptly.

Fads follow the same cycle as fashions do, but their rise in popularity is much faster, their acceptance much shorter, and their decline much more rapid than that of a true fashion. Because most fads come and go in a single season, they have been called "miniature fashions." In recent decades we have had the "punk," multi-colored hair fad of the popstars, the "King Tut" design fad, the "Urban Cowboy" fad, and the "grunge" fad. Fads, like fashions, invade every field: sports, literature, religion, politics, and education.

However, many things that begin as fads become fashions and can carry over for several seasons. In fact, it is very difficult to draw the line between fads and fashions. The chemise, or sack dress, is probably the outstanding example of this phenomenon. After an instant rise to popularity in the late 1950s, it quickly passed from the fashion scene. A few years later, the chemise reappeared as the shift. In 1974, the chemise again appeared in the Paris collections, modified to eliminate its former disadvantages. American manufacturers quickly reproduced it in several versions and in a wide price range. That the chemise, in its various manifestations, again appeared in the late 1980s and the mid 1990s is strong evidence that it, too, will become a fashion classic.

A Trend

A **trend** is a general direction or movement. For example, you will often read in fashion magazines "there is a trend toward longer skirts"; it means that several designers, including some leading ones, are showing longer skirts, leading retailers are buying them, and fashion-forward customers are wearing them. It is often difficult to tell a trend from a fad; even the experts get caught. However, marketers always want to know whether a new development is going to be a trend or a fad—because they want to cash in on trends but avoid getting burned by fads. A trend can originate anywhere, and has a solid foundation that supports its growth; a fad does not.[10]

Components of Fashion

Fashion design does not just happen, nor does the designer wave a magic wand to create a new design. Fashion design involves the combination of four basic elements or components: silhouette, detail, texture, and color. Only through a change in one or more of these basic components does a new fashion evolve. This is true of any fashion-influenced product, from kitchen appliances to automobiles, from apartment houses to office buildings, and from accessories to apparel.

Silhouette

The **silhouette** of a costume is its overall outline or contour. It is also frequently referred to as "shape" or "form." It may appear to the casual observer that women have worn countless silhouettes throughout the centuries. In the 1930s, Agnes Brooke Young's research showed that there are actually only three basic forms—straight or tubular; bell-shaped or bouffant; and the bustle, or back fullness—with many variations.[11] Today, most fashion experts include four variations on the tubular silhouette: slim, rectangle, wedge, and A-line (see Figure 1.4).

Details

The individual elements that give a silhouette its form or shape are called **details**. These include trimmings; skirt and pant length and width; and shoulder, waist, and sleeve treatment.

Silhouettes evolve gradually from one to another through changes in detail. When the trend in a detail reaches an extreme, a reversal of the trend takes place. For example, dresses and suits featured wide shoulders with much padding in the 1940s and 1950s. This was reversed in the late 1960s and 1970s, when the look became casual and unstructured. This casualness reached such extremes that by the start of the 1980s, structured clothing was back in fashion and dress and suit shoulders began once again to grow wider as padding was inserted. By the 1990s, the unstructured look was predominant again; and entering the 2000s, structured suits and wide shoulders were again seen on the runways!

Variations in detail allow both designer and consumer to express their individuality freely within the framework of the currently accepted silhouette. To emphasize a natural-waistline silhouette, for example, a slender woman might choose a simple wide belt, a decorated belt, or a belt in a contrasting color. To express his individuality, a man might emphasize the wide shoulder look with epaulets or heavy shoulder pads.

Texture

One of the most significant components of fashion is texture. **Texture** is the look and feel of material, woven or nonwoven.

Texture can affect the appearance of a silhouette, giving it a bulky or slender look, depending on the roughness or smoothness of the materials. A woman dressed in a rough tweed dress and a bulky knit sweater is likely to look larger and squarer than she does in the same dress executed in a smooth jersey and topped with a cashmere sweater.

FIGURE 1.4
Silhouettes are categorized as belonging to one of three basic groups: (a) bell-shaped or bouffant, (b) bustle or back fullness, and (c) straight or tubular. Variations of the straight silhouette are (d) slim, (e) rectangular, (f) wedge, and (g) A-line.

Texture influences the drape of a garment. Chiffon clings and flows, making it a good choice for soft, feminine styles, while corduroy has the firmness and bulk suitable for more casual garments.

Texture affects the color of a fabric by causing the surface to either reflect or absorb light. Rough textures absorb light, causing the colors to appear flat. Smooth textures reflect light, causing colors to appear brighter. Anyone who has tried to match colors soon discovers that a color which appears extremely bright in a shiny vinyl, satin, or highgloss enamel paint seems subdued in a rough wool, a suede, or a stucco wall finish.

Color

Color has always been a major consideration in women's clothing. Since World War II, color in men's clothing has been regaining the importance it had in previous centuries. Today, color is a key factor in apparel selection for both sexes. Color is important in advertising, packaging, and store decor as well.

Historically, colors have been used to denote rank and profession. Purple, for instance, was associated with royalty, and in some periods, could be worn only by those of noble birth. Black became customary for the apparel of the clergy and for members of the judiciary.

Color symbolism often varies with geographical location. While white is the Western world's symbol of purity, worn by brides and used in communion dresses, it is the color of mourning in India.

Today, a fashion designer's color palette changes with consumers' preferences. In some seasons, all is brightness and sharp contrast, and no color is too powerful to be worn. In other seasons, only subdued colors appeal. Fashion merchants must develop an eye for color—not only for the specific hues and values popular in a given season, but also for indications of possible trends in consumer preference.

The Fashion Cycle

All fashions move in cycles. The term **fashion cycle** refers to the rise, wide popularity, and then decline in acceptance of a style. The word "cycle" suggests a circle. However, the fashion cycle is represented by a bell-shaped curve (see Figure 1.5).

Some authorities compare the fashion cycle to a wave, which shows first a slow swell, then a crest, and finally a swift fall. Like the movement of a wave, the movement of a fashion is always forward, never backward. Like waves, fashion cycles do not follow each other in regular, measured order. Some take a short time to crest; others, a long time. The length of the cycle from swell to fall may be long or short. And, again like waves, fashion cycles overlap.

Stages of the Fashion Cycle

Fashion cycles are not haphazard; they don't "just happen." There are definite stages in a style's development that are easily recognized. These stages can be charted and traced, and in the short run, accurately predicted. Being able to recognize and predict the different stages is vital to success in both the buying and the selling of fashion.

Every fashion cycle passes through five stages: (1) introduction, (2) rise, (3) culmination, (4) decline, and (5) obsolescence. A comparison of these stages to the timetable suggested by Laver would look like this:

Introduction	"indecent/shameless"
Rise	"outré"
Culmination	"smart"
Decline	"dowdy/hideous"
Obsolescence	"ridiculous"

The fashion cycle serves as an important guide in fashion merchandising. The fashion merchant uses the fashion cycle concept to introduce new fashion goods, to chart their rise and culmination, and to recognize their decline and obsolescence.

Introduction Stage

The next new fashion may be introduced by a producer in the form of a new style, color, or texture. The new style may be a flared pant leg when slim legs are popular, vibrant colors when earth tones are popular, or slim body-hugging fabrics such as knit jersey when heavy-textured bulky looks are being worn.

New styles are almost always introduced in higher-priced merchandise. They are produced in small quantities since retail fashion buyers purchase a limited number of pieces to test the new styles' appeal to targeted customers. This testing period comes at the beginning of the buying cycle of fashion merchandise, which coincides with the introduction stage of the fash-

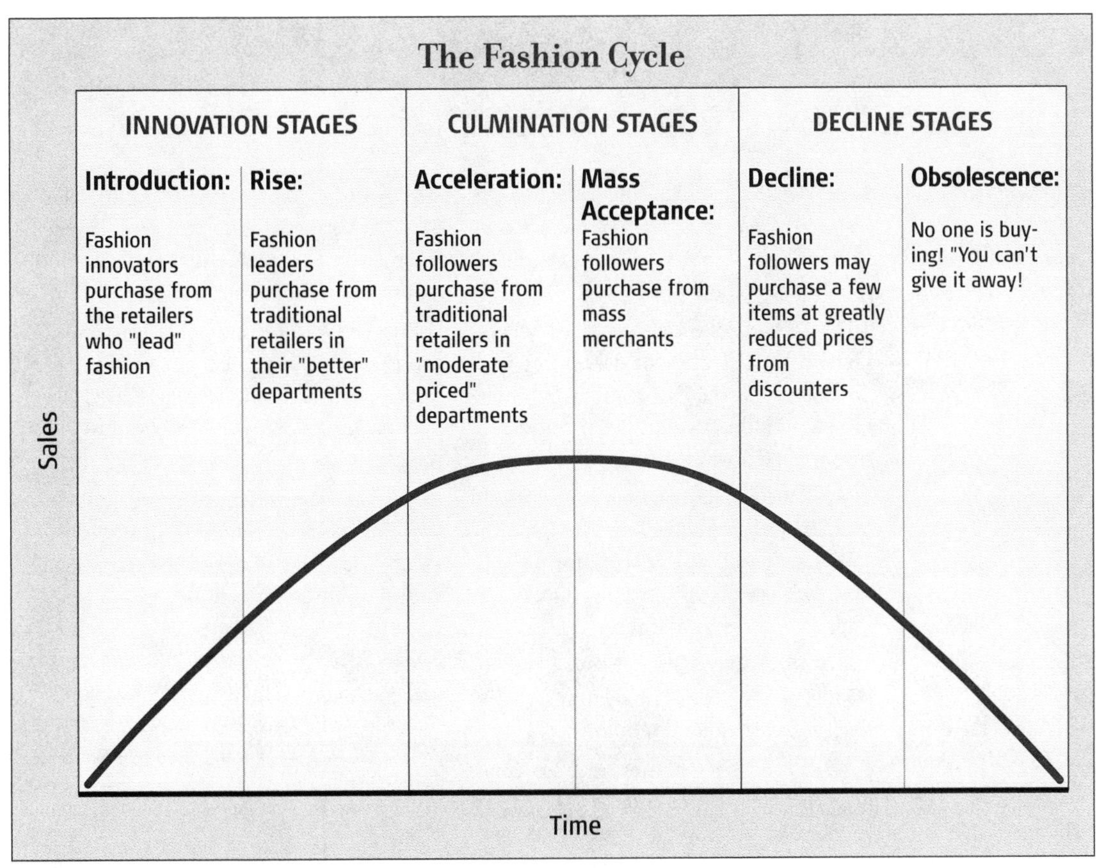

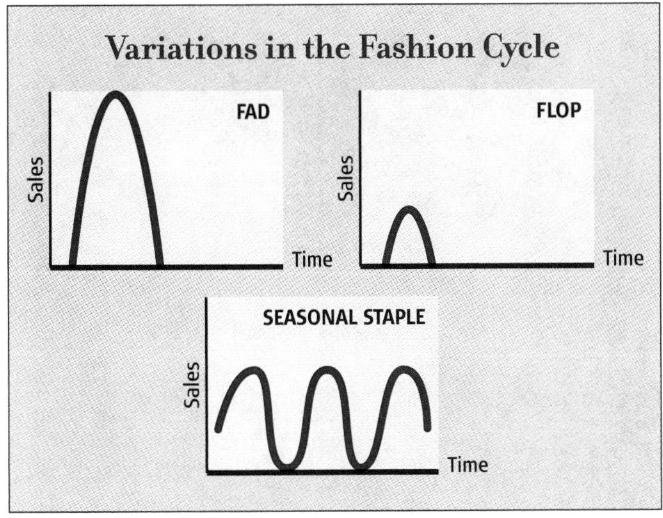

FIGURE 1.5
The basic life cycle of fashion can be represented by a bell-shaped curve. Variations can occur to the height to which a fashion rises at its peak and the length of time it takes to get to that point and then to decline in popularity.

ion cycle. The test period ends when the new style either begins its rise or has been rejected by the target customer. Because there can be many risks, new styles must be priced high enough so that those that succeed can cover the losses on those that don't succeed. Promotional activities such as designer appearances, institutional advertising, and charity fashion shows, which will appeal to the fashion leaders of the community and also enhance the store's fashion image, take place at this point.

Rise Stage

When the new original design (or its adaptations) is accepted by an increasing number of customers, it is considered to be in its **rise stage.**

Then & Now

How Women Have "Worn" Power Through the 20th Century

Successful and powerful women have faced the challenge of "what to wear" ever since the beginning of time. Eve and her fig leaf, Cleopatra and her eye kohl, Amelia Bloomer and her "bloomers"—these were all women who had to make that decision. For many years the only big decision men had to make was which color tie to wear, while women have more questions to answer, and some of those questions are heavy with symbolism. Wear the pants? Let down their hair? Wield that cleavage . . . or conceal it?

THE DECADES:

1900–1909 Dawn of a new century and with it came a new "try-everything attitude.

1910–1919 Fashion changes when society's ideal beauty standard of maturity gives way to youthfulness.

1920–1929 The Roaring Twenties . . . also known as the Jazz Age were a time of hope and idealism. The poster girl of the decade is the Flapper.

1930–1939 Following the Stock Market Crash of 1929 the world is mired in a terrible recession, but a growing entertainment industry acts as a source of fashion inspiration.

1940–1949 The Forties gave us World War II and rationing. In the postwar 1940s, a designer named Dior revolutionizes fashion with a New Look that impacted styles for decades.

1950–1959 From the New Look to poodle skirts, from Hula Hoops to TV, the 1950s are fat and fabulous.

1960–1969 The Sixties see sweeping fashion and lifestyle changes. The Civil Rights Movement, the Women's Movement, the drug culture, long-haired hippies, and their "flower power" costumes.

1970–1979 An era of excess, the classics are out and silhouettes are extreme. Women toss away their bras, and pantsuits become popular.

1980–1989 The era of Conspicuous Consumption when American designers like Ralph Lauren, Calvin Klein, and Donna Karan become household words.

1990–2000 In the workplace, dress codes are shattered, comfort and cocooning dominate lifestyles, and shopping via the Internet becomes a multibillion-dollar venture.

Sources:

Jolie Solomon and Mary Sears, "Dress For Success," *FSB* March 2001 pg.88, 89.

WWD CENTURY, Special Collector Edition, September 1998.

Then, a powerful woman of her time, Mrs. Eleanor Roosevelt broadcasted on NBC Radio in 1948.
Courtesy, AP Wide World Photos.

Today, Hillary Clinton successfully "wears" her power.
Courtesy, Fairdhild Publications, Inc.

At this stage, the buyer reorders in quantity for maximum stock coverage.

During the rise stage of a new original design, many retailers will offer line-for-line copies or, **knockoffs**, as they are referred to in the fashion industry. These are versions of the original designer style duplicated by manufacturers. These copies look exactly like the original except that they have been mass-produced in less expensive fabrics. Because production of the merchandise is now on a larger scale, prices of the knockoffs are generally lower.

As a new style continues to be accepted by more and more of the customers, adaptations appear. **Adaptations** are designs that have all the dominant features of the style that inspired them, but do not claim to be exact copies. Modifications have been made, but distinguishing features of the original, such as a special shoulder treatment or the use of textured fabric, may be retained in the adaptation. At this stage, the promotion effort focuses on regular price lines, full assortments, and product-type ads to persuade the customer of the store's superiority in meeting his or her fashion needs.

Culmination Stage

The **culmination stage** of the fashion cycle is the period when a fashion is at the height of its popularity and use. At this stage, also referred to as the **plateau**, the fashion is in such demand that it can be mass-produced, mass-distributed, and sold at prices within the range of most customers. This stage may be long or brief, depending on how extended the peak of popularity is. The quilted coat, which began as an expensive down-filled style in the late 1970s, reached its culmination stage when mass production in acrylic fill had made a quilted coat available to practically every income level. At the culmination stage, the high-price line fashion buyer stops reordering the fashion and begins reducing stock.

The culmination stage of a fashion may be extended in two ways:

1. If a fashion becomes accepted as a classic, it settles into a fairly steady sales pattern. An example of this is the cardigan sweater, an annual steady seller.
2. If new details of design, color, or texture are continually introduced, interest in the fashion may be kept alive longer. Shoulder-strap handbags are a perfect example. Another example is the continued fashion interest in running shoes, fostered by new colors, designs, and comfort innovations.

Decline Stage

When boredom with a fashion sets in, the result is a decrease in consumer demand for that fashion. This is known as the **decline stage**. It is a principle of fashion that all fashions end in excess.

As a fashion starts to decline, consumers may still be wearing it, but they are no longer willing to buy it at its regular price. The outstanding fashion merchandiser is able to recognize the end of the culmination stage and start markdowns early. At this point, production stops immediately or comes slowly to a halt. The leading fashion stores abandon the style; traditional stores take a moderate markdown and advertise the price reduction. This will probably be followed in a short while by a major price-slash clearance or closeout. At this stage, the style may be found in bargain stores at prices far below what the style commanded in earlier stages.

Obsolescence Stage

When strong distaste for a style has set in and it can no longer be sold at any price, the fashion is in its **obsolescence stage**. At this stage, the style can be found only in thrift shops, garage sales, or flea markets. A style at this stage is often donated to charity or sent to third world countries. Or it may be turned into rags for a variety of industrial and home uses.

Lengths of Cycles

Predicting the time span of a fashion cycle is impossible since each fashion moves at its own speed. However, one guideline can be counted on. Declines are fast, and a drop to obsolescence is almost always steeper than a rise to culmination. At this point, as they say in merchandising, "You can't give it away."

As the world moves into the 21st century, the speed with which products move through their cycles is accelerating. Rapid technological developments and "instant" communications have much to do with this speedup, as do fast-changing environmental factors. The result is an intense competition among manufacturers and retailers to provide consumers with what they want and expect—constantly changing assortments from which to choose.

American society at the end of the 20th century accepts as routine live TV pictures of astronauts working in outer space, of battles being fought in various parts of the world, and of personalities participating in social occasions at every point of the globe. Our appetite for constant newness and change seems to be insatiable. The vast choice of new styles that consumers are offered continuously by the fashion world provides them with an important role in the movement of fashion cycles. Consumers either give a new style enough acceptance to get it started, or they immediately reject it. Since more new fashions are always ready to push existing ones out of the way, it is no wonder that with each passing year, the time required for a fashion to complete its cycle becomes shorter and shorter.

Breaks in the Cycle

In fashion, as in everything else, there are always ups and downs, stops and starts. The normal flow of a fashion cycle can be broken or abruptly interrupted by outside influences. The influence can be simply unpredictable weather or a change in group acceptance. Or it can be much more dramatic and far-reaching—war, worldwide economic depression, or a natural disaster, for example.

Although no formal studies have been made of the phenomenon of the broken cycle, manufacturers and merchants have a theory about it. They believe that a broken cycle usually picks up where it has stopped once conditions return to normal or once the season that was cut short reopens. Consider the effect that a shortage of oil can have on the movement of manufactured fibers. Although the success of manufactured fibers—with all their easy-care attributes—is tremendous, their availability was interrupted by oil shortages in 1973, in 1979, in the late 1980s, and again in the early 2000s. However, when the oil supply increased, the popularity of these fibers returned to what it had been.

Widespread economic depressions also temporarily interrupt the normal progress of a fashion cycle. When there is widespread unemployment, fashion moves much more slowly, resuming its pace only with economic recovery and growth.

Wars also affect fashion. They cause shortages that force designers, manufacturers, retailers, and consumers to change fashions less freely or to restrict styles. People redirect their interests, and fashion must take a back seat. When fashion apparel is in a cycle break, interest in cosmetics usually picks up. Women switch cosmetics or use them differently to satisfy their desire for something new. After wars have ended, interest in fashion picks up and flourishes once again.

Long-Run and Short-Run Fashions

The length of time individual fashions take to complete their cycles varies widely. **Long-run fashions** take more seasons to complete their cycles than what might be considered average; **short-run fashions** take fewer seasons.

Some fashions tend to rise in popular acceptance more slowly than others, thereby prolonging their life. Some stay in popular demand much longer than others do. The decline in popular demand for some fashions may be slower than for others.

Consumer Buying and the Fashion Cycle

Every fashion has both a consumer buying cycle and a consumer use cycle (see Figure 1.6). The curve of the consumer buying cycle rises in direct relation to that of the consumer use cycle. But when the fashion reaches its peak, consumer buying tends to decline more rapidly than consumer use. Different segments of society respond to and tire of a fashion at different times. So different groups of consumers continue to wear fashions for varying lengths of time after they have ceased buying them. While each group is using and enjoying a fashion, the producers and retailers serving that group are already abandoning the style and marketing something newer. Their efforts in this direction are most profitable when they anticipate, rather than follow, the trend of consumer demand. Consumer buying is often halted prematurely. This happens because producers and sellers no longer wish to risk making and stocking an item they believe will soon decline in popularity. Instead, they concentrate their resources on new items with better prospects for longevity. This procedure is familiar to anyone who has tried to buy summer clothes in late August or skiwear in March.

The Intangibles of Fashion

Fashion itself is intangible. A style is tangible, made up of a definite silhouette and details of design. But fashion is shaped by such powerful intangibles as group acceptance, change, the social forces important during a certain era, and people's desire to relate to specific lifestyles.

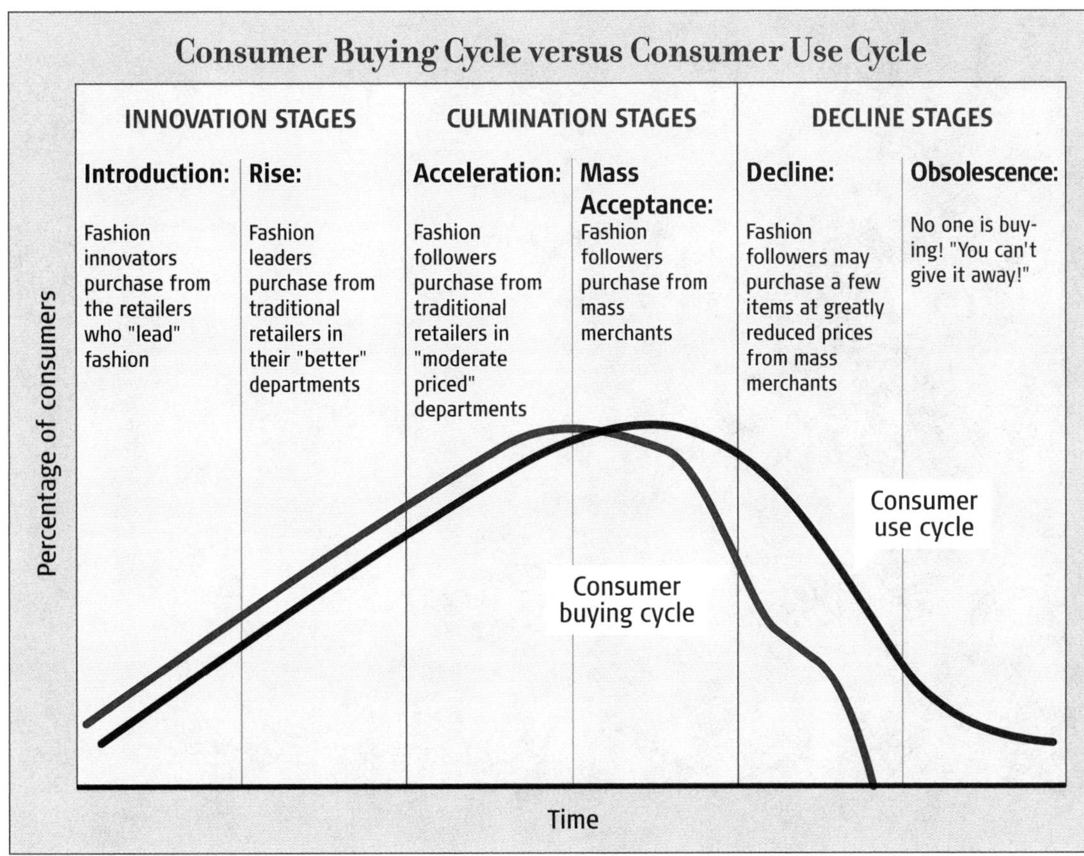

FIGURE 1.6
Consumer use of a fashion product follows a cycle similar to the buying cycle, but the use cycle begins after the buying cycle and endures beyond the buying cycle's decline and obsolescence stages.

Group Acceptance

The fig leaf, the first fashion creation, was widely accepted, and since then we have come a long way. Basically, fashion is acceptance: Group acceptance or approval is implied in any definition of fashion. Most people have a deep-seated wish to express themselves as individuals but also to be part of a group. To dress in the latest fashion means that they are trying to be individual yet also belong.

However, acceptance need not be universal. A style may be adopted by one group while other segments of the population ignore it. As David Wolfe, creative director of Doneger Design Group put it:

> *More people care about fashion than we think, but they don't care about trends. Fashion with a capital "F" is a game played by few people. More people care about presentation. Only 5 percent of Americans are passionate about fashion, while the majority move at a slower pace.*[12]

A style may also be accepted and become a fashion in one part of the world while it is ignored or rejected elsewhere. Each of the following is considered fashionable by its own inhabitants: the igloo of the Inuit, the thatched hut of some African tribes people, and the ranch style house of many American suburbanites. Similarly, many ethnic and religious groups have distinctive styles of dress (see Figure 1.7).

The way we dress is a personal signature. The dress or suit we wear is not just a confirmation of the old adage that "Clothes makes the man . . . or woman," but rather an example of the fact that our need for acceptance is expressed largely in the way we dress. Acceptance also means that a fashion is considered appropriate to the occasion for which it is worn. Clothes considered appropriate for big-business boardrooms would not be considered acceptable for casual weekends.

If any of you should doubt the power of acceptance in fashion, try a simple experiment. Put on clothes worn 10 or 20 years ago, or totally different in style from what is considered the fashion. Then go out casually among your friends, acquaintances, or even strangers, and note their reactions toward you and then your feelings toward yourself. There will be quizzical looks, doubtful stares, and in some cases smirks

FIGURE 1.7
For members of religious groups, conformity to a traditional style of dress is an expression of belonging and adherence to the religion's beliefs and values.
Courtesy, Ruth Fremson/ New York Times.

and laughter. No one can really "belong" to a chosen group and at the same time choose to be completely "out" of present-day fashion. Such is the power of fashion acceptance.

Change

Fashion changes because ideas about politics, religion, leisure, democracy, success, and age change. Fashion is also a complex means for facilitating orderly change within a mass society. This is particularly true when the society is no longer able to provide identity and maintain social order via custom or tradition. In the United States, where different immigrant and ethnic groups must adjust to one another, fashion is one means of providing a social bond.

Fashion is subject to change—both rapid and gradual. Modern communications play a major role in today's accelerated rate of fashion change. The mass media spreads fashion news across the face of the globe in hours, sometimes seconds. Live TV coverage of events around the world enables us to see not only what people are doing but also what they are wearing. Our morning newspapers show us what fashion leaders wore to a party the night before. Even slight fashion changes are given faster and wider publicity than ever before. Consumers who like these changes demand them from merchants, who in turn demand them from manufacturers.

New technology is constantly producing new fibers and blends of fibers. Each seems to offer more than the one before and encourages the discarding of the old.

Clothing is also getting a lot smarter, and high tech clothing is now an integral part of the world of wearable computers. They are so portable that their components are stored on the body in places like lapels, armbands, or eyeglass frames.

In 2000, a new jacket went on sale for about $900 in London and around Europe that featured a built-in combination cell phone and MP3 player. "Clothing is a usable, simple interface," says Jimmy Farringdon, the scientist who collaborated with Levi Strauss & Company to develop the technology used by the jackets.[13]

FASHION FOCUS

Donna Karan Now–True to Herself

Donna Karan was the head designer for Anne Klein when she set out on her own in 1984 with a seven-easy-pieces basic wardrobe for women based on a body-suit that was then layered with jackets and wrap skirts. It was a hit! Women found Karan's styles comfortable both at work and out on the town. From that simple and classic design grew a multi-faceted design house under the leadership and design talent of Donna Karan.

The late 1980's and early 1990's were high-flying days for Donna Karan. But, 1996 proved to be a stumbling step for Donna Karan when it went public. Expenses were high and profits were low. Karan was perceived as spending too much and expanding too quickly into too many new areas. Donna, professional that she is, realized that design skills were not enough to sustain a multi-million dollar company. So she hired John Idol away from Ralph Lauren in 1997. An industry professional with a proven track record of success, Idol focused on the more profitable parts of the business. The strategies he used transformed Donna Karan from a wholesale-driven company to one with revenues coming from licensing ventures and from retail stores. In 1999 a DKNY flagship store opened on Madison Avenue to house the complete line of DKNY products. This store joined the growing number of stores in the United States and 32 other countries.

A deal that married two of the industry's biggest names—Liz Claiborne and Donna Karan—was just one of John Idol's strategies to take Donna Karan back into the limelight with exciting designs and profits. Claiborne, famous for its expertise in distribution, now has the long-term exclusive right to source, market, and distribute DKNY jeans and active sportswear, putting the Donna Karan Jeans in the forefront of the largest, hippest market in apparel.

Another blockbuster deal was the fragrance and cosmetics licensing agreement with the Estee Lauder Company, the dominant force in the prestige cosmetics business. Karan started her own beauty company in 1992 and had originally intended to keep it in house, but losses were substantial and she agreed to the licensing agreement with Lauder. In the years since Lauder has owned the business, the company has expanded. The original Cashmere Mist franchise introduced in 1994 is one of the fastest-growing fragrances in the United States.

In December of 2000, LVMH Moet Hennessy-Louis Vuitton acquired 100 percent of the Donna Karan trademarks becoming part of the LVMH Fashion Group. This group includes Louis Vuitton, Christian Lacroix, Fendi, Givenchy, Kenzo, Loewe, Marc Jacobs, and Thomas Pink, among many other luxury labels.

LVMH planned to significantly grow its presence in the United States and felt that with strong worldwide awareness, Donna Karen International had excellent potential for growth internationally as a global luxury lifestyle brand as part of the LVMH Fashion Group.

In August of 2001 Donna Karan opened a second Manhattan store in Soho. Donna felt that "uptown and downtown is merging." She said, "This store is what New York is all about: eclecticism. This not a clothing store, not a home store, not an antiques store. It's everything." Karen has her mind set on breaking out of the box she feels she has been placed by the fashion press and retailers. When she tries to be creative, reviews are mixed, since "they" expect her wearable, sensible clothes.

On her own now, Karen is ready to take a chance and let the artist run loose. That may require the designer to spend more time in Paris and Milan, but it doesn't mean she will be letting go of New York's energy. "My vision is big," Karen says. "That's what keeps me going! "So she is using her partnership with LVMH as an opportunity to move forward, to build an accessories collection, and to manufacture more of her clothes, and maybe even hand-made shoes in Europe.

Sources

Carrie Donovan, "Conversations with Carrie"- Donna Karan, *New York Times*, December 2, 2001, p. 95.

Donna Karan International, Inc. *Hoover's Online*, February 28, 2002.

Fashion Scoops, "Donna, The Publisher," *Women's Wear Daily*, Online Archive February 19, 2002.

Jane Ozzard, "Getting Down with DKNY," *Women's Wear Daily* Online Archive August 13, 2001.

LVHM, Press Release, "LVHM to Acquire Donna Karan," December 17, 2000

Eric Wilson, "Donna Now," *Women's Wear Daily*, November, 2001, pp. 72-74.

Eric Wilson/with contributions from Miles Socha,Paris/ Julie Naughton, Melanie Kletter, Kristen Larson, New York, "New Role for Donna Karan?," *Women's Wear Daily*, Online Archive, January 28, 2002.

Eric Wilson, "SKNY Pens License For Jeans in Europe," *Women's Wear Daily*, October 10, 2002, p.3.

Eric Wilson, "Wilson Makes Key DKI Moves," *Women's Wear Daily,* October 9, 2002, pp. 2-3.

Vickie M. Young, "DKI Expecting Accelerated Growth," *Women's Wear Daily*, October 30, 2001, p. 2, 7.

Donna Karan.
Courtesy, Fairchild Publications, Inc.

The Futility of Forcing Change

Fashion expresses the spirit of the times, and in turn influences it. Fashion designers are successful or not, depending on their ability to sense and anticipate changes if not to initiate them. Changes can be initiated, but there are as many examples of failures as there are of successful changes. Efforts have been made from time to time to force changes in the course of fashion, but they usually fail. Fashion is a potent force which by definition requires support by the majority.

As an example, in the late 1960s, designers and retailers decided that skirts had reached their limit in shortness and that women would soon be seeking change. So the designers designed and the retailers stocked and promoted the "midi," a skirt mid-calf in length. The designers and retailers were right in theory but wrong in timing and choice of skirt length. Consumers found the midi too sudden and radical a change and did not accept or buy the style in sufficient numbers to make it a fashion. In the late 1980s, designers and retailers did it again—this time they tried to force a change to very short skirts. Again, the public disliked the radical change and refused to buy miniskirts when they were first introduced. In the mid-1990s however, women were wearing both miniskirts and long skirts. By 2003, the runways were full of miniskirts once again.

Occasionally, necessity and government regulation can interrupt the course of fashion. During World War II, the U.S. government controlled the type and quantity of fabric used in consumer goods. One regulation prohibited anything but slit pockets on women's garments to avoid using the extra material that patch pockets require. Skirts were short and silhouettes were narrow, reflecting the scarcity of material.

FIGURE 1.8
After World War II, Christian Dior meet the demand for change from the tailored short-skirted look of the early 1940s by providing women with the full-skirted, feminine "New Look."
Courtesy, Musee des Arts de la Mode © D.A.C.S.

Meeting the Demand for Change

After World War II, a reaction to these designs was to be expected. A new French designer, Christian Dior, caught and expressed the desire for a freer line and a more feminine garment in his first collection, which achieved instant fashion success. Using fabric with a lavishness that had been impossible in Europe or America during the war years, he created his "new look," with long, full skirts, fitted waistlines, and feminine curves (see Figure 1.8).

Dior did not change the course of fashion; he accelerated it—from an evolutionary course to a revolutionary one. He recognized and interpreted the need of women at that time to get out of stiff, short, narrow, unfeminine clothes and into soft, free, longer, feminine ones. Consumers wanted the change, and the lifting of the very limiting wartime restrictions made it possible to meet their demand.

Another example of a consumer demand for change occurred in men's wear just before World War II. Year after year, manufacturers had been turning out versions of a style that had long been popular in England—the padded-shoulder, draped suit. A number of young men from very influential families, who were attending well-known northeastern colleges, became tired of that look. They wanted a change. They took their objections to New Haven clothing manufacturers, and the result was the natural shoulder Ivy League suit that achieved widespread popularity for the next 15 to 20 years.

A Mirror of the Times

Fashion is a nonverbal symbol. It communicates that the wearer is in step with the times. Because fashions are shaped by the forces of an era, they in turn reflect the way we think and live. Each new fashion seems completely appropriate to its time and reflects that time as no other symbol does. A study of the past and careful observation of the present makes it apparent that fashions are social expressions that document the tastes and values of an era just as the paintings, sculpture, and architecture of the times do. The extreme modesty of the Victorian era was reflected in bulky and concealing fashions. The sexual emancipation of the flappers in the 1920s was expressed in their flattened figures, short skirts, "sheer" hosiery (the first time the bare leg was exposed), and short hair. The individualistic fashions of the 1990s and 2000s are a true reflection of the current freedom of expression and lifestyle.

Social Class

Fashions mirror the times by reflecting the degree of rigidity in the class structure of an era. Although such ideas are difficult to imagine today, throughout much of history certain fashions were restricted to the members of certain rigidly defined social classes. In some early eras, royal edicts regulated both the type of apparel that could be worn by each group of citizens and how ornate it could be. Class distinctions were thus emphasized. Certain fashions have also been used as indications of high social standing and material success. During the 19th century, the constricted waists of Western women and the bound feet of high-caste Chinese women were silent but obvious evidence that the male head of the household was wealthy and esteemed.

Today, social classes are far more fluid and mobile than ever before. Because there is no universal way of life today, people are free to choose their own values and lifestyles—and their dress reflects that choice. Many fashions exist simultaneously, and we are all free to adopt the fashions of any social group. If we do not wish to join others in their fashion choices, we can create our own modes and standards of dress. The beatniks of the 1950s and the hippies of the 1960s had their typical fashions, as did the bohemians of the 1920s and the liberated groups of the 1970s. In the 1980s, the phenomenon of the punk rockers existed side by side with the yuppies. In the 1990s, hip-hop fashion coexisted with Ralph Lauren's Polo-Sport. Now in the early 2000s, vintage has found a home alongside celebrity glamour.

Lifestyle

Fashions also mirror the times by reflecting the activities in which people of an era participate. The importance of court-centered social activities in 17th- and 18th-century Europe was in evidence in men's and women's ornately styled apparel. Fashions became less colorful and more functional when a new working class was created by the industrial revolution.

Currently, our clothes also vary according to lifestyle. More casual and active sportswear in wardrobes reflect our interest in active sports and leisure pastimes. The difference in the lifestyle of an urban, career-oriented woman and that of a suburban housewife is totally reflected in their choice of wardrobes (see Figure 1.9).

FIGURE 1.9
Popular television shows, such as Everybody Loves Raymond, *both reflect and influence the variety of clothing styles that people adopt to suit their different lifestyles.*

Principles of Fashion

Diversification of fashion has added new dimensions to the interpretation of the principles of fashion. While the intangibles of fashion can be vague and sometimes difficult to predict and chart, certain fundamental principles of fashion are tangible and precise. For many decades these principles served as the solid foundation for fashion identification and forecasting—they still do—but the astute student of fashion recognizes that in today's vibrant and changing atmosphere, the application of these principles becomes a more intricate and challenging task.

The five principles we will discuss are the foundations upon which the study of fashion is based.

1. **Consumers establish fashions by accepting or rejecting the styles offered.** The popular belief that designers create artistic designs with little regard for the acceptance of these designs by the public is quite false. No designer can be successful without the support and acceptance of the customer.

   It is true that new fashions can be introduced by famous designers, but it is relatively rare. A few examples are the loose, boxy jacket of the Chanel suit, the famous bias cut clothes designed by Vionnet, and the "New Look" by Christian Dior. However, the designers who are considered to be the "creators" of fashion are those who have consistently given expression to the silhouette, color, fabric, and design that are wanted and accepted by a majority of the consumers.

   A **customer** is a patron or potential purchaser of goods or services. Thus, a retail store's dress buyer is a customer of a dress manufacturer, and the dress manufacturer is a customer of a fabric producer. The **consumer** is the ultimate user; the person who uses the finished fashion garment.

   Designers create hundreds of new styles each season, based on what they think may attract customers. From among those many styles, manufacturers choose what they think will be successful. They reject many more than they select. Retailers choose from the manufacturers' offerings those styles they believe their customers will want. Consumers then make the vital choice. By accepting some styles and rejecting others, they—and only they—dictate what styles will become fashions.

2. **Fashions are not based on price.** Just because something is expensive it does not follow that it will be successful. Although new styles that may eventually become fashions are often introduced at high prices, this is happening less and less today. What you pay for an item of apparel is not an indication of whether the item is considered to be fashionable.

   In the fashion diversity offered to consumers today, successful fashions are to be found at every price level. Upper income consumers will accept fashions at very low prices, and consumers at the opposite end of the income scale will often splurge and buy a very expensive item—if it is in fashion. In many cases, consumers coordinate fashions that are both inexpensive and expensive with little regard to the price. For example, an expensive piece of jewelry can be pinned to a inexpensive T-shirt, or conversely, a fashionable piece of costume jewelry can be pinned to an expensive designer suit.

3. **Fashions are evolutionary in nature; they are rarely revolutionary.** In these days of rapid cultural and national revolutions, it is hard to believe that a worldwide phenomenon such as fashion is evolutionary in nature—not revolutionary. To the casual observer it appears as though fashion changes suddenly. Actually, fashion change comes about as a result of gradual movements from one season to the next.

   Throughout history there have probably been only two real revolutions in fashion styles. One of these occurred during the 20th century: the Dior "New Look" of 1947. The other was the abrupt change of styles brought about by the French Revolution when the fashion changed overnight from elaborate full skirts, low-cut daring bodices, and ornate and glamorous fabrics to simple, drab costumes in keeping with the political and moral upheaval.

   Fashions usually evolve gradually from one style to another. Skirt lengths go up or down an inch at a time, season after season. Shoulder widths narrow or widen gradually, not suddenly. It is only in retrospect that fashion changes seem marked or sudden.

   Fashion designers understand and accept this principle. When developing new design ideas, they always keep the current fashion in mind. They know that few people could or would buy a whole new wardrobe every season, and that the success of their designs ultimately depends on sales. Consumers today buy apparel and accessories to supplement and update the wardrobe they already own, some of which was purchased last year, some the year before, some the year before that, and so on. In most cases, consumers will buy only if the purchase complements their existing wardrobe and does not depart too radically from last year's purchases.

4. **No amount of sales promotion can change the direction in which fashions are moving.** Promotional efforts on the part of producers or retailers cannot dictate what consumers will buy, nor can they force people to buy what they do not want. The few times that fashion merchants have tried to promote a radical change in fashion, they have not been successful.

   As the women's liberation movement grew in the late 1960s, women rebelled against the constriction of girdles and bras. The overwhelming majority stopped wearing girdles and began wearing pantyhose instead. Various "counterculture" looks were adopted by some, and a more relaxed look was adopted by nearly everyone. Reflecting this change was the reemergence of the soft, no-seam natural bra. Regardless of promotion by the intimate-apparel industry, nothing could persuade the majority of American women to submit again to the rigid control of corsets and girdles.

   Also, promotional effort cannot renew the life of a fading fashion unless the extent of change gives the fashion an altogether new appeal. This is why stores have markdown or clearance sales. When the sales of a particular style start slumping, stores know they must clear out as much of that stock as possible, even at much lower prices, to make room for newer styles in which consumers have indicated interest.

5. **All fashions end in excess.** This saying is sometimes attributed to Paul Poiret, a top Paris designer of the 1920s. Many examples attest to its truth. Eighteenth-century hoopskirts ballooned out to over eight feet in width, which made moving from room to room a complicated maneuver. The French tried to accommodate these skirts and designed doors that could be opened to a width far beyond that of regular doors. They became known as "French doors" and can still be found in architecture today. Similarly, miniskirts of the 1960s finally became so short that the slightest movement caused a major problem in modesty. This same trend toward excess can be found in men's wear. Just think of the growth of the width of a tie. It will start as a thin string tie, and become wider and wider until it becomes as wide as a bib!

   Once the extreme in styling has been reached, a fashion is nearing its end (see Figure 1.10). The attraction of the fashion wanes and people begin to seek a different look—a new fashion.

FIGURE 1.10
The principle that all fashion ends in excess is still being demonstrated on the runway. This partially see-through dress by designer Marc Bower proves this concept to be true.
Courtesy, Fairchild Publications, Inc.

SUMMARY AND REVIEW

In its narrow sense, fashion is the prevailing way a group of people at a particular time and place dress themselves. The fashion industries, which manufacture the materials and finished products of clothing, also produce related goods, including cosmetics, fragrances, and home fashions. Fashion designers attempt to determine what styles—characteristic appearances of garments and other fashion items—will appeal to their target group of consumers. The designs that are offered to the public are versions of a style that are distinguished by their silhouette, details, texture, and color.

Public acceptance of a fashion follows a course called the fashion cycle, which includes the following stages: introduction, rise, culmination, decline, and obsolescence. A fashion that reaches the culmination stage and then declines over a brief period of time is called a fad. A classic, on the other hand, may not necessarily reach its peak of popularity very quickly, but its decline is gradual, and it never reaches the obsolescence stage.

Typically, the fashion leaders who buy a fashion at the introductory stage are the wealthy clientele of high fashion designers. These consumers can afford to experiment with their wardrobes. When a fashion appears to gain acceptance, it can be mass-produced with less expensive materials for fashion followers. Some fashions have broad appeal, and others attract a smaller segment of the public, for example, a particular age group, an ethnic group, or people with a common lifestyle, such as casual suburbanites or more formally dressed businesspeople.

Any fashion evolves according to the demands of its market. Neither pricing nor promotion by the producers can force consumers to embrace a new fashion. Usually changes evolve gradually, building up to an extreme and then reversing and moving toward the other extreme. The success of fashion merchandisers depends on their ability to predict the changing tastes of their public with scientific accuracy and to use their artistic creativity to satisfy those tastes.

Trade Talk

Define or briefly explain the following terms:

adaptations
classic
high fashion
knockoffs
consumer
culmination stage
customer
decline stage
design
details
fad
fashion
fashion business
fashion cycle
fashion industries
fashion marketing
fashion merchandising
long-run fashions
marketing
mass or volume fashion
obsolescence stage
plateau
rise stage
short-run fashions
silhouette
style
style number
taste
texture
trend

For Review

1. What group ultimately decides whether a style will be "fashionable" or not? Explain your answer.
2. Apparel styles are often named for the period in history in which they were introduced. Name three such styles and the historic period in which they originated.
3. Give two examples of "classics" that are in style today for each of the following groups: (a) men, (b) women, and (c) children.
4. Distinguish between (a) style, fashion, and design, and (b) classic and fad.
5. List and briefly explain the interrelationships among the four components of fashion.
6. Fashion apparel change has accelerated during the past 100 years. Which factors, in your opinion, have had the greatest influence on change? Why?
7. Fashions go through a five-stage life cycle. Name and explain each stage.
8. In what respects does the consumer buying cycle differ from the consumer use cycle? How is such information useful to fashion merchants?
9. Can designers, manufacturers, or retailers force unwanted fashion on consumers? Explain your answer.

10. What are the five basic principles relating to fashion? What are the implications for fashion merchants?

For Discussion

The following statements are derived from the text. Discuss the significance of each, giving examples of how each applies to merchandising fashion goods.

1. Men today are as influenced by and responsive to fashion as women.
2. Predicting the time span of a fashion cycle is impossible since each fashion moves at its own speed.
3. Because there is no universal way of life, people are free to choose their own values and lifestyles.

References

1. George P. Fox, *Fashion: The Power That Influences the World. The Philosophy of Ancient and Modern Dress and Fashion* (London: Lange and Hellman, Printers & Stereotypers 1850–1860–1872), Introduction, p. 20.
2. Collin McDowell, "Fashion Today," Phaidon, September 2000. Taken from "Fade to Greige," by Elaine Showalter, *London Review of Books*, January 4, 2001, pp. 37-39.
3. Rosemary Feitelberg, "The New Look of Work Wear," *Women's Wear Daily*, February 9, 2001, p.4.
4. *Webster's Tenth New Collegiate Dictionary* (Springfield, Mass.: G & C Merriam Company, 1998), p. 450.
5. Peter F. Drucker, *Management Tasks, Responsibilities, Practices* (New York: Harper & Row, 1973), pp. 64–65.
6. Paul H. Nystrom, *Economics of Fashion* (New York: The Ronald Press, 1928), pp. 3–7; and *Fashion Merchandising* (New York: The Ronald Press, 1932), pp. 33–34.
7. Ibid., p. 7.
8. James Laver, *Taste and Fashion*, rev. ed. (London: George C. Harrop & Co., Ltd., 1946), p. 202.
9. Jenny Lyn Bader, "The Miniskirt as a National Security Threat," *New York Times*, September 10, 2000, p. 3.
10. Irma Zandl, "How to Separate Trends from Fads," *Brandweek* Online, October 23, 2000.
11. Agnes Brooke Young, *Recurring Cycles of Fashion; 1760–1937* (New York: Harper & Brothers, 1937; reprint, New York: Cooper Square Publishers, Inc., 1966), p. 30.
12. Holly Haber, "Talking Trends," *Women's Wear Daily*, January 3, 2002.
13. Anne Eisenberg, "A Step Beyond Palmtop: Collartop," *New York Times*, November 20, 2000, p. G8.

CHAPTER 2

The Environment of Fashion

WHAT'S IN IT FOR YOU?

Everything you always wanted to know about the environmental factors affecting fashion, as well as the geographic, demographic, psychographic, and behavioral research tools for market segmentation.

Key Concepts:

- The four major factors affecting fashion
- How research is used by fashion producers and retailers to help them with market segmentation
- The five basic psychological factors that motivate human behavior—and how each affects fashion

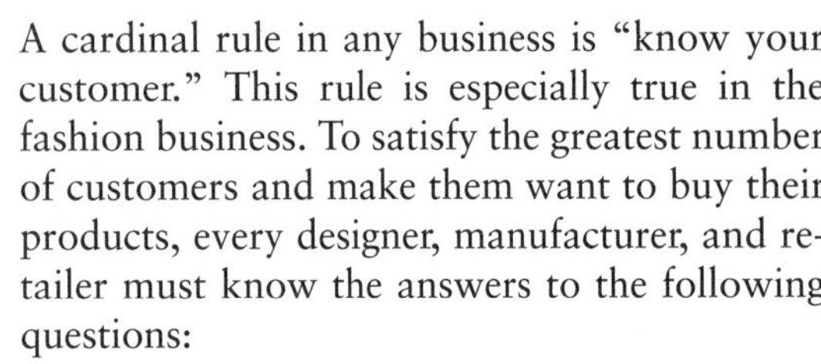

A cardinal rule in any business is "know your customer." This rule is especially true in the fashion business. To satisfy the greatest number of customers and make them want to buy their products, every designer, manufacturer, and retailer must know the answers to the following questions:

- How many potential customers for your products and services are there in a given community?
- How old are these customers?
- How much are they willing to spend on your product?
- What level of service do they expect?
- Are they married or single, homeowners or renters?
- How many children do they have?
- What kind of work do they do?
- What is their annual income?
- What is more important to them—value or style? Prestige or price?
- How much do they have to spend on "extras"?
- Do they like to shop early or late in the day? Weekdays or weekends?
- What motivates them to shop in a particular store?
- How do they spend their leisure time?

In other words: Who are your customers?

Accurate facts about customers, properly interpreted, help designers, manufacturers, and retailers make major decisions about what to offer them. Guesswork and misinterpreted facts can lead to major business failures.

One major source of information about the consumer market is the U.S. Bureau of the Census. The U.S. census produces over three billion separate statistics about how many Americans there are, what work they do, where they live, and how they are doing as measured by income and creature comforts. These seemingly dull statistics are a treasure trove of vital information, not only for government, but also for every business. They help businesspeople who are interested in translating the data and projections drawn from them into new product and profit opportunities.

Used properly, census data provide us with all-important information about conditions that affect our lives and influence our actions. Collectively, the conditions under which we live are called our **environment.** Just as the environment of one nation or society differs from that of another nation or society, so the environment of one neighborhood differs from that of another. In fashion merchandising, it is important to be aware of the conditions that affect a particular customer's environment and to know how the environment differs from one group to another.

Four major environmental factors affect fashion interest and demand:

1. Market segmentation by geographics, demographics, psychographics, and behavior.
2. The degree of economic development and well-being of a country or society.
3. The sociological characteristics of the class structure.
4. The psychological attitudes of consumers.

Each will be discussed in turn in this chapter.

Market Segmentation

Both manufacturers and retailers try to identify and select target markets for their goods. **Target markets** are specific groups of potential customers that a business is attempting to turn into regular customers. Businesses attempt to determine who their customers are, what those customers want, how much the customers are willing to pay for goods, where potential customers are located, and how many targeted customers there are. Today, geographic, demographic, psychographic, and behavioral research studies are a vital part of determining these important factors.

Most manufacturers and designers are concerned with national trends. Retailers, however, must consider the impact of statistics in their local areas as well as statistics from national studies. **Market segmentation** is the separation of the total consumer market into smaller groups. These are known as **market segments.** By identifying and studying each market segment, producers and retailers can target their goods and services to their special markets. Markets are divided or segmented in four major ways: by geographics, demographics, psychographics, and behavior.

Geographics

Geographics are population studies that focus on where people live. These studies organize data by region of the country, by county or city size, by population density, and by climate. See Table 2.1 for an example of geographic data on apparel spending.

Demographics

Demographics are population studies that divide broad groups of consumers into smaller, more homogeneous market segments. The variables covered in a demographic study include:

- Age
- Sex
- Family size
- Stages in family life cycle
- Income
- Occupation
- Education
- Religion
- Race and ethnicity or nationality

Psychographics

Psychographics are studies that develop fuller, more personal portraits of potential customers and their lifestyles. Psychographic studies more fully predict consumer purchase patterns and distinguish users of a product. The variables covered in a psychographic study include social class, values and lifestyle, and personality.

TABLE 2.1 Estimated Household Spending on Apparel (for top five metro areas)

RANK	AVERAGE YEARLY SPENDING
1. Detroit, MI	$2,532
2. Chicago–Gray Lake, County IL–IN–WI	$2,415
3. Denver–Boulder CO	$2,310
4. NY, Northern–Long Island	$2,211
5. Washington, DC–MD–VA	$2,284
Average U.S.	$1,790

Source: U.S. Census Bureau, Statistical Abstract of the United States.

Sometimes researchers request information about the actual product benefits desired by consumers. These studies help greatly in matching the image of a company and its product with the type of consumer using the product.

Many research firms combine geographic and demographic studies for retailers and manufacturers. One such firm, the Claritas Corporation, produces the PRIZM systems, which divides and then clusters the population of the United States into 62 market segments or "clusters" based on postal zip codes, housing, and lifestyle choices. The clusters have catchy names like "Blue Blood Estates." According to Michael Weiss, author of The Clustered World, The residents of Blue Blood Estates are the well-heeled Americans who enjoy the embellishments of money-lavish homes, expensive clothes, luxury cars, and private club memberships—in a gilded suburban setting with others who share the same values.[1] The 62 clusters are then grouped into 15 broader groups, based on degree of urbanization and socioeconomic status. PRIZM's most affluent cluster, Blue Blood Estates, combines the zip codes for Scarsdale, New York; Winnetka, Illinois; Potomac, Maryland; and Rolling Hills, California. One in ten of the residents in these areas is a multimillionaire. They make up only 0.8 percent of the population with a median household income of $113,000.

PRIZM tells you what people buy, but not why. To get closer to that information, many people turn to another widely used research system that uses demographics and psychographics: the VALS 2 system. The VALS 2 (Values and Life Styles) system sorts customers into eight major categories based on psychological attributes. The categories are arranged into a framework that puts consumers with the most resources on the top and those with the fewest, on the bottom. It also arranges consumers into three groups horizontally: principle-oriented, status-oriented, and action-oriented (see Figure 2.1).

Behavior

In an attempt to gather even more insight into customer preferences, some retailers and manufacturers use research on **behavior**. These studies group consumers according to: (1) their opinions of specific products or services or (2) their actual rate of use of these products or services. Behavioral studies help companies understand and predict the behavior of present and potential customers. If you segment your market by behavior, you might be able to identify the reasons for one group's refusal to buy your product. Once you have identified the reason, you may be able to change the product enough to satisfy their objections. A more recent extension of VALS, **GeoVALS**, uses psychographics to identify where customers live and further explain their behavioral trends.

The Economic Environment

The growth of fashion demand depends on a high level of economic development, which is reflected in consumer income, population characteristics, and technological advances. In his book *On Human Finery*,[2] Quentin Bell underscores the relationship between economics and fashion. He explains that most economically

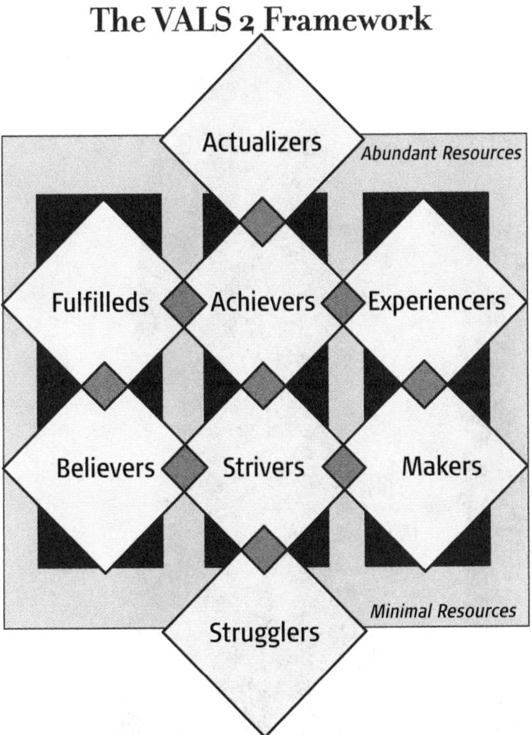

FIGURE 2.1
In the VALS 2 System, each diamond-shaped box represents one of the eight consumer markets.
©1991 Rebecca Piirto Heath, *Beyond Mind Games: The Marketing Power of Psychographics,* American Demographic Books, p. 80. Adapted with permission.

sophisticated countries discard their national costumes long before other nations begin to abandon theirs. England, for example, which led the Western world into the industrial revolution, was the first country to stop wearing traditional national dress. Bell points out that Greece, Poland, and Spain, countries with little in common except for being in similar stages of economic development, retained their national costumes when countries with more industrialized economies—Germany, Belgium, Denmark, and Japan—were abandoning theirs.

A striking example of how countries with swift economic development also move ahead in fashion is the People's Republic of China. Long restricted to the traditional blue Mao jacket and pants for both sexes, the Chinese have increased their interest in contemporary fashions with their increased economic growth, complete with fashion shows and boutiques! With control of Hong Kong restored to China by Britain in 1997, the Chinese fashion industry got a boost from Hong Kong-based companies that moved their manufacturing facilities to the mainland (see Figure 2.2a and b).

A notable example of the reverse situation occurred in Afghanistan in the mid- to late 1990s, when the fundamentalist Taliban faction rose to power and required strict adherence to traditional religious law, including prescribed dress. Men were required to grow their beards and women to wear only the most concealing traditional dress. These laws were a manifestation of a legal code that was particularly severe in its treatment of women, denying them even the right to an education. The political and economic climate of the country at the time of the takeover was one of turmoil, and the repressive regime cut Afghanistan off from participation in the global economy. However, following the U.S.-led invasion in 2001, the country underwent a complicated and uncertain governmental transition that now tries to satisfy the needs of many ethnic and tribal groups, as well as the U.S. demand for stability and transparency in the region.

Consumer Income

Consumer income can be measured in terms of personal income, disposable income, and discretionary income. Many groups of people use the amount of personal income as an indicator of "arriving" in their particular social set. The more personal income they have, the more socially acceptable they consider themselves to be.

At present, many U.S. families may be earning more personal income, but enjoying it less. Statistics have shown sharp increases in personal income in the past decades, but decreases in amounts of disposable and discretionary income.

Personal Income

The total or gross income received by the population as a whole is called **personal income.** It consists of wages, salaries, interest, dividends, and all other income for everyone in the country. Divide personal income by the number of people in the population and the result is **per capita personal income.**

Disposable Personal Income

The amount a person has left to spend or save after paying taxes is called **disposable personal income.** It is roughly equivalent to take-home pay and provides an approximation of the pur-

A

B

FIGURE 2.2
Asian fashion has embraced a contemporary style of dress. From (a) a traditional look to (b) fabulous new fashions, such as this design by Arthur Lam.
(a) Magnum photos © Dennis Stock. (b) Courtesy, The Hong Kong Fashion Designers Association (HKFDA).

chasing power of each consumer during any given year.

Disposable income per household and per capita varies according to age groups and sex (see Figure 2.3). While household after-tax income starts to drop after age 49, individual after-tax income does not peak until ages 60 to 64, showing that consumers in the 50- to 64-year-old age bracket have the highest disposable income of any group.

Discretionary Income

The money that an individual or family can spend or save after buying necessities—food, clothing, shelter, and basic transportation—is called **discretionary income.** Of course, the distinction be-

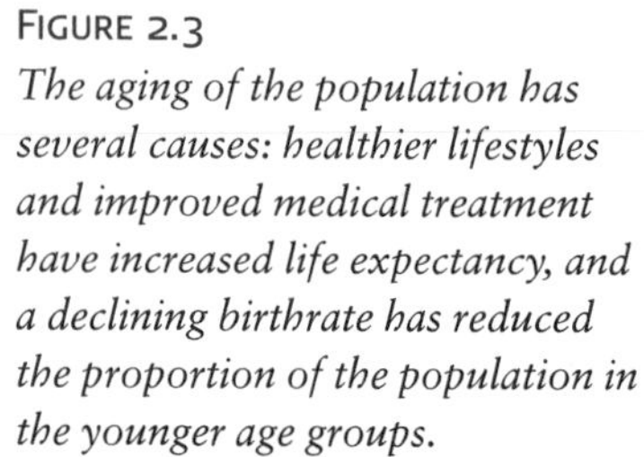

FIGURE 2.3
The aging of the population has several causes: healthier lifestyles and improved medical treatment have increased life expectancy, and a declining birthrate has reduced the proportion of the population in the younger age groups.
Adapted from www.ameristat.org/estproj/aging.

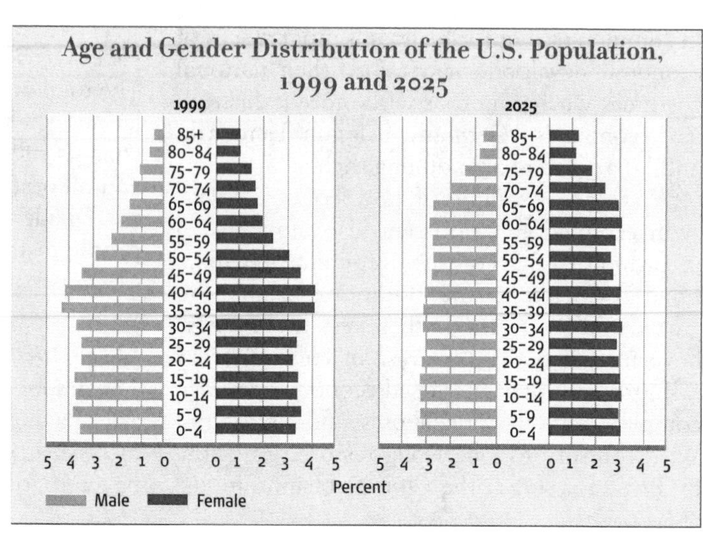

tween "necessities" and "luxuries" or between "needs" and "wants" is a subjective one.

One definition of "middle class" is the middle 60 percent of U.S. households, ranked by income. Between 1968 and 1988, this group's income fell by three percent. Between 1988 and 1993, it lost another two percent. Meanwhile, the average income of the richest households was rising sharply. The average income of the top five percent of households increased almost ten percent. In other words, the vast majority of U.S. households had less discretionary income than they did in 1988, while a lucky few had a lot more.[3] Although the economic gap is still growing, it is imperative to keep the middle class strong, for they are the key factor in fueling the American economy.

The lucky few are like consumer royalty, able to buy a wide variety of goods and services. Although marketers like to target these consumers, it may not be a wise long-term strategy. The super-rich have greater purchasing power, but they are declining in number. While middle-class households have less money, they still have overwhelming strength in numbers.

Purchasing Power of the Dollar

Average income has been increasing each year, but this has not meant that people have an equivalent increase in purchasing power. The reason for this is that the value of the dollar—its purchasing power or what it will buy—has steadily declined since 1950.

A decline in the purchasing power of money is caused by inflation. **Inflation** is defined as an increase in available money and credit, with relative scarcity of goods, resulting in a significant rise in prices.[4] Inflation, therefore, is an economic situation in which demand exceeds supply. Scarcity of goods and services, in relation to demand, results in ever-increasing prices. Table 2.2 shows the changes in the purchasing power of the consumer dollar from 1950 to 1998.

When income taxes increase, the purchasing power of the family income drops; a decrease in income taxes has the reverse effect. With an inflationary economy, the working time required to acquire the necessities of life—basic food, clothing, transportation, and shelter—increases. The increase is not, however, uniform among all items.

In a **recession**, which represents a low point in a business cycle, money and credit become scarce, or "tight." Interest rates are high, production is down, and the rate of unemployment is up. People in the lower-income groups are the hardest hit; those with high incomes are the least affected. Yet these groups are small when compared with the middle-income group. It is the reaction of these middle-income people to any economic squeeze that is the greatest concern of the fashion merchant. For not only is the middle-income group the largest, it is also the most important market for fashion merchandise.

Both inflation and recession affect consumers' buying patterns. Fashion merchants in particular must thoroughly understand the effects of inflation and recession when planning their inventory assortments and promotional

TABLE 2.2 Purchasing Power of the Dollar: 1950–2000

YEAR	AVERAGE AS MEASURED BY CONSUMER PRICES
1950	$4.15
1955	$3.73
1960	$3.37
1965	$3.16
1970	$2.57
1975	$1.85
1980	$1.21
1985	$0.92
1990	$0.76
1994	$0.67
1998	$0.60

Source: *Statistical Abstract of the United States—1999*, U.S. Department of Commerce, p. 493.

Trend Spotter. . . What's That?

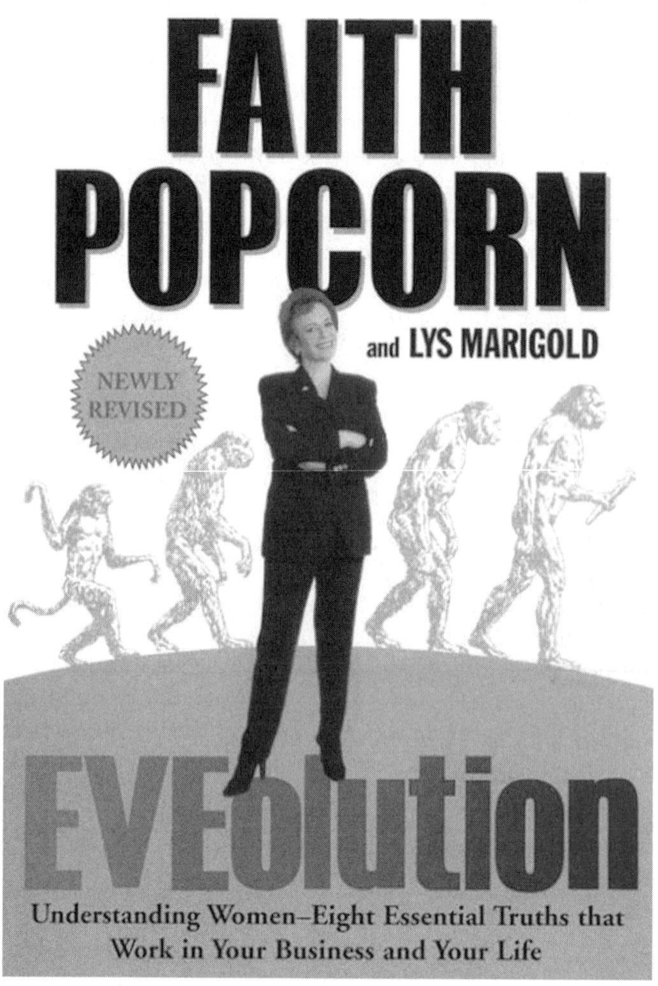

Courtesy, Hyperion Publishers. Jacket design/illustration © Anton Markous. Jacket photograph © Sigrid Estrada. Used with permission.

Nobody knew, much less cared, what a trend spotter was when Faith Popcorn called herself one in 1974 and opened her company, BrainReserve. Her unique talent has established her as the trend spotter of the future. Predicting consumer trends and selling that information to companies who sell to the rest of us has made her a force to be reckoned with! She forecasted the S.U.V. craze and the feeding frenzy over organic food, and was the "trender" who spotted the nesting thing called cocooning! Think Home Depot, home delivery, and home office.

She was the first to spot that women craved treatment from major corporations commensurate with their spending clout—after all, 80 percent of the consumer goods in this country are bought by women! Her best-seller book on that topic, "EVEolution," was an eye opener to corporations like Ford, Kraft, MasterCard, and Wal-Mart, who hired Ms. Popcorn to improve their image with women.

As the key strategist for BrainReserve, Faith applies her "trend spotting" regarding cultural and business trends to help her clients reposition established brands, introduce new products, and define areas of new business opportunities. She is documented as having a 95 percent accuracy rate—an amazing record in the field of predicting.

She is also the author of "The Popcorn Report," published in 1991, which was based on the trends she had researched through the 1980s. Her current book, "The Dictionary of the Future," concerns itself with 21st century trends. She predicts the demise of dating and the rise of "DNA-ing," a process where potential mates compare compatibility via computer chip implants and being "DNA-ed." It is a euphemism for being dumped! This is just a sampling of what is in the book. Other fun definitions are "Bachelor Herds," young men left mate-less when older ones grab trophy wives, and "Baboons," baby boomers with no savings.

Sources:

Robin Finn, "The Future's Paying Off Nicely for a Trend-Spotter," *New York Times, Metro,* June 6, 2001, p. B2.

Hubert B. Herring, "Roll Over, Shakespeare, the Future of Jargon is Here," *New York Times, Markets & Investing,* January 2, 2002.

http://www.faithpopcorn.com/trends/trends.html 2002ll.

activities. Manufacturers must also understand how consumers are affected by economic factors.

Population

The majority of the population of the United States has some discretionary income and thus can influence the course of fashion. Two factors relating to population, however, have an important bearing on the extent of fashion demand:

1. The size of the total population and the rate of its growth
2. The age mix of the population and its projection into the future

Size of Population

The size of the population relates to the extent of current fashion demand. The rate of population growth suggests what tomorrow's market may become. In 1920, the United States had a population of about 106 million. By 1950, that figure had reached 151 million, and by 1980, 227.6 million. In 2000, the population reached 284.7 million, showing the largest increase in one decade in U.S. history. By 2010, U.S. population is estimated to reach 310,900,000![5]

Age Mix

The age mix and its projection into the future affect the characteristics of current fashion demand and suggest what they may be in the future. While the overall population continues to grow, the growth rate is not the same for all age groups or for both sexes. Since each group has its own special fashion interests, needs, and reactions, changes in the age mix serve as vital clues to future fashion demand.

For example, children born between 1946 and 1964 were known as the **baby boom generation**, because they were the largest group ever recorded. The first baby boomers reached 55 in 2000 and the largest and fastest growing age group in the United States was graying. They were followed by the much smaller "baby bust" or **generation X** group. This was in turn followed by the slightly larger "baby boomlet" or "echo-boom" group, known as **generation Y** (see Table 2.3).

TABLE 2.3 A Guide to the Generations

	TOTAL	POST BOOMLET 1995–2025	BABY BOOMLET 1977–94	BABY BUST 1965–76	BABY BOOM 1946–64	PRE-BOOM 1900–44
Age						
1995	—	—	under 19	19 to 30	31 to 49	50+
2005	—	*under 10*	*10 to 28*	*29 to 40*	*41 to 59*	*60+*
2015	—	*under 20*	*20 to 38*	*39 to 50*	*51 to 69*	*70+*
2025	—	*under 30*	*30 to 48*	*49 to 60*	*61 to 79*	*80+*
Number						
1995	262,754	—	72,176	44,602	77,587	68,389
2005	286,324	38,241	76,135	46,264	76,476	49,247
2015	330,376	82,280	73,126	46,788	72,744	30,430
2025	380,400	129,872	79,820	45,452	64,740	14,330
Percent						
1995	100	—	27.5	17.0	29.5	26.0
2005	*100*	*13.4*	*26.6*	*16.2*	*26.7*	*17.2*
2015	*100*	*26.5*	*25.2*	*15.1*	*23.4*	*9.8*
2025	*100*	*38.9*	*23.9*	*13.6*	*19.4*	*4.3*

Adapted from Diane Crispell, "Generations to 2025," *American Demographics*, p. 4. Reprinted from *American Demographics* magazine with permission. © American Demographics, Inc., Ithaca, New York.

Because both men and women are living longer, the over-age-65 group is steadily growing. Those 50 years old and older account for over one-half of all discretionary spending power. This mature group becomes increasingly important in the fashion world as their earlier retirement—and in many cases, increased retirement incomes—allows them to spend many active years wherever and however they choose. They are healthier, better educated, and more active and will live longer. Their interests and discretionary purchases vary radically from those of their younger counterparts, offering a real challenge to businesses to meet the demands of the "new old." The demand of older consumers for items such as package travel tours, cosmetic aids, and apparel that suits their ages and retirement lifestyles will offer growth opportunities for marketers, especially in fashion.

The Sociological Environment

To understand fashion, one needs to understand the sociological environment in which fashion trends begin, grow, and fade away. The famous stage and screen designer Cecil Beaton saw fashion as a social phenomenon that reflects "the same continuum of change that rides through any given age." Changes in fashion, Beaton emphasized, "correspond with the subtle and often hidden network of forces that operate on society . . . In this sense, fashion is a symbol."[6]

Simply stated, changes in fashion are caused by changes in the attitudes of consumers, which in turn are influenced by changes in the social patterns of the times (see Figure 2.4a–f). The key sociological factors influencing fashion today are leisure time, ethnic influences, status of women, social and physical mobility, instant communications, and wars, disasters, and crises.

Leisure Time

One of the most precious possessions of the average U.S. citizen today is leisure time, because it is also one of the most scarce. The demands of the workplace compete with the demands of family and home for much of people's waking hours, leaving less and less time for the pursuit of other activities, whether those activities be a fitness regimen, community work, entertainment, relaxation—or even shopping.

The ways in which people use their leisure time are as varied as people themselves. Some turn to active or spectator sports; others prefer to travel. Many seek self-improvement, while growing numbers improve their standard of living with a second job. The increased importance of leisure time has brought changes to people's lives in many ways—in values, standards of living, and scope of activities. As a result, whole new markets have sprung up. Demand for larger and more versatile wardrobes for the many activities consumers can now explore and enjoy has mushroomed.

Casual Living

A look into the closets of the American population would probably reveal one aspect that is much the same from coast to coast, in large cities and in small towns: Most would contain an unusually large selection of casual clothes and sportswear. The market for casual apparel developed with the growth of the suburbs in the 1950s, and has had a continuous series of boosts in the years since. The "do your own thing" revolution of the 1960s made a casual look for men and women acceptable in what had been more formal places and occasions. The 1970s saw a tremendous surge in the number of women wearing slacks and pantsuits and in the number of men and women wearing jeans just about everywhere.

Even with the return to more formal styles for many occasions in the 1980s, comfortable styling and casual influence continue to strongly influence dress in all segments of society. In the 1990s, "dress-down Fridays" at work became popular from coast to coast. The choice as to what is suitable for an activity is still largely left to the individual, and into the 2000s a shift in the direction of casual dress has begun a reverse trend as an interest in "dressing up" starts to grow again.

Active Sportswear

There is no doubt about it, the superstar of the fashion market in the 1970s, the 1980s, and the 1990s was sportswear. Its growth was phenomenal! While sports clothes have been around since the turn of the century, when they first appeared they were not particularly distinctive. Women's sport dresses for playing tennis or golf were not much different from their regular streetwear, and men's outfits similarly varied little from business suits. By the 1920s, consumers began demanding apparel that was appropriate for active sports or simply for re-

FIGURE 2.4

What a difference a decade makes! Swimsuits show this difference graphically: (a) the covered-up 20s, (b) the sturdy 30s, (c) the flirty 40s, (d) the wild 50s, (e) the "anything goes" 60s-90s, and (f) today back to covering it up!

(a)-(e) UPI Corbis-Bettmann. (f) Courtesy, Fairchild Publications, Inc.

laxing in the sunshine. But it is the emphasis on health and self in the past three decades that has caused the fantastic growth of the active sportswear market.

Today, sports-minded people play tennis in specially designed tennis fashions. Golfers want special golfwear. Joggers want only jogging outfits. And cyclists seem able to bike only in spandex biker shorts and high-tech helmets. Rollerbladers also want helmets, wrist and knee guards, and appropriate fashions. The same goes for ice-skaters, skiers, runners, hang gliders, sky divers, and climbers. Health clubs, exercise classes, and workout gyms exploded in popularity in the 1980s and a whole new and vast world of leotards, exercise suits, warm-up suits, and other self-improvement fashions and accessories were born. Whatever the activity, the specialized fashions—from jogging suits to biker shorts—quickly followed and became *de rigueur.* Today, even those who do not participate in a particular sport beyond watching the pros on television feel the need to look the part!

Ethnic Influences

In recent years, minority groups in the United States, representing over 30 percent of the nation's total population, have experienced vast population increases and sociological changes. The future holds even more change. By 2025, African Americans may slip from the largest minority group in the United States to the second largest. Hispanics outnumber African Americans, and Asians will exhibit a rapid rate of growth (see Figure 2.5). This historic shift in the racial and ethnic composition of the U.S. population will have many long-range implications. For example, the growth of the Hispanic and Asian populations has brought about an increased demand for clothing in smaller sizes because both men and women in these groups are typically smaller in stature than people whose ethnic heritage is Northern European.[7]

Racial and Ethnic Composition of the United States, 1999 and 2025

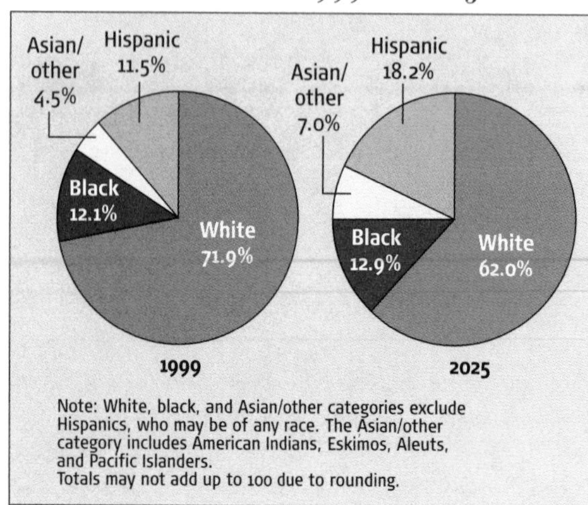

FIGURE 2.5
Projections show the proportion of the non-Hispanic white majority shrinking, the Hispanic population replacing African Americans as the largest minority, and the percentage of Asian Americans increasing at a fast rate.
Adapted from: http://www.ameristat.org/.

African Americans

At 12.3 percent of the population in 2000, African Americans were the largest minority in the United States, with a collective income of $543 billion.[8] They are better educated and hold higher-level jobs than they did in the past. With better education comes a stronger sense of oneself and one's heritage. Many black people show the pride they feel in their African heritage by wearing African styles, fabrics, and patterns. Other ethnic groups have adopted these styles as well. Fashion companies have acknowledged the changes that have occurred among the African American population and have reflected these changes in the products they market and the models they use. Cosmetics are available that emphasize rather than hide the beauty of dark skin. African-American men and women have become world famous modeling clothing and advertising various items in magazines and on television.

Hispanics

The Spanish-speaking market within the United States is growing so fast that market researchers cannot keep up with it. In 1987, there were an estimated 18 million Hispanics, or Latinos, as they are sometimes called, in the United States. In addition, six to ten million undocumented Hispanics were estimated to be here. By 2000, the documented Hispanic population of the United States had increased to 35.3 million. By 2005, Hispanics may become the largest minority group in the nation.[9] Today, the United States follows only Mexico, Spain, Colombia, and Argentina in Hispanic population. By the year 2020, the Hispanic population is expected to be 16 percent of the total U.S. population, or 50 million people.[10]

Until 1930, immigration to the United States was almost exclusively from Europe. For the next three decades, Latin Americans, mostly from Mexico and Puerto Rico, comprised 15 percent of the immigrants. By 1970, that portion had grown to 40 percent, with an influx of Central and South Americans. Since 1980, an estimated 153,000 Haitians and Cubans have also sought refuge in the United States.[11]

The Hispanic population has made its impact on the fashion scene with the introduction of fiery colors, and prints reminiscent of lush South American rainforests. Dance and music styles from mariochi to macarena, have been accepted by the entire American public.

Asians

Asian-Americans are the fastest growing minority group in the United States, with a population that has doubled since 1975. This population, about 10.9 million in 1999, will more than triple again by 2050. But Asian-Americans are not one homogeneous group. They come from more than a dozen countries and speak at least 41 different languages!

About two-thirds of Asians in the United States are recent immigrants and have different characteristics from second, third, and fourth generation U.S.-born Asian-Americans.[12] These refugees joined other Asians who were already part of our country: Chinese, Filipinos, Japanese, and Koreans.

Asians in the United States are more geographically concentrated than blacks or Hispanics. The states that account for roughly half of the Asian population are New York, California, and Hawaii.[13]

The end of the Vietnamese war and the influx of thousands of refugees from Cambodia and Vietnam brought additional traditions and costumes to be shared. This stimulated interest in some of the more exotic fashions of the East and in the everyday comfort of the Chinese sandal and quilted jacket.

Immigration from many Asian countries is up sharply. The number of Pakistanis and Bangladeshi is growing rapidly. But the largest numbers of immigrants have come from India. At a total of 1.7 million, the Asian Indian population in the United States has nearly doubled from 1990 to 2000, fueled by the high demand for high-tech work, as well as an increase in the number of immigrants.[14]

Most Asian Indians who came to the United States in the 1980s were affluent; 30 percent of those in the workforce were in professions, as opposed to 13 percent of all U.S. employees.[15] As with most recent immigrant groups, Asian-Americans tend to live in and around major cities, like New York, Chicago, and Los Angeles.

Status of Women

In the early 1900s, the American woman was, in many ways, a nonperson. She could not vote, serve on a jury, earn a living at any but a few occupations, own property, or enter public places unescorted. She passed directly from her father's control to her husband's control, without rights or monies. In both households, she dressed to please the man and reflect his status.

Profound changes began to occur during World War I and have accelerated ever since. The most dramatic advances have happened since the mid-1960s and the advent of the women's movement. Women's demands for equal opportunity, equal pay, and equal rights in every facet of life continue to bring about even more change. These changes have affected not only fashion but the entire field of marketing.

Jobs and Money

The number of women aged 20 and over who work has increased dramatically since 1975. This represents a staggering increase of over 15 million women who have entered the workforce since 1975. This figure has doubled, despite the fact that women's salaries are still, on average only 73 percent of men's salaries (see Figure 2.6a). Both financial pressures and career satisfaction should keep the number of working women growing.[16] As of 2000, roughly 60 percent of all women were working, and a growing number of women continue to enter the workforce each year (see Figure 2.6b).

The dramatic increase in working women has led to a surge in fashion interest, because a woman who works is continuously exposed to fashion. It is everywhere around her as she meets people, shops during her lunch hour, or is on her way home. As a member of the workforce, she now has the incentive, the opportunity, and the means to respond to fashion's appeal. Magazines such as *Ms.* and *Working Woman* make this market reachable.

Finally, women in general today have more money of their own to spend as they see fit. Approximately four women in every six have incomes, earned and unearned, of their own. These women and their acceptance or rejection of offered styles have new importance in the fashion marketplace.

Education

Often the better educated a woman becomes, the more willing she is to learn new things. She is also more willing to try new fashions, which of course serves to accelerate fashion change. And with more women today receiving more education than ever before, the repercussions on fashion are unmistakable. Today's educated women have had wider exposure than their mothers or grandmothers to other cultures and to people of different backgrounds. Consequently, they are more worldly, more discerning, more demanding, and more confident in their taste and feel for fashion.

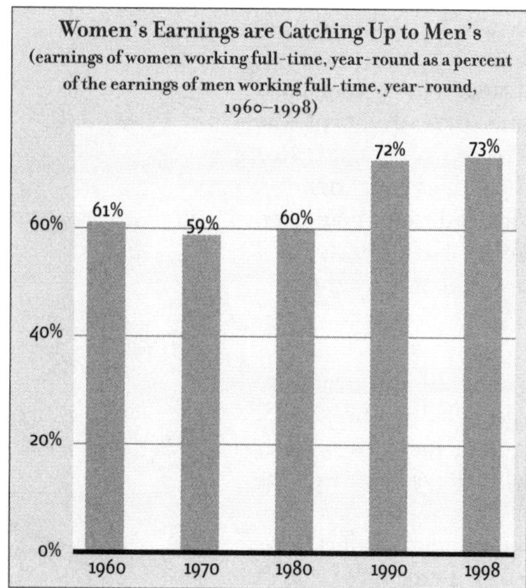

FIGURE 2.6A
The earnings of women working full-time has increased, and statistics show they are catching up to the yearly wages of men. By 1998, women had earned 73 percent as much as men, and this number is still growing today.
Source: Demographics of the U.S.: Trends and Projections.

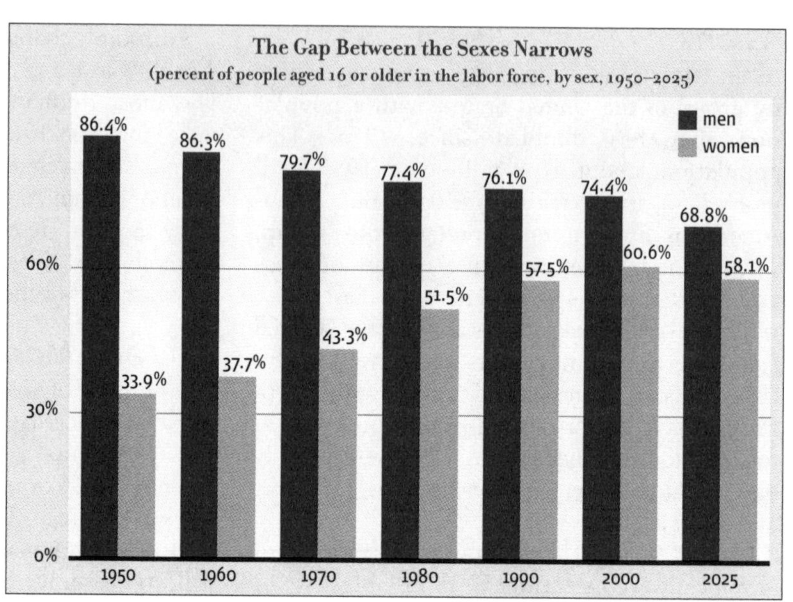

FIGURE 2.6B
The labor force has changed drastically since 1950, and the gap between the sexes is projected to narrow even further as of 2025.
Source: Demographics of the U.S.: Trends and Projections.

No wonder Edward Sapir, a leading social scientist, considered education a major factor in fashion change. "Fashion is custom in the guise of departure from custom," said Sapir.[17] To him, fashion is a resolution of the conflict between people's revolt against adherence to custom and their reluctance to appear lacking in good taste.

Social Freedom

Perhaps the most marked change in the status of women since the early 1900s is the degree of social freedom they now enjoy. Young women today are free to apply for a job, and to earn, spend, and save their own money. They are free to go unescorted to a restaurant, theater, or other public place. Women travel more frequently than they did in the past. They travel to more distant locations at a younger age and often alone. Many own their own cars. If they can afford it, they may maintain an apartment or share one with others. It is difficult to imagine that the social freedoms and responsibilities that today's young women accept as normal were considered unfeminine or outrageous as recently as 30 years ago.

Short skirts, popular in the 1920s, the early 1940s, the 1960s, and the 2000s are commonly interpreted as a reflection of women's freedom. So, too, is the simplicity of the styles that prevailed in those periods: chemises, sacks, tents, shifts, other variations of loose-hanging dresses, and pants.

Different theories exist about why these changes came about. Some people believe that stiff, unyielding corsets went out with a stiff, unyielding moral code. Others believe that the changes had no particular social significance. They believe that women rejected inflexible corsets not because of a change in the moral code, but because the new materials were simply more comfortable. Similarly, pants may be viewed as an expression of women's freedom or merely as suitable garments for hopping in and out of the indispensable car.

Whatever the reasons, the lifestyles of American women, and their opinions and attitudes about fashion, have changed radically in the past three decades. American women have gained hard-won freedoms in their social and business lives. They are just as definite about their freedom of choice in fashion. The thought of today's independent women accepting uncomfortable and constricting clothing or shoes just to follow the dictates of some fashion arbiter, as they did years ago, is ludicrous. Today's busy, active women, whether at home or at the office, have very carefully defined preferences for fashions that suit their own individual needs and comfort. Today's successful designers recognize these preferences and make sure that their drawing boards reflect them.

Social Mobility

Almost all societies have classes, and individuals choose either to stand out from or to conform to their actual or aspired-to class. Bell viewed fashion as the process "whereby members of one class imitate those of another, who, in turn, are driven to ever new expedients of fashionable change."[18]

Bell considered the history of fashion inexplicable without relating it to social classes. He is not alone in his thinking. Other sociologists have related fashion change to changes in social mobility and to the effort to associate with a higher class by imitation.

The United States is sometimes called a classless society, but this is valid only in that there are no hereditary ranks, royalty, or untouchables. Classes do exist, but they are based largely upon occupation, income, residential location, education, or avocation, and their boundaries have become increasingly fluid. They range from the immensely wealthy (self-made millionaires or their descendants—the Vanderbilts, Whitneys, and Rockefellers, for example) at the top through the very wealthy (mostly nouveau riche) through the many middle-income levels and finally to the low-income and poverty levels. At the very bottom are the so-called hardcore unemployed and the homeless (see Table 2.4).

TABLE 2.4 The Six Major Social Classes in the United States

SOCIAL CLASS	CHARACTERISTICS
Upper-upper	These are the people in an area who represent"old families," who are locally prominent, and whose wealth is inherited. Such people usually occupy an old mansion and may have homes in other places. They are deeply interested in cultural events, usually travel extensively, serve on boards of charitable foundations, and are secure in their social position.
Lower-upper	The nouveau riches of the community constitute this class. Their wealth is not usually inherited but has been acquired by aggressive entrepreneurial activities. These people enjoy spending the wealth they have acquired, like publicity, and want to be seen at important events. They seek the news in purchases and lifestyles.
Upper-middle	These are moderately successful doctors, lawyers, or other professional people, or owners of medium-sized businesses, or middle managers in large firms. They are concerned with status, live well, are usually substantial members of their communities, and have an enormous drive for success.
Lower-middle	To this group belongs the large segment of people who teach, work in offices, are small-business owners, successful salespeople, and blue-collar workers with good jobs. As a group, these people strive for success, are relatively conservative and respectable, either own their own homes or aspire to do so, and contribute to the overall stability of the country.
Upper-lower	People with limited education who may have fairly substantial incomes that are derived from semiskilled work or from work in small factories or retail shops, from jobs as police personnel, fire department employees, or sanitation workers, or from work as office clericals are classified in this group. These people often live from day to day, enjoy spending money (easy come, easy go), attend sporting events, and hang out at neighborhood recreation areas.
Lower-lower	This group comprises unskilled, uneducated, unemployed, and unassimilated people who are very poor, often on welfare, and sometimes even homeless.

Source: Based on W. Lloyd Warner, Marchia Meeker, Kenneth Eells, *Social Class in America* (Chicago: Science Research Associates, 1949).

Middle-Class Influence

Most fashion authorities agree that there is a direct relationship between the growth and strength of the middle class and the growth and strength of fashion demand. The middle class has the highest physical, social, and financial mobility. Because it is the largest class, it has the majority vote in the adoption of fashions. Members of the middle class tend to be followers, not leaders, of fashion, but the strength of their following pumps money into the fashion industry. And the persistence of their following often spurs fashion leaders to seek newer and different fashions of their own.

The United States has a very large middle class—roughly the middle 60 percent of U.S. households as ranked by their income.[19] They have both fashion interest and the money to indulge it. Despite fluctuations in the economy, this growth generally means a widespread increase in consumer buying power, which in turn generates increased fashion demand.

Physical Mobility

Physical mobility, like social mobility, encourages the demand for and response to fashion. One effect of travel is "cross-pollination" of cultures. After seeing how other people live, travelers bring home a desire to adopt or adapt some of what they observed and make it part of their environment (see Figure 2.7a and b).

Thus Marco Polo brought gunpowder, silks, and spices from the Orient, introducing new products to medieval Europe. In the 19th century, travelers brought touches of Asian and African fashions to Western dress and home furnishings. In the 20th century, Latin American and pre-Columbian influences were introduced into North America, dramatically changing the direction and emphasis of fashion in this country.

In the United States, people enjoy several kinds of physical mobility. For example, the daily routine for many people involves driving to work or to a shopping center, often in a different city. Among the broad range of influences they are exposed to during their daily trips are the fashions of others and the fashion offerings of retail distributors.

A second form of physical mobility popular among Americans is vacation travel. Whether travelers are going to a nearby lake or around the world, each trip exposes them to many different fashion influences and each trip itself demands special fashions. Living out of a suitcase for a few days or a few months requires clothes that are easy to pack, wrinkle-resistant, suitable for a variety of occasions, and easy to keep in order.

A third form of physical mobility is change of residence, which, like travel, exposes an individual to new contacts, new environments, and new fashion influences. Record unemployment figures caused shifts in population in the 1980s, 1990s, and 2000s in many parts of the United States.

Faster Communications

Related to physical mobility is faster communications. Not many years ago, news of every sort traveled more slowly. This meant that life moved more slowly and fashions changed more slowly. It took weeks or months for people in one section of the country to learn what was being worn in another part of the country. Fashion trends moved at a pace that was as leisurely as the news.

Our electronic age has changed all that. Today, we enjoy rapid communication in ever-increasing quantities and infinite varieties. By means of satellites and round-the-clock broadcasting, television brings the world to our homes. Thus, it has become a most important medium for transmitting fashion information. Famous designers create special costumes for stars, and we all take note. Changes in the dress and hairstyles of our favorite newscasters, talk-show personalities, series characters, and even sports stars have a great impact on us. For instance, in the mid-1990s, the hip-hop look swept the country, as teenagers and young adults tried to emulate the style of their favorite rap stars.

Popular movies also influence fashion. Back in 1983, *Flashdance* caught the fancy of millions of young people. Soon the one-bare-shoulder look was seen everywhere. A few years later, *Top Gun* and its star Tom Cruise helped to popularize aviator-style sunglasses. Film after film shows sophisticated young stars surrounded by high-tech paraphernalia like cell phones, headsets, and high-powered computers, cruising the Internet at warp speed.

At the same time, a continuing enthusiasm for exercise has kept interest in fashions for fitness high. The support of major celebrities in this area influences the public as well. For instance, Jane Fonda has devoted ongoing pro-

A

B

FIGURE 2.7
The ease of travel and communication in the modern world have brought fashion influences from one corner of the globe to another.(a) In India, political figure Sonia Gandhi and daughter Pyriyanka are dressed in the traditional sari. (b) Cheri Blair, wife of British Prime Minister Tony Blair, wore a sari when they visited India.
(a) Magnum Photos © Raghu Rai. (b) Courtesy, Fairchild Publications, Inc.

motion to her enormously popular workout program through exercise studios, a book, and a number of videocassettes. Today, the famous model Christy Turlington's Nuala yoga line is contributing to the appeal of being healthy and fit. Other celebrities, such as Cher and Suzanne Somers enhanced the appeal of exercise equipment and apparel by acting as spokespeople in "infomercials" (program-length advertising on television). While television informs us about fashion on a national and international scale, radio also has a valuable place. Radio is an excellent medium through which local merchants can inform their audiences of special fashion events.

War, Disaster, and Crisis

War, widespread disaster, and crisis shake people's lives and focus attention on ideas, events, and places that may be completely new. People develop a need for fashions that are compatible with changes in their attitudes and also changes in their environment.

Such changes took place in women's activities and in fashions as a result of the two world wars. World War I brought women into the business world in significant numbers and encouraged their desire for independence and suffrage. It gave them a reason to demand styles that allowed freer physical movement. World War II drew women into such traditionally masculine jobs as riveting, for which they previously had not been considered strong enough. It put them in war plants on night shifts. It even brought women other than nurses into the military services for the first time in the country's history. All these changes gave rise to women's fashions previously considered appropriate only for men, such as slacks, sport shirts, and jeans.

The Depression of the 1930s was a widespread disaster with a different effect on fashions. Because jobs were scarce, considerably fewer were offered to women than had been before. Women returned to the home and adopted more feminine clothes. And because money also was scarce, wardrobes became skimpier. A single style often served a large number of occasions. Women who did hold jobs felt pressure to look younger so they could compete with younger applicants. This encouraged an increased use of lipstick and cosmetics.

Then & Now

Matinee Idols

Since Rudolph Valentino tangoed his way across movie screens in the 1920s, male movie stars have been role models for boys and men, made fashion statements, typified suavity or rebellion, and raised havoc in feminine hearts. As they reflect their times, they influence us across the decades, forever preserved on film.

Cary Grant.
Courtesy, The Kobal Collection.

James Dean.
Courtesy, The Kobal Collection.

Sidney Poitier.
Cinerama Releasing Corporation. Courtesy, The Kobal Collection.

George Clooney.
Courtesy, The Kobal Collection.

Leonardo DiCaprio.
Photographer: John Clifford/NewLine. Courtesy, The Kobal Collection.

Denzel Washington.
Courtesy, The Kobal Collection.

Even disruptions of lesser magnitude than war or economic depression can bring about a fashion trend. For example, in response to a transit strike in New York in 1981, businesspeople wore athletic shoes on their way to and from their offices because many of them had to walk great distances to reach alternative forms of transportation. Even after the strike was settled, the combination of athletic footwear and business suits remained a common sight on the streets of New York—and other cities as well. Perhaps the growing interest in physical fitness and the realization that walking provides good exercise helped to keep the trend alive. In the late 1970s and early 1980s, a combination of the energy crisis and exceptionally cold weather brought a mass of warm clothing to the marketplace. Thermal underwear, formerly seen only in sporting goods catalogs, was featured in department and specialty shops. Retailers stocked up on sweaters, tights, boots, mittens, leg warmers, scarfs, coats, jackets, and vests with down fill. Not only the Northeast and West but the normally temperate Sun Belt was struck by bitter-cold weather. Again in 1995, 1997, and 2003, record-breaking cold and unfamiliar snow and sleet created demand for warm clothing in areas formerly not interested in such apparel.

In the early 1990s, the rapid success of the U.S. forces in Operation Desert Storm led to young men wearing army fatigues as leisure wear on the street—whether they had military status or not. More recently, fashion worldwide reacted to the terrorist attacks on the United States in 2001. Many designers began to calm down and the idea of comfort clothing resurfaced. Anything that suggested urban aggression was wiped away, and new roomy corduroys and bright sweaters by designers like Dolce & Gabbana and Versace became popular, not to mention the emergence of a simple, classic style, soothed the uncertainties of war.

The Psychological Environment

"Fashion promises many things to many people," according to economist Dr. Rachel Dardis. "It can be and is used to attract others, to indicate success, both social and economic, to indicate leadership, and to identify with a particular social group."[20] Fashion interest and demand at any given time may rely heavily on prevailing psychological attitudes (see Figure 2.8).

The five basic psychological factors that influence fashion demand are boredom, curiosity, reaction to convention, need for self-assurance, and desire for companionship.[21] These factors motivate a large share of people's actions and reactions.

- *Boredom.* People tend to become bored with fashions too long in use. Boredom leads to restlessness and a desire for change. In fashion, the desire for change expresses itself in a demand for something new and satisfyingly different from what one already has.
- *Curiosity.* Curiosity causes interest in change for its own sake. Highly curious people like to experiment; they want to know what is around the next corner. There is curiosity in everyone, though some may respond to it less dramatically than others. Curiosity and the need to experiment keep fashion demand alive.
- *Reaction to Convention.* One of the most important psychological factors influencing fashion demand is the reaction to convention. People's reactions take one of two forms: rebellion against convention or adherence to it. Rebellion against convention is characteristic of young people. This involves more than boredom or curiosity: It is a positive rejection of what exists and a search for something new. However, acceptance by the majority is an important part of the definition of fashion. The majority tends to adhere to convention, either within its own group or class or in general.
- *Need for Self-Assurance.* The need for self-assurance or confidence is a human characteristic that gives impetus to fashion demand. Often the need to overcome feelings of inferiority or of disappointment can be satisfied through apparel. People who consider themselves to be fashionably dressed have an armor that gives them self-assurance. Those who know that their clothes are dated are at a psychological disadvantage.
- *Desire for Companionship.* The desire for companionship is fundamental in human beings. The instinct for survival of the species drives individuals to seek a mate.

FIGURE 2.8
Outrageous hairstyles and fashion trends can be created based on a person's attitude and their surroundings.
Courtesy, Fairchild Publications, Inc.

Humans' innate gregariousness also encourages them to seek companions. Fashion plays its part in the search for all kinds of companionship. In its broader sense, companionship implies the formation of groups, which require conformity in dress as well as in other respects. Flamboyant or subdued, a person's mode of dress can be a bid for companionship as well as the symbol of acceptance within a particular group.

SUMMARY AND REVIEW

Fashion marketers determine their customers' wants and needs by examining various market segments, identified by geographics, demographics, psychographics, and behavior. Each marketer identifies the group or groups within the general population that are its target customer. Determining the average customer's personal income helps marketers make pricing decisions and estimate sales, especially when population trends are matched with income figures. For example, businesses that target middle-age and retirement-age consumers know that their customers are increasing in number and that the average income for consumers in these age groups is also increasing. The teenage and young adult markets are a smaller portion of the population than they were earlier in the century, but they are an influential market segment, often spending their discretionary income on fashion merchandise. The growing value placed on leisure time and leisure-time activities has increased the market for casual clothing and active sportswear.

Marketers also track trends in the population of targeted ethnic groups. Changing patterns of immigration bring with them new influences from different parts of the world. The Hispanic market is projected to become the largest ethnic minority in the United States in the 21st century, superseding the African-American market in size. The Asian-American market is the fastest growing minority. The non-Hispanic Caucasian population is expected to remain the majority, but by a reduced percentage.

The role of women in society changed dramatically in the 20th century, and their increased freedom, better education, and growing presence in the labor force increased their average income and changed their buying habits.

Other social forces that affect business include greater mobility and more rapid communication, which bring individuals wider choices in their purchases. Political, economic, and natural upheavals also affect fashion marketing, often leading to trends that last beyond the crisis. As consumers become more knowledgeable about their growing choices in their buying behavior, marketers are paying more attention to psychographic factors as they attempt to identify and meet the demands of their target customers.

Trade Talk

Define or briefly explain the following terms.

baby boom generation	GeoVALS
behavior	inflation
demographics	market segmentation
discretionary income	market segments
disposable personal income	per capita personal income
environment	personal income
generation X	psychographics
generation Y	purchasing power
Geographics	recession
	target market

For Review

1. Name the four major environmental influences on fashion interest and demand in any era.
2. Market segmentation is vitally important to producers and retailers of fashion merchandise. Explain why, giving at least two examples of how such information could be used by the fashion industry.
3. How does the size and age mix of a population affect current fashion demand? What does information about size and age mix today tell us about the future of fashion demand?
4. In what ways has increased availability of leisure time affected the fashion market?
5. How has the changing status of ethnic groups affected fashion interest and demand? Cite at least two examples.
6. How does a higher level of education affect fashion interest and demand?
7. What is social mobility? How does the degree of social mobility affect fashion interest and demand? Illustrate your answer with examples.
8. Upon what factors are classes in the United States usually based? Why is it more difficult to identify an individual's social class in this country than it is in other countries?
9. Describe three kinds of physical mobility that people in the United States enjoy today, explaining how each influences fashion demand.
10. Five basic psychological factors motivate much of human behavior. List them, explaining how each affects fashion interest and demand.

For Discussion

1. Is discretionary income or disposable personal income the more significant figure to fashion producers and marketers? Why?
2. Discuss the similarities and differences between the GeoVALS and PRIZM 2 systems.
3. How has the status of women changed during the 20th century? How have these changes affected fashion interest and demand?

References

1. Michael Weiss, *The Clustered World,* (New York: Little Brown and Co.), 2000, c.1.
2. Quentin Bell, *On Human Finery* (London: The Hogarth Press, Ltd., 1947), p. 72.
3. Editorial, "The Great Money Grab," *American Demographics*, January 1995, p. 2.
4. *Webster's Tenth New Collegiate Dictionary* (Springfield, MA: Merriam-Webster, Inc., 1998).
5. Population Estimates Program, Population Division, 1999-2010, U.S. Bureau of The Census, Washington D.C. 20233, release date January 13, 2000.
6. Cecil Beaton, *The Glass of Fashion* (New York: Doubleday & Company, Inc., 1954), pp. 335, 379–381.
7. Jennifer Steinhauer, "A Minority Market With Major Sales," *New York Times*, July 2, 1997, p. D-1.
8. Linda S. Wallace, "As Income Rises, African Americans Go on High Tech Buying Binge," www.Diversity.com, September 13, 2001.
9. U.S. Census Bureau, "Census Bureau Projects Doubling of Nation's Population," United States of Commerce News, Washington D.C., January 13, 2000.
10. Ibid.
11. Carol J. DeVita, Population Bulletin, "The United States at Mid-Decade."
12. John Nasbitt's Trend Letter, September 12, 1996, p. 2.
13. William Frey, "Census 2000," American Demographics, June 2001.
14. Aseem Chhabra, "Asian Indian Population Doubles in a Decade," The Rediff US Special Online, May 16, 2001.
15. Marcia Mogelonsky, "Asian-Indian American," American Demographics, August 1995, p. 34.
16. Demographics of the U.S.: Trends and Projections, Labor Force, 1999.
17. Edward Sapir, "Fashion," *Encyclopedia of the Social Sciences*, vol. VI (London: Macmillan & Co. 1931), p. 140.
18. Bell, *On Human Finery*, p. 72.
19. Editorial, "The Great Money Grab," p. 2.
20. Rachel Dardis, "The Power of Fashion," *Proceedings of the Twentieth Annual Conference, College Teachers of Textiles and Clothing*, Eastern Region, New York, 1966, pp. 16–17.
21. Paul H. Nystrom, *Economics of Fashion* (New York: The Ronald Press, 1928), pp. 66–81.

CHAPTER 3

The Movement of Fashion

WHAT'S IN IT FOR YOU?

Everything you always wanted to know about the theories, and identifications of the movement of fashion.

Key Concepts:

- Factors influencing the movement of fashion
- Predicting the movement of fashion
- Theories of fashion adoption
- Identifying fashion leaders and fashion followers

Fashion is, in many ways, like a river. A river is always in motion, continuously flowing—sometimes it is slow and gentle, at other times rushing and turbulent. It is exciting, and never the same. It affects those who ride its currents and those who rest on its shores. Its movements depend on the environment.

All of this is true of fashion, too. The constant movements of fashion depend on an environment made up of social, political, and economic factors. These movements, no matter how obvious or how slight, have both meaning and definite direction. There is a special excitement to interpreting these movements and estimating their speed and direction. Everyone involved in fashion, from the designer to the consumer, is caught up in the movement of fashion.

The excitement starts with the textile producers. Fully 12 to 18 months before they offer their lines to manufacturers, the textile people must choose their designs, textures, and colors. From three to nine months before showing a line to buyers, the apparel manufacturers begin deciding which styles they will produce and in which fabrics. Then, two to six months before the fashions will appear on the selling floor, the retail buyers make their selections from the manufacturers' lines. Finally, the excitement passes on to the consumers, as they select the garments that will be versatile, appropriate, and suitably priced for their individual needs and wants.

How can all these people be sure their choices are based on reliable predictions? Successful designers, manufacturers, buyers, and consumers have a good understanding of basic cycles, principles, and patterns that operate in the world of fashion. Their predictions are based on this understanding.

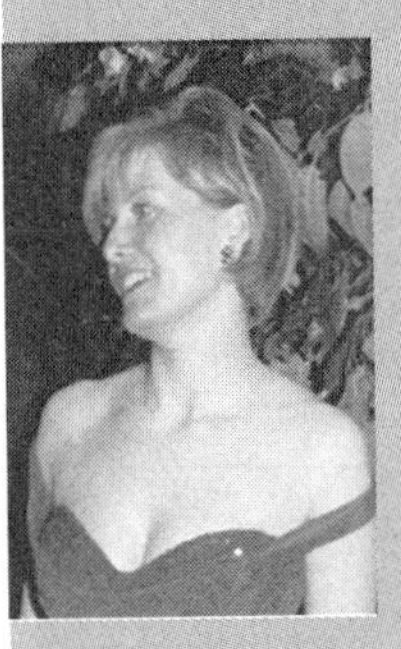

Factors Influencing Fashion Movement

At the beginning of this chapter, the movement of fashion was likened to the movement of a river. As James Laver said, in comparing the fashion cycle to a force of nature, "Nothing seems to be able to turn it back until it has spent itself, until it has provoked a reaction by its very excess."[1] However, just as a river can swell to turbulent flood stage or be slowed or diverted by a dam, so the movement of fashion can be accelerated or retarded by a variety of factors.

Accelerating Factors

There are seven general factors that speed up fashion cycles. These influences are, themselves, ever growing and accelerating in the 21st century as the pace of life becomes more and more rapid and geographically all-encompassing. The accelerating factors are:

- Widespread buying power
- Leisure time
- More education
- Improved status of women
- Technological advances
- Sales promotion
- Seasonal change

Widespread Buying Power

Widely diffused discretionary income means there are more people with the financial means to respond to a fashion change. The more consumers flock to a new fashion, the sooner it will reach its culmination. The more widespread the financial ability of consumers to turn to yet a newer fashion, the sooner the current fashion will plunge into obsolescence.

Leisure Time

In the past, long hours of work and little leisure permitted scant attention to fashion for the great majority of the population. More leisure time usually means more time to buy and enjoy fashion of many kinds. Since 1900, decreases in working hours and increases in paid vacations have encouraged more use of at-home wear, casual clothes, sports apparel, travel clothes, and different types of ordinary business dress. Increased purchases of these types of apparel give impetus to their fashion cycles.

One result of today's frantic pace has been the return to catalog buying and the emergence of other forms of nonstore retailing. Catalog buying originally evolved because people in farming societies lived far from stores and had little leisure time for shopping. Today's leisure time has allowed people to add new physical and mental activities to their lives, such as sports and hobbies, leaving little time for shopping once again. Realizing that their customers are using leisure time in other pursuits, retailers are bringing shopping into the consumers' homes with catalogs, cable TV shopping channels, and Web sites on the Internet. Consumers can browse at any time of day, and with customer service telephone lines and computer connections available all day, every day, customers can place their orders whenever they wish.

More Education

The increasingly higher level of education in the United States helps to speed up fashion cycles in two ways. First, more people's horizons have been broadened to include new interests and new wants. And second, more people are equipped by education to earn the money to satisfy those wants. These two factors provide significant impetus to the adoption of new fashions.

Improved Status of Women

In a society with few artificial social barriers, women with discretionary income can spend it as they choose. No law or custom prevents any woman from buying the newest and most prestigious styles in dresses, hats, or shoes if she can afford to—thus giving impetus to a fashion cycle in its earliest phases. Sex discrimination in the job market has steadily decreased, and social acceptance of women who manage both homes and jobs has steadily increased. As a result, today's women have more discretionary income and are influencing the speed of fashion cycles in the way they use that income.

Technological Advances

Today we live in an "instant" world. The stunning advances in technology in almost every area have put us in immediate possession of facts, fantasies, and fashions. We see news as it happens around the world. Goods are sped to retail stores by land, air, and sea more rapidly than would have been dreamed of just a few decades ago.

New fibers, finishes, and materials with improved qualities are constantly being developed. Computer technology has improved

FIGURE 3.1
Sometimes accelerating factors combine. Here the latest technology and sales promotion produce a Web site home page for Nicole Miller.
Courtesy, Nicole Miller.

production techniques and statistical control and analysis for more efficient product marketing. The result has been control of price increases, and in many cases, reduced prices on fashion goods. All of these technological advances combine to make goods available almost at the instant that the consumer is psychologically and financially ready to buy. Thus, the cycle of fashion becomes more and more accelerated.

Sales Promotion

The impact of sales promotion is felt everywhere in the fashion world today. Magazines, television, newspapers, billboards, and direct mail all expose the public to new fashions in a never-ending procession. While there is no way to force consumers to accept new fashions, nor any way to save a fashion if consumers reject it, sales promotion can greatly influence a fashion's success by telling people it exists. Sales promotion can help to speed up acceptance of a new fashion or sometimes extend its peak or duration. Promotion, therefore, can frequently help a fashion reach its culmination more speedily (see Figure 3.1).

Seasonal Change

Nothing is so consistent in bringing about change in fashions as the calendar. As the seasons change, so do consumer demands. After months of winter, people want to shed their heavy clothing for lightweight spring and summer fashions. In climates where there are radical seasonal changes, this is only natural, even though our homes, schools, cars, and places of business are kept at desired temperatures through central heating and air conditioning. However, even in areas such as Florida and Hawaii, where the weather is moderate year-round, people change their wardrobes with the seasons. Even if the 21st century brings complete climate control, people will never accept the boredom of a year-round wardrobe.

Because people today are so geared to travel at all times of the year to all types of climates, the seasonal changes are accelerated and a kind of preseason testing can go on. Resort wear appears in retail stores in time for selection by the public for winter vacations in tropical areas. The late-June appearance of the first fall fashions in leading stores makes it possible for the style-conscious to make their selections well in advance of the first cold wind. Consumer responses to these early offerings allow manufacturers and retailers alike to know what does and does not appeal.

Retarding Factors

Factors that retard the development of fashion cycles either discourage people from adopting incoming styles or encourage them to continue using styles that might be considered on the decline. Retarding factors include the opposites of the accelerating factors; for example, decreased buying power during recessionary periods. Major retarding factors are habit and custom, religion and sumptuary laws, the nature of the merchandise, and reductions in consumers' buying power.

Habit and Custom

By slowing acceptance of new styles and prolonging the life-spans of those already accepted, habit and custom exert a braking effect on fashion movement. Habit slows the adoption of new skirt lengths, silhouettes, necklines, or colors whenever shoppers unconsciously select styles that do not differ perceptibly from those they already own. It is easy for an individual to let habit take over, and some consumers are more susceptible to this tendency than others. Their loyalty to an established style is less a matter of fashion judgment than a natural attraction to the more familiar.

Custom slows progress in the fashion cycle by permitting vestiges of past fashions, status symbols, taboos, or special needs to continue to appear in modern dress. Custom is responsible for such details as buttons on the sleeves of men's suits, vents in men's jackets, and the sharp creases down the front of men's trousers. Custom usually requires a degree of formality in dress for religious services. The trend toward similarity of dress for men and women in the United States has permitted women to wear trousers, but custom still discourages men from wearing skirts.

A classic example of the influence of custom is the placement of buttons. They are on the right side for men, originating with the need to have the weapon arm available while dressing and undressing. And they are on the left for women, who tend to hold babies on that side and can more conveniently use the right hand for buttons. The stitching on the backs of gloves is another example; it dates back to a time when sizes were adjusted by lacing at these points.

Religion

Historically, religious leaders have championed custom, and their ceremonial apparel has demonstrated their respect for the old ways. In the past, religious leaders tended to associate fashion with temptation and urged their followers to turn their backs on both. Religion today, however, exerts much less of a restraining influence on fashion. Examples of the new relaxation may be found in the modernization of women's dress in most religious orders and in the fact that most women no longer consider a hat obligatory when in church.

In the 1970s and 1980s, a countertrend arose to religion's diminishing impact on fashion. It is particularly evident in the dress adopted by the young followers of Hare Krishna and in the adoption of ancient dress in countries ruled by religious fundamentalists, such as Afghanistan and Iran. In both cases, the religious leaders of these movements have decreed that modern fashions lead to temptation and corruption.

Sumptuary Laws

Sumptuary laws regulate what we can and cannot purchase. Today, there are sumptuary laws that, for example, require that children's sleepwear be flame-retardant. In the past, sumptuary laws have regulated extravagance and luxury in dress on religious or moral grounds. Height of headdress, length of train, width of sleeve, value and weight of material, and color of dress have all at times been restricted by law to specific classes. Such laws were aimed at keeping each class in its place in a rigidly stratified society.[2]

Other laws, such as those of the Puritans, attempted to enforce a general high-mindedness by condemning frippery. An order passed in 1638 by the General Court of Massachusetts stated:

No garment shall be made with short sleeves, and such as have garments already made with short sleeves shall not wear same unless they cover the arm to the wrist; and hereafter no person whatever shall make any garment for women with sleeves more than half an ell wide.[3]

And in the 18th century, a bill was proposed (but rejected) that stated:

All women of whatever age, rank, profession, or degree, whether virgin, maid, or widow, that shall impose upon, seduce, and betray into matrimony any of His Majesty's subjects by scents, paints, cosmetic washes, artificial teeth, false hair, Spanish wool, iron stays, hoops, high-heeled shoes, or bolstered hips, shall incur the penalty of the law now in force against witchcraft and the like demeanours, and that marriage, upon conviction, shall stand null and void.[4]

People have a way of ignoring local ordinances, however, if they conflict with a fashion cycle that is gathering strength. In New York in the 1930s, fines could be imposed on individuals who appeared on the streets wearing shorts, or whose bathing-suit shoulder straps were not in place on public beaches. What was considered indecent exposure then—shorts and strapless bathing suits—is commonplace today. More recently, the mid-1990s saw a dramatic change in school dress codes, in reaction to the laxity of the 1980s "anything goes" dress codes. Many private schools, of course, had maintained strict requirements in regard to acceptable dress through the turbulent late 1960s, 1970s, and 1980s.

FIGURE 3.2
Until the 1930s, modesty prevented Chinese women from undressing for medical examinations. They used figures such as this to indicate where they were feeling pain.
Courtesy, The Museum of Jewelry, San Francisco, California.

School uniforms in public schools were common before the 1960s, however they were largely abandoned in the free-spiritedness of that decade. However, in the 1990s, when school violence and classroom disruption increased across the country, uniforms became popular once again. In his State of the Union address in 1996, President Bill Clinton endorsed uniforms as a way to keep kids "from killing each other over designer jackets."

People in favor of uniforms argued that they would promote a sense of discipline and belonging, and serve as a concrete and visual means of restoring order to the classroom. Sales of school uniforms rose 22 percent, from $900 million in 1999 to 1.1 billion in 2000. Again today there are questions about whether uniforms are such a great idea. The strongest opposition to uniforms comes from two camps: civil libertarians and older students. Civil libertarians argue that uniforms violate students' free expression rights, while students resent the fact that uniforms make all students look alike.[5]

Nature of the Merchandise

Not all merchandise moves at the same pace through a fashion cycle. Often the very nature of the merchandise is responsible for the rate of movement. Over the years it has been accepted as normal that men's fashion cycles move more slowly than women's. In recent years, however, the changing lifestyles of the male population have resulted in accelerating men's wear cycles. Women's apparel generally moves in slower cycles than accessories, though some accessories now have full-run cycles comparable to those of apparel.

Reductions in Consumers' Buying Power

Consumers' buying power has a powerful effect on the movement of fashion cycles. When buying power increases, fashion cycles often speed up. Decreased buying power, conversely, can retard the movement of fashion cycles. During economic recessions and resultant high unemployment, consumers' buying power is sharply reduced. Many people make do with clothes they have, buying only necessities. A similar caution is shown by consumers affected by strikes, inflation, high taxes, or interest rates. All these factors have a slowing influence on fashion cycles. The poorer people are, the less impact they have on fashion's movements. They become bystanders in matters of fashion, and as a result do not keep cycles moving. Laver emphasized the importance of buying power when he said that nothing except poverty can make a style permanent.[6]

Recurring Fashions

In the study of fashion history, we see that styles reoccur, with adaptations that suit the times in which they reappear. Occasionally an entire look is reborn. The elegant, simple look of the late 1940s and early 1950s, for example, was born again for the generation of the 1980s. Nostalgia influenced choices not only in apparel, but also in hairstyles and makeup.

Sometimes a single costume component or a minor detail that had exhausted its welcome stages a comeback, like the "chandelier" earring in the mid-1980s. At other times, a single article of clothing, like the sandals of the ancient Greeks, returns to popularity.

An outstanding example of a recurring men's fashion is the T-shirt. T-shirts originated in France as cotton underwear. They were discovered during World War I by American soldiers who preferred them to their own itchy wool union suits. In the 1940s they reemerged as "tee" shirts for golfing and other active sports. In the sixties they became part of the women's fashion scene as well.

Today, the T-shirt has put ego into fashion. T-shirts are bought for both fashion and antifashion reasons, and in both cases they announce to all what the wearer stands for and where he or she has been. A T-shirt can feature a country or city, a rock concert tour, a traveling art exhibition, the uniform number of one's favorite baseball player, or the name of a designer (Tommy Hilfiger) or manufacturer (Nike). T-shirt wearers can identify themselves outright by names, initials, telephone numbers, or even blown-up photographs of themselves transferred onto the T-shirt.[7] Organizations offer T-shirts as promotional items (Hard Rock Cafe T-shirts featuring the names of cities where the theme restaurant is located) and souvenirs of conventions (corporate sales meetings and class reunions).

Research indicates that in the past, similar silhouettes and details of design in women's apparel have recurred with remarkable regularity. In *Recurring Cycles of Fashion*,[8] Agnes Brooke Young studied skirt silhouettes and their variations in connection with her interest in theatrical costumes. From data she collected on the period from 1760 to 1937, she concluded that despite widely held opinions to the contrary, there were actually only three basic silhouettes, bell-shaped, backfullness, and straight, which always followed each other in the same 100-year sequence. (See Chapter 1 for variations on this theory.) Each silhouette with all its variations dominated the fashion scene for a period of approximately 35 years. Having reached an excess in styling, it then declined in popularity and yielded to the next silhouette in regular sequence.

The anthropologist A. L. Kroeber studied changes in women's apparel from the early 1600s to the early 1900s. His conclusions confirm Young's findings that similar silhouettes recur in fashion acceptance approximately once every 100 years. In addition, Kroeber found that similar neck widths recurred every 100 years, and similar skirt lengths every 35 years.[9] In more recent times, this rate of change has altered. There was the short skirt in the 1940s, the long skirt in the 1950s, the micro-mini in the 1960s, and the mid-length skirt in the 1970s. Interestingly, in the last years of the 20th century, it seems that all lengths—from the super-short skirt to ankle length, and every length in between—are acceptable!

Playing the Apparel Fashion Game

According to Madge Garland, a well-known English fashion authority: "Every woman is born with a built-in hobby: the adornment of her person. The tricks she can play with it, the shapes she can make of it, the different portions she displays at various times, the coverings she uses or discards" all add up to fashion.[10]

Many clothing authorities read a clear message into the alternate exposure and covering of various parts of the body—sex. J. C. Flügel cited sexual attraction as the dominant motive for wearing clothes.[11]

Laver explained fashion emphasis in terms of the sexuality of the body. "Fashion really began," he said, "with the discovery in the fifteenth century that clothes could be used as a compromise between exhibitionism and modesty."[12] Laver also suggested that those portions of the body no longer fashionable to expose are "sterilized" and are no longer regarded as sexually attractive. Those that are newly exposed are **erogenous**, or sexually stimulating. He viewed fashion as pursuing the emphasis of ever-shifting erogenous zones, but never quite catching up with them. "If you really catch up," he warned, "you are immediately arrested for indecent exposure. If you almost catch up, you are celebrated as a leader of fashion."[13]

Men's apparel has long played the fashion game, too, but, since the industrial revolution, in a less dramatic manner than women's. Women's fashions have tended to concentrate mainly on different ways to convey sexual appeal. Men's fashions have been designed to emphasize such attributes as strength, power, bravery, and high social rank. When a male style does emphasize sex, it is intended to project an overall impression of virility.

Pieces of the Game

The pieces with which the women's fashion game is played are the various parts of the female body: waist, shoulders, bosom, neckline, hips, derriere, legs, and feet, as well as the figure as a whole (see Figure 3.3). Historically, as attention to a part of the anatomy reaches a saturation point, the fashion spotlight shifts to some other portion.

In the Middle Ages, asceticism was fashionable. Women's clothes were designed to play down, rather than emphasize, women's sexuality. The Renaissance was a period of greater sexual freedom. Women's apparel during this period highlighted the breasts and the abdomen, particularly the latter.

By the 18th century, however, the abdomen had lost its appeal. Although the bosom continued to be emphasized, a flatter abdomen was fashionable, and heels were raised to facilitate upright carriage. The Empire period, with its high waistline, also stressed the bosom. But the entire body was emphasized with sheer and scanty dresses—some so sheer they could be pulled through a ring. Some advocates of this fashion even wet their apparel so that it would cling to the figure when worn.

During the 19th century, fashion interest shifted to the hips, and skirts billowed. Later, the posterior was accented with bustles and trains.

Early in the 20th century, emphasis switched from the trunk to the limbs, through short skirts and sleeveless or tight-sleeved dresses. Flügel interpreted accent on the limbs, together with the suggestion of an underdeveloped torso, as an idealization of youth. He foresaw continued emphasis on youth and boyishness as a result of women's participation in varied activities, the steady march of democracy, and increasing sexual freedom.[14]

In the 1960s, fashion interest was focused on short skirts and the legs. As the sixties drew to a close, interest shifted from legs to bosom. By the early 1970s, the natural look of bosoms was in. The unconstructed, natural look was followed by the "no-bra" look. This fashion reached its culmination and began its decline when bosoms were only slightly concealed beneath see-through fabrics or plunging necklines. As this excess led to obsolescence, the 1980s ushered in a reemergence of the 1950s bosom. Manufacturers of bras and inner wear featured soft-sided bras, strapless bras, T-back bras, and sports bras to once again give a firmly supported look to the bosom.

According to Garland, the fashions of the 1950s and early 1960s showed off the entire figure:

> *The modern girl manages at the same time to bare her shoulders, accentuate her bust, pull in her waist, and show her legs to above the knees. It is a triumph of personal publicity over the taboos of the past and the previous limitations of fashion.*[15]

Until the late 1960s brought the "youth cult" and its attendant revolt against conventional sexual and political attitudes, previous fashion eras had centered attention only on parts of the body. The "triumph of personal publicity" achieved in the late 1960s and early 1970s broke all records for calling attention to just about every area of the human body. It was, indeed, an allover feast for the eye of the observer.

Rules of the Game

In the game of emphasizing different parts of the female body at different times, as in any game, there are rules.

The first and strongest rule is that fashion emphasis does not flit from one area to an-

FIGURE 3.3
Stella McCartney's "eye-popping" design emphasizes the bosom and reveals just enough cleavage.
Courtesy, Fairchild Publications, Inc. Photographer: Dominique Maitre.

other! Rather, a particular area of the body is emphasized until every bit of excitement has been exhausted. At this point, fashion attention turns to another area. For example, as has been noted, when miniskirts of the 1960s could go no higher and still be legal, the fashion emphasis moved on.

The second rule of the fashion game may well be, as Garland suggested, that only certain parts of the body can be exposed at any given time.[16] There are dozens of examples throughout fashion history that back up this theory: floor length evening gowns with plunging necklines, high necklines with miniskirts, turtlenecks on sleeveless fashions.

A third rule of the fashion game is that, like fashion itself, fashion attention must always go forward. "A fashion can never retreat gradually and in good order"; Dwight E. Robinson said, "like a dictator it must always expand its aggressions or collapse. Old fashions never fade away; they die suddenly and arbitrarily."[17]

Predicting the Movement of Fashion

Producing and selling fashion merchandise to consumers at a profit are what fashion merchandising is all about. To bring excitement and flair to their segment of merchandising, producers and retailers must have a well-defined plan and must follow the movement of general fashion preferences.

The success of fashion merchandising depends upon the correct prediction of which new styles will be accepted by the majority of consumers. The successful forecaster of fashion must:

1. Distinguish what the current fashion trends are.
2. Estimate how widespread they are.
3. Determine when these fashions will appeal to the firm's target customer groups.

With information on these three points, projections—a prime requisite in successful fashion merchandising—become possible.

Identifying Trends

A fashion trend, as discussed in Chapter 1, is a direction in which fashion is moving. Manufacturers and merchants try to recognize each fashion trend to determine how widespread it is and whether it is moving toward or away from maximum fashion acceptance. They can then decide whether to actively promote the fashion to their target customers, to wait, or to abandon it.

For example, assume that wide-leg pants have developed as a fashion trend. At the introduction and rise stages, retailers will stock and promote more and more short wide-leg pants. When customer response begins to level off, retailers will realize that a saturation point is being reached with this style and will begin introducing narrower pants into their stocks in larger and larger numbers. If the retailers have correctly predicted the downturn in customer demand for wide-leg pants, they will have fewer on hand when the downturn occurs. And while some customers may continue to wear the wide-leg style, they will not be buying new wide-leg pants, and certainly not at regular prices.

Sources of Data

Modern fashion forecasters bear little resemblance to the mystical prognosticators of old. Their ability to predict the strength and direction of fashion trends among their customers has almost nothing to do with what is often called a "fashion sense." Nor does it depend on glances into the future via a cloudy crystal ball. Today's successful fashion forecasters depend on that most valuable commodity—information. Good, solid facts about the willingness of customers to accept certain goods are the basis of successful merchandising decisions.

In today's computerized business world, merchants can keep "instant" records on sales, inventories, new fashion testing, and myriads of other contributing factors that aid the fashion merchandising process. In addition, wise merchants keep their eyes open to see what is being worn by their own customers as well as by the public as a whole. They are so familiar with their customers' lifestyles, economic status, educational level, and social milieu that they can determine at just what point in a fashion's life cycle their customers will be ready to accept or reject it. Merchants turn to every available source for information that will help ensure success. They use their hard-earned sales experience but don't just rely on their own judgment; they rely on the judgment of others, too. From the producers of fashion, from resident buying/merchandising/developing offices, and from special fashion groups they learn about the buying habits of customers other than their own (see Figure 3.4). Successful merchants look at the larger fashion picture to predict more ably just where their local scene fits in.

WSRA Presents...
THE MAY EVENT
San Diego
The Shortest Distance Between Vendor & Retailer.
3 days, 2 nights, seminars, golf, food, entertainment, discounts *, and much more!!
Join us & acquire some of the most valuable information offered by both Retailers & Vendors to boost your business!
May 3, 4, & 5.......................$295.00
In San Diego, at the DoubleTree Carmel Highland Resort
Topics Will Include:
Vendor Support • Communications • Merchandising
Computers • Personnel • Insurance • Etc...
For reservations & more Info, contact WSRA
Ask for Linda!
* Receive a minimum 5% discount for any at once, fill-in orders received at this 3-day event!!!
Space is Limited!! Call Today!

FIGURE 3.4
Regional trade shows and seminars like those offered by WSRA are a reliable source of information for retailers—not to mention the opportunities they provide for networking and fun!
Courtesy, The Western Shoe Retailers Association.

Interpreting Influential Factors

An old theater saying goes, "It's all in the interpretation." In other words, written or spoken words gain their importance by the way they are presented to the audience. That is where the special talents of the performer come in. The same is true of fashion forecasting. All the data in the world can be collected by merchants, producers, or designers, but this is of little importance without interpretation. That is where the forecasters' knowledge of fashion and fashion principles comes into the picture. From the data they have collected, they are able to identify certain patterns. Then they consider certain factors that can accelerate or retard a fashion cycle among their target group of customers. Among these factors are current events, the appearance of prophetic styles, sales promotion efforts, and the canons of taste currently in vogue.

Current Events

The news of what is going on in the country or the world can have a long-term or short-term influence on consumers and affect their response to a fashion (see Figure 3.5). For example, in the mid-1980s, many newspapers, magazines, and TV shows were discussing opportunities for women at mid- and upper-management levels. Success in responsible positions in the business world demanded "dressing for success," and career-minded women responded by adopting the severely tailored business suit look. By their very appearance, these women indicated their determination to succeed in the still male-dominated world of business. A reaction to this male-dominated, strictly tailored look occurred in the early 1990s, when women turned to a softer, less tailored look and many men abandoned the business suit "uniform" that had been *de rigueur* for generations.

FIGURE 3.5 *Fashion shows came to a halt and organizers raised the American flag after the September 11th terrorist attacks on the United States in 2001.*
Courtesy, Fairchild Publications, Inc.

Prophetic Styles

Good fashion forecasters keep a sharp watch for what they call **prophetic styles**. These are particularly interesting new styles that are still in the introduction phase of their fashion cycle. Taken up enthusiastically by the socially prominent or by the flamboyant young, these styles may gather momentum very rapidly or they may prove to be nonstarters. Whatever their future course, the degree of acceptance of these very new styles gives forecasters a sense of which directions fashion might go in.

Sales Promotion Efforts

In addition to analyzing the records of past sales, fashion forecasters give thought to the kind and amount of promotion that helps stimulate interest in prophetic styles. They also consider the kind and amount of additional sales promotion they can look forward to. For example, a fiber producer's powerful advertising and publicity efforts may have helped turn slight interest in a product into a much stronger interest during a corresponding period the previous year. The forecaster's problem is to estimate how far the trend might have developed without those promotional activities. The forecaster must also assess how much momentum remains from the previous year's push to carry the trend forward in the current year, and how much promotional support can be looked for in the future. The promotional effort that a forecaster's own organization plans to expend is only one part of the story; outside efforts, sometimes industrywide, also must be considered in forecasting fashions.

Canons of Taste

According to Paul H. Nystrom, fashions that are in accord with currently accepted canons (standards) of art, custom, modesty, and utility are most easily accepted.[18] Today's forecasters are careful to take current canons of taste into consideration as they judge the impact of new styles.

Importance of Timing

Successful merchants must determine what their particular target group of customers is wearing now and what this group is most likely to be wearing one month or three months from now. The data these merchants collect enable them to identify each current fashion, who is wearing it, and what point it has reached in its fashion cycle.

Since merchants know at what point in a fashion's cycle their customers are most likely to be attracted, they can determine whether to stock a current fashion now, one month from now, or three months from now.

Theories of Fashion Adoption

Fashions are accepted by a few before they are accepted by the majority. An important step in fashion forecasting is isolating and identifying those fashion leaders and keeping track of their preferences. Once these are known, the fashion forecaster is better able to forecast which styles are most likely to succeed as fashions, and how widely and by whom each will be accepted.

Three theories have been advanced to explain the "social contagion" or spread of fashion adoption: the downward-flow theory, the horizontal-flow theory or "mass-market" theory, and the upward-flow theory. Each attempts to explain the course a fashion travels or is likely to travel, and each has its own claim to validity in reference to particular fashions or social environments (see Figure 3.6).

Downward-Flow Theory

The oldest theory of fashion adoption is the **downward-flow theory** (or the "trickle-down theory"). It maintains that in order to be identified as a true fashion, a style must first be adopted by people at the top of the social pyramid. The style then gradually wins acceptance at progressively lower social levels.

This theory assumes the existence of a social hierarchy in which lower-income people seek identification with more affluent people. At the same time, those at the top seek disassociation from those they consider socially inferior. The theory suggests that (1) fashions are accepted by lower classes only if, and after, they are accepted by upper classes, and (2) upper classes will reject a fashion once it has flowed to a lower social level.

Thorstein B. Veblen, an economist at the turn of the 20th century, was among the first to observe this type of social behavior and its effect upon fashion. In 1903, French sociologist Gabriel Tarde described the spread of fashion in terms of a social water tower from which a continuous fall of imitation could descend.[19] The German sociologist George Simmel, one of the first of his discipline to undertake a serious study of fashion, wrote in 1904:

> *Social forms, apparel, aesthetic judgment, the whole style of human expression, are constantly being transformed by fashion in [a way that] . . . affects only the upper classes. Just as soon as the lower classes begin to copy their styles, thereby crossing the line of demarcation the upper classes have drawn and destroying their coherence, the upper classes turn away from this style and adopt a new one . . .. The same process is at work as between the different sets within the upper classes, although it is not always visible here.*[20]

The downward-flow theory has had among its 20th-century proponents such authorities as Robinson, Laver, Edward Sapir, and Flügel. Flügel, in fact, suggested that sumptuary laws originated with the reluctance of upper classes to abandon the sartorial distinctiveness that to them represented superiority.

Implications for Merchandising

To some extent, the downward-flow theory has validity. Some fashions may appear first among the socially prominent. Eager manufacturers then quickly mass-produce lower-priced copies that many consumers can afford, and the wealthier consumers seek newer styles.

Because our social structure has radically changed, this theory has few adherents today. The downward-flow theory of fashion dissemination can apply only when a society resembles a pyramid, with people of wealth and position at the apex and followers at successively lower levels. Our social structure today, however, is more like a group of rolling hills than a pyramid. There are many social groups and many directions in which fashion can and does travel.

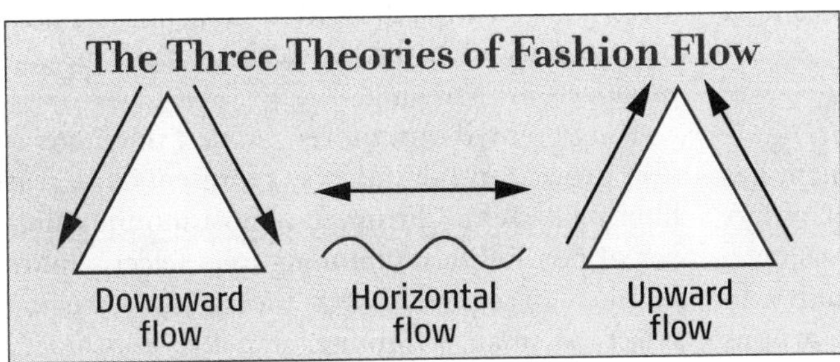

FIGURE 3.6
The three theories of fashion flow.

This altered pattern of fashion acceptance is also a result of the speed with which fashion news now travels. All social groups know about fashion innovation at practically the same time. Moreover, accelerated mass production and mass distribution of fashion goods have broadened acceptance of styles. They are available at lower prices and more quickly than ever before.

Industry Practice

For the reasons given above, those who mass-produce fashion goods today are less likely to wait cautiously for approval of newly introduced styles by affluent consumers. As soon as significant signs of an interesting new style appear, the producers are ready to offer adaptations or even copies to the public.

Horizontal-Flow Theory

A newer theory is the **horizontal-flow theory** (or mass-market theory) of fashion adoption. This theory claims that fashions move horizontally between groups on similar social levels rather than vertically from one level to another.

One of the chief exponents of this theory was Dr. Charles W. King. He proposed that the social environment, including rapid mass communications and the promotional efforts of manufacturers and retailers, exposes new styles to the fashion leaders of all social groups at approximately the same time. King noted that there is almost no lag between the adoption of a fashion by one social group and another.[21] Paris fashions, for example, are now copied for mass distribution sometimes even before the originals are available to the more affluent markets. The designers themselves are bringing out their ready-to-wear lines at the same time as their more expensive custom designs.

This horizontal flow also has been observed by some modern supporters of the older downward-flow theory. Robinson, for example, said that any given group or cluster of groups takes its cues from contiguous groups within the same social stratum. He claimed fashions therefore radiate from a center of each stratum or class.[22]

Implications for Merchandising

The theory of horizontal fashion movement has great significance for merchandising. It points out the fallacy of assuming that there is a single, homogeneous fashion public in this country. In reality, a number of distinctly different groups make up the fashion public. Each group has its own characteristics and its own fashion ideas and needs. The horizontal-flow theory recognizes that what wealthy society people are wearing today is not necessarily what middle-class suburbanites, college students, or office workers will either wear tomorrow or wait until tomorrow to accept. This theory acknowledges that there are separate markets in fashion goods as in any other type of merchandise.

Retailers who apply the horizontal-flow theory will watch their own customers closely rather than being guided solely by what more exclusive stores are selling. They will seek to identify the groups into which customers can be divided in terms of income, age, education, and lifestyle. Among their customers, they will look for the innovators and their style choices as well as the influentials and their selections. King defined a **fashion innovator** as a person who is quicker than his or her associates to try out a new style. A **fashion influential** is a person whose advice is sought by associates. A fashion influential's adoption of a new style gives it prestige among a group. The two roles may or may not be played by the same individual within a specific group.

The news that socially prominent women are wearing plunging necklines in exclusive New York restaurants will have less significance for the retailers in a small Midwestern city than the observation that the leader of the country club set in their community is abandoning bright colors for black on formal occasions. If the latter is a fashion influential in the community, she is a more important bellwether for them than the New York socialites.

Industry Practice

King drew a distinction between the spread of fashion within the industry itself and its adoption by consumers. A vertical flow definitely operates within the industry, he conceded: "Exclusive and famous designers are watched closely and emulated by lesser designers. Major manufacturers are studied and copied by smaller and less expert competitors."[23] And, as any reader of *Women's Wear Daily* knows, the hottest news in the industry concerns what the top designers and the top producers are showing.

King pointed out, moreover, that the innovation process in the industry represents a "great filtering system." From an almost infinite number of possibilities, manufacturers select a finite number of styles. From these, trade buyers select a small sampling. Finally, consumers

FASHION FOCUS

Ralph Lauren: True Blue from a Blue Blood

Colin McDowell, Chairman of the Costume Society of Great Britain, gives his highest praise to American designer Ralph Lauren. "The first designer to base fashion philosophy on American history and their tradition crafts skill, the Long Island Edwardian country life of the Vanderbilts and the Whitneys, the American dream of 1930's movies . . . and added the ice-cool sophistication of Manhattan in the 1950's and 1960's. He has a firm commitment to the past and much confidence in his own beliefs. He literally took the history of nation and re-presented it to itself through his clothes."

Introducing his Polo line of men's ties in 1967, Lauren set off on a mission to bring elegance and style into the lives of his customers—not only in clothes but also in accessories, underwear, jewelry, fragrances, and home fashions. Today, the world of Ralph Lauren includes not only his famous men's wear labels, Purple Label Collection, Polo, Ralph Lauren Menswear, and Chaps, but it also includes Ralph Lauren Womenswear and Ralph Lauren Sports. Not one to rest upon his laurels, Lauren premiered the luxury Ralph Lauren Home Collection in 1983, with linens, tabletop, and beautifully crafted furniture.

Over the years, he also created an entire wardrobe of fragrances and toiletries for men and women, which includes Polo, Lauren, and Safari. In 1995, he added the Ralph Lauren paint collection, allowing customers to coordinate all aspects of their home and wardrobe, from paint color to fragrance to home fashion to a dress or suit.

In 2002, still not resting on his laurels, Ralph Lauren debuted a women's lifestyle sportswear collection, Ralph Lauren Blue Label. A collection with a strong weekend focus, Blue Label consists of modern interpretations of classic Lauren styles. Looks include weathered chinos, corduroy pants and skirts, Shetland and English tweed jackets, Fair Isle hand-knit sweaters, and cashmere blend cable sweaters in an array of colors. Also included in the Blue Label line are the requisite washed oxford shirts and plaid shirtings, as well as came hair Polo coats, toggle coats, and weathered canvas weekend jackets—ah, the beauty of a Blue Label weekend with Ralph Lauren.

Lauren's company went public in 1997 and has been a good performer for stockholders. Overall, Polo generates $4.8 billion in wholesale volume through all its products and licenses. A great portion of his business is driven by licensing, and more than 30 companies pay to manufacture, distribute, and advertise Ralph Lauren products. Lauren provides the design and creative talent and receives royalty fees on the sales of the merchandise. Men's apparel accounts for $2.1 billion, women's apparel accounts for 1.2 billion, accessories is $435 million, home is $402 million, fragrances is $386 million, and children's wear is $282 million.

Lauren is famous for his loyalty to his executives, many of whom have been with him for years. He also welcomes new talent, and nurtures and grows young neophytes into seasoned professionals, a rarity in the frenetic and ever-changing fashion scene.

Ralph Lauren may be one of the most famous names and personalities in the fashion business, but he and his family lead a quiet life and perform many admirable and charitable acts with little fanfare or publicity. He galvanized the fashion industry to support breast cancer and AIDS research and education well before it became "the thing to do." He quietly supports worthy causes that impact many lives, and most recently he donated millions to restore the image of the American flag. To honor his impact on style and culture, he was awarded the prestigious Lifetime Achievement Award from the Council of Fashion Designers (CFDA). "Everything I do has a personal reference . . . It's who I am." So says Ralph Lauren, and we say it is true blue from a blue blood.

Sources

Phyllis Berman, "The Wall Street Fashion Game," *Forbes*, March 4, 2002, pp. 55-60.

Ralph Lauren Web Site, http://www.ralphlauren.com/Biography.

Lisa Lockwood, "Ralph Rebuilds Bridge: Sees $100 Million Biz with New Blue Label," *Women's Wear Daily*, January 24, 2002, pp. 1-4.

Colin McDowell, "Fashion Today," (Phaidon Press), September 2000.

Vicki M. Young, "Polo Gallops Ahead with Swing to Profit in Second Quarter," *Women's Wear Daily*, November 7, 2001, pp. 1-8.

Designer Ralph Lauren.
Courtesy, Fairchild Publications, Inc.

choose from among retailers' selections, thereby endorsing certain ones as accepted fashions.

This process, King maintained, is quite different from the consumer reaction outlined by Simmel and other proponents of the downward-flow theory. The difference lies in the fact that today the mass market does not await the approval of the "class" market before it adopts a fashion.

Upward-Flow Theory

The third theory that attempts to explain the process of fashion adoption is relatively new. It reflects the enormous social changes that have occurred in the past five decades. Because the process of fashion dissemination that evolved in the decades of the 1950s through the 2000s was the exact opposite of that which prevailed throughout much of recorded history, this theory has important implications for producers and retailers alike.

This theory of fashion adoption is called the **upward-flow theory**. It holds that the young—particularly those of low-income families and those in higher-income groups who adopt low-income lifestyles—are quicker than any social group to create or adopt new and different fashions. As its name implies, this theory is exactly the opposite of the downward-flow theory. The upward-flow theory holds that fashion adoption begins among the young members of lower-income groups and then moves upward into higher-income groups.

The decades of the fifties through today have outstanding examples of the upward-flow theory. In the fifties, young people discovered Army/Navy surplus stores and were soon wearing khaki pants, caps, battle jackets, fatigues, and even ammunition belts. In the sixties, led by the Hell's Angels, the motorcycle clubs introduced the fashion world to black leather—in jackets, vests, and studded arm bands. Soon the jet set was dressed in black leather long coats, skirts, and pants. Meanwhile, other young people were discovering bib overalls, railroad worker's caps, and all-purpose laborer's coveralls that were soon translated into jumpsuits. Peasant apparel, prairie looks, and styles and designs from various minority groups followed the same pattern. They began as part of a young and lower-income lifestyle and were then quickly adopted among older people with different lifestyles and incomes.

FIGURE 3.7
Avril Lavigne's rock and punk style studs and ties have impacted teen fashion in the 2000s. Is this an example of the upward flow theory?
Courtesy, Fairchild Publications, Inc.

One of the more dramatic illustrations of this has been the T-shirt. In its short-sleeved version, it has long been worn by truckers, laborers, and farm workers. In its long-sleeved version, it was the uniform of local bowling and softball teams. In the seventies, the T-shirt became a message board and sprouted a brand-new fashion cottage industry. The ultimate T-shirt was the Chanel No. 5; first the perfume, then the T-shirt. Actually, the Chanel T-shirt was a logical application of a tenet long held by the late Coco Chanel, who believed that fashion came from the streets and was then adapted by the couture.

In the eighties, sources of inspiration for fashion styles representing the upward-flow theory were everywhere, especially in the world of rock music. By following the fashion statements of rock-and-roll idols, America's youth were arrayed in worn denim, metal, leather, lace, bangles, spandex, and glitter. Colors ranged from

Cyndi Lauper's peacock looks to Roy Orbison's basic black. Madonna became a style-setter and introduced the country to her underwear worn on the outside.

In the nineties, rap artists not only composed lyrics that spoke of ghetto life in street language; they also introduced and popularized hip-hop clothing styles.

Implications for Merchandising

For producers and retailers, this new direction of fashion flow implies radical changes in traditional methods of charting and forecasting fashion trends. No longer can producers and retailers look solely to name designers and socially prominent fashion leaders for ideas that will become tomorrow's best-selling fashions. They also must pay considerable attention to what young people favor, for the young have now become a large, independent group that can exert considerable influence on fashion styling.

As a result, today fewer retailers and manufacturers attend European couture showings, once considered fashion's most important source of design inspiration. Now producers and retailers alike are more interested in ready-to-wear (prêt-à-porter) showings. Here they look for styles and design details that reflect trends with more fashion relevance for American youth. Young designers in their twenties and thirties complain that the more established, larger companies are copying their innovations.[24]

Industry Practice

Apparently, fashion will never again flow in only one direction. Of course, customers will always exist for high fashion and for conservative fashion. But producers and retailers must now accept that they will be doing a considerable proportion of their business in fashions created or adopted first by the lower-income young and by those who choose to be allied with them.

Fashion Leaders

As different as they may be, the three theories of fashion flow share one common perspective: They recognize that there are both fashion leaders and fashion followers. People of social, political, and economic importance here and abroad are seen as leaders in the downward-flow theory. The horizontal-flow theory recognizes individuals whose personal prestige makes them leaders within their own circles, whether or not they are known elsewhere. Finally, the important fashion role played by young, lower-income groups in the last half of the 20th century is recognized in the upward-flow theory.

The theories of fashion adoption stress that the fashion leader is not the creator of the fashion; nor does merely wearing the fashion make a person a fashion leader. As Quentin Bell explained: "The leader of fashion does not come into existence until the fashion is itself created . . . a king or person of great eminence may indeed lead the fashion, but he leads only in the general direction which it has already adopted."[25] If a fashion parade is forming, fashion leaders may head it and even quicken its pace. They cannot, however, bring about a procession; nor can they reverse a procession.

Innovators and Influentials

Famous people are not necessarily fashion leaders, even if they do influence an individual style. Their influence usually is limited to only one striking style, one physical attribute, or one time. The true fashion leader is a person constantly seeking distinction and therefore likely to launch a succession of fashions rather than just one. People like Beau Brummel, who made a career of dressing fashionably, or the Duchess of Windsor, whose wardrobe was front-page fashion news for decades, influence fashion on a much broader scale.

What makes a person a fashion leader? Flügel explained: "Inasmuch as we are aristocratically minded and dare to assert our own individuality by being different, we are leaders of fashion."[26] King, however, made it clear that more than just daring to be different is required. In his analysis, a person eager for the new is merely an innovator or early buyer. To be a leader, one must be influential and sought after for advice within one's coterie. "A fashion influential," said King, "sets the appropriate dress for a specific occasion in a particular circle. Within that circle, an innovator presents current offerings and is the earliest visual communicator of a new style."[27]

Royalty

In the past, fashion leadership was exclusively the province of royalty. New fashions were introduced in royal courts by such leaders as Empress Eugenie and Marie Antoinette. In the

20th century, the Duchess of Windsor, although an American and a commoner by birth, was a fashion innovator and influential from the 1930s through the 1960s. When the King of England gave up his throne to marry "the woman he loved," style and fashion professionals throughout the world copied her elegance. The Sotheby auction in the late 1980s of the Duchess of Windsor's jewelry sparked new interest in her style, and designers are still showing copies of her jewelry.

Until Princess Diana (see Figure 3.8) and Sarah Ferguson married into the British royal family, few royal personages in recent years had qualified as fashion leaders. Despite the belief held by some that kings and queens wear crowns and ermine, the truth is that modern royalty has become a hard-working group whose daily life is packed with so many activities that sensible and conservative dress is necessary for most occasions.

An outstanding example of a current royalty is Sophie, the Countess of Wessex (see Figure 3.8) and wife of Prince Edward, the youngest son of Queen Elizabeth. Having run a successful public relations firm for several years, Sophie balances career and marriage. Although not known as a fashion plate, she has her own sense of style combining her busy business life with her royal chores. Although Sophie still suffers in comparison to Diana's fashion image, they share a striking resemblance of one another, allowing the image of Diana to hold its lasting impression on the public.

The Rich

As monarchies were replaced with democracies, members of the wealthy and international sets came into the fashion spotlight. Whether the members of "society" derive their position from vast fortunes and old family names or from recent wealth, they bring to the scene a glamor and excitement that draws attention to everything they do. Today, through the constant eye of television, magazines, and newspapers, the average person is able to find fashion leadership in a whole new stratum of society—the jet set.

What these socialites are doing and what they are wearing are instantly served up to the general public by the media. As far as fashion is concerned, these people are not just in the news; they *are* the news. Any move they make is important enough to be immediately publicized. What they wear is of vital interest to the general public. The media tell us what the social leaders wear to dine in a chic restaurant, to attend a charity ball, or to go shopping. Because they are trendsetters, their choices are of prime interest to designers and to the world at large.

Of course, this inundation of news about what social leaders wear influences the public. The average person is affected because so many manufacturers and retailers of fashion take their cue from these social leaders. Right or wrong, fashion merchants count on the fashion sense of these leaders. They know that the overwhelming exposure of these leaders in the

A

B

FIGURE 3.8 *The fashion limelight continues to shine on Britain from the royal lineage of (a) Princess Diana to (b) Sophie, the Countess of Wessex.* Courtesy, Fairchild Publications, Inc.

media encourages people of ordinary means to imitate them—consciously or unconsciously.

The Famous

Fashion today takes its impetus and influence from people in every possible walk of life. These people have one thing in common, however: they are famous. Because of some special talent, charisma, notoriety, or popularity, they are constantly mentioned and shown on television, in fashion magazines, and in newspapers. They may or may not appear in the society pages.

In this group can be found presidents and princesses, movie stars and religious leaders, sports figures and recording stars, politicians and TV personalities (see Figure 3.9 and 3.10). Because they are seen so frequently, the public has a good sense of their fashions and lifestyles and can imitate them to the extent of the public's means and desires.

Prominent individuals have been responsible for certain fashions that continue to be associated with them. Many times, however, these individuals are not what would be considered fashion leaders. Although the cornrow braiding of hair had been practiced among blacks in Africa and America for decades, it was adopted by many young black women only after Cicely Tyson appeared with the hairstyle in the movie *Sounder* in 1972. In 1979, Bo Derek wore cornrows in the film *10* and gave the style new impetus. In the 1930s, a tremendous impact was felt by an entire men's wear industry when Clark Gable appeared without an undershirt in the film *It Happened One Night*. Practically overnight, men from all walks of life shed their undershirts in imitation of Gable. In the late 1930s, women dared to wear slacks after seeing Greta Garbo and Marlene Dietrich wearing them in the movies. In the early 1960s, when Mrs. John F. Kennedy appeared in little pillbox hats, both the style and the hat market blossomed under the publicity. Some styles are so closely associated with the famous people who wore them that they bear their names (see Table 3.1).

FIGURE 3.9
Brad Pitt and Jennifer Aniston are celebrity figures; their every business move or mundane activity is avidly reported.
Courtesy, AP Wide World Photos © Kevark Djansezian.

FIGURE 3.10
Music sensation Eminem is in the "public eye" for not only his music, but his style of fashion as well.
Courtesy, AP Wide World Photos © Marc J. Ternll

TABLE 3.1 Fashion Styles Named for the Famous

TRENDSETTERS	STYLES
Amelia Bloomer	Bloomers
Earl of Chesterfield	Chesterfield jacket
Dwight D. Eisenhower	Eisenhower jacket
Geraldine Ferraro	"Gerry cut" (hairstyle)
Mao Tse Tung	Mao jacket
Jawaharlal Nehru	Nehru jacket
Madame de Pompadour	Pompadour (hairstyle)
Nancy Reagan	"Reagan plastics" (costume jewelry), colon red
Duke of Wellington	Wellington boots
Earl of Cardigan	Cardigan sweater
Duke of Windsor	Windsor knot (tie)
Duke of Norfolk	Norfolk jacket
Nelson Mandela	Madiba smart (shirt)
The Beatles	hairstyle

FIGURE 3.11
Athletes, like Venus Williams, are often used in advertisements to sell sportswear.
Courtesy, Fairchild Publications, Inc.

Athletes

Today, there is strong emphasis on sports. And what prominent sports figures wear is of great importance to the people who seek to imitate them (see Figure 3.11). Television has increased the public acceptance of several sports. For example, people have enjoyed going to baseball, football, or basketball games for years. But sports of a more individual nature, such as tennis and golf, were of minor interest. Now these sports are brought into the living rooms of an increasing number of viewers. As a result, fashions for participating in these sports have grown remarkably in importance. Tennis is now a very popular participation sport and has given rise to an entire specialized fashion industry. Today, every aspiring tennis player has endless fashion styles, colors, and fabrics to choose from. A wide selection of fashion is also available for golf, jogging, running, swimming, skating, cycling, snorkeling, snowboarding, and other sports. The names of Michael Jordan, Tiger Woods, and Venus Williams are known to most Americans.

Fashion Followers

Filling out forms for his daughter's college entrance application, a father wrote of his daughter's leadership qualities: "To tell the truth, my daughter is really not a leader, but rather a loyal and devoted follower." The dean of the college admissions responded: "We are welcoming a freshman class of 100 students this year and are delighted to accept your daughter. You can't imagine how happy we are to have one follower among the 99 leaders!"

Most people want to be thought of as leaders, not followers. But there are many people who are followers, and good ones. In fact, followers are in the majority within any group. Without followers the fashion industry would certainly collapse. Mass production and mass distribution can be possible and profitable only when large numbers of consumers accept the merchandise. Though they may say otherwise, luckily, more people prefer to follow than to lead. The styles fashion leaders adopt may help manufacturers and retailers in determining what will be demanded by the majority of consumers in the near future. Only accurate predictions can ensure the continued success of the giant ready-to-wear business in this country, which depends for its success on mass production and distribution. While fashion leaders may stimulate and excite the fashion industry, fashion followers are the industry's lifeblood.

Reasons for Following Fashion

Theories about why people follow rather than lead in fashion are plentiful. Among the explanations are feelings of insecurity, admiration of others, lack of interest, and ambivalence about the new.

Feelings of Insecurity

Flügel wrote, "Inasmuch as we feel our own inferiority and the need for conformity to the standards set by others, we are followers of fashion."[28] For example, high school boys and girls are at a notably insecure stage of life. They are therefore more susceptible than any other age group to the appeal of fads. A person about to face a difficult interview or attend the first meeting with a new group carefully selects new clothes. Often a feeling of inadequacy can be hidden by wearing a style that others have already approved as appropriate.

Admiration

Flügel also maintained that it is a fundamental human impulse to imitate those who are admired or envied. A natural and symbolic means of doing this is to copy their clothes, makeup, and hairstyles. Outstanding illustrations of this theory have been provided by movie stars and models—Mary Pickford, "America's Sweetheart" of the 1910s; Clara Bow, the "It" girl of the 1920s; Ginger Rogers, Katharine Hepburn, and Rosalind Russell of the 1930s; Veronica Lake and Ann Sheridan, the "Oomph Girls" of the 1940s; Doris Day and Marilyn Monroe in the 1950s; Twiggy in the 1960s; Farrah Fawcett in the 1970s; Christie Brinkley in the 1980s; Elle McPherson and Cindy Crawford in the 1990s; and Jennifer Lopez, Cameron Diaz, and Britney Spears at the beginning of the 21st century. Their clothes and hairstyles were copied instantly among many different groups throughout this country and in many other parts of the world. On a different level, the young girl who copies the hairstyle of her best friend, older sister, or favorite aunt demonstrates the same principle, as do college students who model their appearance after that of a campus leader.

Lack of Interest

Edward Sapir suggested that many people are insensitive to fashion and follow it only because "they realize that not to fall in with it would be to declare themselves members of a past generation, or dull people who cannot keep up with their neighbors."[29] Their response to fashion, he said, is a sullen surrender, by no means an eager following of the Pied Piper.

Ambivalence

Another theory holds that many people are ambivalent in their attitudes toward the new; they both want it and fear it. For most, it is easier to choose what is already familiar. Such individuals need time and exposure to new styles before they can accept them.

Varying Rates of Response

Individuals vary in the speed with which they respond to a new idea, especially when fashion change is radical and dramatic. Some fashion followers apparently need time to adjust to new ideas. Merchants exploit this point when they buy a few "window pieces" of styles too advanced for their own clientele and expose them

Then & Now

T.V. WOMEN

The evolution of the female TV character, from Moms to single girls, has come a long way. From the 1950s through the 1970s, we were bombarded with TV women who were perfect in every way. Perfect, that is, for the modes and morals of those times.

But times are changing . . . and so are the women of TV. Let us look at the differences.

MOTHERS IN OZZ

THEN

Harriet Nelson, Ozzie's devoted wife & homemaker on 1950's TV.

Courtesy, AP Photo.

NOW

Sharon Osbourne, Ozzy's potty-mouthed wife & manager on MTV

Courtesy, AP Photo/Kim D. Johnson

PEACE KEEPERS

THEN

Edith Bunker, lovable dingbat who melted Archie's tough exterior.

Courtesy, The Kobal Collection.

NOW

Carmela Soprano, loving wife, who keeps the peace in her family.

Courtesy, Fairchild Publications, Inc.

SINGLE CITY GIRLS

THEN

Mary Richards, spunky TV producer with a grumpy big boss.

Courtesy, AP Photo.

NOW

Carrie Bradshaw, flirty sex columnist with a hunky Mr. Big.

Courtesy, Fairchild Publications, Inc.

SPY GIRLS

THEN

Emma Peel, a master of espionage with sass, class, and sex appeal.

Courtesy, The Kobal Collection.

NOW

Sydney Bristow, a secret agent with spy tricks, high kicks, and sex appeal.

Courtesy, Fairchild Publications, Inc.

in windows and fashion shows to allow customers time to get used to them. Only after a period of exposure to the new styles do the fashion followers accept them.

Fashion as an Expression of Individuality

As the 21st century entered its first decade, a strange but understandable trend became apparent across the nation. People were striving, through their mode of dress, to declare individuality in the face of computer-age conformity.

People had watched strings of impersonal numbers become more and more a part of their lives—zip codes, bank and credit card account numbers, employee identification numbers, department store accounts, automobile registrations, social security numbers, and so on. An aversion to joining the masses—to becoming "just another number"—began to be felt. So while most people continued to go along with general fashion trends, some asserted their individuality. This was accomplished by distinctive touches each wearer added to an outfit. A new freedom in dress, color and texture combinations, use of accessories, and hairstyles allowed people to assert their individuality without being out of step with the times. Most social scientists see in this a paradox—an endless conflict between the desire to conform and the desire to remain apart.

We have all known people who at some point in their lives found a fashion that particularly pleased them. It might have been a certain style of dress, a certain shoe, or a hairstyle. Even in the face of continuing changes in fashion, the person continued to wear that style in which she or he felt right and attractive. This is an assertion of individuality in the face of conformity. Although superbly fashion conscious, the actress Joan Crawford never stopped wearing the open-toed, slingback, wedge shoe of the 1940s. When the pointed toe and stiletto heel of the fifties gave way to the low, chunky heel of the sixties, she continued to wear the same style. She was perfectly in step with fashion when the wedge shoe finally returned to popularity in the early 1970s. Woody Allen achieved special recognition for wearing—anywhere and everywhere—sneakers! At formal occasions he conforms by wearing appropriate formal attire. But his feet remain sneakered, and Woody retains his individuality.

Most people prefer to assert their individuality in a less obvious way, and today's ready-to-wear fashions lend themselves to subtle changes that mark each person's uniqueness. No two people put the same costume together in exactly the same way.

Fashion editor Jessica Daves summed up the miracle of modern ready-to-wear fashion. It offers, she said, "the possibility for some women to create a design for themselves . . . to choose the color and shape in clothes that will present them as they would like to see themselves."[30]

The Paradox of Conformity and Individuality

For decades, experts have tried to explain why people seek both conformity and individuality in fashion. Simmel suggested that two opposing social tendencies are at war: the need for union and the need for isolation. The individual, he reasoned, derives satisfaction from knowing that the way in which he or she expresses a fashion represents something special. At the same time, people gain support from seeing others favor the same style.[31]

Flügel interpreted the paradox in terms of a person's feelings of superiority and inferiority. The individual wants to be like others "insofar as he regards them as superior, but unlike them, in the sense of being more 'fashionable,' insofar as he thinks they are below him."[32]

Sapir tied the conflict to a revolt against custom and a desire to break away from slavish acceptance of fashion. Slight changes from the established form of dress and behavior "seem for the moment to give victory to the individual, while the fact that one's fellows revolt in the same direction gives one a feeling of adventurous safety."[33] He also tied the assertion of individuality to the need to affirm one's self in a powerful society in which the individual has ceased to be the measure.

One example of this conflict may be found in the off-duty dress of people required to wear uniforms of one kind or another during working hours, such as nurses, police officers, and mail carriers. A second example is seen in the clothing worn by many present-day business executives. Far from the days when to be "The Man in the Gray Flannel Suit" meant that a man had arrived in the business world, today executives favor a much more diversified wardrobe. While suits of gray flannel are still worn, so are a wide variety of other fabrics and patterns. And some top executives favor a more relaxed look altogether, preferring to wear appropriately fashioned separate jackets or blazers with their business slacks.

Retailers know that although some people like to lead and some like to follow in fashion, most people buy fashion to express their personality or to identify with a particular group. To belong, they follow fashion; to express their personality, they find ways to individualize fashion.

Fashion and Self-Expression

Increasing importance is being placed on fashion individuality—on expressing your personality, or refusing to be cast in a mold. Instead of slavishly adopting any one look, today's young person seeks to create an individual effect through the way he or she combines various fashion components. For instance, if a young woman thinks a denim skirt, an ankle-length woolen coat, and a heavy turtlenecked sweater represent her personality, they will be considered acceptable by others in her group.

Forward-looking designers recognize this desire for self-expression. Designers say that basic wardrobe components should be made available, but that consumers should be encouraged to combine them as they see fit. For instance, they advise women to wear pants or skirts, long or short, according to how they feel, not according to what past tradition has considered proper for an occasion. They suggest that men make the same choice among tailored suits, leisure wear, and slacks, to find the styles that express their personalities.

Having experienced such fashion freedom, young people may never conform again. Yet despite individual differences in dress, young experimenters have in common a deep-rooted desire to dress differently from older generations.

Summary and Review

It is the nature of fashion to change, but the speed and direction of its changes are difficult to predict. Some factors that accelerate the pace of change are widespread buying power, increased leisure time, increased education, the improved status of women, technological advances that bring new and improved products to the market, and seasonal changes. However, the pace of change can be slowed by habit and custom, religious restrictions, and sumptuary laws (laws placing limits or requirements on the construction of apparel).

Some types of fashion merchandise change more slowly than other types. For example, men's fashions change more slowly than women's. Some fashion historians have tracked the basic shapes of apparel, particularly women's wear, and concluded that three basic silhouettes dominate fashion in turn, each for about 35 years, creating a cycle that lasts about 100 years. Other details of line, such as sleeve shape and skirt length have similar cycles.

Fashion also focuses on different parts of the body at different times, accentuating the seductive appeal of each part in turn. For fashion merchandisers, success depends on the accuracy of predictions of trends and judging when and to what degree a fashion will be adopted by the producer's or retailer's target market. Inventory and sales records and a careful following of current events, the reception of new styles at the introductory stage of the fashion cycle, sales promotion, and current canons of taste help forecasters make accurate predictions.

Three theories attempt to explain the movement of fashion; they are the downward-flow, horizontal-flow, and upward-flow theories. The acceptance of a fashion depends on innovators, who are the first to wear it, and influentials, whose personal style is copied by others. On a broad scale, public figures are often innovators and influentials. The buying public watches the fashions of royalty, high society, athletes and other entertainers, and other celebrities. On a smaller scale, individual communities have their own fashion innovators and influentials, but a fashion's acceptance ultimately depends on fashion followers. They are the people who spread a fashion and account for the number of sales. Each person adjusts his or her wardrobe to balance a sense of belonging to a group and being an individual.

Trade Talk

Define or briefly explain the following terms:

downward-flow theory	horizontal-flow theory

erogenous
fashion influential
fashion innovator
prophetic style
sumptuary law
upward-flow theory

For Review

1. Describe the theory of fashion cycles and explain why it accelerated in the 20th century.
2. List the "pieces" of the women's fashion game, according to Madge Garland. What happened to these "pieces" in the 1960s and 1970s?
3. According to leading fashion authorities, what are the three basic rules that govern the fashion game?
4. What basic resources are available to the fashion merchant to predict fashion?
5. Explain the term "prophetic style."
6. Is the downward-flow theory of fashion adoption as valid today as it was in years past? Explain your answer.
7. How does the horizontal-flow theory of fashion adoption affect fashion merchants today? How are merchants today affected by the upward-flow theory?
8. Explain why (a) rich people, (b) famous people, and (c) athletes are prime candidates for positions of fashion leadership.
9. Give four reasons why most people follow, rather than lead, in regard to fashion. Explain each.
10. How can fashion be used as a means of expressing individuality?

For Discussion

1. Give at least one current example of each of several factors that are accelerating the forward movement of fashions today.
2. Certain factors tend to retard the development of fashion cycles by discouraging the adoption of newly introduced styles. List these factors and give at least one example of how each factor exerts a braking influence on fashion development.
3. Why do people today seek both conformity and individuality in fashion? How does this affect the fashion designer or manufacturer? The fashion retailer?

References

1. James Laver, *Taste and Fashion*, rev. ed. (London: George G. Harrop & Co., Ltd., 1946), p. 52.
2. Pearl Binder, *Muffs and Morals* (London: George G. Harrop & Co., Ltd., 1953), pp. 162–164.
3. Elisabeth McClellan, *History of American Costume* (New York: Tudor Publishing Company, 1969), p. 82.
4. John Taylor, *It's a Small, Medium, and Outsize World* (London: Hugh Evelyn, 1966), p. 39.
5. Glori Chai, "School Uniforms: Panacea or Band Aid?," 1999. Available www.education-world.com/a_admin130.html
6. Laver, *Taste and Fashion*, p. 201.
7. Clara Pierre, *Looking Good: The Liberation of Fashion* (New York: Reader's Digest Press, 1976), p. 149.
8. Agnes Brooke Young, *Recurring Cycles of Fashion: 1760–1937* (New York: Harper & Brothers, 1937; reprint New York: Cooper Square Publishers, Inc., 1966), p. 30.
9. A. L. Kroeber, "On the Principles of Order in Civilizations as Examplified by Change in Fashion," *American Anthropologist*, vol. 21, July–September 1919, pp. 235–263.
10. Madge Garland, *The Changing Form of Fashion* (New York: Praeger Publishers, 1971), p. 11.
11. J. C. Flügel, *The Psychology of Clothes* (New York: International Universities Press, 1966), p. 163.
12. Laver, *Taste and Fashion*, p. 200.
13. Ibid., p. 201.
14. Flügel, *Psychology of Clothes*, p. 163.
15. Garland, *Changing Form of Fashion*, p. 20.
16. Ibid., p. 11.
17. Dwight E. Robinson, "Fashion Theory and Product Design," *Harvard Business Review*, vol. 36, November–December 1958, p. 128.
18. Paul H. Nystrom, *Fashion Merchandising* (New York: The Ronald Press, 1932), p. 94.
19. Gabriel Tarde, *The Laws of Imitation* (New York: Henry Holt and Company, 1903), p. 221.

20. Georg Simmel, "Fashion," *American Journal of Sociology*, vol. 62, May 1957, p. 545.
21. Charles W. King, "Fashion Adoption: A Rebuttal to the Trickle-Down Theory," *Proceedings of the Winter Conference*, American Marketing Association, New York, December 1963, pp. 114–115.
22. Dwight E. Robinson, "The Economics of Fashion Demand," *The Quarterly Journal of Economics*, vol. 75, August 1961, p. 383.
23. King, "Fashion Adoption," pp. 114–115.
24. Gregory Beals and Leslie Kaufman, "The Kids Know Cool," *Newsweek*, March 31, 1997, p. 91.
25. Quentin Bell, *On Human Finery* (London: The Hogarth Press, Ltd., 1947), p. 46.
26. Flügel, *Psychology of Clothes*, p. 140.
27. King, "Fashion Adoption" p. 124.
28. Flügel, *Psychology of Clothes*, p. 140.
29. Edward Sapir, "Fashion," *Encyclopedia of the Social Sciences*, vol. V1 (London: Macmillan & Co. 1931), p. 140.
30. Jessica Daves, *Ready-Made Miracle* (New York: G. P. Putnam's Sons, 1967), pp. 231–232.
31. Simmel, "Fashion," pp. 543–544.
32. Flügel, *Psychology of Clothes*, p. 140.
33. Sapir, "Fashion," p. 140.

CHAPTER 4

The Business of Fashion

WHAT'S IN IT FOR YOU?

Everything you always wanted to know about the levels of the fashion business.

Key Concepts:

- The four levels of the fashion business
- The three common forms of business ownership
- The role of franchising and licensing
- The role of the designer, the manufacturer, and the retailer in the fashion business

Fashion is a business, affected by the same technological advances, investment patterns, and economic forces that affect other major businesses in the world. Fashion is not just limited to apparel, and impacts our complete lifestyle and as well as the products that we buy. Fashion influences the automobile, housing, and entertainment industries, and like these industries, it is shaped by the basic principles of business and economics.

What is business? Business is the activity of creating, producing, and marketing products or services. The primary objective of business is to make a profit. **Profit**, or net income, is the amount of money a business earns in excess of its expenses. Consequently, in the United States, **business** can be defined as the activity of creating, producing, and marketing products or services for a profit.

Economic Importance of the Fashion Business

The business of fashion contributes significantly to the economy of the United States, through the materials and services it purchases, the wages and taxes it pays, and the goods and services it produces. The fashion business is one of the largest employers in the country. However, employment has declined almost by half since the industry boom in the early 1970s. Now, roughly 670,000 people in the United

States are employed either in factories that produce apparel for men, women, and children or in textile plants that produce the materials from which garments are made.[1]

More people are employed in apparel production than in the entire printing and publishing business or the automobile manufacturing industry. In addition, more than 62,000 people are employed in producing such fashion items as fur and leather garments and accessories, jewelry and cosmetics; hundreds of thousands more are employed by the retail organizations that distribute these goods. When we add to this a share of the total number of jobs in finance, transportation, advertising, computers, electronics, and other services that devote part of their efforts to the fashion industry, it becomes obvious that the fashion industry has a tremendous impact on our economy.

The growth and development of mass markets, mass-production methods, and mass distribution have contributed to the creation of new job opportunities in the fashion industry—not only in the production area, but in design and marketing as well. Young people are entering the fashion business in greater numbers each year and are having a marked effect on the business. Innovation and change have become increasingly important factors in the economic growth of the fashion business.

Scope of the Fashion Business

The fashion business is composed of numerous industries all working to keep consumers of fashion satisfied (see Figure 4.1). A special relationship exists among these industries that makes the fashion business different from other businesses. The four different levels of the fashion business—known as the primary level, the secondary level, the retail level, and the auxiliary level—are composed of separate entities, but they also work interdependently to provide the market with the fashion merchandise that will satisfy consumers. Because of this unique relationship among the different industries, the fashion business is unusually exciting.

The Primary Level

The **primary level** is composed of the growers and producers of the raw materials of fashion—the fiber, fabric, leather, and fur producers who function in the raw materials market. The earliest part of the planning function in color and texture takes place on the primary level. It is also the level of the fashion business that works the farthest in advance of the ultimate selling period of the goods. Up to two years'

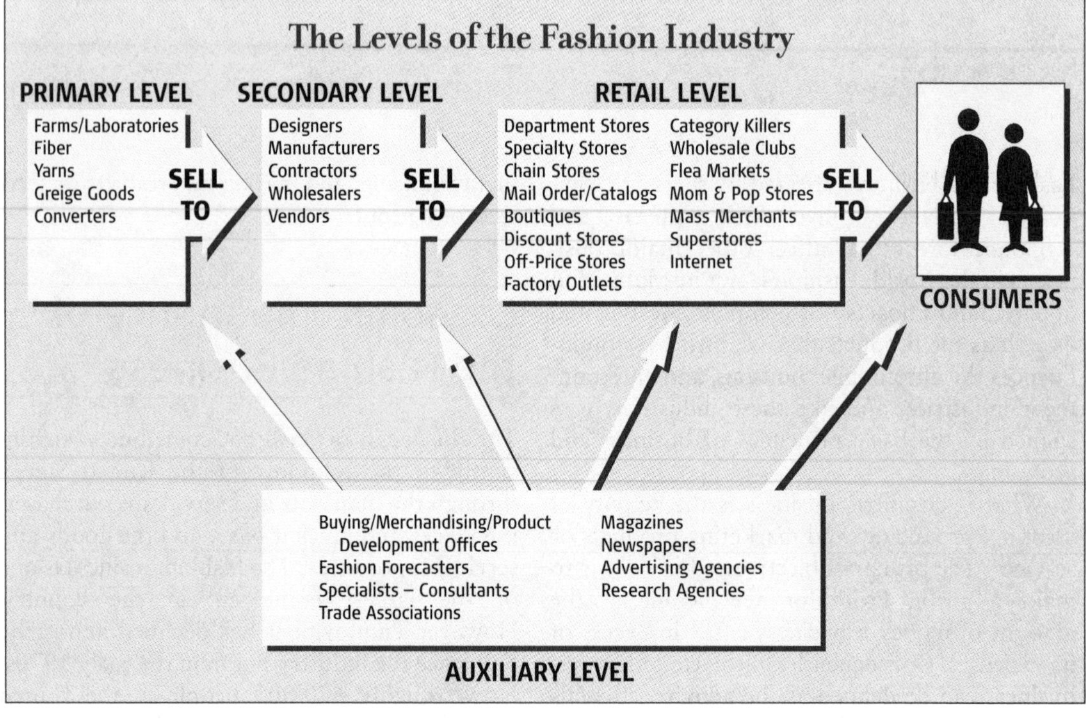

FIGURE 4.1 *The fashion industry operates collaboratively on four levels to serve the customer.* Source: The Fashion Institute of Technology, New York.

	3/6/2002	3/7/2002	3/8/2002	3/9/2002	3/10/2002	3/11/2002	3/12/2002	
12am	This is HSN	Maggie Sweet by Daniel Kiviat	Diane Gilman	The Look by Randolph Duke	USA Gold	Serious Skin Care	Spring Into Absolute 1st Anniversary	9pm
1am	Best of Ireland	Slinky Brand Fashions		Betula by C. Birkenstock				10pm
2am	Jewelry Outlet	Cervelle Casual Fashions	Storybook Knits	Spring Fashion Forecast	HSN Sports Weekly	Amber Jewelry		11pm
3am		Marvilleous Fashions	Technibond Outlet	Cynthia Taylor Fashions	The Doll Shop		Terry Lewis' Classic Luxuries	12am
4am				Cervelle Casual Fashions		Gemstone Outlet		1am
5am		Curve Appeal Premiere	Spring Fashion Forecast	The Denim Collection	Seymour Mann Dolls		Curve Appeal	2am
6am		Cynthia Taylor Fashions	The Denim Collection	Storybook Knits	Plug It In		Take Care Of Yourself	3am
7am	Sunrise	Sunrise	Sunrise	Monzo & Franco Premiere	Take Care Of Yourself	Sunrise	Sunrise	4am
8am				Spring Fashion Essentials	Spring Home Week Preview			5am
9am	Home Solutions	Spring Fashion Forecast	Cynthia Taylor Fashions	Anthony Mark Hankins		Amber Jewelry	Take Care Of Yourself	6am
10am	Maggie Sweet by Daniel Kiviat	Home Solutions	Diane Gilman	Due Per Due Premiere			Spring Into Absolute 1st Anniversary	7am
11am		Hoover 3rd Anniversary		Sharif Studio	USA Gold	Serious Skin Care		8am
12pm	Doll Collecting with Tina	Monzo & Franco Premiere	Christine Alt Premiere	The Look by Randolph Duke				9am
1pm		Maggie Sweet by Daniel Kiviat	Susan Lucci Collection	Slinky Brand Fashions		USA Gold	Take Care Of Yourself	10am
2pm	Silver Reflections		Jewelry Under $50	Storybook Knits	Colors of Sapphires		The Denim Collection	11am
3pm		Diane Gilman		Terry Lewis' Classic Luxuries		Giovanni	USA Gold	12pm
4pm	Samsonite Luggage	Cynthia Taylor Fashions	The Watch Hour		Take Care Of Yourself	Serious Skin Care		1pm
5pm	Trade Secrets	Home Solutions	Ann Marino Shoes	Christine Alt Premiere	Plug It In	Amber Jewelry	Take Care Of Yourself	2pm
6pm	Home Solutions	Hoover 3rd Anniversary	Susan Lucci Collection	Due Per Due Premiere			Spring Into Absolute 1st Anniversary	3pm
7pm	At Home	The Denim Collection	Storybook Knits	Betula by C. Birkenstock	USA Gold	Serious Skin Care		4pm
8pm	Office@Home	Susan Lucci Collection	Harve' Benard Fashions	The Look By Randolph Duke				5pm
9pm	Simply The Best Jewelry	Maggie Sweet by Daniel Kiviat	Diane Gilman	Maggie Sweet by Daniel Kiviat		USA Gold		6pm
10pm			Christine Alt Premiere		Take Care Of Yourself			7pm
11pm	Samsonite Luggage	Sharif Studio	The Look By Randolph Duke	Harve' Benard Fashions	Serious Skin Care	Giovanni	Take Care Of Yourself	8pm

FIGURE 4.2
The retail level includes nonstore retailers, such as HSN, the Home Shopping Network, which also publishes a magazine that does double duty as a program listing and a mini-catalog.
Adapted from the Home Shopping Network.

lead time is needed by primary-level companies before the goods will be available to the consumer. Primary-level goods may often be imports from third world emerging nations, where textiles are usually the earliest form of industrialization.

The Secondary Level

The **secondary level** is composed of industries—manufacturers and contractors—that produce the semifinished or finished fashion goods from the materials produced on the primary level. On the secondary level are the manufacturers of women's, men's, and children's apparel and also legwear, bodywear, and underwear; accessories; cosmetics and fragrances; and home furnishings.

Manufacturers who function on the secondary level may be based in the United States or overseas. Fashion goods are now produced in the Far East, the Caribbean, South America, and Europe. Secondary-level companies work from six months to one and one half years ahead of the time that goods are available to the consumer.

The Retail Level

The **retail level** is the ultimate distribution level. On this level are the different types of retailers who buy their goods from the secondary level and then supply them directly to the consumer. In many cases, the retail level works with both the primary and secondary levels to ensure a coordinated approach to consumer wants. The interrelationship among the primary, secondary, and retail levels is vertical. The farther removed a level is from the consumer, the farther in advance it must plan. Retailers make initial purchases for resale to customers from three to six months before the customer buying season.

The Auxiliary Level

The **auxiliary level** is the only level that functions with all the other levels simultaneously. This level is composed of all the support services that are working constantly with primary producers, secondary manufacturers, and retailers to keep consumers aware of the fashion merchandise produced for ultimate consumption. On this level are all the advertising media—print, audio, and visual—and fashion consultants and researchers.

Diversity and Competition

The enormous variety and diversity that exist in the kinds and sizes of firms that operate on each level of the fashion industry make it a fascinating and competitive business. There are giant firms, both national and international, and small companies with regional or local distribution, doing business side by side as privately or publicly owned corporations, partnerships, or sole proprietorships. Fashion-producing companies may also be part of conglomerates, which also own, for example, entertainment companies, oil wells, professional sports teams, or consumer foods and products divisions.

Whether large or small, the different types of producers have one need in common—the need to understand what their ultimate customer will buy. Only through complete understanding and cooperation can the four levels of the fashion business be aware of new developments in fashion and apply them to satisfy the wants of their customers. This cooperation allows them to have the right merchandise at the right price, in the right place, at the right time, in the right quantities, and with the right sales promotion for their customers.

However, when you begin to try to sell a product or service in our economic system, chances are that someone else will be trying to sell something similar. No matter what the size of the firm involved, potential customers are free to buy where they please and what they please. Each company must compete with the others for those customers' business. A company can choose to compete in one of three ways: price, quality, or innovation.

Competition and Price

Selling blue jeans for less than your competition may bring you more business. However, you are taking in less money than your rival does on each pair sold, and you still have to cover the same cost and expenses. The hope is that your lower price will attract more customers, sell more jeans than your competition, and so come out with a good overall profit. Head-to-head competition like this tends to keep prices down, which is good for the buying public. At the same time, it allows a company to look forward to a promise of profits if it can sell more of its product or service than competitors do.

Competition and Quality

Rather than sell your jeans for less than your competition, you may choose to compete for customers by offering higher-quality goods. Although you may charge more for your jeans, you offer a better fit, more durable fabric, or better styling. This possibility provides a practical incentive for businesses to maintain high standards and increases the choices available to consumers.

Competition and Innovation

Our economic system not only encourages variations in quality and price, it also encourages immense variety in the types of merchandise and services offered to the public. Changes in taste and new technology bring about innovation, so that your jeans could be trimmed or untrimmed, designer-made, or French cut. The economy and the competitive environment are constantly creating new business opportunities. The result is an astonishing diversity of businesses.

Government Regulation of Business

The right of government to regulate business is granted by the U.S. Constitution and by state constitutions. There are two basic categories of federal legislation that affect the fashion industry: (1) laws that regulate competition, and (2) labeling laws designed to pro-tect consumers. Table 4.1 lists the key federal laws that affect and/or regulate the fashion industry.

Forms of Business Ownership

Ownership of a fashion business—or of any business—may take many different legal forms, each carrying certain privileges and

TABLE 4.1 Key Federal Laws Affecting the Fashion Industry

LAWS AFFECTING COMPETITION	PURPOSE AND PROVISIONS
Sherman Antitrust Act—1890	Outlawed monopolies. Outlawed restraint of competition.
Clayton Act—1914	Same purpose as Sherman Act but reinforced Sherman Act by defining some specific restraint—e.g., price fixing.
Federal Trade Commission (FTC) Act—1914 (Wheeler–Lee Act of 1938 amended the FTC Act.)	Established the FTC as a "policing" agency. Developed the mechanics for policing unfair methods of competition, e.g., false claims, price discrimination, price fixing.
Robinson–Patman Act—1936	Designed to equalize competition between large and small retailers (i.e., to reduce the advantages that big retailers have over small retailers—outgrowth of 1930 depression and growth of big chain retailers in 1920s.) Examples of provision of law: 1. Outlawed price discrimination if both small and large retailers buy the same amount of goods. 2. Outlawed inequitable and unjustified quantity discounts (e.g., discounts allowable if (a) available to all types of retailers and (b) related to actual savings that vendor could make from quantity cuttings or shipments.) 3. Outlawed "phony" advertising allowance monies—i.e., advertising money must be used for advertising. 4. Outlawed discrimination in promotional allowances (monies for advertising, promotional display, etc.)—equal allowances must be given under same conditions to small and large retailers alike.
Cellar–Kefauver—1950	This law made it illegal to eliminate competition by creating a monopoly through the merger of two or more companies.
PRODUCT AND LABELING LAWS DESIGNED TO PROTECT CONSUMERS	**PURPOSE AND PROVISIONS**
Wool Products Labeling Act—1939; amended in 1984	Protects consumers from unrevealed presence of substitutes or mixtures. FTC responsible for enforcing law.
Fur Products Labeling Act—1951	Protects consumers and retailers against misbranding, false advertising, and false invoicing.
Flammable Fabrics Act—1954; revised in 1972	Prohibits manufacture or sale of flammable fabrics or apparel.
Textile Fiber Identification Act—1960; amended in 1984	Protects producers and consumers against false identification of fiber content.
Fair Packaging and Labeling Act—1966	Regulates interstate and foreign commerce by prohibiting deceptive methods of packaging or labeling.
Care Labeling of Textile Wearing Apparel Ruling—1972; amended in 1984, 1997	Requires that all apparel have labels attached that clearly inform consumers about care and maintenance of the article.

TABLE 4.2 Advantages and Disadvantages of Each Form of Business Ownership

FORM OF OWNERSHIP	ADVANTAGES	DISADVANTAGES
Sole proprietorship (single owner)	• Ability to keep all profits • Simple to form and easiest to dissolve • Ownership flexibility	• Unlimited financial liability • Limited capital • Management deficiencies • Lack of continuity
Partnership (a few owners)	• Ease of formation • Complementary management skills • Greater financial capacity than sole proprietorship • Less red tape than corporation	• Unlimited financial liability • Interpersonal conflicts • Lack of continuity if partner dies • Harder to dissolve than sole proprietorship
Corporation (Inc.) (many owners)	• Limited financial liability • Specialized management skills • Greater financial capacity than other forms of ownership • Economies of larger-scale operation • Easy to transfer ownership	• Difficult and costly ownership form to establish and dissolve • Tax disadvantage • Legal restrictions • Depersonalization

responsibilities. The three most common forms of business ownership are the sole proprietorship, the partnership, and the corporation. Corporations tend to be large-scale operations that account for the greatest share of the profits earned by U.S. business. However, sole proprietorships are more numerous, accounting for almost 70 percent of all business.

Each form of ownership has a characteristic structure, legal status, size, and field to which it is best suited. Each has its own advantages and disadvantages and offers a distinctive working environment with its own risks and rewards (see Table 4.2).

Business Growth and Expansion

For the past few years, business activity has focused on the change in forms of business growth and expansion. The news media is filled with reports of businesses buying and selling other businesses and seeking new methods to make themselves more efficient and competitive.

One of the most distinct changes in the fashion business has been the rise of corporate giants which grew through mergers, acquisitions, and internal expansion. The growth of these giants has changed the methods of doing business, and has led to the demise of old-time famous-name sole proprietorships, partnerships, and small companies that could no longer compete.

Growth and expansion are fundamental to today's business world. Corporate growth has become a major economic, political, and social issue in recent years. Growth and expansion can occur in a variety of ways—internal growth, mergers, and acquisitions. Many large corporations grow by more than one of these methods. For example, cosmetics giant Estée Lauder developed the Prescriptives brand to expand to a more upscale consumer market. The company also acquired several smaller companies that cater to a younger market, including Bobbi Brown and MAC.

Internal Growth

A company's ability to grow internally determines its ability to offer more service and broader assortments of merchandise, and to increase profits. This is true because internal growth is real growth, in terms of creating new products and new jobs. Internal growth can be accomplished through horizontal means, or vertical means, or both. When a company has **horizontal growth**, it expands its capabilities on the level on which it has been performing successfully. An apparel company could add new lines to diversify its product offerings; a retail store could open new branches. When a company has **vertical growth**, it expands its capabilities on levels other than its primary function. An apparel company could begin to produce its own fabric, or could retail its manufactured

FIGURE 4.3
Donna Karan's DKNY store is an example of vertical growth from the secondary to the retail level.
Courtesy, Fairchild Publications, Inc.

goods in stores that the apparel company owns (see Figure 4.3).

Mergers and Acquisitions

In a **merger** (or acquisition) a sale of one company to another company occurs, with the purchasing company usually remaining dominant. Companies merge to form a larger corporate organization for many reasons. They may wish to take advantage of a large corporation's greater purchasing power, or they may want to sell stock to obtain the financial resources needed for expansion. The desire to constantly increase sales is often able to be fulfilled only by a merger. At the retail level, for example, the acquisition of Macy's by Federated Department Stores extended the conglomerate's market to include Macy's customers.

Operating economies can often be achieved by combining companies. Many times duplicate facilities can be eliminated, and marketing, purchasing, and other operations can be consolidated. **Diversification**, the addition of various lines, products, or services to serve different markets, can also be a motive for a merger. For example, the acquisition of Banana Republic by the Gap broadened the Gap's market to reach customers for clothing at higher price points. Then the Gap started Old Navy to reach to even lower-price points. Now the company covers three price points.

The Franchise

A rapidly growing business arrangement is the **franchise.** This arrangement is a contract that gives an individual (or group of people) the right to own a business while benefiting from the expertise and reputation of an established firm. In return, the individual, known as the franchisee, pays the parent company, known as the franchisor, a set sum to purchase the franchise and royalties on goods or services sold. Franchises may be organized as sole proprietorships, partnerships, or corporations, although the form of business organization that the franchise must use may be designated in the franchise contract.

Franchises generate one-third of all retail sales in the United States today and are steadily growing in volume according to industry reports. Although the franchise arrangement is most widespread among fast-food restaurants, convenience stores, and automobile dealers, franchises can be found at many levels of the fashion business, especially in retailing.

The growth in the number of manufacturer-franchised shops is phenomenal. One of the outstanding examples of this is the very popular Athlete's Foot stores (see Figure 4.4). Although we will learn much more about designer-name franchising when we cover the apparel industries, it is important to note that Ralph Lauren, Donna Karan, and Oscar de la Renta are all involved in designer-franchised boutiques and shops in major cities throughout the United States, Europe, and Asia.

Advantages

Franchising offers advantages to both the franchise and the franchisor. The franchisee can get into business quickly, use proven operating methods, and benefit from training programs and mass purchasing offered by the franchisor. The franchise is provided with a ready market that identifies with the store or brand name, thus assuring customer traffic. The franchisor has a great deal of control over its distribution network, limited liability, and less need for capital for expansion. Expansion is therefore more

FIGURE 4.4
Athlete's Foot is a popular franchise that is well-known for its footwear collection.
Courtesy, The Athlete's Foot.

rapid than would be possible without the franchising arrangement. Royalty and franchise fees add to the profits of the parent company, and the personal interest and efforts of the franchisees as owner-managers help to assure the success of each venture.

Disadvantages

Franchising also has drawbacks for both parties. The franchisee may find profits small in relation to the time and work involved, and often has limited flexibility at the local level. In addition, there is the risk of franchise arrangements organized merely to sell franchises, rather than for their long-range profitability to all parties involved. The franchisor may find profits so slim that it may want to own stores outright rather than franchise them. Attempts to buy back franchises often lead to troubled relations with the remaining franchises.

Licensing

Licensing is an increasingly popular method of expanding an already existing business. **Licensing** is a legal arrangement whereby firms are given permission to produce and market merchandise in the name of the licensor for a specific period of time. The licensor is then paid a percentage of the sales (usually at the wholesale price) called a **royalty fee**. The royalty fee usually ranges from 2 to 15 percent.

Licensing grew tremendously in the late 1970s and through the 1980s and 1990s. By 2000, retail sales of licensed fashion merchandise in the United States and Canada reached almost $12.7 billion. Of that total, apparel accounted for $4.23 billion, accessories for $1,821 billion, footwear for $88 million, and health and beauty aids for $2.5 billion.[2]

The first designer to license his name to a manufacturer was Christian Dior, who lent his name to a line of ties in 1950. Today, many of the best-known women's and men's apparel designers are licensing either the use of their original designs or just their names without a design for a wide variety of goods, from apparel to luggage. Many fashion labels—Ralph Lauren and Laura Ashley, for example—also extend into home furnishings through licensing. Among the many American designers involved in licensing are Bill Blass, Calvin Klein, Ralph Lauren, John Weitz, and Oscar de la Renta. Most customers are not aware that some of the fashion merchandise they buy is licensed. For example, to customers every J.G. Hook product is made by J.G. Hook. In fact, this licensor manufactures *no* merchandise in house.

The licensing phenomenon is not limited to name designers. Manufacturers of athletic shoes expand their business enormously by licensing their logos and names to producers of active sportswear. Nike, Reebok, and Adidas have been particularly successful. Popular movies and TV shows have spawned apparel and other products based on their themes or characters. Disney's sales of licensed merchandise are $7.5-8 billion annually.[3] Comic or movie characters like Mickey Mouse, Garfield, Teenage Mutant Ninja Turtles, and Snoopy are also frequently licensed, as are most professional sports teams and many players or athletes. The National Hockey League sold $7 billion of licensed merchandise in fiscal 1998.[4]

The advantage of a licensing arrangement to a manufacturer is that the merchandise is identified with a highly recognizable name, which

FASHION FOCUS

Young Designers: Where Does Their Garden Grow?

Today, when most of us think of designers, we think of Oscar de la Renta, Ralph Lauren, Donna Karan, Carolina Herrera, and Diane Von Furstenberg. These, and many other famous foreign and American designers, are all 40 years old, and in some cases way over the rainbow.

Design by Zac Posen.
Courtesy, Fairchild Publications, Inc.

The phenomenon of today's design talent is youth. There is Esteban Cortazar, whose 2002 fashions were influenced by the glamorous lives of his artist father and singer mother. Cortazer took off time from—of all places—high school, to put on his 2003 Spring Collection show!

The energy of these young designers infuses the fashion industry with excitement and creative promise. Designers like Hushi Mortezaie of Michael and Hushi did a collection inspired by "a modern-day Auntie Mame starved for fast fashion and fast food." But these fresh new faces do not necessarily equal downtown mayhem. Peter Som is bringing the ease of the 1920s Riviera where "you can wear your pajama pants to dinner," to the lifestyle of his 2003 customers.

This new group of designers, mostly under 30 years old, are stepping up to the plate and showing that American designers are a force to be reckoned with! They design clothes that are beautiful, feminine, and sexy. Among this group are Jeremy Scott, Zac Posen, Alvin Valley, Michael Soheil, and James Thomas. Another phenomenon among these new American designers is the diversity of their birthplaces. Valley comes from Cuba, while Soheil comes from Tehran, Iran. Diego Benetti is from Buenos Aires, Argentina. This global background offers an international flair to their fashion outlook and designs.

With the press, retailers, and most importantly, the customers recognizing the talent of this new youth brigade, you can be sure that international success is on the horizon for them. Watch out world, the Americans are coming—and bringing American fashion for everyone!

Designs by the Indigo People.
Courtesy, Fairchild Publications, Inc.

Sources

Rose Apadaca Jones, "New York: The Collections-the Best of Both Coasts," *Women's Wear Daily*, February 6, 2002, p. 16.

Samantha Conti, "Primed for the Limelight," *Women's Wear Daily*, February 6, 2002, p.6.

Joshua Greene, "CMG Hosts Designer Showcase," *Women's Wear Daily*, August 28, 2002.

Miles Socha, "They'll Take Manhattan," *Women's Wear Daily*, February 6, 2002, p.14.

"GenArt's Corset Crusaders," *Women's Wear Weekly*, August 6, 2001, p. 26.

"New York Collections: Wild or Wild," *Women's Wear Weekly*, Section II pp. 8–22.

www.about.com Young/New Fashion Designers.

"Gen Arts' Fresh Faces," *Women's Wear Daily*, October 10, 2002.

FIGURE 4.5
Retail sales of fashion brands declined 6% due to a soft apparel market and continuous consolidation within the licensor and licensee ranks.
Adapted from the Gladys Marcus Library, Fashion Institute of Technology.

Retail Sales of Licensed Fashion Merchandise, by Product Category, U. S. & Canada, 2000 (in millions of dollars)

Product Category	Retail Sales 2000	Retail Sales 1999	Product Category	Pct. Change '00/'99	Share of Total ('00)
Accessories	$1,840	$1,975	Accessories	−7%	14%
Apparel	$4,225	$4,510	Apparel	−6%	33%
Footwear	$880	$950	Footwear	−7%	7%
Health/Beauty	$2,550	$2,630	Health/Beauty	−3%	20%

also generally connotes high quality (see Figure 4.5). Of course, the manufacturer also runs the risk of the designer's popularity fading. However, many manufacturers produce licensed goods for several designers.

The recognition factor can be valuable to retailers in presenting their own fashion image. And to consumers, the designer name not only indicates a certain quality of merchandise, but symbolizes status or achievement as well. Because of that built-in appeal, stores have stocked up on designer goods from socks to fragrances and jewelry.

Designers' Retail Programs

A famous designer name is a strong selling point at retail. Licensing spreads a designer's name, while giving the financial responsibility—and risk—to licensees who are specialists in their respective product categories. For example, under licensing agreements, Calvin Klein improved its sales of jeans and underwear by 73 percent over the previous year in 1996. It was also able to expand into eyewear, handbags, and several home fashion categories.[5]

Designers' International Programs

Licensing is also crossing international borders, as an increasing number of designers, foreign and domestic, are making licensing agreements in other countries. The need to grow internationally is driven by an oversaturated U.S. market.

Birth of a Fashion

But how do fashions generally begin? Who starts them, who sponsors them, and what influences customers to accept them? Answers to these questions are complex and involve designers, manufacturers, retailers—and most of all—customers.

The myth that every change in fashion is caused by a designer seeking a new way to make money is, of course, not true. As we saw in Chapter 1, it is consumers who bring about changes in fashion. The needs and wants of consumers change. Their ideas about what is appropriate and acceptable change, as well as their interests in life. These are all reasons that influence fashion designers and manufacturers to produce new and different styles for consumer's consideration. The charting, forecasting, and satisfaction of consumer demand are the fashion industry's main concerns.

Current trends in consumers' purchasing, lifestyles, and attitudes are noted and analyzed. Subsequently the trends are interpreted and presented to consumers in the form of new styles. Designers and manufacturers influence fashion by providing an unending series of new designs from which consumers choose how best to express their individual lifestyles.

Many precautions are taken to ensure that designers are presenting what customers want. Even so, at least two-thirds of the new designs introduced each season by the fashion industry fail to become fashions. Some designs are introduced too early, before the public is ready to accept them. Other designs fail because they are too extreme for consumer acceptance. Still other designs fail to become fashions because although they are commonly accepted in many places, they meet pockets of resistance in certain areas of the country. What is worn in New York is not necessarily what consumers in less urban areas of the United States are ready to accept. Think about the hot pants, the harem pants, the peasant looks of the 1970s, and the punk-rock extremes of the 1980s! Only a trend that reflects a nationwide mood will successfully cross the United States from ocean-to-ocean and affect the lives and wardrobes of all those in-between.

The Designer's Role

The days when the design world was populated by a few visionaries whose ideas produced all the designs for the public are long gone. Today, there are unlimited opportunities in the field of design for those who have the special talents, both artistic and practical, that are needed to shape the consumer's world. Designers are everywhere and they design everything—fashions, furnishings, housewares, and office equipment. Their tools range from pencil and sketchpad to computer programs.

Designers must continually study the lifestyles of those consumers for whom their designs are intended. Because designers work far in advance of their designs' final production, they must be able to predict future fashion trends. Designers must be aware of the effects of current events, socioeconomic conditions, and psychological attitudes on fashion interest and demand.

In creating designs that will not only reflect consumer attitudes and needs but also give expression to artistic ideas, fashion designers are continually influenced and limited by many factors. Of particular importance are practical business considerations. All designs must be produced at a profit and within the firm's predetermined wholesale price range. Consequently, designers must consider the availability and cost of materials, the particular image that the firm wants to maintain, available production techniques, and labor costs. Great designers use their creativity to overcome all these limitations and to produce salable, exciting designs.

Types of Designers

Most designers can be classified in one of the following three categories:

1. *High-fashion or "name" designers* are responsible for the full range of decisions of a fashion house as well as for establishing the image and creating designs for the company. They design ready-to-wear lines as well as custom designs, and many license the use of their prestigious names to manufacturers of accessories, fragrances and cosmetics, and home fashions. Some, like Ralph Lauren in the United States, run houses that bear their

FIGURE 4.6
Sometimes it seems as if designer logos are taking over the world.
EEK & MEEK reprinted by permission of Newspaper Enterprise Association, Inc.

Then & Now

Partners: Someone to Watch Over Me!

Part guardian angel, part therapist, part entrepreneur, and part best friend, business partners of famous designers have served as the foundation of the success of famous names for years. The names of these partners are barely known, and they like it that way—the name to be nurtured, polished, and become a business success, is that of the designer.

Ben Shaw, Stuart Kriesler, Barry Schwartz, Robert Duffy, and Bud Konheim are certainly not recognized names by the general public. But Oscar de la Renta, Ralph Lauren, Calvin Klein, Marc Jacobs, and Nicole Miller bring immediate recognition and all carry the glamorous image of fashion.

Back THEN, Ben Shaw had the title of "Mr. Seventh Avenue" gaining his reputation by introducing the famous designer names of his time—Donald Brooks, Norman Norell, Stephen Burrows, Dominic Rompollo, Giorgio Sant'Angelo, Halston, and the then little known Oscar de la Renta—and turning their companies into successful business enterprises. Stuart Kreisler was the business genius who boosted the careers of Clovis Ruffin, Albert Capraro, and, at that time, the unknown Ralph Lauren! Stuart was the one who convinced Ralph to design women's wear, and the legacy of Ralph Lauren was launched.

But NOW, Barry Schwartz is chairman and chief executive officer of Calvin Klein. Inc., where Calvin's name has become a household word, and Calvin Klein fashions are sold all over the world. In 2003 they sold their privately held company for more that $700 million, not bad for boyhood friends from the Bronx that started their business with $10,000! Robert Duffy, a dress salesman for Rubin Thomas, attended a school fashion show and was impressed by the talent of a young student designer, Marc Jacobs. Today, these partners have built a successful business and a worldwide reputation for the Marc Jacobs name. Bud Konheim is the business end of the partnership with Nicole Miller. Nicole does the designing and creative thinking for the company, while Bud takes care of the business and makes sure that everything results in a successful bottom line.

Whether these partners were mentors or advisors, shrewd businessmen or flashy wheeler-dealers, they shared a common passion to succeed by placing someone else's name in the spotlight, building an image around it, and making fortunes along the way.

Sources:

Arthur Friedman, "Someone to Watch Over Me," *Women's Wear Weekly* Special Section "The Americans", May 2002, pp. 40, 42.

Eric Wilson, "Triple Crown," *Women's Wear Weekly* Special Section, pp. 62, 64, 66.

Ben Shaw was partners with Oscar de la Renta, and also gave numerous designers their start, including Donald Brooks, Norman Norell, and Stephen Burrows.
Courtesy, Fairchild Publications, Inc.

Marc Jacobs and Robert Duffy have been partners through thick and thin.
Courtesy, Fairchild Publications, Inc.

For over 20 years, Bud Konheim and Nicole Miller have been partners.
Courtesy, Fairchild Publications, Inc.

own name. Others take over a design company at the death or retirement of its founder. For example, Karl Lagerfeld took over the designing reins at Chanel, in addition to running his own studio.

2. *Stylist-designers* work for manufacturers and adapt the designs of others, typically of name designers. Usually they create variations in less expensive fabrics to appeal to a market for lower-priced merchandise at the late rise or early culmination stage of the fashion cycle.
3. *Freelance designers* sell sketches of their original designs or adaptations to manufacturers. Freelancers typically work out of design studios. They are not involved in the selection of fabrics and colors or in the business decisions that are required to manufacture the products based on their designs. Donna Karan, now an internationally recognized name designer, got her start designing for Anne Klein.

Insight and Intuition

A designer takes a fashion idea and embodies it in new styles. Even the most creative designers, however, disclaim any power to force acceptance of their styles. Few have said so more effectively than Paul Poiret, one of the 20th century's great Parisian couturiers. He once told an American audience:

I know you think me a king of fashion . . . It is a reception which cannot but flatter me and of which I cannot complain. All the same, I must undeceive you with regard to the powers of a king of fashion. We are not capricious despots such as wake up one fine day, decide upon a change in habits, abolish a neckline, or puff out a sleeve. We are neither arbiters nor dictators. Rather we are to be thought of as the blindly obedient servants of woman, who for her part is always enamoured of change and a thirst for novelty. It is our role, and our duty, to be on the watch for the moment at which she becomes bored with what she is wearing, that we may suggest at the right instant something else which will meet her taste and needs. It is therefore with a pair of antennae and not a rod of iron that I come before you, and not as a master that I speak, but as a slave . . . who must divine your innermost thoughts.[6]

Insight and intuition always play a large part in a designer's success. Constant experimentation with new ideas is a must. As one fashion reaches the excess that marks its approaching demise, a designer must have new styles ready and waiting for the public.

Sources of Design Inspiration

Where does the designer get ideas and inspiration for new fashion? The answer, of course, is: everywhere! Through television, the designer experiences all the wonders of the entertainment world. In films, the designer is exposed to the influences of all the arts and lifestyles throughout the world. Because consumers are exposed to movies through international distribution, films prime their audiences to accept new fashions inspired by the costumes. Museum exhibits, art shows, world happenings, expositions, the theater, music, dance, and world travel are all sources of design inspiration to fashion designers (see Figure 4.7). The fashions of the past are also a rich source of design inspiration.

While always alert to the new and exciting, fashion designers never lose sight of the recent past. They know that consumers need to anticipate something new each season. But they also

FIGURE 4.7
Museum exhibits often inspire new trends, such as this modern day toga dress inspired by the Metropolitan Museum of Art's exhibit called "Goddess."
Courtesy, Fairchild Publications, Inc.

recognize that whatever new style is introduced will have to take its place with what consumers already have in their wardrobes. No one starts with all new clothes each season. Rarely does a revolutionary new style succeed. Instead, it is the evolutionary new style that so often becomes the best-selling fashion.

The Manufacturer's Role

Manufacturers would agree with Dwight E. Robinson that "every market into which the consumer's fashion sense has insinuated itself is, by that very token, subject to [the] common, compelling need for unceasing change in the styling of its goods."[7]

Even in such mundane items as writing paper, the need for change has produced rainbows of pastels, brilliant deep shades, and the traditional white with dainty or bold prints. Similarly, in basics such as bedsheets or men's dress shirts, the once traditional white has yielded to a variety of colors, stripes, and prints. There is scarcely an industry serving consumers today in which the manufacturer's success does not depend, in part, upon an ability to attune styling to fashion interest and demand. A current trend is to hire merchandisers who do market research for the manufacturer, specializing in identifying the correct customer and his or her needs and wants.

Types of Manufacturers

In general, manufacturers of fashion goods can be divided into five groups, differentiated by styling and price. One group is made up of designers or firms that produce innovative, high-fashion apparel that is very expensive. Another group bridges the price range between custom designs and high quality but less expensive merchandise. Hence the name **bridge market.** Some high-fashion designers also produce bridge lines. The next group is usually identified as the **better market.** Its price range is just below that of the bridge lines. A third group of firms sometimes produces originals. But it usually turns out adaptations of styles that have survived the introduction stage and are in the rise stage of their fashion life cycle. This group of firms is usually identified as the **moderate-priced market.** A fifth group of manufacturers makes no attempt to offer new or unusual styling. Rather, these firms mass-produce close copies or adaptations of styles that have proved their acceptance in higher-priced markets. This group is usually identified as the **budget market.**

Fashion Influence

In the field of women's apparel, manufacturers are committed to producing several new lines a year. A **line** is an assortment of new designs with a designated period for delivery to the retailer. Some of these may be new in every sense of the word and others merely adaptations of currently popular styles. Producers hope that a few of the designs in a given line will prove to be "hot"—so precisely in step with demand that their sales will be profitably large.

For the most part, the fashion industries are made up of manufacturers whose ability to anticipate the public's response to styles is excellent. Those who do badly in this respect, even for a single season, usually reap small sales and large losses. Unless they are unusually well financed, they quickly find themselves out of business. In the fashion industry, the survival of the fittest means the survival of those who give the most able assistance in the birth and growth of fashions that consumers will buy.

The Retailer's Role

Although retailers do not usually create fashion, they can encourage or retard its progress by the degree of accuracy with which they anticipate the demands of their customers. They seek out from manufacturers styles that they believe are most likely to win acceptance from these target groups.

Some large retailers work directly with manufacturers and firms at the primary level to develop styles for exclusive sale at their stores. Thus, retailers such as The Gap and The Limited can stock only their own labels. Others, such as Federated Department Stores, sell private label merchandise along with national brands. (We will examine the practice of product development by retailers in more detail in Chapter 16.)

Types of Retailers

There are many ways to classify retail firms. However, when firms are evaluated on the basis of their leadership positions, they tend to fall into three main categories.

First, there are firms that are considered "fashion leaders." They feature newly introduced styles that have only limited production

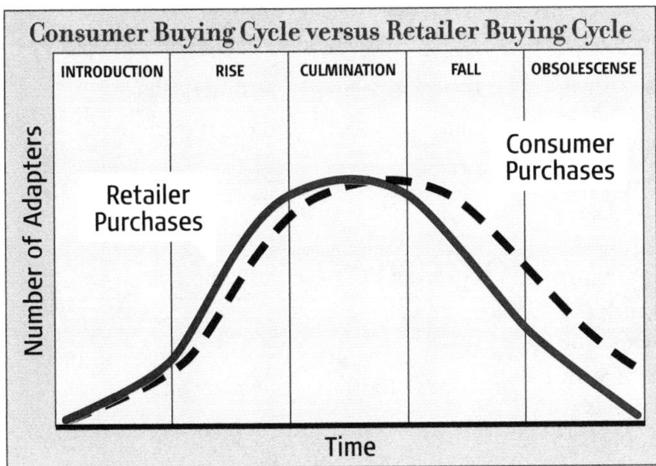

FIGURE 4.8
Retailers have to stay just a step ahead of their target customers. Retailers need to have sufficient stock available when customers are ready to buy a new fashion, but need to avoid being overstocked when customers interest shifts to a new fashion.

and distribution. These styles, called "Designer Collections," are usually very expensive. Examples of these firms include Bergdorf Goodman, Neiman Marcus, and Nordstrom.

A second group, called "traditional retailers"—by far the largest in number—features fashions that have captured consumer interest in their introduction stage and are in the late rise or early culmination stage of their life cycles. These styles are from designers "Bridge Collections" or from "Better" or "Moderate" manufacturers. Since these styles are usually widely produced by this time, they are most often offered at more moderate prices. Examples of these firms include Macy's, Dillard's, and the May Company. The distinction between the traditional retailers and fashion leaders is somewhat blurred in that the fashion leaders may also carry "traditional" merchandise, and the traditional retailers may have designer departments.

A third group of retailers, often called "mass merchants," features widely accepted fashions that are well into the culmination phase of their life cycles. Since fashions at this stage of development are usually mass-produced, mass merchants can and do offer fashions at moderate to low prices. Examples of these firms include J.C. Penney and Sears. At the low end of the mass market are the discounters, like the off-price Dress Barn, for example, which sold more than $695 million in merchandise in 2001 at discounted prices. Other examples include Wal-Mart and Kmart.

Fashion Influence

Sometimes, because of their constant and intimate contact with their customers, retailers are so intuitive or creative that they lead their suppliers in anticipating the styles their customers will accept (see Figure 4.8). Such retailers accelerate the introduction and progress of new fashions by persuading manufacturers to produce styles that answer an upcoming need or demand. Because of this ability, retailers are doing more and more product development for their own customers. (This trend is discussed in detail in Chapter 16.)

However, most retailers simply select from what is offered to them by producers that they have been successful with in the past. There is a constant flow, back and forth, of information about the styles that the customer is buying. The systems that producers and retailers have today for this purpose are rapid and accurate, mainly because of the development of the computer.

Because of these instantly available and accurate records, retailers can monitor sudden or gradual changes in the preferences of their own customers. The variations in what consumers are buying at a particular store are reflected in what the store buys from the manufacturers of fashion merchandise. From these manufacturers come information about customer preferences that flows in several different directions. One flow is back to the retail stores to alert them to trends they may not have noticed themselves.

Retailers can influence fashion by failing to stock styles that consumers are ready to buy if given the opportunity. Conversely, retailers can make the mistake of exposing new styles prematurely. No amount of retail effort can make customers buy styles in which they have not yet developed interest or in which they have lost interest. The more accurately a retailer understands his or her customers' fashion preferences, the more successful the operation will be. And the more successful the operation, the more important the retailer's fashion influence will be.

Summary and Review

The fashion industry is a major business sector in the United States and around the world. It employs people at four levels: (1) producers of materials, such as natural and manufactured textiles, leather, fur, and materials used in decorative trimmings; (2) manufacturers of apparel, accessories, cosmetics and fragrances, and home fashions; (3) fashion retailers; and (4) auxiliary services to the other three levels, including market research and forecasting and promotional services. Businesses at all four levels collaborate to capture their share of the market.

Companies compete with others at their level by offering advantages of price, quality, and innovation. The federal government regulates the production and sale of fashion goods to ensure safe, functional products for consumers and fair marketing practices among competitors.

Like other businesses, fashion businesses at all levels may be sole proprietorships, partnerships, or corporations. Fashion companies grow horizontally by getting into new markets or vertically by expanding into levels beyond the level of their original business. They may expand internally, acquire or merge with other companies, or franchise or license a part of their business. Continuing into the 21st century, licensing is an important part of virtually every major designer's business strategy, and businesses outside the fashion industry license their names and logos to apparel producers.

At all levels, fashion business executives must be able to predict the tastes of the consumers who wear and use their merchandise. Depending on level, a company must anticipate consumer demand from 6 months to more than a year in advance of the day a new fashion becomes available at retail.

Trade Talk

Define or briefly explain the following terms:

auxiliary level
better market
bridge market
budget market
business
diversification
franchise
horizontal growth
licensing
line
merger
moderate-priced market
primary level
profit
retail level
royalty fee
secondary level
vertical growth

For Review

1. What is the primary objective of all businesses? Explain your answer.
2. Describe the four levels of the fashion business; give examples.
3. How does the auxiliary level differ from the other levels?
4. Compare the advantages and disadvantages of a sole proprietorship and a partnership as a form of business for a fashion retailer.
5. Why do companies seek growth through mergers and acquisitions?
6. What are the practical obstacles that limit fashion designers? What additional factors must be considered in developing each fashion design?
7. List the three types of designers commonly serving the U.S. fashion industry today. Give the responsibilities of each.
8. If you were the president of a national chain of shoe stores, what are five laws and regulations that would affect how you do business? Which of these laws would *not* affect a small, privately owned bridal shop?
9. Differentiate between a license agreement and a franchise.
10. How is a licensed designer name an advantage to the manufacturer? To the consumer? To the retailer?

For Discussion

1. What initial decisions need to be made by an individual or group of individuals who plan to form a company with regard to the form of ownership which will be most beneficial to all?
2. What does the statement "You're only as good as your last collection," mean in regard to fashion designers?

References

1. U.S. Department of Commerce, *U.S. Industrial Outlook 2000,* (Lanham MD: Bernan Press) 2000, pp. 33-33-34.
2. *The Licensing Letter*, 2001, EPM Communications, Inc., April 2000, p. 4.
3. Karen Ragust, *The Licensing Business Handbook* (Brooklyn, NY: EPM Communications, 1995), p. 8.
4. Ibid.
5. Jennifer Steinhauer, "Firm Grasp of Fashion," *The New York Times,* November 4, 1997, p. D1.
6. Quentin Bell, *On Human Finery* (London: The Hogarth Press, Ltd., 1947), pp. 48–49.
7. Dwight E. Robinson, "Fashion Theory and Product Design," *Harvard Business Review*, vol. 36, November–December 1958, p. 129.

UNIT ONE

Exploring a Career in Fashion

The person who embarks on a fashion career today enters a field that is far-flung and many faceted. In this field there is freedom to grow, freedom to change jobs or direction, and freedom to move to different cities or even to different countries without having to begin anew in a different industry or an unrelated type of work.

Career Planning Skills

As you explore the many possible careers in the fashion industry, you will be engaged in the same kinds of career planning activities that apply to people entering the workforce in any industry. If you want your work to provide an exciting and satisfying part of your life as well as your livelihood, you should approach the task of finding your first full-time fashion job and your subsequent jobs seriously and systematically. Basically, planning your career means learning about yourself and about the job market in your chosen field of work and then finding the best available match.

Planning a career is an ongoing process. Your first job has special importance because it sets the direction of your career, but as you gain skill and experience, you change. What you can offer to an employer changes, and what you can expect from your work—in terms of job satisfaction as well as income—changes, too.

Evaluating Career Goals

An individual's career is usually the single most important factor in determining his or her lifestyle. You should therefore consider the effect career choice will have on such things as geographic location, family life, monetary compensation, degree of pressure an responsibility the job requires, and number of hours devoted to the job.

Too often dissatisfaction with a job is not the fault of either the job or the worker, but rather the result of a mismatch between the two. The scope and variety of job opportunities within the fashion field means that there is a fashion-related position for almost anyone who is interested, and a realistic evaluation of career goals will help eliminate many future disappointments.

In-Depth Job Study

Obviously, you cannot make a wise decision until you know your options. The importance of making an in-depth study of the career you are considering cannot be overemphasized. As is true with many glamour jobs, there are a great many unrealistic perceptions of what a fashion career is really like. college graduates often expect to become buyers within a year and are very surprised when they are asked to sell and do stock work, literally starting from the bottom in what might seem to be painfully slow progress toward their ultimate goal. You have already taken the first step toward choosing a career in fashion by taking this course and studying this textbook.

Importance of First Jobs

First jobs in any industry can be critical, and the fashion business is no exception. Obviously, experience and training can be gained in any job, but will the job be a real plus on a résumé? What is the reputation of the firm or individual? What type of training program or apprenticeship is offered? The value of a good reference from an individual who is well respected in the industry cannot be overemphasized! And, it is often better to accept a lower-paying job that offers outstanding training, rather than a higher-paying position with narrower opportunity in the long run.

In some ways, first jobs are easier to get than position at a higher level. There are more entry-level positions available, and the requirements are less demanding. However, there are also more applicants, and without experience, it is difficult to stand out in the crowd as being especially well qualified.

What can you offer a prospective first employer? Recruiters of entry-level employees typically look for general work habits and skills that will enable the applicant to learn and grow on the job. As you develop your résumé and prepare for job interviews, compare your background with the job descriptions. Make the connections between your skills and experience and the demands of the work you are seeking. For example, if you are interested in a career in advertising, you will want to point out your relevant education, not only your fashion and marketing courses, but also English composition. Sales experience in the fashion industry is obviously a big plus on your résumé, but even sales experience in a different industry, say, fast-food, is relevant; it demonstrates your ability to deal with customers, your physical stamina, and your conscientious work habits. Similarly, volunteer work and extracurricular activities tell something about you as a person and potential employee.

Not the least important attribute that you can demonstrate is enthusiasm based on a realistic assessment of the job. Yes, it may pay little and require you to spend a lot of time on menial chores, but yes, you are willing to accept these negative aspects *if* the job will help you fulfill your ambition to develop your talents, learn the business, and advance. Let your résumé, application forms, and interviews demonstrate that you are a serious candidate for a career in the fashion industry.

Career Paths

A **career** is a lifelong activity, involving all of the jobs an individual may have, both paid and unpaid. An aspiring designer may, for example, begin by designing his or her own clothes and those of family and friends. As opportunities for education and experience occur, choices are made, and so an occupational **career path,** the order of occupations or periods of work in a person's life, is formed. With planning, a career path can take the direction of a **career ladder,** an upward-moving progression of jobs, each building on the experience, responsibilities, and financial compensation of the last.

A **job** is a specific position within an industry. In fashion retailing, for example, typical **entry-level jobs,** requiring little or no specific training and experience, include salesperson, cashier, and stock person. **Mid-management positions,** requiring some experience and training and involving a higher degree of responsibility, include department manager and manager of a small store. **Management positions** include buyer, merchandise manager, and manager for a large store.

Individuals who do some advance planning, who determine the goals they wish to pursue in the fashion industry, and who analyze the education, training, and experience necessary to achieve these goals are more likely to recognize a good opportunity when they see it. They make things happen!

Planning a Career in Fashion

One of the advantages of the fashion industry as a center for your career is its sheer size. Fashion is big business with lots of jobs to fill and abundant opportunity for advancement for those who commit themselves to a career in the industry. Another advantage is its scope. In the production and retailing segments and in fashion-related auxiliary services, positions are available for people with a variety of skills and interests. The industry utilizes the talents of people in management, marketing, and science and technology, as well as the artistic or "creative" side of the business.

Personal Qualities and Skills Required in Fashion Fields

The fashion field is many faceted, and the positions open to people starting a career are numerous and diverse. Some fields, such as designing, advertising, and display, usually demand a high degree of artistic creativity and originality. Others, such as fiber and fabric research and development, require an interest and education in scientific subjects. Still others, such as plant management and retailing management, call for in-depth business know-how and administrative skills.

A pleasing personality, a genuine interest in people, and a willingness to work and learn are indispensable in the fashion field. A strong constitution and healthy feet are also helpful in the market work of retail buyers, resident office representatives, magazine editors, fashion coordinators, and their assistants. Skills in writing, sketching, word processing, and photography are much in demand in the fashion field. Sewing and draping skills, even without a designer's creativity, can lead to such interesting work as sample making. In personnel, supervisory, and training work, an ability to teach is very helpful. This ability can also lead to a position as a teacher in one of the many schools devoted to fashion training.

Education and experience requirements vary even between one company and another within the same industry. Many large retail organizations, for example, will not even interview a job candidate who does not have a baccalaureate degree. Others will accept associate degrees and certificates from specialized fashion schools. Still others hire for management training primary those individuals on their sales staff who show the most promise. The wide variation in requirements, therefore, makes advance planning and research doubly important to the individual planning a fashion career.

Finding a Job in Fashion

One of the first steps in career selection should be a self-evaluation to determine what you truly want from a career. Listed below are some of the questions that should be answered to narrow the many choices available to the fashion graduate to the ones that are suitable for you.

Self-Evaluation

Rank the following things that you want from a career in their order of importance to you. There is no right or wrong order, just one that fits you. Add any other things important to you.

money	self-satisfaction
prestige	security
challenges	interesting experiences
chance to be creative	pleasant environment
independence	free time
chance for advancement	

1. ________	6. ________
2. ________	7. ________
3. ________	8. ________
4. ________	9. ________
5. ________	10. ________

Circle the word or words that best describe what you want from your career.

casual or formal	live in same area
workplace	or willing to move
full- or part-time	relaxed or hectic
work	pace
work weekends or not	home-based work or work outside home
travel on job or not	

Consider each response in light of various careers you have contemplated. When you have narrowed your career choices, make a thorough investigation of each to determine how well a career area meets your needs.

Part-time experience is an excellent way to explore job possibilities. Field experience and internship programs in colleges provide such opportunities, and students have the advantage of being able to share experiences with other students.

Looking for Opportunities

Where can you look for full-time jobs in fashion? One possible source—and often the best—is the campus interview. Each spring, retailers from all over the United States send recruiters to various campuses in an effort to select personnel for executive training programs in their stores. Your former part-time employers can also be an excellent source of information for employment; often if they have no position available, they can give leads to other sources.

Many personnel agencies specialize in specific types of job placement. A telephone survey of possible agencies can save time and make job hunting much more effective. Also check the classified listings in newspapers and trade periodicals. Companies that are looking for employees use these resources; so should you.

Finally, networking among friends in the fashion field can be one of the best ways to pick up leads. Let everyone know that you are actively looking for employment. This multiplies the effort and can therefore often shorten the search.

After You Are Hired

The true professional never stops growing, whether by participating in professional organizations, taking advanced courses and seminars, or reading journals and other publications. It is also important to stay aware of opportunities for growth through promotion or moves to other firms. Such information is often acquired through a network of professional friends—valuable assets to any career. Such a network must be cultivated, however, which means at least in part that the policy to follow when moving from one organization to another is "Don't burn your bridges behind you!"

Assignments

1. Prepare your résumé for a potential job in the general field of fashion. Follow the sample résumé on page 91. Be sure to include any work experience, as well as any education you have had. By the end of this book, you will have studied a number of career areas. At that point, you will revise your résumé, with a specific job in mind.
2. Begin a Career Journal, with a section for each of the four levels of the fashion industries. Many students prefer a three-ring binder for this activity.

"I see some of the most outlandish women—big fat slobs—wearing tight skirts and pants on the street. There really should be a law against what they wear."
NORMAN NORELL, 1963

"The change is already happening in decorating, where homes are developing a personal, individual feeling. Today, the women look the same but the homes look different. It used to be the homes were the same, but the people were different."
ARNOLD SCAASI, 1963

"I live for the day fashion ceases to be a spoof. It's an enormously serious business and should be treated as such. To an extent it has. We're covered in Time, in Fortune now. Yet that doesn't mean we have to be safe or dull. You can be just as serious about whimsy."
BILL BLASS, 1964

"If only American designers would create their own designs, we'd be so strong. We'd influence the world. I want to scold American designers, and myself included."
NORMAN NORELL, 1965

"I think this trend of fashion being public, amusing and spread out is very healthy. There's a real chance for individualism. You can wear what you want—long or short skirts, long or short hair. I even think women who aren't beautiful are now Individualists. Take Barbara Streisand or Penelope Tree, even Julie Christie is basically plain and she's made herself into something special.
HALSTON, 1968

"I predict that by the turn of the 21st century clothes will be extremely simple and functional. Not only in American rtw but also in French and English clothes."
GEOFFREY BEENE, 1969

Another Winner

MR. RUDI GERNREICH CHALLENGES THE IMAGINATION — STARTS THE NEW — HE'S OFF — LIKE A FLASH — FOR NEW DIMENSIONS.

His Swimsuit: More of the bosom exposed . . . and not far off — no tops at all just bare bosoms. Side-exposed maillot for Harmon Knitwear in black wool knit with elastic.

His Clown Dress: Very ruffled and very soft in white crinkled voile, dotted in black.

His Hemp with Crocodile: Off in another direction — strictly tailored blazer suit in natural colored Italian hemp, with brown crocodile piping.

His 1930s Prints: Nuts about purple—nuts about the wonderful way women wore crepe prints in the '30s — so Mr. Gernreich shows a series for resort — this one in black with splashes of pink and yellow and a draped cowl neckline.

Great idea for the flat-chested.

9/25/63

Drawings by Kenneth Paul Block
Photo by Tony Palmieri

Rudi Gernreich and one of his designs.

color
movement
texture
feel
classic
quality

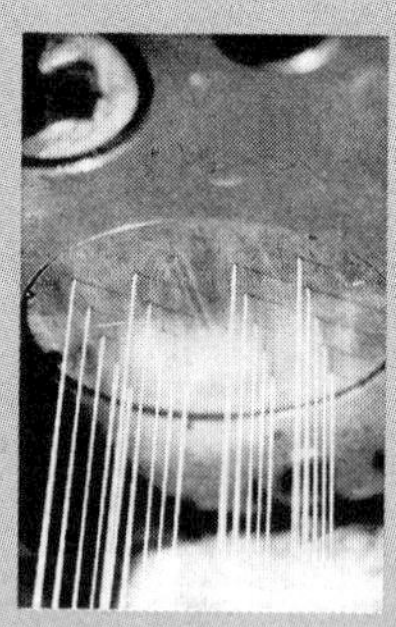

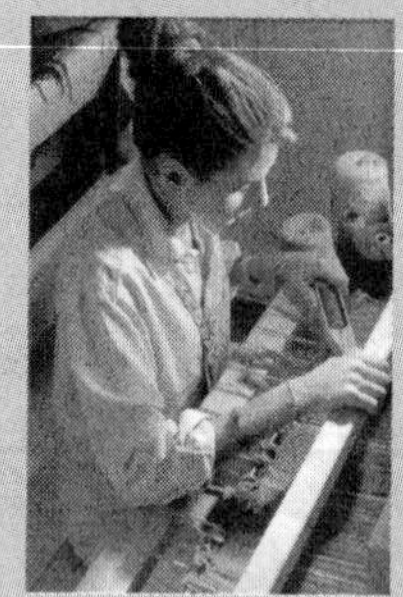

UNIT 2

The Primary Level—The Materials of Fashion

All good stories have a terrific beginning. If the beginning of the story is interesting, intriguing, exciting, and beautiful, it makes you want to read to get to the end of the story. So it is with fashion—all good fashions have good beginnings. They are the fibers, fabrics, leather, and fur industries known in fashion as the primary markets. Unit Two covers these primary market suppliers—the growers and producers of the raw materials of fashion.

The earliest part of the planning function—in both color and texture—takes place on the primary level. It is also the level of the fashion business that works the farthest in advance of the ultimate selling period for the finished goods. Primary-level companies need up to two years lead-time before the goods will be available to the consumer. Goods at the primary level may often be imports from third world emerging nations, where textiles are usually the earliest form of industrialization.

More fashion apparel and accessories are made of textiles than any other kind of material. Fashion textiles are the product of a network of primary industries, such as the cotton industry, the wool industry, the various industries producing manufactured fibers, and the fabric industry.

Changes in the textile industries have been rapid and important particularly in recent years. Not only have there been radical new methods of producing and blending fibers, but also advances have been made in the methods of making and finishing fabrics. All of these new and fast-moving advances have contributed to an increasing variety of fashion goods.

In contrast to the methods used for producing textiles, the processing of fur and leather appears primitive and slow. Yet changes are taking place at a dizzying pace, and these changes are giving designers a wider range of products to work with. These current changes may be the indicators of the exciting course that fashion in leather and fur may take to satisfy the fashion needs of the future.

The primary level is the foundation upon which the merchandisers and marketers of fashion products build their ideas and designs that will answer the needs and wants of the customer.

CHAPTER 5

Textiles: Fibers and Fabrics

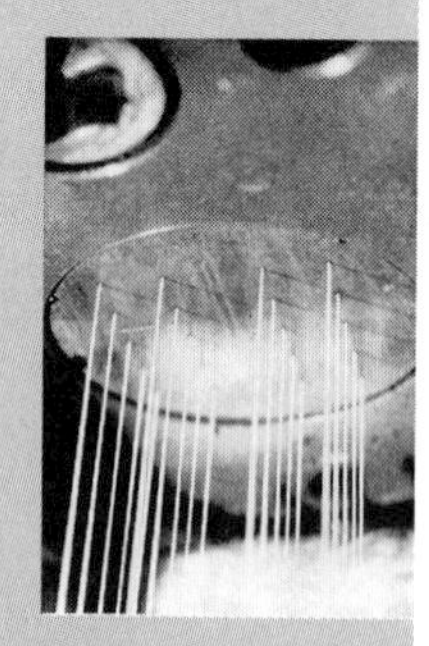

WHAT'S IN IT FOR YOU?

Everything you always wanted to know about fibers and fabrics.

Key Concepts:

- The difference between a natural fiber and a manufactured fiber
- The major steps in the production of most fabrics
- The effect of imports on the U.S. fiber and fabric industries
- The effects of new technology on textiles

Fashion and the materials from which they are made are inseparable. Have you ever bought a fashion product simply because you loved the feel of it? Perhaps it was rough and coarse, or silky and smooth. Maybe it was incredibly soft to the touch. If so, then you, like almost every else, have responded to a fabric rather than to the style or color of a fashion product.

The designer creating a style at the drawing board must consider the material best suited for the particular silhouette and details of design. The manufacturer must then consider the various weights of material currently desired as well as the cost factors.

Finally, the retailer must select fashions made of those materials considered appropriate and desirable by their target customers.

So important is the material or fabric a garment is made of that Christian Dior, the world-famous haute-couture designer, once said of it: "Fabric not only expresses a designer's dream, but also stimulates his own ideas. It can be the beginning of an inspiration. Many a dress of mine is born of the fabric alone."[1]

The enormous appeal of fabric—and the fibers of which it is composed—lies in its many varied textures, finishes, uses, and colors. These are created, as we shall learn, by the fiber and fabric industries that work closely together to produce an end product, which is called **fashion textiles**.

The production of fiber and fabrics is the first step in the manufacture of clothing, accessories, and home fashions. As a result, textile fiber and textile fabric manufacturers are considered **primary suppliers**. The makers of **trimmings**, such as Criscone, Brooklyn Bow International, and Velcro USA Inc., are also at the primary level of the fashion business. (Other primary suppliers, who create fur and leather, will be explored in the next chapter.)

THE FIBER INDUSTRY

A **fiber**—an extremely fine, hairlike strand almost invisible to the eye—is the smallest element of a fabric. It is also the starting point of a fabric. Fibers can be spun or twisted into continuous threads called **yarn**, and yarns can be knitted, woven, or bonded into **fabrics.** Although tiny, fibers have enormous influence on fashion. They are what gives a fabric its color, weight, texture, and durability.

Fibers are either natural or manufactured. **Natural fibers** are found in nature, that is, they come from plant or animal sources. In contrast, the **manufactured fibers** are made in a chemist's laboratory. They may be made from substances that occur in nature, such as wood pulp, air, petroleum, or natural gas, but these natural substances must be converted into fibers before they can be made into fabric. Manufactured fibers are sometimes called "man-made" or "synthetic fibers." Because manufactured fibers are invented in the laboratory, they are more plentiful than natural fibers. Currently, 26 manufactured fibers are available. Some of the manufactured fibers whose names you may recognize are rayon, nylon, acetate, acrylic, spandex, and polyester.

History and Development

The use of natural fibers is ancient, whereas most of the manufactured fibers have been invented in the past 50 years. Despite their relatively short life span, however, very rapid advances have been made in the use of manufactured fibers. In contrast, the natural fiber industry has developed much more slowly. In fact, many of the recent developments in natural fibers are actually advances made in the manufactured fiber industry that were transferred to the natural fiber industry.

The Development of Natural Fibers

The use of natural fibers predates written history. Prehistoric humans are known to have gathered flax, the fiber in linen, to make yarns for fabrics. There are four major natural fibers: cotton, silk, flax (linen), and wool. Two other minor natural fibers are ramie and hemp. In addition, there are many other natural fibers that are in short supply, and so limited to luxury items (see Table 5.1).

Cotton, the most widely used of all the natural fibers, is the substance attached to the seed of a cotton plant. Cotton fibers are composed primarily of cellulose, a carbohydrate that especially lends itself to the manufacture of fibrous and paper products. Cotton fibers absorb moisture quickly, dry quickly, and have a cooling effect that makes cotton a good fiber for hot or warm weather. Usually the fluffy cotton boll is white, but new growing methods have brought about naturally colored cotton. This new cotton can be grown in at least 22 colors, thus eliminating the need for dyes. Long and extra long cotton fibers (or staple), produce the finest fabrics. The United States leads the world in the production of long staple Pima cotton, while Egypt is a close second.[2]

Wool is the fiber that forms the coat of sheep. Sheep produce one of the few replenishable natural commodities. Shear a sheep's coat time after time, and it quickly grows a new one. An animal fiber, wool is composed mostly of protein. Wool fiber is a natural insulator and is used to make warm clothes. Wool fiber, in fact, has a natural crimp that is ideal for the production of bulky yarns that trap air to form insulating barriers against the cold. Wool absorbs moisture more slowly and dries more slowly than cotton. A new lightweight summer wool has been developed to be machine washable.

Silk comes from a cocoon formed by a silkworm. The silkworm forces two fine streams of a thick liquid out of tiny openings in its head. These streams harden into filaments, or fibers, upon contact with the air. Silk, best known for its luxurious feel, is a breathable fabric that can be worn year-round. For many years silk required dry cleaning, but much of today's silk is washable.

Silk all but disappeared from the U.S. fashion market during and after World War II. It has made a dramatic comeback! In the late 1970s, a group of U.S. and Hong Kong businesspeople worked with Chinese manufacturers to develop cheaper silk. Within ten years, the Chinese had a high-quality, washable silk that became a low-cost substitute for polyester. Silk imports from China to the United States reached 1.92 billion in 2000, more than doubling the figure since the early 1990s.[3]

TABLE 5.1 Natural Luxury Animal Fibers

NAME	SOURCE	CHARACTERISTICS AND USES
Alpaca	Member of llama family found in Andes Mountains in South America	Fine, hollow-core fleece; annual shearing yields 6–12 lbs of fibers; 22 natural shades; strongest, most resiliant wool; scarce
Angora	Rabbit hair	Soft fiber; dyes well; sheds easily
Camel hair	Camel	Usually left in natural tones; used in coats, jackets, artists' brushes
Cashmere	Kashmir goat (60° found in China but also bred in United States)	Rare (1/100 of wool crop); sheared annually; one goat produces enough for one-quarter of a sweater
Goose down (often mixed with goose feathers to cut cost)	Goose	Most compressible insulation; lightweight warmth for jackets, vest, comforters, pillows, sleeping bags, feather beds
Llama	Llama found in Andes Mountains of South America, United States, Canada, Australia, and New Zealand	Coarser, stronger than alpaca; used in utilitarian items such as sacks
Marabou	African marabou stork or turkey	Soft, fluffy material from feathers
Mohair	Angora goat, originally from Turkey, now from South Africa, Texas, and New Zealand	Twice-yearly shearing; 2½ times as strong as wool; less allergenic than sheep's wool
Ostrich feathers	Ostrich	Used in high-fashion apparel, feather dusters
Pashmina	Mountain goats from Himalaya	Softer than cashmere-fiber equivalent to Merinque
Qiviut	Musk ox down from Canada, Alaska	Natural taupe color; soft, light, 8 times warmer than sheep's wool; rare ($20–$25/oz)
Vicuna	Rare llama-like animal from Peru	World's finest natural fiber

Flax, used to make linen, comes from the stem of a flax plant. Only after the flax fiber is spun into yarn and woven or knit into fabric is the product called **linen**. Flax is the strongest of the vegetable fibers (it is twice as strong as cotton), and like cotton, it absorbs moisture and dries quickly. These features make linen an excellent fabric for warm-weather apparel (see Figure 5.1). However, even with new technology that makes linen less apt to wrinkle, it still has a tendency to wrinkle and is harder to iron than cotton. Most flax is imported from Europe, especially Belgium and Ireland.

Ramie comes from a woody-leafed Asian plant grown mostly in China. It has been available in the United States only since 1979, when the United States and China reopened trade with one another. A linen-like fabric suitable for warm weather apparel, ramie is also inexpensive.

Hemp is a fibrous plant with an interesting history in the United States. It was an agricultural staple in America for hundreds of years.

FIGURE 5.1
Trade associations sometimes promote fibers by extolling the virtues of the fiber and by including their association logo in their advertising materials.
Courtesy, Masters of Linen.

In fact, the Declaration of Independence was written on hemp paper. The crop was so important then that three colonies had laws requiring farmers to grow hemp.[4] Today, laws make it illegal to grow hemp in the United States. Raising it in the United States (and most industrialized nations) has been illegal since the 1970s, because lawmakers feared that growers would plant illegal marijuana, which looks very similar to industrial hemp (although industrial hemp lacks hallucinatory power), making the illegal weed harder to find. Imports of finished hemp garments are allowed, however, and demand is soaring. Not only are its ecological, or "green," properties high selling points, but its aesthetic, comfort, and performance have made it a very popular and viable fiber for home furnishings and fashion.[5]

A number of other natural fibers are used in apparel and home furnishings. They are relatively rare and thus expensive. A few are outlined in Table 5.1.

The Development of Manufactured Fibers

Manufactured or synthetic fibers have been improving the quality of our lives since rayon, the first synthetic fiber, went into production in 1910. Since then, many other manufactured fibers have been introduced in literally thousands of new apparel, upholstery, and industrial applications (see Table 5.2).

Manufactured fibers offer a variety of characteristics that are mostly unavailable in natural fibers. Each year, manufactured fibers find new uses in our wardrobes, homes, hospitals, and workplaces. Designers like Armani, Calvin Klein, and Joseph Abboud all use high tech, stretch, and classic fabrics to illustrate the constant innovation of their product lines.[6]

All manufactured fibers start life as thick liquids. Fibers of continuous, indefinite lengths are produced by forcing the liquid through the tiny holes of a mechanical device called a **spinnerette.** This is similar to the way pasta dough is pushed through a pasta machine to make spaghetti (see Figure 5.2).

Fibers are then cut into short lengths and spun into yarn, as is the case with natural fibers, or they are chemically processed into yarn directly. In the latter case, the production of fiber and yarn occurs simultaneously.

There are two basic types of manufactured fibers: cellulosic and noncellulosic.

Cellulosic Fibers

Cellulose, the same fibrous substance found in the natural fibers of plants, is also used to manufacture **cellulosic fibers.** The cellulosic fibers are made with a minimum of chemical steps. They include rayon, acetate, triacetate, and lyocell. Triacetate is now produced only in small quantities in Europe. The cellulose used to make these fibers comes mostly from soft woods, such as spruce.

Noncellulosic Fibers

Petroleum, coal, natural gas, air, and water are used to make **noncellulosic fibers.** They are produced from various combinations of carbon, hydrogen, nitrogen, and oxygen. Fiber chemists working in laboratories link the molecules into long chains called **polymers.** Nylon, acrylic, and polyester are in this category.

TABLE 5.2 Manufactured Fibers

DATE	FIBER	FIRST COMMERCIAL PRODUCTION
1910	Rayon	The first manufactured fiber. The first commercial production of rayon fiber in the United States was in 1910 by the American Viscose Company. By using two different chemicals and manufacturing techniques, two basic types of rayon were developed. They were viscose rayon and cuprammonium rayon. Today, only viscose rayon is being produced in the United States.
1924	Acetate	The first commercial production of acetate fiber in the United States was in 1924 by the Celanese Corporation.
1938	Nylon	The first commercial production of nylon in the United States was in 1939 by the E. I. Du Pont de Nemours & Company, Inc. It is the second most used manufactured fiber in this country, behind polyester.
1950	Acrylic	The first commercial production of acrylic fiber in the United States was in 1950 by E. I. Du Pont de Nemours & Company, Inc.
1953	Polyester	The first commercial production of polyester fiber in the United States was in 1953 by E. I. Du Pont de Nemours & Company, Inc. Polyester is the most used manufactured fiber in the United States.
1954	Triacetate	The first commercial production of triacetate fiber in the United States was in 1954 by the Celanese Corporation. Domestic triacetate production was discontinued in 1985.
1959	Spandex	The first commercial production of spandex fiber in the United States was 1959 by E. I. Du Pont de Nemours & Company, Inc. It is an elastomeric manufactured fiber (able to stretch at least 100% and snap back like natural rubber). Spandex is used in filament form.
1961	Polyolefin/ polypropylene	The first commercial production of an olefin fiber manufactured in the United States was by Hercules Incorporated. In 1966, polyolefin was the world's first and only Nobel-Prize winning fiber
1993	Lyocell	The first commercial production of lyocell in the United States was in 1993 by Courtaulds Fibers, under the Tencel trade name. Environmentally friendly, lyocell is produced from the wood pulp of trees grown specifically for this purpose. It is specially processed, using a solvent spinning technique in which the dissolving agent is recycled, reducing environmental effluents.
2002	Polyatide	The first commercial production of PLA in the United States was in 2002 by Cargill Dow Polymers. PLA is a plastic derived from natural plant sugars, bridging the gap between natural fibers and conventional synthetic fibers.

Source: Adapted from Fabric Link/Fabric University, http://www.fabriclink.com/Fabric University/Man-made Fibers and http://www.Fibersource.com.

Generic Names for Manufactured Fibers

The Federal Trade Commission has assigned **generic names**, or nontrademarked names, to 26 manufactured fibers. Within any of these broad generic categories, fiber producers can modify the composition to produce a new fiber, called a **variant**. The variant is then given a brand name by the producer. There are hundreds of **brand names**, or trademarks, which are registered with the U.S. Patent Office; only the manufacturer of a variant is allowed to use

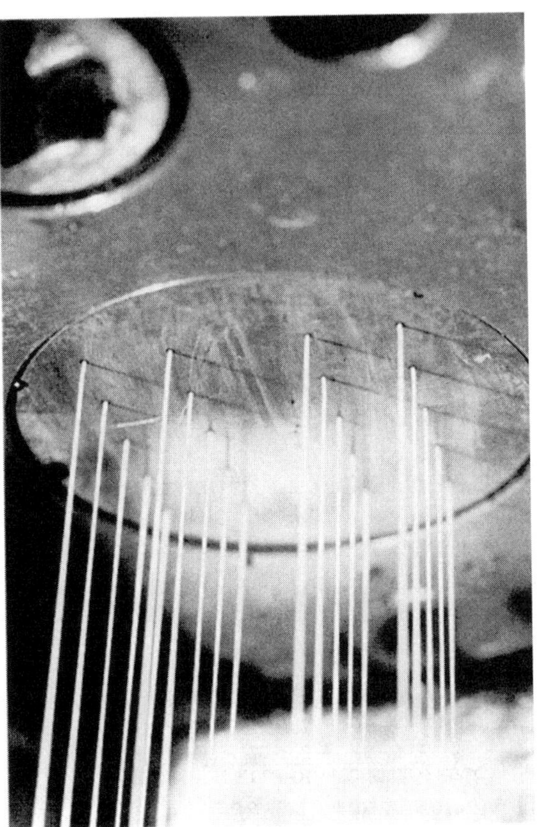

FIGURE 5.2
Manufactured fibers of varying lengths are produced by forcing thick liquids through the tiny holes of a devise known as a spinnerette.
Courtesy, Fairchild Publications, Inc.

the registered name. For example, polyester is the generic name, and Dacron is the Du Pont trademark for polyester (see Table 5.3).

The properties of these fibers greatly influences the behavior of the finished fabric made from them. Polyester, for example, is strong and wrinkle-resistant, which contributes to its durability and washability. Once scorned as the dull material of inexpensive leisure suits, today's polyester has the subtle sheen of fine silk.

Microfibers

A major technological breakthrough occurred in 1989 with the first commercial production of microfiber in the United States by Du Pont. A **microfiber** is a fiber that is two or three times smaller than a human hair—smaller than wool, cotton, or silk fibers (see Figure 5.3). Microfiber is the thinnest and finest of all manufactured fibers. It has a touch and texture similar to silk or cashmere, but is wrinkle-resistant and can usually be machine washed and dried. Today, microfiber is produced in a number of manufactured fibers—for example, nylon, acrylic, and polyester. Designers have used it widely in women's wear, men's wear, activewear, outerwear, and home furnishings.

Organization and Operation

Because of the differences in the origin and characteristics of fibers, each industry—the natural fiber industry and the manufactured fiber industry—is organized along different lines.

The Natural Fiber Industry

Cotton is produced in four major areas of the United States: the Southeast; the Mississippi Delta; the Texas–Oklahoma panhandle; and New Mexico, Arizona, and California.

Nearly all cotton growers sell their product in local markets, either to mill representatives or, more typically, to wholesalers. The cotton wholesalers bargain at central markets in Memphis, New Orleans, Dallas, Houston, New York, and Chicago.

The wool produced in the United States comes from relatively small sheep ranches in the Western states. Boston is the central marketplace for wool, both domestic and imported.

Linen, silk, and ramie are not produced in any great quantities in the United States. Like hemp, these fibers are imported from foreign sources.

The natural fiber industry in the United States has been greatly affected by the advent of manufactured fibers. The ability to tailor the manufactured fibers to the demands of the ever-changing marketplace has forced the natural fiber industries to become more attuned to the needs of their customers. To compete, the natural fiber industries have become more aggressive about developing new uses for their products and have aggressively promoted themselves. Cotton, usually a warm-weather fiber, is now promoted as a year-round fiber, largely through the use of heavier cotton fibers used to make cotton sweaters. And wool, usually designed for cold-weather wear, is now being treated to make new, lightweight fibers suitable for year-round wear. Through advanced technology and innovative chemical processing, many natural fibers are treated with special finishes to give them care-and-wear properties equal to those of manufactured fibers.

TABLE 5.3 Generic Names and Trade Names of Manufactured Fibers Used in the United States

GENERIC NAME	TRADENAMES
Acetate	Celanese, Chromspun, Estron, Microsafe
Acrylic	Acrilan, Bio Fresh, Bounce-Back, Creslan, Cystar, Cystar AF, Duraspun, Fi-lana, Pil-Trol, Sayelle, So-Lara, Smart Yarns, Wear-Dated, Wintuk
Aramid	Kevlar, Nomex
Lyocell	Lenzing Lycocell, Tencel
Modacrylic	SEF Plus
Nylon	A.C.E., Anso, Antron, Assurance, Avantige, Cantrece, Capima. Caplana, Caprolan, Captiva, Cordura, Creme de Captiva, Crepeset, DuraSoft, DyeNAMIX, Eclipse, Hardline, Hydrofil, Hytel, Matinesse, Microsupplex, No Shock, PowerSilk, Resistat, Shimmereen, Silkey Touch, Solution, Sportouch, Stainmaster, Stay Gard, Supplex, Tactel, Tru-Ballistic, Ultra Image, Ultra Touch, Ultron, Wear-Dated, Wellon, Wellstrand, WorryFree, Zefsprot, Zeftron
Olefin	Alpha, Essera, Impressa, Inova, Marvess, Patlon III, Polystrand, Spectra, Synera, Trace
Polyester	A.C.E.., Ceylon, Comfort Fiber, Compet, Coolmax, Corebond, Dacronfi, ES.P, Fortrel, Hollofi, Kodaire, Kodel, KodOfill, KodOsoff, Pentron, Premafill Plump, Premafill Soft, Trevira, Trevira Finesse, Trevira Microness, Universe
PBI	PBI Logo
Rayon	Beau-Grip, Fibro, Galaxy
Spandex	Lycra
Sulfar	Ryton

Adapted from: http://www.fibersource.com/fiber info/"A Quick Guide." Washington, D.C.: American Fiber Manufacturers Association.

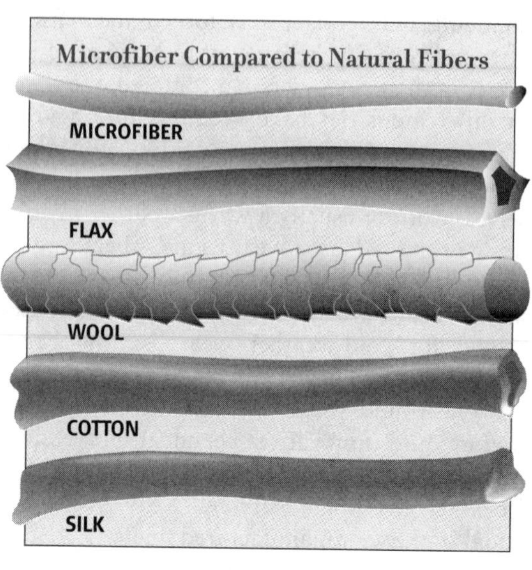

FIGURE 5.3
A microfiber compared to silk, cotton, wool, and flax.
Courtesy, Fairchild Publications, Inc.

The Manufactured Fiber Industry

Obviously, climate and terrain have nothing to do with the production of a manufactured fiber. Indeed, chemical plants are extremely adaptable, requiring only supplies of raw chemicals, power, and labor. Chemical companies have thus erected their plants in every part of the United States—up and down the East Coast, in the South, the Midwest, and increasingly on the West Coast. Operations are located wherever companies have found raw materials or railroads and waterways for convenient shipment of those materials. Most of these plants are huge.

With manufactured fibers, it is also possible for the producing plant to serve as its own market. It purchases fibers from chemical companies, spins them into yarn and then knits or weaves the yarn into fabric. Burlington Industries and Galey & Lord, Inc., are two of the giants that consolidate all operations, from spun yarn manufacture to finished fabric (see Figure 5.4).

FIGURE 5.4
The J. Jill catalog features many styles of Tencel clothing, identifying Tencel as a registered trademark, and pointing out that it is a soft and silky fabric that drapes beautifully. It is also processed in an environmentally way.
Courtesy, © J. Jill Catalog.

Fiber Development

Limited quantities of a new or modified manufactured fiber are usually first produced in a pilot plant on an experimental basis. If research indicates that both industry and consumers will accept the new product, mass production begins. New applications of the fiber are then explored and new industries are consulted and encouraged to use it.

While this procedure is going on in one chemical company, there is always the possibility that another company may be working along similar lines to develop a competitive fiber. The company that is first to develop a new fiber has no assurance that it will have the field to itself for long. There are many brands of such manufactured fibers as nylon, rayon, and acetate on the market and a roster of companies producing various acrylics and polyesters (see Table 5.2).

The fierce competition among various producers of manufactured fibers is tied to the fact that in one season, a need may arise for fiber that is stretchable, offers warmth without weight, and is also wrinkle-resistant. Armed with a list of customer preferences, competing laboratories go to work to develop new products. It is no wonder that several of them come up with the same answer at the same time.

Under the Textile Fibers Products Identification Act of 1960, consumer products that use textile fibers are required to label their products by the country where processed or manufactured and by the generic names and percentages of each fiber that is used, assuming that it is more than 5 percent, in order, by weight (see Figure 5.5). Brand names or trademarks may also be used on the label, but they are not required by law.

SCOTT
SUPERLABEL™
Laser Care Label
50% COTTON
50% POLYESTER
STYLE 12345
LOT #100
RN# 00000

Machine Wash Warm
Gentle Cycle
Tumble Dry Low
Use Non-Chlorine
Bleach if Required
Made in USA

MEDIUM

SUPERLABEL™
The Laser
Care Label.

FIGURE 5.5
Even unbranded fibers must be carefully identified on labels, along with International Care Symbols, bar codes, and, of course, the manufacturer's name and logo.
Courtesy, Scott Tag and Label Company.

Fiber Distribution

Producers of manufactured fibers sell their fibers to fabric manufacturers in one of three ways:

1. As unbranded products, with no restrictions placed on their end use and no implied or required standards of performance claimed

Then & Now

Stretch for Freedom—What Gives?

Linked by comfort, control, and sex appeal, the bond between stretch fabrics and fashion continues to strengthen and evolve. If Coco Chanel hadn't created a sportswear collection in 1913 made of jersey, a stretch knit, would we still be wearing whalebone and laces in order to show off our figures?

Chanel wanted women to move their bodies without constriction, and using stretch in clothing was the best way to do it. In the 1940s and 1950s, Claire McCardell used stretch jersey knits in her comfortable and stylish spotswear and swimwear. And thanks to DuPont's revolutionary spandex fiber that came upon the scene in 1958 as a replacement for rubber in girdles, the shape of modern style and fit has never been the same.

Fashion insiders credit a cadre of forward-thinking designers of the 1970s and 1980s for introducing stretch to readey-to wear, including Azzededine Alaia's bondage-inspired corset dresses, Jean Gaultier's edgy styles, Norma Kamali's body-conscious retro-dresses, and Betsy Johnson's flamboyant, clingy dresses.

Over the past decade, stretch fibers have introduced women to an even wider variety of fabrics, causing some ready-to-wear and sportswear designers to rethink their basic approach to designing and making clothes. Look how DuPont has time-lined the use of LYCRA® . . . then and now!

LYCRA® Timeline

1958
DuPont invents "Fiber K" and LYCRA® will soon be trademarked.

1959
LYCRA® replaces rubber in corsets for a more comfortable look and feel.

1962
LYCRA® gives a real lift to support hose for the first time.

1974
LYCRA® gives saggy swimwear a new look!

1979
LYCRA® is added to sheer pantyhose. It really gives a lift to hosiery.

1985
Athletes make LYCRA® part of their wardrobe and a new look in streetwear is born.

1994
The new LYCRA® logo is introduced to the public and quickly becomes an icon.

1995
New LYCRA® Soft shapes up intimate apparel by adding comfort and soft control.

1997
"Real men do wear LYCRA®" Stretch fabric enhances classic men's suits and sportswear.

1999
The LYCRA® Soft fibers extends to ready-to-wear, hosiery, activewear and swimwear.

2000 and beyond
With over 40 years of expertise, LYCRA® has and continues to create innovative forms of stretch material for everyone!

Adapted from: www.lycra.com/Lycra/knowledge/dupont.html.

Sources

"DuPont: Celebrating the Body," Innerwear Report, *Women's Wear Daily*, September 9, 2002, p. 10.

Daniela Gilbert, 'What Gives?," *Women's Wear Daily*, June 12, 2001, p.8.

Julee Greenberg, "Stretching Designers' Ideas on Fit," *Women's Wear Daily*, June 12, 2001, p. 15.

Georgia Lee, "Mills Weave Their Way In," *Women's Wear Daily*, June 12 2001.

Rusty Williamson, "Stretch Fibers: The Freedom Factor," *Women's Wear Weekly*, June 12, 2001, p. 16.

"WWD 90th Anniversary/The Early Years," *Women's Wear Daily*, July 2001, p. 59.

Claire McCardell's lightweight swimwear was popular in the 1940s.
Courtesy, © Genevieve Naylor/Corbis.

Today stretch fibers are also being used for activewear.
Courtesy, Fairchild Publications, Inc.

2. As branded or trademarked fibers, with assurance to consumers that the quality of the fiber has been controlled by its producer, but not necessarily with assurance as to either implied or required standards of performance in the end product
3. Under a licensing agreement, whereby the use of the fiber trademark is permitted only to those manufacturers whose fabrics or other end products pass tests set up by the fiber producer for their specific end uses or applications

Licensing programs set up by different fiber producers and by processors of yarn vary considerably in scope. The more comprehensive programs entail extensive wear testing to back up the licensing agreement. The fiber and yarn producers exercise considerable control over fabric products that have been licensed, sometimes specifying blend levels, and offer technical services to help correct a fabric that fails to pass a qualifying test. The trademarks used under such licensing agreements are referred to as **licensed trademarks.** Fiber Industries' Fortrel is an example of a licensed trademark.

Merchandising and Marketing

No matter how familiar producers and consumers may be with the qualities of each fiber, there is always the need to disseminate information about the newest modifications and their application to fashion merchandise. To do this, producers of both natural and manufactured fibers make extensive use of advertising, publicity, and market research. They also extend various customer services to manufacturers, retailers, and consumers.

Usually a producer of manufactured fibers, such as Du Pont or Monsanto, undertakes these activities on behalf of its own individual brands and companies. The Acrylic Council is a nonprofit trade association of 13 leading U.S. acrylic fiber producers, yarn spinners, and ingredient suppliers that promotes the features and benefits of acrylics. The American Fiber Manufacturers Association (AFMA), a domestic trade association that represents more than 90 percent of the U.S. producers of manufactured fibers, filaments, and yarns, also carries on a very active program of consumer education about manufactured fibers in general.

So that they can better promote their new products (and themselves), the natural fiber industries also have organized trade associations that carry their message to the textile industry as well as to the customer (see Table 5.4).

Advertising and Publicity

As you might suspect, given their greater potential for competition, the manufactured fiber industries spend considerably more money on advertising than do the natural fiber industries. They maintain a steady flow of advertising and publicity directed at both the trade and consumer markets (see Figure 5.6). Sometimes an advertising campaign will promote an entire range of textile fibers; at other times, it will concentrate only on a single fiber. Fiber companies give most of their advertising dollars to support the manufacturers who use their fibers.

Some natural fiber groups are putting more effort and money into campaigns to combat the growing domination of manufactured fibers.

TABLE 5.4 Natural Fiber Trade Associations

FIBER	ORGANIZATION
Cotton	Cotton Incorporated National Cotton Council, Supima Assn of America
Linen	Masters of Liner (European)
Mohair	The Mohair Council of America
Silk	International Silk Association
Wool	America Wool Council The Woolmark Company

Source: Hemp Industries Association, 1999. Available at http://www.thehia.org/.

FIGURE 5.6
She has it! DuPont, the manufacturers of Lycra®, features music sensation Jessica Simpson in their ad for denim jeans that "have" Lycra®.
Courtesy, DuPont.

Because these campaigns are mainly handled by trade associations, they promote the fiber itself, not the products of an individual natural fiber producer. One of the most eye-catching campaigns is that of Cotton Incorporated. The ads and posters not only emphasize cotton's advantages as a fiber but also point to the cotton industry's importance in the economy and to cotton's ecological appeal.

Fiber sources also provide garment producers and retailers with various aids that facilitate mention of their fibers in consumer advertising, adding to the recognition already achieved by the fiber producer's name, trademark, slogan, or logo. For example, the Wool Bureau encourages the use of its ball-of-yarn logo in producer and retailer advertising of all wool merchandise, as well as in displays.

Fiber industry producers and trade associations continually provide the press with new information, background material, and photographs for editorial features. Some of this publicity effort is accomplished by direct contact with the press; some of it is done by supplying garment producers and retailers with materials they can use for promotion.

Advertising undertaken by fiber producers in cooperation with fabric and garment manufacturers and retailers benefits the fiber industry in two ways. First, consumers begin to associate the fiber name with other names that are already familiar, such as the name of the fiber source or the name of the retail store selling the garment. This is particularly important in introducing a new manufactured fiber. Second, fabric and garment producers, as well as retailers, are encouraged to use and promote the fiber because the fiber producer's share of advertising costs subsidizes its local or national advertising.

Research and Development

Both natural fiber producers and manufactured fiber producers are constantly seeking ways to improve their products. Individual large manufactured fiber producers conduct research and development. The natural fiber producers, which tend to be small in size, often work through the trade group for a particular fiber.

Customer Services

All major producers of manufactured fibers and many smaller firms offer a number of services to direct and secondary users of their products. Producers of natural fibers, working through their associations, also offer many such services. These include:

- Technical advice as well as technical know-how on weaving and knitting techniques
- Assistance to textile and garment producers and retailers in locating supplies
- Fabric libraries that include information about sources, prices, and delivery schedules (Research in a fabric library saves precious time spent shopping the market for trend information)
- Fashion presentations and exhibits for the textile industry, retailers, garment manufacturers, the fashion press, and occasionally, the public
- Extensive literature for manufacturers, retailers, educators, and consumers about fiber properties, use, and care
- Fashion experts who address groups of manufacturers, retailers, or consumers, staging fashion shows and demonstrations
- Educational films and audiovisual aids for use by the trade, schools, and consumer groups

Trends in the Fiber Industry

The most dramatic trend in the fiber industry is the increasing use of blends of natural and manufactured fibers. This trend will be discussed in more detail in the next section of this chapter, as will the second most widespread trend, the use of microfibers.

The fiber industry is fighting hard to overcome a major problem: the encroachment of imports into its domestic markets. Since manufactured fibers account for over 75 percent of fiber usage annually in the United States, it is obvious that this will be a continuing and ongoing problem. The U.S. fiber industry will have to fight harder than ever for its share of the international and even the domestic market.

Computers are also playing an important role in the fiber industries' abilities to service their customers more quickly and efficiently. In addition to facilitating communications, computers offer important linkages between the various industries and enable them to do such things as coordinate delivery schedules and provide bar coding.

To many observers, the manufactured fiber story is just beginning, and the next half-century promises to be even more exciting than the previous one. Productivity rises by 3.4 percent per year with fascinating new products emerging from the laboratories. With approximately $2 billion spent annually on automated technology in the past decade, today's looms require less workers, raising the competition among plants.[7]

THE TEXTILE FABRIC INDUSTRY

Midway between the fiber and the finished apparel, accessory, or home furnishing product is the fabric. **Textile fabric** is any material that is made by weaving, knitting, braiding, knotting, laminating, felting, or chemical bonding. It is the basic material from which most articles of apparel, accessories, and home fashions are made (see Figure 5.7).

FIGURE 5.7 *A hand-shuttle loom is used by many designers to create unique fabrics.* The Fashion Institute of Technology, New York/Photograph: John Senzer.

Americans use a lot of textile fabric. Each person consumes nearly 86 pounds of textile fabric annually, an all-time record.[8] We use fabric for clothing and home furnishings; in transportation, industry, defense, recreation, and health care; and for space exploration.

The production of most fabrics begins with the creation of yarn from fibers. With the exception of felted fabric and a few other nonwoven fabrics, fibers cannot be made into fabrics without first spinning or twisting them into yarn. Yarns are then woven or knit into **greige** (pronounced—and sometimes spelled—"gray") **goods**, or unfinished fabrics. Greige goods are converted into finished fabrics for consumer or industrial use.

History and Development

The earliest step toward the mechanization of the textile fabric industry was the introduction of the spinning wheel. It was brought to Europe from India in the sixth century. Even with the spinning wheel, yarn-making remained tedious work that was mostly done in the home. Not until the 18th century did the British develop mechanical methods of spinning cotton fibers into yarn.

The result of mechanized spinning—large quantities of yarn—increased the need for better looms to weave the yarn into fabric. The first power loom was invented by an English clergyman, Dr. Edward Cartwright, and patented in 1785. It used water as a source of energy.

The new mechanization soon spread to America. In 1790, Samuel Slater established a yarn mill in Pawtucket, Rhode Island. The present-day giant in the textile fabric field, J. P. Stevens and Company, is descended from Slater's mill. For decades, though, fabric production remained both a hand operation and a home industry, totally inadequate to meet the demand. Then Francis Cabot Lowell, a New Englander, visited a textile factory in England and memorized the detailed specifications of its power-operated machinery. In 1814, Lowell built the first successful power loom and the first textile fabric mill in the United States. The demands of a rapidly growing country provided an eager market for the output of American textile mills, and the young industry flourished. Even more automation and mechanization followed.

One of the biggest changes in the U.S. textile industry in the past two decades has been the massive shift to shuttleless looms. These looms are much faster and quieter. They are also wider and less likely to break the yarns. While the initial cost is high, they are usually cheaper to operate. In 1972, only 3 percent of the looms in the United States were shuttleless. By 2000, 95 percent of looms were shuttleless.[9]

Today it is possible for a single operator to oversee as many as 100 weaving machines, if the fabric is not too detailed. Similarly, today's dyeing and finishing plants can produce over one million square yards of finished textiles per week.

Organization and Operation

For decades, there was no pattern of organization in the textile fabric industry. Some textile fabric companies were large corporations employing thousands of people, but many remained small operations with only a few dozen employees.

Imports decimated the U.S. textile industry in the late 1970s and 1980s. In 1985, a wave of mergers occurred, involving half of the nation's

15 biggest textile mills. Unfortunately, imports continued to impact the industry in the 1990s. Currently, industry experts predict that the merger mania will continue and result in fewer but stronger companies. The pace of mergers and acquisitions continues to accelerate at a dizzing rate. An example is Springs Industries, Inc., which since 1991 has bought a bath group (Wamsutta), two Canadian companies (C.S. Brooks Canada and Griffiths-Kerr), a towel maker (Dundee Mills), a blind and shade maker (Bali), a shutter maker (Nanik Window Coverings), and a rug maker (Regal Rugs Inc.). In addition, Springs sold two industrial products units.[10]

Many companies have adopted a strategy of economies of scale; they see "big" as vulnerable and seek to be "giants." Other companies aim to fill in gaps in their product offerings quickly through acquisitions, rather than developing new products more slowly themselves. Table 5.5 shows the five largest textile companies in the United States.

Industry mergers generally assume one of two forms. The first strategy is for a company to buy all or part of a competitor in order to dominate a segment of the market. The second and less popular strategy is for a company to diversify by buying an apparel company that manufactures clothes out of imported apparel fabric.

Textile mills are widely dispersed throughout the country. The industry has tended to seek areas where labor and land costs are low. There has also been little advantage in concentrating production in any one area through the construction of giant mills or complexes. Textile mills used to be concentrated in the northeastern states, but in recent years the southeastern part of the country has offered cheaper labor and land.

Because commitments to specific weaves, colors, and finishes must be made 6 to 18 months in advance, the textile fabric industry is extremely well-informed about fashion and alert to new trends. Information about these trends comes from fashion designers, predictive services, fashion directors for fiber or yarn companies, and advance textile shows throughout the world. But because they are geared to mass-production methods, most mills were reluctant to produce short experimental runs for individual designers. This is changing as new technology comes online.

The market centers for textile fabrics are not at the mills but in the fashion capital of the country, New York City. There, on the doorstep of the garment industry, every mill of importance has a salesroom. A fabric buyer or designer for a garment maker, or a retail store apparel buyer or fashion coordinator, has only to walk a block or two to obtain firsthand information on what the fabric market offers.

Types of Mills

Some mills sort and select the fibers to be used, spin them into yarn, then weave or knit them and finish the fabric. Finishing may include dyeing, napping, adding fire retardants, glazing, waterproofing, and pressing. It may also include treating the fabric to ensure such attributes as nonshrinkage and permanent press. Fashion influences decisions every step of the way.

TABLE 5.5 The Largest Textile Companies in the United States

COMPANIES	REVENUES IN $000	PROFITS AS % OF REVENUES
1. Mohawk Industries	3,256	5
2. Springs Industries	2,275	3
3. Westpoint Stevens	1,816	–4
4. Burlington Industries	1,620	–53
5. Interface	1,284	1
6. Unfi	1,280	3
7. Pillowtex	1,451	–4
TOTAL	**12,982**	

Adapted from: "Fortune 500 Largest Corporations," Fortune, 2000. Available at http://www.fortune.com.

Some mills produce only the yarn. Others weave or knit fabric from purchased yarn but do not carry the process beyond the greige state. There are also plants that bleach, dye, preshrink, print, or in other ways impart desired characteristics to fabrics produced by other mills. The plants that handle the various stages may or may not be under common ownership, and may or may not be geographically close to one another.

For richer and deeper color, yarns may be dyed before being woven or knitted. This process is known as **yarn-dyed**. However, most fabrics are knitted or woven first and then dyed. This process is known as **piece-dyed**. The piece-dyed process gives manufacturers maximum flexibility.

Many mills no longer limit themselves to working with yarns made of a single fiber. Fibers may be used alone or with other fibers, as demand dictates. Any of the types of mills described above may combine a natural fiber with another natural fiber, or, more commonly, a natural fiber with a manufactured fiber, to achieve a desired effect. For example, polyester is the most blended manufactured fiber. It is strong and resists shrinking, stretching, and wrinkling. Best of all, it is easily washed and machine dried. A blend of 65 percent polyester with 35 percent cotton yields an easy-care fabric widely used for shirts, blouses, and sheets.

FIGURE 5.8
Fabrics come in a wide range of patterns and colors, such as this exciting mix of checks and stripes.
Courtesy, Park B. Smith, Ltd.

The Converter

It is probably correct to say that the textile converter is the real middleman of the textile industry. **Textile converters** buy greige goods from the mills, have the goods processed to order by the finishing plants, and then sell the finished goods to garment makers. Therefore, textile converters must be on top of trends in colors, patterns, and finishes. They must fully understand fashion and must be able to anticipate demand. Converters work very quickly since they come on the production scene toward the end of the operation and are primarily interested in the finish and texture applied to the greige goods.

In recent years, converters' know-how has helped U.S. textile producers meet the competition from foreign textile producers who offer more fashion-oriented goods in small yardages. Converters can supply apparel producers with fewer yards of selected fabrics than can larger fabric mills. The latter must produce tremendous yardages of a designated pattern or design in order to maintain a profitable operation. While many converters are small operators, others, such as Springs Industries, are large. As the industry continues to consolidate, the converter function is still important, but it is done within the corporation, rather than by an outside firm.

Merchandising and Marketing

Many designers let the fabric act as the creative impetus for their designs. Good designers respond to new fabrics and search for that special fabric that will drape in the way they want or has just the color or texture they need. It is the job of the fabric industry to introduce designers to the particular fabric needed.

The textile industry works several seasons ahead. Fiber producers usually work two years ahead of a season. They must present their products this early to textile mills and converters so they will have enough lead time to plan their color and fabric lines. The fabric market presents its products a year ahead of a season.

New Horizons–Fabrics that Travel Well for Adventure

The adventure travel market incorporates a variety of activities including walking/ trekking/hiking, fly fishing, cycling, camping, and kayaking/rafting/ sailing. The crossover of technical fabric products into comfortable, lightweight, easy-care clothing for the traveling consumer provides functional qualities for all types of weather conditions, whether packing for a weekend getaway or an extended vacation.

In today's world of lifestyle choices, both men and women are becoming part of the health and fitness movement. No sport or leisure activity has the sole ownership of male or female users, whether it is swimming, soccer, basketball, or the marathon. The need for clothing that services the new needs of this group has taken fabrics into a new horizon.

One major trend is the influx of technical clothing for travel and leisure activities providing a wide range of features to consumers. Garments can now address any challenge that might occur during an outdoor experience, including built-in bug repellent, moisture management, anti-microbial properties, and sun block protection. Janine Robertson, spokesperson for Ex Officio, an adventure travel manufacturer noted, "With the spread of West Nile Virus, the launch of our new 'Bug-Away' apparel was very timely.

Current examples of categories that are using the new horizons of treated fabrics are footwear, socks, and functional sportswear that are easy to pack and comfortable to wear.

One of the more important functions of fabrics for consumers is moisture management. Dri-release, a patented technology from Optimer Performance Fibers, enhances the performance attributes of synthetic fibers, while maintaining the look and feel of natural fibers. Dri-release is engineered for permanent performance, enhances body comfort, moves moisture and dries quickly. It is soft and breathable with a natural fiber feeling, and is easy- care. It is also available with Freshguard to neutralize body odors, and remains effective for over 50 washings. Among the well-known apparel manufacturers who use these new horizon fabrics are Nike, REI, The North Face, Adidas, Levi, Tommy Hilfiger, Asics, and Saucony.

Many of the new horizons fibers and fabrics are developed to handle the new needs and wants of the very active consumer. Yoga practitioners, cross-country-skiing enthusiasts, African Safari Trekkers, Alaskan Explorers, and our Military are better dressed and better served with the continuing work of the fiber and fabric manufacturers who are constantly experimenting and testing for newer horizons.

Source

"New Horizons," KnitAmericas, Fall 2002, pp. 25–27.

Dri-release fabric for soccer apparel from Optimer Performance Fibers.

Courtesy, Knit Americas.

I. Spiewak & Sons uses fashionable fabrics for outerwear, such as this polyester bubble jacket.

Courtesy, I. Spiewak & Sons Inc.

Their first presentation is to the manufacturers of apparel and accessories, after which they present their finished products to retail stores and the press—all ahead of season—so they can publicize upcoming trends.

Since the textile industry must work several seasons ahead of consumer demand, it must also take the lead in recognizing new fashion directions.

The Industry's Fashion Experts

To guide them in future planning, textile firms employ staffs of fashion experts. These experts work with textile designers to create fabrics in the weights, textures, colors, and patterns that they anticipate consumers will want. Since most of the early decisions in both the fiber and the fabric market are based on color, the industry's fashion experts also work closely with specialized associations within the fashion industry that provide advance research and trend information.

Most prominent among these groups are the ones that work exclusively with color, such as the Color Association of the United States, the International Color Authority (ICA), the Color Box, and Pantone. Pantone is revamping its 19 year old textile color system. It is now called Pantone for fashion and home. It is done chromatically.

Color forecasting services provide their clients with reports and newsletters, color swatches, palette predictions, and color-matching services—all geared to each of the apparel markets (men's, women's, children's).

In addition to making decisions about color, the fabric industry must also consider fabrication and texture. If the trend is toward structured clothing, firm fabrication will be necessary, but when a soft, layered look is in, fabrication can be lightweight and soft.

Since trends must be spotted so far in the future, the fashion experts play an important role as they work with fiber and fabric mills as well as designers and buyers.

Textile Trade Shows and Fairs

New trends are also introduced at trade shows and fairs held throughout the world. Usually semiannual events, these shows are attended by designers, manufacturers, and retailers. The most important of these shows are:

- Interstoff Textile Fair in Asia
- Premiere Vision (First Look) in Paris, France
- Ideacomo (Ideas from Como) in Como, Italy
- Pitti Filati (Pitti Yarns) in Florence, Italy
- Canton Fair in Guangzhou, China
- Yarn Fair International in New York City
- International Fashion Fabric Exhibition (IFFE) in New York City

The failure to identify and act on a trend seen at a major textile show, for example, would mean that retailers and apparel manufacturers would be unable to supply the fashions that consumers want.

Advertising and Publicity

Unlike fiber producers, fabric manufacturers rarely advertise these days. But when they do, their advertising usually features the brand names of their products and frequently the names of specific apparel manufacturers that use their goods (see Figure 5.9). Either with the cooperation of fiber sources or on their own, these fabric houses run advertisements in a wide variety of mass-circulation magazines and newspapers and share the cost of brand advertising run by retail stores. Their advertising generally makes consumers aware of new apparel styles, the fabrics of which they are made, and often the names of retail stores where they may be purchased.

Fabric producers compete among themselves for the business of apparel producers. They also compete for recognition among retail store buy-

FIGURE 5.9
This ad for Gore-Tex fabric stresses its trademark status.
Courtesy, W.L. Gore & Associates, Inc.

ers and for consumer acceptance of products made of their goods. They publicize brand names and fabric developments, and stage seasonal fashion shows in market areas for retailers and the fashion press. They provide hang-tags for the use of garment manufacturers. These tags may bear not only the fabric's brand name but also instructions relating to its care. In accordance with federal regulation, fabric producers also supply manufacturers with the required care labels that must be permanently sewn into all garments. Many fabric firms supply information to consumers and the trade press and make educational materials available to schools, consumer groups, and retail sales personnel.

Research and Development

Fabric producers, like fiber producers, now devote attention to exploring the market potential of their products and anticipating the needs of their customers. Success in the fashion industry depends on supplying customers with what they want. Swift changes are the rule in fashion. Anticipation of such changes requires close attention to the market and a scientific study of trends. Market research is used to identify changing lifestyles as well as geographic demands.

Many of the large fabric producers maintain product- and market-research divisions. Their experts work closely with both the trade and consumer markets in studying fabric performance characteristics. Many fabric producers provide garment manufacturers with sample runs of new fabrics for experimental purposes. The market researchers conduct consumer studies relating to the demand for or acceptance of finishes, blends, and other desired characteristics. Such studies also help fabric and garment producers to determine what consumers will want in the future, where and when they will want it, and in what quantities.

Environmental Concerns

Textile manufacturers are collecting plastic drink bottles, used clothing, and cotton and wool scraps, then turning them into first-quality fleece fabrics. As Karen Deniz of Dyersburg Fabrics said: "We've used ordinary garbage to make an extraordinary product . . . . We can't burn plastic soda bottles, we can't bury them and we can't sink them, so it's time we started wearing them."[11]

Wellman, one of the handful of companies that make recycled fibers, estimates that it recycles 2.5 billion bottles annually. That saves enough petroleum to power the city of Atlanta for a year! Wellman developed Fortrel EcoSpun from recycled soda bottles; it is being used in backpacks, ski hats, and work gloves.[12] The French company Rhovyl produces an apparel textile fiber called Rhovyl'Eco from recycled mineral water and cooking oil bottles. It takes 27 recycled water bottles to make enough fabric for a sweater.[13]

The U.S. floorcovering industry has responded to the issue of decreasing space in existing landfills by collecting used carpets and researching new ways to recycle them. Hoechst Celanese has created a new polyester carpet without a latex backing; this carpet can be easily reprocessed.

The American Textile Manufacturers Institute (ATMI) launched an environmental protection program called E3 (Encouraging Environmental Excellence) in 1992. It has ten guidelines for member companies to follow, including environment audits and developing spill prevention and control plans.[14]

Unfortunately, the United States is not in the forefront of the environmental movement. In 1988, German companies voluntarily stopped the production of some azo dyes that were thought to cause cancer in textile workers. By 1996, Germany had banned the import of 150 azo dyes and any textiles made using these dyes. The search continues for new dyes that do not cause cancer or pollute.[15]

Antibacterial Finishes

Chemically imparting antibacterial finishes to cotton, rayon, and polyester/cotton blends can produce fabrics having durable germ-killing properties. In addition, a new bacteria is being designed by a scientific SWAT team at the University of Massachusetts, Dartmouth, that will feed on bodily secretions like sweat.[16]

Customer Services

Today's well-integrated and diversified fabric companies speak with great fashion authority. They also employ merchandising and marketing staffs whose expertise in fashion trends is available to apparel manufacturers, retailers, the fashion press, and frequently to consumers. Fashion staffs attend fashion forecasts. They conduct in-store sales training programs, address consumer groups, and stage fashion shows for the trade and press. They help retail stores arrange fashion shows and storewide promotions featuring their products, and they

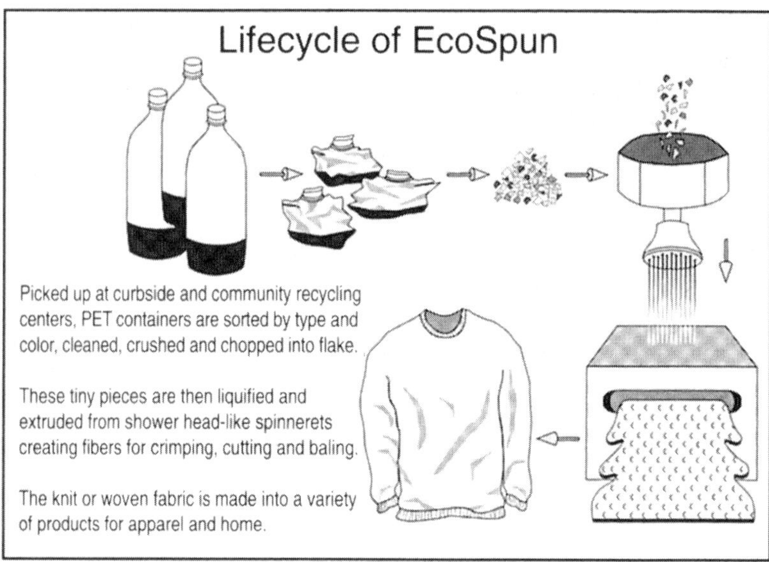

FIGURE 5.10
From garbage to garments: this diagram demonstrates how attractive sweaters have been made from EcoPile, which is produced from recycled plastic bottles.
Courtesy, Draper Knitting.

assist buyers in locating merchandise made from their fabrics.

Trends in the Textile Fabric Industry

A dramatic change in the mindset of the textile producers and marketing managers has broadened the product mix, quickened the response time required to meet customer demand, and made possible shorter runs of more innovative and fashionable fabrics. Currently, retailers, apparel manufacturers, and the fiber and fabric industries are working together to explore new and innovative ways to move textile products through the pipeline to the ultimate consumer more quickly and efficiently (see Figure 5.10).

Fortunately, the consumption rate of textiles increases every year. Economists forecast that this trend will continue and even accelerate into the 2000s. The role of the textile fiber and fabric industries in the U.S. economy is an important one. These industries employ 1.4 million people from all 50 states, making this the largest U.S. manufacturing sector. However, from 1997-1998, the Asian currency began to fall, making their extremely low-priced textile and apparel products very attractive to U.S. buyers. As a result of a continued fall in currency, over 100 textile plants in the United States have closed, making for the worst industry downturn in 50 years.[17] In spite of industry problems, the textile business is still one of the nation's essential industries.

Some of the major trends that affect both the fiber and fabric industries are:

- The production of high-tech fabrics
- Growing global competition
- Increasing exports
- Greater diversification of products
- Increased government regulations
- New technology in equipment

Production of High-Tech Fabrics

We live in a high-tech age, when almost every new product is a result of combined effort and sophistication in research and development. Fabric is no exception, as evidenced by the frequent introduction of new textiles endowed with some novel and valuable property, characteristic, or performance.

A fabric that has been constructed, finished, or processed in a way that gives it certain innovative, unusual, or hard-to-achieve qualities not normally available can be defined as **high-tech fabric.**[18]

Protective Uses of High-Tech Fabrics

Many common fabrics have been transformed into high-tech fabrics by coating or laminating them, or by making them with innovative yarns such as Kevlar, Nomex, Spectra, and so on. These fabrics are engineered to resist extreme temperature changes, or to have superior strength, or to have resistance to radiation, corrosive chemicals, and other stresses (see Figure 5.11a and b).

A bright future is forecast for these specialized fabrics in a variety of situations:

- *Activewear*—Apparel for jogging, golfing, cycling, skating, sailing
- *Rainwear*—Raincoats, capes, hats
- *All-weather wear*—Apparel for hunting, fishing, skiing, mountaineering, and so forth
- *Swimwear*—Bathing suits, bodysuits for diving, life vests
- *Protective clothing*—Garments to protect the wearer from hazardous waste; medical contamination; bullets or shrapnel; radiation; cutting or abrasion; electronic, computer, and pharmaceutical manufacture
- *Heat and fire protection clothing*—Occupational clothing for firefighters, blast furnace workers, car racers, tank crews
- *Chemical protection clothing*—Occupational clothing for chemical workers, workers at toxic waste sites and spills

An outstanding example is a knit fabric blending Hydrofil, polyester, and Lycra spandex that moves moisture away from the body. It is currently being used in cross-country ski tights, sports tops, cycling jerseys, jackets, face masks, and gloves. High-tech fabrics can help to keep an athlete's or worker's mind and body more comfortable, thus allowing the person to improve his or her performance or make that extra effort.

Other new high-tech fabric developments are having a major impact on home furnishings. For example, KromaLon, an olefin fiber, is used to make carpets that are antimicrobial as well as stain and bleach resistant.[19]

Designers Use of High-Tech Fabrics for Apparel

Designers at all price points are incorporating a range of materials besides natural fibers—metallic threads, plastic, vinyl, rubber, and reflective material. In one of his early collections, Alexander McQueen attracted a lot of attention when he cut out pieces of lace, backed them with latex, and splattered them on nude chiffon. The late Gianni Versace used clear vinyl extensively, as well as a chain-mail fabric that drapes easily. "I have always been in love

A

B

FIGURE 5.11A AND B *I. Spiewak & Sons seeks different features in fabrics for its core business, industrial outerwear, exemplified by this (a) police officer's uniform and (b) fashionable sporty jacket .* Courtesy, I. Spiewak & Sons, Inc.

with antique armors," Versace said. "I wanted to use metal in a dress as though it were fabric."[20] Helmut Lang adopted the reflecting strips commonly found on backpacks, running shoes, and firefighters' uniforms, into reflective jeans. Fredric Molenac, designing for the Madam Gres collection, used Lycra with neoprene, a rubber-like fabric. Cynthia Rowley incorporated stainless steel organza into some of her designs. Miuccia Prada uses mostly synthetics in her Miu Miu line; some of her jackets have Velcro fastenings. As the expanding field of new fabrics grows, more and more designers are finding inspiration and esthetic value in high-tech fabrics.

Growing Global Competition

The major concern of the U.S. textile industry is the growth of a global competition that shows every promise of being permanent. Although the domestic fiber and fabric industries produce a huge amount of goods, the United States still imports vast quantities of fiber, yarn, and fabric from around the world. From 1980 to 1986, imports of apparel and apparel textiles doubled! Since the WTO went into effect in 1995, U.S. imports of textiles and apparel have increased 90 percent. A recent study by Kurt Salmon Associates (KSA), a leading textile and apparel consulting firm, stated that imports control 90 percent of the U.S. apparel market.[21]

Like other American industries, the fiber and fabric mills have been adversely affected by overseas competition. Wages are so much cheaper in those markets that U.S. apparel makers have turned to such countries as Korea and China for fabrics. As a result, most domestic textile companies have restricted their production of apparel fabrics and gone into the production of industrial and household goods.

The United States is still the world's leading exporter of raw cotton. Sluggish world economic growth has kept the world's consumption of cotton relatively even from 1990 to 2000. But the even world numbers mask the changes that have occurred in the spinning of cotton and its distribution since 1995. Cotton consumption in China and Pakistan has had the largest increase while the United States experienced the greatest decrease. Consumption of raw cotton is forecast to rise in China, while declining in the United States, Mexico, and India.[22]

Not surprisingly, another trend, limited to fabric producers, is toward the acquisition or establishment of mills abroad. Such foreign-based mills may be wholly owned by a U.S. firm or jointly owned by a U.S. firm and a host-country firm. Most mills are located close to the fiber sources. The engineers may be American or American-trained, but the rest of the staff are local workers who are paid according to local wage scales. Advantages to the host-country firm are the availability of the facilities, the fashion knowledge gained, the technical skill of the U.S. owners or part owners, and increased employment opportunities for its citizens. By producing some goods abroad, domestic manufacturers are able to defend themselves against the competition of foreign-made fabrics. They can also put themselves in a more favorable position to sell in countries where tariffs limit or keep out goods made in the United States. An example is Guilford Mills, Inc., which was founded in 1946 in Greensboro, North Carolina, and went public in 1971. In 1994, the company increased its stock in Groupo Ambar, a leading manufacturer of knit textiles in Mexico. In 1995, Guilford opened its first office in Central America, in Guatemala City. Due to the industry's tough economic state over the past several years, Guilford has shut down all but two of their U.S. mills and will retain an apparel operation only in Mexico.[23]

Another trend involves foreign business firms buying into fabric or finishing plants here. Some of these firms are becoming partners in, or sole owners of, new facilities being built in the United States. An example is Hoechst, a West German company which bought Celanese, a major U.S. producer.

Despite these trends, domestic producers, particularly given their closeness to their customers, still have a number of important advantages over importers. They can react more quickly, provide shorter lead time, structure shorter production runs, and in general, remove much of the guesswork that used to hinder the industry.

Increasing Exports

The industry has nearly tripled its exports over the past decade, exporting 20 percent of its output—roughly $16 billion a year.[24] The textile industry is now directing more of its efforts toward capturing a share of the global market. A number of corporate strategies for the years ahead include:

- Increasing the focus on foreign markets and operations for apparel fabrics, since most studies indicate that the major growth in apparel markets will be outside the United States

- Developing overseas manufacturing operations, or exploring licensing in conjunction with foreign mills, to attain a stronger foothold on the international scene
- Devoting increased resources to market research
- Continuing technological advances

For example, the United States is currently a world leader in home-furnishing textiles, offering more diversified products than any other country. In an attempt to expand this trade, the U.S. textile industry is focusing more of its manufacturing and marketing activities abroad on fabrics for home furnishing and industrial end uses, which are projected to gain larger market shares in the future.

Another relatively new concern for U.S. companies that want to export to European countries are the ISO 9000 standards. These are a set of international standards that companies must meet to be "ISO certified." These standards are generic and apply to any industry. Basically, in order to be certified, companies must have systems in place to judge quality. Many European companies will not buy from a company that is not ISO certified.

The ISO 14000 was a set of standards that was developed after the success of the ISO 9000. It was designed to assess the need for international environment management standards.[25]

Greater Diversification of Products

Today, the textile industry produces a more diversified range of fibers and fabrics than ever before. The specialization that once divided the industry into separate segments, each producing fabrics from a single type of fiber, has all but faded. To meet the needs of consumers, it is often necessary to blend two or more fibers into a yarn or to combine yarns of two fibers. Mills are learning to adjust their operations to any new fiber or combination of fibers.

One of the largest firms in the field illustrates how the industry is moving toward greater product diversification. Burlington, originally a rayon mill specializing in bedspreads, now produces and sells spun and textured yarns of both natural and manufactured fibers. Its new products include a variety of finished woven and knitted fabrics, some unfinished fabrics, and hosiery for men, women, and children. It also produces domestic and home furnishings ranging from bed linens to rugs and furniture.

Another bright spot for the domestic textile market is **geotextiles**, or manufactured permeable textiles that are currently used in reinforcing or stabilizing civil engineering projects.[26] Two examples of industrial fabrics are Kevlar and Tyvek, which are used for diverse applications such as book covers and wrapping houses to prevent moisture penetration.

An example of an industrial protective coating is Teflon—yes, the coating used on nonstick frying pans—which is now being used to protect delicate fabrics. With fashion designers searching for new fabrics every day, can apparel applications for industrial and geotextiles be far behind?

Increased Government Regulation

One of the biggest impacts on the textile industry in the past decade has been the intervention of the federal government in every aspect of the industry: health and safety, noise levels and chemical pollution, consumer product liability, environmental impact, and hiring practices.

Until recently, federal regulation of the textile industry was mainly concerned with the fiber content labeling of fabrics and products made of those fabrics. In 1953, the Flammable Fabrics Act was passed, but it served to ban from the market only a few very ignitable fabrics and apparel made from them. The increasing strength and direction of the consumerism movement, however, resulted in more government regulation of the textile industry on both the federal and state levels.

In July 1972, two important changes in federal textile regulations took effect: the Federal Trade Commission's (FTC's) rule on Care Labeling of Textile Wearing Apparel and the revision of the Flammable Fabrics Act. The FTC's care-labeling rule requires that all fabrics—piece goods as well as apparel and accessories made of fabric—be labeled to show the type of care they require. In 1997, the FTC again changed the rules by introducing new care label symbols. They indicate whether the fabric can be hand washed or machine washed or should be dry-cleaned. The symbols also indicate whether ironing is required, and if so, at what temperature. The manufacturer must sew a permanent label with these care symbols into each garment.

Other trends in the textile industry that are a result of government environmental and consumer regulations include:

- Fibers and textile products will be made by larger producers with a resulting decrease in the number of small concerns and marginal operations. This will result primarily from the higher production costs related to complying with the new government regulations and the greater capital investment required to stay competitive in a period of continually rising costs.
- Manufacturing operations will function at higher efficiencies, recycling as much material as possible and converting waste to energy.
- New chemical processes will be developed to recover, recycle, and reuse fibers, dyes, and other chemicals.
- Fibers with built-in environmental disadvantages will slowly give way to more suitable replacements, or new processing techniques will be devised to allow their continued use.
- Transfer printing may be an important way to reduce some of the dye-house stream-pollution problems.
- Consumers will be increasingly protected, with particular emphasis on children's apparel and home furnishings.
- Consumers will be better advised on the characteristics of their purchases.

New Technology in Equipment

"New technology is totally revolutionizing the textile industry," says Jack Lenor Larsen, an eminent textiles designer in the home furnishings industry.[27] The trend toward increased mechanization and automation is clearly apparent throughout the industry as it has changed from one that is labor-intensive to one that is equipment-intensive.

In recent decades the textile industry has experienced a number of technological developments; for example, the shuttleless loom and computer design of fabrics. In the mills, new machines combine higher production speeds with lower energy consumption. Automated weaving and knitting machines produce more with fewer operators.

The industry is also experimenting with new printing techniques. Rotary-screen printing is truly the technology of the 21st century and will replace flat-screen and roller printing techniques. Powerful computers will enable the industry to set the cost and price of fabrics before they are knitted or woven. These elements are needed to be competitive in the global textile market.

Computer technology is playing a key role in quick response programs that improve communications among fiber, fabric, apparel, and retail businesses (see Figure 5.12). Quick response shortens the time between the placement of orders by retailers and the delivery of goods. Bar codes have been established by the Fabric and Supplier Linkage Council so that vendors can label shipments with standard bar codes that purchasers can enter immediately into inventory records. This reduces inventory costs, warehouse time, forced markdowns, and stock outs.

FIGURE 5.12
A CAD system can be used to experiment with producing innovative fabric designs.
Courtesy, Fairchild Publications, Inc.

FIGURE 5.13
Manufacturers show their products at the annual Bobbin Show months in advance of the season when they will appear on new lines of apparel.
Courtesy, BobbinBlenheim Media.

The industry experimented widely with robots in the 1980s, and will probably employ them with increasing frequency into the next century.

Although the new technology has created job losses, it will ultimately help the industry by attracting bright, ambitious young workers and leaders who want to work in a progressive environment.

Today, U.S. textile plants are characterized by computer-run looms that feed a mile of yarn per minute, as well as completely automated yarn spinning plants that can run 24 hours a day, 7 days a week. Technological advances have long been introduced at the Bobbin Show, a 3-day event held annually in the United States. In 1998, the Bobbin Show became Bobbin World, a triennial international show, which alternates with the Bobbin Show (see Figure 5.13). Other major shows are the International Machinery Show in Germany and the Japanese International Apparel Machinery Show.[28]

SUMMARY AND REVIEW

Textiles begin with fibers, which may be natural (cotton, wool, flax, and silk) or manufactured. Manufactured fibers are either cellulosic (made of cellulose, which is also the substance of natural plant fibers) or noncellulosic (combining chemicals in a laboratory). Variants of generic manufactured fibers bear the trade name of the manufacturer. For example, Dacron is Du Pont's brand of polyester.

The main market for fibers is the textile fabric industry, which weaves, knits, or otherwise turns fibers into greige goods. These goods are then finished by either the textile mill or converters, who add such treatments as dye, waterproofing, and fire-retarding and permanent-press finishes. Finishes added to natural fibers allow them to compete more effectively with manufactured fibers by taking on some of the properties that consumers demand in apparel and other textile products.

Textiles are sold primarily to manufacturers of apparel and home fashions, but marketing of fibers and textiles is directed at retailers and consumers, too, to build demand. U.S. textile manufacturers compete with foreign imports through technological advances that speed production, minimize pollution, and improve the performance of fabrics in terms of colorfastness, insulation, and other desirable features. Computerized systems expedite order fulfillment.

Trade Talk

Define or briefly explain the following terms:

brand names	microfiber
cellulosic fibers	natural fibers
cotton	noncellulosic fibers
fabrics	piece-dyed
fashion textiles	polymers
fiber	primary supplier
flax	ramie
generic names	silk
geotextiles	spinnerette
greige goods	textile converters
hemp	textile fabric
high-tech fabric	trimmings variant
licensed trademarks	wool
linen	yarn
manufactured fibers	yarn-dyed

For Review

1. What is the difference between a natural and a manufactured fiber? Give five examples of each, and indicate the source of each natural fiber you name.
2. What has the natural fiber industry done to counteract the effects of manufactured fibers in the marketplace?
3. Trace the steps through which a new or newly modified manufactured fiber passes as it goes from conception to general availability.
4. Name and explain the three ways in which producers of manufactured fibers usually sell their products to fabric manufacturers.
5. Describe the three major merchandising and marketing activities of natural and manufactured fiber producers.
6. Describe the major steps in the production of most fabrics.
7. What is the function of the textile converter? What are the advantages of dealing with a converter for (a) a fabric mill, and (b) an apparel producer?
8. How do textile fabric producers keep informed about new fashion trends?
9. How have increased fiber, yarn, and fabric imports affected the American textile industry?
10. What are the provisions of the Flammable Fabrics Act of 1953 and the FTC's rule on Care Labeling of Textile Wearing Apparel of 1972?

For Discussion

1. What is the role of trade associations in the marketing of fibers and textile fabrics?
2. When a major designer designed his collection for a mass merchandiser, he went directly to the textile mills with specifications for his fabrics in regard to width, pattern repeats, and so on. Can most designers do this? Why or why not?
3. Discuss the relationship of the designer and the manufacturer of fashion merchandise to the textile industry.

References

1. Jane Dorner, *Fashion in the Forties and Fifties* (New Rochelle, NY: Arlington House, 1975), p. 38.
2. http://www.supimacotton.org/faq/.
3. Asia Pulse News, March 20, 2001, p. 248.
4. Loren Kruse, "The World Grows Hemp, U.S. Waits," *Successful Farming*, December, 2000, v98, i13, p. 3.
5. Faye Musselman, "Fabric Vendors are High on Hemp in Home Fashions," *Home Furnishing News*, May 7, 2001, p. 23.

6. Stan Gellers, "CMA Seminar Addresses Global Issues for Millenium," *Daily News Record*, September 1999, p. 1B.
7. Alicia Hills Moore, "U.S. Textiles Hang in with High Tech," *Fortune*, April 16, 2001, V43, No. 8.
8. ATMI, 2000 Scope and Importance of the U.S. Textile Industry, p. 6, http://www.atmi.org/econTradeData/si2000.pdf.
9. ATMI 2001, U.S. Department of Commerce & Bureau of Labor Statistics, Quick Facts About U.S. Textile Industry.
10. *Hoover's Company Profiles* (Austin, TX: Hoover's, Inc., 2000).
11. Karen Kaplan, "The Cutting Edge/Computing/Technology/Innovation: A New Idea in Trashy Clothes," *Los Angeles Times*, April 26, 1995, p. B4.
12. http://www.wellmaninic.com/RawMaterialPurch/recyclingstory.asp, 2001.
13. http://www.rhovyl.com/pageshtml-gb/labels/rhovyleco.html
14. "E3—Encouraging Environmental Excellence," ATMI press release, 1996.
15. Michael Roberts, "Germany Restricts Imports for Azo Dyes," *Chemical Week*, August 23, 1995, p. 20.
16. David Kirby, "Designer Bacteria May Have a Future in Fashion," August 19, 2001, *Stores*, p.5.
17. ATMI, *Crisis in U.S. Textiles,* prepared by Office of the Chief Economist and the International trade Division of ATMI, August 2001, p. 5.
18. A. Reisfeld, "High-Tech Apparel: Growing Area for Knit Applications," *Knitting Times*, June 1996, pp. 70–71.
19. Warren S. Perkins, "AATCC Presenters Detail New Research—Part Two," *American Textiles International*, November 1996.
20. Martha Duffy, "Neoprene? Pewlon? Designers Are Giving Synthetic Fabrics New Looks—and Vice Versa," *Tiime*, February 17, 1997, p. 52.
21. ATMI, *Crisis in U.S. Textiles,* prepared by Office of the Chief Economist and the International trade Division of ATMI, August 2001, p. 18.
22. National Cotton Council, *Economic Outlook for U.S. and World Cotton Markets*, May 24, 2002.
23. *Hoover's Company Profiles* (Austin, TX: Hoover's, Inc., 2001).
24. ATMI, *Crisis in U.S. Textiles,* prepared by Office of the Chief Economist and the International trade Division of ATMI, August 2001, p. 2.
25. Quality Standards ISO: http://www.engineers-international.com/quality.html.
26. Matthew Hein and Maria Corey, *Textiles*, Office of Textiles and Apparel, September 1993, p. 9.
27. Michael Sand, "Fashion Nerd," *Wired*, June 1996, p. 43.
28. Erin Moriarty, "Bobbin Loss a Blow to City's Latin Hopes," April 2000.

CHAPTER 6

Leather and Fur

WHAT'S IN IT FOR YOU?

Everything you always wanted to know about the leather and fur industry.

Key Concepts:

- The three major types of companies in the leather industry and their functions
- The nine different categories of leather and the special finishes used on leather
- The history and development of the fur industry in the United States
- The functions of the three major groups in the fur industry
- The steps in transforming fur pelts into finished garments

The most glamorous and sought-after textiles—leather and fur—are also the two oldest. Prehistoric people discovered that the animals they killed for food could serve another purpose, that of providing them with warmth and protection from the elements. One side of an animal skin could be worked into leather; the other furnished fur. Today leather and fur are vital to the apparel, home furnishings, and automotive industries, contributing the raw materials for coats and jackets, handbags, shoes, gloves, and an ever-widening range of fashion products.

The leather industry is currently in the process of expanding its markets in ways that no one even dreamed of ten years ago. New processing methods have created leathers so thin and supple that designers can use them for everything from bikinis to shirts to evening wear—all available in an incredible array of colors.

After several years of decline because of environmental concerns over the use of scarce or rare animal skins, furs are making a comeback, especially with the young, first-time customer. The demand for furs has never been greater, at the very time when the fur industry is experimenting with new colors and styles.

THE LEATHER INDUSTRY

Leather-making is a highly specialized and time-consuming operation. Because of the time involved, the leather industry must anticipate and predict trends far in advance of other textile suppliers. Leather producers typically decide what production method, textures, finishes, and colors they will use 8 to 16 months before a leather will reach apparel and accessory manufacturers. As a result, those in other fashion industries often look to the leather industry for leadership, particularly in terms of color and texture.

Since leather is a by-product of the meatpacking industry, it is not the target of environmentalists as is the fur industry. Few animals are raised specifically for their hides. Most animals are raised to feed people, and their skins and hides, which have no food value, are then sold to the leather trade.

History and Development

Archaeologists have found leather thong sandals in the tombs of ancient Egypt. They were the prized possessions of priests and pharaohs more than 5,000 years ago (see Figure 6.1). From the earliest times, leather was valued as clothing, but as tanning methods improved, leather became important for armor, helmets, and saddles. In Europe in the Middle Ages, leather was considered a luxury product within the reach of the rich and noble only.

In the many years that Indian tribes roamed the North American continent, long before the arrival of the first European colonists, the tanning of leather was an important part of tribal life. Indians used deerskins to make clothing, soft yet sturdy moccasins, and tepee homes. By today's tanning standards, their methods would be considered limited and primitive, yet the techniques they used to transform raw animal hides into a variety of products certainly served them well.

In 1623, not long after the arrival of the Pilgrims in Massachusetts, the first commercial tannery in the American colonies was established in Plymouth by an Englishman with the fitting name of Experience Miller. Later Peter Minuet, Governor of New Amsterdam, invented the first machinery used for tanning in the colonies. His invention was a horse driven stone mill that ground the oak bark then used to convert animal skins into leather.

Many years passed before more important mechanization of the leather industry occurred. But in 1809, a giant step was taken. Samuel Parker invented a machine that could split heavy steer hides 25 times faster than people could do it by hand. The machine also produced a lighter and more supple leather; just what people wanted for their shoes, boots, and other clothing.

Today, new machines do much of the manual work formerly required to stir hides and skins as they soaked. Other machines dehair and de-

FIGURE 6.1
Working with leather dates back to 1550 B.C. in Ancient Egypt. The figure on the left is soaking the hide in large jar; the figure on the right is stretching and kneading a skin on a trestle to soften it. The figures at the center bottom are cutting a skin with a knife. At the top right is the completed skin of an animal.

flesh them. Still others split the skins and emboss patterns on them. Machinery has taken much of the human labor out of the processing of leather. In addition, chemistry has provided new tanning agents that reduce the time required to transform hides and skins into leather. These new tanning agents also help achieve a greater variety of finishes. This variety is possible in spite of restrictions on the commercial use of the skins of some animals that have been placed on endangered-species lists.

Organization and Operation

Although tanning was once a cottage industry in the United States, it quickly became, relatively speaking, big business. By 1870, there were over 6,600 small tanneries in the United States. By 1979, only 4,500 tanneries operated in the United States. Like the textile industry, the leather business has been subjected to its share of mergers since the late 1970s. A combination of factors hit the American tanning industry then: overwhelming shoe imports, stronger environmental regulations, and sharply increased exports of hides. Today, there are only about 343 tanneries in the United States, but they are large plants that produce tens of millions of square feet of leather! The Northeast dominates the industry with 146 establishments, 66 that are located in New York City. The majority of the other tanneries are located in Massachusetts, Texas, California, and Wisconsin.[1] Wisconsin has a cluster of 20 tanneries (see Table 6.1).

The American leather industry is divided into three major types of companies: regular tanneries, contract tanneries, and converters. **Regular tanneries** purchase and process skins and hides and sell the leather as their finished

TABLE 6.1 U.S. Balance of Trade—Leather (in $ Millions)

	Hides and Skins		Leather		Shoes and Leather Products[A]		Net
	Imports	Exports	Imports	Exports	Imports	Exports	Deficit
1981	101	691	354	275	3,785	269	3,005
1982	71	769	318	279	4,476	273	3,580
1983	63	791	298	252	5,288	239	4,367
1984	70	1,149	403	313	6,745	250	5,506
1985	73	1,071	394	284	7,626	205	6,533
1986	65	1,293	406	313	8,540	229	7,176
1987	82	1,413	563	396	9,898	350	8,384
1988	102	1,603	748	506	11,001	379	9,363
1989	98	1,562	744	625	11,260	396	9,519
1990	93	1,607	683	751	12,451	527	10,342
1991	109	1,270	571	680	12,335	649	10,416
1992	124	1,250	631	705	13,002	733	11,069
1993	120	1,189	736	764	13,857	837	11,923
1994	126	1,382	960	812	14,791	839	12,834
1995	140	1,237	1,089	870	15,298	844	13,536
1996	131	1,235	1,139	951	15,858	9223	14,936
1997	126	1,491	1,376	1,146	17,288	942	15,211
1998	109	1,113	1,571	1,289	17,322	897	15,703

Source: *U.S. Leather Industries Statistics.*

product. **Contract tanneries** process the hides and skins to the specifications of other firms (mainly converters), but are not involved in the final sale of the leather. **Converters** buy the hides and skins from the meat packers, commission the tanning to the contract tanneries, and then sell the finished leather. In recent years, converters have been buying finished leather from both regular and contract tanneries.

The leather industry has remained specialized. Calfskin tanners do not normally tan kidskin, and gloveskin tanners do not work with sole leather.

Like textile producers, most leather firms maintain sales offices or representatives in New York City for the convenience of their customers.

Categories of Leather

Almost all leather comes from cattle. But the hides and skins of many other animals from all parts of the world are also used in fashion apparel and accessories. There are nine major categories of leather (see Table 6.2).

The Equine Group

Horses provide a rugged leather. Some horsehide is tanned into cordovan leather, which makes extremely durable and sturdy shoe uppers. The hide is also used for leather jackets. But it is important to know that most of what is called "pony skin" is really stenciled calfskin, which is used because it is more pliable than real pony skin. Real top-quality pony skin comes from wild horses in Poland and Russia.[2]

The Exotic Leathers

Supplies of the so-called "exotic leathers" are diminishing worldwide, driving prices up sharply. There is some good news, however. From 1967 to 1987, the American alligator was listed as an endangered species. Today the alligator is out of danger because of a policy called **sustainable use**. This refers to an environmental program that encourages landowners to preserve alligator eggs and habitats in return for the right to use a percentage of the grown animals. In Louisiana, for example, which supplies 40 percent of the world's alligator and crocodile skins, 184,189 hides were sold in 1999, up from only 53,000 in 1989.[3]

In a related development, Native American Indian tribes are raising bison (American buffalo) and have opened a tannery in Billings, Montana to tan the hides with the hair on them to make them into buffalo robes. They use an environmentally friendly process known as brain tanning, which leaves the hides softer than chemical tanning, and easier to sew.[4]

Leather Processing

Animal pelts are divided into three classes, each based on weight. Those that weigh 15 pounds or less when shipped to the tannery are called **skins**. This class consists mostly of calves, goats, pigs, sheep, and deer. Those weighing from 15 to 25 pounds, mostly from young horses and cattle, are referred to as **kips**. Those weighing more than 25 pounds, primarily cattle, oxen, buffalo, and horse skins, are called **hides**.

The process of transforming animal pelts into leather is known as **tanning**. The word is derived from a Latin word for oak bark, which was used in early treatments of animal skins. Tanning is the oldest known craft.

Three to six months are needed to tan hides for sole leather and saddlery. Less time is required for tanning kips and skins, but the processes are more numerous and require more expensive equipment and highly trained labor. The tanning process involves minerals, vegetable materials, oils, and chemicals, used alone or in combination. The choice of a tanning agent depends on the end use for which the leather is being prepared.

Minerals

Two tanning methods use minerals. One uses alum; the other uses chrome salts. Alum, used by the ancient Egyptians to make writing paper, is rarely used today. Chrome tanning, introduced in 1893, is now used to process nearly two-thirds of all leather produced in the United States. This is a fast method that takes hours rather than weeks. It produces leather for shoe uppers, garments, gloves, handbags, and other products. Chrome-tanned leather can be identified by the pale, blue-gray color in the center of the cut edge. It is slippery when wet. It is usually washable and can be cleaned by gentle sponging.

Vegetable Materials

Vegetable tanning, which is also an ancient method, uses the tannic acids that naturally occur in the bark, wood, or nuts of various trees and shrubs and in tea leaves. Vegetable tanning is used on cow, steer, horse, and buffalo hides. The product is a heavy, often relatively stiff leather used for the soles of shoes, some shoe uppers, some handbags and belts, and saddlery.

TABLE 6.2 Nine Major Categories of Leather

CATTLE GROUP

Steer, cow, and bull hides, producing leather for:

- Shoe and slipper outsoles, insoles, uppers, linings, counters, welts, heels, etc.
- Traveling bags, suitcases, briefcases, luggage straps, etc.
- Gloves and garments
- Upholstery for automobiles, furniture, airplanes, buses, decoration
- Handbags, purses, wallets, waist belts, other personal leather goods
- Harnesses, saddles, bridles, skirting (for saddles), etc.
- Machinery belting, packings, washers, aprons, carders, combers, pickers, etc.
- Footballs, basketballs, volleyballs, and other sporting goods
- Laces, scabbards, holsters, etc.

Kips or kipskins (from large calves or undersized cattle), producing leather for:

- Shoe and slipper uppers and linings
- Handbags and other personal leather goods
- Gloves and garments
- Sweat bands for hats
- Rawhide and parchment
- Athletic helmets
- Bookbindings
- Handicrafts, etc.

SHEEP AND LAMB GROUP

Wooled skins, hair skins (cabrettas), shearlings, producing leather for:

- Shoe and slipper uppers and linings
- Gloves and garments
- Chamois
- Handbags and other personal leather goods
- Moutons and shearlings (skins with wool on)
- Parchment
- Textile rollers
- Hats, hat sweat bands, millinery, and caps
- Bookbindings
- Piano actions
- Sporing goods (balls, gloves, etc.)

GOAT AND KID GROUP

Skins producing leather for:

- Shoe and fancy uppers, linings
- Gloves and garments
- Fancy leather goods, handbags
- Bookbindings

EQUINE GROUP

Horse, colt, ass, mule, and zebra hides, producing leather for:

- Shoe soles and uppers
- Luggage
- Gloves and garments
- Belts
- Aviator's clothing
- Sporting goods (baseball covers and mitts, etc.)

BUFFALO GROUP

Domesticated land and water buffalo (not American Bison, whose hide is not tanned for their leather) producing leather for:

- Shoe soles and uppers
- Handbags
- Fancy leather goods, luggage
- Buffing wheels

PIG AND HOG GROUP

Pig, hog, boar, peccary, carpincho (a Brazilian rodent) skins, producing leather for:

- Gloves
- Innersoles, contours, etc.
- Fancy leather goods, luggage
- Saddlery and harnesses
- Shoe uppers
- Upholstery

DEER GROUP

Fallow deer, reindeer, elk, and caribou skins, producing leather for:

- Shoe uppers
- Gloves
- Clothing
- Piano actions

Moccasins
Mukluks
Fancy leather goods

KANGAROO AND WALLABY GROUP

Skins producing very strong leather for:

- Shoe uppers, including track and basketball shoes

EXOTIC LEATHERS

Aquatic Group—frog, seal, shark, walrus, and turtle
Land group—camel, elephant, ostrich, and pangolin
Reptile group—alligator, crocodile, lizard, and snake

Source: Leather Industries of America, *Dictionary of Leather Terminology,* 8th ed. (Washington, D.C.: Leather Industries of America).

Vegetable-tanned leather can be identified by a dark center streak in the cut edge. It is resistant to moisture and can be cleaned by sponging. Vegetable tanning is the slowest tanning method and takes months to complete. Because it is so labor-intensive, relatively little vegetable tanning is done in the United States.

Oil

Processing with oil is one of the oldest methods of turning raw animal skins into leather. A fish oil—usually codfish—is used. Today, oil tanning is used to produce chamois, doeskin, and buckskin—relatively soft and pliable leathers used in making gloves and jackets.

Chemicals

The most widely used and quickest method of tanning relies primarily on formaldehyde. Because the processing turns the leather white, it can easily be dyed. Formaldehyde-tanned leather is washable. It is often used for gloves and children's shoe uppers.

Combinations

It is possible to combine tanning agents. A vegetable and mineral combination is used to "retan" work shoes and boots. Combinations of alum and formaldehyde or oil and chrome are common.

Finishing

The finishing process gives leather the desired thickness, moisture, color, and aesthetic appeal. Leather can now be dyed in nearly 500 different colors! Dyed leather is also sometimes finished with oils and fats to ensure softness, strength, or to waterproof it. Special color effects include sponging, stenciling, spraying, or tie dyeing. Other finishes include matte, luster or pearl, suede, patent, or metallic. It is important to note that suede is a finish, not a kind of leather. Table 6.3 describes the characteristics of different leather finishes.

Merchandising and Marketing

Because of the lead-time needed to produce leather, the leather industry not only must stay abreast of fashion, it must be several steps ahead of it. Months before other fashion industries commit themselves to colors and textures, leather producers have already made their decisions. They have started the search for the right dyes and treatments to meet expected future demand. As a result, the leather industry's forecasters are considered the best and most experienced in the fashion industry.

TABLE 6.3 Special Finishes for Leather

FINISHES	CHARACTERISTICS
Aniline	Polished surface achieved with aniline dyes
Matte (mat)	Flat eggshell-surface look
Luster or pearl	Soft, opaque finish with a transparent glow
Antiqued	Subtle two-toned effect like polished antique wood
Burnished	Similar to antiqued, but with less shadowing
Metallic	Surface look of various metals—copper, gold, silver, bronze
Waxy	Dulled, rustic look, as in waxy glove leathers
Patent	Glossy, high-shine finish
Napped	Buffed surface such as in suede or brushed leather
Suede	Leather finish that can be applied to a wide variety of leather
Washable	Waterproof finish that can be applied to some leathers

Source: William A. Rossi, "What You Should Know About Leathers," *Footwear News Magazine*, June 1982, p. 16 and Rohm-Hass, *Leather Technicians Handbook of Furnishings*, 1994.

Then & Now

The Looks of Leather–20th Century to 21st Century

At the beginning of the 20th century, leather was used mainly for accessories like shoes, boots, belts, and bags, but not apparel. There were a few exceptions. Cowboys had long worn leather or shearling chaps to protect their legs from long days in the saddle. In the East, as in England, many riders wore jodphers with leather insets to protect their legs. Blacksmiths wore leather aprons to protect themselves from the open fire.

Animal skins suggested sensuality in the 1920s, when movie stars were photographed lying on bear and tiger skins. In the 1930s, leather and shearling jackets were worn mainly by cowboys, outdoor laborers, and a few pilots. Both pilots and football players wore leather helmets for protection. Brown leather "bomber jackets," often lined with shearling, were worn by U.S. airmen in the 1940s to protect them from the cold at high altitudes. Many men liked the look, the fit, and the practicality of this style. It has been popular ever since.

The black leather jacket acquired a sinister edge in the 1950s after it was worn by James Dean in the film *Rebel Without A Cause* and by Marlon Brando in the film *The Wild Ones*, which was about a violent motorcycle gang. In the 1960s, Diana Rigg played on this image of power and sex appeal when she wore a skintight black leather bodysuit in the TV series, *The Avengers*. Yves Saint Laurent was the first high-fashion designer to take up the motorcycle jacket; in 1960 he showed it in crocodile skin with a mink collar! British designer Ossie Clark played up the dark side image of the black leather jacket by fitting it so tightly that the zipper looked like a scar. In the 1970s, the "perfecto" jacket was being worn as a badge of rebellion by many rock stars, including Sid Vicious.

Claude Montana took the leather jacket upmarket in the 1980s with butter-soft leather and very wide shoulders. In the early 1990s, Gianni Versace was putting sexually suggestive black leather on his runways. In the late 1990s, leather came back strongly, often combined with other fabrics. Anna Sui showed suede with silk, and Versace showed leather with lace for evening wear.

Roaring into the 21st century, leather is leading the fashion pack. A favorite with designers, editors, and consumers, leather is the fashion fabric of choice, from casual vests for weekend dressing, to cropped blouson jackets to an embroidered suede peasant shirt. Leather in now the hottest fashion look for all seasons.

After three years of research and development washable leathers are truly washable and can be cared for at home using a washing machine. We've come a long way! Once upon a time, leather was synonymous with hard edges, tough men, and the great outdoors; these days it comes in softer styles, some so supple they look like lace.

The new look of leather can be hammered, embossed, metallic, pearlized, hard or soft finished, and cut-out. It can be fashioned into cold weather rugged wear or sophisticated, sexy evening wear. American and international designers think leather, and not only for the usual products such as shoes, handbags, gloves, and other accessories—they think leather for FASHION!

Sources:

Melanie Kletter, "Sensational Leather," *Women's Wear Daily*, March 5, 2002.

www.leatherassociation.com/trends.html

Melanie Kletter, "Textured Looks on Tap for Leather Goods," *Women's Wear Daily*, July 22, 2002.

"Leather and Lace," *Women's Wear Daily*, January 14, 2003.

A

B

Wearing leather has long typified rebellion. (a) Marlon Brando wore a black leather motorcycle jacket in The Wild Ones, a 1950s film about a motorcycle gang. (b) Today, a lacelike leather jacket is an urbanite's way to stand out from the crowd.

(a) Columbia. Courtesy, The Kobal Collection.
(b) Courtesy, Fairchild Publications, Inc.

Fashion Information Services

Because they make their assessments of fashion trends so far in advance, others in the industry look to the leather industry for information. Like other fashion industries, the leather industry retains experts to disseminate information about trends and new products in the leather industry. They often produce booklets that forecast trends, describe new colors and textures, and generally promote the leather industry. Samples of important textures and looks are included.

Fashion experts also work directly with retailers, manufacturers, and the press to help crystallize their thinking about leather products. One-on-one meetings, seminars, and fashion presentations are used to educate the fashion industry and consumers about leather.

Despite all this activity, individual tanners are not known by name to the public. Nor is a fashion editor, in describing a leather garment, likely to mention its manufacturer. Leather producers are not named in retail stores or in leather manufacturers' advertising. Consumers who can name several fabric and fiber producers would have a difficult time naming any leather tanners.

Trade Associations and Trade Shows

Much of the information collected and disseminated by the leather industry comes through its strong trade association, Leather Industries of America (LIA). LIA has worked hard to broaden the market for all types of leathers, often in the face of serious competition. For example, shoe manufacturers, who were important leather users a few years ago, have now turned to other products as well. This has compelled the leather industry to promote and defend its products, and LIA has taken the lead in this activity.

LIA sponsors semiannual color seminars and sells a packet of each season's color swatches to industry members. It supports a Hide Training

FIGURE 6.2
Leather products are shown at the Asian Pacific Leather Fair, which runs during April at the Hong Kong Convention Center.
Courtesy, Fairchild Publications, Inc.

School and sponsors a student design award. LIA's weekly newspaper, Council News, covers the leather industry.

Trade shows are another important source of information within the leather industry. Two years before the ultimate consumer sees finished leather products in retail stores, the leathers are introduced in several industry trade shows. The oldest and most established show, the Semaine du Cuir, is held in Paris in the fall, usually September. The Hong Kong International Leather Fair is held in June, and the Tanners' Apparel and Garment Show (TAG) is held in New York City in October.

Research and Development

The leather industry retains and expands its markets by adapting its products to fashion's changing requirements. Before World War II, relatively few colors and types of leather were available in any one season, and each usually had a fashion life of several years. Today, a major tannery may turn out hundreds of leather colors and types each season, meanwhile preparing to produce more new colors and textures for the next season.

To protect and expand their markets, leather producers constantly broaden their range of colors, weights, and textures. They also introduce improvements that make leather an acceptable material where it formerly had either limited use or no use at all.

Leather has the weight of tradition behind it; people have regarded fine leather as a symbol of luxury for centuries. But today, leather shares its hold on the fashion field with other and newer materials. Through product research and development, producers are attempting to meet the competition not only among leathers but also from other materials.

Trends in the Leather Industry

Until just a few decades ago, the leather industry concerned itself primarily with meeting consumer needs in relatively few fashion areas—mainly shoes, gloves, belts, handbags, luggage, and small leather goods. The use of leather for apparel was restricted largely to a few items of outerwear, such as jackets and coats. These were stiff, bulky, and primarily functional in appeal. Now designers offer colorful, supple leather vests, jeans, pants, blazers, anoraks, skirts, and suits of every description, in addition to jackets and coats (see Figure 6.3a and b).

Today, the leather industry has changed. These changes are the result of three trends: enlarging market opportunities, increased competition from synthetics, and increased foreign trade.

Enlarging Markets

Improved methods of tanning are turning out better, more versatile leathers with improved fashion characteristics. In general, these improvements fall into three categories:

1. The new leathers are softer and more pliable. Tanners' ability to split full-grain leather thinner and thinner creates this new suppleness.
2. The new leathers can be dyed more successfully in a greater number of fashion colors.
3. Washable leather finishes and improved cleaning techniques have made it easier for consumers to care for leather garments.

In cowhide leathers, the demand is high for the lighter-weight, mellow, natural-looking, full-grain leathers. Especially desirable are the glazed, rich-colored, aniline-dyed types that accentuate the natural beauty of the grain. These leathers are used predominantly in luggage, portfolios, and furniture.

Sheep and lamb tanners are encouraged by the sustained demand for glazed and suede leathers in the leather apparel market. They are also very pleased by customers' enthusiastic response to the new lighter-weight shearling used in coats, jackets, and vests. Some new shearling styles are also reversible. The nonwool side is traditionally finished as suede, but it can also have a napped finish.[5]

Prada and Gucci are two upscale fashion companies built on leather. They continue to expand their offerings season after season. Other designers working with leather include Vakko, Donna Karan, Ralph Lauren, Escada, and more recently Michael Kors and Calvin Klein, seen prominently in their 2002 Spring collections.[6]

Increased Competition from Synthetics

In the past few decades, the leather market has been eroded by synthetics. Leather heel lifts, which used to be commonplace, are now more

A

B

FIGURE 6.3A AND B *The beauty and versatility of soft leather is a hit on the runway. Such as, (a) Dominic Bellisimo's long-haired shearling coat and camel leather pants with pink shell by Sisters and (b) skirt by Tommy Hilfiger.* Courtesy, Fairchild Publications, Inc.

often than not replaced with plastic. Synthetics that look and feel like leather but are less susceptible to scratches and easier to maintain are used to make handbags and other small leather goods.

Since most synthetic leather products were not as attractive as leather, synthetics did not offer leather any real competition for a long time. Over a decade ago, however, imitation leathers and suedes that were true substitutes began to be marketed. The most important one, Ultrasuede, quickly became a fashion classic. Although a washable synthetic, Ultrasuede does not have an image of being fake or cheap, and it is used by high-fashion designers. Another more recent artificial suede, called Facile, has improved suppleness. It is also widely used by high-fashion designers. Vinyl is widely used for shoes, handbags, and other accessories, and its appearance has improved over the years.

Increased Foreign Trade

An increased worldwide demand for leather has enabled American hide dealers to obtain higher prices for their products in countries where demand outstrips supply. This, in turn, has led to sharp increases in the export of hides since foreign tanners are able to produce leather more cheaply than their U.S. counterparts (see Table 6.1). However, with the outbreak of Mad Cow and foot and mouth disease infecting cattle throughout Europe in 2001, production of leather is down and prices have risen. As a result, leather will most likely become a luxury product once again.

While the United States has been inundated with cheap leather products in the past few years, its own tanners have turned to exporting their own products. American tanners, known for the high quality of their tanning process and their excellent finishing techniques, have had no trouble expanding into foreign markets.

Industry Growth Factors

Several factors point to overall industry growth. Foremost among these is the trend toward a classic and elegant fashion look with an emphasis on quality. When quality is desired, consumers want real leather with all its mystique and will not settle for substitutes. Another hopeful sign is the fact that the supply of raw hides is large enough to allow for growth in production. Actively supported by a federal export program, the industry's aggressive efforts to develop foreign markets ensures future growth for the industry, as does the industry's expanded research programs.

THE FUR INDUSTRY

Long before prehistoric people learned how to plant crops, weave cloth, or build shelters, they figured out how to use fur. They spread it on the floor and used it as rugs. They used it to cover and create walls, thus bringing some warmth into an otherwise cold and drafty cave.

By the Middle Ages, the wearing of fur announced one's wealth and status. Sable, marten, ermine, and fox were the favored furs of nobility. Italian cardinals wore ermine as a symbol of purity; English nobles wore it as a sign of power. Fur was also a valued commodity; something that was used in trading. For centuries in Northern Europe, furs were valued more than gold and silver. Fur was still as good as gold in 1900 when Chile banked chinchilla skins as security for a loan.

Fur is still big business in the United States. There are approximately 1,500 retailers and 100 manufacturers in the United States, 85 percent that are small, independently run businesses. The United States ranks among the top countries for retails sales of fur.[7] In 1996, family fur farms in the United States produced about 3.6 million mink and fox pelts with a value of nearly $127 million, or ten percent of the worlds's mink supply.[8]

History and Development

The search for a northwest passage that would shorten the route between Europe and the Orient led to the establishment of the fur trade in North America. When French explorer Jacques Cartier arrived at the mouth of the St. Lawrence River in 1534, he traded furs with the Indians. The next year, when he sailed even farther up the river, he realized what a vast wealth of fur-bearing animals existed on the continent. English and Dutch explorers soon joined the French in setting up trading posts. The first posts were situated along the St. Lawrence and Hudson rivers, but they soon dotted the continent. Early fur-trading posts played a role in establishing such cities as St. Louis, Chicago, Detroit, St. Paul, and Spokane.

The plentiful supply of furs helped the colonists in other ways. They were able to export furs and use the money to bring European necessities—and even some luxuries—to the New World. Furs were an important source of clothing and furnishings. For a while in the mid-18th century, furs were virtually the currency of North America.

It is the beaver, however, that truly deserves a special place in North American history. The discovery of this fur led to a "fur rush" that rivaled the Gold Rush. Beaver was used mostly to make men's hats, but in Canada in 1733, one beaver pelt could also buy a pound of sugar or two combs or six thimbles or eight knives. Settlers pushed west in search of beaver, leaving behind communities with names like Beaver Creek, Beaver Falls, and Beaver Lake. Fortunes were made. John Jacob Astor was among the first to become a millionaire in the beaver trade. He dreamed of a beaver-fur empire stretching from New York to the Northwest Territory.

Ironically, just as beavers were becoming scarce, the fashion changed. Abraham Lincoln wore a silk top hat to his inauguration, and men stopped wearing beaver hats and began to buy hats made of silk and felt. The demand for beaver ceased overnight.

The interest in women's furs remained strong, however, and during the Civil War, the first mink ranch was established by T. D. Phillips and W. Woodstock. In 1880, silver fox fur farming began on Prince Edward Island, off the eastern coast of Canada. Fur farming and ranching have undergone renewed expansion in the past half century.

Fashions in furs do change, although they change less quickly than do other apparel styles because furs are expensive. While mink coats account for half of all furs sold today, 50 years ago, a woman who wanted to look glamorous chose an ermine cape. Today, an ermine cape would be valuable only as a theatrical prop—and it could be picked up fairly cheaply in a secondhand store.

More than at any other time in the history of fur fashion, the current list of furs is long and varied. Mink is the overwhelming favorite among consumers. Sable is a distant second,

FASHION FOCUS

We're Just Wild About...Furs

What goes together better than peanut butter and jelly, ham and eggs, and love and kisses? It's movie stars and mink! A mink coat has been an incomparable symbol of luxury and glamour and status and security—not to mention warmth and sensuality—for over 100 years. Today's stars still swath themselves in fur, but not just mink. And you don't have to be a movie star to wrap yourself into a fur coat, fur vest, fur hat, or fur suit to become a "star."

The fur industry—from breeder, to manufacturer, to retailer, to customer—has changed dramatically in the last decade. This is most evident from a style standpoint, where more playful and youth-oriented styles are being paraded down the runways, such as a pink Mongolian lamb poncho, a reversible patchwork coat, or a mink rugby shirt. This kind of pizzazz is luring more and more eclectic crowds to fur shows and fur stores.

Thanks partially to all the furs seen in rap videos, more women in their twenties and thirties are frequenting fur stores . "Young people think it is cool to wear fur, and that's great for us," said Jeffrey Lehman, president of Edwards-Lowell, a Beverly Hills boutique.

Today, names like Dennis Basso, Gilles Mendel, Anne Dee Goldin, and Sherry Cassin who design primarily in fur, mix with famous couture designers names like Michael Kors, Dolce & Gabbana, Prada, Gucci, and Sean Jean in the exciting world of fur design and fashion. Although most of the press and public relations people photograph the movie, music, and video stars at the fashion shows, there are many other places these stars can wear their fur. Chanel offers a knee length baby-blue sheared mink perfect for the Aspen slopes, Sean Jean has a black fur lined and fur collared leather bomber jacket for the hip look, and Fendi designs a wrap around fur coat that could double as a blanket—talk about doing double duty!

Fur is flying again! Still, the revival of fur fashions has stopped short of a rejection of animal rights. PETA (People For The Ethical Treatment of Animals) is still active in its fight for the right of animals, but more and more consumers want the right to choose for themselves to wear fur...or not!

Sources:

Rosemary Feitelberg, "A Novelty Look," *Women's Wear Daily*, February 28 , 2002.

Alex Joseph, "Taking Fashion Fur-ward," NETWORK, February 2003, pp. 16-17.

www.furs.com.

Ready-to-Wear Report, "Wild for Fur in High Places," *Women's Wear Daily*, January 2003, p. 10.

Eric Wilson, "PETA to Sponsor Show," *Women's Wear Daily*, January 29, 2002, p. 2.

From stoles to coats to capes; from mink to fox to chinchilla; furs steal the spotlight for both day and evening.
Courtesy, Fairchild Publications, Inc.

TABLE 6.4 Selected Popular Furs and Their Characteristics

FUR	CHARACTERISTICS	YOU SHOULD LOOK FOR
Beaver		
Sherared	Soft, plushy texture.	Silky texture. Well-matched, pelts, evenly sheared.
Natural	Long, lustrous guard hairs over thick underfur.	Lustrous sheen of guard hairs and thickness of underfur.
Calf	Short, sleek, flat hairs. Comes in many natural colors and patterns and may be dyed.	Lustrous, supple pelt with bright luster. Marking should be attractive.
Chinchilla	A short, dense, very silky fur. Originally from South America, but now wholly ranch-raised.	Lustrous slate-blue tiop hair and dark underfur, although mutaion colors are now available.
Coyote	A long-haired fur, often pale gray or tan in color. Durable and warm.	Long guard hair and thick, soft underfur.
Ermine	A fur with very silky white guard hairs and dense underfur.	Clear white color.
Fox	The widest range of natural mutation colors of any fur except mink; silver, blue, white, red, cross, beige, gray, and brown. Cna also be dyed in a wide variety of colors.	Long, glossy guard hairs and thick soft underfur. Also clarity of color.
Lamb		
American Processed	Pelts of fine wool sheep sheared to show the pattern near the skin. Naturally white but may be dyed.	Silky, lustrous moire pattern, not too curly.
Broadtail	A natural (unsheared) flat moire pattern, Color may be natural browns, gray, black, or dyed in more exotic colors.	Silky texture and uniformity of pattern.
Mongolian	Long, wavy, silky guard hiar. May be natural off-white, bleached, or dyed in more exotic colirs.	Silky texture, with wavy—not frizzy—hair.
Mouton	Pelts are sheared, hairs are straightened for soft, water-repellent fur, generally dyed brown.	Uniformity of shearing.
Shearling	Natural sheepskin (lamb pelt), with the leather side sueded and worn outside. The fur side (or inside) is often sheared.	Softness of leather side and even shearing.
Persian lamb	From karkul sheep reaised in Southwest Africa, or central Asia. Traditionally black, brown, and gray, new mutaion colors available; also dyed.	Silky culs or ripples of jur and soft, light, pliable leather.

followed by fox and beaver. A new category, called "sport" or "contemporary," includes such furs as raccoon, fox, beaver, coyote, muskrat, tanuki (Japanese raccoon), and nutria (a South American beaver-like animal). Table 6.4 lists furs and their characteristics.

In addition to the use of newer furs such as tanuki and nutria, fur manufacturers often reintroduce older ones. Persian lamb, shunned by fur buyers for over two generations, has now made a comeback. Remembered as a fur that was used for grandmother's conservative coat, Persian lamb, which is flat enough to be cut almost like cloth, is now being put to new uses. It is a prime choice in new fur garments such as scarves, sweaters, and jackets.

Sometimes an interest in a fur comes about because fur manufacturers invent a finishing

FUR	CHARACTERISTICS	YOU SHOULD LOOK FOR
Lynx	Russian lynx is the softest and whitest of these long-hired furs, with the most subtle beige markings. Canadian lynx is next, while Montana lynx has stronger markings. Lynx cat or bobcat is reddish black fading to spotted white on longer belly hairs.	Creamy white tones and subtle markings.
Marten	See also sable.	Texture and clarity of color.
American	Long silky guard hairs and dense underfur. Color ranges from blue-brown to dark brown.	
Baum	Softer, silkier, and shinier than American marten.	
Stone	The finest marten has soft, thick guard hairs and a bluish-brown cast with pale underfur.	
Mink	Soft and lightweight, with lustrous guard hairs and dense underfur.	Natural luster and clarity of color. Fur should be full and dense.
Mutation	Most colors of any natural ranched fur, from white to grays, blues, and beiges.	
Ranch	Color ranges from a true, rich brown to a deep brownish black.	
Wild Pieced*	Generally brown in color. Color and pattern depends on pieces used. This is the least expensive mink.	Pattern and well-made seams.
Nutria	Similar to beaver, often sheared for a sporty, more lightweight feel. Popular for linings and trims. Often dyed in a variety of colors.	Clarity of color.
Rabbit	Generally long hair in a variety of natural colors, including 14 natural mutation colors in ranch rabbit. May be sheared and grooved. Not very durable, shed easily.	Silky texture and uniformity of
Raccoon	Long silver, black-tipped guard hairs over wooly underfur. May also be plucked and sheared and dyed.	Silvery cast. Plenty of guard hair with heavy underfur.
Sable	Member of marten family. Russian sable has a silver cast; the most expensive. Crown sable is brown with a blue coat. Canadian golden sable, an amber tone, is less expensive.	Soft, deep fur in dark lustrous brown, with silky guard hairs.
Tanuki	Also called Japanese raccoon. Color is light amber brown with distinctive cross markings.	Clarity of color and dense, full texture.

*The same piecing technique can be used for almost any fur. The most common pieced furs are mink, sable, marten, fox, Persian lamb, raccoon, and beaver. Adapted from a number of sources, including the booklet *Choosing Fur* published jointly by The Fur Council of Canada and the Fur Information Council of America, Herndon, Virginia, pp. 4–5.

technique that makes a fur seem new (see Figure 6.4a). A renewed interest in raccoon can be traced to a technique that eliminated much of its bulkiness. In the 1940s, beaver was invariably sheared to look like a short fur; today it is sometimes left unplucked, giving it a totally new look. Or beaver may be sheared and have multicolored insets (see Figure 6.4b).

Animal Rights Groups

Over the past 30 years, animal rights groups have protested the wearing of animal fur as cruel and inhumane. Some groups are opposed to trapping fur-bearing animals in the wild. Others also protest fur farming. Some groups, like **PETA** (People for the Ethical Treatment of Animals) and The Friends of Animals have

A

B

FIGURE 6.4A AND B *A fur coat is not necessarily a classic coat; (a) Eric Gaskins' coyote jacket and (b) Zuki's swing coat in reversible dyed sheared beaver are eye-popping.* Courtesy, Fairchild Publications, Inc.

staged confrontations and demonstrations to get media attention. Long-standing activists Carnie Wilson, Pamela Anderson, Kim Basinger, Tyra Banks, and Joaquin Phoenix were all used as endorsements in the 2001 PETA anti-fur campaign that coincided with the New York Fashion Week. Some activists have thrown paint at women wearing furs. Others have picketed fur stores and industry trade fairs. Still other groups, like the Animal Liberation Front, have raided mink and fox farms and let the animals loose. They also destroyed pedigree cards containing irreplaceable genetic data.[9]

The industry response has been strong on a number of fronts. It is working with the U.S. and Canadian governments and the International Standards Organization to develop global humane trapping standards. Fur farmers are proposing legislation to make the crime of releasing fur-bearing animals a felony. Associations of American and Canadian fur farmers have also offered rewards for information leading to the arrest of fur raiders. Fur auction houses are offering farmers vandalism insurance. The industry has done a great deal of consumer education to stress that today's farmed furs come from only nonendangered species. They also stress that:

- Fur farms do not remove animals from the wild.
- Ninety-five percent of U.S. mink production comes from farms certified as humane.[10]
- Unlike manufactured (fake) fur, real fur does not use nonrenewable petroleum by products.[11]

Manufactured Furs

Manufactured, synthetic, or "fake" furs were long regarded as beneath the notice of serious designers and were limited to inexpensive garments. Technological developments in the 1980s and animal rights activism changed that. The new manufactured furs looked so good that fashion writers dropped the word "fake" and began calling them "faux" furs. (*Faux* is the French word for false.)

The improved synthetic furs quickly were used by a wide range of designers for higher-priced garments that still cost less than real fur.

Oleg Cassini unveiled a 100-piece fake fur line in a show sponsored by the Humane Society. The event was videotaped so that many people could view the show. Named the "Evolutionary Fur," the fake fur line retails from $500 to $1,000 and is carried in major department stores. Some designers, like Calvin Klein and Betsey Johnson, still shun real fur as a matter of principle and use fakes instead. However, many industry observers feel that the fur industry has profited from the popularity of both real and manufactured fur.[12]

Organization and Operation

The fur industry in the United States is divided into three groups, which also represent the three stages of fur production: (1) the trappers, farmers, and ranchers who produce the pelts and sell them at auction; (2) the fur-processing companies; and (3) the manufacturers of fur products.

Pelt Production

The first step in the production of fur is to obtain the necessary pelts. A **pelt** is the skin of a fur-bearing animal.

Trappers are the primary source of wild-animal pelts, which must be taken only during the coldest season of the year in order to be of prime quality. In 2000, there were 80,000 licensed fur trappers in Canada.[13] Trappers sell pelts to nearby country stores or directly to itinerant buyers. In some areas, collectors or receiving houses accept pelts for sale on consignment from trappers or local merchants. When enough pelts have been gathered, a fur merchant exports them or sends them to an auction house, or they are sold at a private sale through a broker.

The majority of furs come from farms or ranches, where fur-bearing animals are bred and raised strictly for their fur. Almost all mink, rabbit, fox, and more recently, chinchilla, Persian lamb, and broadtail are ranched. **Fur farming** offers two important advantages. First, animals can be raised under controlled conditions. Second, they can be bred selectively. When wild mink roamed North America, they came in one color, a dark brown with reddish highlights. Today, many beautiful colors, some of which are trademarked and denote a manufacturer's private label, are available. Among the better-known names are Azurene, Lunaraine, Rovalia, Lutetia, Jasmin, Tourmaline, Cerulean, and the most recognizable name of all, Blackgama.[14]

The number of mink and fox ranches in the United States dropped by half between 1989 and 1996. Over the same period, the number of pelts obtained fell by 42 percent to 2.7 million in 1995. Reasons for this rapid decline include an outbreak of diseases, low prices in 1990–1991, and farm raids by animal activists. As a result, by 1996, prices hit $53 a pelt, the highest price in more than 20 years[15] (see Figure 6.5).

Fur Auctions

Fur pelts are sold at auctions today, much as they were in the 13th century. Fur buyers and manufacturers bid on the pelts, which are sold in bundles. Buyers look for bundles that are matched in quality and color. This enables a manufacturer to make up a garment of uniform beauty.

Recently, competition has increased among buyers to purchase a "top bundle"—that is, an unusually beautiful bundle that goes for an unusually high price. This, in turn, results in a much-touted coat—often costing $100,000 or more—that is made from the top bundle.

The auction trail is an international one, although except for England, Tokyo, and more recently, Beijing, each market sells indigenous furs. Fur buyers from the United States travel to Canada, Scandinavia, China, and Russia. Though demand for furs in Russia is climbing, production at Russia's more than 70 fur farms is down 50 percent since 1995.[16] To buy North

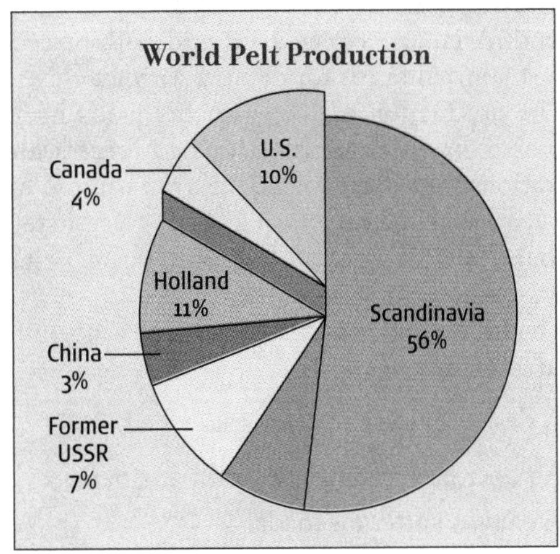

FIGURE 6.5

Adapted from: www.furcommission.com/farming/pelts.htm.

American furs, fur buyers travel to auction houses in New York, Seattle, Toronto, and North Bay, Canada.

Fur Processing

After manufacturers of fur goods buy the pelts, they contract with fur-dressing and fur-dyeing firms to process them.

The job of fur dressers is to make the pelts suitable for use in consumer products. The pelts are first softened by soaking and mechanical means. Then a flesher removes any unwanted substances from the inner surface of the skin. For less expensive furs, this is done by roller-type machines. At this point, the pelts are treated with solutions that tan the skin side into pliable leather. The fur side may be processed at the same time. This involves either plucking unwanted guard hairs or shearing the underfur to make the fur more lightweight. Although fur dressing has traditionally been a handcraft industry, modern technology is turning it into a more mechanical process.

After dressing, the pelts may go to a dyer. Fur dyes were once made from vegetable matter, but are now mostly derived from chemical compounds. New dyes are constantly being developed, making it possible to dye fur more successfully and in more shades than ever before.

Fur Manufacturing

Most fur manufacturers are small, independently owned and operated shops, although a few large companies have emerged largely as a result of the explosion in the number of fur products. New York City's fur district on Seventh Avenue between 23rd and 30th Streets is the main center for fur manufacturing.

The production of fur garments lends itself neither to mass production nor to large-scale operations. Skill and judgment are required at every stage of manufacturing. Doing each step by hand lets a worker deal with each pelt's color, quality, and peculiarities.

The following steps transform pelts into finished garments:

1. A design of the garment is sketched.
2. A paper pattern is made of the garment.
3. A canvas pattern is made.
4. The skins are cut in such a way as to conform to the designer's sketch, exhibit the fur to its best advantage, and minimize waste.
5. The cut skins are sewn together.
6. The skins are wetted and then stapled to a board to dry, a process that sets them permanently.
7. The garment sections are sewn together.
8. The garment is lined and finished.
9. The garment is inspected.

For some luxurious furs, the cutting operation becomes extremely complex. Short skins must be **let out** to a suitable length for garments. Letting out mink, for example, involves cutting each skin down the center of a dark vertical line of fur (the grotzen stripe). Each half skin must then be cut at an angle into diagonal strips one-eighth to three-sixteenths of an inch wide. Then each tiny strip is resewn at an angle to the strips above and below it to make a long, narrow skin. The other half-skin is sewn in a similar manner (see Figure 6.6).

The two halves are then joined, resulting in a longer, slimmer pelt that is more beautiful than the original. Considerable hand labor is required to do all of these operations. Ten miles

FIGURE 6.6

The making of a fur coat involves many painstaking steps. Here, the letting-out process elongates fur and avoids cross-seaming.

Courtesy, Fairchild Publications, Inc.

of thread and over 1,200 staples may be used in a single coat.

In an industry that for generations has produced furs in much the same way as in ancient times, a revolutionary process was developed through technology in 1989. The famous Fendi sisters of Italy showed an entire collection of furs based on a new process that made them all, from sables to squirrels, reversible. Interfacing, lining, and construction are all eliminated, and the result is fur coats of incredible lightness and minimal bulk. These coats are so light in fact, that a full-length fur coat can be folded up and put into a knapsack. Changing from the fur side to the leather side can be done in a minute and there is no bulky look—no matter which side is outside. The fact that all inner construction was eliminated changed the look of the coats themselves. Eliminating the shoulder pads makes everything fit naturally, and the lightness of the fur make them swing and swirl as if made of chiffon.

Retail Distribution of Furs

There are more than 1,500 retail stores across the United States that specialize in furs. While some are chain operations, 85 percent of fur retailers are small, family-owned businesses.[17] That said, the line between manufacturing and retailing is less clear in the fur industry than in most other industries. Retail fur merchants, for example, typically make up an assortment of garments to sell off the rack to customers, but they also maintain a supply of skins in their workroom for custom work.

In retail stores, fur departments are either leased or consignment departments. Both operations permit a retail store to offer its customers a large selection without tying up a lot of capital in inventory.

A **leased department** is situated in the store but run by an independent merchant (such as Maximillian at Bloomingdale's), who pays a percentage of sales to the store as rent. The operator either owns or leases the stock. Lessees often run several similar departments in many stores and can, if necessary, move garments and skins from one location to another. Lessees, who are a unique kind of retailer, are usually well capitalized and have expert knowledge in both furs and retailing.

In **consignment selling**, a fur manufacturer supplies merchandise to a retail store, which has the option of returning unsold items. In effect, the manufacturer lends stock to a store. Consignment selling is influenced by the state of the economy. When interest rates are high, stores tend to buy less stock. Ritz is an example of a consignment seller.

Merchandising and Marketing

Fur traders, dressers, producers, and their labor unions all work through their various trade associations to encourage the demand for fur.

Trade Associations

Trade associations mount their own campaigns to promote furs, and they also work with retailers. The leading trade association is the Fur Information Council of America (FICA), which represents fur retailers and manufacturers. It has placed ads in various fashion magazines to counter some of the animal-rights arguments.

The ranch mink association, American Legend, is a nonprofit cooperative formed through the combination of two major mink-producing groups: Emba Mink Breeders Association (EMBA) and Great Lakes Mink Association (GLMA). With more than 1,000 members, American Legend now markets about 70 percent of the total American mink production at the Seattle Fur Exchange.[18] It has a program to protect its trademarks from infringement. The association supplies labels and other point-of-purchase materials only to retailers and manufacturers who can prove they purchased the group's pelts at an American Legend auction.

Trade associations not only monitor the industry, but they help to educate consumers. Fur is a product that is most successfully purchased when the consumer has some specialized knowledge about what he or she is buying. Consumers need to know, for example, that the rarer the breed, the more expensive the fur. Mink is sold at a wide variety of price points, with the commercial mink coat in the early 2000s priced anywhere from $2,499 to $5,999. The moderate mink can be purchased for $6,000-$9,999, while on the upper end, one can expect to spend as much as $50,000.[19]

Another important factor in the quality of fur is whether the pelts are female or male. Most female skins are softer and lighter. Although there are exceptions, such as fitch, for which the male skins are preferred, a coat of female mink costs more than one of male skins.

International Fur Fairs

As the demand for fur increases, and the world supply of fur pelts decreases, people are traveling farther than ever before to get the best buys. Designers, manufacturers, retailers, importers/exporters, wholesalers, and the media all attend one or more of the leading international fur fairs listed in Table 6.5.

Labeling

The Fur Products Labeling Act of 1952 requires that all furs be labeled according to:

1. The English name of the animal
2. Its country of origin
3. The type of processing, including dyeing, to which the pelts have been subjected
4. Whether or not parts have been cut from a used garment or from the less desirable paw or tail sections

Years ago, such labeling would have been helpful, for example, to prevent a customer from buying a less expensive, dyed muskrat that was touted as the much rarer and more expensive Hudson seal. Today, such labeling is helpful in distinguishing one fur from another in an industry that, without intending to defraud, has learned to capitalize on fashion trends by treating less expensive furs to look like more expensive ones.

Trends in the Fur Industry

As a general rule, the demand for furs is related to the economy. During the Depression, fur sales dropped off dramatically. After World War II, when the economy was expanding, fur sales boomed. In the early 1970s, conservationists' concerns about the diminishing wild-life species put a temporary damper on fur sales, but the industry rebounded in the 1980s. Mid-1987 saw the highest point, the $2 billion mark. But in the early 1990s, a combination of antifur activism and mild winters brought a rapid downturn in fur sales. Synthetic fur sales rose rapidly. But then the record-breaking bad weather in the mid-1990s saw a renewed interest in real fur. Sales in 2000 increased 21 percent over 1999, to $1.69 billion.[20] Industry experts say the outlook for the fur industry continues to be good.

Growth will be affected by the following four major trends:

- Renewed fashion interest in furs
- Increased foreign trade
- Restrictive legislation that actually helps the industry
- New channels of retail distribution

Renewed Fashion Interest

Once worn only by the rich or for formal occasions, furs are now bought and worn by many kinds of consumers for many occasions. The average customer no longer buys one conservatively cut coat, either. Furs are now sporty and casual, elegant and classic, or faddish and trendy—and with such choices, many customers have been persuaded to buy more than one. As fur designer Michael Kors has said: "At this point, people who think of fur as a separate category make it very old-fashioned. It's getting rid of that idea of my one great mink coat of my lifetime, and instead treating fur like another fabric, another texture."[21]

TABLE 6.5 Leading International Fur Fairs

SITE	NAME OF FAIR	MONTH HEAL
Tokyo	Japan International Fashion Fair Outerwear	February
Hong Kong	Hong Kong International Fur & Fashion Fair	February
Milan	Mifur Fur & Leather Exhibition	March
Lausanne	Comispiel	March
Moscow	Moda Spring & Mexa Fall	March, October
Frankfurt	Frankfurt International Outerwear Fair	March, October
Montreal	North American Fur & Fashion Outerwear Expo	May

Source: "1996 Fur Fairs: Retail Growth Should Spur Successful Season," *Fur Age,* January 22, 1996.
*Note: months may change according to calendar.

FIGURE 6.7
Comeback star Liza Minelli reinforces her starship in a glamorous lynx full-length coat by Dennis Basso.
Courtesy, Fairchild Publications, Inc.

Not only have older women—the traditional market—continued to buy furs, but the market has expanded to young and working women as well. In the 1970s and 1980s, a new market opened up for fur—namely, women themselves. For many years, women received fur coats only as gifts. They seldom bought this luxury item for themselves. But in the 1970s and 1980s, when more women started working, and also began to get paid more for their work, they started buying furs for themselves, thus creating, in effect, a new market—one that the fur industry has been quick to recognize and expand upon. Odd as it seems today, fur advertising had always been directed at men buying fur coats as gifts for women.

Fur manufacturers are exploring other new markets as well. For most of history, men as well as women wore furs, but in the past 100 years, the fur coat became almost exclusively a woman's garment. In the early 1980s, men once again began wearing fur coats. The fur industry is also expanding into new products, using fur to make garments, such as vests, sweaters, and dresses, that have not traditionally been made of fur.

Finally, the growing excitement and sales of fur have led to big-name designers entering the field or expanding their fur collections. In 1985, only 42 fashion designers created fur garments. By 2000, over 300 designers were working with fur.[22] French designers—among them Christian Dior, Yves Saint Laurent, and Karl Lagerfeld—are also presenting furs. Italian designers such as Fendi, Valentino, and Soldano are known for their innovative techniques.

Saga Furs of Scandinavia is a company formed by fur breeders' associations in Denmark, Sweden, Finland, and Norway. It has a worldwide market share of 66 percent of farm-produced mink and 66 percent of farmed fox skins.[23] Saga produces top-of-the-line traditional fur garments.

Some American designers, like Oscar de la Renta and Jerry Sorbara, have produced fur collections for years. A trio of designers—Marc Jacobs, Byron Lars, and Michael Kors—have developed signature looks over the past few seasons and have already established a following of fashion insiders. An important addition to this group is Dennis Basso, who retails his fur designs (see Figure 6.7).

Canadian designers have traditionally worked with fur. D'Arcy Moses presents themes of Canada's indigenous peoples in furs inset with patterns of forest and eagle feathers. Fellow Canadian Paula Lishman is famous for her knit fur and washable fur-with-cotton knits. And Zuki made waves with his eye-popping "op-art" sheared beaver coats.

Increased Foreign Trade

The export market is strong for the American fur industry, not only because of the variety of furs that are available but also because of the reputation for quality in U.S. pelt dressing. The United States produces innovative, high-style furs that are in great demand around the world.

In the mid-1990s, Russia removed its trade barriers for imported furs and began a boom in imported Canadian and American pelts. With the growing economic conditions in Russia, fur has only continued to be in high demand, as more and more people can afford nice coats.

China is potentially the world's greatest market for furs. In 1999, China and Hong Kong were the biggest fur buyers in the world, and accounted for over 50 percent of skins sold.[24] China is already the largest consumer of fox

FIGURE 6.8
Helen Yarmuk's tiered black leather coat and red fox scarf is a fabulous fashion combination.
Courtesy, Fairchild Publications, Inc.

skins, used for fur-trimmed leather jackets that are widely worn in China (see Figure 6.8).

The importation of fur garments produced primarily in the Far East posed a serious problem for the domestic fur industry in the 1980s. China has become one of the top three buyers of pelts at auction, but most of that country's low-price fur garments were sold abroad, especially in the United States. This situation is expected to change as more Chinese are able to afford fur. One of the largest manufacturers in the Far East is Jindo, Inc., of Korea. Not only does Jindo manufacture and sell coats to retail stores around the world, but the company has its own retail stores in Hong Kong and the United States. Its brands are Jindo Fur and Antonovitch, which uses leather and double-sided lamb.

In 1995, buyers from the United States, Canada, Europe, South America, and the Far East traveled to New York to attend the first Fur Fashion Week. In 2000, the Fur Fashion Week featured over 50 designers' fur collections and attracted worldwide media attention. It has become an important catalyst in bringing foreign fur buyers to the doorstep of domestic fur manufacturers.

New Legislation

The Federal Trade Commission and the fur industry are constantly engaged in talks about fur labeling. Ironically, the most important recent legislation, which was intended to restrict the fur industry, has actually been a boom to sales. The Endangered Species Act of 1973 forbade the sale of furs made from endangered species such as leopard, tiger, ocelot, cheetah, jaguar, vicuna, and a few types of wolf. Since women no longer have to worry about wearing an endangered species, many have returned to the fur market.

New Channels of Retail Distribution

Fur manufacturers have sought other distribution channels in addition to the retail outlets that they have opened (see Figure 6.9).

Hotel, armory, and arena fur sales are held almost every fall and winter weekend in New

FIGURE 6.9
Even old furs can be fashionable: this ad suggests transforming an old coat into a fur-lined one.
© Bergdorf Goodman.

York City and other large cities. Fur manufacturers can conduct these sales for a fraction of the cost in wages and rent that would be required if they were to maintain comparable facilities year-round. Even better, the average hotel ballroom, armory, or arena showroom is suitable for displaying thousands of coats, far more than the average fur salon can attractively exhibit. The sales appeal to customers, who like the hands-on approach and lower prices. The same customers who frequent weekend sales also can shop in manufacturer-leased discount and off-price stores such as Filene's, Syms, and Loehmanns.

Summary and Review

In America, the tanning of leather for clothing and footwear dates back to the pre-colonial Indian populations. Today, the industry consists of three major types of businesses: regular tanneries, contract tanneries, and converters.

Most leather comes from cattle as an offshoot of the meat-packing industry, but leather is also produced from the pelts of eight other animal groups. Tanneries tend to specialize according to the end use of the leather. Tanning may involve one or more processes using minerals, vegetable materials, oils, and chemicals, alone or in combination, to achieve the desired color and textural finish.

Leather Industries of America (LIA), the industry's trade association, advises its members on fashion and technical issues and promotes the industry to its markets.

Fur has been used for warmth in clothing and shelter since prehistoric times. Fur trading, especially in beaver skins, was a major industry in the European colonization of America, and it remained so well into the 19th century. For much of the 20th century, fur was considered a luxury fashion item for women, but in recent years, fur has been used as a trim for various types of apparel, and men's furs have become a growing market. The efforts of animal rights activists, periods of economic downturn, and competition from imports and from faux furs have challenged the industry, but most recently, economic prosperity and industry campaigns to educate the public about humane industry practices have had a positive effect on sales.

The fur industry is made up of three groups: (1) trappers, farmers, and ranchers, (2) fur-processing companies, who buy furs at auctions, and (3) manufacturers of fur products. Processing pelts and turning them into fashion products require skilled labor although some mechanization has been introduced into processing. The distinction between levels in the fur industry is less precise than in other segments of the fashion industry. Because of the specialized knowledge and the financial investment required, furs are often sold to consumers by consignment or leased departments in retail stores, by mail order, or in manufacturers' shows in hotels or other large spaces.

Trade Talk

Define or briefly explain the following terms:

consignment selling
contract tannery
converter
fur farming
hide
kip
leased department
let out
pelt
PETA
regular tannery
skins
sustainable use
tanning

For Review

1. In what ways have technological advances in machinery and chemistry benefited the leather industry?
2. Name and describe the three major types of companies in the leather industry.
3. What are the nine major groups of fur-bearing animals?
4. What has Leather Industries of America done to broaden the leather market and soften the impact of competition from synthetics?
5. What factors point to growth for the leather industry?
6. Describe the history and development of the fur industry in the United States.
7. Into what three groups is the fur industry divided? Briefly describe the function of each.
8. What are the advantages of fur farming over trapping?
9. Outline the steps in transforming processed fur pelts into finished garments.

10. Differentiate between leased departments and consignment selling as these terms apply to retail distribution of fur garments. What major advantages does each have for retail merchants?

For Discussion

1. Discuss the following statement from the text and its implications for leather merchandising: "The leather industry not only must stay abreast of fashion, it must be several steps ahead of it."
2. Discuss current trends in the leather industry that relate to (a) enlarging markets, (b) competition from synthetics, (c) increased foreign trade.
3. Discuss the pros and cons of trapping and raising animals for their fur. Explain your support or rejection of the arguments advanced by animal rights activists and by the fur industry.
4. Discuss current trends in the fur industry as they relate to (a) fashion interest, (b) increased foreign trade, (c) new channels of retail distribution, (d) low-cost imports, (e) rising overhead, and (f) lack of skilled workers and managers

References

1. U.S. Department of Commerce. The Market for Leather Accessories and Travelware c. Business Trend Analysis, Inc., 2000, p. 571.
2. Robin Givhan, "Equine Finery for Fall, Designers Gallop Toward the Tony Pony," *Washington Post*, October 23, 1996, p. D1.
3. Louisiana Department of Agriculture & Forestry; August 25, 2000.
4. Jerry Reynolds, "Inter-Tribal Bison Co-op Enters Tannery Relationship," *Indian Country Today (Lakota Times)*, May 25, 1994, p. 1.
5. Renee Minus White, "Surely Shearling," *New York Amsterdam News*, July 16, 1994, p. PG.
6. Daniela Gilbert, "Leather's Luxurious Spin," *Women's Wear Daily*, June 19, 2001, p. 14.
7. The Fur Industry at a Glance," Fur Information Council of America, 2001. Available online at http://www.fur.org.
8. National Agricultural Statistics Service, USDA. Mink. July 20, 2000, Lv Gn3 (7–00).
9. "Carnie Wilson Sheds Pounds & Clothes, Poses for PETA," 2001. Available online at http://www.furisdead.com.
10. UPI, "Animal Rights Extremists on Midwest Spress," September 18, 200 p. 1008261 u 4868.
11. Kathryn Bold, "In Fur Frankly," *Los Angeles Times*, March 9, 1995, p. 4.
12. Alison Maxwell, "Oleg Cassini Launches Fake-Fur Line," *Women's Wear Daily*, November 9, 1999, p. 12.
13. "Facts About Fur." Economic Importance of the Fur Trade to Canada. Can be found online at http://www.fur.ca.com.
14. The American Legend. Can be found online at http://www.americanlegend.com/alcompany.html.
15. James Brooke, "Anti-Fur Groups Wage War on Mink Farms," *New York Times*, November 30, 1996, p. 9.
16. N.A. Balakirev, "Fur Farming in Russia: The Current Situation and the Prospects," Report from Research Institute of Fur and Rabbit Breeding, p. 7.
17. The American Legend. Can be found online at http://www.americanlegend.com/alcompany.html.
18. Ibid.
19. "Price Schedule," Can be found online at http://www.furs.com/price.html.
20. Fur Information Council of America, "US Fur Sales Up in 2000," Press Release, May 21, 2001.
21. "Who Where," Saga Furs of Scandinavia, 2001. Can be found online at http://www.sagafurs.com.
22. "Facts," Fur Information Council of America, 2001. Can be found online at http://www.fur.org.
23. "Who Where," Saga Furs of Scandinavia, 2001. Can be found online at http://www.sagafurs.com.
24. Richard Heller, "Where the Fur Flies," *Forbes*, November 1, 1999.

Exploring Careers at the Primary Level

The principal manufacturing industries in the fashion field require fashion-oriented and fashion-trained people to guide their production, market their products to the industries they serve, and keep both their customers and fashion consumers informed about their products.

Raw Materials Industries

The greatest number and variety of fashion careers in the raw materials field are found among the producers of fiber and fabrics. Similar positions, but in smaller numbers, are also to be found with other raw materials producers, such as leather, furs, and trimmings, and their respective industry associations.

Fashion Expert

Fiber producers and fabric firms have fashion departments headed by individuals with a variety of titles who attend worldwide fashion openings, keep in close touch with all sources of fashion information, and disseminate the fashion story throughout their respective organizations. Candidates for such positions may have already acquired fashion expertise in other areas of the fashion business or may be employees of the firm who have demonstrated an ability to handle such responsibilities.

In the fur and leather industries, fashion forecasters for individual firms or the trade organizations must be especially adept at predicting trends in color, prints, and textures. This is because finishing treatments needed to achieve the desired qualities in fur and leather sometimes require months.

The fashion department's activities usually require personnel with the ability to coordinate apparel and accessories, to stage fashion shows, to work with the press, to assist individual producers and retailers with fashion-related problems, and to set up fashion exhibits for the trade or for the public.

Fabric Designer

It takes both technical and artistic skills to produce a fabric. Fabric companies employ designers who have not only technical knowledge of the processes involved in producing a fabric but also artistic ability and the ability to successfully anticipate fashion trends. The fabric designer, who works months ahead of the apparel trades, needs fashion radar of superlative quality. The chief designer for a fabric mill makes fashion decisions that can involve vast capital investments every time a new season's line is prepared.

Fabric Stylist and Colorist

Many fabric companies employ a fabric stylist, a colorist, or both to revise existing fabric designs for a new seasonal line, try out various color combinations for an existing design, or adapt designs for specific markets.

Fabric Librarian

Most major synthetic fiber sources maintain libraries of fabrics that are made from their fibers. These libraries consist of fabric swatches clipped to cards on which detailed descriptions and sources of supply are recorded. The librarian in charge is expected to be thoroughly capable of discussing fashion trends and fabric matters with interested designers and manufacturers.

Publicity Executive

In both fiber and fabric companies, the publicity staff keeps in close touch with technical as well as fashion matters and makes information about company products readily available to the trade and consumer press. Usually product stories can be tied to fashion information, enhancing their appeal to editors and readers alike.

In the major fiber-producing companies, there may be a corps of publicity executives, each specializing in one or two closely related industries. One may concentrate on the use of specific fibers in apparel fabrics, for instance, while another may specialize in the use of the company's fibers in rugs and carpeting. In smaller organizations, there may be only one such executive.

The leather and fur industries rely more heavily on their trade associations for publicity because most of their companies are small and lack a publicity staff. Publicists for the leather industry, and even more so for the fur industry, must not only promote their products but must also be able to counter the opposition of animal rights activists and to allay the concerns of environmentalists about protection of endangered species.

Jobs in Textile Technology

Positions within the industry are also available for individuals with technical training in the production of textile products. Converters oversee the various processes in the transition of greige goods to finished fabric. Lab technicians perform tests on fabrics, yams, fibers and garments to determine durability, colorfastness, and shrinkage. Other positions involve responsibility for quality control, design of graphs for knits, fabric analysis, and color research.

Marketing Fibers, Fabrics, Leather, and Fur

All of the industries at the primary level offer career opportunities in sales, market research, and promotion. These are not always fashion jobs, however, and they are rarely open to beginners. Some experience within the company and some specialized skill in the field are likely to be more important in getting such jobs than a knowledge of fashion alone. These requirements apply especially in the leather and fur industries. Because of the retailing activities of producers, marketing personnel in these industries must be able to translate their considerable product knowledge into benefit statements that consumers will understand.

Jobs in Trimmings

Careers in the trimmings industries for fashion-oriented employees are found mostly in sales and marketing. Representing one's company to producers of apparel, accessories, and home fashions involves working with clients to produce custom-designed trimmings as well as selling the employer's own lines. To be successful in meeting customers' needs, one must be aware of trends in color and fabric prints and textures. A complementary career at the secondary level of the fashion business is trimmings buyer. This job provides experience with a whole range of decorative and functional trimmings.

Jobs in Leather and Fur

The production positions in the leather and fur industries require specialized skills that are learned on the job. Pride in craftsmanship and an eye for quality in monitoring the finishing processes are developed through training.

The fur industry offers opportunities, unique in the fashion business, for people interested in breeding and wild-life management. These highly specialized careers require extensive knowledge about the animals whose fur is the raw material of the business, about the laws governing the industry, and about the production of pelts with the desired fashion properties.

Assignments

1. Prepare the first unit in your Career Journal by finding help wanted advertisements for positions within the fiber, textile, trimmings, leather, and fur industries. These openings may be found in general circulation newspapers, trade publications, online resources, or notices in your school's career development office. For each position, list the positive and negative aspect for you personally. Consider your interests, career goals, training, and experience. If you do not yet meet the job requirements, what further training or experience would you need to qualify?
2. Environmental factors affect each primary level industry of the fashion business. For each industry discussed in Unit Two—fibers, fabric, trimmings, leather, and fur—give a current example of the effects of the natural, economic, social, and political/legal environment.

UNIT TWO: THE 1970s

Clovis Ruffin • Liz Claiborne • Anne Klein • Halston • Calvin Klein • Diana Vreeland • Ralph Lauren

"We are like Detroit—big business—and can't afford to experiment the way they do in Europe. They have a small business and they appeal to a smaller audience, and this goes all the way down the line...fabrics as well as clothes.

LIZ CLAIBORNE, 1971

"[Classics have returned so strongly because] of the bad business a lot of people have experienced. Possibly it is a very presumptuous thing to say, but SA has always been known to follow the leader, and our success has been almost legendary. Also, the world is becoming more casual. We live more casually, we entertain more casually. How many women really dress to go to the theater these days?

ANNE KLEIN, 1971

"You're only as good as the people you dress."

HALSTON, 1971

)esigns by Anne Klein.

If department stores are going to keep up with the times, they will have to change their oats, dress and suit departments to 'resource' departments. Buyers will shop resources ather than markets. Everything I have to offer—coat or dress—should be sold in the same lepartment."

CALVIN KLEIN, 1973

You can't take yourself too seriously. I believe in lots of looks. Part of clothes is playing. For nstance, one day I like to be an English gentleman and the next day I think I'm a cowboy."

RALPH LAUREN, 1974

'Boy, was I in the greatest seat, at the greatest hour of the greatest time. I went into Vogue n 1962—the year of the jet, the Pill. A completely different social world was being created."

DIANA VREELAND, 1979

'I want to be the all-American boy dressing the all-American girl. I'm not dressing a French girl. I'm dressing an American girl who hops into coffee shops, who works in offices every day...she takes five courses a week—carpentry, plumbing, writing and furniture refinishing. She takes furniture refinishing more times a week when 'Peyton Place' was on the tube. And she needs clothes for that kind of life."

CLOVIS RUFFIN, 1973

Designer Anne Klein.

IEW
CHANEL 25-32 of 242

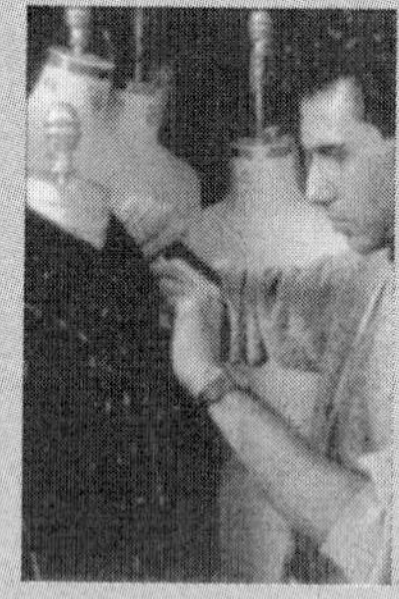

CK
CK Calvin Klein

A FEW REASONS TO DONATE TO K.I.D.S.
"There are millions of children who desperately need our donations."
"Up to twice your cost of the donation may be deducted from your taxes."
"K.I.D.S. is our industry's charity endorsed by the CMA, the TMA, and the JPMA."
CALL 1-800-266-3314

FRENCH CUFFS

UNIT 3

THE SECONDARY LEVEL: THE PRODUCERS OF APPAREL

Fashion has many faces—different faces for different places, different looks for different years. Fashion is also products—products with a past. The past of a product includes all the designers and manufacturers who have watched their customer, and are always trying to give them what they want.

Fashion fascinates, it holds our interest, and even appears in our dreams. Back in 1982, Perry Ellis declared, "Ultimately, I feel clothes have to be beautiful by my own standards, and that means stimulating, creative, controversial, and always with wit." This is quite an extraordinary challenge for the producers of fashion.

In the past few decades, the fashion apparel manufacturing business has changed from an industry composed of many small companies into a far larger one, dominated by a growing group of giants. This has changed the way that apparel is designed, manufactured, and merchandised. Large companies can afford to invest in the newest technology. Technology, in turn, has helped make high style and quality accessible to everyone. This unit explores several aspects of apparel production.

Chapter 7 explains the six-stage process of developing and producing a line, introduces the concept of Quick Response, and discusses major industry practices of licensing, private label, specification buying, offshore production, factors, and chargebacks.

Chapter 8 gives the history of the women's apparel industry and details the categories, size ranges, and price zones as well as the roles of brand names and designer names in the marketing of women's apparel. Chapter 9 compares and contrasts all the factors that are common to both men's and women's apparel and explains the differences that exist in producing and marketing men's wear.

The unit concludes with Chapter 10, which explains the impact of demographics on children's apparel, the influence of fashion on children's wear, and the impact of licensing. Industry trends and responses to social issues are also explored in this chapter.

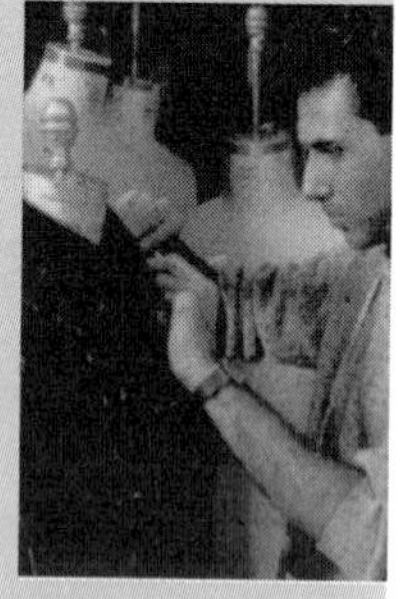

CHAPTER 7

Product Development

WHAT'S IN IT FOR YOU?

Everything you always wanted to know about the product development process in the apparel and fashion related industries.

Key Concepts:

- The major advantages and disadvantages of the contractor system
- The six-stage process of developing and producing a line.
- The major industry practices of licensing, private label and specification buying, offshore production, CAD/CAM use of factors, and chargebacks
- Industry trends, such as brand extensions, globalization, and industry cooperation
- The Quick Response movement and the mass customization theory and their effects on the product development chain
- The new SIC/NAICS codes and how manufacturers and retailers can use them

The level of activity in textile and apparel product development has been steadily increasing. This increase in activity together with the global manufacturing and assembly practices, have integrated product development into the mainstream business decision structure of all fashion industry firms, from manufacturers to retailers.

If new apparel and fashion related products are not developed, sales and profits decline, technology and markets change, or innovation by other firms makes the original product obsolete. All of this points to the importance of product development for the continued success of a company.

Product development is the teaming of market and trend research, with the merchandising, design, and technical processes that develop a final product. Product development is used by both wholesale manufacturers, who develop products for a signature brand, and retailers who use it for private label development for their own stores.

Whether making plain T-shirts or elaborate evening gowns, the men's, women's, and children's apparel industries in the United States have managed to settle into a basic cycle of design and production that repeats itself more or less unchanged from season to season. However, before an article of clothing reaches the retail store racks, a great deal of work and planning are involved. (There are similar cycles for accessories, cosmetics and fragrances, and home fashions; they will be discussed in Unit Four.) This chapter will focus on the design and production of apparel for men, women, and children; subsequent chapters will examine each area in detail.

What Is a Product Line and Who Develops It?

Product lines of apparel are created and styled for wholesale presentation several times, or seasons, per year. In the fashion industries a product line is referred to simply as a "line." A line not only encompasses the individual item of apparel or accessories but the entire season's production from that manufacturer as well. The term "line" is used for moderate- and popular-priced apparel (see Figure 7.1). The term **collection** is used to describe an expensive line in the United States or in Europe. Lines are divided into **groups** of garments, linked by a common theme like color, fabric, or style. Each garment is known as a style number or "number," such as 401 or 57.

FIGURE 7.1
This Web site shows garment lines for different seasons by dozens of leading designers. Here is one page showing numbers 25-32 of Chanel's Fall 2002 Ready to Wear collection.
© 2002 firstVIEW.com

It is important to note here that in the United States, designs cannot be copyrighted, as they are in France. Copying from creative designers is common throughout the fashion industry; it is not considered piracy. At some firms, few if any designs are original, rather they are copied **line-for-line** in a similar fabric, or adapted from another designer in a cheaper fabric (knock-offs), or reworked from a previous season in a different color or fabric (**anchors**).

Designers typically work on three seasonal lines at a time. They monitor the sales of the *current* season's line, put the finishing touches on *next* season's line, while they begin to develop the new line for the *following* season. Clearly, this is a challenging balancing act!

Clothing manufacturers produce between four and six lines every year. For women's wear, these are spring, summer, transitional or fall I, fall or fall II, resort, and holiday (see Table 7.1).

Many firms, however, add new styles to lines throughout the year in order to keep buyers "shopping" their lines to see what is new. Or, at a minimum, they update styles or change the fabrics used in the line. Conversely, as new styles are added, old ones are dropped.

Manufacturers start work on their new lines anywhere between 3 to 12 months before presentation to retail buyers. This means clothes are planned and designed as much as a year before customers will see them in the stores.

Now we will examine the roles played by the merchandiser, the designer, and the producer.

Role of the Merchandiser

The merchandiser is the person who channels the creativity of the designer and design staff so that the six "rights" of merchandising can be successfully accomplished. These rights are: the right merchandise, at the right price, at the right time, in the right place, in the right quantity, with the right promotion. To these rights must be added another one—the right customer! Because this customer is so important, the merchandiser is given the responsibility to research who the "right" customer is. Bud Konheim, CEO of Nicole Miller, Ltd., has stated:

> *You've got to know who you're designing for. But we take another step. First of all, we figure out which stores have a Nicole Miller customer. To the ones who don't, our answer to them is don't buy it, because you don't have our customers, plain and simple. We're not for everybody, and we understand it . . . . This is what we do. We don't sell [to] any discount stores, we have no outlet stores, we have no secondary ways to buy the product, and we establish credibility with our customer 100 percent.*[1]

Some people in the industry have described the merchandiser as the "glue" that holds the whole product development concept together. In fact, the merchandiser is the liaison among the design staff, the production facilities, and the sales staff. The merchandiser has to view the line from the design point of view and also has to be knowledgeable about production and sales efforts.

Role of the Designer

Designers can create by sketching (croquis) or by drawing on a computer (computer-aided design [CAD]), or by draping cloth on a model. In addition to looking for artistic excellence, designers must keep practical business considerations in mind. All designs must be produced at a profit and within the firm's wholesale price range. Consequently, designers must keep in mind the availability and cost of materials, the cost of cutting and sewing the garment, and labor costs.

TABLE 7.1 Seasonal Lines

NAME OF LINE	WHEN SHOWN
Spring	October and November
Summer	Early January
Transitional or fall I	February
Fall or fall II	Early April
Resort	August
Holiday	August

Most U.S. designers who are using their artistic and innovative talents to design fashion-oriented merchandise fall into one of three categories:

- High-fashion or "name" designers
- Stylist-designers
- Freelance artist-designers

High-fashion designers are usually referred to in this country as "name" designers. Because of the success and originality of their designs, name designers are well-known to fashion-conscious customers. High-fashion designers are responsible not only for creating the designs, but also for the choice of fabric, texture, and color in which each design is to be executed. They may often be involved in development of the production model, as well as in plans for the promotion of a firm's line. Some name designers work for fashion houses, as does Tom Ford for Gucci. Others, like Oscar de la Renta, and Anna Sui, own their own firms or are financed by a "silent partner" outside the firm. Still others, like Ralph Lauren and Donna Karan, are publicly owned corporations that are listed on a stock exchange.

Designer names were once associated only with original, expensive designs in apparel. Then, beginning in 1922 with Chanel, many designers licensed their names to fragrances. Today, most name designers also license their names to manufacturers of accessories and home furnishings.

Stylist-designers use their creative talents to adapt or change the successful designs of others. A stylist-designer must understand fabric and garment construction as well as the manufacturing process, because designs are usually adapted at lower prices. Stylist-designers usually create designs at the late rise or early culmination stages of the fashion cycle. They are usually not involved in details relating to the production of the firm's line or in the planning of its promotional activities. Rather, their focus is on designing within the limits of the firm's production capacity and capability. Stylist-designers who work in a firm that sells to major retail store chains often accompany the firm's salespeople to define the look or to learn firsthand what the retail store buyer wants.

Freelance artist-designers sell their sketches to manufacturers. They may work independently at home or from a design studio. These sketches may be original designs by the freelancer, or adaptations of a design furnished by the manufacturer. The sketches may reflect the freelancer's own ideas, or the manufacturer's detailed specifications. With the delivery of a sketch to the manufacturer, a freelancer's job ends, and he or she goes on to another project.

Role of the Producer

The fashion apparel industry consists of three types of producers: manufacturers, jobbers, and contractors. A **manufacturer** is one who performs all the operations required to produce apparel, from buying the fabric to selling and shipping the finished garments. An **apparel jobber** handles the designing, the planning, the purchasing, usually the cutting, the selling, and the shipping, but not the actual sewing operation. A **contractor** is a producer whose sole function is to supply sewing services to the industry, where it is sometimes called an **outside shop**. Contractors that specialize in the production of one product are sometimes referred to as **item houses**. Increasingly, the term "manufacturer" is being used more loosely to describe any firm that handles any part of the cutting or sewing process, and the terms "jobber" and "contractor" are used less often.

Manufacturers

A manufacturer, by definition, is a producer who handles all phases of a garment's production. The staff produces the original design or buys an acceptable design from a freelance designer. Each line is planned by the company executives. The company purchases the fabric and trimmings needed. The cutting and sewing are usually done in the company's factories. On certain occasions, however, a manufacturer may use the services of a contractor if sales of an item exceed the capacity of the firm's sewing facilities and if shipping deadlines cannot otherwise be met. The company's sales force and traffic department handle the selling and shipping of the finished goods. One great advantage of this type of operation is that close quality control can be maintained. When producers contract out some part of their work, they cannot as effectively monitor its quality.

Apparel Jobbers

Apparel jobbers handle all phases of the production of a garment except for the actual sewing and sometimes the cutting. A jobber firm may employ a design staff to create various seasonal lines or may buy sketches from freelance designers. The jobber's staff buys the fabric and trimmings necessary to produce the styles in each line, makes up samples, and grades the patterns. In most cases, the staff also cuts the fabric for the various parts of each garment. Jobbers, however, do not actually sew and finish garments. Instead, they arrange with outside factories run by contractors to perform these manufacturing operations. The sales staff takes orders for garments in each line, and the shipping department fills store orders from the finished garments returned by the contractor. (Note that apparel jobbers are involved in manufacturing, whereas most other "jobbers" buy finished goods and sell them to small users who are not able to place large orders.)

Contractors

Contractors usually specialize in just one phase of the production of a garment: sewing. In some cases contractors also perform the cutting operation from patterns submitted by a jobber or a manufacturer. Contractors developed early in the history of the fashion industry, with the beginning of mass-production techniques. Contractors serve those producers who have little or no sewing capability of their own as well as those whose current business exceeds their own capacity. Sometimes a "subcontractor" is used by the initial contractor to perform specialized work that the initial contractor is not equipped to perform, such as beading or embroidery. When there is a very large order, a subcontractor may be used to produce the over-booked production.

If a contractor is used, cut pieces of the garment are provided by the manufacturer. For an agreed price per garment, the article is sewn, finished, inspected, pressed, hung, or packaged, and returned to the manufacturer for shipment to retail stores.

In the mass production of ready-to-wear, a single sewing-machine operator rarely makes a complete garment. Each operator sews only a certain section of the garment, such as a sleeve or a hem. This division of labor, called **section work** or **piece work**, makes it unnecessary for an operator to switch from one highly specialized machine to another or to make adjustments on the machine. Any change or adjustment in equipment takes time and increases labor costs. In the fashion trade, time lost in making such changes also causes delays in getting a style to consumers. Delays in production could mean the loss of timeliness and sales appeal before an article reaches market.

A contractor may arrange to work exclusively with one or more jobbers or manufacturers, reserving the right to work for others whenever the contractor's facilities are not fully employed. Such agreements are necessarily reciprocal. If a contractor agrees to give preference to a particular jobber's or manufacturer's work, the jobber or manufacturer gives preference to that contractor when placing sewing orders.

The advantages and disadvantages of the contractor system for the manufacturer are as follows:

Advantages:

- Large amounts of capital are not required for investment in sewing equipment that may soon become obsolete.
- Difficulties in the hiring and training of suitable workers are minimized.
- The amount of capital necessary to meet regular payrolls is greatly reduced.
- By providing additional manufacturing facilities in periods of peak demand, contractors help speed up delivery of orders.
- It is unnecessary to keep one factory busy year-round.

Disadvantages:

- No individual has full responsibility for the finished product.
- Other "manufacturers" (jobbers) may use the same facilities and get preferential treatment, because they place larger orders, or offer repeat business, or even guarantee future business.
- The quality of workmanship and inspection tends to be uneven.

The Product Development Process

In a recent study published in the *Journal of Textile and Apparel Technology and Management*, the authors listed the following functions for an effective integrated system of product development:[2]

- Marketing
- Forecasting
- Merchandising
- Product Line Development
- Product Design and Specifications
- Material Requisition Planning
- Inventory Control

- Costing
- Production Planning and Scheduling
- Sourcing and Manufacturing
- Quality Control
- Human Resources
- Purchasing
- Logistics
- Warehouse Inventory Movement Systems
- Finance
- Sales
- Field Sales Support
- Performance Measurement
- External Communication

Currently there are many variations in the product development process. We will discuss a simple six-stage process that covers the functions performed at every firm, regardless of size. The major differences are the number of people involved, and how they communicate and interact.

The six-stage product development process is outlined below and illustrated in Figure 7.2:

- Stage 1. Planning the line
- Stage 2. Creating the design concept
- Stage 3. Developing the designs
- Stage 4. Planning production
- Stage 5. Production
- Stage 6. Distributing the line

Stage 1: Planning a Line

The first step of the product development process involves the work of a designer or a product development team, working under the direction of a merchandiser. It is these people who are charged with creating a line (see Figure 7.3). Their first task is research. They review information on trends, colors, fabrics, and other materials, often using fashion forecasting services, such as Sputnik, Promostyl, or Color Box. Of course, team members must keep in mind previous fashion successes or failures, so past sales records are reviewed, as well as markdown reports. Some firms develop "trend boards" that contain visual or graphic representations of developments that are affecting their target customer. All of this research helps designers or product development teams to formulate some idea of what the new line will contain.

Using all their merchandising and marketing skills, merchandisers or designers help to form and maintain a positive image in the marketplace for the manufacturer. It is this image that influences a specific consumer group to buy a particular line at the retail level.

In most cases, design has to be disciplined and directed so that the particular image of the manufacturer and the merchandise that is produced will continue to fit the needs and wants of a specific consumer group.

There are three major types of firms that develop a line of apparel:

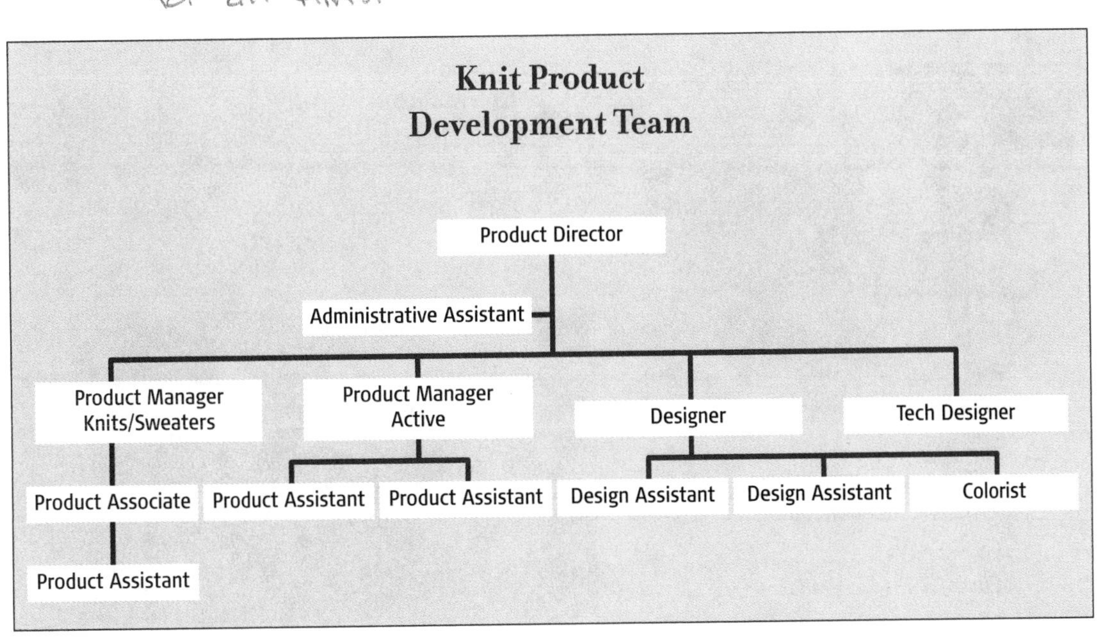

FIGURE 7.2
This organizational chart outlines the hierarchy of a product development team.

FIGURE 7.3
The Product Development Process.
The Fashion Institute of Technology, New York/Photographs: John Senzer.

1. PLANNING A LINE
Researching past sales and trends
Researching the market
Identifying key trend
Developing a strategy
Budgeting for the season
Planning for advertising

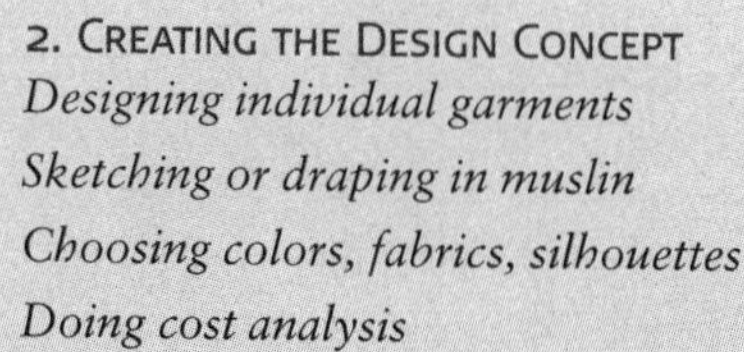

2. CREATING THE DESIGN CONCEPT
Designing individual garments
Sketching or draping in muslin
Choosing colors, fabrics, silhouettes
Doing cost analysis

3. DEVELOPING THE DESIGN
Developing styles
Drawing up specifications for each garment
Making a pattern
Producing a sample
Getting approvals on designs, color, and fabrics

4. PLANNING PRODUCTION
Sourcing
Ordering piece goods (fabric)
Placing orders
Tracking orders
Costing out each garment

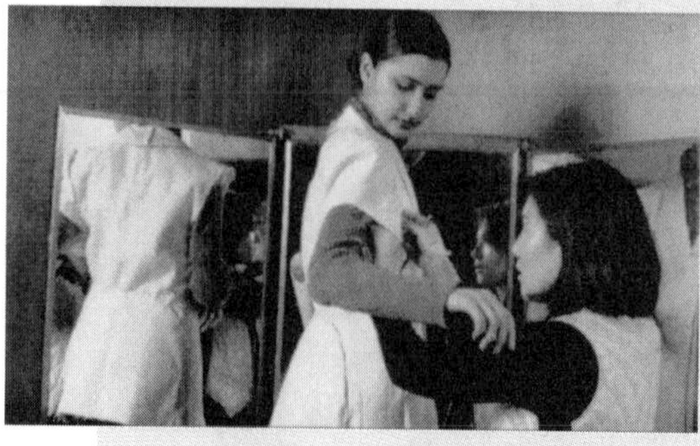

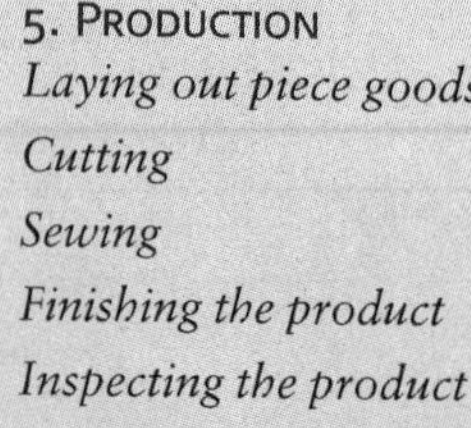

5. PRODUCTION
Laying out piece goods
Cutting
Sewing
Finishing the product
Inspecting the product

6. DISTRIBUTING THE LINE
Ticketing and bar coding
Consolidating
Distributing to retailers

1. *Large Manufacturers*. In a large apparel firm, such as Liz Claiborne, Vanity Fair, Carter's, and Levi Strauss, merchandisers are responsible for developing new lines. They plan the overall fashion direction for the coming season and direct a design staff about the kinds of garments to be designed. They may also determine color choices. The design staff is generally not known to the public. Together with the marketing and sales departments, the merchandiser and designer form a **product development team**, which is responsible for a particular product line or brand.
2. *Designer-Owned Firms*. In firms where the designer is also the owner (or part owner) of the firm, the designer may design all or part of a line, using other designers to fill out the line. Examples of this kind of firm are Donna Karan, Ralph Lauren, and Vera Wang.
3. *Small Manufacturers*. In small firms, all the activities in the product development process may be done by the owner, with one or more assistants. Most designers, with the exception of Tommy Hilfiger, began this way. Small companies still predominate in the U.S. apparel industry, especially in women's wear, so it is important to note that the designer/product developer/owner ends up performing a wide variety of tasks (see Figure 7.4).

Stage 2: Creating the Design Concept

Next come designs for individual garments. Each one is sketched or developed in muslin. At this stage, the designer or design staff considers his or her work, and weighs it on two points: first, on its own individual merit and, second, for its suitability in the line as a whole. Many designs are discarded at this point.

Price is also a critical factor in determining whether or not a design is deleted from a line. A cost analysis is often done at this stage, and designs that are too expensive to produce profitably at the desired price point are rejected.

Stage 3: Developing the Designs

Those designs that seem most likely to succeed are made up as finished sample garments. A patternmaker creates a production pattern in the garment size the company uses to produce its samples. From this pattern, one or more samples are cut. Finally, the garment is sewn by a designer's assistant who is also a seamstress. This person is called a **sample hand**.

Now the design is presented to various executives and managers of the company—people in sales, purchasing, production, and cost accounting. Both the cost of the fabric and the

FIGURE 7.4
Members of a product development fashion design team are hard at work creating new products.
Courtesy, ©Anthony Redpath/Corbis.

cost of producing the garment are carefully analyzed. Many designs are discarded at this point, while others are sent back to the design department for modification. A few are accepted. The accepted design is assigned a style number. At this point, it is officially part of a manufacturer's line.

Computer-Aided Design

Although the day has not yet arrived when designers will throw away their sketch pads and pencils, the advent of **computer-aided design (CAD)** is giving designers new freedom to explore and manipulate their designs in relatively easy, quick, and inexpensive ways. A designer no longer has to take a chance that he or she is having a sample made up in the best color. Now CAD is used to test various colors and color combinations, fabrics, and styles. CAD allows three-dimensional (3-D) contouring of objects on screen (see Figure 7.5). Folds, creases, and textures are simulated so that CAD-generated garments drape and hang accurately. Once the design is set on the computer, the computer image is used to create a pattern that is complete with darts, seams, and tailor's markings. Because the computer can create the design in 3-D, the computer image can be rotated to see all sides of the garment. Many companies are thus reducing the number of costly sample garments that they produce. Instead of a physical sample, they use the computer image in merchandising and sales presentations.

Linked CAD/CAM/CIM

But that is no longer the end of the road for CAD systems. Instead, CAD is now being linked to **CAM (computer-aided manufacturing)**, and **CIM (computer-integrated manufacturing)** systems to provide information internally and to suppliers and even to retailers across the country and across the world.[3] Linked CAD/CAM/CIM technology will be discussed in more detail later in this chapter.

Stage 4: Planning Production

This stage of the product development process begins with **sourcing**, or determining where the components of a garment (fabric, thread, linings, facings, buttons, trim, etc.) will be purchased and, in some cases, where the garments will be cut and sewn. It is now that the vital question of domestic or foreign manufacture must be decided. (The role of Quick Response in this decision is discussed later in this chapter.)

FIGURE 7.5
Many designers use CAD systems to change, clarify, and perfect their designs.
Courtesy, Noten Marketing/CADTEX Corporation.

The Name Game—Who Remains a Legend?

Designers brands have as many lives as the proverbial nine lives of a cat, as a new generation of young designers is setting its sights on fashion avenue stardom, there is now a tremendous interest in the "old" designers – vintage brands that have outlasted their founding namesakes. Houses like Perry Ellis, Anne Klein, Chanel, Christian Dior, Bill Blass, and Halston are now assuming interest from the public.

The recipe for the continued success of a brand following the departure of its founders is complicated, and many have tried it with disastrous results. Anne Klein is in its sixth recarnation since her death in 1974, and recent flops at Blass and Perry Ellis preceded their latest success. But with the right combination of mastery and creativity, it can succeed. The crucial ingredient is the ability to recognize what customers once valued in the name, and then to recreate it for a contemporary audience.

Karl Lagerfield continues to win accolades for his modern interpretations of the Chanel signature style. John Galliano overhauled the Christian Dior label, and Tom Ford has brought new life and success to the Gucci and Yves Saint Laurent Rive Gauche brands. Certain designer brands have second and third lives. Five years ago, Burberry and Yves Saint Laurent Rive Gauche were out of favor, but look at them now!

The most classic name game brand has been Halston. A number of designers have come and gone at the brand since it was relaunched in 1997—Randolph Duke, Kevin Hall, Craig Natiello, and Bradly Bayou, who was hired in 2003 to reinvigorate the image. Bayou has had Halston as his idol ever since 1978 when he met Halston at Studio 54, where Halston held court for the leading ladies of fashion. "Everything I do there's some Halston in it," he said. "I'm not going to literally translate what he did and might bring back some materials, like jersey and ultrasuede, but what I really like about Halston was that he dressed all types of women's body types."

There are other great American names, like Rudi Gernreich, Claire McCardell, and Pauline Trigere that are ripe for a fashion resurrection, as well as Norell, Mainbocher, or Galanos.

The only way to be successful in continuing a designer's label is to truly understand why the label was successful with the customers and why it was valuable to them. Only time will tell who will return again and again to keep the fickle fashion customers interested in a name!

Sources

Eric Wilson, "The Name Game," *Women's Wear Daily*, New York Collections, Section II, September 10, 2002, pp. 4-6.

Eric Wilson, "Fifth Times a Charm? Halston Taps Bayou," *Women's Wear Daily*, December 5, 2002 pp. 4–18.

Still a legend, Halston has created beautiful designs from early on in his career.
Courtesy, Fairchild Publications, Inc.

Reservations for production must be made, so that the garments will be available when needed. The fabric must be ordered, along with orders for the other components of the garment. Finally, each garment must be costed out, so that the exact cost and selling price can be set. See Figure 7.6 for an illustration of how a typical garment is costed. The samples are used to determine the cost of producing the garment. The money needed to finance production must be obtained. Only when all of these steps have been completed can actual production begin.

The samples, each with its style number, are then presented to retail buyers at the manufacturers' seasonal shows. The retail buyers either accept or reject parts of the line, or more rarely, the entire line. The buyers usually place orders for some of the individual designs. Sometimes they test a line by buying a small number of styles in small quantities. If these styles sell; they reorder them. Most manufacturers have set **minimum orders** for the quantity, number of styles, and/or dollar amount required to accept the retail buyer's order.

Because the manufacturer usually has not yet begun production when a line is shown to the buyers, it may be possible to fine-tune production to the buyers' orders. When a particular style receives a lot of attention from buyers, it is then scheduled for production. Items that generate little or no enthusiasm are dropped from the line.

Production contracts are often being finalized while the manufacturer's representatives are selling the line to retail accounts. If these two things can be done simultaneously, the manufacturer has a better chance of moving to the next step or "cutting as close to paper as possible," which means limiting the risk of investing in fabric, trim, and production costs while negotiating quantity discounts.

Stage 5: Production

Cutting

One of the most important steps in the mass production of apparel is the cutting of the garment pieces. Once a garment is slated for pro-

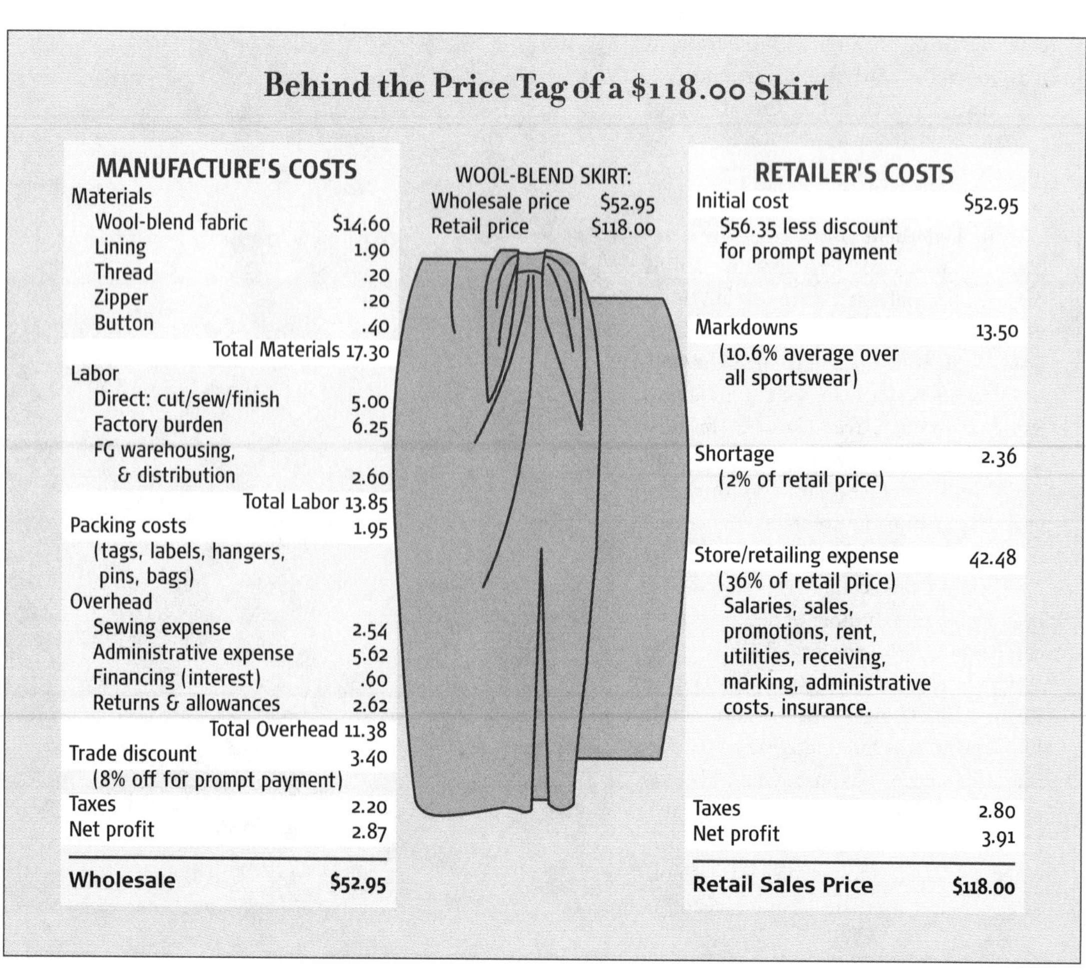

Behind the Price Tag of a $118.00 Skirt

WOOL-BLEND SKIRT:

Wholesale price	$52.95
Retail price	$118.00

MANUFACTURE'S COSTS	
Materials	
Wool-blend fabric	$14.60
Lining	1.90
Thread	.20
Zipper	.20
Button	.40
Total Materials	17.30
Labor	
Direct: cut/sew/finish	5.00
Factory burden	6.25
FG warehousing, & distribution	2.60
Total Labor	13.85
Packing costs (tags, labels, hangers, pins, bags)	1.95
Overhead	
Sewing expense	2.54
Administrative expense	5.62
Financing (interest)	.60
Returns & allowances	2.62
Total Overhead	11.38
Trade discount (8% off for prompt payment)	3.40
Taxes	2.20
Net profit	2.87
Wholesale	**$52.95**

RETAILER'S COSTS	
Initial cost $56.35 less discount for prompt payment	$52.95
Markdowns (10.6% average over all sportswear)	13.50
Shortage (2% of retail price)	2.36
Store/retailing expense (36% of retail price) Salaries, sales, promotions, rent, utilities, receiving, marking, administrative costs, insurance.	42.48
Taxes	2.80
Net profit	3.91
Retail Sales Price	**$118.00**

FIGURE 7.6
A costing sheet for a garment includes each component and its cost.
The Fashion Institute of Technology, New York.

duction, it is **graded**, or sloped, to each of the various sizes in which it will be made. After a pattern has been graded into the various sizes, the pieces are laid out on a long piece of paper called a **marker** (see Figure 7.7). The success of cutting depends on the accuracy with which each of the many layers of material are placed on top of one another. A **spreader**, or laying-up machine, carries the material along a guide on either side of the cutting table, spreading the material evenly from end to end. The marker is laid on top of these layers.

For many years, material was cut by hand, but today, the cutting process is either computer-assisted or totally computerized. Computers are programmed to feed instructions to laser, blade, or high-speed water jet machines that do the actual cutting.

FIGURE 7.7
Laying out and grading a garment in a factory require both great care and skill; mistakes are costly.
Courtesy, Gerber Technology, Inc.

Once the cutting is completed, the pieces of each pattern—the sleeves, collars, fronts, and backs—are tied into bundles according to their sizes. This process is called **bundling**; it must be done by hand. The bundles are then moved to the manufacturers' sewing operators, who may be on the premises or in contractors' shops.

Sewing

Technology has dramatically changed the sewing stage of production. The industrial sewing machine sews much faster than a home sewing machine because it has an engine with a clutch and brake, rather than a motor. Home sewing machines perform many functions, while industrial machines perform specialized functions. Some sew only seams, while others sew blind hems. Button machines sew on buttons. Computerized sewing machines that do embroidery can be set up to stitch whole patterns without a machine operator. Robotic sewing equipment is being developed. A completely automated sewing assembly line is under development in Japan. The only thing humans will do in this new system is supervise.

Meanwhile, **single-hand operations** still exist, in which one operator sews the entire garment. These are used for very high-priced garments that are produced in very small quantities. Today, most manufacturers use a combination of mass production systems, including the popular **modular manufacturing system**, in which teams of seven to nine workers produce entire garments, passing them on to each other, until the garment is complete. This system requires extensive cross-training, so each team member can learn all the tasks involved, and do them as the flow of work demands.

Finishing the Product

The sewn garment is still far from ready for the retail floor. Pants, for example, are sewn with the legs inside out. They must be turned right side out. A label must be sewn in. Buttons and buttonholes may be added at this stage.

Some fabrics are washed at this stage to prevent shrinkage. Others have a wrinkle-resistant finish applied. Still others are dyed at this point, called garment-dyeing, which gives the manufacturer last-minute control of color.

The garment is then pressed and folded or hung on a hanger with a plastic bag over it. Some manufacturers also offer services that make their apparel **floor ready**; that is, with bar-coded price tickets attached, cartons labeled, and shipping documents attached. Of course, this adds to the cost, but many retailers find that this portion of the Quick Response strategy makes up in speed for the cost. See "Stage 6: Distributing the Line."

Inspecting the Product

Garments are inspected many times during the production process. First the fabric and the dye quality are checked. Cutting is checked for pattern matching and size specs, among other things. Sewing is also checked repeatedly along the way, for stitch length, seam type, buttonhole stitching, and hem stitching. **Quality assurance**, or **QA**, which refers to the product meeting the standards established for it, includes the inspection of each ingredient of the garment: fabric, thread, buttons, snaps, or zippers, hem tape, linings, shoulder pads, and so forth.

Stage 6: Distributing the Line

Once the line is completed, it still requires more work before the retailer can sell it. Sales tickets and bar codes must be added; these time-consuming tasks are frequently done by the manufacturer, except for the smallest stores. Then shipments must be consolidated, and finally sent to retailers by truck, rail, or air.

As the season progresses, manufacturers remain sensitive to retail sales. For example, when reorders come in, they recut only the garments that are most in demand—and therefore, the most profitable. Manufacturers may also recut "hot sellers" in different fabrics and colors to maximize the sales generated by high customer demand.

Specializing by Product

Apparel producers have typically been specialists, producing apparel for a particular gender and age, a particular size range, and a specific price range. A women's blouse manufacturer, for example, seldom makes dresses, and a dress manufacturer usually does not turn out dresses in both women's and junior sizes. A coat and suit manufacturer does not usually produce both expensive and popular-priced lines.

By Gender, Age, and Size Categories, and by Classification

Historically, the U.S. apparel industry has been divided into three major categories: women's, men's, and children's. These three categories are discussed in detail in Chapters 8, 9, and 10. Within these three categories, are smaller subcategories, divided by age. For example, children's wear is subdivided into infants', toddlers', girls' and boys', preteen (girls), and young men's. Within infants' wear, sizes include 0 to 3 months, 6 months, 12 months, 18 months, and 24 months.

Another way that apparel is organized is by the type of garment produced, or classification. Examples for girls' wear include:

- Outerwear—coats, jackets, and raincoats
- Dresses
- Blouses
- Sportswear—pants, sweaters, shirts
- Active sportswear—swimsuits, skiwear, bike shorts
- Underwear
- Sleepwear
- Socks
- Tights
- School uniforms

Despite a move toward greater diversification, producers and retailers still have to think and work like specialists. For instance, a producer must of necessity choose an inexpensive fabric for a popular-priced line and a more expensive fabric for a better-priced line. Retail buyers still shop one group of producers for sportswear, another for coats, and still another for bridal wear—and this is not likely to change in the near future.

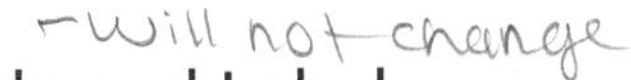

Brands and Labels

A special *Infotracs* supplement to *Women's Wear Daily* and the *Daily News Record* listed five distinct kinds of brands or labels used by apparel industry insiders:[4]

1. National/designer brand
2. Private label
3. Retail store brand
4. All other brands
5. Nonbrands

Customers, of course, realize few of these distinctions; they think of them all as "brands" or "nonbrands." But to retailers and manufacturers, these distinctions are vital, impacting heavily on their profits, and offering differentiation in an era when customers complain of the "sameness" of many stores and the goods they offer (see Figure 7.8).

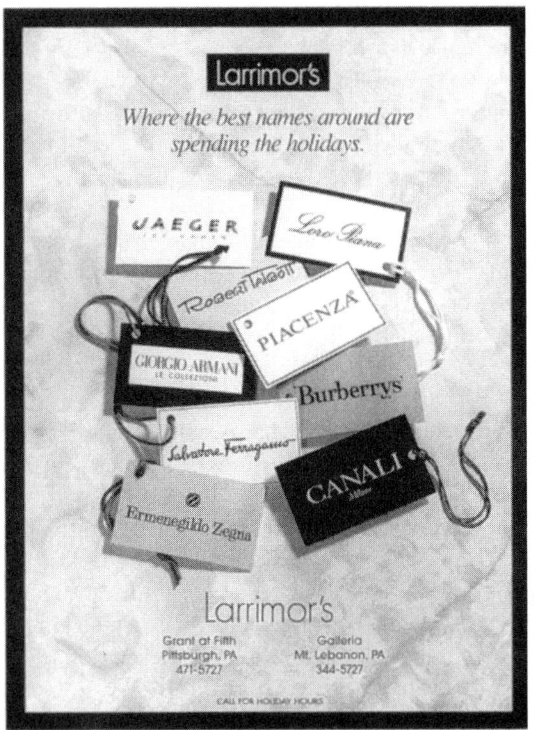

FIGURE 7.8
In this ad directed at local customers in Pittsburgh magazine, a savvy men's wear retailer uses the brands he or she carries to convey the store's image.
Larrimors. Reprinted with permission.

National/Designer Brands

National brands are those that are owned by a manufacturer who advertises them nationally. Some of the first apparel brands to gain national recognition were the Arrow Shirt Company and the B.V.D. Company, a maker of men's underwear, in the 1930s. National brands continued to grow in number over the next five decades, but the 1980s and 1990s saw a tremendous leap in sales for national brands. In part, this resulted from a huge increase in the number of national advertising campaigns directed at consumers. National brands are expected to continue to predominate in the industry, while private labels "fill in the cracks."[5] Examples of national brands include Pendleton, Fruit of the Loom, Levi's, Carter's, Koret, Reebok, Hanes, Revlon, and Dan River.

Designer labels carry the name of a designer; they have grown enormously in number and importance since the 1940s. As mentioned previously, the four U.S. mega-designers are Ralph Lauren, Calvin Klein, Donna Karan, and

Tommy Hilfiger. Hundreds more are working in the United States today (see pages 477–481 for a detailed list of designers). Many other designer names continue to be featured, although the original designer has retired or died; examples include Anne Klein, Liz Claiborne, and Halston.

Designer labels are no longer limited to apparel; they are frequently found on accessories of every kind, on fragrances and cosmetics, and on home furnishings.

Private Labels

A **private label** is one that is owned by a retailer and found only in its stores. Examples of private label apparel are the Kathie Lee Gifford line sold by Wal-Mart, the Jaclyn Smith line sold by Kmart, the Charter Club line sold by Federated Department Stores, and the Original Arizona Jeans Company line sold by JCPenney. These labels are sold alongside national/designer brands. The proportion of private labels to national and designer brands varies from retailer to retailer. As Jim Hodges, a veteran label specialist said:

> *A carefully defined private label program gives a retailer control of design, specification, fabric, trim, and production to assure that delivery be up to established standards and tailored to merchandising goals. The result should be product that differentiates the chain from its rivals, allowing it to more effectively compete, and earn higher margins.*[6]

Retail Store Brand

A **retail store brand** is the name of a chain that is used as the exclusive label on most of the items in the store or catalog. Examples of retail store brands for apparel and accessories include the Gap, The Limited, Ann Taylor, Victoria's Secret, Talbots, L.L. Bean, and Lands' End. Examples of store brands for home furnishings include Pier 1, Crate & Barrel, and Williams-Sonoma. Few, if any, national or designer brands are carried by these stores or catalogs.

Other Brands

This catchall category includes labels not in the preceding three categories; for example, cartoon characters, like Disney's Mickey & Co. and Warner Brothers' Looney Tunes; sports teams, like the Chicago Bulls; colleges, like the University of California at Berkeley; and museums, like The Museum of Fine Arts—Chicago. These brands are often licensed.

Nonbrands

This is a label to which customers attach little or no importance. These labels are usually used by firms that manufacture low-priced goods and do little or no advertising to consumers. These labels are found in discount and off-price stores.

Industry Practices

Every industry has its own particular way of conducting business; the apparel industry is no exception. Some of the practices discussed in this section grew as responses to specific industry problems. These practices were once considered "trends," but are so established now that they are no longer trends, but business as usual. The six major industry practices that we will discuss are: manufacturers acting as retailers, licensing, private label and specification buying, offshore production, the use of factors, and chargebacks.

Manufacturers Acting as Retailers

An increasing number of clothing manufacturers are opening their own stores. Disappointed by the sales, service, and space allotted to them in retail stores and wanting to create the "right" atmosphere for this clothing, they are choosing to enter the retail business themselves. Of course, larger profits are also part of the attraction. The manufacturer can sell the product to consumers at full retail price, rather than at the wholesale price required by retail customers.

Designer Ralph Lauren was the first to take this step. Frustrated by the way department and specialty stores were selling his clothes, he opened the first Polo/Ralph Lauren shop on Rodeo Drive in Beverly Hills in 1971. Since then, he has built an empire of Polo/Ralph Lauren shops that stretches coast-to-coast in the United States and across the oceans to Europe and Asia.

Calvin Klein, Donna Karan, Adrienne Vittadini, Marc Jacobs, and Vivienne Tam have also opened their own retail outlets. As Vivienne Tam put it: "It's a trend to have a vertical business. Instead of relying on other buyers you do your own thing. You relate to the customer in a direct way so you know what they want."[7]

But whether all manufacturers and designers will be successful retailers remains to be seen. A producer first has to compete for good retail

Then & Now

The Names That Have Stood the Test of Time

What apparel and accessory brand names do consumers know best? The Fairchild 100 Survey, published each year in *Women's Wear Daily*, charts the public's name recognition in all categories of apparel and accessories. The survey shows clearly that mass market labels far outpace designer names. For example, in the 2000 survey, Timex captured the number 1 spot. Let's take a look at a few favorites:

- **L'eggs®**—Despite dwindling sales of sheer hosiery business, it remains the best-selling hosiery brand in mass marketers. It ranked second in the 2000 survey.
- **Levi Strauss**, the world's largest apparel manufacturer, has been shaking things up recently. Levi's jeans were a success *then*, while its Slates and Dockers are the success stories of *now*. Levi's ranked fifth in the 2000 survey.
- **Vanity Fair** began in 1911 and went public in 1952 . In 1968, the giant parent company was formed. This famous name has reinforced itself through the years by hefty advertising, and by introducing new products. It ranked 39th in the 2000 survey.
- **Catalina**, a staple of the beauty pageant for decades, was brought back to life in 1993, when Authentic Fitness bought them. *Now* into sleek suits, a children's division, and a plus-size line, Catalina reigns as number 62 in the 2000 survey.
- **Capezio**, once known mainly for ballet shoes and leotards for aspiring ballerinas, has modified its line to appeal to a broader customer base that pursues exercise and fitness. In addition, *now* the company has several free-standing stores, and it is developing lines for figure skating and ballroom dancing. Capezio also sells products through its Web site. It was number 66 in the 2000 survey.
- **Calvin Klein**, the only designer name among the top 35 in the 2000 survey, has become a licensing giant in three key areas: fragrance, jeans, and underwear. Klein continues to extend his CK brand into new areas; for example, watches. He has many international free-standing stores; his plans call for 100 CK stores in Europe and the Mideast by 2001.

These six companies are a small cross-section of the names the public is familiar with and which keep the cash register ringing!

Source

Based on *The Fairchild 100: A Special Report*, January 2000.

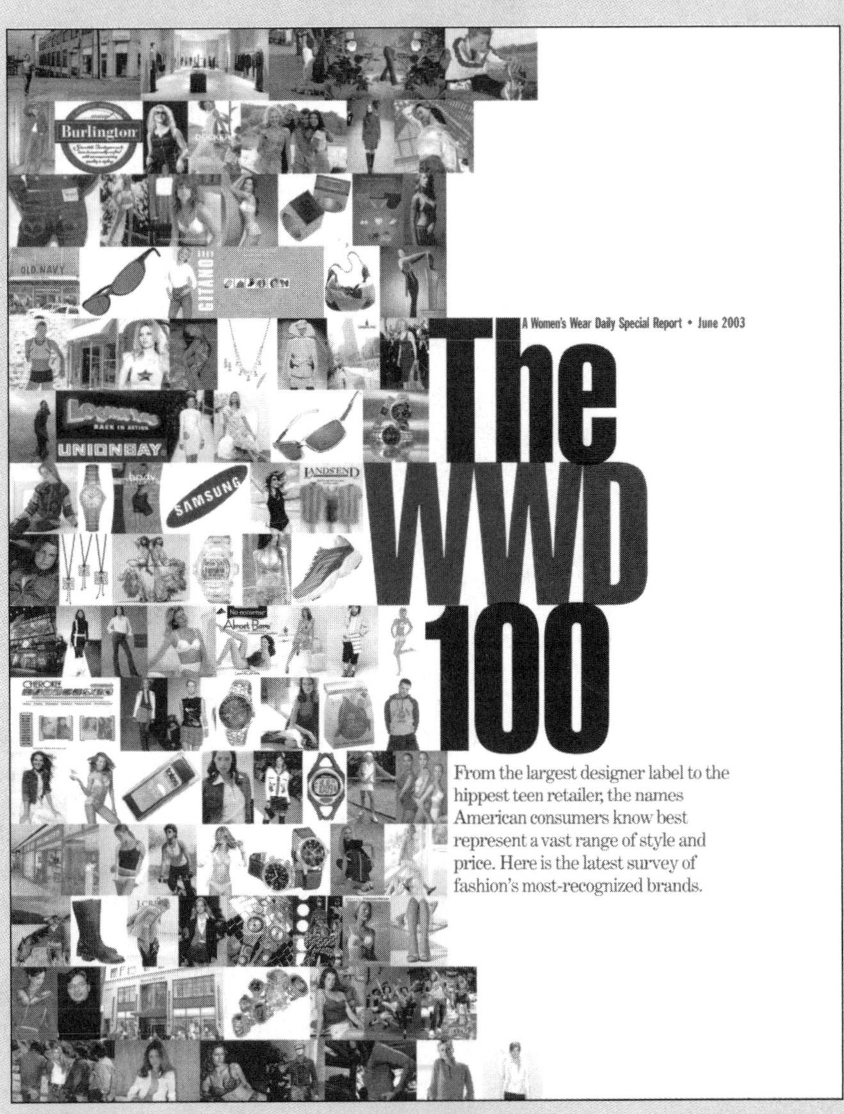

"The Fairchild 100," Women's Wear Daily: WWD Special Report, *June 2003*. Courtesy, Fairchild Publications.

talent, which can be expensive, as well as retail space in a prime location. The risks escalate if the manufacturer franchises, which many must do when they cannot personally oversee their retail empire.

Another problem is the reaction of the department and specialty stores that carry the manufacturers' lines. They feel such competition is unfair, and many have decided to stop carrying lines that are sold in manufacturers' own outlets. Other stores have learned to live with the new outlets.

Manufacturer's outlet stores, called "factory outlets," have also grown at a rapid rate. They allow manufacturers to dispose of poor sellers, overstocks, and "seconds" and still make more money on them than they could by selling them to discount retailers as "closeouts" (see Figure 7.9).

Many industry experts feel that the industry cannot sustain everyone, and that ultimately only the strongest manufacturer/retailers will succeed. But designers and manufacturers continue to open their own stores at a dizzying rate. Kari Sigerson, who with Miranda Morrison designs Sigerson Morrison shoes, which opened a small shop in Soho in New York, said:

> *A department store buyer is one person making one decision. Here we get to have fun with color, and we see that people do buy color and things department stores are afraid to do. It's a big laboratory. You get to experiment. And the stores love it. They call us and ask how things are selling, and what our customers are talking about.*[8]

FIGURE 7.9
Closeouts are a fact of life in manufacturing.
Courtesy, Hudson Distributing Enterprises, Inc.

The opposite of manufacturers acting as retailers is retailers acting as manufacturers, through the private label programs of department stores and discounters, and through the retail store brands of specialty chains like the Gap and Talbots. These strategies will be discussed in depth in Chapter 18.

Licensing

Licensing, which was described in Chapter 4, experienced a boom in the United States in the 1980s and 1990s. This was largely due to the emergence of an important new market segment—working women. As a group, they are not quite in the income bracket to buy designer clothes, but designers have learned that they can capitalize on the market these women represent through licensing ventures.

The great appeal of licensing is that merchandise is identified with a highly recognizable name. Licensed products are estimated at $107 billion annually.[9] The advantages for designers include the royalties they receive on the sale of each product (usually from 2 percent to 15 percent), greater exposure of their name, and little investment in product development and manufacturing.

The disadvantages in licensing are few. When designers turn over control to a manufacturer as they do when they license a product, they may lose some quality control. A bigger problem is that a designer will move too far afield for his or her more exclusive customers, but considering the potential profits in licensing, this is unlikely to worry many designers.

Christian Dior was a pioneer in licensing, having granted his first license in 1949. Even though Dior died in 1957, his name still appears on many products. Beside the Christian Dior shoe, jewelry, perfume, and cosmetic products that are owned and produced under the umbrella of Dior's parent company LVMH, the brand also has a license with Sanofi Eyewear.[10] Pierre Cardin used licenses to create a fashion empire—the largest of its kind—with over 800 products, from perfumes to pencil holders!

The first landmark deal in licensing in the United States occurred in the 1930s when Mickey Mouse products flooded the market. Later in the 1930s, Shirley Temple was the first human to find a windfall in selling her name for use on dresses, dolls, and an assortment of other products.

One of the pioneers of designer apparel licensing in the United States was Bill Blass, who had 42 licenses for men's and women's apparel and accessories and home fashions. Anne Klein has many licenses for accessories, such as with Swank for jewelry, and other manufacturers for eyeglasses, watches, and coats.

In 2001, Vera Wang started building a business that covered everything from accessories to tabletop. Her first product launch was the fragrance "Vera Wang" in the spring of 2002, which was followed by the introduction of china, crystal, and shoes. Wang explains her license development like this:

> *When I began the business and realized this was my own money I would be spending, it took on a whole new meaning. This business is a lifetime of my own savings. I know that I'm not able to fund everything in house. I don't have that sort of infrastructure nor the financial ability. So, licensing was a way for my business to make money.*[11]

A final note on the importance of a company's brand name: **corporate licensing**, or the use of a company's name on related merchandise, is the fastest-growing segment of licensing today. Overall, corporate licensing reached $982 million in sales in 2000, according to the International Licensing Industry Merchandisers' Association.[12] The Nike "swoosh" is seen worldwide. Harley Davidson has licensed its name for T-shirts and children's wear, Dr. Scholl's has expanded from foot care to pillows, and Jeep now has a line of sunglasses.

Private Label and Specification Buying

The terms "private label" and "specification buying" may be used to describe the same items of merchandise, but the meanings are slightly different. If the retailer agrees, the manufacturer may design **private label merchandise** for the retailer. Federated Department Stores' private labels include Jennifer Moore, Charter Club, and Badge. On the other hand, **specification buying** is a type of purchasing that is done to the store's rather than the manufacturer's standards. JCPenney and the Gap are two examples of stores that make extensive use of specification buying. These retailers provide the standards and guidelines for the manufacture of clothes they order. Standards cover everything from the quality of materials and workmanship to styling and cost.

Specification buying has become so specialized that many stores now employ a **specification manager** or **product manager** who is trained in specification buying. While keeping an eye on industry and government standards, specification managers work closely with manufacturers to ensure that their products will be economically successful for both the retailer and the manufacturer.

As they grow more successful with specification buying, stores have begun to use it for their private label lines. Initially intended as a way to keep production at home, a growing amount of private label is now purchased offshore. (See the following section and Chapter 16).

Because retailers often place large orders for a few related lines, the private labels are a growth area for the manufacturers and may account for 20 to 45 percent of the manufacturer's output. According to the individual agreement between retailer and manufacturer, product development can be in the hands of either party. To maintain the separate, distinctive images of their retailer clients' private brands and their own national brands, some manufacturers have separate teams of designers. The manufacturer can achieve ecomomies of scale by sourcing both their national brand and their retailer clients' brands from the same offshore supplier.

Offshore Production

American manufacturers are increasingly turning to **offshore production**, that is, the manufacture of American goods in cheap-labor foreign countries. Offshore production is seen as a way to generally lower costs and therefore compete more effectively with low-cost imports. Some industry insiders view this practice as a threat to the health of American labor; others regard it as a necessity in order for U.S. manufacturers to remain competitive.

Offshore production is appealing under certain conditions because the federal government gives domestic producers a special tariff advantage, provided only part of the production is done offshore. Under Section 807 of the Tariff Classification Act, for example, manufacturers can cut and design their own garments and finish them domestically, sending only the sewing to a labor-cheap offshore country. Duty is paid only on the value added to the garment by the work done abroad. Under the North American Free Trade Agreement (NAFTA), a substantial amount of offshore production has shifted from Asian countries to Mexico, where wages are low and shipping costs less.

Use of Factors

Apparel manufacturers and contractors need cash or credit to produce garments the season before they are sold. Some banks have been reluctant to lend money to apparel companies because of the high risks involved. So an alternate system of financing has developed for the apparel industry. Called **factors**, these companies either purchase a manufacturer's accounts receivable or advance cash on the basis of the accounts receivable. Their interest rates are generally higher than those of a bank.

Another more recent development is the use of credit insurance by firms that do not use factors. Credit insurance, used for decades in Europe, protects the insured company from losses as a result of a customer's bankruptcy or very late payment. Credit insurance is also useful for a U.S. manufacturer with international business, since it is cheaper than international letters of credit.[13]

Chargebacks

As retail chains have grown in size, their power over their suppliers has also increased. Apparel manufacturers are increasingly hit with demands for **chargebacks**, which are financial penalties imposed on manufacturers by retailers. The reasons for chargebacks include errors like mistakes in purchase orders or ticketing. Sometimes retailers request chargebacks for partial or late shipments, or even for poor-selling products. Chargebacks are also used for cooperative advertising. Naturally, chargebacks can cause financial problems for designers and manufacturers, especially small ones.

Advanced Technologies and Strategies

A number of advanced technologies and the strategies used to harness them have been implemented by the U.S. apparel industry. These technologies have already had a profound impact on the profitability of the business, and are poised to increase it further in the 21st century. They include the use of computer-integrated manufacturing, Quick Response, bar codes and scanners, electronic data interchange (EDI), mass customization, and body scanning.

Computer-Integrated Manufacturing

Standalone computerized equipment is now common in most manufacturers' plants. This is known as **computer-aided manufacturing (CAM)**. It includes such things as programmable sewing machines, patternmaking machines, and cutting machines.

But the enormous power of the computer lies in its ability to be linked to other computers, so that the computers can direct the entire production process from design to finished garment. In **computer-integrated manufacturing (CIM)**, data from many computers within a manufacturing company is linked from design through production stages. The potential for cost savings is tremendous, since repeated data entry is eliminated, along with entry errors.

In the apparel industry, CAD and CAM are linked into a CIM system, so that a design, patternmaking, and grading are linked to cutting equipment as well as to computers that prepare costing reports and specification sheets. In some plants, these computers are even linked to stitching machines.

One example of a software product that helps manufacturers harness CIM to quickly search for information is called ConceptManager97. It allows users to search for, display on screen, and print any visual element. For example, a manufacturer can search for all fabrics priced below $10 a yard, a primary color of blue, and sourced in Hong Kong.[14]

The specialty retailer/cataloger Talbots is using a groupware computer program combined with the Internet to share critical information among members of its product development team: the product manager, who is responsible for developing new clothing lines;

a source, who is responsible for getting an item manufactured once it has been designed; and a buyer, who decides on quality and price. As Annie Stobbs, project manager at Talbots said: "All these people need to collaborate on product development, and we need to be able to track the progress."[15] Since Talbots designs and manufactures 90 percent of all the merchandise it sells, this tracking is especially crucial.

Quick Response

Quick Response—the industry buzzword is bandied about at trade conferences, seminars, boardrooms, and back rooms. Many say this is where all textile, apparel, and retail industries are headed. Simply put, it aims at delivering the right product at the right time!

Quick Response, or **QR**, is a business strategy that shortens the time from raw materials to design to production to finished product to the consumer. It was developed to give U.S. manufacturers a potent weapon against imports and foreign competitors. The necessary partnerships and electronic high-tech mechanisms are in place to link all parts of the supply pipeline directly to the nation's retailers. As Richard Feldman of the Feldman Manufacturing Company in Queens, New York, a maker of private label swimwear for J. Crew, Eddie Bauer, and Victoria's Secret, said:

It's all about speed. The buzzword is Quick Response. The swimwear can go from here to a wearhouse to a distribution center in 48 hours. If you go to the Orient, you need three or four months.[16]

What QR really means is a far closer association between manufacturer, supplier, retailer, and customer. QR requires the development of trust and communication, and that goes all the way from the cash register to the apparel people and the textile suppliers.

As Kurt Salmon Associates, a prestigious consulting firm which was in on the birth of Quick Response in 1985 put it:

From a manufacturer's point of view, QR can be defined as having in place an operating strategy which has been designed to enable the company to profitably supply its chosen markets with the right product at a competitive price, in the right quantities, at the right time, and with minimum commitment to inventory. Certainly there is nothing new about such a formula. What is new is the change of emphasis and timing, plus the fact that for many companies survival is at stake.[17]

QR had evolved from a theoretical concept in 1985 to a comprehensive integrated system by 1995; one that has shortened total cycle time and improved service. But there is more to QR than moving goods more quickly to a retailer's shelf, and ultimately more quickly into the consumer's hand. Once belittled as the pipedream of a few idealistic textile and apparel executives, QR has proved effective. In a study conducted by North Carolina State University, domestic QR resulted in better overall retail performance than did a strategy of importing apparel. The key advantage of QR was that it allowed retailers to reorder during the season, as customer demand was being revealed to them. The retailers could look at their point-of-sale data and make small, frequent reorders. This prevented both big oversupply of inventory and stockouts (being out of stock).[18]

The growing segment of companies that has tried QR is gleeful about the payoffs. The point of QR is not only to restock but also to let both the retailer and manufacturer see what the customers like and what sizes they wear—tools for planning and implementing the next season's line. Thus QR is a change from the "push" system strategy of the past, in which products were produced and then "pushed" on the consumer. Instead, QR is a "pull" system strategy, because information about what consumers want flows from the consumers to the producers.

Bar Codes and Scanners

Bar coding, scanning, and computer-to-computer communications have become integral parts of QR. Bar coding makes tracking merchandise—from fabric rolls to designer dresses—easier, faster, and more accurate (see Figure 7.10).

The **universal product code** (**UPC**) is one of a number of bar codes used for automatic identification of items scanned at retail cash registers. UPC is the symbol that has been most widely accepted by retailers and manufacturers.

Bar codes are made up of a pattern of dark bars and white spaces of varying widths. A group of bars and spaces represents one character. Scanners "read" the bar code. The UPC symbol does not contain the price of the merchandise; that information is added by the retailer to the store's computerized cash registers. It can be easily changed.

FIGURE 7.10
Bar codes give vital product information.

The Role of Technology in Getting the Right Product to the Right Place at the Right Time

1. Scanning at the Point of Purchase
When a 5-ounce package of Countryside Lavender Bouquet Potpourri is purchased, its Universal Product Code (UPC) is scanned and information is entered into the Elston Specialty Store's database. Elston's is a chain of 225 specialty stores around the country. The data recorded includes the stockkeeping unit number (SKU 51093 07203) for one particular kind of potpourri, the retail price, and the cost to Elston's. Elston's uses this data to manage its inventory. Is a store in Portland, Oregon sold out? Are sales poor in Portland, Maine? Is the reason the season? Shipping? The price? The competition? Elston's can monitor the status of SKU 51093 07203 instantly, and take prompt action to correct any problems.

2. Using Locator Computer Programs
If an Elston store runs out of SKU 51093 07203, managers or salespeople can pick up one of Elston's hand-held computers and enter into Elston's Locator Computer Program to find the closest Elston's store with a supply of SKU 51093 07203 to spare. After a telephone call to that store, the merchandise will be sent to the store where it is needed.

3. Transmitting Data by Sattellite
Elston's hand-held computers communicate by sattellite with Elston's headquarters in Babson Park, Florida every day. Store managers track SKU 51093 07203 and can order display changes when, for example, Countryside Herb Farms advertises the potourri in *Redbook* magazine.

4. Using Supplier/Retailer Computer Links
The Supplier/Retailer Computer Link is a database that Elston's shares with 91 of its 148 suppliers, including Countryside Herb Farm Brands, the manufacturer, which is based in Seattle, Washington. The sales history of SKU 51093 07203 at Elston's is instantly available to Countryside Herb Farms, which can meet Elston's needs as they change.

5. Forecasting by Computer
To improve coordination between retailers and its suppliers, Elston's and Countryside Herb Farms are using a strategic alliance (see Chapter18) to form a mutual forecasting computer program that takes into account such factors as season. This computerized forecasting program has cut the time it takes Countryside Herb Farms to get SKU 51093 07203 to Elston's from two months to three weeks.

Electronic Data Interchange (EDI)

Electronic Data Interchange (EDI) is the electronic exchange of machine-readable data in standard formats between one company's computers and another company's computers. It replaces a large number of paper forms that were the primary link between manufacturers and their retailer customers. These included forms like purchase orders, invoices, packing slips, shipping documents, and inventory forms.

EDI is faster than mail, messenger, or air delivery services. By eliminating paper-based transactions, large companies can save clerical time, paper, and postage. EDI goes beyond bar code scanning to include handheld laser scanners, satellite links, and wireless systems. This technology results in both increased productivity and improved customer service. Using EDI, Federal Express and UPS, for example, can trace any of the millions of packages they ship anywhere in the world. EDI also offers shops an avenue to e-commerce. The EDI system supplies a business with the infrastructure necessary to take the business on to the Internet. However, since the configuration process is complicated, fewer than 30,000 shops have actually implemented the technology.[19]

Mass Customization

For the past 80 years, we have lived in a world where mass production was the model for products and services, because standardized products meant lower costs. The mass customization concept is being explored by author/researcher B. Joseph Pine II, who says it is "efficiently serving customers uniquely."[20] He urges manufacturers and retailers to find out what customers like and then to build those attributes into all the products and services a company offers. Every time a customer takes home an attribute that he or she really does not want in the product, it is a form of waste. In **mass customization**, the idea is to tailor the product to fit one particular customer—not one size fits all—and to supply thousands of individuals, at mass prices, not custom-made prices (see Figure 7.11).

Applying the mass customization concept to apparel and accessories would result in a huge shift in the fashion industries. Half of all the people in the United States buy ill-fitting clothes, and only half of them bother with alterations, according to David Bruner of TC2, a research and development company in Cary, North Carolina.[21]

Obviously, this problem is an opportunity for manufacturers and retailers. Some have already begun to respond. Perhaps the best-known response was Levi Strauss & Company's introduction of its Women's Personal Pair Jeans program in 1994. Levi Strauss sends four measurements taken by "personal fit specialists" in its stores to a factory in Tennessee that turns out a custom-fit pair of jeans and sends them to customers within 2 weeks, for about $55. Levi's aimed to offer hard-to-fit customers—large and small—a custom fit. It found many customers beyond this group; the PPJ program accounted for 25 percent of women's jean sales in only three years.[22] Another effect of the PPJ program has been to eliminate inventory completely! Levi Strauss has built new distribution centers that can pick and ship one item as easily as they can thousands.[23] The VF Corporation soon followed Levi's lead, and announced its own made-to-measure jeans program in 1997. It is available at stores where VF products are sold.[24]

Body Scanning

The Interactive Custom Clothes Company, known as IC3D, in Westchester County, New York, has pioneered software that customizes patterns to fit an individual's body. It operates from an Web site that instructs customers in how to take 11 of their own measurements and then order jeans in a combination of hundreds of styles, colors, and finishes, for $90 to $300. TC2 is also developing a device that will scan the entire body to produce a 3-D portrait, and a custom pattern.[25] Another manufacturer/retailer that is doing well with an individually crafted product is Custom Foot of Westport, Connecticut, which uses a scanner to create custom-made shoes to fit a customer's feet.

As technology continues to improve and to become cheaper, scanning of the entire body will become common, resulting in the kind of fit previously available only to the wealthy or to home sewers (see Figure 7.12).

Industry Trends

The fashion industry is moving closer to traditional marketing models for consumer goods. We will focus on three trends that prove this point: brand extensions, industry cooperation, and globalization.

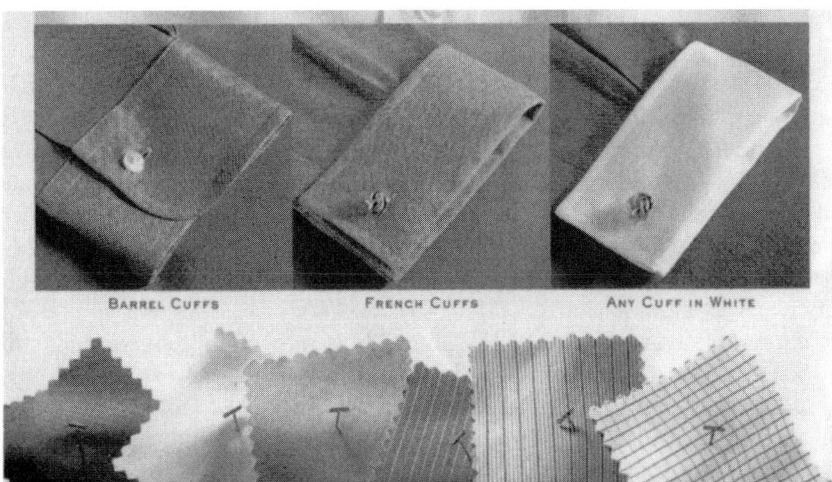

FIGURE 7.11
The mass customization trend, now available at Brooks Brothers, is expected to sweep the apparel industry in the 21st century.
Courtesy, Brooks Brothers.

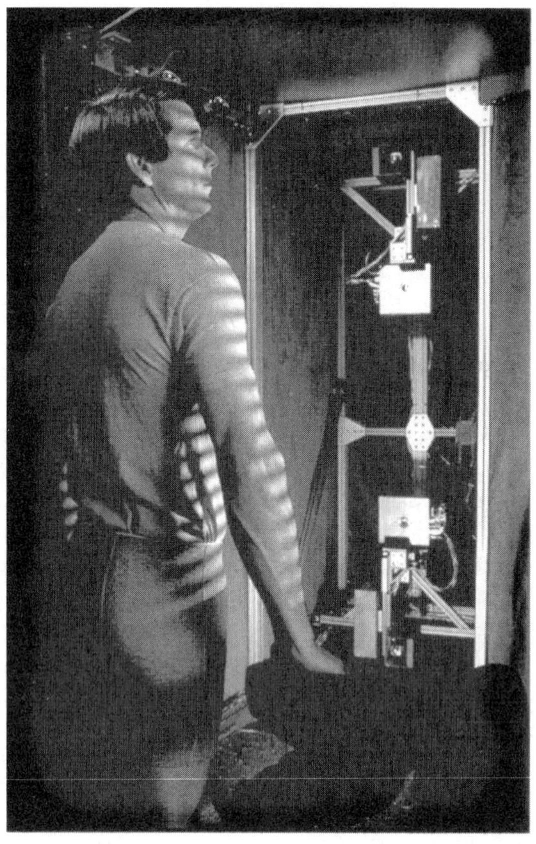

FIGURE 7.12
Body scanning on a computer will allow better-fitting clothes for everyone; once available only to the rich or to home sewers. [TC]²
© 1998. Photographed by R. A. Flynn, Inc.

Brand Extensions

A common technique in consumer goods marketing is **brand extension**, which is a strategy in which a company uses a successful brand name to launch new or modified products. Brand extension saves the company the high cost of promoting a new name and creates instant brand recognition of the new product line (see Figure 13a and b). It is one way in which a company can diversify its product line. This is a common strategy of packaged goods manufacturers; for example, the Dial brand of the Armour conglomerate was used on a variety of products beyond the original bar soap. One fashion company that extended its line is Fossil, which was successful with watches, and then branched out into handbags and belts.

In the apparel industries, a move into a related category of apparel is the easiest and cheapest way to diversify. A company that makes T-shirts may add a line of cotton sweatshirts, which are also sized small, medium, large, and extra-large. A designer of men's suits may add coats. A children's wear manufacturer may add an infants' line. A woman's shoe manufacturer may add matching handbags.

The move to an unrelated line has traditionally been more difficult—and more costly. One of the first brand extensions by designers was expanding into fragrances and cosmetics.

Fragrances and Cosmetics

Chanel and Schiaparelli had paved the way into fragrances in the 1920s and 1930s. After World War II, Pierre Cardin and Christian Dior launched new perfumes. In the United States, what was once a trickle of designer fragrances has become a torrent—with many introductions each season. The move into color cosmetics, however, has been much slower, because of the high cost of entry into this line, and the established competition. (See Chapter 13).

Accessories

The next natural product extension for many designers was accessories. Scarfs or ties, jewelry and watches, leather shoes, belts, or handbags, furs, hoisery or socks—it sometimes seems that every name designer does it all. This helps them create a "total concept" or look, that distinguishes their merchandise. This also ties into the licensing trend, which is the low-cost, low-risk way that most designers choose to move into specialized areas, like leather apparel or shoes, or fur. (See Chapter 12).

Men's and Women's Wear

Designers who have been successful in either men's or women's wear now regularly turn to designing for the opposite sex. This has become so routine that it is difficult for newcomers to the fashion industries to appreciate what a dramatic change this is from the practice of the past.

For many decades (1930s to the mid-1950s) women wore men's jeans, because manufacturers did not make jeans in women's sizes. Adding women's sizes to a jeans line was a bold, unprecidented move at the time—but it succeeded. Today, manufacturers and designers both move easily into unisex wear. The move from men's wear to women's wear was made first; only in 1991 did a women's wear designer (Donna Karan) dare to move into men's wear.

Children's Wear

While expanding into children's wear is still done less frequently than the expansions discussed previously, it is becoming more common. Children's lines such as Italy's Moschino, with both Moschino Bambino for infants and toddlers, and Moschino Junior for 2 to 15 year

A

B

FIGURE 7.13A AND B *Kate Spade extended her popular line of (a) handbags with the creation of a (b) beauty line.* Courtesy, Fairchild Publications, Inc.

olds, are well-known. American and European designers are aiming to differentiate themselves from the frilly, fussy dress clothes available from established children's wear firms, as well as from the casual basics offered by Polo Ralph Lauren, Tommy Hilfiger, and CK Calvin Klein.

Many retailers of adult apparel have also expanded into children's wear; examples include Baby Gap, Talbots Kids, and The Limited Too.

Home Furnishings

Once limited to Bill Blass in the United States, this extension exploded in the 1990s because of a downturn in women's wear and growing sales of home furnishings. Ralph Lauren is perhaps the most successful designer in this field, but he is getting lots of company, as many name designers make licensing agreements with established manufacturers. In fact, the largest dollar growth area for designer licensing is in home fashions. Designers such as Calvin Klein, Alexander Julian, and Liz Claiborne have had great success in home fashions. Interior designers are also entering the field via licensing, such as Christopher Lowell and Lynette Jennings. Martha Stewart, also known for her domesticity, has licensed a line of sheets and towels with Kmart.

Adding Different Price Lines

The practice of moving into different price levels is now widely accepted by both manufacturers and name designers. As price lines blur, the distinctions of yesteryear are blurring too. Most name designers now have several price levels, none of which is perceived by customers as cheapening the image of the others. Examples abound: one is Donna Karan's signature collection. Its sales have not been adversely affected by the huge sales of her lower-priced DKNY line.

Unusual Brand Extensions

One unusual example of brand extension is Eddie Bauer's alliance with the Ford Motor Company to offer special Eddie Bauer versions of select Ford vehicles. Over 700,000 cars were sold over 10 years.[26] Now Eddie Bauer is getting into the travel business with a travel agency that is also owned by Spiegel, Inc. The new company, called Eddie Bauer Travel, will sell adventure travel packages.

Industry Cooperation

It is necessary for companies in the fashion industry to harness technology as they strive to push costs out of the entire product distribution pipeline, rather than to just push costs onto their trading partners. Bill Gates, president of Microsoft, predicts that:

> *By 2005, the supply chain is going to be a lot more efficient, and the apparel and retail industries are not going to have to invent their own technologies to make that happen . . . . The real advances in supply-chain management are coming from PC technology and the Internet.*[27]

Industry cooperation, already at an all-time high, continues to grow. The issue of partnerships, or strategic alliances, between textile producers, apparel and accessories manufacturers, and retailers is discussed in more detail in Chapter 18. Two current examples of industry cooperation follow: VICS and ANSI X.12.

FIGURE 7.14
Alexander Julian, a well-known designer, shows how fashion trends can update and add flair not only to sheets but also to old-fashioned mattress "ticking" material.
Courtesy, Alexander Julian, Inc.

VICS

Voluntary Inter-Industry Communications Standards Committee (VICS) was formed in 1986 by retailers and producers to establish common standards of communication, including the current UPC system. This group grew out of the Crafted With Pride program, and has members from Wal-Mart, Kmart, Dayton Hudson, Sears, Levi Strauss, and VF Corporation. This group also developed a retail-specific version of ANSI X.12, the standards for electronic documents.

ANSI X.12

ANSI X.12 is the backbone of the Quick Response movement, because it is the set of standards that govern creating an electronic document (EDI). Since all the documents use the same format, the entire apparel industry can use the ANSI standards, whether they are sending or receiving documents, whether the company is small or huge. For example, the first three-digit number describes the type of document being sent (like a purchase order) and the next ten numbers give the sender's name, and on and on through every line of the document.

Globalization

Globalization of the marketplace—finding both foreign competitors and foreign customers—has happened to a wide range of U.S. heavy manufacturing industries; for example, cars, televisions, electronics, steel, and computers. From the 1970s to the 1990s, globalization occurred in the apparel industries. In this chapter, we have explored several high-tech responses to protect U.S. manufacturers: CAD/CAM/CIM, EDI, QR, and mass customization, among others. In Unit Five we will explore the opportunities presented by global markets.

Meanwhile, in the words of apparel industry expert Karen Ann Zimmermann: "The Internet is shaping up as the key global communications tool for retailers, manufacturers, and raw materials suppliers seeking to streamline most supply chains and logistics."[28] For example, most leading manufacturers are already communicating with raw materials suppliers in Asia using the Internet.

SIC/NAICS Codes

Another reflection of globalization is the change from the Standard Industrial Classification (SIC) codes to North American Industry Classification System (NAICS). SIC was originally developed in the 1930s to classify U.S. establishments by the type of activity in which they primarily engage, and to create a data base of comparable information that would describe the parts of the U.S. economy.

Over the years, the SIC was revised periodically to reflect the changes in the businesses that make up the U.S. economy. The last major revision of the SIC was in 1987. In 1997, the SIC was replaced by the NAICS, which is also being used by Canada and Mexico.[29] The NAICS will provide industrial statistics produced in the three countries that will be comparable for the first time, reflecting the interrelated nature of these economies. This data will be extremely useful for businesses, and the fashion industry will be at the forefront of those using the information to aid in decision-making. Table 7.2 shows one section of the old SIC and the comparable new NAICS codes. The new codes are much simpler.

TABLE 7.2 Comparison of Selected NAICS and SIC Codes

NAICS Codes		SIC Codes	
315	Apparel Manufacturing		
3152	Cut and Sew Apparel Manufacturing		
31521	Cut and Sew Apparel Contractors		
315211	Men's and Boys' Cut and Sew Apparel Contractors	*2311	Men's and Boys' Suits, Coats, and Overcoats (contractors)
		*2321	Men's and Boys' Shirts, Except Work Shirts (contractors)
		*2322	Men's and Boys' Underwear and Nightwear (contractors)
		*2325	Men's and Boys' Trousers and Slacks (contractors)
		*2326	Men's and Boys' Work Clothing (contractors)
		*2329	Men's and Boys' Clothing, NEC (contractors)
		*2341	Women's, Misses', Children's, and Infants' Underwear and Nightwear (boys' contractors)
		*2361	Girl's, Children's, and Infants' Dresses, Blouses and Shirts (boys' contractors)
		*2369	Girl's, Children's, and Infants' Outerwear, NEC (boys' contractors)
		*2384	Robes and Dressing Gowns (men's and boys' contractors)
		*2385	Waterproof Outerwear (men's and boys' contractors)
		*2389	Apparel and Accessories, NEC (contractors)
		*2395	Pleating, Decorative and Novelty Stitching, and Tucking for the Trade (men's and boys' apparel contractors)
315212	Women's and Girls' Cut	*2341	Women's, Misses', and Juniors' Blouses and Shirts (contractors)
		*2335	Women's, Misses', and Juniors' Dresses (contractors)
		*2337	Women's, Misses', and Juniors' Suits, Skirts, and Coats (contractors)
		*2339	Women's, Misses', and Juniors' Outerwear, NEC (contractors)
		*2341	Women's, Misses', Children's, and Infants' Underwear and Nightwear (contractors)
		*2342	Brassieres, Girdles, and Allied Garments (contractors)
		*2361	Girls', Children's, and Infants' Dresses, Blouses and Shirts (girls' contractors)
		*2369	Girls', Children's, and Infants' Outerwear, NEC (girls' contractors)
		*2384	Robes and Dressing Gowns (women's, girls', and infants')
		*2385	Waterproof Outerwear (women's, girls', and infants' contractors)
		*2389	Apparel and Accessories, NEC (contractors)
		*2395	Pleating, Decorative and Novelty Stitching, and Tucking for the Trade (women's and girls' apparel contractors)

Source: *Federal Register*/Vol. 62, No. 68, pp. 17308–17309.

SUMMARY AND REVIEW

The men's, women's, and children's apparel industries develop and produce lines of apparel following a standard cycle. The six-stage process of developing and producing a line involves: (1) planning a line, (2) creating the design concept, (3) developing the designs, (4) planning production, (5) production, and (6) distributing the line.

Types of producers include manufacturers, apparel jobbers, and contractors. Producers specialize by gender, age, and size categories, as well as by classification. While consumers generally do not know the differences, industry insiders distinguish between five major types of brands and labels: (1) national/designer brands, (2) private labels, (3) retail store brands, (4) other types of brands, and (5) nonbrands.

Major industry practices that directly affect profitability include licensing, private label and specification buying, offshore production, the use of factors, and chargebacks.

Advanced technologies affecting product development of apparel include computer-integrated manufacturing, Quick Response, the use of bar codes and scanners, electronic data interchange, mass customization, and body scanning computers.

Product development is also affected by the major industry trends of brand extensions, globalization, and industry cooperation. A reflection of globalization is the new NAICS codes used by Canada, the United States, and Mexico, which replace the SIC codes that classified industries and made company comparisons possible.

Trade Talk

Define or briefly explain the following terms:

anchor
apparel jobber
brand extension
bundling
chargeback
collection
computer-aided design (CAD)
computer-aided manufacturing (CAM)
computer-integrated manufacturing (CIM)
contractor (apparel)
corporate licensing
Electronic Data Interchange (EDI)
factor
floor ready
freelance artist-designer
graded
group
high fashion or name designer
item house
line-for-line copy
manufacturer (apparel)
marker
mass customization
minimum order
modular manufacturing
off-shore production system
outside shop
piece work
private label merchandise
product development
product development team
product manager
retail store brand
quality assurance (QA)
Quick Response (QR)
sample hand
section work
single-hand operation
sourcing
specification buying
specification manager
spreader
stylist-designer
universal product code (UPC)

For Review

1. How does EDI differ from CIM?
2. How does a jobber differ from a manufacturer?
3. What are the major advantages of the contractor system? What is the key disadvantage?
4. What are the six stages of the product development process?
5. What is a chargeback?
6. What is the goal of Quick Response?
7. Why do most fashion producers sell directly to retail stores rather than through wholesalers?
8. What is the difference between a national brand and a private label?
9. What role do factors play in the fashion industry?
10. Discuss the major problems facing a manufacturer who is also a retailer.

For Discussion

1. Compare and contrast the roles of the designer, the merchandiser, and the product manager in developing a line.

2. Give current examples of brand extensions in apparel, accessories, fragrances and cosmetics, and home furnishings.

References

1. Robin Lewis, "Partner or Perish," *WWD Infotracs*, November 1995, p. 9.
2. Muditha M. Senanayake, Trevor J. Little, "'Measures' for New Product Development," *Journal of Textile and Apparel Technology and Management,* Volume 1, Issue 3, Spring 2001, p. 9.
3. "Lisa Schultz: Fashion Arbiter," *Time*, April 21, 1997, p. 56.
4. Robin Lewis, "What's In a Name?", *WWD Infotracs*, November 1995, pp. 1–35.
5. Robin Lewis, "Manufacturers Say: Brands Still King, Private Labels Fill In," *WWD Infotracs*, November 1995, p. 28.
6. Jim Hodges, "If the Label Fits," *Private Label Development*, May 1996, p. 30.
7. Amy M. Spindler, "Designers Discover Small Is Beautiful," *New York Times*, September 19, 1996, p. B6.
8. Ibid.
9. Robert Grey, "Brands Profit From Loaning Out Kudos," *Marketing*, October 4, 2001, p. 9.
10. Marcy Medina, "Shades of Spring at Vision Expo," *Women's Wear Daily*, September 23, 2002, p. 12.
11. Julee Greenburg, "Vera Wang Steps On the Gas," *Women's Wear Daily,* December 7, 2001.
12. Gerry Khermouch, "Whoa, Cool Shirt, Yeah It's a Pepsi," *Businessweek*, September 10, 2001.
13. John Metzger, "Credit Insurance for Non-factored Firms," *The Fashion Manuscript*, August 1997, p. 86.
14. "Animated Images," *Apparel Industry Magazine*, May 1997, p. 56.
15. Kim Ann Zimmermann, "Talbots Groupware Strategy," *Women's Wear Daily*, July 9, 1997.
16. Lisa W. Foderaro, "Made in New York Is Coming Back Into Fashion," *New York Times*, January 13, 1998, p. B7.
17. Kurt Salmon Associates, "A $13 Billion Success Story: Quick Response," *Bobbin*, June 1997, p. 46.
18. Ibid.
19. "EDI offers Bridge to XML, e-commerce," *I-S Analyzer*, June 2002, pp. 1-3.
20. Tom Brown, "Efficiently Serving Customers Uniquely," *Management Review*, April 1, 1996, p. 60.
21. Susan Carpenter, "Technology Fashions a Fit Accompli," *Los Angeles Times*, February 20, 1997, p. 1, Life & Style.
22. Ibid.
23. Annie Gowan, "The Data Game," *Women's Wear Daily*, March 20, 1996, p. 12.
24. Ibid.
25. Carpenter, "Technology Fashions a Fit."
26. Christy Fisher, "Have Clothing Business, Will Travel," *American Demographics*, April 1997.
27. Kim Ann Zimmermann, "Internet: The Vital Link," *Women's Wear Daily/Global*, July 1997, p. 78.
28. Ibid.
29. *The Federal Register*, April 9, 1997, p. 17228.

CHAPTER 8

Women's Apparel

WHAT'S IN IT FOR YOU?

Everything you always wanted to know about the history, organization, and operation of women's apparel.

Key Concepts:

- Categories, size ranges, and price zones of women's apparel
- Roles of brand names and designer names in the marketing of women's wear.
- Advertising and promotional activities in the marketing of women's apparel
- Trends in the women's apparel industry

Located in the heart of midtown Manhattan, the Fashion District is the capital of American fashion. It is a vibrant and diverse community where more than 80,000 people work at over 6,500 companies in the 450 buildings that make up the neighborhood. To celebrate the fashion designers whose innovative and distinctive styles helped shape the course of American fashion, the Fashion Walk of Fame was created in 2000. The series of 30 commemorative sidewalk plaques run the length of "Fashion Avenue" between 35th and 41st Streets, highlighting the names and designs of these national fashion treasures.[1]

The manufacturing and merchandising of women's apparel is a giant multibillion dollar industry employing hundreds of thousands of people. Its influence on the economy is so strong that retail sales figures are one indicator of the health of the nation's economy.

Of necessity, the industry exists in a constant state of change, reacting on an ongoing basis to women's tastes and styles, to an increasingly global economy, and to new technology. It is an industry that truly thrives on change and novelty.

History of the Women's Apparel Industry

For thousands of years, people made their own clothes, often producing their own raw materials and converting them into textiles with which they

could sew. A farmer might grow cotton, for example, and his wife would spin and weave it into cotton fabric, which she then used to make the family's clothes. Until the mass manufacturing of clothing began, sewing was considered women's work, except for the wealthy man, who "bespoke" hand-made garments from a male tailor, who specialized in men's high-fashion apparel.

The first step in moving the manufacture of clothes out of the home came around 1800, when professional male tailors began to make more men's clothing. These clothes were still **custom-made**, that is, fitted to the individual who would wear them and then sewn by hand. A few professional dressmakers began to make women's clothes, but only rich women could afford these custom-made designs. Most women still sewed their own clothes at home.

Growth of Ready-to-Wear

The mass production of clothing did not begin until the mid-19th century. After the Civil War, some manufacturers began to mass-produce cloaks and mantles for women. These garments were not fitted, so they could be made in standard sizes and produced in large numbers.

By the turn of the century, limited quantities of women's suits, skirts, and blouses were being made in factories. Around 1910, someone had the idea of sewing a blouse and skirt together in what was called a *shirtwaist*, and the women's ready-to-wear dress business was born. In contrast to custom-made clothes produced by professional dressmakers or tailors or made by home sewers, **ready-to-wear** (RTW) refers to clothing produced in factories to standardized measurements. In the first decade of the 20th century, growing numbers of women began to substitute store-bought clothes for home-sewn ones.

Acceptance of Ready-to-Wear in the 20th Century

By the 1920s, most women shopped for their wardrobes in department and women's specialty stores. Mass production and distribution through retail outlets accelerated the fashion cycle of styles produced in the following three decades and made the latest fashions available to the vast middle and working classes. With technological improvements in machinery and the development of synthetic fabrics, fashion producers were able to respond quickly to the changing needs of women for clothing that suited changing social, economic, and political conditions.

FIGURE 8.1
The ups and downs of fashion: in free-wheeling decade of the 1960s, women were for the first time encouraged to wear any length of skirt they desired-not what the "pundits" of fashion decreed.
© Archive Photos.

Growth of the Fashion District

Crucial in the evolution and success of the American ready-to-wear business is New York's fashion district. This fashion center was created early in the century by a committee of clothing manufacturers working with investors and a major real estate developer. The manufacturers had outgrown their small shops and factories on the Lower East Side and needed to expand. They wanted to move into a new, mostly undeveloped area of the burgeoning city. Between 1918 and 1921, 50 to 60 manufacturers moved uptown to Seventh Avenue along the west side of Manhattan. With more room for expansion in the new area, these entrepreneurs were able to parlay a baby business into a mature industry.

New York City, already a major industrial center, was well positioned to capitalize on the ready-to-wear boom. A large pool of cheap, immigrant labor was available. In addition, New York was ideally located near the textile producers in New England and the South. It was also a port city, so imported textiles could be brought in when needed. By 1923, the city was producing 80 percent of all women's apparel, with 20 percent still being done by home sewers and custom tailors. The 1920s and 1930s saw the emergence of several large clothing manufacturers.

Although New York remains the fashion capital of the United States and an international fashion center, sportswear and activewear manufacturers are booming in California, especially in Los Angeles.

Unionization

The history of the women's apparel business cannot be told without also describing the growth and influence of the clothing unions. The success of the industry in the early 20th century came about largely because the manufacturers were able to draw upon a substantial supply of immigrant labor. The industry was dominated by Jewish and Italian workers. In 1910, 55 percent of garment workers were Jewish, 35 percent were Italian, and 10 percent were from other groups. Many of the immigrants had no skills, but a sizable number had trained as dressmakers or tailors in their homelands. Skilled and unskilled labor was needed in the garment industry, which seemed to have gotten big overnight. The opportunity to turn a large and quick profit was enormous, at least for the owners.

At the other end of the scale, unfortunately, were the workers, who worked long hours for very little pay under conditions that were totally unregulated. A typical garment factory was dark, overcrowded, unsanitary, and unsafe (see Figure 8.2).

In 1900, the workers began to unionize, a move they saw as their only chance to improve their working conditions. The International Ladies Garment Workers Union (ILGWU) was formed, and it remained the major garment industry union until its merger with the Amalgamated Clothing and Textile Workers

FIGURE 8.2
Early apparel factories, called sweatshops, used hand sewers. Very few of these factories even had sewing machines.
Corbis-Bettmann.

Union in 1995. The Union of Needletrades, Industrial, & Textile Employees, or UNITE, as the new organization is known, now represents the vast majority of workers in basic apparel and textiles, as well as millinery, shoes, and gloves.

Unionization did not happen overnight, and employers resisted the new union's demands as much as they could. Strikes in 1909 and 1910 paved the way for collective bargaining, but public sympathy for the ladies' garment workers was not aroused until the devastating Triangle Shirtwaist Factory fire in 1911. One hundred forty-six workers, most of them young women, were killed. A tragedy of massive proportions, it nonetheless lent strength to the union movement.

At last people began to realize that the union stood for more than collective bargaining, that indeed many of its demands revolved around matters of life and death. The union's new strength opened the door to many concessions that helped the workers, such as strict building codes and protective labor laws. Child labor was outlawed.

The ILGWU managed to survive the Depression years. Under the guidance of David Dubinsky, who took the helm in 1932 and held it for 34 years, the ILGWU enjoyed a period of expansion, and the garment industry underwent a period of innovative growth. ILGWU negotiated a 35-hour, 5-day work week and paid vacations. It instituted health, welfare, and pension programs and financed housing projects and recreation centers.

From 1975 until the 1995 merger, the ILGWU fought imports—the first real threat to the American women's apparel industry in several decades—with its "Look for the Union Label" campaign. As part of UNITE, it actively supports the current "Crafted With Pride in U.S.A." campaign and the movement to abolish sweatshops at home and abroad (see Chapter 16).

Organization and Operation of the Women's Apparel Industry

For many decades, the typical women's apparel company was a small, independently owned, and often family-run, business. Unlike the automobile industry, no Ford or General Motors dominated the women's apparel industry. In the early 1970s, about 5,000 firms made women's dresses. The industry's power came from its collective size. Its 5,000 firms did $3 billion in business every year.

All this changed in the 1970s. An expanding economy led to increased demand for everything, including clothing. Many of the textile companies had grown into huge businesses, as had several major retailers. Pushed from both directions, the clothing manufacturers responded by merging to create large publicly owned corporations.

Within a few years, it became obvious that many of the large corporations and conglomerates were not as successful as the smaller companies had been. The major problem was that the giants lacked the ability to respond quickly, a necessity in the fashion industry. Those that have survived and prospered have combined the advantages of large and small size by having divisions and subsidiaries function independently within the larger structure.

Regardless of whether a company is part of a conglomerate or a family-owned shop, the way in which clothes are produced does not vary. The operation of the apparel industry remains remarkably similar from business to business. The organization of the industry is currently undergoing changes, however. After years of specialization, the emergence of giant apparel producers has brought diversification. A number of the giants have divisions manufacturing men's wear, children's wear, home fashions, and accessories. Some began by serving a discreet segment of the women's apparel market. For example, Liz Claiborne started with fashionable but affordable business dresses and branched out into Liz Sport, Liz Wear, Elisabeth (for plus-size), shoes, accessories, and even men's wear. Other fashion businesses branched *into* women's wear. Ralph Lauren, who began his career designing neckties, subsequently began a women's line to parallel his men's wear designs. Nike and Reebok expanded from manufacturing athletic footwear to producing men's and women's activewear to go with their lines of shoes.

Size of Producers

The legacy of the mergers and acquisitions of the 1980s is a bottom line mentality. The trend toward giantism shows no signs of letting up. It will continue, if for no other reason than the economy demands it. This means that as some firms strive to become giants, many small- and medium-sized firms will be swallowed up or will go out of business because they cannot compete. But those giants that give their subsidiaries and divisions the autonomy needed to serve their markets and thereby get to the bottom line can expect to continue to prosper. One example of a giant apparel firm that is growing is the VF Corporation, which designs, manufactures, and markets apparel for women, men, and children, with the following brand names: Lee, Wrangler, Riders, Rustler, Chic, Gitano, Vanity Fair, Vassarette, Bolero, Healthtex, North Face, Jantzen, and Jansport, among others.

Specialization by Product

Apparel producers have typically been specialists, producing apparel for a particular lifestyle, for a particular size range, and a specific price range. Nowhere in the industry is this more true than in women's wear, the segment with the largest, most varied, and fastest changing market. A woman's coat manufacturer, for example, seldom makes dresses, and a dress manufacturer does not turn out bathing suits. This is completely hidden from the customer by the growing practice of putting national brands and licensed designer names on a wide variety of merchandise—from evening gowns to bathing suits to shoes to perfume to sheets.

Despite a move toward greater diversification, producers and retailers still have to think and work like specialists. For instance, retail buyers still shop one group of producers for formals, another for rainwear, and still another for maternity wear—and this is not likely to change in the future.

The Role of Designers

Designers, too, must balance diversification with specialization. From superstars to the new generation struggling to be recognized, all designers specialize to the extent that they are marketing their own artistic identity to a segment of the population that shares their vision (see Figure 8.3).

Today, as designers from the United States show in Paris and Milan, and European and Japanese designers show in New York, fashion conscious consumers have a virtually limitless choice of looks they can adopt. There is the street-smart hip-hop style of P. Diddy; the casual, gentrified elegance of Ralph Lauren; the spare, clean look of Jil Sander; the meeting of Asian and Western sensibilities in the designs of Issey Miyake; and the luxury and sumptuousness of Giorgio Armani. The established designers of upscale lines not only cater to the people who can afford their clothing but also lead the way for producers of more moderately priced fashion in interpreting trends in fashion and popular culture.

FIGURE 8.3
At the end of another successful show, Oscar de la Renta receives applause for his unique designs in women's apparel.
Courtesy, Fairchild Publications, Inc.

Categories in Women's Apparel

The following are the basic categories in women's apparel and the types of garments generally included in each are organized in Table 8.1.

The categories of outerwear, suits, dresses, and blouses, have been fixtures in the women's ready-to-wear industry from the beginning, and sportswear and separates has been an important category since the 1930s. Jeans are considered a separate category by many manufacturers and retailers, because of their unique position in Americans' wardrobes. The uniforms and aprons category fills a consumer need but does not set fashion trends. The same is true of the category for special needs.

Increasing attention to the categories of activewear, formal or after-five wear, bridal wear, and maternity deserve further discus-sion. Along with apparel for the physically-challenged, these categories may be thought of as small market segments or "niche" markets, that can be grouped by lifesyle and interests.

TABLE 8.1 Basic Categories in Women's Apparel and the Types of Garments Included in Each Category

CATEGORY	TYPES OF GARMENTS
Outerwear	Coats, rainwear, jackets
Dresses	One- or two-piece designs and ensembles (a dress with a jacket or coat)
Blouses	Dress and tailored
Suits	Jacket/skirt and jacket/pants combinations
After-5 and evening clothes	Formal and prom gowns, and other dressy apparel; this is often called "special occasion"
Bridal wear	Gowns and dresses for brides, attendants, and mothers-of the-bride and groom
Sportswear and separates	Town-and-country and spectator sportswear, such as pants, shorts, tops, sweaters, skirts, shirts, jackets, casual dresses, and jumpsuits
Activewear	Clothing for participatory sports and athletic activities such as swimwear, tennis dresses, running suits, cycling shorts, exercise apparel, and skiwear
Uniforms and aprons	Aprons, smocks, housedresses, and a variety of uniforms
Maternity	Dresses, sportswear, evening clothes, suits, and blouses designed to accommodate the special needs of pregnant women
Innerwear	Brassieres, panties, shapewear, bodywear, sleepwear, and other intimate apparel (see Chapter 11)
Special needs	Dresses, slops, nightgowns, hosiery, and other intimate apparel designed with snaps or Velcro for ease of use by elderly or physically-challenged women

Activewear

The "fitness craze" that emerged in the 1980s with workout programs on television and videotape intensified in the 1990s. People began flocking to gyms to work out before and after work, and travelers maintained their exercise routines in health clubs that became an essential hotel service. Jogging gained favor, and the New York and Boston marathons became national news. Women's sports received a boost in public attention with the formation of the Women's National Basketball Association and the Supreme Court ruling that universities accepting federal funding must offer equal athletic opportunities for male and female students.

All of these developments contributed to the growth of the market for comfortable and fashionable apparel for specific sports and exercise activities (see Figure 8.4a and b). Leading producers of activewear are the athletic shoe companies Nike, Reebok, and Addidas, all of which have developed lines of clothing. By the late 1990s and early 2000s, their women's apparel divisions were given equal attention with the men's. Performance features are emphasized in the styling and fabrication; spandex, nylon, and polyester are favored for their durability, light weight, and water resistance. The growing popularity in women's sports, coupled with women-specific fitness Web sites and awareness, has been a key tool in the promotion of this merchandise.[2]

Swimwear has been an important segment of the women's apparel industry for decades, and the business has evolved somewhat differently from that for other activewear. Fashion features are much more important than they are for some of the sport-specific activewear because

A

B

FIGURE 8.4A AND B *(a) Yogini Shiva Rea with The Weekend Exercise Co. and (b) Nike have developed popular yogawear apparel for women.* Courtesy, Fairchild Publications, Inc.

the look is a primary function. As Kim Ross, Lands' End's swimwear merchandiser put it, "Swimwear is the most revealing piece of apparel that we wear."[3]

Some of the fabrics that are used in other activewear are also used in swimsuits, but for a different purpose. Lycra, for example, provides control that improves the appearance of the fit. The biggest U.S. manufacturers of swimwear continue to be such specialists as Cole of California, Jantzen, and Catalina, which produce designer brands through licensing agreements, as well as producing their own lines.

Skiwear for women is a growing business, providing better fit, appealing colors, and female-friendly "bathroom zippers."[4] Now that women make up a quarter of the snowboarder market, specialized clothes to accommodate the active moves of this new sport are being produced by small new companies like Cold As Ice and Betty Rides. Larger companies that produce men's gear are also entering this market, among them Burton's and Sims.

Formal Wear

Despite the growing casualness of everyday apparel, people all over the world still like to mark special occasions by wearing formal clothing. Elegant fabrics, trim, and silhouettes—worn with more elaborate jewelry, watches, and other accessories—mark most formal wear. This category is often called "after-5" or "special occasion."

Designers like Bob Mackie and Roberto Cavalli specialize in dressing Hollywood stars for opening nights and award ceremonies; thousands of women across the country want similar looks for weddings, dances, and formal dinners.

It is interesting to note that evening wear gets more media coverage than any other category; especially at the Oscars, the Tony Awards, the VH1 awards, and similar events.

Picking out a prom dress has become a coming-of-age ritual in many parts of the United States, not unlike the formal "coming out" party ritual for debutantes—as well as a solid source of income for many manufacturers and retailers.

Bridal Wear

Bridal wear has always been a category for a personal fashion statement, both for brides and designers. The tradition of the haute couture runway shows in Paris is to conclude with the modeling of a bridal gown, and some designers, such as Vera Wang, are known primarily for their work in this category (see Figure 8.5). Weddings of movie stars, royalty, and other celebrities often inspire trends in bridal fashions, but the range of available styles runs from modern interpretations of Victorian designs to

FIGURE 8.5
Vera Wang offers a wide range of fashionable gowns for the modern bride.
Courtesy, Fairchild Publications, Inc.

unadorned slip dresses. Hemlines range from the traditional floor length to street length to mini, and variety appears even in color. The rising age of first-time brides and the increase in the number of second weddings in recent years has contributed to the popularity of sophisticated styles.

The average bride who has a formal wedding spends more than $800 for her gown,[5] and it may be the only clothing purchase she ever has custom-fitted. If her taste is for beading or other details that require extensive handwork, the price may rise to several thousand dollars. Thus, compared to other apparel categories, the business depends more on the high price of one-time purchases and less on volume. Bridal wear is typically retailed in bridal salons in department stores and in specialized apparel stores, some of which also carry lines of evening wear. Kleinfeld, one of the best-known bridal stores located in Brooklyn, New York, has added petite and plus-size styles, in addition to enlarging the store's assortment of shoes and evening wear. Discounted and rental gowns remain a small percentage of wedding dresses, but they are growing.

Maternity

Now that two out of three pregnant women stay on the job almost the entire nine months of their pregnancies, pregnant career women have become an important and growing submarket, and the whole maternity category is receiving new emphasis. The large number of women of childbearing age has also contributed to renewed interest in maternity fashion (see Figure 8.6).

Mothers Work is the leading designer, manufacturer, and marketer of maternity fashion in the United States, with over 750 locations nationwide and growing. They own leading brands Motherhood Maternity, Mimi Maternity, Mimi Essentials for Maternity, A "Pea in the Pod," and Motherhood Outlets. They offer online Internet retailing at www.maternitymall.com.

Maternity clothing is one of the merchandise categories that has benefited from online sales. Some retailers, like the Gap, sell maternity clothes online only where the merchandise can attract an audience nationwide.

Size Ranges

Women's apparel is divided into several size ranges. Unfortunately, the industry has not yet developed standard industry-wide size measurements for each of these ranges, although exploratory work has been undertaken in this direction. In many cases, the manufacturer has the pattern made to fit its targeted customer's approximate size measurement. This is why one manufacturer's misses' size 12 is likely to fit

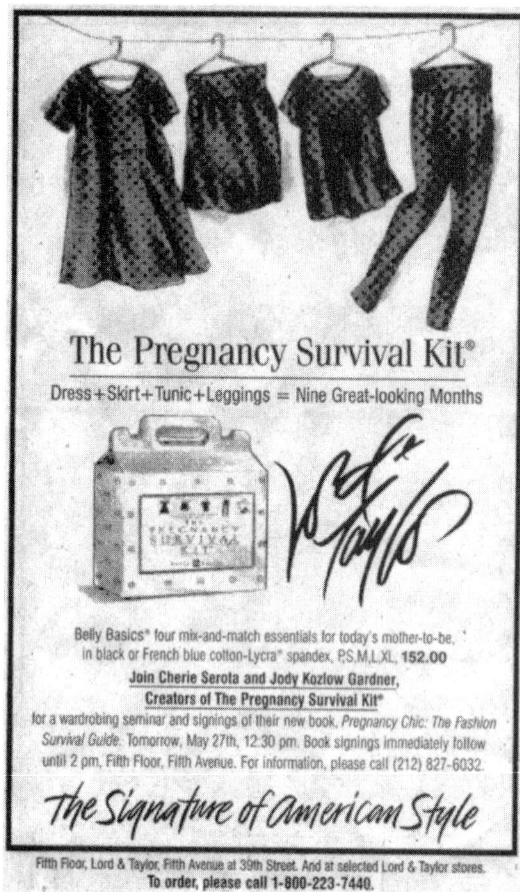

FIGURE 8.6
Style, sophistication, and comfort are the major points in today's maternity wear. There are styles to fit many lifestyles!
Courtesy, Lord & Taylor.

quite differently from another manufacturer's misses' size 12. With licensing agreements and offshore production playing an increasing role in apparel manufacturing, even two different styles bearing the same label in the same size may fit differently.

Women's wear is produced in the following size ranges:

- *Misses*—Includes regular even-numbered sizes 4 to 20, tall sizes 12 to 20, and sometimes sizes as small as 0-2.
- *Juniors*—Includes regular sizes 5 to 17 and petite sizes 1 to 15.
- *Petites*—Includes misses' even-numbered sizes 2P to 16P and junior sizes 1P to 15P.
- *Womens and Women's Petites*—Includes even-numbered sizes 12WP to 26WP, straight sizes 26 to 52, and XL to 5X.

Misses

Misses' sizes are cut to fit the average adult woman's figure. Most women who are between 5 feet, 5 inches and 5 feet, 9 inches tall and of average weight can find suitably proportioned sizes in this range. You may hear the term "missy" used to describe this size range.

Juniors

The juniors' range was introduced in the 1950s by Anne Fogarty, whose Anne Fogarty Five was designed to fit a slimmer, shorter-waisted figure than the women's size 6, which was the smallest readily available size at the time. Because the junior figure is more common among teenagers than fully developed women, much of the apparel in this range has youthful styling, and many of the customers in junior departments and stores are teenagers.

Because many of the first baby boomers had their children at a relatively late age, the teen population began to grow rapidly in the mid-1990s, and it is expected to continue to do so well into the 21st century. American teenagers, especially the girls, typically spend a third of their income on clothes. In 1996, junior apparel sales amounted to $9.7 billion.[6] Companies like Wet Seal/Contempo, Rampage, and XOXO are responding to the growth of the junior market, as is the specialized junior's catalog, dELiA. Clearly, this segment of market promises great opportunities for producers and retailers.

Petites

Forty-seven million women are estimated to be under 5 feet 4 inches tall and thus in need of small sizes; a statistic that has caused rapid growth in market for this size range.

Proportioned for short, small-boned women who wear sizes zero to eight, petite sizes are worn by both junior and misses' customers. Not only are the skirts and pants legs shorter than in regular-sized apparel; the sleeves are shorter, and details such as collars, and pockets are scaled down.

In 1980, Evan-Picone, Inc., created a separate division of petite-sized apparel, and other manufacturers, including Jones New York, Liz Claiborne, and Levi Strauss, quickly followed this example. Separate petite departments in department stores and women's wear specialty stores are now the norm, and stores devoted entirely to apparel in this size range have been around since the 1975 opening of Petite Sophisticate.

The influx of immigrants from Southeast Asia after the Vietnam War and the growing population of Hispanic Americans indicate that this size range will continue to be profitable.

Women's and Women's Petites

Approximately one third of all women in the United States wears women's sizes 16 through 20, 26-52, and XL to 5X, and women's petites sizes 12WP to 26WP which are designed to fit shorter women with a fuller bust and shorter waistline (see Figure 8.7). Until recently however, apparel in these sizes made up a small percentage of production, and were notable for their lack of style. This has all changed! Designers and manufacturers got on the bandwagon, and labels like Liz Claiborne, Dana Buchman, and Eileen Fisher began making stylish clothes for larger-sized women.

The large size apparel market rose 10 percent in 2000 to $27 billion and is expected to top $35 billion by the mid-2000s. Industry watchers say the plus-size apparel market for women is one of the fastest growing sectors in retails. Department stores took the lead, moving larger sizes to their main apparel shopping floors. It is estimated that 30 percent of clothes in larger sizes are private-label or store brands.

Many specialty retailers have also begun to woo this customer. Talbots started "Talbots Woman" as a store dedicated to larger sizes, and the Gap and Old Navy are offering clothing through size 20. Lands' End and L. L. Bean, leading catalog companies, have devoted special catalogs to these customers and their business has been overwhelming. Both Catherine's and Lane Bryant, part of the Charming Shoppes Co., have had a staggering increase in their plus-size business.

With celebrities like Rosie O'Donnell, Delta Burke, and Star Jones appearing on television regularly, the new look of the stylish and sophisticated plus-size woman has been reinforced. Adding to the availability of stylish plus-size fashion is the one-stop shopping offered on the Internet. One Web site—www.Plusssize.com—features over 35 plus-size merchants, including Liz Claiborne and Lands' End, as well as merchandise from Nordstrom, Chadwicks, and Spiegel. This Web site offers fashion conscious, plus-size women around the world a welcoming community where they can share their joys and frustrations about being full figured in a "thin is in" world.[7]

FIGURE 8.7 *Emme provides stylish apparel geared toward the plus-size consumer.* Courtesy, Fairchild Publications, Inc.

Wholesale Price Points

Women's apparel is produced and marketed at a wide range of wholesale prices. Major factors contributing to the wholesale price of a garment are:

- The quality of materials
- The quality of workmanship
- The amount and type of labor required in the production process
- The executive and sales position structure of the organization
- Showroom rent and business overhead

Major Price Zones

Within the wide range of prices, however, there are certain traditional **price zones**, or series of somewhat contiguous price lines that appeal to specific target groups of customers. The women's ready-to-wear market has six major price zones. In order from the most to least expensive, they are as follows:

1. *Designer Signature.* The highest price zone includes lines by such name designers as Ralph Lauren, Oscar de la Renta, Calvin Klein, Donna Karan, Jean-Paul Gaultier, and John Galliano. A jacket alone costs more than $1,500.
2. *Bridge.* This zone is so named because it bridges the price ranges between designer and better prices. Bridge merchandise usu-

ally costs one-third to one-half of designer prices; or $800 to $1,000 for a three-piece outfit. A jacket alone costs about $300.[8] Some designers who produce lines at the designer signature zone or at lower zones also have bridge lines. Examples include Tommy by Tommy Hilfiger, Donna Karan's DKNY, Calvin Klein's CK, Armani's Mani, and Emanuel Ungaro's Emanuel. Ellen Tracy, Tahari, Dana Buchman, Eileen Fisher, and Andrea Jovine are positioned as bridge companies.

3. *Contemporary.* This new zone is favored by young designers who want to enter the market with innovative, designer-quality lines but, at the same time, seek a broader market than that of the designer signature zone. By using less expensive fabrics and locating in lower-rent spaces, they can offer their lines at lower prices.[9] Jackets wholesale from $90 to $120. "Contemporary is definitely growing at the store level, but it is sandwiched in between bridge and better," says Mark Mendelson of Laundry by Shelli Segal.[10] Labels in this zone include Laundry by Shelli Segal, Vivienne Tam, Cynthia Rowley, Geronimo, Susan Lazar, Catalyst, and Misc.
4. *Better.* Apparel in this zone is usually medium to high in price. Familiar labels include Liz Claiborne, Chaus, Nautica, Evan-Picone, Harvé Benard, J. H. Collectibles, Karen Kane, and Jones New York. They appeal to a middle-class market, offering fashionable clothes at an affordable price. A jacket sells for about $160.[11]
5. *Moderate.* As the name suggests, this zone includes lines of nationally advertised makers, such as Guess, Esprit, Levi Strauss, Jantzen, Alfred Dunner, J.G. Hook, Ellen Figg, Inc., and Leslie Fay, which have less prestige than lines with designer names but still appeal to middle-class consumers. More firms are moving into this price zone, among them are Halston's Lifestyle sportswear line and the Emma James line from Liz Claiborne. Wholesale prices for a two-piece outfit run about $39.[12] Moderate merchandise is sold mostly in chain stores or in main-floor departments in department stores.
6. *Budget.* The lowest price zone is sometimes referred to as the "promotional" or "mass" market. It includes some national brand names such as Wrangler, Donkenny, and Judy Bond Blouses, but is primarily a mass market retailer private label such as JCPenney's Arizona line of jeans or Sears' Canyon River Blues line of jeans, or Kmart's Jaclyn Smith line.

A recent development is the emergence of a seventh price zone, the new high end, for the super-rich. Some designers are trading up, offering special pieces in very limited quantities, at astronomical prices. This range is aimed at people who crave exclusivity, and have the means to afford it. Ralph Lauren calls his line of hand-tailored women's classic suits and sportswear in luxury fabrics the Purple Label Custom Collection (see Figure 8.8). Donna Karan offers a Limited Edition label with her signature, on dresses costing $5,000 to $6,000.[13] Carolyn Herrera, Bill Blass, and Oscar de la Renta are also known for developing exclusive designs for special customers.

Multiple Price Zones

Some producers offer merchandise in several price zones to capture a share of the business in each of several market segments. Manufacturer/retailer firms such as The Limited and the Gap cater to different price zone markets in each of their

FIGURE 8.8
This print ad for Ralph Lauren's Purple Label Collection stresses the high quality appropriate for a high-end designer label.
Courtesy, Ralph Lauren.

Then & Now

Celebrity Apparel: The Survival of the Fittest

Jennifer Lopez is about to find out if she is a survivor! J. Lo is a collection named for her in the latest in a long string of celebrity named fashion lines. Back in the 1950s, Gloria Swanson licensed a "Forever Young" dress line, and celebrities have been at it ever since. While the past 50 years have been filed with a number of success stories, the fashion graveyard is filled with star names that were not able to parley their fame into a major apparel success.

The winners, although with varying life spans and degrees, have been Jacklyn Smith, Kathy Ireland, Kathi Lee, Cheryl Tiegs, Esther Williams, Gloria Venderbilt, and Delta Burke.The losers, usually short lived, have been Diahann Carrol, Nike Taylor, Marilyn Monroe, and Roseanne. Despite such failures, or the risk that a celebrity's off screen activities might cause some embarrassment, the allure of fashion continues to entice them. The celebrity phenomenon seems more prevalent in the men's market, where Arnold Palmer, Jack Nicklaus, Bruce Jenna, Michael Jordan, and Tiger Woods are among the scores of athletes to lend their names to sportswear.

Newcomers to the celebrity apparel scene include Christy Turlington, Emma, and Venus Williams who signed a reported $40 million, five-year deal with Reebok. In 2002, the Venus collection — apparel that can be worn on or off the tennis court—was offered at retail stores throughout the country.

With all the problems along the road to a successful star-powered brand, it's not as easy as putting a celebrity name on a line and collecting royalties. According to industry executives, the most important ingredient in the success of the line is the products' integrity. The line must stay true to its customers, and it's a big plus when the celebrity gets a lot of media exposure, has input into the line's design, and helps with marketing and advertising.

Celebrity apparel deals depend mostly on the cultural appeal of the celebrity. Jennifer Lopez certainly has broad appeal—teens and adults, and male and female—all love her and want her to succeed. Let's see how J.Lo makes it—in five years – in ten years– or more!

Source:

Lisa Lockwood, "Celebrity Apparel: Survival of the Fittest," *Women's Wear Daily*, March 3, 2001.

Gloria Swanson, 1950.

Courtesy, © Sunset Boulevard/Corbis Sigma.

"J.LO" models her own line of clothing.

Courtesy, © AP Photo/Jill Connelly.

member store chains. Merchandise at The Limited stores appeals to a higher income customer than that at Lerner's. The Gap's stores have a somewhat overlapping price zone structure with Banana Republic merchandise at its highest zones, the Gap catering to the middle of its market, and Old Navy at its low end.

Designers also produce lines segmented by price zone. For example, DKNY is the label of Donna Karan's bridge collection; the Donna Karan label is reserved for her lines in the designer price zone, and the Limited Edition label for her custom-made collection. Ralph Lauren is another designer with lines in several different price zones. In descending order a partial list of his lines are Ralph Lauren Purple Label Collection, Ralph Lauren, RL, Polo Sport, Black Label, and Polo.

Off-price apparel stores, which sell name-brand and designer merchandise at prices well below traditional department store levels, are putting increasing pressure on all the traditional price zones, especially moderate to better. These outlets, such as Marshalls, T. J. Maxx, Filene's Basement, and Loehmanns, are thriving because customers are aware of the price zones associated with the labels and realize they are getting a bargain, though perhaps not this season's look (see Figure 8.9). Factory outlets offer prices similar to those found in off-price stores, but the merchandise is limited to the goods of a single producer.

Perhaps the most compelling reason a consumer would be willing to pay full retail price at a traditional department or specialty store is the availability of a broad assortment of styles, sizes, and colors from the beginning of each season. Generally the stock in off-price and factory outlets is limited to merchandise that was not ordered earlier by stores charging full retail price.

Private Labels

Traditional department and specialty stores can also compete in pricing by developing their own private labels. Much of this merchandise is priced in the better price zone but the quality is comparable to that of designer signature or bridge apparel. Some of the same manufacturers who produce the name-brand merchandise that a store is selling at higher prices also make the store's private label goods. Private label merchandise is vigorously promoted to develop brand recognition, and some customers do not distinguish between private and national brands when they shop. For example, when the Federated conglomerate bought Macy's, it distributed Macy's Charter Club and other private labels in some of its other member stores. Many shoppers are only dimly aware of these stores' connection with each other, but those who develop brand loyalty automatically become loyal customers of the stores that carry the private label.

Seasonal Classifications

In addition to classifying women's apparel by function, size, and price zone, retailers and producers also pay attention to season. This classification is different from the others, however, in that few businesses specialize in just one season. Even swimwear is sold in the winter resort season as well as the summer.

The major apparel seasons correspond to the calendar, with the semiannual designer runway shows introducing fall/winter and spring/summer

FIGURE 8.9
Filene's Basement Stores, an off-price apparel retailer, keeps the merchandise coming and going—coming from apparel manufacturers, going as purchased by customers.
Ad provided by Filene's Basement.

FASHION FOCUS

American Trailblazers

From Hollywood to the White House to Madison Avenue, American designers have cleared an impressive path to success. Along every step of the journey of American fashion, there have been trailblazers—those designers who stepped out from the back rooms to greet their clients, the ones who followed their own design instincts rather than the dictates of Paris, those who forged their own retail paths, and those who created the first megabrands. These American fashion trailblazers inspired and carved a path for future generations.

The Dreamers

In the 1920s, American fashion was more about textile and garment manufacturing than a concept of design. But on the West Coast, there were dreamers. Costume designers like Edith Head, Travis Benton, and Irene Sharaff created the inspiration for a generation of designers who grew up watching movies, from the *Wizard of Oz* with Dorothy's gingham pinafore designed by Adrian, to *All About Eve* with Sharaff's elegantly wicked designs for Bette Davis.

In the 1920s, 1930s, and 1940s people went to the movies to see clothes they never had imagined before, and before they knew it, the clothes were in the stores.

The First Wave

During World War II, designers in New York came into their own, led by names like Claire McCardell, Hattie Carnegie, Adele Simpson, Vera Maxwell, Adrian, and Charles James. McCardell and Bonnie Cashin designed easy, utilitarian sportswear that was an early example of the difference between the Americans and the structured, more formal European designers.

The Founding Members

Most labels made before the 1960s bore the name of the manufacturer, not that of the designer. Oscar de la Renta from Elizabeth Arden and Bill Blass from Maurice Rentner were among the first to challenge the system, a change that precipitated the founding of the Council of Fashion Designers of America in 1962. Among the founders were designers who through their efforts established fashion as an art form, and went on to become celebrities.

Rudi Gernreich shocked the world with his topless swimsuit and became famous! "What was important to us was that fashion would be perceived as an art form," said de la Renta.

The Politicians

American First Ladies have been style inspiration for many decades. They have brought fame to designers like James Galanos, Arnold Scassi, Adolpho, and Oleg Cassini. The First Ladies most imitated in recent times have been Nancy Reagan, Jackie Kennedy, and Laura Bush. However, Mami Eisenhower and her "pie-crust" hat, Bess Truman and her matronly dress, Eleanor Roosevelt and her "upswept" hairdo, and Hiliary Clinton vacillating between glamorous and dowdy have not had an impact on the style inspiration of American women.

The Practicals

Liz Claiborne, Perry Ellis, Kasper, Anne Klein, and Willi Smith pioneered the concept of branding affordable clothes, leading to the rise of moderate, better, and bridge-price categories. Claiborne became famous for dressing career women with a new interrelating-separates concept. Ellis, one of the industry's most endearing legends, believe that people show not take fashion too seriously, and Anne Klein, who started her career in juniors, was an early proponent of building the American sportswear concept went on to help launch the careers of other important designers, including Donna Karan, Louis Dell'Orio, and Narciso Rodriguez.

The Megabrands

Donna Karan, Ralph Lauren, Calvin Klein, and Tommy Hilfiger have built fashion empires based upon carefully designed lifestyle aesthetics. For Donna Karan it is refined elements of luxury. Calvin Klein drives a clean ideal of minimalism and sexuality. Ralph Lauren is the preppy, moneyed dreamer, aspiring to the good life. And Tommy Hilfiger is the all-American kid next door, waving the red, white, and blue. For these four pioneers, success hasn't always been easy, but they built the business blueprints for today's approach to the rewards of success.

Bonnie Cashin

Oscar de la Renta

Tommy Hilfiger

collections, each a half-year in advance of the time when the new fashions appear on the retail selling floor. Within the fall season are the holiday season, which features evening wear for New Year's Eve, and the resort season, when cruise wear and swimsuits are the focus of attention. The spring/summer season has its emphasis on summer. In temperate climates with seasonal temperature changes, spring weather does not last long. Therefore, lightweight topcoats and linen suits in dark colors have less of a market than apparel designed for warmer weather.

Merchandising and Marketing

Most fashion producers sell directly to retail stores rather than through intermediaries. The pace of fashion in all but a few staple items is much too fast to allow for the selling, reselling, or warehousing activities of wholesale distributors or jobbers.

As a result, women's apparel producers aim their sales promotion efforts at both retailers and consumers. Such efforts take the form of advertising, publicity, and sales promotion. (Chapter 18 discusses the collaborative marketing efforts of producers and retailers from the retailers' perspective.)

Advertising

Today most retail advertising of women's fashion apparel carries the name of the manufacturer. But this was not always the case. Until the 1930s, many retailers refused to let manufacturers put any tags or labels on the clothes they made. Merchandise shortages during World War II, coupled with government regulations, helped to reverse this situation. Most merchants are now happy to capitalize on the producers' labels that are attached to clothes. They feature manufacturers' names in their own advertising and displays and set up special sections within stores that are exclusively devoted to individual producers' lines.

The apparel manufacturing industry spends less than one percent of its annual sales on advertising, but the exposure given to its products is impressive. After all, that one percent is usually based on very healthy sales figures.

The 1980s saw a tremendous growth in sales for national brands and nationally known designer labels. In part, this resulted from national advertising campaigns directed at consumers. National brands and designer labels continued to predominate in the industry in the 1990s and 2000s, with no signs of a change in this trend.

Print Advertising

Fashion and general-interest magazines and newspapers are prime outlets for apparel advertising, as are trade publications such as *Women's Wear Daily*, with its large circulation among retailers. Fashion magazines provide another forum for exposure, largely directed to the customer, with editorial reports about clothes and fashion trends of the season and with both United States and international coverage.

Considering the amount of money that goes into advertising, and the use that retailers are now willing to make of manufacturer's names, it is not surprising that cooperative advertising appears both in magazines and newspapers and now also in store catalogs, such as those from Federated Department Stores.

Broadcast Advertising

Because radio is dominated by local stations and because it lacks the visual element, it is not the medium of choice for product advertising of apparel. Mention of brand names or categories of clothing usually take the form of retailers' spot commercials advertising a sale or the arrival of new seasonal merchandise.

Television advertising of women's wear is dominated by large producers, such as Levi Strauss, and national retail chains, such as Sears and JCPenney, which can afford the expense of producing the commercials and purchasing network air time. Locally broadcast spot announcements are sometimes paid for with cooperative advertising dollars. The commercial is produced for the manufacturer with a voice track that can be changed to name the retail outlet that is advertising as a source of the brand.

Cable TV advertising is less expensive than network TV, and is used by smaller manufacturers and retailers of women's wear, especially on cable channels with programming directed to women, such as Lifetime Cable.

Large producers are also showing ads that look like movie trailers in movie theaters across the country.

Other Electronic Advertising

The Internet is exploding with advertising for apparel of all kinds, as even very small manufacturers and retailers develop their own sites.

Designers are offering their fans more detailed information on their collections, and pushing their lifestyle visions. See the discussion under "Industry Trends" at the end of this chapter.

Publicity

In addition to the enormous amount of money spent on advertising, apparel producers also use publicity to promote their names. Many manufacturers, especially in the designer area, retain the services of a public relations firm, whose primary job is to ensure coverage in the editorial pages of magazines and newspapers. Cable television is another source of editorial coverage for designers; C-Span, MTV, and VH-1 broadcast fashion programs that feature designers who cater to their audiences' tastes. VH-1 gives annual Fashion Awards that are extremely influential.

Manufacturers also supply sports personalities and other celebrities with clothes in an attempt to attract public attention. One rarely watches a sports event these days without seeing and hearing mention of the brand names, not only of the equipment being used but also of the apparel that is worn, along with endorsements from leading athletes.

Fashion Shows, Press Weeks, and Trade Shows

The major public relations effort in women's wear goes into the presentations and fashion shows at which designers show their new collections for retailers and the fashion reporters for the press, and the broadcast and Internet media.

The shows provide the country's newspaper, magazine, radio, television, and Internet fashion editors and reporters an opportunity to examine the newest American designer collections as well as those of leading European manufacturers. Editors are deluged with press releases and photo and interview opportunities that will help them tell the fashion stories to their readers. Initially, there were "press weeks" that followed the formal line openings where designers exhibited merchandise lines in all price categories specially to the press rather than to buyers. Gradually, however, the lower-priced merchandise was eliminated. Press weeks as exclusive showcases for high-priced fashion continued; then, as a result of cost and timing factors, they were eliminated. Now the press sees the collections at the same time as the retailers do.

To coordinate shows of their new lines during market weeks, the manufacturers who lease permanent or temporary showroom space at the major regional markets in Los Angeles, Dallas, Miami, Atlanta, and Seattle depend on the services of the management of their market buildings. New York designers (including foreign designers with New York showrooms) are not housed in a single site, so they have joined together to form 7th on Sixth, an organization that manages the fashion week shows that are staged in Bryant Park in New York City. IMG sponsors an annual award show that attracts international press and broadcast coverage. The giant MAGIC show for women's wear is held semiannually in Las Vegas. The B.A.T. Woman Show for plus and tall sizes has become an international hit. Other major international women's wear shows include those held semianually in Paris, London, Milan, Tokyo, and Hong Kong. These shows are discussed in more detail in Chapter 15.

Trunk Shows

Trunk shows are another excellent form of publicity for the women's apparel industry. **Trunk shows** present a manufacturer's line to a retail store's sales staff and its customers (see Figure 8.10). A representative of the company, sometimes a designer, typically mounts a fashion show of sample garments. After the show, he or she meets with customers to discuss the styles and their fashion relevance. The retail store's customers may review items they have seen and order them.

Everyone benefits from trunk shows. Customers see clothes as the designer planned them and coordinated them, and they experience some of the glamour of the fashion industry. The retailer enjoys the dramatic influx of customers who come to such personal appearances and shows and any profits that result as clothes are ordered. The manufacturer tests the line on real customers and in order to understand real consumers' needs *firsthand*! If customer response is enthusiastic, the designer achieves new status—and bigger orders—from the retailer than otherwise expected.

Although trunk shows may mean headaches for designers, they still pack a punch when it comes to selling high-priced clothes. Designers say that trunk shows account for anywhere from 20 to 43 percent of a line's business. They also give the designer an opportunity to make a personal statement directly to the consumer. Oscar de la Renta says that trunk shows are

FIGURE 8.10
This "trunk show" by designer Donna Karan features the designer herself explaining her latest line.
Courtesy, Fairchild Publications, Inc.

very important because of the promotional impact, especially if the designer is working with licensees. At Linda Dresner's Boutique on Park Avenue, Luisa Beccaria sold $54,000 worth of merchandise during her two-day trunk show.[14]

Donna Karan joined the trunk show circuit when she began designing under her own name. Besides being good for profits, trunk shows seem to have a great effect on the designer's designs. Being able to see their clothes on the women who wear them, in the part of the country where they live, helps the designer find out what works and what does not.

Most of these clothes retail for over $500, making them investment dressing. Many designers say that store buyers have a limit on how much they may purchase from any one designer. At a trunk show, the consumer can see almost everything that the designer has created and is given a much larger choice and selection.

Videotapes and CD-Roms

Videotapes and CD-Roms that show off a manufacturer's line are another promotional tool. The manufacturers' and designers' seasonal premiers are videotaped with live models; a running commentary is then added by the manufacturer or designer. Videotapes are primarily shown to retailers' sales staffs to explain the fashion importance of items and to give tips on selling, but they are also sometimes shown on the selling floor.

Unfortunately, in-store showings of videotapes have not been the potential goldmine that manufacturers had hoped, perhaps because women who are already in the store to shop do not want to stand around and look at a videotape. Videotape producers have begun to zero in on their market, though, and fashion videotapes are now showing up in restaurants, hospitals, airports, doctors' and dentists' offices, and discos—all places that seem to be more conducive than the store to this form of entertainment. There is no charge to the apparel producer (the video user on location pays a use fee), so this amounts to another form of publicity for the fashion industry. But apparel manufacturers have not given up entirely on the idea of fashion videotapes.

Promotion Aids

Manufacturers also provide retailers with an assortment of other promotional aids designed to assist them and speed the sale of merchandise. A firm may offer any or all of the following:

- Display ideas
- Display and stock fixtures
- Advertising aids
- Reorder forms and assistance in checking stock for reordering purposes
- Educational and sales training assistance for salespersons and customers
- Promotional talks by producers' representatives
- Assistance in giving in-store fashion shows
- Statement enclosures or other ads designed to reach customers by mail
- Special retail promotions to tie in with national advertising campaigns
- Advertising mats for smaller stores
- Cooperative advertising funds from the manufacturer or the fiber association

Industry Trends

Throughout the coming decades, the U.S. women's apparel industry and the U.S. apparel industry overall will face dramatic changes. American designers have finally succeeded in rivaling designers from Paris and Milan as definers of high fashion. However, the American manufacturing industry faces what may be its toughest competitive challenge ever: the growth of a global clothing market out of which U.S. manufacturers must carve their market share, since a rise in imports has threatened the market they had enjoyed within the United States.

After decades of domination at home, the American wholesale market has been inundated with imports from countries with cheap labor. More and more U.S. manufacturers are using foreign labor, a process called global sourcing, in factories they own or lease in low-wage countries around the world. The U.S. apparel industry is taking steps, however, to enable it to compete more effectively in an increasingly global marketplace. Some of its tactics include:

- Emergence of manufacturers as retailers (see Figure 8.11)
- Greater emphasis on licensing
- Increased offshore production
- Increased emphasis on Quick Response
- Use of computers and the Internet

Manufacturers as Retailers

As discussed in Chapter 7, designer Ralph Lauren was the first designer to open his own retail store. Frustrated by the way department

FIGURE 8.11
Coach both manufactures and retails—a prime example of vertical integration.
Courtesy, The Coach Factory Store, San Marcos, Texas. Design: Brand + Allen.

and specialty stores were selling his clothes, he opened the first Polo/Ralph Lauren shop in 1971. Since then, his empire has grown to shops throughout the United States, Europe, and Asia. Because of his investment in the design and interior decoration of his stores, particularly the Madison Avenue store, Ralph Lauren's foray into retailing has benefitted his business more as a promotional tool for his fashion collections than as a source of income.[15] He still exercises tight control over the sale of his collections in stores-within-stores in the major department store chains. Today, dozens of designers have followed Ralph Lauren's example.

Other producer/retailers sell at retail exclusively through their own outlets. Benetton is one example; Talbots is another.

Which manufacturers will succeed as retailers remains to be seen. A producer first has to compete for good retail talent, which can be expensive, as well as retail space in a prime location. The risks escalate if the manufacturer franchises, which many must do because they cannot personally oversee their retail empire.

Licensing

As was discussed in Chapter 4, licensing, selling the right to produce merchandise bearing a designer's name, is a strategy of virtually every major American designer. In women's wear, some designers, like Donna Karan, have relatively few licensed products, while others, like J.G. Hook, are full-time licensors that produce nothing in house. Still others offer an extensive range of licensed accessories and home furnishings, while producing most apparel in house. Sometimes the revenue from licensed products exceeds that of the main business; it is rumored that some designer fragrances bring in far more than their signature apparel lines! Some manufacturers see licensing as a way to test market a new product category in a relatively low-risk way. If the new category succeeds, it may be brought in house for manufacture, once it has proved that it will sell.

See Table 8.2 for a list of selected fashion licenses in women's apparel.

Offshore Production

With their promise of delivering low cost, imports have made inroads into women's wear. Producers' associations such as the Crafted With Pride Council and labor unions such as

TABLE 8.2 Selected Fashion Licenses for Women's Apparel

Adrienne Vittadini
Anne Klein
Armani
Arnold Scaasi
B.U.M. Equipment
Benetton
Bill Blass
Bob Mackie
Bonjour
Calvin Klein
Carolina Herrera
Christian Dior
Donna Karan
Givenchy
Guess?
Halston
J.G. Hook
Jones New York
Natori
Nautica
Nicole Miller
Oscar de la Renta
Pierre Cardin
Ralph Lauren
Rampage
Todd Oldham
Wrangler

Source: Karen Raugust, *The Licensing Handbook* (Brooklyn, NY: EPM Publications), p. 24.

UNITE have been diligently applying the same anti-import pressure on behalf of the women's wear industry that they have applied on behalf of the textile, men's, and children's wear industries. Imports—particularly those involving textile and apparel—are seen as a major threat to the survival of the U.S. clothing industry.

The federal government is reluctant to impose any curbs on offshore production that might interfere with its role in keeping clothing prices (and inflation) down, and U.S.-owned manufacturers that benefit from the lower labor costs of overseas assembly naturally support policies that favor their operations. As good corporate citizens, however, many apparel manufacturers were quick to recognize the need for self-regulation when sweatshop conditions in third-world countries—and even in some domestic factories employing illegal aliens—came to light in the mid-1990s.

Buying foreign-made women's wear has many limitations. Very early commitment—as much as eight to nine months lead time, for example—is necessary. Usually there is no opportunity for reorders. These limitations have been siezed upon by U.S. manufacturers anxious to stem the tide of imports.

Increased Emphasis on Quick Response

American manufacturers who rely on domestic production facilities have several advantages over those who use global sourcing. Some of the cost savings of manufacturing in countries where labor is cheaper are reduced by import duties, so American manufacturers have learned to have the less labor-intensive operations performed at home. American garment workers trained to operate computerized equipment are skilled employees, and the difference between their wages and those of factory workers in low-income countries represents a difference in the job performed. Furthermore, the automation of production processes means that they can be completed more quickly. Add the speed of production to the time saved by not having to ship goods overseas, and the producer can offer retail customers Quick Response, a crucial consideration in the fashion business.

Use of Computers and the Internet

Another way U.S. fashion manufacturers attract business is through their use of computers, especially the Internet. As we have already discussed in Chapter 7, computerization is now an integral part of the production process, starting with designing. But with the Internet, it is also a selling and promotional tool. Even small producers such as Whole Nine Months, a maternity-wear manufacturer in Poway, California, have their own Web sites, which connect them with retail clients, potential employees, and consumers. As Bill Fields, president of the Wal-Mart Stores division, said: "I'm not really sure what the benefits of all this technology are, but the ability to understand what the customer wants is perhaps the biggest asset a retailer can have in the future."[16] This holds true for designers, producers, and manufacturers as well.

Summary and Review

Women's wear is the largest segment of the fashion industry, and it sets the trends for other segments. In the 20th century, merchandising of ready-to-wear apparel has in the United States has been centered in the fashion district of New York City, with other major markets in Los Angeles, Dallas, and Atlanta. Mass production has depended on a unionized labor force, represented by UNITE.

The production of women's wear is segmented in several ways, and companies may specialize according to use categories, such as activewear or bridal wear; sizes, including misses, junior, petite, women's, and half sizes; price zones, ranging from designer signature to bridge to better and contemporary to moderate and budget. Manufacturers and designers change their goods by selling season.

Merchandising and marketing activities include advertising; publicity; fashion shows, press weeks, and trade shows; trunk shows; videotapes; and other promotion aids.

Five major industry trends include manufacturers acting as retailers, more and more licensing, increasing offshore production and imports, increased emphasis on the Quick Response strategy in the United States, and the widespread use of computers and the Internet.

Trade Talk

Define or briefly explain the following terms:

custom-made
plus-sizes
price zones
ready-to-wear (RTW)
trunk show

For Review

1. Why did New York City become the center of the garment industry in the United States?
2. Discuss the growth and contributions of UNITE to the apparel industry.
3. Name some specialized market segments served by apparel manufacturers.
4. List the traditional basic categories of women's apparel, giving types of garments in each category.
5. Into what size ranges is women's apparel traditionally divided?
6. List and describe the six major price zones into which women's apparel is divided. What are the major factors contributing to the wholesale price of garments?
7. Why do most fashion producers sell directly to retail stores rather than through wholesalers?
8. Discuss the merchandising activities of women's fashion producers today.
9. How does a manufacturer or designer benefit from attending a trunk show in a retail store?
10. Discuss the major problems facing a manufacturer who is also a retailer.

For Discussion

1. Discuss the advantages and disadvantages of standardization of women's apparel sizes.
2. What are the repercussions of a name-brand or designer manufacturer selling current-season apparel to off-price outlets as well as to department and specialty shops?

References

1. The Fashion Center Business District Office.
2. Elise Ackerman, "She kicks, She scores, She sells," *U.S. News & World Report*, July 26, 1999, v127, i4, p. 42.
3. Rachel Beck, "Swim Suits Accommodate More People," *Associated Press*, May 5, 1997.
4. Barbie Ludovise, "By Design: Cool Customers," *Los Angeles Times*, November 25, 1995, p. 3.
5. LaMont Jones, "Stylewise: Guides for Brides," *PG News*, August 6, 2000.
6. Ylonda Gault, "Junior Mint in Teeny-bopping Shopping," *Crain's New York Business*, February 24, 1997, p. 45.
7. Constance L. Hays, "Advertising," *New York Times*, February 27, 2002, C10.
8. Eric Wilson, "Bridge at an Impasse, Looking for Direction," *Women's Wear Daily*, July 11, 2001.
9. Janet Ozzard, "Bridge, Contemporary Create a New Lure For Young Designers," *Women's Wear Daily*, October 23, 1996, pp. 1, 8–9.
10. Anne D'Innocenzio, "Contemporary Gets a Lift From Fashion," *Women's Wear Daily*, July 9, 1997, p. 9.
11. Anne D'Innocenzio, "Better's Space Race Accelerates," *Women's Wear Daily*, July 9, 1997, p. 9.
12. Anne D'Innocenzio, "Moderate Report: The Push for Sharper Pricing, Fashion," *Women's Wear Daily*, July 9, 1997, p. 12.
13. Anne Marie Shiro, "For the Rich, a New High End," *New York Times*, April 29, 1997, p. B11.
14. Anamaria Wilson, "Beccaria Nets $54k at Dressner," *Women's Wear Daily*, February 12, 2002.
15. Susan Caminiti and Joe McGowan, "Ralph Lauren: The Emperor Has Clothes," *Fortune*, November 11, 1996.
16. Annie Gowen, "The Data Game," *Women's Wear Daily*, March 20, 1996, p. 1.

CHAPTER 9

Men's Apparel

WHAT'S IN IT FOR YOU?

Everything you always wanted to know about trends in the men's apparel industry.

Key Concepts:

- The history of the men's wear industry
- Categories of men's apparel
- Roles of brand names and designer names in the marketing of men's wear
- Advertising and promotional activities in the marketing of men's apparel

Clothes have been part of the story of man—yes, "man"—because most of the world's great clothes have been worn by men to express power, wealth, and glory. Such male clothes are shown in museums around the world. These clothes represented the tribal chief, the warrior, the cleric, and the monarch—in a word, the male.

In fact, the men's business outfit in the 21st century has retained a basically conservative style that evolved in the late 1700s. Over the years, neutral colors have prevailed, and changes in style have occurred mostly in the details. Jackets are longer or shorter, with wider or narrower lapels; jacket vents and trouser cuffs come and go. Shirt collars mutate into various shapes, and ties are invented and reinvented. But overall, men's clothing has changed very little (see Figure 9.1).

History of the Men's Apparel Industry

The oldest of the domestic apparel industries, the men's wear industry gave birth to the women's and children's wear industries. It got its start in the late 1700s. Prior to that the rich

A

B

C

FIGURE 9.1
Presidents (a) Lincoln, (b) Clinton, and (c) Bush—all reflect the fashions of their eras.
(a) Corbis-Bettmann. (b) AP/Photo, (c) AP/Photo/Pablo Martinez Monsivais.

patronized tailor shops, where their clothing was custom-made or fitted to them. Everyone else wore homemade clothing.

Birth of Ready-to-Wear

The first ready-to-wear men's clothing was made by tailors in port cities along the Atlantic Coast. Seamen arrived in these cities in need of clothes to wear on land but without the time to have them tailor-made. To meet their needs, a few astute tailors began anticipating the ships' arrivals by making up batches of suits in rough size groupings. Sailors, who could put on the new clothes and walk away in them, liked the idea. These early ready-to-wear stores were called **slop shops**, a name that was appropriate to what they sold. Ready-to-wear clothing offered none of the careful fit or detail of custom-tailored clothes. But the price was right and the convenience was important, so ready-to-wear clothing gradually gained acceptance in ever-widening circles.

Although never considered slop shops, some distinguished men's wear retail operations got their start on waterfronts. Brooks Brothers' first store opened in 1818 in downtown New York, and Jacob Reed's Sons first store opened in 1824 near the Philadelphia waterfront.

Role of the Industrial Revolution

The market for ready-to-wear clothing was further increased by the industrial revolution. Ironically, though, the industrial revolution also helped to create the new conservative look that prevailed for so long. The industrial revolution led to the introduction of machinery in all areas of production and replaced the absolute dependence on human hands in the making of goods. Clothing, like much else, could be mass-produced. This, in part, led to standardization in people's tastes. Mass-produced clothes were made for the lowest common denominator, which in men's wear led to a conservatively cut, dark-colored suit.

The look, however, was not entirely the result of mass production. The idea of conservative men's suits also had its origins in a new role model that emerged during the industrial revolution—the industrialist. On the one hand, these newly rich tycoons had working-class roots and were not about to dress like the rich peacocks. On the other hand, they had finally gained access to something long denied them—power and money—and they wanted this to show in their dress. Sober and conservative themselves, they chose to wear clothes that were sober and conservative.

The industrial revolution also helped to create a managerial class made entirely of men who were happy to emulate the look of the rich industrialists. Soon all men who worked in offices wore the look, and the tailored, dark-colored work suit that men would wear for the next 150 years was born.

The industrial revolution helped to move the production of clothing out of the home. The demand for people to operate the new machines was so great that entire families often went to work. This left no one at home to sew, and further boosted the demand for ready-to-wear clothing.

Mid- to Late 1800s

As late as the mid-1800s, rich people still did not consider buying their clothes off the rack in shops that had been slop shops, but had become respectable. The middle class, usually the most important element in making a style acceptable, patronized the stores.

Advances in Production Techniques

The introduction of the sewing machine in 1846 was another important advance in men's apparel; it sped up production. During the Civil War, when manufacturers scrambled to make uniforms according to specification, standardized sizes for a variety of figure types developed. The invention of paper patterns by Ebenezer Butterick and his wife in 1863 improved the consistency of the sizing, assuring a better fit in ready-to-wear clothing—the last thing that was necessary to make them popular with all classes.

Use of Contractors

As the men's ready-to-wear business grew, so did its attractiveness as a profitable investment. But going into business as a men's wear manufacturer required considerable capital in terms of factory construction, equipment, and labor costs. This situation led to the birth of the contractor business, described in Chapter 7. By hiring a contractor to do the sewing and sometimes the cutting as well, manufacturers eliminated the need for their own factories, sewing machines, or labor force. They could function with just a showroom or space for shipping.

Early contractors of men's wear operated in one of two ways. Usually, they set up their own factories where the manufacturing was done. But sometimes they distributed work to operators who would work at home, either on their own machines or on machines rented from the contractors. These workers were paid on a piecework basis.

Right after the Civil War and for the next two decades or so, men's wear was manufactured in three different ways:

1. In **inside shops**, or garment factories, owned and operated by manufacturers
2. In contract shops, or contractors' factories, where garments were produced for manufacturers
3. In homes, where garments were made usually for contractors but sometimes for manufacturers

The Rise of Unions

As the men's wear market and industry grew, so did competition among manufacturers. To produce ready-to-wear clothing at competitive prices, manufacturers and contractors demanded long hours from workers and yet paid low wages. In addition, factory working conditions, which had never been good, deteriorated further. Contractors were particularly guilty, and their factories deserved the names *sweat* shops or "sweaters" that were given to them. According to an official New York State inspection report of 1887:

> *The workshops occupied by these contracting manufacturers of clothing, or "sweaters" as they are commonly called, are foul in the extreme. Noxious gases emanate from all corners. The buildings are ill smelling from cellar to garret. The water-closets are used by males and females, and usually stand in the room where the work is done. The people are huddled together too closely for comfort, even if all other conditions were excellent.*[1]

What happened next was inevitable. Workers finally rebelled against working conditions, hours, and pay. Local employee unions had existed in the industry since the early 1800s, but none had lasted long or wielded much power. The Journeymen Tailors' National Union, formed in 1883, functioned mainly as a craft union. A union representing all apparel industry workers, the United Garment Workers of America, was organized in 1891, but it had little power and soon collapsed. Finally, in 1914, the Amalgamated Clothing Workers of America (ACWA) was formed. It remained the major union of the men's wear industry until the 1970s, when it merged with the Textile Workers of America and the United Shoe Workers of America to form the Amalgamated Clothing and Textile Workers Union (ACTWU). Then, in 1995, the Amalgamated joined with the International Ladies Garment Workers Union (ILGWU) to form UNITE, the Union of Needletrades, Industrial, & Textile Employees.

UNITE represents the workers in virtually all domestic plants in the tailored-clothing segment of men's wear manufacturing. The common beginnings of both the union and the factories in the Northeast may account for this strong presence. However, its influence in factories producing men's work clothes, furnishings, and sportswear in other parts of the country was almost nonexistent until the famous strike during the early 1970s at the El Paso, Texas, factory of the Farah Company, one of the largest manufacturers of men's pants and work clothes. The company had resisted the attempt of the Amalgamated to organize the Farah workers for many years, and only after a long court battle were the plant and its workers unionized. However, the influence of UNITE is still not as strong in other segments and regions as it is in tailored clothing in the Northeast.

Acceptance of Ready-to-Wear in the 20th Century

Store-bought clothes finally broke the class barrier during the last half of the 19th century. Financial crises such as the panics of 1869, 1873, and 1907 sent men who had formerly worn only custom-tailored clothes into the ready-to-wear clothing stores. Even though custom-tailoring remained a vital part of the men's wear industry far longer than it lasted in women's wear, it was dealt a final blow during the Great Depression. Today, it represents only a small segment of the industry.

World War II

The Great Depression of 1929 brought about a decline in demand for all consumer products, and the economy did not get back on its feet again until World War II.

During the war, of course, the entire apparel industry was given over to the war effort. The men's wear industry ground to a halt and turned its attention to making uniforms. Restrictions were placed on the design and use of fabric. Trouser cuffs, which required extra fabric, disappeared. Once the war ended, however, the restrictions were lifted, and even more important, a long era of post-war prosperity began.

The returning servicemen were eager to get out of their uniforms. The demand for "civvies," or civilian clothes, was so great that for a few years clothing manufacturers worked—with little thought for changing styles—simply to keep up with the demand. By the late forties, manufacturers were meeting demand and could even stand back and consider style.

The Post-War Era

The major change in the men's wear industry in the post-war period was the emergence of a new class of clothes called sportswear. It originated in Southern California in the late 1940s, where suburban living and a climate conducive to leisure created a demand for clothes to be worn outside work.

For a while, the demand for sportswear was filled by a group of former New York manufacturers who had gravitated to the West Coast. Not only did they give sportswear to California, but to the entire nation. The California market, as sportswear came to be known in the business, gained further momentum when buyers from major department stores such as Marshall Field, Hudson's, Macy's, and Lord & Taylor traveled to the West Coast to attend the spring sportswear show held every October in Palm Springs. New York clothing manufacturers wasted no time cashing in on the trend. By the mid-1960s, men's sportswear was as much a part of the East Coast market as tailored clothing.

What later become known as "designer clothes" also got their start in California in the 1940s. Hollywood motion-picture costume designers such as Don Loper, Orry-Kelly, Howard Greer, and Milo Anderson created lines for California sportswear manufacturers. Oleg Cassini and Adrian began licensing agreements with New York neckwear producers.

Designer clothes, à la California, proved to be an idea born before its time, a rare occurrence in the trendy fashion world. The designer sportswear could not compete with the new Ivy League or continental look that emerged on the East Coast. Designer clothes faded away and did not reemerge until the 1960s when designers like Pierre Cardin and John Weitz would try again, with much greater success.

Fashions of the 1960s and 1970s

Little happened in men's fashion until the 1960s, when suddenly men's wear blossomed, cultivated by the costuming of such British rock groups as the Beatles and the Rolling Stones. The "Mod look" brought color to men's wear after a 150-year-old absence. It was followed by the "Edwardian look," which changed the shape of men's wear for the first time in decades. Other styles, such as the Nehru jacket, were little more than fads.

Revolutionary Fashion. The social revolution of the 1960s was reflected in the hippies' all-occasion dress code. For men, it prescribed long hair and beard; jeans; a choice of tie-dyed T-shirt, denim work shirt, or a colorfully flower-powered shirt with no tie; love beads; and, weather permitting, sandals. The civil rights movement was expressed in fashion by the adoption of African clothing, especially the *dashiki*, a colorfully printed, loose-fitting, collarless woven shirt.

In Europe, Pierre Cardin's "Peacock look," with its peaked shoulders, fitted waist, and flared pants, transformed the male uniform and blazed the trail for current men's fashions.

Revolutionary Fabrics. For the first time since the development of the sewing machine, technology influenced men's wear fashions. Knits, made from synthetic fibers, enjoyed a boom in the 1970s. Suddenly a man could outfit himself entirely in knit clothes—a double-knit suit, circular knit shirt, interlock knit underwear, a knit tie, and jersey knit socks.

The overexposure of knits, often in poorly designed and constructed clothing, gave polyester a bad image. Its use fell off in the women's apparel industry, but men's wear manufacturers continued to use it in a low-key way in woven fabrics. Today, 95 percent of men's tailored clothing is made with polyester, most typically blends combining polyester with wool or cotton. Sixty-five percent of men's finer quality suits are made of 55/45 polyester/wool blend; it is the most popular suiting fabric in the United States.

Another technological development of the period that has had staying power is the permanent press finish of cotton. Home laundering of no-iron shirts has made a difference in the maintenance of men's wardrobes.

The Last Decades of the 20th Century

In the 1980s men's fashion took on new life once again, as it had in the 1960s. For the first time, magazines devoted exclusively to men's fashion appeared. Men's fashion types emerged, and a variety of styles became acceptable. A man could be the continental type or the Ivy League type; he could be Edwardian, if he chose (see Figure 9.2a and b).

A

B

FIGURE 9.2
Both (a) the Edwardian look and (b) the hippie look were worn in the 1970s.
(a) UPI/Corbis-Bettmann.
(b) Baldwin H. Ward/Corbis-Bettmann.

A

B

C

FIGURE 9.3
Power suits: (a) in the 18th century, (b) in the 1980s as interpreted by Armani, and (c) in the future, perhaps—Darth Vader—in Star Wars: Episode V-The Empire Strikes Back.
(a) Corbis-Bettmann. (b) Fairchild Publications, Inc. (c) LUCASFILM LTD. © 1980 and 1997. Lucasfilm Ltd. & TM. All rights reserved.

For those who did not trust their own judgment, scientifically confirmed "dress for success" guidelines were suggested in John Malloy's book of the same name. The book prescribed style and color details to create the right combination of authority and friendliness for a variety of business negotiations. Intentionally conservative in its advice, it promoted what came to be known in the 1980s as the "power suit" and "power tie" for "power lunches" (see Figure 9.3).

The Casual Look

The look that really took off among more self-confident dressers was one of casual elegance, personified by the stars of the popular television show *Miami Vice*. The clothes were designed by big designer names, which ensured their elegance, and they were casual, which basically added up to T-shirts worn under Italian sports jackets, classic loafers with no socks, and ever-present designer sunglasses. For the first time, the American men's wear market was segmented as the women's market always had been by age, education, and income.

Dress-Down Fridays

In the 1990s, the casual look was officially welcomed to the corporate office, sometimes without the elegance. It began with "dress-down Fridays" in the summer, when companies made allowance for the quick weekend getaway to the beach. Gradually the trend expanded to the cooler months and to other days of the week. Each firm that followed the trend had to make up its own rules—or decide not to. By 1995, *Fortune* magazine was ready to declare, "In short, there is no corporate uniform anymore."[2] Suddenly men actually had to think about what they would wear. This in turn led to men taking an interest in shopping for their own wardrobes, instead of relying on their wives or girlfriends. As Paula Ausick, director of brand equities for Foot, Cone & Belding observed:

> *Men like to shop, but men hate to shop the way women shop. They don't like to perceive themselves as aimless wandering. Men see themselves as more purposeful.*[3]

The effect of the dress-down trend on the men's wear business has been profound. Sales of men's suits fell 11 percent between 1994 and 1996, while sales of sports coats grew 14 percent. Sales of casual slacks grew 14 percent over that period, while sales of dress pants fell 4 percent.[4]

Demographic Influences

The popularity of casual business wardrobes may be attributable to the coming of age of the baby boomers. The young adults and teenagers of the 1960s were beginning to reach middle age and the height of their earning power. Many male baby boomers have been worrying more about aging, and doing something about it. As Sheron David, SVP of BBDO, New York, said, "Men are much more concerned about grooming than they used to be. It used to be considered not masculine. That's no longer the case."[5]

The young adults of the 1990s are the children of these baby boomers. For both age groups, alternate lifestyles with untraditional wardrobes are not news. Urban "hip-hop" styles popularized by rap stars exploded into dozens of new manufacturers like Phat Farm, Fubu, Karl Kani, Shabazz Brothers, and Third Rail. Inevitably, some of their merchandise found its way into the newly informal office, along with earrings and nose studs. Currently there is as much room for the conservatively casual dresser as for the man who wants to express a uniquely personal style. What is news is the expanded range of choices that comes with the relaxing of the rules. And with freedom to choose comes responsibility for evaluating the options and making decisions.

Style is expected to remain an important factor in men's wear. It should be noted, however, that in the midst of the interest in new styles, the classic look, popularized in the 1980s by designers such as Ralph Lauren and Giorgio Armani, continues to be strong. The conservative men's suit remains the outfit of choice for formal business and social occasions, and not only for the president.

Organization and Operation of the Industry

The men's wear industry traditionally has been divided into firms making different kinds of clothing:

1. *Tailored clothing*—Suits, overcoats, topcoats, sports coats, formal wear, and separate trousers
2. *Furnishings*—Dress shirts, neckwear, sweaters, headwear, underwear, socks, suspenders, robes, and pajamas
3. *Outerwear*—Raincoats, coats, jackets, and active sportswear
4. *Work clothing*—Work shirts, work pants, overalls, and related items
5. *Other*—Uniforms and miscellaneous items

A

B

C

FIGURE 9.4
The popular television sitcom Frazier reflects how the21st century man defines himself by his fashion statement. They may be related, but (a) tweedy Frazier, (b) designer-suited brother Niles, and (c) Dad in his flannel shirt wear no family resemblance.
(a) © Ross Frank/Corbis Sygma (b) NBC-TV/Courtesy, the Kobal Collection.

FIGURE 9.5
High fashion designers like Donna Karan are showing men's tailored clothing the way they have shown women's wear—and sometimes in the same show.
Courtesy, Fairchild Publications, Inc.

The federal government uses these five classifications. Although it is not an official classification, sportswear (including active sportswear) has become a vital portion of the business, and should be considered a men's wear category.

Size and Location of Manufacturers

Men's wear, led by the booming sportswear segment, represents a $34.7 billion market.[6] Unlike women's apparel, the business has been dominated by large firms at the manufacturing level.

In recent years Levi Strauss, Blue Bell, Cluett, Peabody, and Interco have been the four largest manufacturers of men's wear and boys' wear. Their combined volume has been estimated to count for approximately one-third of the total volume of the top 30 firms. In tailored men's wear, the largest producer is the Hartmarx Corporation, the Chicago-based manufacturer of 20-plus brands, including some women's wear lines. Hartmarx's 2001 sales totaled $601.6million.[7] Oxford Clothes, Inc., is another example of a hard-pressed U.S. men's high-end suit maker. To increase sales, Oxford added a new model of suit, called Renaissance, which has a more contoured silhouette and broader shoulders, that is closer to the Italian suit.[8] Because of diversification, mergers, and acquisitions by top men's wear producers in the past few years, it has become more difficult to ascertain company size and production figures.

Although there are men's wear manufacturers in almost every section of the country, the greatest numbers of plants are in the mid-Atlantic states. New York, New Jersey, and Pennsylvania form the center of the tailored-clothing industry. Over 40 percent of all men's wear manufacturers are located in this area.

However, the industry's center is gradually moving. A number of northeastern manufacturers have set up plant facilities in the South, where both land and labor are less expensive. These include not only apparel manufacturers from the mid-Atlantic states but also some men's shoe manufacturers, who were once found almost exclusively in New England. Some men's wear manufacturers have always been located in the South, which has always been a center for manufacturers of men's shirts, underwear, and work clothes.

The number of firms located in the West is also steadily growing. For instance, two of the largest firms manufacturing separate trousers—a segment of the tailored clothing industry—are located in Texas: Farah in El Paso and Haggar in Dallas. Other areas of the West are also popular; for example, Guess? and L.A. Gear are located in Los Angeles and Levi Strauss, Nautica, and Patagonia are headquartered in San Francisco. In the Pacific Northwest, Portland, Oregon, is the home of White Stag and Pendelton, while Eddie Bauer and R.E.I. are located in Seattle, Washington. Most of these companies produce sportswear or casual attire. The upper Midwest (Lands' End in Wisconsin) is also important for sports outerwear and activewear such as parkas, skiwear, and hunting and fishing gear (see Figure 9.6).

New York City is the capital of manufacturers' showrooms. Many are located at 1290 Sixth Avenue, and others are situated on 51st, 52nd, and 53rd Streets between Fifth and Seventh Avenues. The showrooms for men's furnishings are concentrated in the Empire State Building at Fifth Avenue and 34th Street.

Dual Distribution

It is far more common in the men's wear industry than in women's apparel for clothes to be distributed on a two-tier system called dual distribution. In **dual distribution**, apparel is made available through both wholesale and retail channels; that is, the manufacturer sells it in its own retail stores, as well as to retail stores owned by others. The practice got its start in the first half of the 19th century when the ready-to-wear business, along with the country's population, was expanding. Its popularity has proven to be cyclical. Interest last peaked in the 1960s and 1970s but subsided when the industry was threatened with antitrust suits. Federal law forbids the domination by any one company of a segment of any industry.

Designing a Line

For generations, tailored-clothing manufacturers in the United States were known as slow but painstakingly careful followers, rather than leaders, in men's wear styling. The typical tailored clothing manufacturer had a staff of tailors to execute existing designs or bought freelance designs. Designers' names were known only within the trade and were seldom considered important by consumers.

Traditionally, the leading fashion influence was English styling. Designers in this country would study the styles currently popular in England (specifically Savile Row), decide which might be acceptable here, and gradually develop a line based on those styles. Production was a slow process because of the amount of handwork involved in making tailored clothing. Usually, a full year passed from the time a style was developed until a finished product was delivered to a retail store.

The first signs of male rebellion against traditional styling came during the late 1940s and early 1950s. As described earlier, year after year manufacturers had been turning out versions of a style that had long been popular on Savile Row—a draped suit with padded shoulders, based originally on the broad-chested uniform of the Brigade of Guards. A number of young men attending well-known northeastern colleges became tired of the traditional look. They took their objections to New Haven clothing manufacturers, and the result was the natural-shoulder, Ivy League suit.

FIGURE 9.6
This Lands' End ad for Pima Lisle Golf Polo shirts show men's activewear can have a silky and soft feel.

A radical shift in attitudes in the 1960s finally made men willing to wear suits as fashion. The antiwar protests, student activism, black power, and other political movements encouraged American men to express themselves in a nonmainstream manner. They led to the era of the "Peacock revolution," when men once again took great pride in their appearance, as in days long ago. Some favored long hair, bold plaid suits, brightly colored shirts, wide multicolored ties, and shiny boots. Others dressed, even for work, in Nehru and Mao jackets, leisure suits, white loafers, polyester double knits, and the "Las Vegas look"—shirts unbuttoned to the waist and gold necklaces in abundance around their necks.

Importance of Name Designers

By the late sixties, designer names in the men's wear industry mushroomed. Most of them were women's wear designers, often from Europe, who decided to exploit their renown by trying out their creativity in the men's field. So popular was the European designer image that even an American designer like Bill Kaiserman gave his firm an Italian name, Raphael.

Among the first American designers who made no bones about being American were Oleg Cassini, John Weitz, Bill Blass, and Ralph Lauren. In fact, Bill Blass won the first Coty Award ever given for men's wear design, in 1968.

Since most of these designers were famous as designers of women's apparel, there was a question about whether men would buy their designs. The movement of men into fashion during the sixties and seventies dispelled that doubt. As reported in the *New York Times*:

The idea that men would wear clothes designed by a woman's apparel designer was never considered seriously, and one thing that men have arrived at today is that being interested in clothes does not carry a stigma.[9]

The fact that much men's wear, particularly furnishings and sportswear, is bought by women for men also aided in the acceptance of name designer styles. Women were familiar with the names and had confidence in the designer's taste.

Although the first foreign country that influenced the design of men's wear was England, French and Italian designers became as important in men's wear as the traditional English. Pierre Cardin signed his first contract for men's shirts and ties in 1959 and did his first ready-to-wear men's designs in 1961. Christian Dior, Yves Saint Laurent, and other famous women's designers followed his example. One important men's wear designer who did not come from the ranks of women's wear is Ralph Lauren. He began his career in men's wear, designing for women only after he became successful and famous designing for men.

Designer Names Today

Currently, an entirely new world of men's wear has emerged in which designer labels are promoted as heavily as well-established brand names used to be. A designer who licenses his or her name in suits may also license men's jeans, shirts, jackets, sportswear, activewear, or ties. The manufacturer pays for the design or name of the designer in royalties based on gross sales. Royalties average from five to seven percent on men's suits and five percent on men's sportswear, according to industry sources.

Manufacturing companies that license name designers usually establish separate divisions and in many cases allocate separate manufacturing facilities for them. Among the designer brand names of Hartmarx are Burberry, Evan Picone, Kenneth Cole Perry Ellis, Pierre Cardin, and Tommy Hilfiger. In licensing agreements, the extent of designer involvement varies; designers are not necessarily responsible for all the designs that bear their name. Some licensing agreements simply pay for the use of the designer's name, and the name designer has no design input at all.

Today the "name game" is big business in all segments of the men's wear industry. While there are no hard figures on the amount of designer business alone at the wholesale level, the best market estimates for retail sales are over $1 billion for all categories combined.

One reason for the continuing popularity of designer names is that they are so easily promoted. Consumers associate them with prestige and fashion and recognize them when they see them. Designers have helped by becoming highly visible. Their names are household words, and their faces frequently appear in newspapers and magazines. They lend themselves to the fantasy of the customer who longs for wealth and excitement.

Leading Italian designers of men's wear include Armani, Brioni, Donatella Versace, Dolce & Gabbana, Romeo Gigli, Kiton, and Ermenegildo Zegna, not to mention Americans Tom Ford of Gucci and Stephen Fairchild of Valentino. Four Belgian designers achieved widespread popularity in the late 1990s; Raf Simons, Wim Neels, Dreis Van Noten, and Walter van Beirendonck. Other influential European designers include Helmut Lang, Paul Smith, Heidi Slimane of Saint Laurent, Comme des Garçons, Yohji Yamamoto, and Jean-Paul Gautier.

American designers of men's wear include, of course, the "Big Four": Ralph Lauren, Calvin Klein, Donna Karan, and Tommy Hilfiger. Other popular designers include John Weitz, Mossimo, Gene Meyer, John Bartlett, Alexander Julian, Richard Edwards, and Jhane Barnes. A recent entry into men's sportswear is Nicole Miller, already well-known for her ties.

Designer names also get more exposure than brand names in stores because they often appear on many different kinds of goods displayed in several different departments. Designers often have their own boutiques within stores.

FASHION FOCUS

Urban Brands Gain Spotlight

Classic clothing labels like Tommy Hilfiger and Nautica are getting some real competition from names like Sean John, Phat Pharm, Ecko, and Enyce – and they are getting it in unexpected places – department stores.

Urban clothing brands, which up until now were showcased in small clothing stores and inner-city chains, are now gaining more space and attention in department stores. These urban "bad boy" brands have added energy and fashion assortment to young men's apparel areas. The number of department stores that carry urban brands has grown by over 50 percent. "I see this as a big opportunity to reinvent the department stores model. Department stores haven't been on the top of the minds for young men," said George Jones, President and Chief Executive of Saks, one traditional department store chains that includes Proffets and Passion.

The popularity of the urban brands in not new, but what is new is their appeal to suburban youths rather than just those in the inner city. However, the executives of companies like Phat Pharm and Sean John say they don't want to be stereotyped as urban brands, given their multi-cultural appeal. They emphasize that each of the lines feature their own design aesthetic. Phat Pharm, for example, is known for classic style argyle sweaters and denim sportswear. Sean John, meanwhile, has more flamboyant clothing that includes pinstriped suits, shearling coats, and suede pants and shirts.

The mixing of music and clothing is not new, as styles of particular music genres have always had an influence on how the world dressed. However, music is now taking this relationship a step further by not only influencing fashion, but designing as well. The most well known are Sean "Puffy Combs" John, Busta Rhymes, Def Jam co-founder Russell Simmons, Rapper Jay-Z, and Rapper Nelly. Pop band NSYNC band member Chris Kirkpatrick started a line called FuMa Skeeto that is sold in Nordstrom and Bloomingdales. Where will it all end? The big question still remains—can these musicians sew as well as they sing? That's up to the public to decide. Among the hottest urban lines are:

Platinum Fubu
Iceberg
Coogi
Ecko
Ruff Ryders
Johnny Blaze
Enyce
Snoop Dogg
Outkast
PhatFarm
Sean John
Maurice Malone

Sources

Anne D'Innocenzia, "Urban Brands Gain Spotlight in Department Stores," *The Salena Journal/Life*, October 1, 2002.

C. E. Pelc, "Flavaful Fashion," www.Funkybitch.com, September 13, 2002.

Austin Silver, "The Male Celerity Trendsetters," http://www.askmen.com , February 3, 2003.

Roundtable Discussion, http://www.students.sup.edu /360/Winter, 2001

The Phattest Gear – Urban Apparel, 2002

New York customers check out a Hard Knocks brand shirt in Macy's.
Courtesy, AP Photo/Toyokazu Kosugi.

Market Segments

Most market segments are based on style differences, but some exist because they involve different production methods. The five main market segments in men's wear are: (1) tailored clothing, (2) sportswear, (3) activewear, (4) contemporary apparel, and (5) bridge apparel.

Tailored Clothing

Tailored-clothing firms produce structured or semistructured suits, overcoats, topcoats, sports coats, formal wear, and separate slacks that involve hand-tailoring operations. This kind of clothing once dominated the market, but in recent years, the demand for tailored clothing has steadily declined. The higher price of tailored clothing makes the difference all the more striking. Despite the decline, tailored suits have long been—and still are—considered the backbone of the men's wear industry.

A tailored suit is structured, or three-dimensional, which gives it a shape even when it is not worn. Until very recently, tailored clothing was graded according to the number of hand-tailoring operations required to make it. The grades were 1, 2, 4, 41, 6, and 61, with a grade 1 suit representing the lowest quality.

At the top of the quality scale, the number of hand-tailoring operations has been reduced by machinery that can produce stitching of a similar caliber. However, the finest suits still have hand-sewn details representing hours of work by skilled tailors.

Designer Suits. Another difference between an inexpensive, low-grade suit and an expensive designer suit is the way each is cut. Designer suits are typically sized on a "7-inch drop." **Drop** refers to the difference between the chest and waist measurements of a jacket. Some jackets designed for young men and other customers who keep in shape may have an even greater drop. Nondesigner suits, in contrast, have a 6-inch drop, which gives a suit jacket an entirely different look and fit.

Differences also exist between traditional suits, which have a natural shoulder, and suits with **European styling**, which feature a more fitted jacket, built-up shoulders, and a higher armhole.

Production. The production of tailored clothing, as you have probably guessed, is a long, complicated process, although it does parallel the production process for women's apparel. Styles are selected for a new line, after which a manufacturer orders fabrics for the line. Delivery of the fabric may take up to 9 months, so it must be ordered far in advance of when it will be used. Next, the line is presented to buyers. Manufacturers do not start to cut suits until enough orders have accumulated to make production of a style worthwhile.

Men's tailored clothing is produced in the following proportioned sizes, with the number ranges representing chest measurements:

- *Short* (36–44)
- *Regular* (35–46)
- *Long* (37–48)
- *Extra long* (38–50)
- *Portly short* (39–48)
- *Large* (46, 48, 50)

Not every style is cut in every size range, but the most popular styles are made up in at least half the size ranges.

Suit Separates. The steady decline in structured and semistructured tailored men's wear has been offset by an increased demand for **suit separates**—sports jackets and trousers that are worn much as the tailored suit used to be. Tailored suits are now the business uniform only in large, sophisticated cities, and even there, only in some firms and industries and for some levels of management. Elsewhere, suit separates are often worn to work—or for almost any occasion except where formal wear is required.

Although an attempt was made in the 1960s to sell men's wear consumers on the idea of coordinated sportswear, that is, jackets, vests, and pants that could be mixed and matched with one another, the idea never took hold. Today, suit separates refers to sports jackets and trousers.

Suit separates are usually machine-made and as a result, can be significantly lower-priced than tailored garments. When they are made for better-priced lines, they can also be expensive. Because each item is bought separately, the expensive alterations that manufacturers and retailers must often make on tailored clothes are avoided. One industry expert believes that men who buy separates are more fashion-aware than those who need the reassurance of a preassembled look.

Sportswear

Sportswear, or casual wear, which runs the gamut from unconstructed jackets, knits and woven sports shirts, slacks, and leisure shorts, to coordinated tops and bottoms, has been the fastest-growing segment of the men's wear industry since the 1970s. Changes in lifestyle, plus men's growing interest in having more variety and fashion in their wardrobes, have created a demand for leisure clothes.

A generation ago, tailored clothing was office or formal wear, and sportswear was strictly weekend or vacation wear. Today, the real difference between the two lies in the construction rather than the occasion or the styling, colors, or fabrics of the garments.

Sportswear is unstructured, or at minimum, less structured than tailored clothing. Few if any hand-tailoring operations, for example, are required to make a sports jacket. Sportswear lacks padding, binding, and lining, and takes its shape (if indeed it has any shape these days) from the person who is wearing it.

Sportswear production also differs from that of tailored wear. Unlike tailored-wear manufacturers, who want staying power for their styles and a lot of lead time, sportswear manufacturers are interested in short runs and a quick response to customer demand. A **short run** is the production of a limited number of units of a particular item, fewer than would normally be considered an average number to produce. Producers of men's sportswear sometimes rely on contractors to keep up with the fast-moving fashion cycles of this market segment. The quality of workmanship is much less important than the quick production of the styles, colors, and fabrics that customers want.

In addition, unstructured sportswear, regardless of the kind of firm producing it, is likely to be made up in a much narrower size range than tailored clothing. For instance, a sport shirt is not produced in the wide variety of neck sizes, sleeve lengths, and collar and cuff styles in which a dress shirt is made. Instead, a sport shirt is usually produced in four basic sizes (small, medium, large, and extra large), with a choice between short and long sleeves.

This is the kind of production work that contractors handle most successfully. When contractors are used, the sportswear manufacturer may be the designer, a designer may be hired, or a design may be bought from a freelancer. The manufacturer buys the needed fabric. Then sometimes the cutting and all of the sewing are done by the contractor, as in the women's apparel field. Finally, the finished goods are returned to the manufacturer, who handles the distribution.

Activewear

Another phenomenon emerging in the 1980s and continuing in the 1990s was the rapid growth of the **activewear** market, which consists of clothing worn during active sports participation as well as during leisure time. In fact, the larger segment of this market is men who want to look as if they are doing something athletic, even when they are ambling to the store for the Sunday paper or flopping down in front of the television set to watch a ball game. As a result, the active sportswear producers make running suits for men who run and men who do not, but want to look as if they do. Sportswear was also responsible for making color a permanent part of men's wardrobes. Colorful skiwear dominates the slopes. Golf wear has become popular on and off the links, with licensed apparel and accessories by players like Tiger Woods (for Nike) and Greg Norman (for Reebok) (see Figure 9.7a and b). These major brand names in athletic shoes have become big names in activewear as well.

Contemporary Apparel

Contemporary men's wear refers to a special type of styling that provides high quality and fashion. Contemporary men's wear, which produces clothing in all categories, can often be distinguished by its use of bright colors.

Initially, the typical consumer was a young, educated man with the verve to look fashionable. Today, contemporary men's wear no longer belongs exclusively to the young but is worn by elegant, style-conscious men of all age groups.

Contemporary merchandise is produced by both tailored-clothing and sportswear firms. It is usually produced under a name designer's licensing agreement, rather than styled by a manufacturer's in-house or freelance designer. When this type of merchandise is produced by a firm already making other types of apparel and furnishings, new operating divisions are usually created to handle the product, give it identity, and enhance its marketability.

Bridge Apparel

In the 1980s, the term **bridge apparel** came into play in the men's wear industry to define clothing that spanned the style gap between young men's and men's collections, and the price gap between contemporary and designer apparel. In broad terms, the bridge customer is an aging baby boomer who has grown out of young men's clothing but can't yet afford designer

A

B

FIGURE 9.7
(a) Tiger Woods and (b) Greg Norman are fashion leaders on and off the golf course.
(a) AP Photo/Kevork Djansezia. (b) Courtesy, the Greg Norman Collection.

clothes. Bridge customers are between 25 and 40 and have sophistication and style.

Unlike the bridge concept in women's sportswear, for which certain manufacturers and designers have developed collections specifically created as bridge lines, men's bridge apparel is defined much more by retailers than by manufacturers. Each retailer may interpret bridge differently in order to fit its own customer profile. Therefore, one store might have bridge lines while another might call them contemporary. Whatever their definition of bridge apparel, retailers that identify a portion of their men's wear assortment as bridge apparel are seeking to balance fashion with price.

Merchandising and Marketing

Like the women's wear producers, men's wear producers back their lines with advertising and publicity. Men's wear fiber and textile producers sometimes promote their products. The largest percentage of promotion is done, however, by the men's wear producers, who rely on agencies, freelancers, and less often, on an in-house department for advertising and publicity.

Advertising

Men's apparel producers began advertising in the late 1800s. Initially, they used trade advertising to establish contact with retailers. Strong, stable relationships were built, and in many large towns and small cities, major manufacturers maintain an exclusive arrangement with one retailer. Not surprisingly, the producers tend to put a lot of their advertising money into cooperative advertising for their long-term retail accounts. Brand-name and designer name producers also sponsor national advertising campaigns.

Sportswear houses, relative newcomers to the marketplace, do not have long established or exclusive ties with retailers, so they compensate with large national advertising campaigns as well as cooperative advertising with retailers.

Publicity in Newspapers and Magazines

The only trade newspaper devoted to men's wear is the *Daily News Record*, published by Fairchild. Consumer magazines devoted to men's fashions also provide an interesting forum for publicity for men's wear products. They include *Gentlemen's Quarterly* (*GQ*), a recognized leader in the field; *Esquire*, once the leader in

FIGURE 9.8
Men's fashion periodicals frequently feature attractive celebrities, not professional models, on their covers.
Courtesy, Fairchild Publications, Inc.

men's fashion and now reasserting itself; *Details*; and an assortment of ethnically oriented publications such as *Ebony Man* and *Modern Black Man*. Producers make excellent use of the editorial pages of these various publications, and also supply clothes to be modeled. See Figure 9.8 for some samples of popular men's periodicals.

Visual Merchandising

Wendy Liebmann, president of WSL Strategic Retail, a marketing research firm, reports:

Men's retailers have to do more of what we see in better women's stores, and [realize] that we need to see more outfits merchandised together instead of having the pure selection of 50 shirts stacked up by size, or a hundred ties laid down in a glass case or hanging on racks. It's becoming more and more important to show how different items work together, the jacket with the shirt and and the tie.[10]

Trade Associations

The major publicity efforts, however, are still undertaken by the trade associations, which sponsor market weeks, trade shows, and other promotions designed to publicize individual producers and the industry as a whole (see Fiugre 9.9). New York is the largest U.S. market center for all kinds of men's wear, including tailored clothing, sportswear, contemporary lines, and furnishings. Regional markets in other parts of the country—Chicago, Los Angeles, and Dallas, for example—are growing in importance, but the largest number of permanent showrooms are still located in New York.

A number of trade associations support the men's wear industry. The following have a major role:

- *The Fashion Association (TFA)*. Founded as Men's Fashion Association of America in 1955, TFA expanded to other areas of the apparel industry. TFA represents the industry to the media with press kits and seminars as well as its two press preview weeks. In 2001 it merged with American Apparel and Footwear Association (AAFA). The TFA remains a lobbying group based in New York City.
- *National Association of Men's Sportswear Buyers (NAMSB)*. As the name suggests, this is an organization of men's wear retailers. Since its 1953 founding, it has expanded beyond sportswear to other men's apparel. Its market week trade shows give members access to more than a thousand producers exhibiting at each show. NAMSB also provides seasonal fashion-trend slide kits for members' use in merchandising and marketing. It has a scholarship program for children of members and their employees.
- *Men's Apparel Guild of California (MAGIC)*. This group was founded in the late 1930s as the Los Angeles Men's Wear Manufacturers Association to promote California-style men's sportswear. It has since expanded beyond California to an

FIGURE 9.9
The ASR Trade Show—the granddaddy of surf, skateboarding, and streetwear—not only shows the newest sportswear, but also provides entertainment.
Courtesy, Fairchild Publications, Inc.

international show and to other segments of the men's wear industry. Currently it includes women's and children's trade shows in addition to its semiannual extravaganzas in Las Vegas.

- *Clothing Manufacturers Association (CMA).* This organization of manufacturers of tailored clothing was founded in 1933. It represents management in negotiations with the industry labor union, UNITE. CMA acts as a liaison to the federal government on such issues as labeling. With *Newsweek*, it publishes an internationally distributed trade periodical twice a year. CMA also prepares statistical and technical reports for its members.
- *Big and Tall Associates.* Founded in 1971 for manufacturers and retailers who cater to men over five feet, 11 inches tall, and/or with chest measurements over 48 inches, this organization conducts semiannual market weeks.

Table 9.1 lists the major men's wear trade shows in the United States. As the market for imports and exports has grown in size and im-

TABLE 9.1 Major U.S. Trade Shows for Men's Wear

WHEN	WHO	WHERE	WHAT
January	NAMSB	New York City Hilton and Sheraton	Producers show retailers all types of men's and boys' wear, furnishings
January/February	CMA	New York City	Fall/Winter showings by producers of tailored men's wear
	TFA	West Coast	Press show by whole apparel industry
March	NASMB	New York City Javits Center	Same as January show
June	TFA	Near New York City	Same as January/February West Coast show
	NASMB	New York City	Same as January show
August/September	CMA	New York City	Summer/spring showing by producers of tailored men's wear
September	MAGIC	Las Vegas	All men's product lines (also produces women's and children's shows)
October	NASMB	New York City Javits Center	Same as January show

portance, more and more domestic manufacturers now attend the important international shows, most notably Pitti Uomo in Italy, IMBEX in London, and SEHM in France.

Industry Trends

The dynamics of population growth as well as lifestyle changes and developments in the economy are bringing about changes in all segments of the men's wear industry. Some of the most noteworthy trends include a diversification of products on the part of producers, the automation of production processes, an increase in foreign production and sales, and a proliferation of specialty stores. Consumers are showing greater interest in style and are demanding quality in fabric and construction. All of these trends relate to the growing informality of American culture.

Trends in Production

The manufacturing side of the men's wear industry has grown increasingly complex as individual firms find new ways to compete. The major producers that dominate the tailored clothing, sportswear, and activewear segments are expanding through mergers and acquisitions in each other's markets. Technological advances are speeding production, and offshore contracting is being used to control costs.

Diversification of Product

In addition to mergers and acquisitions, diversification is occurring through expanded product lines. Producers that for years were highly specialized, often producing only a single type of garment in one grade, are now expanding into other grades and product lines.

Some of the biggest changes have taken place in an area that was one of the most specialized, that of work clothes. Firms like H. D. Lee and Levi Strauss, which for years never varied their products, began to expand when the casual market took off. In addition to designer jeans, which had saturated the market by the mid-1970s, Lee, Levi Strauss, and similar manufacturers moved into slacks, casual pants, and jackets—and even tailored clothing.

Increased Automation

New equipment and computer systems are helping manufacturers combat one of the more serious problems faced by apparel producers: labor. The rising cost of labor is pitted against a dwindling skilled labor force. The men's wear industry has also experienced a turnover rate of between 60 and 70 percent for the past few years. Good tailors and sewers take time to train, and supply has not kept up with demand.

Automation has also invaded the labor-intensive, better-tailored-clothing industry (see Figure 9.10). In the past, 1 to $1^1/2$ hours were required to hand-press a man's grade 6 or 61 suit. Today that time is reduced to a matter of minutes by means of a computer-controlled, automated system that steam-presses each part of the suit. In fact, with computer-assisted machines to mark and cut cloth, manufacturers of tailored clothing can, and sometimes do, turn out a garment entirely by machine.

In general, the industry is gradually becoming more machine-oriented than operator-oriented. This is a vast change for an industry that, throughout most of its history, prided itself on the individual workmanship that went into many of its products.

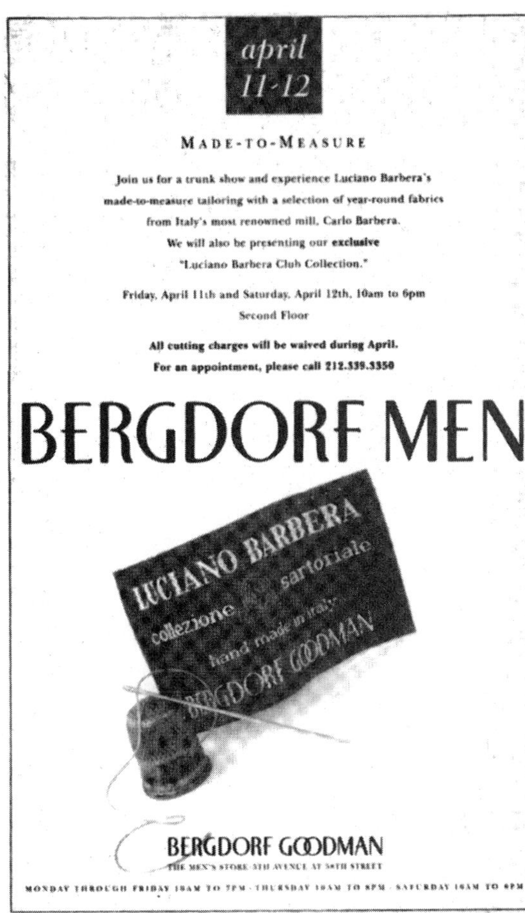

FIGURE 9.10
Computer technology has taken over some hand-tailoring operations, even in top quality tailored suits.
© Bergdorf Goodman.

Then & Now

Go Get a Job – Go Buy a Suit

"Everyone wants to be Cary Grant, Even I want to be Cary Grant," so said Cary Grant! After two decades of flared, flowered, and flak, traditional styling is back in fashion.

For the past 20 years, men have experimented with a variety of looks in their wardrobes. From the mid 1970s to the mid 1990s, men have tried a variety of "looks." There was the post-hippie look (flowered shirts and matching ties with velvet jackets), the quasi-military look (flak jackets, safari jackets, duck-hunting jackets), the Milanese deconstructed look (two sizes too large), and the casual Friday look (jeans to the office Friday, downsized on Monday).

Then came the new millennium, and the fashion trends and media hailed it as the "sartorial" look, (go buy a suit!). After all the fuss about "casual Fridays" many young men have discovered suits and all the cool accessories that go with them. For the past few years, the American white-collar worker has been anything but white-collar. Trickle-down techie casual, of course, led legions of managers and executives to the racks in search of VC-blue dress shirts and chinos. But with White House suit-and-tie dress code in place, dot-coms gone from status to stigma, and men more in touch with their "sartorial" side, suits are enjoying a renewed interest.

The suit carries an air of success, taste, and sophistication. In the hierarchy of style, a good suit remains a man's trump card. It is designed to make men look better, to break the boundaries between social classes, and to make a small man tall or a fat man slim. t is, in its best form, an outfit that will never fail! But remember—no one can be Cary Grant, but everyone will try.

Assuming you are not an investment banker, you don't need ten suits; you only need four and here they are:

The Fab Four

The Standard Blue: Great for business, lunches, New York Mayors, summer dinners, or casual parties. Can be worn with black or brown shoes, even white if you're daring. Reflects well by a pool. Standard blue means navy, with no room for paler shades, even if you went to UNC

The Classic Gray: Appropriate for everything and even makes a redhead look dandy. Grays also are the best patterns, especially in the chevron family. Start with plain, move to window-pane. Even such, gray is never controversial. It's the Switzerland of suits.

The Basic Black: Our favorite and the perennial classic, it's fit for the Oscars or your sister's wedding, the perfect compliment to a good white shirt, beloved by gangsters, designers, and undertakers (those jobs with the highest doses of fashion-conscious aptitudes; respectively, aggression, vanity, and wisdom). If you only own one suit, this is it.

Any of the above, with pinstripes.

Sources

G. Bruce Boyer, "Classic Conscious," The Good Life. Source: http//www.CIGA-RAFIONARDO.COM, 8/1998.

The Editors, "Men's Fashion", *The Morning News*, April 15, 2002. Source: http//www.themorning... al/mens,

The Charlotte Observer, August 7, 2000, reprinted in The First Choice by Crystal Dempsay. Source: http//www.searchproinc.com

Ethan Smith, "Go Buy a Suit," *The Industry Standard*, June 12, 2001. Source: http//www.thestandard.come.

The blue pinstripe suit is perfect for the professional man.
Courtesy, Fairchild Publications, Inc.

Foreign Production and Imports

Price competition is very strong in the men's wear market. A very important factor in setting prices at wholesale is the cost of labor. Because of this an increasing number of men's wear producers, particularly sportswear firms, are building plants or contracting to have work done in areas outside the country, where land and labor costs are lower.

Traditional men's wear manufacturers had turned away from contractors and stayed away until recently for several reasons.

1. The men's wear industry had a pattern of very slow style change, and contracting was not as economical as inside-shop production.
2. Improved equipment and cheaper electric power helped make production in inside shops more practical and efficient.
3. As quality became increasingly important, men's wear manufacturers found it easier to control work within their own factories than in the contractors' factories.

Imports have also made inroads in the U.S. men's wear market. Their promise of lower production prices and solid quality, plus a demand for exclusivity, have led more retailers to build up their direct-import programs and buy indirect imports (clothing made abroad for U.S. manufacturers).

Specialty Trends in Retailing

Men's wear producers may no longer be specializing as much as they once did, but this does not mean that specialization is dying out. In fact, there are several interesting new trends toward specialization, mostly on the retail side of the business.

The number of men's wear stores rapidly increased in the 1960s and then decreased in the early 1970s. The 1980s saw a slight increase, most notably in stores specializing in active sportswear in response to the health and fitness craze.

In the early 1990s, Army/Navy stores attracted a whole new customer age group during the height of the "grunge look." The 1990s also witnessed the expansion of national chains catering to the needs of men and women for casual and dress-casual wardrobes. The Gap has segmented this market by price with its Banana Republic subsidiary at the high end, Gap stores in the middle, and Old Navy at more moderate prices.

In addition, retailers that had traditionally catered exclusively to the women's market began to take advantage of the new fashion-oriented men's market by opening specialty stores. In 1987, The Limited, for example, opened a chain of men's sports and leisure wear stores called Express Man.

Also gaining in popularity are men's clothing discounters. Popular discounters are Syms, Today's Man, BFO (Buyer's Factory Outlet), and NBO (National Brands Outlet) on the East Coast; The Men's Wearhouse; National Dry Goods in Detroit; and The Suitery in Chicago. Loehmann's, the venerable women's discount chain, opened men's departments in selected stores around the country.

Catalog sales are another specialty trend. Major retailers, as well as specialty stores, have begun to send out catalogs geared exclusively to men, and stores such as L.L. Bean, which always sold by catalog, report an increase in business. Catalogs are typically slated for a specific market; that is, they specialize in low prices; certain styles or fashions, such as golf or western; a certain size range, such as big and tall; or exclusivity. Those specialty catalogs that have done thorough market research and have offered their customers exactly what they want have been quite successful.

Style and Lifestyle

The most important trend in men's apparel is the continuing boom in casual and sportswear. As early as 1987, a vice president and director of men's clothing at Neiman Marcus summed up the men's market, saying: "The clothing business hasn't changed, but the lifestyle has."[11] At least the second half of that observation remains true more than a decade later. The first half is debatable: Many of the major players remain the same, but their continuing success has been correlated with their ability to adapt to the changes in the buying behavior of the ultimate consumer. Because men are now interested in fashion, they are buying different kinds of clothes. Most men's wardrobes today can be divided into three categories according to use: suits for formal business and social occasions, activewear for sports (spectator as well as participatory) and for the most casual situations, and slacks and sports coats for everyday office wear and after-work socializing. Matching the category to the occasion is not always a clearcut, easy decision, however. Separates may be acceptable for client meetings, depending on the firm and the client, for example. And at some social events, men dressed in the three categories may mingle comfortably.

The daily decision about what to wear to work is probably the most important wardrobe choice because of its relationship to career success. The question plagues employers as much as employees. When dress codes began to be relaxed, the certainty about image that was associated with the business suit faded. Deliberately or by chance, new dress codes are being created. Savvy men's wear marketers among both producers and retailers are coming to the rescue with seminars and brochures.

When men do wear traditional tailored clothing these days, they favor quality in fabric and workmanship and styling that flatters their build and expresses their taste. Spending $700 to $800 for a tailored suit is not unusual. Since many men no longer need an assortment of suits for business wear, they can afford to invest more in each suit they do buy. And they want value for their money.

Separates

Although the popular-priced blazers, vests, and slacks produced by such companies as Levi Strauss and Haggar have found a permanent place in the men's wear market, with the renewed emphasis on quality, better-priced tailored clothes are once again selling well. They are unlikely, however, to edge out separates. Even Hartmarx, the giant maker of men's suits, introduced sportswear lines under the Hickey-Freeman and Hart Schnaffner & Marx names. Colors are lighter and brighter in these new lines and the items are meant to be mixed and matched, as women have done for decades with separates.[12]

Shirt Styles

Producers have recently made some changes in shirt sleeve sizes. Men's long-sleeved dress shirts are made in neck sizes 14 1/2 to 17 inches, graduated in half-inches. In each size, the sleeve length has, until recently, also been graduated from 32 to 35 inches. In an effort to reduce inventories and increase stock turnover, though, producers have begun making dress shirts in two sleeve lengths—regular (32–34 inches) and long (34–35 inches). Over 50 percent of all men's dress shirts are now produced only in regular and long sleeve lengths.

Whether this trend will prevail is unclear. Not all shirtmakers have converted to the new sizing, and with the renewed interest in quality, there has also been a reverse trend among some producers toward making exact sleeve sizes again.

Fitted dress shirts, tapered through the torso, or with darts to make them fit close to the body, resurfaced in the late 1990s after an absence of more than a decade. They were widely supported by designers, led by Ralph Lauren, and including Perry Ellis and Tommy Hilfiger.

At the opposite end of the fashion spectrum, interest in short-sleeved dress shirts blossomed, with the cartoon character Dilbert leading the way.

Designer and Brand-Name Labels

Although designers such as Ralph Lauren, Calvin Klein, Giorgio Armani, and Helmut Lang have made an enormous impact on men's fashion, few believe that their impact on men's fashion will equal that of women's fashion. In most American stores, national brands and private labels are more likely to be in competition for retail space than are designer clothes. Yet this too may be changing. For the first time, there are more influential designers with serious men's wear collections than without them.[13]

National brands, which have already had considerable impact, are expected to remain strong in the foreseeable future. In tailored men's wear, brand names are seen as a sign of quality. Private label merchandise is also making inroads. As is the case with women's private labels, they provide men's wear retailers with exclusivity and higher profit margins.

Retail operations strive to provide their customers with a mix of designer names, brand names, and private labels. For manufacturers, representation in the men's department of a department store may mean supplying fixtures and promotional videos for their own store-within-a-store or for sections within such areas as activewear or sportswear.

Summary and Review

Designer and brand names are part of the push to provide men with up-to-date fashion. And while there will always be a market for classic or traditional men's clothes, industry forecasters predict that men's wear will continue to be ever more fashion oriented. The Europeanization of the American tailored clothing market has brought an appreciation of quality and fit. Comfort and convenience remain important to the average man, especially in casual wear and active wear.

While men's wear changes more slowly than women's wear, the industry saw dramatic change and growth in the 1990s, as dress-down Fridays were adopted by most businesses in the United States. The activewear category also saw dramatic growth as firm, toned bodies became the goal of tens of thousands of men. As the baby boomers aged, more and more men turned to plastic surgery and cosmetics to hide the signs of aging.

The industry was quick to capitalize on the new interest in men's wear, offering increasingly diverse products by using increased automation. Meanwhile, foreign production and imports continued to climb. Retailers jumped on the bandwagon, offering improved visual merchandising, and increased advertising in newspapers, magazines, and on the Internet.

Trade Talk

Define or briefly explain the following terms:

activewear	European styling
bridge apparel	inside shop
contemporary men's wear	short run
	slop shop
drop	suit separates
dual distribution	tailored-clothing firm

For Review

1. What effect did the industrial revolution have on male apparel? What socioeconomic factors were responsible for the drastic changes that occurred?
2. What three developments in the mid-19th century were largely responsible for the development of the men's ready-to-wear industry in this country? How did each help to accelerate those developments?
3. Discuss the development of sportswear and casual wear in the men's market and the influence they have had on the men's wear industry as a whole.
4. For what three reasons did early manufacturers of men's tailored clothing give up the use of contractors?
5. What role have unions played in the production of men's wear? Why were unions formed in the 19th and early 20th centuries? What role do they play in the industry today?
6. Name the different segments into which the men's wear industry is subdivided, on the basis of the type of product lines each produces. What specific products are produced by each segment?
7. How has the sizing of men's suits and dress shirts been simplified in recent years?
8. What is the role of trade shows in promoting men's fashions? Name and describe five trade shows that command national attention.
9. How have men's wear producers tried to compensate for the rising cost of labor and the shortage of skilled workers in the United States?
10. Describe two men's wear style trends that are likely to continue.

For Discussion

1. Is the conservative men's suit dying out, or is it taking on a new life in the wake of more casual business dress codes? In what situations are tailored suits commonly worn in your community? What local trends do you see?
2. What is the role of designer names in men's wear? Which men's designer fashions are currently popular?
3. Discuss the influence of modern production techniques on the manufacturing of men's wear. What are the effects on costs and pricing?

References

1. Harry A Cobrin, *The Men's Clothing Industry* (New York: Fairchild Publications, 1970), p. 67.
2. William Nabers, "The New Corporate Uniforms," *Fortune*, November 13, 1995, p. 132.
3. Nancy Brumback, "Men Like Shopping After All; Two-Year Study Finds They Shop With a Purpose," *Daily News Record*, February 26, 2001, p. 1B.

4. Jennifer Steinhauer, "What Vanity and Casual Fridays Wrought," *New York Times*, April 9, 1997, p. D5.
5. Carol Angrisani, "Today's Man," *Brand Marketing*, January 2001, p. 32.
6. Ira P. Schneiderman, "Friday Wear Trend Far From Over," *Daily News Record*, August 19, 1996, p. 24.
7. *Hoover's Company Profiles* (Austin, TX: Hoover's, Inc., 2001).
8. Robert Berner, "An Old Clothier Learns Some New Tricks," *Wall Street Journal*, July 24, 1997, p. B1.
9. Barbara Ettore, "Business and Buttonholes," *New York Times*, October 28, 1979, p. F1.
10. "Menswear Feature," *SportswearNet International*, November 1996.
11. Herbert Blueweiss, "Clothing at Neiman-Marcus," *Daily News Record*, November 29, 1987, p. 10.
12. Steinhauer, "What Vanity," p. D5.
13. Amy M. Spindler, "A New Symbiosis Between Men's and Women's Wear," *New York Times*, December 24, 1996, p. B6.

CHAPTER 10

Children's and Teen's Apparel

WHAT'S IN IT FOR YOU?

Everything you always wanted to know about the influence of fashion on the children's and teen's apparel industry.

Key Concepts:

- The impact of demographics on the children's apparel industry
- The history of the children's apparel industry
- Size categories of children's wear
- Unique features of infants' and toddlers' wear
- Merchandising and marketing of children's apparel
- Licensing in the children's apparel industry
- Industry trends and responses to social issues

We are all familiar with the phrase, "Out of the mouth of babes." Today, as media bombards children with grown-up images, new demands are heard "out of the mouths of babes"—demands for all things that are presented to them on television, in movies, and in books. Gone are the days when children were seen and not heard—producers of products such as soft drinks, candy, food, music, movies, and apparel heed the newly acquired sophistication of children. Everything presented to children is entertainment, and children want it all! This presents a wonderful opportunity for designers and producers of children's apparel to adapt to the wants of these savvy new customers. A classic example of this is the way that Burberry, the famous London fashion house, decided to continue their brand extension. They produced two new products featuring their famous signature plaid—a luxury children's line featuring shearling coats, plaid duffle bags, and a Burberry Barbie. Burberry outfitted this legendary doll icon with a plaid skirt and classic trench coat, plus a plaid messenger bag. Ah,

FIGURE 10.1A
Barbie, the famous fashion doll, has a wide variety of clothing and style—much like today's teen fashion!
Courtesy, © Corbis Sygma/Scott Houston.

FIGURE 10.1B
Inspired by plus-sized model Emme, this fashion doll shows a new, stylish image for full fashioned teens.
Courtesy, Fairchild Publications, Inc.

to be young, fashionable, and in love with Barbie![1] (See Figure 10.1a).

Making clothing fun for pint-sized consumers and the adults who pay for their wardrobes is a serious business, generating more than $25.4 billion annually in U.S. retailing.[2]

Psychological Importance of Children's, Tween's, and Teen's Clothes

The apparel industry is not the only beneficiary of the growing interest in dressing children well. Psychologists believe that clothes play an important role in shaping and guiding a child's self-image. As parents understand the role that clothes play at various stages of a child's growth, they can help to ensure that a child's appearance will enhance his or her striving to become a mature, self-confident adult.[3]As California designer Maline Gerber said:

> *A customer who had dressed her daughter in my line throughout the girl's childhood recently thanked me for the influence that my clothes had on her child's development. The girl received consistent positive attention, which contributed significantly to her confidence. This comment made me realize that my work really has an impact on the development of children's personalities.*[4]

Proponents of the idea of school uniforms argue that uniforms foster a sense of belonging to a group and encourage neatness. Their opponents point out that selecting one's own attire is a form of self-expression.[5] Both views recognize the importance of clothing to a child's self-identity.

Demographics and the Children's, Tween's, and Teen's Apparel Industry

This apparel industry is unusual in the extent to which it has been shaped by demographics. Patterns of childbearing tend to be cyclical. Although the birth rate had been steadily declining since the end of the 19th century, the aftermath of World War II brought about a baby boom. Women who had been working to support the war effort turned over their jobs to the returning soldiers and went home to become full-time housewives—and mothers. The birth rate soared. Three to four children per family was not unusual. Between 1953 and 1964, a whopping four million births occurred every year.

In the 1970s, many people became concerned that the world population was growing too rapidly and advocated that families have fewer children. More women began to work outside the home again. The birth rate declined and the average number of children per family sank to fewer than two.

The 1980s did not bring about another baby boom, with three to four children per family, but because the baby boom babies had themselves reached child-bearing age, the number of babies born increased for the first time since the 1960s. This increase occurred even though women continued to have a statistical average of 1.5 children and many postponed motherhood to continue their careers. Over 3.5 million babies were born in 1987, and almost 3.9 million were born in 1988. Besides the increasing number of children, the culture of spending in the 1980s contributed to the success of the children's apparel industry. The number of mothers who worked soared, and two-income families generally had more discretionary income. People not only bought more for each child, but they purchased more expensive goods than in the past.

In the 1990s, parents reined in their family clothing budgets. For single mothers and for couples whose sense of job security was diminished by mergers and downsizing, the mother's income came to be viewed as essential to the family's financial well-being rather than "extra" money. But parents' more cautious spending behavior has not caused a downturn in the children's apparel industry. What has happened instead is that new markets for children's wear have emerged. In 1996, the first wave of baby boom babies turned 50, and the population of *their* elders was growing, thanks to life-prolonging improvements in health care. All those doting grandparents have made the over-50 age group the top spenders on children's retail clothing. Toward the other end of the age spectrum, children themselves, especially those over age 12, have become a formidable group of shoppers. They spent more than $124.2 billion in 2001, much of it on clothing, and their style- and brand-consciousness contributes significantly to the success of such brands as Tommy Hilfiger, Calvin Klein, Guess, Levi's, and Gap.

The teen market also reached a fever pitch in 2000, when annual teen spending rose to a dizzying height of over $140 billion, much of it on clothing. Although a slower economy lowered the figures in 2001 to $124 billion, teenagers still consumed more than they had before the boom years (in 1998, annual sales figures were $91.5 billion). This indicates that teens largely stick to their consumer habits even in a tougher economic climate.[6]

What should we expect to happen to the children's apparel business in the 21st century? Demographers project a steady increase in the actual number of people under the age of 20 through the first few decades, but they will comprise a smaller portion of the total population of the United States because the over-65 age group is expected to grow at a faster rate than the birth rate. The market for children's clothing is expected to remain steady, as it was in the last decades of the 20th century. The markets for women's and men's wear are expected to decline, but the dollar amounts spent on adults will continue to be greater than the amounts spent to clothe children (see Figure 10.2).

History of the Children's Apparel Industry

Although boy's wear is considered part of the men's apparel industry, for our purposes it will be considered as part of children's wear and described in this chapter.

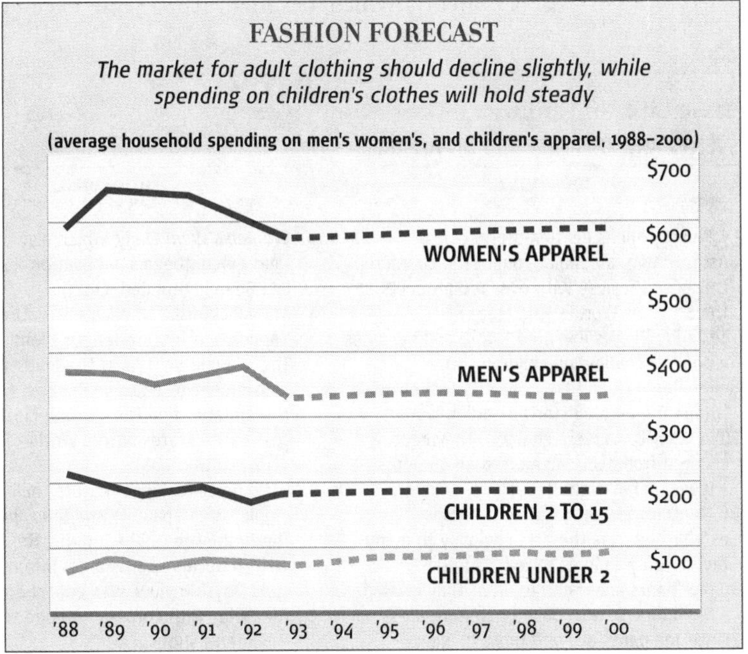

FIGURE 10.2

The average family spends less on children's clothing than on adults, but this comparison does not suggest child neglect. Children's clothing is typically less expensive than comparable adult clothing. Teens may wear adult sizes. Can you think of other reasons for the difference in spending?

Sources: U.S. Bureau of Labor Statistics' Consumer Expenditure Surveys and American Demographics projections.

As a commercial activity, the children's wear industry is a phenomenon of the 20th century. For most of history, children were dressed like miniature adults. Study a portrait from the Renaissance or the American colonial era, and you will see children wearing the same low necklines, bustles, and pantaloons that were currently stylish with adults.

When children's clothes finally began to look different from those that adults wore toward the end of the 1800s, they took on the look of uniforms. All little girls, for example, dressed in a similar drab outfit—dark high-button shoes, a mid-calf length skirt, and dark stockings.

Clothes were made extra large so children could grow into them. Their construction was sturdy so they could be handed down to younger children. Many children's clothes were hand-sewn or made by a few apparel manufacturers who seldom offered any variations on the clothes, nor, for that matter, experienced any growth in their businesses. It did not matter that children's clothes were dull and unattractive because no child would dare to protest what parents wanted him or her to wear. One 1800s success story was the William Carter Company, which began in 1865 and became one of the largest children's underwear companies. It is still in business today.

Although a few designers specialized in high-priced children's wear in the early 1900s, it was not until after World War I that the commercial production and distribution of stylish children's wear began. Not surprisingly, the growth of the children's wear industry followed in the wake of the developing women's wear industry. When women stopped making their own clothes, they also stopped making their children's clothes.

The children's wear industry also grew because manufacturers found ways to make factory-produced clothing sturdier than homemade clothes. The development of snaps, zippers, and more durable sewing methods were important contributions.

Another important step in the manufacture of children's clothes occurred after World War I, when manufacturers began to standardize children's wear sizes. What began as a very primitive method of sizing children's clothing has since turned into a highly sophisticated sizing operation, with many categories and subdivisions.

The next major change in the children's wear industry was the introduction of radio and movies into Americans' lives in the 1920s,

Time Line for Children's Wear—1900 to 2000

EVENTS AND THEIR EFFECTS ON APPAREL

1900–1910

J.C.Penney opens his first store. (1902)
Buster Brown, a popular comic strip character, is licensed for use with over 100 products at the St. Louis World's Fair. (1904)
The Teddy Bear is invented (1905) and becomes a popular emblem on children's wear.
Sears, Roebuck and Co. opens its first store. (1906) The catalog started earlier.
Child labor Laws were enacted. They kept children from working more than 66 hours a week and at night. (1907)
Dr. Denton's Sleeping Garment Mills is established; It is the first company to manufacture only children's wear. (1909)
Rubber pants are manufactured. They caused a revolution in how baby boys were dressed, since the pants allowed them to wear trousers instead of skirts before they were potty trained. (1910)
OshKosh'B Gosh introduces overall for boys. (1910)

1910–1920

Women's Wear Daily, which also covers girl's wear, begins publication. (1910)
L.L. Bean is founded. (1913)
Mary Pickford, "America's Sweetheart," appears in feature-length silent films.
The Triangle Shirtwaist fire leads to the movement to end sweatshops. (1911)
The athletic shoe is invented. (1916)
The United States enters World War I. (1917–1918)
Little boys' fashions feature "military look," with epaulets and brass buttons.
The first issue of The Infant's Department, which became Earnshaw's Infants', Girls', and Boys' Review, was published. (1917)
The Stride Rite Corp. is founded to make children's shoes. (1919)

1920–1930

The first Miss America is crowned. (1921) Thousands of girls aspire to become beauty queens.
The Health-Tex Company is founded. (1921)
The first commercial radio broadcast is made. (1922)
The romper is invented. (1923)
The first Macy's Thanksgiving Day parade is held. (1924)
Winnie-the-Pooh by A.A.Milne is published. (1926)
The Lee Company invents the zipper jean. (1926)
The sunsuit is invented to provide children with maximum exposure to sunlight, which was thought to be healthful. (1927)
The first "talking" motion picture is made. (1927)
Walt Disney introduces Mickey Mouse. (1928)
The Stock market crashes, ushering in the Great Depression. (1929) As a result, millions of children wear hand-me-down adult cast-off clothing, and patched garments.

FIGURE 10.3

Based upon numerous industry publications and company histories.

1930s, and 1940s. All across the country mothers dressed their little girls like Shirley Temple and their boys like cowboy western heros. Teens wanted to dress like Judy Garland and Mickey Rooney, stars of countless teen musicals.

In the 1950s, another change—really a revolution—was brought about by the introduction of television into Americans' homes. It did not take advertisers long to discover that children, among the largest group of consumers of television, could be targeted directly. From *Howdy Doody* to the *Mickey Mouse Club*—and their innumerable followers through the 1990s—kids loved TV, shows and commercials alike. Then it was a short step to gear the advertising in other media—radio as well as magazines and newspapers—toward children. See Figure 10.3 for a time line of children's wear in the 20th century.

Television programs geared to audiences of different ages help to establish the popularity of clothing styles for each age group, from the preschoolers playing on *Sesame Street* to the high school students on *Dawson's Creek* and *Buffy the Vampire Slayer*. Interestingly, it is the Los Angeles area manufacturers and retailers who are taking the lead in providing teen fashions tailored to the less developed proportions of preteen girls.[7]

Organization and Operation of the Children's, Tween's, and Teen's Apparel Industry

There are close to 1,000 companies that make children's apparel. Despite the prominence of such giant companies as Carter's, OshKosh B'Gosh, Bugle Boy, Gerber Children's Wear, and Health-Tex, most children's clothes are still made by small, family-owned businesses. Notable among them are the following multigenerational firms: Quiltex, Celebrity International, Will'Beth, Raj Manufacturing, and Spencer's of Mount Airy.

Many adult apparel producers, including Levi Strauss, Patagonia, Old Navy, Gap, and Reebok, also operate children's apparel divisions. Many adult apparel designers have also begun children's divisions.

Like adult clothing, children's wear is divided into categories based on price, size, and

1930–1940

Shirley Temple, age 6, makes her first movie, and her long licensing career begins. Little girls want to look just like her—from her 52 bouncy curls to her short, frilly dresses. (1934)
The Dionne Quintuplets are born and everything is licensed in their name. (1935)
Walt Disney makes *Snow White and the Seven Dwarfs,* which becomes the top-grossing movie of the year and a licensing bonanza. (1938)
Judy Garland and Mickey Rooney star in Love Finds *Andy Hardy,* the first of their many teenage films together. (1938)
Superman (1938) and Batman (1939) comics are published.
Nylon is invented by DuPont, (1934) and nylon stockings are introduced. (1939)

1940–1950

The Child Labor Law restricts employment for those under 16. (1940)
An embargo is placed on Japanese silk. (1940)
The United States enters World War II, (1941–1946) and there is a new austerity in children's wear. Clothes and shoes are rationed. The short Eisenhower jacket becomes popular in boy's wear.
Florence Eiseman Inc. founded; influential designer of children's wear. (1945)
Baby and Child Care by Dr. Benjamin Spock is published. (1946)
Teen girls wear saddle shoes, sweater sets, and pageboy hairdos. They swoon over "crooners' like Frank Sinatra. Teen boys wear "zoot suits" after the war.
Hopalong Cassidy is the first western shown on a new invention called "television." (1949) It's only in black and white, but a bright new era in licensing has dawned.

type of merchandise. Children's clothes are produced in budget, moderate, better-priced, and designer price ranges. Most children's clothes bought by parents are in the budget and moderate price ranges, although, as previously noted, better-priced and designer merchandise is a common gift purchase by grandparents and other adults. The retailer giant Wal-Mart has taken tween TV culture one step further by launching a clothing brand from teenybopper twins Mary-Kate and Ashley Olsen (from *Full House* and *Two of a Kind)* in 2001.

Size Categories

Children's wear is divided into seven basic size ranges (see Table 10.1) to accommodate the differences in body proportions and ranges of height and weight of children in different age groups.

As Dr. William J. Kish, a professor of pediatrics and Chairman of the American Academy of Pediatrics' nutrition board pointed out: "American children over the past decade have been getting significantly heavier." This trend has led manufacturers and retailers to respond. As fashion writer Dana Canedy said:

After years of neglect, the children's industry is recognizing that overweight children make up an increasing segment of the fashion market, and retail chains from the JC Penney Company to Kids "R" Us are rushing to add larger sizes . . . and special departments for pudgy pre-adolescents.[8]

Although the actual size range is the same, the preteen sizes for girls offer more sophisticated styling than the girls' sizes. Similarly, the **young men's** category (also called **prep, student,** or **teen**) stresses sophisticated styling more than boys' sized apparel does.

Special Features of Infants' and Toddlers' Wear

Clothing in infants' and toddlers' sizes is designed to meet needs that are unique to the youngest children. For example, pants are available with snaps along the inseams to facilitate diaper changes. Undershirts may have snaps to open at the front so that they don't have to be pulled over the baby's head. Elasticized waistbands—rather than buttons or zippers—make changing pants or skirts easier for adults or for toddlers who are learning to

Time Line for Children's Wear—1900 to 2000

EVENTS AND THEIR EFFECTS ON APPAREL

1950–1960

Acrylic fibers introduced; Orlon sweaters quickly become popular. (1950)
Color TV is introduced. (1950) It is very expensive at first.
Charlotte's Web by E.B. White is published. (1952)
The Cat In The Hat by Dr. Seuss is published. (1957)
The United States enters the Korean War. (1950–1953)
Howdy Doody is an early TV show for kids; its popularity licensed playwear. (1947)
Girls wear short "poodle cut" hairdos, and circle skirts with crinoline petticoats. Saddle shoes are "out" and "ballerina" flats are "in."
Polyester fibers introduced. (1953)
Davy Crockett becomes a hit song, movie, and TV show; kids all over America wear coonskin caps. (1954)
Polio vaccine developed by Dr. Jonas Salk. (1955)
The Mickey Mouse Club starts on TV and Disneyland, in California, opens. (1955)
Rebel Without A Cause raises James Dean to stardom; he becomes a symbol of rebellion to the young. (1955)
Elvis Presley appears (from the waist up) on *The Ed Sullivan Show,* becomes "The King of Rock and Roll" (1956)
Spandex fiber is introduced by DuPont; it is widely used in swimwear, hosiery, and intimate apparel. (1958)
The first Barbie doll is introduced by Mattel. (1959)
Peanuts and Snoopy become national icons.
The Hush Puppies Company opens. (1958)

1960–1970

The Communists erect the Berlin Wall. (1961)
The disposable diaper is invented. (1961)
The first Wal-Mart and the first K-Mart open. (1962)
The United States Enters the Vietnam War. (1965–1975)
Spandex yarns are introduced. (1964)
The Gap opens its first store in San Francisco. (1969)
Star Trek begins on TV. (1966)
The Beatles conquer the music world.
Sesame Street begins on TV. (1969)
The Brady Bunch begins on TV. (1969)
The first Earth Day is held; environmental awareness grows; issue fascinates children. (1970)
"Flower children" protest war, wear jeans, tie-dye T-shirts, long hair, beads. Unisex look trickles down to kids.

FIGURE 10.3 (CONTINUED)

TABLE 10.1 Size Ranges of Children's Wear

SIZE CATEGORY	AGE RANGE	SIZES
Infant's	Newborn–1 year	0–24 months (0–3 months, 6-, 9-, 12-, 18-, and 24-months Newborn, small, medium, large, extra-large
Toddler's	2–3 years	2T–4T
Children's	3–6 years	3–6X for girls 3–7 for boys
Girl's	7–14 years	7–16
Preteen	7–14 years	6–16 for girls
Boy's	6 or 7–14 or 15 years	8–20 (available in husky, regular and slim)
Young men	8–20 years, concentrating on 14–20 years	8–20

dress themselves. Stretchy suits and snowsuits for infants and sleepwear for infants and toddlers may be fitted with soft-soled "feet" to offer extra warmth and protection. Mitten-like flaps on newborns' sleepwear help to prevent babies from scratching themselves with their fast-growing fingernails. Bonnets and caps tie under the chin, and bootees have elastic around the ankles to keep these clothing items on the baby.

Layettes, collections of crib and bath linens, sleepwear, and underwear for infants, include

1970–1980

Disney World opens in Orlando. (1971)
The Muppets. (1976)
Star Wars opens and The Empire begins. (1977)
Soccer becomes the fastest growing sport in the United States (1977)
Skateboards introduced. (1977)
The *Annie Hall* (1977) men's wear look for women and girls.
Saturday Night Fever starts disco craze. (1977) Teen boys wear white polyester leisure suits and black shirts.
Fruit of the Loom introduces Underoos, decorated boys underwear 1978); girl's Undaroos follow.
Superman: The Movie (1978) and *Superman II* (1980) are mega-hits, and little boys begin wearing caped pajamas and undershorts like Superman's.
Sony introduces the Walkman. (1979)
Hip-huggers, bell-bottoms, granny gowns, tube tops, vests.
Designer jeans with back pocket logos sweep the world.

1980–1990

French Toast opens. (1980)
Michael Jackson's "Thriller" album is bestseller ever. (1982)
VCRs and home videos are popular.
Roller blades, bike shorts–active wear takes off.
Yuppies and the "baby boomlet"
California surf wear with bold colors and graphics.
ET: The Extra-Terrestrial is a hit with kids all over the world, and another licensing frenzy begins. (1982)
Cabbage Patch Kids introduced. (1983)
The "ribbon dress" for girls. (1983)
Miami Vice on TV has huge impact–unconstructed jackets with T-shirts and sunglasses. (1984)
Baby Guess/Guess Girls begin. (1985)
Cotton Caboodle, Flapdoodles, and Joe Boxer Corp. open. (1985)
L.A. Gear opens. (1986)
The Limited Too opens. (1987)
Natural fibers preferred; polyester scorned.
Catalog shopping increases dramatically.
Backpacks appear on kids; adults want them, too.
Tommy Hilfiger opens. (1989)
Little Mermaid, Disney's film, opens. (1989)

1990–2000

Barney starts on TV and toddlers love him. (1992)
Home computers proliferate and surfing the Internet is "in." Fleece and shearling newly popular as cold winters occur.
"Grunge" music and look sweep the country.
Cow & Lizard opens. (1990)
Jurassic Park and dinosaurs everywhere. (1993)
Toy Story opens. (1996)
Manufactured fibers blended with natural fibers. Spandex is blended with almost every fiber!
Home Alone opens and spawns sequels. (1990)
The Lion King is a blockbuster hit for Disney. (1994)
Nicole Miller for Kids opens. (1995)
School uniform legislation. (1995–1997)
Michael Jordan and Air Jordans super popular.
The *Star Wars Trilogy* returns. (1997–2000)

some unique items, such as sleeping sacs with drawstrings at the bottom. A one-piece undergarment, known as a "onesie," consisting of a shirt with a long tail that extends under a diaper and snaps to the front of the shirt, is another item designed specifically for infants.

Product Specialization

Children's wear manufacturers typically specialize by product. One producer will make only girls' knits, while another makes only girls' dresses, and another makes only preteen sportswear. But unlike the producers of adult wear, children's wear producers often make a single type of clothing in several size ranges. For example, a producer may make boys' sportswear in sizes 8 through 20, while a producer of girls' dresses may make a product in toddlers through girls sizes.

A few observations about the fabrics used in children's wear are worth keeping in mind. One is the enduring popularity of knits for infants' wear and for tops in the everyday wardrobes of girls and boys through the larger size ranges. Another is the demand for natural fibers, especially cotton. Anyone interested in the children's apparel industry should be aware of the Flammable Fabrics Act of 1972 and its subsequent modifications, which require that sleepwear for children be treated with flame-retardant finishes.

The same design and production methods that are used in the manufacture of adult apparel are used in children's wear, although they are often simplified. While children's garments require less fabric, they are usually more expensive to make, because they require more labor.

FIGURE 10.4
Fashion consciousness starts with the very youngest.
Courtesy, Fairchild Publications, Inc.

The Role of Fashion in Children's, Tween's, and Teen's Wear

Even the most basic lines of children's clothing reflect attempts to make the clothes fashionable, and the demand for style, once primarily an urban phenomenon, is now felt in every area.

The demand for stylish children's clothes, which has escalated every year, has most recently culminated in designer clothing for children. Children's wear, however, must still be viewed as a business that is a *fashionable* rather than a *fashion* business. The difference is that while the children's wear industry produces fashionable clothing, the styles adapt men's and women's styles. They are not in and of themselves innovative, nor does new fashion start in children's wear lines. The backpack is one recent exception.

The children's wear industry also does not operate with the intensity of the adult clothing industry. Children's clothes, for example, do not follow a ready-to-wear production and design schedule.

Producers of children's clothing have typically operated on a one line per season production schedule, and four lines—spring, summer, winter, and fall—are typical. Lines are not updated during a season. Once a line has been shown and accepted, that is all the manufacturer produces. An exciting and very hot new look might appear at midseason, but this is still rare. Most manufacturers could not produce a new look until the following season, at which point demand may even have begun to decline.

The children's wear business has begun to make the kinds of operational changes that are necessary to permit it to stay more on top of changing fashion. Styles in children's wear used to trickle down from the adult fashion world, and typically lagged a year or more behind adult fashions. Today, however, the lag is shrinking.

Increasingly, children look to their own peers and to the group just ahead of them, young adults, for pace-setting styles and trends. Successful children's wear producers have learned that they too must look to the young adult fashion world for inspiration. This means watching fads as well as trends. Popular young adult fads and styles are increasingly being translated into children's wear lines (see Figure 10.5).

The industry has also begun to use fashion forecasting specialists to enable manufacturers to incorporate new styles into their lines as soon as a trend is spotted. At this point, the smaller (and trendier) manufacturers are still quicker to incorporate new styles and fashion than are the larger companies. The leading designers of adult fashion who have developed lines of children's apparel and the retailers whose store brands extend to the children's market—Talbots Baby and Talbots Kids, for example—can bring out corresponding lines of adult's and children's fashion concurrently.

FIGURE 10.5
Even children and teens know the Calvin Klein label.
1998 © Calvin Klein Jeans Kids, photo by Perry Ogden.

Merchandising and Marketing

Many of the features and activities of the children's wear industry are similar, if not identical, to those of the women's and men's apparel industries. Sales promotion and advertising activities for children's wear, however, are considerably more limited.

The few giants in the industry—Carter's, Health-Tex, and OshKosh B'Gosh—advertise aggressively to consumers. Smaller firms—the majority of firms producing budget and moderately priced children's wear—leave most consumer advertising to retailers. Firms producing higher priced, name-designer merchandise do a limited amount of consumer advertising. The high cost of this advertising is often shared with textile firms.

In general the industry limits its advertising to the trade press. Specialized publications that are concerned with children's wear include *Children's Business*, *Earnshaw's Infants'*, and *Girls' and Boys' Wear Review*. Trade publications that report on adult fashions, such as *Women's Wear Daily* and the *Daily News Record*, also carry children's wear advertising and news reports of interest to retailers on a regular basis. More and more companies are going on the Internet, often combining information about the company with a catalog.

FIGURE 10.6
More and more parents are seeking clothing that offers sun protection for their children. Koala Konnection's press kit shows one Australian manufacturer's response.
Courtesy, Koala Konnection™.

Market Centers

Most of the children's wear firms are located in the North Atlantic states, particularly in New York City. As is the trend in the women's and men's apparel industries, some factories have moved farther south in order to obtain lower production costs. In many cases goods are produced in foreign countries—the Far East primarily for outerwear, jeans, woven shirts, and sweaters; Greece, Spain, and Israel for infants' knits and apparel items. These countries offer lower production costs than do France, Italy, and Switzerland, which produce prestige merchandise. But the design, sales, and distribution centers of such firms remain in New York City. While New York continues to be the most important market center for children's wear, many producers maintain permanent showrooms in the large regional apparel marts, especially in Miami, and schedule showings there. Los Angeles, too, has emerged as a children's apparel center, not only because of its enormous manufacturing base, but also for the fashion trends that originate there. Dallas has Anthony Mark Hankins, for example, who sells his budget line of children's wear to Target Stores, among other retailers.

FIGURE 10.7
This trade show advertisement is an important place for children's apparel manufacturers to reach retail store buyers.

Trade Shows

Coast 2 Coast is a children's wear association sponsored by the CaliforniaMart in Los Angeles. It promotes through direct mail, floor displays, and caravans that bring in retailers from surrounding counties (see Figure 10.7). It also sponsors the Los Angeles Kids Show, held three times a year. The huge MAGIC International shows for men's, women's, and children's apparel and accessories are held in Las Vegas twice a year.

Other popular children's wear trade shows include the New York-based Children's Kids World Expo, Kids World Expo that runs concurrent with Magic in Las Vegas, and Style Max, a biannual women's and children's apparel show in Chicago.

Designer Labels

Children's designer-label clothing and accessories are highly visible in stores across the country. The appeal of these items seems to rise above income levels. Designer labels are available in stores geared to middle-income as well as high-income customers. Although designer wear for children has been around for a while—Izod introduced a boys' line in the late 1960s—the explosion in designer-label children's wear took off in the late 1970s with the designer jean craze.[9]

Designer labels are expected to continue to grow in children's wear. An interesting British Lifestyle Survey by Mintel in 2001 showed that parents continue to indulge their children with brand name clothing even when the economy is slow and they have less money for themselves. The study found that many parents sacrificed their own wardrobe to buy designer labels for their children.[10]

Well-known brand names in children's wear include Flapdoodle, Gymboree, Little Me, Absorba, Tickle Me!, Joe Boxer, Cotton Caboodle, and, of course, GUESS? and the Gap. Because they have designer-name status, some children's wear designers, following in the pioneering footsteps of Florence Eiseman and Ruth Scharf, have acquired celebrity status. These include Hanna Anderson and Sylvia Whyte.

Adult designers have also entered the children's wear arena. As David Wolfe, creative director of Doneger Group, a New York buying office said:

Status is definitely trickling down to kids. They are looking at their mothers and older sisters, and they want to wear the same brands. They are also looking at pop icons and want to dress just like them.[11]

Several companies, including Esprit, GUESS?, Patagonia, Ralph Lauren, and Jessica McClintock have launched separate divisions of children's wear. Other designers offering children's lines are Gucci, Donna Karan's DKNY and Moschino, which markets Moschino Bambino for infants and toddlers and Moschino junior for 2 to 15 year olds.

Status names are also changing the shape of the boys' wear industry. It is difficult to tell which came first, though—the boys' demand for designer clothes or the designers' efforts to enter the boys' wear market. Whatever the case, well-known fashion designers are now competing for space alongside traditional branded merchandise in boys' wear departments. Boys' wear, in fact, has become a prime area for designers such as Pierre Cardin, Yves Saint Laurent, Ralph Lauren, Tommy Hilfiger, and Calvin Klein. Of course, not all designers actually design and manufacture all the products sold under their labels. One example is Perry Ellis, whose girl's and boy's wear is designed and produced by J.A. Besner & Sons of Canada, which has the licensing agreement.

Licensing

Like designer labels, other kinds of licensed names provide a sense of fashion rightness, in addition to giving a garment or line instant identification in consumers' minds. As a result, as the children's wear industry became more fashion-conscious, manufacturers were quick to produce licensed goods. Today, in addition to designer names, the ever-popular cartoon and toy character licenses share the spotlight with a growing number of sports and corporate licenses.

Character Licensing

The first licensed cartoon character was Buster Brown, in 1904. Licensed cartoon and toy characters, long a staple with children, are still thriving in the 1990s. Younger children especially enjoy wearing representations of their favorite characters. A widespread example is Barney, whose plump purple picture adorns toddlers coast to coast.

Character licenses dominate in children's T-shirts, sweatshirts, and sleepwear, and are also strong in accessories and sportswear. Their impact is not as great in dresses, suits, and outerwear, but some of these items are available. Even with the recent boom, children's character licenses, especially those associated with feature-length movies, tend to be short lived, like the Dick Tracy merchandise. Only a few reached the ranks of true stardom (and big profit). As a result, many retailers, particularly department store buyers, have become cautious about overinvesting in them. Department stores, whose promotion is necessary if a licensed character is to be truly successful, tend to stick with classics like Pooh, Snoopy, and Mickey Mouse. In the popular-priced lines of children's apparel, a licensing agreement between Kmart and Children's Television Workshop, creators of *Sesame Street*, is likely to be profitable to both parties for a long time. Even the American Society for the Prevention of Cruelty to Animals (ASPCA), is getting into character licensing. It has introduced two "spokespets": Purcilla, a cat who speaks with Mary Tyler Moore's voice, and Fremont, a dog who speaks with Matthew Broderick's voice.

Two major studios that produce cartoons, Disney and Warner Brothers, have established their own retail outlets, where the mix of apparel, accessories, and toys may help to extend the lives of the movie characters. Warner Brothers owns both Superman and Batman, perennial favorites with boys on sleepwear, underwear, and T-shirts. Warner Brothers made a licensing agreement with Spalding Sports Worldwide to put its Looney Tunes characters (Bugs Bunny, Daffy Duck, Road Runner, and Wile E. Coyote) on its leisure products line, including backpacks. Warner Brothers also oversees licensing arrangements for the Hanna-Barbera studio (the Flintstones, Scooby Doo, and Tom & Jerry). Kmart's exclusive Disney Kids and Sesame Street clothing licenses have been so successful, that the otherwise ailing discount chain store was the number two retailer in children's clothing in 2002.[12]

Sports Licensing

Sports licensing is another prospering area of licensing. Sports figures and teams both have high media visibility and thus enjoy instant recognition among children and young adults.

Then & Now

Toys are—Kids Big Business

The 1940s
Mattel Company is born (1945)

Launched out of a garage workshop in Southern California by Ruth and Elliot Handler.

The 1950s
Barbie doll makes her debut (1959)

Inspired by her daughter's fascination with cutout paper dolls Ruth Handler makes a tree-dimensional doll. She names the doll "Barbie" after her daughter Barbara's nickname.

The 1960s
Ken doll joins Barbie (1961)

Barbie's one and only boyfriend! Ken is named for the Handler's son, Ken. Barbie and Ken are joined by friends Midge doll (1963) and Skipper (1965).

Mattel rolls out the Hot Wheels® die-cast vehicles (1968)

The number one name in die-cast vehicles roars into the toy world. More than 41 million kids grow up with the brand over the years.

Christie, an African-American doll, is introduced (1968)

She is the first of many ethnic friends of barbie, which include Theresa (1988) and Kira (1990) Barbie Latina and Asian friends.

The 1970s
Mattel Children's Foundation is established (1978)

Viewing philanthropy as an investment, The Foundation seeks exemplary nonprofit partners that demonstrate the same belief.

The 1980s
He-Man and the Masters of the Universe take the stage (1982)

To help balance the success of the Barbie Doll with a boy's toy. He-Man was so successful he eclipsed Barbie in demand in the year 1985.

Mattel and Disney Company form alliance (1988)

Mattel signs agreement to produce infant and preschool toys, dolls, games and puzzles based on classic Disney characters.

The 1990s
Fisher-Price joins the Mattel Company (1993)

Mattel designs and manufactures high quality, imaginative products for children from infancy to age five.

Mattel distributes Cabbage Patch Kids (1995)

Cabbage Patch Kids become one of the popular brand names in large dolls.

Tickle Me Elmo is introduced and is an immediate hit (1996)

Barbie introduces Share a Smile Becky, her friend in a wheelchair (1997)

The 2000s
Mattel is granted the licensing agreement for Harry Potter (2000)

Fashion Editor Barbie was launched by Mattel (2002)

Fashion Editor Barbie gets a pal in the business, when Fashion Editor Ken is created (2003)

Sources

http://www.mattel.com

Conti, Samantha. "Marks & Spencer Net Drops to $790M in '02," *Women's Wear Daily,* May 21, 2003, p. 9.

Treybay, Guy. "Memo to Barbie: *You Aren't The Only Model Ken Knows,*" *The New York Times,* Sunday, June 1, 2003, p. 1, 14.

The sister Britten happily sits among her cherished collection of Barbie Dolls.
Courtesy, Elaine Stone.

Mattel signed a licensing agreement with Nickelodeon in 1996. Here, Leah admires a Dora the Explorer doll.
Courtesy, Elaine Stone.

In areas with professional or school teams, college stores, airport shops, and stadium concessions increase the availability of licensed apparel at retail. Sports figures, who have successfully put their names on sports equipment for years, are now adding them to jogging and running suits, tennis clothes and accessories, as well as less active casual and sportswear lines, with great success. And producers of athletic shoes, sweatshirts, and sports equipment feature their names and logos on active sportswear.

Professional hockey, football, basketball, and baseball teams, as well as college and university athletic teams, now routinely license their names for use on clothes, mostly T-shirts and sweatshirts. The National Football League, to increase the already intense popularity of the game with children, launched a "Play Football" promotional campaign with competitions and programs for boys and girls in different age groups, advertising in *Sports Illustrated for Kids* and at the Superbowl, and promotions with 45 national and regional retailers. The results: Kids are not only playing football; they are wearing millions of dollars worth of related apparel.

Sportswear companies are also quick to capitalize on trends. Soccer is the fastest growing sport among young Americans. Not surprising, Nike introduced a children's soccer line in 2001. But it's not only sportswear companies that try to profit from juvenile soccer fever. In 2002, British chain department store Marks & Spencer launched a boys clothing line with British football captain and fashion icon David Beckham.[13]

Industry Trends

Like women's apparel manufacturers, children's wear producers are constantly on the lookout for ways to increase productivity and reduce—or at least minimize—costs while still maintaining quality. Computerized operations have become the norm for manufacturers. Even portions of the design process are now computerized in children's wear, mostly because this helps producers respond more quickly to fashion trends in the industry.

Suppliers, manufacturers, and retailers of children's wear are also interacting on the Internet. Although freestanding e-commerce sits never reached the level of success projected in the late 1990s and still don't have a strong presence on the market, there are Web sites that offer multi-brand clothing for children. Some popular sites include Baby Style (www.babystyle.com) and Totshop (www.totshop.com). However, the e-commerce sites that attract the most traffic are already attached to a major retail brand, like The Disney Store (www.disneystore.com) and Warner Brothers (www.wbshop.com) for younger children and Abercrombie and Fitch (www.abercrombie.com) and Hot Topic (www.hottopic.com) for teens.

Production costs have risen in recent years, and this has forced producers of budget goods to move into moderate lines. Most of the budget-priced children's clothing is produced offshore in labor-cheap foreign countries, but even this expense is growing as the standard of living improves in developing nations.

Price Lines

The clear distinctions that once existed between budget, moderate, and better-priced children's wear were eroded in an era of heavy inflation in the 1970s, and the disintegration has continued. Several major moderate-priced sportswear producers such as Pandora and Girlstown were driven out of business by inflation and rising operating costs.

Had they stayed in business, they would have been forced to raise their prices beyond the upper limits of the moderate price range. This would have placed them in competition with established producers of higher-priced apparel and put them in a much smaller segment of the children's wear market—thus making it likely that they would ultimately fail anyway.

Although there was no room for expansion in the upper-priced categories during the upheaval of the 1970s, this was not the case in moderate-priced children's wear. To fill the vacuum created in this price range, many budget manufacturers opted to trade up. At the same time, many moderate-priced manufacturers such as Health-Tex and OshKosh B'Gosh known as suppliers of children's basics, began to supplement their lines with more up-to-date, fashion-oriented garments, a gesture that moved them closer to the better-priced category. And to come full circle, the vacuum created in the budget market by the upgrading of companies such as Health-Tex and OshKosh B'Gosh is now being filled to a large extent by lower-cost imports.

Offshore Production

Promising low cost and decent quality, imports have made substantial inroads into children's wear. Of special interest to manufacturers of

FASHION FOCUS

That's Entertainment ... Kid Style

What makes kids want to wear something special? What makes him carry his dinosaur-design pillow everywhere? What makes her insist on drinking only from a cup illustrated with her favorite cartoon character? What excites and pleases everyone, especially the young, is fun and entertainment!

Book, movie, and TV companies all spending millions of dollars so that titles of works, individual characters' names, and of course their corporate logos are very visible as their products enchant children every waking hour (and sometimes even in their dreams.)

Classic children's books are a source of many licensed characters. Beatrice Potter's animal figures, depicted in her own original charming drawings, adorn children's cereal bowls and mugs sold by Tiffany's. Many characters from American children's literary classics—the whimsical creatures of Dr. Seuss, for example—have also been extended beyond the bookshelves into a larger world of clothing, lunch boxes and backpacks, and bedding.

Corporations that produce movies and TV shows look for "properties" that will help sell apparel, accessories, and home fashions. Video sales and cinema screenings of cartoons that grown-ups grew up with have created a new, nostalgic market for tie-in products that may not have even existed when a favorite character was first created.

"Action" figures from comic books are especially popular with three–to–ten year olds. Pajamas or underwear that resemble the colorful uniform of a powerful figure, make getting dressed that much more an exciting experience. Evil, alien characters are especially attractive to imaginative youngsters. In addition to everyday wear, manufacturers and merchants alike report a growing volume in Halloween costumes that allow children to transform themselves into their favorite book, film, or television character.

Corporate licenses beyond those generated by the media may seem a strange choice for children's wear, but they have been popular since the 1940s. Once limited to pennants and adults' caps, T-shirts, and sweatshirts, such licenses have expanded into lines of kids' sportswear, sleepwear, and home fashions. It is now possible to buy a young sports fan a complete set of coordinated sheets, spreads, curtains, and pillows for a number of professional baseball, basketball, and football teams, as well as NASCAR licensed bedding.

And there is no end in sight. "That's entertainment!"

Sources

Groce, Vanessa. "Hot Spots," *Earnshaw's Infants', Girls' and Boys' Wear Review*, August 1996, pp. 71–77.

Socha, Miles. "Star Power," *WWD Century: 100 Years of Fashion*, Fall 1998, p. 250.

Verble, Barbara. "Eight Decades of History," *Earnshaw's Infant's, Girl's, and Boy's Wear Review*, November 1996, pp. 77–79.

From earlier childhood until today, the Brothers Britten happily pose among the "stars" they love.
Courtesy, Elaine Stone.

children's apparel are the White House Apparel Industry Partnership's age standards for child labor. These standards are also of increasing concern for children in developed countries, who are dismayed to learn of the existence of child labor in many less-developed countries. Balancing the reliance of families in developing countries on their children's contributions to the family income against the protection of the children, the White House task force set the minimum age for hiring at 15 years, reduced to 14 only in countries which allow the employment of factory workers younger than age 15.

Buying foreign-made children's wear does have some drawbacks. Very early commitment—as much as eight to nine months' lead time, for example—is required and there is usually no opportunity for reordering. Despite this, children's retail buyers still favor imports, because foreign-made goods satisfy consumer demand. In fact, retail buyers not only have been buying imports, but they have often been ordering them to their specifications. In response, manufacturers have also sought out global sourcing.

Specialty Retail Outlets

Increasing attention is being given to children's wear by apparel retailers whose main lines are men's and women's clothing. A related trend is the prominence of clothing in the merchandise mix of retail outlets carrying a broader array of children's goods. Even among clothing stores that have not opened freestanding children's outlets, distinctive stores-within-stores are now selling children's wear exclusively. Carrying the trend to its logical conclusion, the infants' and toddlers' departments of the children's stores and stores-within-stores are being set up as separate outlets.

Separate Stores

Typical of this trend are the Gap's GapKids and BabyGap. Begun in 1969 as a retailer of jeans for adults, the Gap expanded into a private-label specialty store featuring casual wear for men and women. In 1986, the first GapKids store opened, offering Gap customers basic but fashionable children's wear that catered to the same tastes as the adult lines. The BabyGap line, begun in 1990, became a separate department within GapKids stores and departments, and in 1996, the flagship freestanding BabyGap store opened in New York. However, the Gap's overall sales started to decline in 2001, perhaps because the company's core customers felt alienated by the store's fashion forward merchandise. The decreasing traffic also hurt the label's children's wear.[14]

Benetton is another producer/retailer that has developed a successful chain of children's wear stores. Called Benetton 0–12, they are packed with miniversions of the same stylish merchandise sold to adults. In the late 1980s, Laura Ashley began translating her classic English clothing for adults into children's sizes and opened stores called Mother and Child, which effectively cater to two major markets. The Limited Too, which sells hip children's clothes, now also offers infants' and toddlers' sizes. Another major success story is Gymboree, with over 250 stores in the United States, and sales of an astonishing $850 per square foot.

Catalogs

Major catalog retailers such as Lands' End, Eddie Bauer, Talbots, and L.L. Bean have also increased their offerings for children in recent years. They now offer specialized catalogs, such as Talbots Kids and Talbots Baby. JCPenney has long had a separate Kid's Book; it now also offers JCPenney For Baby, with furniture and accessories; JCPenney Class Favorites, for school uniforms; and JCPenney For Scouts, for both Boy and Girl Scouts. Gymboree began a catalog operation in 1996. dELIA's, a catalog for girls and women aged 10 to 24, is another success story. Figures continued to grow until a costly expansion into e-commerce generated major losses in 2000. But the company survived the dot com crash, and today, dELIA's is a leading multichannel retailer for teenage girls with a Web site (www. dELIAs.com) and 65 retail stores in addition to its circulation of 40 million catalogs.[15]

The Internet

Though children and teens are generally very Internet savvy, they still spend most of their time shopping off-line. Research from Jupiter Communications predict that kids and teens will spend almost $5 billion on the Internet in 2005, but they are expected to spend $21.4 billion off-line, based on information that Jupiter found on the Internet. Although the Web sites for companies like Disney, Nike, and Hot Topic offer merchandise online, their most important role is to push the store's image and establish a relationship with their young shoppers, so they will be enticed to buy more products from brick-and-mortar retailers.[16]

FIGURE 10.8
K.I.D.S. (Kids in Distressed Situations) is the children's apparel manufacturers' national charity. It is a way that the industry can demonstrate its concern for the welfare of its market. Members provide clothing and other essentials for disaster victims and other children in need at home and abroad.
Courtesy, K.I.D.S.

FIGURE 10.9
The Children's Orchard, a franchiser for resale shops for children's clothing and accessories, supplies its franchisees with ads they can run in local newspapers. The franchisee just needs to add the store's address, phone number, and business hours.
Courtesy, The Children's Orchard ® Designed by Wagner Design.

Resale of Children's Wear

Another important trend in the retailing of children's wear is the growth of secondhand resale or consignment stores. For parents who are concerned about the price of their children's wardrobe basics, secondhand clothes received as "hand-me-downs," or purchased at garage sales or nursery school bazaars have always been a good source of clothing. Since children—especially infants and toddlers—so quickly outgrow their clothes, more and more budget-minded parents are using this kind of outlet.

In the 1990s, resale shops have emerged as a popular source of "lightly used" children's wear. Two franchise chains, The Children's Orchard and Once Upon A Child, have become prominent resale outlets (see Figure 10.9). Their growth in sales from $5.2 million in 1990 to $10 million in 1995 shows that this trend bears watching.[17]

The appeal of these stores to budget-conscious parents is twofold: They can sell their children's outgrown clothing and get paid for it immediately. This distinguishes resale shops from consignment shops, which pay a percentage of the retail price only when the item is sold.

These stores also have a successful online business with Web sites www.ouac.com and www.childorch.com. Interestingly, resale of children's clothing has become a very popular form of online shopping. There are hundreds of small and large Web sites that offer "gently used" children's clothing.

School Uniforms

With school districts cracking down on dress codes and politicians lauding the virtues of eliminating "dress competition" in schools, uniforms are steadily becoming the norm in classrooms nationwide (see Figure 10.10a

A

B

FIGURE 10.10
Students nationwide are converting to school uniforms.
(a) AP Photo/Joey Garcia. (b) Courtesy, Elaine Stone.

and b).[18] School officials believe the uniforms have contributed to improved behavior, including reductions in lateness, cutting classes, fighting, and robberies and other crimes. As the principal of a middle school in Long Beach, California said: "Uniforms are an effective method of reducing unwanted behavior, because the more formal clothing puts students in the right mind-set to learn. It's about dressing for success."[19]

President Clinton's 1996 State of the Union address included a pitch for school uniforms. The U.S. Department of Education sent every school district in the United States a pamphlet which began with "School Uniforms: Where They Are and Why They Work."[20] Uniforms have become so common at elementary and middle schools that in many areas of the country they are the rule, not the exception.

Supporters of uniforms point out that uniforms also help students identify with their school and make intruders not in uniform easier to spot. They cite the positive associations of children with other uniformed groups, such as scouts, teams in children's athletic leagues, private and parochial schools, and public schools in other countries. Stylish but functional uniforms are presented as a superior alternative to the unofficial uniforms of street gangs.

Answering the objections of opponents, supporters point out that uniforms equalize affluent and low-income students and that a set of uniforms need not be more expensive than an ordinary school wardrobe.[21] Children can be encouraged to participate in the selection of uniforms as a way of expressing their tastes.

Public school uniforms have the potential of greatly expanding a specialized market segment for children's wear manufacturers and retailers. However, because they must be tailored to the individual specifications of small groups of customers, uniforms cannot generate the kinds of profits that large-volume sales do. Becoming the local uniform supplier can promote goodwill for a retailer. Whether or not this exposure will increase sales of the other goods or help to compensate for the reduction in sales of what would have been a school wardrobe remains to be seen. In any event, national retailers from budget-minded Target, Wal-Mart, and Kmart through Sears, JCPenney, and Macy's are working locally to get the business.

As uniforms are becoming more and more common, many schools have updated the traditional (and itchy) blue blazers, plaid skirts, and white knee socks. An increasing number of students are sporting "business casual" clothes like pants, jumpers, and denim shirts from brands like Lands' End, Old Navy, Target, and Wal-Mart instead.[22]

For manufacturing, some stores are turning to French Toast, whose large presence and experience in the market allows for a broad assortment of styles and colors and good depth in sizing. Other respected resources are Girls Will Be Girls! and Longstreet's Genuine School Uniform collection. School Apparel, Inc., sells its products only through authorized school uniform dealers, which sell mainly to schools. The company does not sell to department or discount stores. Some schools are using traditional dealers/distributors of adult uniforms, since these companies have long made quality clothes designed and constructed for daily wear.[23]

Summary and Review

The children's wear market is segmented by gender and by size categories. The special features of infants' and toddlers' apparel must be taken into consideration by designers and manufacturers.

Designer labels, which are often licensed to manufacturers that specialize in children's products, are becoming increasingly important in this industry, as are character and sports licensing.

Established trends that bear watching are manufacturers offering multiple price lines, and steady offshore production. The trend toward school uniforms for grade school students and some high school students also demands attention. Retail trends include establishing separate stores, the widespread use of catalogs, and establishing Internet sites.

In conclusion, most experts are optimistic that the two prevalent trends—a move toward greater fashion in children's and teen's wear and another move toward buying better children's and teen's wear—are unlikely to reverse themselves in the coming years. This situation should serve to make this industry one of the more stable divisions in the fashion industry. The segment that has simply been called children's wear can now rightly be called children's and teen's fashion.

Trade Talk

Define or briefly explain the following terms:

boys' sizes
children's sizes
girls' sizes
infants' sizes
preteen sizes
teen sizes
toddlers' sizes
young men, prep, student, or teen sizes

For Review

1. How did the children's wear industry adjust to demographic changes between the 1980s and 1990s?
2. What three developments occurred after World War I to cause the growth of the children's wear industry?
3. Name and briefly describe the seven size categories of children's wear. What distinguishes girls' from preteen sizes and boys' from young men's sizes?
4. Explain the statement, "Children's wear . . . must still be viewed as a business that is a *fashionable* rather than a *fashion* business." Do you agree with this statement? Explain your reasons.
5. How is consumer advertising handled by different types of firms in the children's wear business?
6. What accounts for the popularity of character licensing in children's wear?
7. What is the appeal of designer-label children's clothing?
8. What has been the attitude of U.S. retailers and manufacturers toward the growth of imports in the children's wear industry?
9. Describe the current trend toward specialty retail outlets for children's wear.
10. Explain the popularity of resale shops for children's wear.

For Discussion

1. Discuss the importance of licensing in today's children's wear market. How does the licensing system work? Why is it particularly popular with children?

2. Discuss the pros and cons of school uniforms. What impact does this issue have on the children's wear industry?
3. What trends do you see in the young adult market today that have filtered into the design of children's clothing?

References

1. "Plaid City," *Woman's Wear Daily*, February 14, 2001.
2. "The Annual Children's Wear Report," *Earnshaw's Infants', Girls' and Boys' Wear Review*, May 2002, p. 25.
3. Joyce Brothers, "How Clothes Form a Child's Self-Image," *Earnshaw's Infants', Girls' and Boys' Wear Review*, November 1979, p. 48.
4. Tammy LaGorce and Kristen Bentz, "Coming of Age in the Kid's Business," *Earnshaw's Infants', Girls' and Boys' Wear Review*, November 1996, p. 152.
5. Jim Urban, "Spending Retirement Dollars...on the Grandkids," *Executive Report* (Riverview Publications, Inc.), June 1, 1996, vol. 14, p. 7.
6. "Teen Spending Down" (Perspectives) Chain Store Executive with Shopping Center Age, April 2002, p. 32.
7. Gail Robinson, "Because Sizes Aren't Written In Stone; Clothes for Girls Who Just Can't Wait to Grow Up," *Los Angeles Times*, January 19, 1995, p. E-1.
8. Dana Canedy, "Letting Out the Seams for Chubby Children: Retailers Fill a New Apparel Niche," *New York Times*, May 30, 1997, p. D1.
9. Susan Ferraro, "Hotsy Totsy," *American Way*, April 1981, p. 61.
10. "Children Dressed Better Than Mum," *The Evening Mail*, January 2001, pp. 5–15.
11. Anne D'Innocenzio, "Designers Think Small: Kid's Wear Shaping Up As New Status Market," *Women's Wear Daily*, February 6, 1997, pp. 1–7.
12. "Top 10 Children's Wear Retailers, (The Children's Business list.)" *Children's Business*, July 2002, p. 7.
13. "It's Time to Play Soccer!" *Sporting Goods Business*, February 12, 2001, p. 29.
14. Top 10 Children's Wear Retailers, (The Children's Business list.)" *Children's Business*, July 2002, p. 7, 23.
15. Julee Greenberg, Katherine Bowers, and Kristin Young, "What the Girls Like and Want, A Look Into the Next Generation," *Women's Wear Daily*, March 28, 2002.
16. "Targeting Teens is a Gender Game, Focus on Marketing to Girls and Programming to Boys," Jupiter Communications, August 30, 2000.
17. Shari Sanders, "Resale Retailers Rebirth," *Children's Business*, November 1996, p. 30.
18. "French Toast Hankers for School Uniforms—Again," *Footwear News*, July 30, 2001, p. 32.
19. Kathyln Swantko, "Students Go to the Head of the Class In Uniforms From School Apparel," *American Sportswear & Knitting Times*, October 1997, p. 12.
20. Tamar Lewin, "In Public School, Uniforms as Dress for Success," *New York Times*, September 25, 1997, p. A1.
21. Yvette Jane Cartes, "Thank You, Mr. President," *Made to Measure Magazine*, Fall/Winter, 1996–1997.
22. Angela Key, "Uniforms are Runway Ready," *Fortune*, October 16, 2000, p. 76.
23. Swantko, "Students Go to the Head of the Class."

UNIT THREE

Exploring Careers at the Secondary Level: Apparel

Apparel Trades

For creative people, the plum of the fashion apparel trades is the designer's job. But the climb to this top job is often laborious and uncertain, and the footing at the top may be slippery. New talent is always elbowing its way in, and even the most successful couture designers are haunted by the prospect of a season when their ideas do not have customer appeal.

The first step in a career at the secondary level of the fashion business may be a position at the retail level. Direct contact with consumers is an invaluable background for fashion professionals, whether they aspire to design, produce, market, or sell apparel for a secondary level firm. And the retailer who is your employer in your first full-time fashion job may be a useful contact or customer when you move into the apparel production business.

Designing

Because so much of an apparel firm's success depends on the styling of its line, the designing responsibility is rarely entrusted to a beginner, even a highly talented one. Fashion designing is an applied art; the designer's sketches, however beautiful they may be as drawings, are primarily a means of communication about how the finished garment will look on a human body. More and more, designers are relying on computer programs that enable them to adjust line, color, and decorative detail and to simulate the draping properties of different fabrics. They can convey this information to their suppliers of fabrics and other materials, to their staffs, and to their customers. Designers must be knowledgeable about matters of cost and mass-production techniques, and they must be able to judge accurately the point in the fashion cycle at which the firm's customers will buy.

For moderate-priced and mass-market producers, the designer's job may be one of adapting rather than creating. Immense skill may be required, nevertheless, to take a daringly original couture idea and modify it so that it appears bright and new but not terrifyingly unfamiliar to a mass-market or middle-income customer.

The beginner, aside from offering designs on a freelance basis, can seek a number of jobs below the designer level in hopes of working up to that top level. Entry-level design jobs include assistant designer, sketcher-stylist, junior designer, pattern maker, sketcher, and sample maker.

CAD Specialist

Combining their artistic talent and computer skills with increasingly versatile computer assisted drafting programs, CAD specialists create and revise apparel designs. CAD-generated designs have such a finished look that they can be used in place of prototypes to present new lines to retailer customers. Adjustments can be shown on the screen to meet the customers' needs, saving time and money that would otherwise be spent producing samples.

At the entry level, technical designers help to develop and evaluate specifications to ensure that the construction, fit, styling, and sizing of the line reflect the designer's concept.

Graphic Designer

Depending on the size of their employers and the equipment available, graphic designers produce hand-drawn or computer-generated designs or both for fabric prints and colors. They maintain a library of design elements—prints, patterns, color combinations, and so on—as a resource for the development of new lines. Graphic designers may also be involved in producing visual aids to promote the designs in their companies' new seasonal lines.

Apparel Production

Positions in this field are with apparel manufacturing plants or offices. Skilled jobs for fashion graduates are available in both apparel production management and in pattern making.

Apparel Production Management

Managing the production of an apparel line take more than an organized person and problem-solver. An entire staff of such people is needed. They must keep track of incoming orders from their suppliers and schedules of their factory workers to ensure the timely fulfillment of orders from their retailer customers. Entry-level positions in this field include junior engineers, costing engineers, assistant plant managers, production assistants, and quality control engineers. A degree in business or engineering is a good background for these jobs. Advancement to higher level positions is frequently based on job performance and demonstration of readiness to take on more responsibility.

Pattern Making

Preparation for careers in pattern making is available in fashion design schools or departments. In addition to an eye for apparel design, pattern makers need an understanding of mathematics and technical training in the use of computerized pattern-making programs. They are responsible for ensuring that each pattern is true to size and that the pieces can be assembled for an attractive and comfortable fit. Entry-level positions in this field include assistant pattern maker, cutting assistant, grader trainee, and marker trainee.

Advertising and Publicity

An advertising manager, with possibly an assistant or two, may handle the advertising and publicity for an apparel manufacturer. Publicity, usually a part of the advertising job, involves sending out press releases to interest consumer publications in some of the firm's new styles. Promotion kits for retailers are prepared under the direction of the advertising manager, as are statement enclosures and other direct-mail pieces offered for retail use. More and more, apparel producers, like other businesses are communicating with their customers and with consumers on their own web sites on the Internet. The job of web page designer is a burgeoning area of employment opportunity, and in the fashion business, presenting the desired image in this new medium is important work.

Sales Opportunities

Sales representatives who call upon retail stores or assist retail buyers in their employers' showrooms should know the fashion points as well as the value points of their merchandise. Today, sales representatives are expected to be able to address retail salespeople, if invited to do so, or even to take part in consumer forums and clinics.

An understanding of retail merchandising, promotion, and fashion coordination is extremely helpful in all sales jobs in the apparel field. As consumers become more educated about fashion, retailers must stay at least a step ahead of their customers to win the customers' business. The sales representatives of an apparel firm are the retailers' source of product information about the producer's lines, so the sales representatives' success depends on helping the retailer become a knowledgeable fashion advisor to the consumer market. When selling to retailers, it is important to understand their needs, problems, and methods of operation, as well as what stage of the fashion cycle is of major interest to their customers. With such a background, sales representatives can present a line more effectively and can also gather and develop sound retail merchandising and promotion ideas for their accounts. The apparel sales representative is essentially a wholesaler, and as such is the link between the manufacturer and the retail client. This relationship exists for reps who are employees of a single manufacturer as well as for independent contractors who represent several producers.

Showroom Sales Representative

For the sales representative who thrives on the excitement of city life, a position in a manufacturer's showroom in New York, Los Angeles, or one of the regional markets should provide a satisfying career. The busiest times, of course are market weeks, but there is scarcely a dull moment between the seasonal presentations. Showroom representatives are in constant contact with resident buying/merchandising/product development offices, and they are also responsible for following up with retailers to be sure that the orders secured as a result of the retailers' buying trips are fulfilled. A position as sales assistant or associate in a manufacturer's showroom is a good first step on this career path.

Outside Sales Representative

For apparel marketers who prefer travel to being based in an office, becoming an outside sales representative may be a good career option. This position also provides an opportunity to operate independently. An entrepreneurial outside sales rep may show the lines of several noncompeting manufacturers who serve the same market. Typically, the rep will call on retailers in smaller cities and towns and will show the lines of smaller manufacturers who do not want the expense and responsibilities of running showrooms. Growth in this career may occur through an increase in the size of one's territory or through an increase in the number of firms one represents.

Account Executive

Major retailing firms—chains like JCPenney and conglomerates like Federated Department Stores—with outlets across the country warrant the attention of an account executive. Since these retailers are significant sources of income for a manufacturer, it is vital to win their trust and to establish a personal relationship through an account executive with a proven record of service. If you are interested in a career in professional selling, this is a position to which you might aspire.

Entrepreneurship Opportunities

Entrepreneurial opportunities in apparel production are limited by the expenses of real estate, equipment, and labor, but there is a market for handcrafted apparel, and adventuresome businesspeople who have skills in design and production as well as marketing may welcome the risk. Others who wish to be fashion entrepreneurs may focus on one aspect of the secondary level of the fashion business, such as freelance designing, multiline sales representation, or import and export. Each of these fields offers ample rewards for those willing to assume the risks.

Careers in the Home Sewing Industry

The resurgence of home sewing as a hobby and a way of building a unique personal wardrobe has expanded the job market for pattern makers and graders. They can apply their skills to preparation of patterns for sale to consumers as well as for apparel manufacturers. Advertising and promotion specialists, fashion illustrators, and copywriters are needed to prepare the seasonal catalogs of patterns from which consumers make their selections.

Assignments

1. Prepare Unit Three in your Career Journal by comparing job opportunities within a single segment of apparel manufacturing, women's, men's, or children's wear. Select as subjects for research two companies that cater to different subsegments within your chosen market. For example, you may compare a manufacturer of men's business wear to a firm specializing in casual wear or a high fashion women's wear designer to a firm that produces mass merchandise lines. Read about your chosen firms in trade publications, and visit their Web sites. Considering your own career goals, compare the job opportunities in design, production, sales, or advertising in the two firms.
2. Environmental factors affect each secondary level industry of the fashion business. For each industry discussed in Unit Three—women's, men's, and children's apparel—give a current example of the effects of the natural, economic, social, and political/legal environment.

UNIT THREE: THE 1980s

Donna Karan • Tom Ford • Perry Ellis • Kal Ruttenstein • David Cameron • Michael Kors • Ralph Lauren

Designer Perry Ellis with his models.

"Ultimately, I feel [clothes] have to be beautiful by my own standards, and that means stimulating, creative, controversial and always with wit...this is as opposed to being pretentious, which I think a lot of fashion is."

PERRY ELLIS, 1982

"Perry [Ellis] took some of the seriousness out of fashion and convinced a new generation of women to wear designer clothes. His clothes represented youthful vigor, spirit, humor and a casual attitude that quickly became Perry's style."

KAL RUTTENSTEIN UPON PERRY ELLIS' DEATH IN 1986

"I see my customer as I see myself—a woman who doesn't have time to shop, a mother, a traveler, perhaps a company owner. I will design only clothes that I myself would wear."

Donna Karan, 1984

"How many more fashion shows can people watch without going bonkers? There are just so many ways you can show clothes on a runway and still make it interesting. That's the fine line between a show and a product. The show is bull, no matter how you look at it.

DAVID CAMERON, 1986

"Sure, there are fashion editors who think I'm not creative and that I only copy L. L. Bean and Brooks Brothers. My answer to that is you don't stay around for so many years if you have nothing new to say."

RALPH LAUREN, 1988

"I don't think clothes should be from totally out in left field. That's not modern. When you consider the price of clothes, people are not as quick to dispose of them. They should be more timeless..."

"Women used to shop for entertainment. Well, all that's changed. Women need clothes they can live in."

MICHAEL KORS, 1989

"This can be a nasty industry to work in. A lot of designers are expected to compromise their creativity to guarantee the bottom line."

TOM FORD, 1989

MANOLO
BLAHNIK

BVD

Sox and the City
While you are in NYC, come visit our showroom.
Soxland
dAvco®
Showroom 347 Fifth Ave Suite 906 New York City 10016

The Crate and Barrel
Summer Sale,

UNIT FOUR

The Secondary Level: The Other Producers

No matter how chic, exquisite, or hip your apparel may look, it is the finishing touches that make your outfit something special, something that says . . . YOU! For years intimate apparel, accessories, and cosmetics and fragrances were simply something that you thought of as "maybe yes, maybe no." They were not the most important part of your fashion look. Things have really changed, and today producers of accessories, innerwear, cosmetics and fragrances, and home fashions must stay on the cutting edge of fashion trends that affect apparel, because the customer expects them to support and refine each new fashion trend.

Today, these producers have evolved from their original role of coordinating with apparel, becoming innovators and fashion- and trendsetters on their own. What we wear underneath is as important to fashion as what we wear outside. How we choose our accessories, cosmetics, and fragrance, and the items we surround ourselves with at home all add up to our own personal fashion feel and look. The four chapters in this unit explore the history and current activities of these other producers.

Chapter 11, "Innerwear, Bodywear, Legwear," covers the history, merchandising, and marketing of these constantly growing and changing industries. Chapter 12 explores the ever-expanding accessories industries, which today are taking advantage of the newest technology, from their history to current merchandising and marketing techniques. In Chapter 13, on cosmetics and fragrances, we discuss the "Dreams versus Science" debate and explain new market segments. Chapter 14, "Home Fashions," is the newest addition to our coverage of the fashion industries. This chapter outlines the growing fashion influence of top apparel designers, who are increasingly producing looks for home as well as apparel.

CHAPTER 11

Innerwear, Bodywear, Legwear

WHAT'S IN IT FOR YOU?

Everything you always wanted to know about the innerwear, bodywear, and legwear industries.

Key Concepts:

- History of the women's intimate apparel industry
- Categories of intimate apparel
- Merchandising and marketing of intimate apparel
- Merchandising of men's and children's underwear and sleepwear
- History and organization of the hosiery industry
- Branding of women's legwear
- Trends in the hosiery industry

Innerwear, bodywear, and legwear used to be a personal and secret choice, hidden from everyone except for your closest and dearest. What supported our bodies, glorified our figures, and made us feel wanted was a secret weapon we shared with no one. Today, all that has changed! Men, women, and children flaunt the "intimate apparel" that was once hidden from view. What is hidden under clothing can never make a name for itself, so innerwear, bodywear, and legwear designers decreed that it should all "hang out." Today, bras, corsets, slips, nightgowns, underwear, and hosiery are a very important part of a person's total fashion look. People enjoy the luxurious array of styles and colors provided by these industries and consider them an important part of their wardrobes. The importance of designer names in these industries has helped to ensure that the interpretation of changes in silhouette, fabrication, and color is reflected in these industries.

When you shop for boxers, do you think of Calvin Klein or Joe Boxer? Do you associate Nike or Russell with activewear? And is Hanes or Donna Karan your choice for hosiery? If you are looking for a leotard, do you think of Danskin or Capezio? Do you buy "no brand" socks or Gold Toe? All these manufacturers are vying for your business. They and their competitors also want their names in the forefront of your mind. Manufacturers and retailers have long recognized that the intimate apparel and hosiery segments of the fashion industry operate in support of the women's, men's, and children's apparel segments. Consumers maximize the versatility of their wardrobes and enhance the look of each outfit by coordinating their underwear and legwear with their clothing. Therefore, the way for a designer, manufacturer, or retailer to grow is to provide the components of a total fashion statement.

An Overview of the Underwear and Innerwear Industries

In the past, the manufacturing and marketing of men's and children's underwear was driven by considerations of practical functionality, but lately, these segments of the apparel industry have also felt the impact of fashion. Through mergers and acquisitions, producers of men's and children's underwear have become divisions of more diversified apparel firms. This trend will be discussed later in this chapter.

Women's underwear or **innerwear**, sometimes called "inner fashions," "intimate apparel," or "body fashions," is the trade term for women's underwear; usually divided into foundations (bras, shapewear), lingerie, and loungewear. Originally these three groups of products were separate industries. In recent years, a single industry called **intimate apparel** has evolved as a result of business mergers, diversification of products, technological advances in fibers and fabrications, and a growing relationship between these industries and women's ready-to-wear.

Innerwear or Intimate Apparel

The wearing of undergarments probably grew out of practical need as people sought something to protect their skins from the chafing of harsh animal skins. And indeed, for many years the purpose of underwear was primarily utilitarian. Foundation garments were for shaping and support, lingerie provided warmth and protection, and loungewear marked the boundaries of propriety for at-home entertaining. As the distinctions among these categories have blurred, new fashion features of intimate apparel, new types of undergarments, and new uses of innerwear as outerwear, have emerged—literally.

History and Development

The foundations industry began after the Civil War with the opening of Warner Brothers corset factory in Bridgeport, Connecticut. The bell-shaped silhouette was then at the height of its popularity. To achieve the tiny waist demanded by the bell and its successors, the bustle back and Gibson Girl silhouettes, women wore corsets made of sturdy, unyielding cotton. Reinforced with vertical stays of whalebone or steel, the corsets laced up the front or back. They were tightly laced to achieve the extreme (in many cases) constriction of the waist and internal organs that fashion required.

Variations on these stiff corsets were worn by all women until the 1920s, when the rounded and bustled silhouettes that had prevailed for decades gave way to the straight, loose styles of the "boyish" flappers. Stiff, full-torso corsets were no longer required. The new silhouette demanded that the bosom and hips be minimized. Bandage-like bras were created to flatten the bust, and new girdlelike corsets controlled any conspicuous bulges below the waist.

By the 1930s, soft, feminine curves were back in style. Rubberized elastic was introduced, and the corset became known as the "girdle." Women now coaxed their bodies into two new types of foundations, the two-way stretch girdle and the cup-type brassiere, both of which were more comfortable than any of their predecessors.

These innovations set a precedent in the foundations industry and in women's lives. Women would henceforth wear inner garments that molded the figure more gently. Undergarments would now permit freedom of movement.

The 1930s also marked the introduction of rayon, changing the face of the intimate apparel industry. Until then, most mass-produced lingerie and loungewear were made of cotton, with wool being used in extremely cold climates. Silk, which was expensive and tedious to care for, appeared in custom-made, luxury styles affordable only by the rich. Rayon had the luxurious feel of silk, but it was washable and inexpensive. Other similar fibers followed, culminating in the 1950s with the reintroduction of nylon, a synthetic fiber that was softer and longer wearing than rayon and even more easily maintained. (Its use had been limited during the war years—1940 to 1945.) Innovations in fabrics continued over the next four decades, with the introduction of polyester, acrylics, microfibers, Tencel, and Lycocel. Stronger sheer fabrics, more pliable leathers, and Ultrasuede also helped transform the intimate apparel industry, especially loungewear.

Repeated improvements in elasticized fabrics have led to softer, more comfortable, and increasingly lightweight foundation garments that retain their shape even after many washings. Spandex body shapers mixed with nylon or polyester microfibers are the latest episode in this ongoing saga, and Nancy Ganz, whose Lycra Bodyslimmers were introduced in 1990, is the heroine. Depending on the area they want to reshape, women can rely on her hipslip, thighslimmer, buttbooster, or knee beater.

Brassieres offer the best example of the massive style changes that the intimate apparel industry has undergone in the past half century. They have evolved from the original bandage-type bra to a cup form; from plain weave cotton, to polyester fiber-filled, to spandex; from the "no-bra" (unconstructed) look to the molded (unseamed) bra.

An important development of the 1940s was the introduction of padded bras to enhance the figure. In the 1960s, feminist activists rebelled against this focus on creating a standard of female beauty, which they characterized as treatment of women as sex objects. Bra-burning became a symbol of the social revolution of the decade (see Figure 11.1). As the movement matured and women felt less compelled to demonstrate their independence from physical stereotypes in such dramatic ways, they adopted natural-looking soft cups and seamless styles of bras that became available in the 1970s. Gradually, more structured styles of foundations were reintroduced to support the power dressing of the business woman of the 1980s.

FIGURE 11.1 *Women protesters took off their bras in honor of the social revolution of their time.* Courtesy, Globe Photos/ Bob West. Reprinted with permission.

In 1986, the Wacoal Company of Japan, a leading manufacturer of foundations, pioneered in the computer "mapping" of the female body, which permitted them and other manufacturers to design undergarments that truly supported and enhanced the female figure. The push-in-and-up bra, introduced in 1994 by Sara Lee Foundations as the Wonderbra, was the foundation fashion story of the 1990s.

While Wonderbra continues to be a big seller, lingerie in the new millennium has focused less on ostentatious curves and more on comfort. Seamless bras like those featured in Victoria's Secret Body by Victoria collection and the Body Revolution bra by Barely There® are examples of the new products that promote a feel-good and streamlined silhouette.[1]

Innerwear has become increasingly luxurious over the decades. And fashion has finally invaded this segment of the market, so much so that some beautifully designed undergarments are now worn as outer garments. A lacy silk camisole is used as a dressy top to wear under a suit jacket—or alone. A sexy slip becomes an evening garment, and lounging pajamas are elegant components of any ensemble (see Figure 11.2). Driving the market are teenage and young adult shoppers, who demand variety to meet their disparate needs from sports bras for the gym to body shapers for form-fitting fashions. Today's innerwear also meets the needs of aging baby boomers, who want to retain a shapely, sexy look.

Categories of Intimate Apparel

Items traditionally classified as **foundations** support either the bust (brassieres) or the lower torso (girdles, which have evolved into shapewear). **Lingerie** is the term for less structured innerwear and sleepwear, and **loungewear** refers to the loose-fitting apparel designed for home entertaining and, more recently, an evening out.

Bras

Brassieres are the most important foundation item for the bust. Their practical features are designed to fit different body types and suit a

FIGURE 11.2
Glamorous sleepwear can often double for evening wear.
Courtesy, Fairchild Publications, Inc.

variety of purposes and occasions. Wide straps, banding or underwires under the cups, and closures with three or more hooks offer extra support and comfort for buxom women. Padding adds shaping and increased size for women with smaller bustlines, and the Wonderbra lifts the bust, creating a different silhouette. Cups cover the breasts completely or not, sides are wide or narrow, and straps are positioned strategically or removed so that the bra will not show unintentionally under the top.

In addition, materials and design accommodate special needs: *training bras* gently support the developing breasts of young teens; *sports bras* move with the body, give support, and absorb perspiration; *nursing bras* have cups that unfasten to allow a mother to breast feed without undressing; and *mastectomy bras* have pockets for prostheses. A *bustier* is a foundation garment that extends over the waist or hips. It serves more often as outerwear, making a provocative fashion statement for evening wear, when covered with satin, crushed velvet, or sequins.

Bras are complicated to make, and their production requires careful management. They may contain 20 pieces, and come in more than a dozen sizes and colors for each style. Fit is critical; no one wants to have a bra altered. Bra manufacturers have to wring the most they can out of each component—such as getting the same kind of strap to work for five different bras. The major offshore bra production center is the Philippines, followed by Costa Rica.

The jewelry designer Jill Weiner is often called upon by bra manufacturers to provide custom-designed closings, hooks, slides, and sew-on accents. She says: "Some manufacturers want jewelry on a bra as a personal statement."[2] While bra straps of the past were designed to be hidden under clothes, today they have become somewhat of an accessory. "With all the transparent clothes out there, a woman has to show a little lingerie," says French luxury underwear designer Capucine Puerari, but she also adds, "In that case, the lingerie has to be pretty and sophisticated."[3]

Shapewear

Girdles, corsets, and *corselettes* (one-piece combinations of a brassiere and girdle) are traditional foundation items designed to smooth and flatten the lines of the stomach, buttocks, hips, and thighs. As with *garter belts*, they also have fasteners to hold up a woman's stockings. With the advent of pantyhose and a growing casualness in everyday dress, these items have been replaced in many women's wardrobes by **shapers**, or shapewear, lightweight undergarments that control problem areas with spandex. Control briefs serve the purpose of the old-fashioned girdle; and for more focused control, waist cincher briefs, butt boosters, tummy toners, and thigh trimmers are available.

Lingerie

The lingerie segment of intimate apparel has typically been divided into daywear (slips, petticoats, camisoles, and panties) and nightwear (nightgowns, sleepshirts, nightshirts, chemises, baby dolls, pajamas, wraps, and robes). *Chemises* are sleep gowns with no waistlines, while *baby dolls* are short, sheer gowns with matching panties. *Wraps* are short robes that cross and tie in front.

The latest revolution in lingerie is the rise of the thong panty. Thongs have come a long way from being a slightly scandalous item that could be found only on showgirls and Brazilian carnival dancers, but today they have become a mainstream lingerie basic worn by women of all ages. Clever new products, like the "control thong" from Donna Karan, hold in the tummy and eliminate bumps and lumps of underwear lines. These new products are likely to become a lingerie drawer staple.[4]

Panties run the gamut from sporty, such as Calvin Klein's 1983 "reinvented lingerie"—men's underpants reproportioned for a woman's body—to filmy, lacy styles, to seductive bikinis and thongs that offer minimal coverage. The fact that they are often merchandised as a set with matching bras indicates the blurring of the distinction between subcategories of intimate apparel. Camisoles are also often paired with panties.[5]

In the nightwear classification, styles also range from sporty and casual to romantic and seductive. Chenille robes, seemingly dead since the 1950s, revived in late 1990s, as TV sitcom stars began wearing updated versions decorated with amusing motifs, such as coffee cups and cats with fish bones. At the elegant end of the style spectrum are the *peignoir* (a sheer robe, often with lace detail) and gown set, popular as a Valentine's Day gift, and the *kimono*, an adaptation of the traditional Japanese garment. The Westernized version is often made of rich silk or less expensive synthetics that imitate silk's luxurious appearance; the kimono can also serve as loungewear.

Loungewear

Loungewear is the trade term for robes, lounging pajamas, hostess gowns, bed jackets, and housecoats or dusters. *Dusters*, which usually have buttons or snaps down the front, are especially popular with the elderly and handicapped, because they are easy to put on and off. Leggings and fleece pants and tops are also popular attire for at-home wear for women of all ages, especially in cold areas. Activewear is also increasingly worn as leisurewear (see Figure 11.3), especially by the young and trim, influenced by TV shows such as *Friends* and *Will and Grace*.

Designs from other cultures are also popular, such as the Hawaiian *muumuu* or float, a short-sleeved garment, which slips on over the head, and comes in several lengths. *Caftans*, ankle-length garments with long sleeves, came originally from Turkey, and are widely worn throughout the Middle East. The African *dashiki*, a loose fitting pullover garment, is also seen increasingly in the United States.

FIGURE 11.3
Today, loungewear is made for relaxing at home, while still suitable for casual sportswear and activewear.
Courtesy, Fairchild Publications, Inc.

Market Centers

New York City is the principal market center for the intimate apparel industry. The major firms maintain permanent showrooms there, as well as in most of the regional apparel marts, like Dallas, Chicago, Los Angeles, and Atlanta. Market weeks are held five times a year:

- Early Spring—August
- Summer—January
- Fall and Holiday—May
- Spring—November
- Early Fall—March

The Intimate Apparel Council is a trade group that is part of the American apparel manufacturers association that organizes subsidiary, promotional activities for market weeks. One of their endeavors is Intimate Apparel Market Week, which is held five times a year and has greatly increased business. The Intimate Apparel Council also organized the first every industry-sponsored lingerie fashion show in the Bryant Park tents during the Mercedes-Benz Fashion Week in September 2001. U.S. trade shows include the Intimate Apparel Salon and Lingerie Americas in New York, and International Lingerie show in Las Vegas (see Figure 11.4).[6]

Merchandising and Marketing

In the merchandising and marketing of innerwear, an emphasis on brand names is concurrent with a trend toward greater promotion of individual styles, colors, fabrics, textures, and designer names. Producers and designers aim to coordinate their innerwear and outerwear lines and to offer a range of images that will offer a complete look for a variety of occa-sions and moods. Market segmentation by age groups enables producers and retailers to target their merchandising and marketing efforts.

Brand Names

Since Warner Brothers opened its first factory in 1874, brand names have been important in the intimate apparel industry. (Warner's is now one of the brands of Warnaco, which also produces Olga.) Many of its merchandising and marketing activities, such as cooperative advertising with retailers in consumer publications and advertisements in trade publications, are geared toward promoting brand names.

These strategies have met with considerable success, as women have identified intimate apparel as a category in which they rely on brand names as an indicator of durability and consistency of fit. As mergers, acquisitions, and licenses of designer names join several brands under a corporate umbrella, parent companies are retaining the individual names to keep their loyal customers. Jockey, the men's and boys' underwear firm started Jockey for Her in 1982. In 1997, it acquired Formfit seamless panties and the Formfit name, re-launching FormFit in the summer of 2000 under the slogan "Fashion, Fit, Comfort."

Market Segments

Teenagers and young adults are a very influential segment of the intimate apparel business. In leisurewear, their interests in working out—or looking as if they do—has popularized such fabrics as fleece, jersey knit, flannel, and flan-

FIGURE 11.4 *Revealing the latest fashion in intimate apparel, models applaud at the end of the Salon International de la Lingerie Show.* Courtesy, Fairchild Publications, Inc.

Then & Now

Pull It In or Push It Up!

Women's bodies have been shaped and reshaped over the centuries. Corsets for pulling it in bras for pushing it out! Think of Scarlett O'Hara battling the corset get to her 14" waist—or Barbra Streisand in her push-up bra.

After the bralessness of 1960s, think of Madonna in her Jean Paul Gaultier's "up and at you" bra in the late 1980s to the caged and corseted looks of 2000+ by such designers as John Galianos, Tom Ford, and Nicolas Ghesquire. Long live curves!

Sources

Nandini D'Souza, "Caught on Film," *Women's Wear Daily*, INTIMATES, August 2001, pp. 12, 16, and 18.

"Hourglass Facts & Figures," *Women's Wear Daily*, INTIMATES, August 2001, p. 22.

Scarlett O'Hara is being pulled in to get her 14" waist popular in her day.
Courtesy, The Kobal Collection.

While in today's fashion market, it has moved from the waist to the bust.
Courtesy, Fairchild Publications, Inc.

nelettes, all of which inject a sportswear attitude into these casual styles. The trend is carried out in underwear in cotton crop tops and matching boyleg briefs or boxers, and in sports bras. Such companies as Natori, with its popular Josie line, and Intimate Resources, with its Max and Eddie and Everlast store brands and Jordache for the mass market, cater to this segment. The trend toward wearing briefer briefs under formfitting pants has boosted sales of junior size hiphugger styles with bikinis, thongs, and high French-cut legs.

The under-25 shopper has also supported the metamorphosis of the girdle into a variety of body shapers. In the market for these products, baby boomers, who are gaining weight as they age, are also an influential segment. Despite increasing interest in health food and exercise, many women find it easier, faster, and more comfortable to shape up with the help of spandex.[7] The large-size woman is a focus of many designers, who are creating attractive and form-fitting leotards, sports bras, and shorts for this emerging market. Playtex has added both the Eighteen Hour Comfort Strap bra and the Cross Your Heart bra with side shaping to its very successful lines to appeal to the plus size woman.

FIGURE 11.5
La Perla's Green Street Shop in New York displays temporary fixtures to show their merchandise to customers.
Courtesy, Fairchild Publications, Inc.

Visual Merchandising

In-store displays for innerwear departments and specialty stores demonstrate the importance of brand names and the close connections between product classifications. In contrast to earlier eras, when intimate apparel was stocked in closed drawers rather than displayed, contemporary fixtures allow for the grouping of bras and panties by brand and, within a brand display, by style and color. Price tags color-coded by size help the customer select her size within each style and color grouping. Although bras and panties are sometimes displayed by size, with different brands and colors on the same rack, this practice is giving way to the more visually appealing displays arranged by brand, style, and color, which promote the fashion features of the merchandise (see Figure 11.5).

Victoria's Secret stores are a good example of the role of visual merchandising in producing a coordinated fashion image. The interior design of the stores, with elegantly appointed alcoves, allows for separate displays of related items in an intimate space, and the Victorian style dressers that serve as storage and display fixtures reinforce the upscale, feminine look of the merchandise.

Industry Trends

Variety is the watchword in every aspect of the intimate apparel industry. Not only are firms that once specialized in foundations, lingerie, or loungewear joining together to produce complete and complementary lines of intimate apparel, but these companies are becoming part of larger firms with other holdings in related segments of the apparel industry. For example, Playtex, Bali, and Wonderbra are siblings of Champion activewear and hosiery manufacturers Hanes and L'eggs, under the umbrella of the parent corporation of Sara Lee. Intimate brands operates 1,799 specialty stores through Victoria's Secret and Bath and Body Works brands, in addition to Victoria's Secret's tremendous catalog business. It is part of the apparel retail group The Limited Inc., which also owns a variety of retails brands including Express, The Limited, and White Barn Candle Company.

These alliances allow the parent corporation to coordinate its appeals to different market segments, offering styles and price points that

FASHION FOCUS

The Natori Story—A Business Sense Combined with a Fashion Flair

With a background in finance not fashion, Josie Natori left a top position at Merrill Lynch as the first woman vice president to pursue her dream of designing, manufacturing and merchandising. There is nothing ordinary about Josie Natori—or the products that bear her name.

The House of Natori ranked 58th among the top 100 luxury brands in the world in a recent *Women's Wear Daily* special report on what consumers considered to be the most prestigious labels. Much of Natori's success can be attributed to her hands-on approach to her business.

Founding her company with husband and co-chairman Kenneth Natori in August 1977, she envisioned a tremendous opportunity, "innerwear that is outerwear." The result of this innerwear-outerwear concept built a company that generates annual sale of over $50 million dollars. Working in a very specialized and competitive industry, Josie says, "I've been through everything—recessions, consolidations, the onslaught of designer names and mega brands that have come and gone —and I'm still around."

The company comprises two brands Natori and Josie. The Natori label which features signature prints and embroideries, is divided into two entities—Natori Black Label dedicated top the sophisticated women who loves luxury and elegance, and Natori White Label aimed at consumers who want feminine, but modern-looking items. The Josie label has a "young, hip point of view."

Further expanding the Natori empire is its foundation and bra licenses with Bestform and a sister company called Kefco Inc. which acts as the manufacturing arm for private label as well as for the new Cruz label. The Cruz label features modern looks in sleepwear that is different from the Natori designer collection and Josie's contemporary looks.

Josie Natori.

Natori—who is always dressed to the nines and wears wonderful jewelry and accessories that make a statement—described herself as an "accessories freak." The company added a selection of scarves and wraps in 1999, and in 2001 launched a full line of handbags and belts. Natori said, "We really are focused on developing our accessory business as carefully as we have built a lingerie powerhouse. Shoes, jewelry, fragrance and eveningwear may follow as the company seeks to maximize the Natori line.

But it is not all work and no play for Natori. The couple jets around the world, have homes in Manhattan and Pound Ridge, New York, and Ken is kept busy at the nearby Glen Arbor Golf Course which he recently bought. Josie herself, who is a type A personality, seems to run on pure adrenaline. She burns the midnight oil with famous designers, financiers, manufacturers, and retailers exchanging fashion facts and gossip. All this in a fantastic lady who rarely eats a full-course meal preferring scrambled eggs or baked potatoes with caviar and champagne—a tiny dynamo who generates excitement wherever she goes.

Sources

Filipino Fashion Web Site/Josie Natori available at http://nes.net/asia/natori

Melanie Kletter and Karyn Monget, "Natori's 25 Years Mystique," *Women's Wear Daily*, November 25, 2002, pp. 6–7.

Karyn Monget, "The Natori Story," *Women's Wear Daily*, Intimates, Special Section, August 2001, pp. 36, 52.

Karen Monget "Natori's New Deal," *Women's Wear Daily*, April 21, 2003, p. 10.

Designs by Natori.
Courtesy, Fairchild Publications, Inc.

attract different age and income groups and retain brand loyalty.

Market Expansion

Intimate apparel producers are expanding their markets in aggressive and innovative ways, including launching crossover product lines and licensing. Crossover products include the Hanes Her Way brand of underwear, which was spun off the Hanes men's underwear brand in 1986. Hanes Her Way has become a big hit, especially in the panty line, which is now the best selling panty line in the entire Sara Lee organization. The equally famous Jockey for Her underwear crossover discussed earlier in this chapter is being futher extended to include lines of hosiery and sleepwear.

Through the licensing of designer names, producers are coordinating their products with ready-to-wear. Licensing is equally advantageous to the designer in associating his or her name and fashion image with this apparel category. For example, Oscar de la Renta's lingerie line is completely licensed to Carole Hochman, a small, family-owned company that started in 1930. Besides the de la Renta line, Carole Hochman produces a signature collection of sleepwear. Jennifer Brodlieb, Ralph Lauren's public relations manager for licensees, expressed that design house's attitude toward licensing in the innerwear market this way: "We don't think of it as licensing; we think of it as an extension of the collection."[8]

As in the ready-to-wear departments, sections of intimate apparel departments feature the lines of individual designers and manufacturers, such as Vanity Fair, Chanterelle, La Perla, Eileen West for Charles Romar and Sons, and Donna Karan Intimates by Wacoal.

Paradoxically, as conglomerates are expanding through acquisitions and mergers of producers that serve various segments, the brands, whether part of a larger organization or not, are focusing on precisely defined segments to increase market share. Rapidly changing selections of colors and prints appeal to the desire for something new among these young customers. For the same market segment, Hanes Her Way offers high-cut and bikini panties in bright colors and retro prints and styles the garments to fit the not-yet-curvy preteen figure.

More and more designers and manufacturers are using TV home shopping channels like QVC and the Home Shopping Network (HSN) to sell their products. Many women appreciate the detailed product information these channels offer; in addition, they like listening to other women calling in to discuss similar purchases.

Junior Innerwear Departments

Recognizing the growing influence of teenage and young adult shoppers (ages 13 to 32) on the intimate apparel market, department stores as well as national chains and discounters are starting to merchandise junior innerwear as collection concepts, much like the shops-within-a-shop for designer label outerwear.[9] Although consumers in this segment typically have less income than their elders, they are more prone to impulse buying of items they consider "fun." They want merchandise they will not find in their mothers' wardrobes. Growing up with the idea that fashion features as well as functionality are important criteria for their innerwear buying decisions, young shoppers are responding favorably to the junior innerwear departments.

Catalogs and the Internet

Manufacturers such as Vanity Fair are marketing their brands directly to retail customers through catalogs. Many department stores send out special intimate apparel catalogs, and they regularly include high-fashion intimate apparel in their seasonal catalogs. The Victoria's Secret catalog, with its provocatively posed models, is a separate company from the stores of the same name. It has a distribution of 365 million and releases 15-20 catalogs a year. Private Lives by Spiegel, the giant mail-order house, marked that company's entrance into the intimate apparel specialty-catalog field. Even L.L. Bean, with its focus on the great outdoors, features silk and thermal long underwear for men and women in its winter catalogs.

Another growing form of nonstore retailing of intimate apparel is the Internet. Even the smallest producer cannot afford to be without a Web site through which it can market directly to consumers as well as communicate with its retailer customers. Virtually every fashion magazine ad for a brand of intimate apparel includes an invitation for a virtual visit to the producer's Web site.

Men's and Children's Underwear and Sleepwear

Even more than women's intimate apparel, men's and children's underwear have been considered utilitarian rather than fashion apparel categories. Today, however, the fashion influence has taken hold (see Figure 11.6).

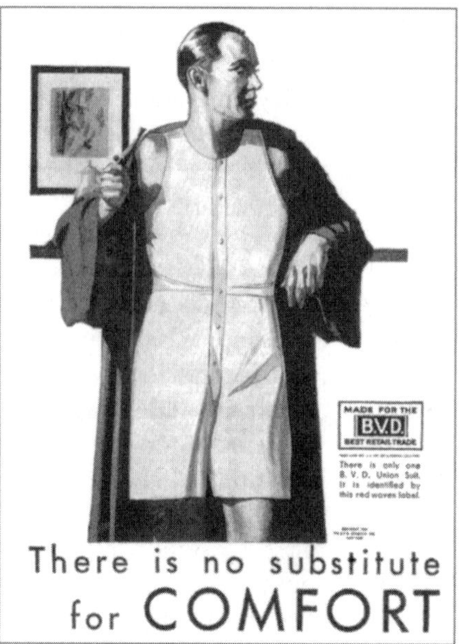

FIGURE 11.6 *Men's underwear styles change more slowly than women's, but still come under the influence of fashion.* The B.V.D. Company, New York. Reprinted with permission.

Men's and Children's Underwear

Much of the history of men's underwear is the history of the biggest name in the industry, Fruit of the Loom.[10] Founded as Union Underwear in 1926, the company began with one-piece underwear known as "union suits." The company was one of the finished-garment licensees of the Fruit of the Loom textile company, and it introduced boxer shorts and knit underwear under that label in the 1940s.

The knit styles of briefs and undershirts were also produced by two famous manufacturers of men's and boy's underwear: Jockey, founded in the late 1800s, and Munsingwear, founded in 1909. Undershirt styles were limited to short-sleeved crew- and V-necks and sleeveless, U-necked ribbed vests. Virtually all men's knit underwear was white, and woven boxers were made in limited colors and patterns.

Not until the 1970s did a wide choice of colors and patterns become available. About the same time, bikini styles in briefs were introduced to the newly fashion-conscious male shopper. In 1982, Calvin Klein's men's underwear collection made white seem boring. By the mid-1990s, casual pants styles with low-slung waists allowed men to show their allegiances to their favorite designers and brands by revealing the elastic waistbands of their underpants, inscribed with such names as Calvin, Tommy Hilfiger, or Jockey.

A trend to watch is the crossover of shapers from women's foundations. Tummy-toners have already won some adherents among men who want to maintain a fit, trim silhouette. Young men have adopted loose-fitting, comfortable boxer shorts and have made them a fashion item for at-home and sleepwear. Boxers are made in a limitless variety of colors and prints and in woven silks, cotton flannel, and jersey knit cotton/polyester blends, as well as the traditional lightweight woven cotton. Women have incorporated boxers into their own wardrobes. In addition to the established men's underwear brands, Joe Boxer enjoys a large market for this item, as does the licensed Tommy Hilfiger Intimates at Bestform, a unit of VF Corporation.

Fashion joins function in the market for long underwear, available in silk, wool, and Duofold, for skiing, snowboarding, and other winter sports. Waffle-knit thermal underwear, also designed for warmth, has a second life as loungewear.

The marketing of men's underwear as a fashion item benefits retailers' private label merchandise as well as national and designer brands. A study of men's shopping habits found that 24 percent of dollar sales and 15 percent of unit sales of men's underwear, sleepwear, and loungewear went to private label brands. Since customers see the merchandise as a brand, comparable to national brands but available exclusively through a particular store, loyalty to private labels translates into store loyalty.

Children's underwear has also evolved from merely functional to fashionable. Girl's panties were available in pastel colors for decades, but the range of colors and prints has exploded to match the variety available to adult women. Thanks to Fruit of the Loom's Underoos line, which first appeared in 1978, little boys also have the chance to express their tastes and to sport the images of favorite cartoon characters, like Batman and Superman. Other manufacturers have joined this trend; for example, Hanes features Spiderman and Toy Story characters on its briefs for boys. Little girls also have cartoon characters, like Minnie Mouse and 101 Dalmatians, made by Hanes Her Way.

The Web site Ecobaby (www.ecobaby.com) exemplifies another trend in children's underwear: parents' preference for natural, environment-friendly products for infants. The Web site sells products like organic diapers and natural disposable diaper liners.

Men's and Children's Pajamas and Robes

Cotton, batiste, flannel, and silk, all in a variety of colors and patterns, have added a fashion element to men's sleepwear. Perhaps the most ubiquitous robe of the last 50 years is the terry cloth robe—worn by men, women, and children and as famous for its comfortable cotton fabric as for its loose fit and easy belt. At the other end of the price spectrum is the classic men's silk robe, by designers such as Fernando Sanchez, and by private labels such as Saks Fifth Avenue.

Children's sleepwear, like adults', includes pajamas, nightgowns, and nightshirts, as well as *Dr. Dentons*. This brand name for sleepers with feet—and sometimes with a back flap for convenience in using the toilet—has come to be used as a generic term for such garments. Special finishes are applied to children's sleepwear to improve its flame resistance, in compliance with the Flammable Fabrics Act. However, the Consumer Products Safety Commission loosened its regulation in 1996, allowing the use of cotton and cotton blends and holding tight-fitting sleepwear in sizes 9 months to 14X and infants' sizes 0 to 9 months to general apparel standards rather than the more stringent children's sleepwear standards.[11]

Bodywear

The physical fitness boom of the 1980s and 1990s, which lured millions of Americans into aerobic classes and bodybuilding activities, also was responsible for producing a new fashion category, **bodywear**. It encompasses coordinated leotards, tights, unitards, wrap skirts, sweatsuits, leg warmers, shorts, T-shirts, and crop tops. The line between bodywear and activewear is constantly shifting—especially as stretch fabrics find their way into more and more activewear.

Originally, bodywear was sold in hosiery departments, but most stores are now selling it in separate shops or boutiques. Some department stores, such as Nordstrom and Dillard's, have focused even more attention on bodywear by staging fashion shows, scheduling personal appearances by designers, and even sponsoring in-store exercise and dance classes. More sporting goods stores and specialty stores are adding bodywear, especially if it has performance features, such as antimoisture fabric. Some gyms have become bodywear retailers as a sideline to their exercise businesses.

Many fashion-conscious women insist on being stylish while they stretch, strain, and sweat to get in shape. Longtime bodywear manufacturers, such as Danskin, capitalized on this market by creating new exciting leotards with coordinating tights, cover-ups, and other workout apparel necessities. Many designers, including Ralph Lauren and Donna Karan, created bodywear lines that have sold very well. Another manufacturer, the Weekend Exercise Company, produces two lines of bodywear: Marika, and the Mikhail Baryshnikov line. Carushka, Inc. of California sells its line of bodywear and yogawear for women on the Internet.

Yoga has become more and more popular, and according to recent reports, 15-18 million Americans practice it regularly.[12] This trend has naturally launched new lines of yogawear, with garments like cotton tank tops, stretching pants, and cashmere shorts and cardigans. In 2001, supermodel Christy Turlington launched the upscale yogawear line Nuala with Puma. Nike released the yoga-inspired clothing line Tek Zen for women in 2002, and the yoga-practicing Donna Karan includes yogawear in her DKNY sportswear line.[13]

In the dancewear category, Capezio, long famous as a manufacturer of ballet and pointe shoes, added lines of leotards, unitards, and dance dresses for women, as well as tights and body and legwarmers. Capezio products, available in more than 3,000 stores or "doors," have been expanded to include lines for figure skating and ballroom dancing.

FIGURE 11.7 *Hosiery from Nine West is a big hit with this actress from the musical 42nd Street.* Courtesy, Kramer & Kramer/ Mark Andrews.

Legwear

The ancient Greeks were among the first to wear cloth legwear. By the late 1500s, European men and women wore stockings made from a single fabric width that was knitted flat, with the two edges sewn together to form a back seam. This technology remained essentially unchanged for centuries. Because of wear at the heels and toes, socks often developed holes that had to be mended; a process that was called "darning." For centuries, darning socks was an everyday task for women.

The hosiery industry in the United States today is undergoing massive changes as fewer women are wearing pantyhose every day, and more women are wearing socks. Sheer hose sales have fallen, while sales of tights and opaques have risen. Socks, especially athletic socks, have seen an enormous surge in popularity in the 1990s.

The Evolution of Women's Hosiery

Until World War I, women's legs were concealed under floor-length skirts and dresses. When skirt lengths moved up and women's legs became visible, interest in adorning them increased, and the hosiery industry began to grow. Hanes, Trimfit, Berkshire, and Round the Clock were all introduced in the 1920s. But it was not until the introduction of nylon that hosiery as we know it today became a fashion accessory. Before the introduction of nylon in 1938, women wore seamed silk, cotton, or rayon stockings. Because of its easier care and greater durability, the new nylon hosiery was eagerly accepted despite its high price. Still a "run" or "ladder" in a nylon stocking was an expensive accident, and women went to great lengths to prevent them. Sales women routinely donned gloves before showing stockings to a customer.

Fashion first entered the hosiery picture in the 1950s with the introduction of colors other than black or flesh tones. But it was not until the 1960s that hosiery became a major fashion accessory. To accessorize the shorter skirt—eventually evolving into the miniskirt and micromini—colors, textures, and weights of stockings were created in great variety. Women wore "pettipants" in the early 1960s to cover the garters of their garter belts or girdles—and to show a bit of lace under the shorter skirts. Then pantyhose were introduced and became a fantastic success. In turn, their popularity led to the introduction of seamless pantyhose and figure-control or support pantyhose.

In the 1970s, when women began wearing pants to work, knee-high and ankle-high hosiery were introduced. Together with pantyhose, they captured the major share of the hosiery business. The sale of stockings plummeted and has never recovered. In addition, with elasticized bands on knee-high and over-the-knee hosiery, garters became unnecessary, and garter belts and pettipants became passe.

In the 1980s, changes in lifestyle produced a new set of customer needs and wants that were met with textures in pantyhose and tights. Socks in ribs and knits, leg warmers, and many kinds of athletic socks, revitalized the industry.

The 1990s saw a drop in the sales of pantyhose, brought about in part by the advent of casual dress days in 90 percent of U.S. businesses. Even with more tailored pants, women may opt for *trouser socks*, a type of knee-high hosiery that is slightly heavier than sheer knee-highs and is available in a variety of colors and textures. Another influence is the impact of teenage customers, who shop for hosiery more frequently than adult women. Reacting to the latest fashion news on MTV, the young shoppers have boosted the sales of brightly colored tights and designer brands. Teens and adults are also wearing hosiery with patterns at the ankles, known as "docks."

Girls also have tights and sheer pantyhose made in girls' sizes by a number of manufacturers; for example, Little L'eggs.

The Recent History of Socks

The influence of teenage shoppers has also boosted the women's sock business. Women of all ages have responded well to the combination of fashion design and comfort features offered in socks for casual wear and for extensive physical activity, such as sports. Dress-down Fridays have also led women to expand their sock wardrobes. Women's socks generally come in three lengths: ankle, crew, and knee.

For work and athletic socks, the comfort features are also emphasized. Cushioning may be designed for very specific activities, with differences between, say, tennis and running.[14] **Wicking**, the ability to carry the moisture of perspiration away from the skin, is offered by various synthetic fibers. Cotton and wool are often combined with nylon, acrylic, and spandex to add elasticity, shape retention, and ventilation.

These comfort features are also an important selling point for men's athletic socks. A new development to reduce blister-causing friction is the interweaving of Teflon fibers with polyester and cotton at pressure points in socks. Inventor Bob Gunn has worked with DuPont's Teflon and Chipman Union, a sock making firm, to market Blister Guards socks.

Fashion is less of an issue in men's hosiery than in women's, but it is not totally ignored. For high school athletes of both sexes, the length of one's socks distinguishes the fashion-savvy player from the object of ridicule. In an ironic turnabout of gender-based concerns, the over-the-calf length of men's dress socks has become a popular way to avoid the exposure of bare leg above the ankle.

Color, patterns, and weight of socks are dictated by use. Dress socks are typically dark in color. Narrow ribbing, sometimes with a cable on either side of the leg, is a common pattern, and the socks are relatively lightweight. Fashion-forward men are choosing patterned socks, including argyles, dobby knits, dots, diamonds, and plaids. The patterns are chosen to coordinate with the shirt, slacks, or suit. Casual socks, designed to be worn with casual trousers and a sport jacket, may be somewhat heavier than dress socks. Athletic and work socks are the heaviest. They are most often white, sometimes with two or three bands of color at the top or a company logo, such as the Nike swoosh. A work sock that has been popular for generations is the famous *monkey sock*, which has a heather brown foot, a red heel, and a white top. These socks can be made into a stuffed monkey toy for children. *Tube socks*, which are knit without a defined heel, are popular as a functional everyday sock. The one-size-fits-all design is almost impossible to outgrow. Tube socks are less expensive to produce than conventional socks, and the savings is passed on to the consumer. Packaging of three or six pairs at a reduced per-pair price also appeals to the budget-minded shopper.

More expensive *ragg socks*, which are very thick, warm socks designed for wear with boots or sandals, are increasingly popular for work or winter sports. Similarly, Polar fleece socks in various lengths are also good for keeping the feet warm, even when wet.

Organization and Operation

The hosiery industry consists primarily of large firms, many of which are divisions of huge textile or apparel conglomerates. The largest concentration of hosiery plants is found in the Southern states, with more than half of them in North Carolina.

Since hosiery is knitted in the greige (unfinished) state, most manufacturers can produce branded and unbranded hosiery in the same mill. The greige goods are then dyed, finished, stamped, and packaged to specification for national brand, private brand, or unbranded hosiery.

FIGURE 11.8
This ad for Soxland brings fashion to functional items, while simultaneously promoting a fun image of the company.
Courtesy, Soxland ®dAVCO.

Merchandising and Marketing

Traditionally, the women's hosiery industry concentrated its merchandising activities almost exclusively on the promotion and sale of nationally advertised brands. Recently, however, the industry has been merchandising its products for private labeling or for sale from self-service displays in supermarkets and drugstores. Designer labeling has also become increasingly important. The world's largest hosiery manufacturer, Sara Lee Hosiery, has annual sales of over $1.5 billion with its designer (Donna Karan), national (Hanes), and mass-merchandise (L'eggs) brands. Hanes alone is the largest hosiery brand in the world (see Figure 11.9). Parent company Sara Lee Corporation is also a major marketer of socks; L'eggswear is just one of their lines of socks and tights.

National Brands

Major hosiery producers sell their brand lines to retail stores across the country. Producers aggressively advertise their lines in national magazines and newspapers and on television. They also usually supply cooperative advertising, display aids, and fashion assistance to help promote these national brands at the store level. Major national brands include Hanes, Burlington, Round the Clock, Trimfit, and Kayser Roth.

Designer-Label Brands

Because designer labeling adds an aura of couture and prestige to any item, designer labels have appeared on a variety of hosiery items, including pantyhose, socks, and leg warmers. Almost all of the designer-label hosiery is the result of licensing agreements between the designer and manufacturers of national brands. In hosiery and pantyhose. In hosiery and pantyhose, Kayser Roth uses Calvin Klein, Pennaco Hoisery uses Givency, and Leg Resource uses Adrienne Vittadini. In socks, The Great American Knitting Company uses Perry Ellis.

FIGURE 11.9
Body Enhancers is a popular collection by Hanes, which enhances your shape and eliminates the sight of pantylines.
Coutresy, Hanes ®.

Private Brands

Chain organizations, retail stores, and some individual stores have developed their own private or store brands that compete with nationally advertised brands. A private label offers many advantages for the retailer. The cost of the hosiery is usually less because there is no built-in charge for advertising as there is for national brands. The private brand can be made up in colors and construction that will match customer profile specifications. Because the private brand is not available elsewhere, price promotions are easier. Customer loyalty can also be built upon the exclusivity of the private brand. Charter Club hosiery, tights, and socks for example, are the private label of Federated Department Stores.

Mass-Merchandised Brands

For self-service stores such as supermarkets, discount stores, and drug chains, hosiery manufacturers have developed low-priced, packaged hosiery. Each mass-merchandised brand offers a good choice of styles and colors. Each manufacturer supplies attractive, self-service stock fixtures and promotes its brand through national advertising. When L'eggs pantyhose, made by Sara Lee Hosiery, were introduced, their distinctive packaging in plastic eggs brought immediate name recognition, but by the early 1990s, a more conventional package was adopted to meet the objections of environmentalists. By then, the name was nationally established as one of the best-selling mass-merchandised brands along with competitor Kayser Roth's No Nonsense pantyhose. Surprisingly, nearly half of the doors that distribute No Nonesense are food stores, drugstores, and other mass merchandisers. There is also A Little Nonsense brand for infants' and toddlers' socks.

Industry Trends

Trends in the legwear industry are similar to those in the innerwear industry. Licensing agreements enable designers and manufacturers to produce and market lines of legwear that coordinate with a designer's ready-to-wear lines. Special packaging also promotes brand loyalty. Manufacturers offer retailers help with visual merchandising to help them stimulate sales. In manufacturing, the trend is toward offshore production.

Fashion Trends

Fashion trends have a tremendous influence on sales in the hosiery industry. For example, when skirts are shorter or have leg-revealing silhouettes, texture and color in hosiery become important. Apparel manufacturers have recently worked with hosiery manufacturers to design pantyhose that are both texture- and color-coordinated to their sportswear. The hosiery is displayed with the apparel to promote a total fashion look.

The inventory of most hosiery departments includes ankle-length, knee-high, and over-the-knee stockings; sheer and opaque pantyhose, leg warmers, bodywear, and casual footwear. Bodywear and casual footwear are relatively high-priced retail items, while packaged hosiery is low-priced. As a result, some stores have made separate departments out of these two different categories.

The needs and wants of customers prompt hosiery manufacturers to design entirely new items. Control-top pantyhose, support hose, and queen-sized pantyhose cater to the demands of an aging population that is also growing heavier. A new nylon and Lycra (spandex) hosiery by Victoria's Secret is promoted as wearing longer and not running easily—even when a tack is pushed through it.

Men's, women's, and children's sock sales are predicted to increase steadily in the next decade. Athletic, sport, and work socks are the sources of growth in the men's area. New textures, colors, and patterns are fueling the market in women's socks, as more spandex content is added to tights and pantyhose. Children are emulating their sports heros and requesting their specific brand of sport socks.

Special Packaging

More and more manufacturers are turning to special packaging as a way to make their products stand out in this very competitive industry. As Paul Kubrie of Gina Hosiery says:

> *In tights and socks, special packaging is an important way to go. It's a necessity now because socks and tights have become a basic, and you have to entice the customer to make a purchase*[15]

Bonuses are popular in sock merchandising. Hue's marketed their sport socks through a Three-for-12 program, which allowed customers to pick and choose three pairs of socks at a discounted price. While each pair retailed for $5, a selection from any of the sport sock lines cost $12. Some of the special packaging success stories include the Gold Toe gift-with-purchase program of Great American Knitting Mills. The company packaged a one-ounce radio with a six-pair pack of boy's crew socks.

This promotion was so successful that the package was prominately displayed at the entrance of many legwear stores.

Visual Merchandising

In-store displays and other point-of-purchase materials are being offered by manufacturers to retailers to add some color to hosiery departments. While increasingly casual dress codes among office workers have caused a decline in sales of sheer pantyhose, the women's sock market has blossomed. Fishnets, animal prints, luxury yarns, and novelty styles, such as the super-low sock traditionally used only by athletes, have given new life to the category.[16] This light-hearted approach has also inspired sock vendors to promote holiday- and Halloween-themed socks with matching retail displays. When Hanes introduced Donna Karan's new Evolution line of hosiery, which offers waist-to-toe compression, they offered retailers a videotape of Donna discussing her view of hosiery; the video was widely played in hosiery departments across the country.[17]

Summary and Review

The categories of women's intimate apparel, men's and children's underwear and sleepwear, and hosiery for all three market segments were long considered strictly utilitarian, but today all of these categories have taken on fashion features. A consumer can develop a wardrobe that is coordinated from the inside to the outside and from head to toe.

Women's intimate apparel includes foundation garments (bras and shapewear), lingerie (such as panties, camisoles, slips, and sleepwear), and loungewear. These formerly separate categories are now coordinated and are often promoted as distinctive designer or producer lines.

Men's underwear and sleepwear also features a broad choice of colors and a variety of styles, ranging from bikini briefs to loose boxers, and children's underwear and sleepwear is decorated with favorite cartoon characters.

The growing awareness of the need for exercise to be physically fit has generated the development of a separate apparel category called bodywear, which includes spandex shorts and tops for both women and men, leotards, and other apparel suitable for wearing while working out.

Hosiery categories include women's pantyhose and tights and a variety of styles of socks for men, women, and children. Through licensing, apparel designers have gained customer loyalty for brands of hosiery coordinated with their apparel lines. Private labels and mass-merchandised brands also have their adherents among consumers, who identify brand names with a particular fashion and quality image. Hosiery manufacturing is carried out wholly or partly overseas by many producers.

FIGURE 11.10

Moschino's bra dress of 1994 spoofed the importance of the bosom in the "Wonderbra Era" of the 1990s.

Photo by Irving Solero. Courtesy of the Museum of the Fashion Institute of Technology, New York.

Trade Talk

Define or briefly explain the following terms:

bodywear
foundations
innerwear
intimate apparel
lingerie
loungewear
shapers
wicking
women's underwear

For Review

1. How does the foundations industry respond to trends in ready-to-wear?
2. How does the intimate apparel industry relate to the ready-to-wear industry?
3. How does the display of women's underwear and intimate apparel demonstrate the growing influence of fashion features? How do current visual merchandising practices differ from those of the past?
4. Why is the junior market important to the women's intimate apparel industry?
5. What fashion features have been emphasized in the merchandising and marketing of men's underwear?
6. What is bodywear, and how did it grow into a separate apparel category?
7. Why is the development of new fibers so important to the women's hosiery industry?
8. Identify and describe four categories of brands of women's hosiery.
9. What is the influence of fashion trends in ready-to-wear on the fashion features of women's, men's, and children's hosiery?
10. How does special packaging help hosiery producers increase market share?

For Discussion

1. Discuss current trends in the intimate apparel industry as they relate to (a) mergers, (b) diversification of product lines, and (c) styling.
2. How has the increasing informality of dress in the 1990s affected the innerwear and hosiery industries?

References

1. Karyn Monget,"Search for Seamless Secret," *Women's Wear Daily*, May 21, 2001.
2. "As You Like It Faced," *Body Fashions Intimate Apparel*, September 26, 1997.
3. Robert Murphy, "Bring Back That Sex Appeal," *Women's Wear Daily*, July 9, 2001.
4. Karyn Monget, "Strong Spring Lifts Outlook," *Women's Wear Daily*, June 17, 2002, p. 8.
5. Charla Krupp, "The Control Thong," *Time*, March 19, 2001, p. 14.
6. Karyn Monget, "It's Showtime!" *Women's Wear Daily*, Intimates, August 2001, p. 20.
7. Patricia Braus, "Boomers Against Gravity," *American Demographics*, February 1, 1995, p. 50.
8. Karyn Monget, "Firming Up the Finishing Touches," *Women's Wear Daily*, April 29, 2002, p. 14.
9. Karyn Monget, "Junior Looks Seek Their Own Homes," *Women's Wear Daily*, August 25, 1997, p. 14.
10. Hoover's Company Profiles, 1997.
11. James A. Morrissey, "CPSC Liberalizes Children's Sleepwear Regs.," *Textile World*, June 1, 1996, p. 18.
12. Stephanie Loughran, "Retailers Fit Yoga Tapes into Whole Health Aisle," *Supermarket News*, December 3, 2001, p. 45.
13. "Nike Plans Yoga Clothing Line," *Marketing to Women*, March 2002, p. 5.
14. "Fashion & Styling," *Spotlight on Socks, A WWD Special Report*, September 1996, p. 4.
15. "Boxing Lessons," *Woman's Wear Daily*, November 1997, p. 42.
16. Marc Karimzadeh, "Socks Lead Surprise Holiday Action," *Woman's Wear Daily*, January 22, 2001, p. 26.
17. Ibid.

CHAPTER 12

Accessories

WHAT'S IN IT FOR YOU?

Everything you always wanted to know about the classifications of accessories. These include footwear, handbags, gloves, belts, millinery, eyewear, and jewelry.

Key Concepts:

- History and development of the accessory industries
- Organization, operation, merchandising, and marketing of the footwear and jewelry industries.
- Manufacturing, merchandising, and marketing of handbags, belts, gloves, hats, neckwear, and eyewear
- Trends in the various classifications of accessories

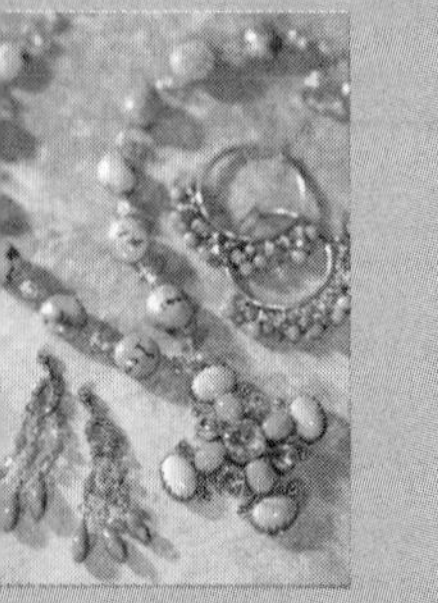

The accessories business, one of fashion's hottest categories in the 2000s, has gotten its biggest boost from graying baby boomers and not from the darlings of the media—Generations X and Y. Citing the old adage, *clothes may make the man or woman, but accessories make the clothes*, baby boomers are buying accessories with an eye to giving life to an old outfit or dynamite pizzazz to a new one.

The manufacturers of accessories must constantly forecast the changes in cycles of fashion, so that their accessories are perfect for new fashions. This includes not only the changes in silhouette, but also fabrications and color. The marketing of accessories gained an enormous boost with the entrance of well-known designers' names into the business. Today, the fame of the accessories designer is as important as the fame of the clothing designer; and in many cases, it is the same famous name. It is only through constant alertness to trends and degrees of customer acceptance that fashion accessory designers succeed. They must be prepared to design and produce styles that blend, follow or lead, and innovate. The fashion accessories category includes footwear, handbags, gloves, hats, neckwear, eyewear, and jewelry.

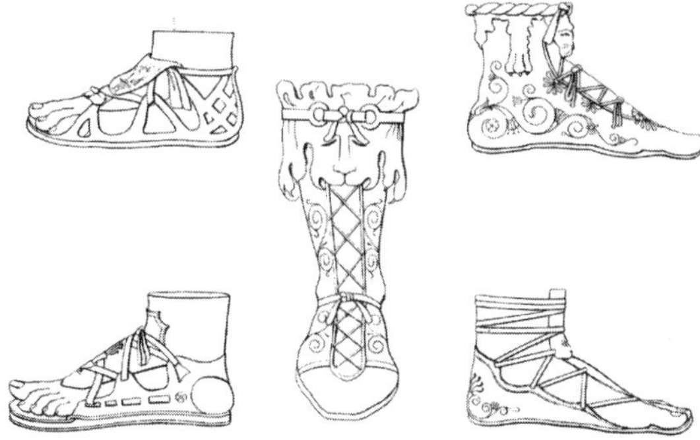

FIGURE 12.1
This drawing shoes ancient Roman styles of sandals.

Footwear

Footwear has always conjured up exciting, glamorous, and amusing times in history and literature. We read about gallant heros in sevenleague boots, princesses in glass slippers, Mercury with winged feet, and, of course, the magic red shoes that took Dorothy from the land of Oz back home to Kansas.

Feet, the base upon which our bodies stand, have been wrapped, covered, or left uncovered since the beginning of time. Primitive people wrapped their feet in fur, and later people strapped them into sandals. Chinese women bound their feet. Footwear often was—and still is—dictated by profession: Arctic trappers wore snowshoes, while ballet dancers wore *pointes*, or toe shoes; cowboys wore leather boots, and firefighters wore rubber boots.

Making shoes was once a painstaking handicraft. But the commercial production of shoes has developed into an industry providing over 300 variations in shoe lengths and widths and over 10,000 different shapes and styles. The footwear category includes shoes, slippers, athletic shoes, and boots. Most shoe styles originated in Europe, keeping pace with the growth of European fashion. However, a classic shoe style that originated in America is the moccasin. Favored by both men and women and adored by most children, the moccasin style of shoe still retains its popularity and stands as one of the first examples of unisex fashion.

Organization and Operation

Footwear production was once a major industry in New England, but many of that region's factories have downsized or closed. Among those remaining are Nine West of Stamford, Connecticut, primarily a manufacturer of women's shoes, and Timberland of Stratham, New Hampshire, best known for its work boots. Timberland boots have become the signature footwear of the hip-hop community, and are immensely popular with young men and women worldwide. The shoe industry moved west when the Midwest became an important source of hide supplies and cheaper labor, and another large center of production grew around St. Louis, Missouri. Brown Shoe Company, producer of Buster Brown children's shoes, Regal shoes for men, and Air Step shoes for women, is based there.

The largest shoe producer in the United States today is Nike. Nike actually does not own any of the manufacturing facilities that produce the shoes and apparel it sells; rather it acts more like a wholesaler, and focuses on marketing its products.

Imports are also a factor in dress shoes at higher price points. A longstanding reputation for quality craftsmanship and styling has contributed to the success of Italian manufacturers, such as Ferragamo, Prada, Gucci, and Diego Della Valle. Italy is the number one producer of high-end designer shoes, with world-famous designs and quality craftsmanship. The bulk of less expensive imported shoes comes from Asia, mainly China. Other countries that export low price shoes are Brazil, Portugal, and Spain. The domestic shoe production declined considerably over the second half of the 20th century. American shoe factories now produce less than 25 percent of the merchandise that was made here in the 1960s. Most of the surviving U.S. manufacturers in the 21st century that have been successful have turned to niche markets.

Shoe production begins with a **last**. Lasts were originally wooden forms in the shape of a foot, over which the shoes were built. Today most modern factories, American and foreign, make lasts of plastic or aluminum. Lasts made from these materials provide more exact measurements, and are easier to handle than the old wooden ones.

The variety of lasts, the quality of materials, and the number and type of manufacturing operations required determine the quality and price of the finished shoe. As many as 200 to 300 operations performed by highly skilled workers are required to make an expensive, high-quality shoe. Shoe manufacturers produce shoes in an enormous range of sizes. The normal range of women's shoe sizes involves 103 width and length combinations. And this does not include sizes shorter than 4, longer than 11, or wider than D.

Inventories, production problems, and capital investments in the shoe business are tremendous compared with those of other fashion-related industries. Thus, it is not surprising that giant companies dominate the industry. Among the fashion industries, only cosmetics has a higher percentage of production by giant companies.

Women's Shoes

For centuries, little attention was paid to the styling of women's shoes. Their purpose was regarded as purely functional. Since the 1920s, however, women's feet have been plainly visible, and shoes have developed both in fashion importance and variety. After World War II, the black or brown all-purpose shoes designed to be worn with any wardrobe disappeared. New and varied leather finishes, textures, plastic and fabric materials, and ranges of colors provided shoe styles that not only kept pace with changes in fashion but in many cases originated fashion trends.

Styles have run the fashion gamut from pointed to square toes, from high to flat heels, and from naked sandals to thigh-high boots. Typically—but not always—broad toes and low, chunky heels go together, and narrow, pointed-toe shoes are more likely to have stiletto heels. The slim, elegant designs have been popular when apparel fashions have emphasized formality, and the heavier, more down-to-earth styles have been the rage in seasons when more casual clothing styles prevailed.

Recently, the market has segmented along age and income lines. The tapered lines featured in high-fashion designer shoes have won some favor with society leaders, while Hollywood stars and models favor the stiletto heel. Working women and younger women, the customers of such manufacturers as Nine West and Kenneth Cole, opted for comfort and solid footing. Even the once outré Hush Puppies returned—in wild new colors. In London, Patrick Cox designed the Wannabe loafer, a chunky, square-toed, unisex shoe that was an immediate hit with movie and TV stars and fellow designers. Perhaps the warnings of orthopedists and fitness trainers have gained attention: Constant wearing of high heels shortens the Achilles tendon, "hammer toes" can result from wearing shoes with very pointed toes, and feet that become accustomed to wide, roomy shoes resist being stuffed into narrower styles. Nevertheless, stiletto heels and pointed toes have made a huge comeback. Young fashion conscious women eagerly follow the example of Sarah Jessica Parker's character, Carrie, in the popular TV series *Sex and the City*, and wear fragile stiletto shoes and sandals as their everyday footwear, regardless of weather and temperature.

Men's Shoes

A shift in thinking and lifestyle on the part of American men has had a dramatic effect on the merchandising of men's shoes. Dress shoes were once the most important sales category in men's shoe departments in retail stores. They are now being replaced by dress/casual and casual shoes, which were once considered appropriate only for the 18-to-25 age group but now are preferred by men of all ages (see Figure 12.2). The dress shoe business is now considered a niche market.

Timberland, Sebago, and Rockport are examples of casual shoe manufacturers whose reputation for durable work shoes has benefited from this trend. Sperry Top-Siders, made by Stride Rite, were once limited to boat owners; today they are much more widely worn for casual wear. Red Wing Shoes of Red Wing, Minnesota, continues to grow in its niche, specialized work shoes for letter carriers, loggers, welders, firefighters, and electrical linemen. Fastlane Footwear of Jackson, Michigan, produces casual shoes and boots bearing the NASCAR emblem and logos from other racing associations, teams, and car makers Ford, Chevrolet, Dodge, and Pontiac. As company chairman John Lefere says: "Our niche is what I call the American icons of the motor and racing industries."

Well-known U.S. brand names for men's dress and casual shoes include Florsheim, Johnston & Murphy, Allen-Edmonds, Alden, and Stuart McGuire. L. B. Evans has been making slippers and sandals in New England since 1804. At the high-end of the market are Gokey boots and shoes, which are handmade in the United States to customer's exact specifications; they are sold by Orvis through its catalog and stores.

American designer dress and dress/casual shoes are also predominately produced abroad. High-end imports from Europe include Clark's of England, Bally of Switzerland, and Ferragamo, Gucci, and Bruno Magli of Italy.

Children's Shoes

From an early age, both boys and girls take a serious interest in their shoe wardrobes. Perhaps they are influenced by stories about

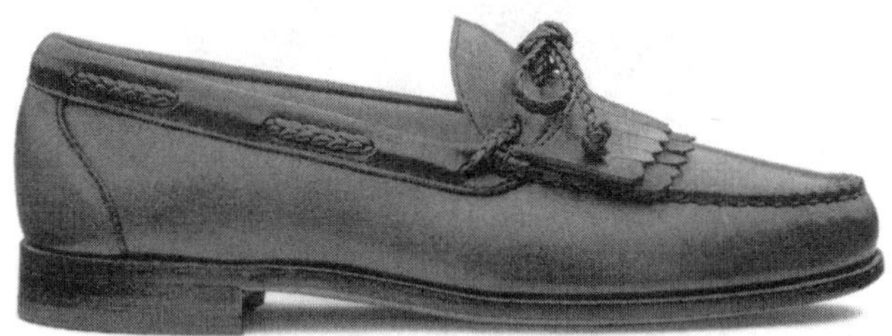

FIGURE 12.2
To stay in the mainstream of fashion, manufacturers of men's dress shoes have branched into casual styles.
© Allen-Edmonds Shoe Corporation.

shoes with magical powers, as in *Cinderella*, *Puss in Boots*, and *The 12 Dancing Princesses*.

Shoes, especially everyday shoes, are subject to wear and tear, so even though they are outgrown as quickly as apparel, they are not as suitable for handing down or buying secondhand. Furthermore, a professionally fitted new pair of shoes are more likely to ensure health and comfort than are used shoes. Children thus must be active participants in the purchase decision. Having a deciding vote on the comfort of their shoes, children can easily make the next step to expressing opinions on appearances. Dressing in conformity with their peers and older children is an obvious way of showing that they fit into their social group.

The styles of children's dress shoes are adaptations of adult styles, with *oxfords* being popular for boys and the classic *Mary Janes* for girls. The use of leather distinguishes higher

Then & Now

Heels, Toes, and Away We Go!

The two fashion points that have changed shoe styles over the years, are the heels and toes. Heels go from low and chunky, to high and stiletto. Toes comes in all shapes—from square to round, to narrow and pointy.

Platform shoes are "retro" indeed.
Courtesy, Fairchild Publications, Inc.

Popular pointy-toed shoes from designer Manolo Blahnik's collection.
Courtesy, Fairchild Publications, Inc.

priced lines from less expensive lines of vinyl and other leather substitutes. For casual wear, a popular low-priced choice is *jellies*, a sturdy style sandal in brightly-colored plastic. Jellies are a rare example of a children's style that became popular for adults. Many teens wear *Doc Martens*, hiking boots with lug soles.

As athletic shoes evolved from canvas sneakers, they became the preferred shoe for school wear. Practical features, such as Velcro fastenings; purely decorative features, such as L.A. Gear's briefly popular light-up shoe; and brand and style identification, such as that provided by Nike's Air Jordans, all influence children's preferences. But the trend to school uniforms for public school students is slowing the switch to athletic shoes for school wear, and leather oxfords or T-straps are reemerging.

Athletic Shoes

Sneakers, the original athletic shoe, were made possible by Charles Goodyear, who invented the vulcanizing process for rubber in the late 1800s. Keds were the first shoes to use this process, bonding rubber soles to canvas tops. In 1917, Converse, Inc., of North Framington, Massachusetts, introduced the All Star, which has sold more than 500 million pairs! From these humble beginnings a huge industry has grown—and shod the world.

Perhaps the most significant development in shoes since the 1980s—affecting men's, women's, and children's shoes—has been the proliferation of athletic footwear. Spurred by the trend toward more casual dressing, this separate category is now considered a mature market.

Athletic shoes have become ever more specialized. Manufacturers make special shoes for virtually any sports activity—walking, running, climbing, aerobics, racquetball, biking, hiking, golf. Most of the "super-specialty" shoes are carried in specialty sporting goods stores, while department stores and other general retailers stock a less specialized and more fashion-oriented range of athletic shoes.

Merchandising and Marketing

As with most fashion industries, New York City is the major U.S. market center for shoes. It is there that most producers maintain permanent showrooms, and it is also home to the industry's trade shows. The Fashion Footwear Association of New York (FFANY), with a membership of 300 corporations and 800 brand names, stages the international footwear trade show New York Shoe Expo four times a year.

The shoe industry has an active national trade association known as the National Shoe Manufacturers Association. Together with the National Shoe Retailers Association, it disseminates technical, statistical, and fashion trend information on footwear. In addition, the leather industry and its associations operate as sources of fashion information for shoe buyers and other retail store executives.

Brand names are important in the footwear industry, and manufacturers advertise extensively in national fashion magazines and on national television. Designer names are also growing in importance, especially at the mid-price to high end of the market. One low-price designer name is that of Anthony Mark Haskins, whose shoes are sold on the Home Shopping Network (HSN). On the low-price retail end, Payless ShoeSource is the largest family footwear retailer in the United States. The company sells more than 200 million pairs yearly to around 160 million customers.[1]

In contrast with most other fashion industries, many of the large shoe manufacturers operate retail chain organizations of their own. This practice is known as *dual distribution*. Another industry that practices dual distribution is the men's wear industry (see Chapter 9). Examples of dual distribution in the shoe industry include the Brown Group, the Melville Corporation, which manufactures Thom McAn shoes, and U.S. Shoe Corporation. All of these shoe brands are sold in retail stores owned by the shoe manufacturers. Frequently these shoe chains also stock related accessories, such as handbags and hosiery.

Some shoe manufacturers also operate in the retail field through leased departments in retail stores. Because of the tremendous amount of capital required to stock a shoe department and the expertise needed to fit and sell shoes, many department and specialty stores lease their shoe departments to shoe manufacturers. Surveys by the National Federation of Retailers have repeatedly shown that women's shoe departments are among those most commonly leased by its member stores. Examples of manufacturers of shoes who operate leased shoe departments in stores are the U.S. Shoe Corporation, which features Cobbies, Red Cross, and Pappagallo lines, and the Brown Shoe Company, which features Buster Brown shoes for children, Naturalizer shoes for women, and Regal shoes for men. The Morse Shoe Company and the

Edison Shoe Company are chain-store retailers that import shoes and also operate leased shoe departments in other stores.

For most men's shoe retailers, space limitations make meeting consumer demands a challenge. Even stores that deal exclusively in men's shoes tend to be small, with less than 1,700 square feet of space for both selling and stocking. The manufacturers' retail outlets that predominate among freestanding units cannot compete on availability of many brands. Catalog retailers such as L. L. Bean, Lands' End, and Orvis, who have less of a space problem, are realizing a golden opportunity to attract customers, so long as they maintain an easy return policy.

Because of the tremendous consumer demand for athletic shoes, many retailers have begun paying extra attention to the category, often creating a separate department for athletic shoes. Athletic shoe stores, such as The Athlete's Foot, Foot Locker, and Foot Action chains, which carry a variety of brands and related fashion-oriented merchandise, have sprung up across the country.

American designer dress and dress casual shoes are also commonly produced abroad.

Industry Trends

Americans purchase more than 1 billion pairs of shoes a year, and at least 95 percent of them are manufactured overseas, mainly in Asia. Like apparel manufacturers, some U.S. shoe companies rely on factories overseas, particularly in third world countries where the labor is cheaper. About 65 percent of the footwear that goes on American's feet is made in China.[2]

Whether in athletic or other footwear, there is a strong relationship between shoes and the clothes with which they are worn. Increased emphasis on fashion continues to be the major trend in the footwear industry. Shoe designers and manufacturers regularly attend the Shoe Fair in Bologna, Italy, or the GDS exhibition in Germany. They also attend European apparel openings, as do shoe buyers from retail stores, gathering information on international trends in styling. More and more, apparel fashions influence both the styling and color of footwear. Skirt lengths, silhouette, pants, and sporty or dressy clothes are the fashion keys to women's shoe designs. It is therefore essential for retailers to coordinate shoes and apparel wherever and whenever they can.

For designers and manufacturers, coordination has meant licensing of names in both directions between shoe and apparel producers. The Nike "swoosh" appears on baseball caps and sweatshirts as well as shoes, for example, and Calvin Klein's CK brand of shoes, produced by Nine West, coordinates with his apparel lines.

Handbags

Today the way that people choose to carry their belongings often makes a statement about them, but this was not always the case. Throughout most of history, small, nondescript sacks vied with pockets as places to store one's personal belongings. Even when handbags were invented, they said little about their owners for quite a long time. But the modern handbag, once a mere receptacle for money and makeup, now sends a distinct fashion message as well as statement about its owner's personality and individual style.

As fashion statements, handbags are used to dramatize, harmonize, or contrast with whatever else one is wearing. Styles vary from the most casual, used for sportswear, to the more formal, used for dress-up evening occasions. A handbag may be small or large; its shape, a pouch or a tote, draped or boxy. So important are handbags as fashion accessories that most women own a wardrobe of them. The late Princess Grace of Monaco favored the Hermès bag, now called the Kelly bag in her honor. The late Princess Diana was often photographed with one of her more than 20 Ferragamo clutch purses. Perhaps the most-copied handbag of this century was Chanel's "2.55" diamond-quilted bag, with the shoulder strap that slides through golden chains.

As personal statements, handbags also send a message. A woman who chooses to carry a leather briefcase, for example, sends a professional message, while a woman who uses a backpack sends one of functionalism. Whether a woman opts for a small, delicate beaded handbag at night or something far more exotic, perhaps a gold box set with unusual jewels, says something about her. The woman who carries a tailored, expensive leather purse creates an image that has more chic than that of the woman who settles on a vinyl tote.

Organization and Operation

Compared with other fashion industries, the handbag industry is small. The number of domestic firms producing handbags diminishes

A Lifetime Achievement—The Women's Jewelry Association

Although jewelry is worn primarily by women, (men are catching up), and jewelry is often purchased by women (me for me), only recently has the female gender begun to be part of the executive ranks of the jewelry and watch industry in a significant way. Much of this progress is because of the efforts of the Women's Jewelry Association (WJA), which celebrated its 20th Anniversary in 2003. It began as an informal networking group in 1983 and now counts more than 1000 members among its ranks.

Reflecting the changing role of women in the 1980s and 1990s when women began to enter the workforce in great numbers, the rise of the WJA, and the changing role of women in the jewelry industry, was a direct result. Today, the list of women who have moved into management positions and through the glass ceiling to the "corner office" has grown dramatically.

Among the WJA's key events and activities are the annual Awards of Excellence dinner event, a biannual newsletter, two national meetings a year, a jewelry design competition, scholarships, mentor programs, and a variety of chapter events held around the country. The Award of Excellence dinner honors women in the following categories: design, manufacture, dealer/supplier, sales, retail, marketing, editorial/reporting/publishing, and special services. It also raises money through a silent auction for its scholarship programs.

Another key WJA activity is the DIVA Award, a national contest that was created to promote jewelry design by the women from all walks of life. It is open to all designers, whether they have a jewelry background or not.

Reflecting the times, the WJA is now online and supplies general information about the group through its Web site. Though the WJA has national headquarters, many female jewelry executives have started regional chapters. These individual chapters aim to give women in the jewelry industry an opportunity to network, enhance their business skills, help newcomers to the business – and have some fun. There are ten chapters: Florida, Las Vegas, Los Angeles, Midwest, New England, Pennsylvania, San Diego, San Francisco, Seattle, and Southwest.

The WJA scholarship and mentor programs are an important part of the organization's mandate and are consistent with its mission to empower women to achieve their highest goals in the jewelry world and related industries. On the scholarship side, money for female students has been distributed for the past 17 years in amounts ranging from $500 to $2,500. In 2002, a new grant program for WJA members was started to help those already in the industry and want to continue their education, even if it's not in jewelry-related subjects.

In that first year, $500 grants were awarded to 15 women, one for every WJA area in the country. It has become so popular that each chapter now adds to the money amount and is giving out several extra awards. But, money isn't everything! Sometimes information, advice, and contacts are what are most needed and that is where the WJA's mentor program comes in. When women are just starting out in the industry and don't know where to turn, knowing a more experienced member to steer them in the right direction can be invaluable—and that is the goal of the mentoring program.

Sources

Sharon Edry, "Scholarships: Investing in the Future," *Women's Wear Daily* Milestones, Section II, January 2003, p. 15.

Marc Karemzadeh, "Saronity Jesters," *Women's Wear Daily* Milestones, Section II, January 2003, pp. 8-12.

Melanie Kletter, "WJA's Price: Women on the Move," *Women's Wear Daily* Milestones, Section II, January 2003, p. 4.

each year, as imports made in Europe, South America, and the Far East increase. Although U.S. manufacturers' brand names are relatively unimportant in the handbag industry (except for certain classics such as Coach Bags, Le Sportsac, and Dooney & Bourke), designer handbags have become popular (see Figure 12.3). Famous names like Anne Klein, Ralph Lauren, Donna Karan, and Marc Jacobs have entered licensing agreements with handbag manufacturers. Judith Leiber, now retired from her namesake company, is still famous for her handmade beaded bags in animal shapes and her metal ***minaudières*** (small evening bags). Kate Spade is a U.S. designer who has won several awards for her striking handbag designs. Today, not all quality handbags are made of leather; microfiber and nylon are key materials, with minibags popular.

Several foreign manufacturers such as Louis Vuitton, Hermès, Ferragamo, Bottega Veneta, and Gucci have always enjoyed enormous status at the high end of the market, and the names of Chanel and, more recently, Prada are associated with distinctive styles of handbags.

Backpacks

Some of the larger manufacturers have recently diversified their lines, reaching out to men, who have flirted with the idea of carrying handbags since the 1960s. The backpack has gained favor with men who do not have enough room in their pockets or briefcases for everything they want to carry. Perhaps the backpack's acceptance is a carryover from its use as a school bookbag. For that purpose, it remains popular with boys and girls from kindergarten through college. Canvas is the most popular material, and names such as L. L. Bean, Lands' End, and Jansport carry status as well as school supplies (see Figure 12.4). Meanwhile, smaller leather backpacks or Prada's nylon backpack have become a trendy handbag style among women.

Small Leather Goods/Personal Goods

The category called **small leather goods** or **personal goods** includes wallets, key cases and chains, jewelry cases, briefcases, and more recently, carrying cases for cell phones and laptop computers. Similarly, men and women with busy schedules are increasingly seen with leather-covered appointment books or "organizers." Of course, despite the name, not all of these items are made of leather. Fabrics, particularly nylon and microfibers, have assumed great importance in this category. Leading manufacturers of these items in the United States include Coach, Nine West, and Dooney & Bourke. More and more

FIGURE 12.3
Valentino's bracelet bag is appropriate for daytime or evening use.
Courtesy, Fairchild Publications, Inc.

FIGURE 12.4
The Jansport backpack is a fashionable way to transport one's valuables.
Courtesy, Fairchild Publications, Inc.

designers are moving into this category, among them are Kate Spade and Anne Klein.

Merchandising and Marketing

Few handbag manufacturers are large enough to advertise on a national basis in newspapers and television. The customer's impression of what is new and fashionable in handbags is mostly gleaned through store displays and advertising in magazines. Catalogs, home shopping networks, and the Internet are also increasingly popular ways of reaching customers.

Industry Trends

Faced with severe competition from foreign imports, many domestic handbag manufacturers have themselves become importers of foreign-made handbags. These importers employ American designers to create styles and then have the handbags made in countries with low wage scales.

The industry's trade organization—the National Fashion Accessories Association (NFAA)—has worked closely with government agencies to promote the domestic handbag industry both here and abroad. The NFAA also formed the Fashion Accessories Shippers Association (FASA) to support the interests of importers as well as manufacturers of handbags and related accessories (including belts, small leather goods, gloves, and luggage).

The leather goods trade fair, Mipel, held in spring and autumn in Milan, attracts handbag buyers from all over the world.

Belts

For dressing an outfit up or down to suit the occasion, a belt is an easy solution. Since belts are not absolutely essential—if you need one to hold up your pants, you can have your pants altered or buy a better-fitting pair—their appeal as a fashion accessory is of primary importance. Although belts are categorized and sold with small leather goods, they are also made of a host of other materials, including cloth, plastic, metal, and straw.

The price of a belt can be less than $10 or more than $500, depending on the materials, the precious metals or jewels used in the belt buckle, and the amount of hand-craftsmanship involved in its production. Designer names and logos—often appearing on the buckle or other metal trim—add to the fashion status of a belt and often to its price.

The fashion district of New York City is the home of belt manufacturing, though small manufacturers like Gem Dandy of Madison, North Carolina, can be found across the country. Manufacturers who produce belts to be sold as separate fashion accessory items are said to be in the **rack trade**. They are distinguished from the **cut-up trade**, which manufactures belts to be sold as part of a dress, skirt, or pair of trousers. **Self belts**, with bands and sometimes buckles covered in the same fabric as the apparel item with which they are sold, are produced by this segment of the industry.

In the rack trade, most men's and women's belts are sized according to waist measurements, with women's belts ranging from 22 to 32 inches and men's, from 28 to 44 inches. Sometimes they are grouped as small, medium, large, and extra large. Plus sizes in belts have become more important. Belts manufactured for the cut-up trade are made in lengths to fit the size of the garment.

The U.S. belt industry generates just under $800 million annually at wholesale, according to industry analysts. Refer to Chapter 6 for more information on leather belts.

Gloves

Crude animal-skin coverings were the forerunners of mittens, which, in turn, evolved into gloves with individual fingers. Gloves are not new, though; leather gloves were discovered in the tombs of ancient Egyptians.

Gloves have enjoyed a long and varied history, at times even taking on symbolic value. To bring them luck, knights once wore their ladies' gloves on their armor as they went into battle. So long as women wore modest dress, men often cherished the gloves of their beloved as erotic objects. Gloves were once exchanged when property was being sold as a gesture of good faith. And in dueling days, one man would slap another across the face with his glove as an invitation to a duel. Gloves have also been used to denote rank or authority. Until the 16th century, only men of the clergy or of noble rank were allowed to wear them.

For centuries, gloves were coordinated in styling, detail, and color with current apparel styles. To be specific, glove styles correlated to the currently popular sleeve length, especially in coats and suits.

In the first half of the 20th century, the glove business flourished largely because no self-respecting, let alone fashionably dressed, woman went out without wearing gloves. The untrimmed, white, wrist-length glove was de rigueur for dress occasions, as was the suit glove, which extends a few inches above the wrist, often made up in leather and used for general wear. The 1960s, which saw the onset of a long period of casual dress, also saw the end of gloves as a requirement for a well-dressed woman. White cotton gloves as an accessory for dress or business wear disappeared. When leather became expensive in the 1980s, manufacturers began to make gloves of knit and woven fabrics, which now dominate the market. Currently, in winter, when gloves are worn for warmth, they are coordinated with dress or casual outfits (see Figure 12.5).

Organization and Operation

The production of gloves varies, depending upon whether they are made of leather or fabric. Leather gloves are among the most difficult accessories to manufacture. Most leather gloves are made, at minimum, with hand-guided operations, and some are still made entirely by hand.

FIGURE 12.5
Gloves combine functionality and fashion.
Courtesy, Aris Isotoner, a division of Saramar Corporation.

Leather gloves are typically made in small factories, since few machines and workers are required to run such a factory. Glove producers tend to specialize, performing only one manufacturing operation, such as cutting or stitching. Other operations are farmed out to nearby plants, each of which, in turn, has its own specialty.

In contrast to the methods used to make leather gloves, the fabric-glove industry is much more mechanized. The cheapest gloves and mittens have only two parts—a front and a back—sewn together. More expensive gloves have separate small pieces that fit the fingers and thumbs. Most fabric gloves are made of some kind of double-woven fiber because this gives them great durability. Knit gloves and mittens are made of wool, acrylic, and cotton—even cotton string—usually in one-size-fits all. Chenille and Polar Fleece are popular for cold weather wear, along with fake fur.

New York City was once the center of the glove-manufacturing industry. Today, glove manufacturers have turned to offshore production, and most gloves are made in China, the Caribbean, and the Philippines. Some specialist glove manufacturers in the United States are Aris Gloves, which produces a line of leather gloves and the Isotoner line of fabric gloves. Other fashion glove makers in the United States are Fownes, Grandoe, and LaCrasia.

Merchandising and Marketing

Compared with the dollars spent on consumer advertising for other accessories, the industry outlay for glove advertising is quite modest. Only a few large producers with nationally distributed brand names actively promote their products or offer even limited merchandising support services to retail stores.

Manufacturers have learned to make gloves more creatively. Gloves are lined—and sometimes even made of—a wide array of knitted fabrics, lace, cashmere, fur, and silk. Wonderful colors—like orange, purple, acid yellow, and lime green—are often matched to winter hats or scarfs.

Finally, while many fashion industries have turned to diversification, the glove industry has moved in the opposite direction, toward specialization. Glove manufacturers, for example, have created markets for gardening gloves, driving gloves, and gloves for specific sports. Men and women can choose from an array of gloves designed for use at tennis, baseball, bicycling, and golfing—to name just a few. Gloves for skiing and winter gloves and mittens are made of high-tech materials, like Gore-Tex, Thinsulate, and Polartec, to maximize their insulating properties.

Industry Trends

Sales of domestically produced leather gloves have suffered considerably in recent years from the competition of less expensive imports. To meet this challenge, the industry is trying to improve manufacturing procedures in order to reduce costs. Manufacturers have reduced the number of glove sizes, preferring to sell gloves in only small, medium, and large. Stretch fabric gloves, in which one size fits all, are made as well. In addition, improved materials are resulting from product research and development in the leather industry. These are expected to increase the market potential of domestically produced leather gloves. For example, many leather gloves today are hand washable and come in a wide range of fashion colors.

The fabric glove industry is exploring innovative packaging techniques, such as packaging matching hats and gloves (or mittens) together, or matching scarfs and gloves, or matching headbands and gloves for winter wear.

Millinery

According to an old saying, whatever is worn on the head is a sign of the mind beneath it. Since the head is one of the more vulnerable parts of the body, hats do have a protective function. But they are also a fashion accessory.

The man's hat of the 19th and 20th centuries in Europe, which was derived from the medieval helmet, protected its wearer both physically and psychologically. The heavy crown kept the head safe from blows, and the brim shaded the face from strong sunlight and close scrutiny. In 19th-century America, the cowboy hat became an enduring national icon. Late in the century, the top hat was a status symbol of a special kind. This was the time of European immigration, and those who wanted to distinguish themselves from the immigrant peasants took care to wear hats.

After decades of prosperity and popularity, the men's hat industry began to collapse in the years following World War II. This was soon true for the women's hat industry, called the **millinery** industry, as well. Because of the more casual approach to dressing and the popularity of women's beehive and bouffant hairstyles, men's and women's hat sales hit bottom in 1960. During the freewheeling 1960s and 1970s, a hat was worn only on the coldest days—strictly for warmth, not for fashion.

During that time, the millinery industry and its active trade association, the National Millinery Institute, researched, publicized, and campaigned in an extensive effort to reverse the trend, with little success. This was not surprising, since, as we have already learned, no amount of sales promotion can change the direction in which fashion is moving.

However, the pendulum has begun to swing back toward the popularity of hats for men, women, and children. Several factors have contributed to this development. One was the fierce winters of the late 1990s, which led to the increased popularity of all types of winter hats and caps. David Chu of Nautica designed a polyester fleece cap and scarf that provide warmth while wicking away moisture. The fleece stocking cap for kids was a runaway bestseller. A variation like a jester's cap was also popular on the ski slopes and city streets.

With the rise of hip hop fashion and "ghetto fabulous" clothing styles, a new range of headwear, from streetwise Kangol hats, berets, and caps, to elegant fedoras, have become must-haves among young fashion addicts. Many leading luxury houses like Gucci, Louis Vuitton, and Burberry are enjoying tremendous success with their logo-embellished newsboy caps, bucket hats, and fedoras.

Another factor was the featuring of flamboyant hats in designer shows, especially on the runways of Paris and Milan. Although these extreme styles are presented more as a display of the designer's imagination than as an attempt to introduce a trend, they remind fashion arbiters and consumers that hats can be a fun accessory, and can make or break an outfit. Philip Treacy, a well-known British hat designer, has designed hats for the runway shows of Chanel, Valentino, and Versace. Treacy has also expanded into handbags.

Well-known U.S. millinery designers include Patricia Underwood, Eric Javits, and, at a lower price point, Betmar. Makins Hats designs for both men and women; its clients include Bill Cosby and Arsenio Hall. August Accessories of Oxnard, California, uses neoprene in a line of reversible, weatherproof hats.

The third factor contributing to the increased popularity of hats is the awareness of the dangers of overexposure to the sun. Dermatologists recommend the wearing of hats for protection in all seasons. Straw and canvas hats with large bills or brims offer shade without undesired warmth. Hats are also available that are made of fabrics with an SPF (sun protection factor). Baby hats that tie under the chin, or bonnets, have long been popular for infants; they are now widely used for toddlers as well. Along with the popular safari hat for men, hats with neck guards, once only seen in French Foreign Legion movies, have become popular in retirement communities across the country.

As with many fashion trends, the growing popularity of baseball caps as a fashion accessory started with young consumers. In this instance, boys and young men have worn them as a mark of support for their favorite teams. Soon the caps became promotional items for businesses, clubs, and other organizations. Designers took up the trend, putting their names and logos on this activewear accessory, often adding sequins, beading, or braid trims. Caps have proliferated, worn backwards or forward, by men, women, and children (see Figures 12.6 and 12.7).

The men's felt hat industry in the United States is still alive. Cowboy hats and "Indiana Jones" hats are the most popular styles, though derbies, pork pies, hombergs, snap brims, and fedoras are being made by a few firms. The largest manufacturer is Hatco of Garland, Texas. It owns the famous Stetson brand of cowboy or western hats as well as the Dobbs and Resistol brands. A few men's custom hatters can still be found, among them are O'Farrell Hats in Durango, Colorado; Rand's Custom Hatters in Billings, Montana; and The Custom Hatter in Buffalo, New York. Well-known European brands for men include Kangol and James Lock & Co. of England and Borsalino of Italy.

The center of the women's millinery industry is in New York City in the West 30s, between Fifth and Sixth Avenues, with some smaller firms in Los Angeles and St. Louis. One-person millinery shops can be found in many cities, since millinery involves a great deal of handwork and is ideal for custom work.

Neckwear

With the introduction of foreign designer's signature scarfs in the 1970s, women's neckwear began an upswing, which continued in the 1990s. (Note that the industry uses the unusual spelling of scarfs, rather than scarves.) Customers are wearing scarfs to change the look of an outfit. Squares and oblongs of varying sizes can be tied in different ways, sometimes with the help of specially designed scarf clips. Neckerchiefs, the hottest trend in the late 1990s, energized the scarf category by bringing

FIGURE 12.6
Today, more women are adding caps to their wardrobes.
Courtesy, Fairchild Publications, Inc.

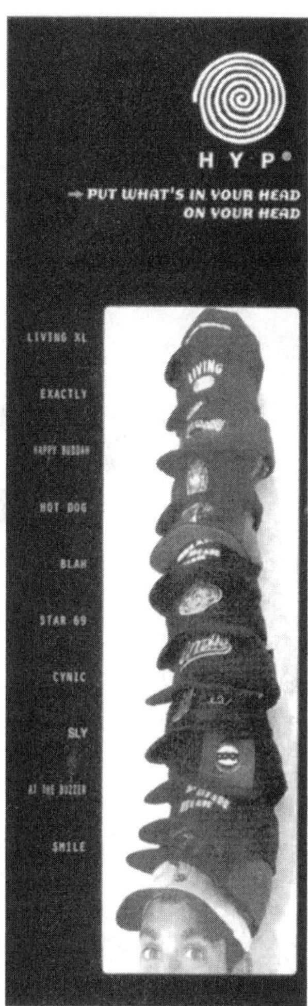

FIGURE 12.7
Baseball caps have become a literal means of making a fashion statement. Check out their Web site at http://www.hyponline.com.
Courtesy, Hyp®

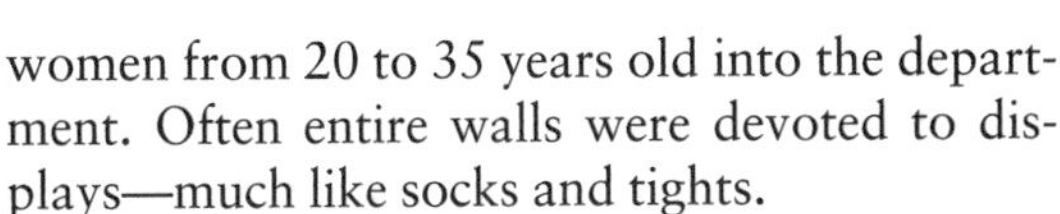

women from 20 to 35 years old into the department. Often entire walls were devoted to displays—much like socks and tights.

Echo is one of the largest manufacturers of scarfs in the United States. In addition, a number of leading American designer names have become associated with neckwear, further enhancing the category's appeal. Among them are Perry Ellis and Anne Klein, Ellen Tracy, Oscar de la Renta, and Liz Claiborne (both under license to Randa Corp). Some high-end imported scarfs, like those of Hermès (France) and Pucci and Gucci (Italy), are famous worldwide.

For men, ties have been a standard accessory for business suits for more than a century. They have provided an opportunity to brighten the business uniform with a small splash of bright colors and lively patterns. The necktie or four-in-hand and the bowtie are the two most common styles. The *bolo* or string tie is popular in the Southwest United States. The *ascot*, or broad neck scarf, is rarely seen today.

Among patterns, the *regimental stripes* have been popular for decades; they began with military regiments in England. *Club ties* have small embroidered emblems. Today most ties are made of woven silk or polyester. Knit ties and ties of leather or other specialty fabrics are only a small percent of total production.

At the height of power dressing in the late 1970s and 1980s, the color, print, and fabric of a necktie became a silent language, communicating the wearer's status. In the more casual office of the 1990s, where ties are not always required, "conversational" or whimsical ties—shaped like a fish or printed with cartoon characters—can contribute to the informal atmosphere.

Top names in the United States include Countess Mara, Ralph Lauren (who began his career designing ties), Salant Corp., Nicole Miller (see Figure 12.8), Vicky Davis, Tabasco,

FIGURE 12.8
Pepperoni or plain? This sketch shoes a "fun" or "conversational" tie. Such ties have revolutionized the once-staid men's neckwear business.
Courtesy, Nicole Miller.

and Ralph Marlin (of fish tie fame), which is now the leader in licensed neckwear.

In addition to neckties, men wear neck scarfs of wool in winter. The knit variation of these scarfs is called a *muffler*. Some men wear silk neck scarfs with formal dress coats.

The Neckwear Association of America is a 100-member international trade association of tie manufacturers and suppliers.

Eyewear

In recent years, consumers have become increasingly aware of the need to protect their eyes from the sun's harmful ultra violet (UV) rays. Even for children, sunglasses are now considered more than a cute wearable toy. Bausch and Lomb has added ten new designs to its children's sunglasses line called Covers. The line features UV protection, impact-resistant lenses, and durable plastic frames in a wide range of colors. Swiss Army Brands entered the high-tech sunglass market with a print ad campaign that said: "Navy Seals bring our knives on every one of their underwater missions. Now they'll be equipped to hit the beaches too."

At the same time, manufacturers of sunglasses have made a concerted effort to produce styles that are high fashion. Wrap-around frames, clear frames, and lenses that are reflective or tinted different colors are some of the distinctive design features. Combine these factors with the high visibility of sunglasses on prominent celebrities and on MTV, and it is no wonder that sales of this category exploded (see Figure 12.9).

Dozens of styles are popular at the same time: from aviators to "Jackie O" types, to John Lennon grannies, to cat-eyes, to "alien eyes." Riding the current wave of popularity are many designer names, among them DKNY, Christian Dior, Gucci, Chanel, Kenneth Cole, and Calvin Klein.

Top-tier sunglass sales are estimated at $490 million a year, with about six million frames sold at an average of $82 a pair.[3] The leading brand name, Ray-Ban (made by Bausch & Lomb), has even managed to achieve designer-name status itself through high-quality standards and well-planned product placement. Ray-Ban sunglasses figure prominently in movie posters for *Risky Business*, *Pearl Harbor*, and *Men in Black I* and *II*.[4] Oakley, Inc., is best-known for cutting-edge, high-tech sunglasses that use polycarbonate, a shatter-proof glass that is preferred for sports use, such as in tennis, golf, and baseball. When Nike released its line of performance-oriented sunwear under the umbrella of Marchon Eyewear in 2001, the brand's sales quickly soared to number three among the top sellers in the category.[5]

FIGURE 12.9
Sunglasses are both fashionable and practical.
Courtesy, Fairchild Publications, Inc.

Designer frames for prescription eyeglasses are another important segment of the fashion eyewear category. Despite the popularity of contact lenses, optometrists now fit their customers to improve their looks as well as their vision. Aging baby boomers have spurred growth in the market for nonprescription reading glasses, or **readers**. The industry has responded with fashionable styles available at different price points. Designer readers are available from such famous names as Donna Karan, Hugo Boss, Perry Ellis, and Calvin Klein. Lower-priced readers are available in drugstores.

Fisher-Price Eyewear for kids is positioned at the other end of the age spectrum, offering eyeglasses and sunglasses for children in a variety of bright colored frames.

In addition, glasses have become a fashion accessory with its own array of accessories, including cases, chains, sports leashes, magnifying pendants, eyeglass holders, and repair kits.

Jewelry

Jewelry has always played a significant and varied role in people's lives. In ancient times, some articles of jewelry were worn as amulets to ward off evil. Jewelry was popular among ancient Greeks, Romans, and Africans. The beautiful Roman women who still live in the old frescoes wore long, thin necklaces that encircled their necks two or three times, strands of pearls braided in their hair, and engraved belts decorated with precious stones.

A symbol of wealth and importance, jewelry was at certain times worn only by nobility. Laden with gold chains, their clothing adorned with gems, their fingers covered with rings, they carried on their persons the fortunes of their ruling houses. Medieval noblemen displayed elaborate heraldic emblems symbolizing their knighthood, and military men, another privileged class, used to make a great display of their decorations, which were once jewel-encrusted. Jeweled tiaras were in vogue among the upper classes in the Napoleonic era, because they simulated the laurel wreaths of antiquity. Tiaras saw an unexpected revival among brides in the early 1980s when Lady Diana Spencer wore a Spencer family heirloom tiara at her wedding to Prince Charles. Tiaras resurfaced again in the late 1990s, when designers like John Galliano and Vivienne Westwood featured them in their fashion shows. Suddenly tiaras were seen at proms and debutante balls around the United States.

Organization and Operation

Methods of making jewelry have changed little over time. Modern jewelers melt and shape metal, cut and carve stones, and string beads and shells much as jewelers have been doing for centuries. Jewelry designers have always used enamel, glass, ceramic, and natural mineral formations as their raw materials.

Based on the quality of their products, the jewelry industry in the United States can be divided into two primary groups: fine jewelry and costume or fashion jewelry. A third group, bridge jewelry, has gained in importance, as has a fourth group, ethnic jewelry.

Fine Jewelry

Fine jewelry is the counterpart of haute couture. Only precious metals such as gold and platinum are used to make fine jewelry. Sterling silver is also considered a precious metal, although its intrinsic value is far less than that of gold or platinum. Too soft to be used alone, these precious metals are **alloyed**, or combined, with one or more other metals to make them hard enough to be fashioned into jewelry.

Platinum (which includes palladium, rhodium, and iridium) is the most expensive metal. It was first used for jewelry by Cartier, and became a hallmark of the Art Deco movement of the 1920s and 1930s.

The gold content of jewelry is measured by weight in **karats**; which are abbreviated as "K." An item called **solid gold** actually has only 24 karats of gold; or 1/24 gold to 23/24 alloy. Less costly 14K gold is popular in the United States, while 18K gold is popular in Europe, and 22K gold is popular in India. *Gold-filled* jewelry is made of an inexpensive base metal with a heavy layer of gold on top. *White gold* is a substitute for platinum; it is an alloy of gold and another metal, usually nickel. **Vermeil** (pronounced ver-MAY) is a composite of gold over sterling silver. The term **sterling silver** is used for jewelry (and flatware) with at least 92.5 parts of silver; the remaining 7.5 parts are usually copper. Not all sterling silver is equal; thicker items are generally more valuable than thin ones.

The stones used in fine jewelry are called **gemstones** to distinguish them from lower-quality stones that are used for industrial purposes. Gemstones, which always come from natural mineral formations, have traditionally been classified as either precious or semiprecious. Precious stones include diamonds, emeralds, rubies, and sapphires. Stones are measured by weight, in a unit of measure called a **carat**, which equals 200 milligrams or 1/142 of an ounce. Carats are subdivided into points; there are 100 points to a carat. Thus a half-carat stone is a 50-point stone.

Diamonds are the hardest substance known, and are in limited supply. From 250 tons of ore, only one carat of rough diamonds can be recovered, and only 20 percent of them are suitable for gemstones. Diamonds are found in South Africa, Siberia, Australia, and Arkansas. The world supply is dominated by the DeBeers cartel of South Africa. It has spent millions to promote the romance of diamonds with its ad slogan "A diamond is forever."

Diamonds are usually cut into 58 *facets*, which are small, polished planes that are precisely placed to reflect the maximum amount of light. Traditional cuts or shapes of diamonds are round, emerald, marquise, pear, oval, and heart (see Figure 12.10). A relatively new cut, called the radiant cut, was developed in 1976.

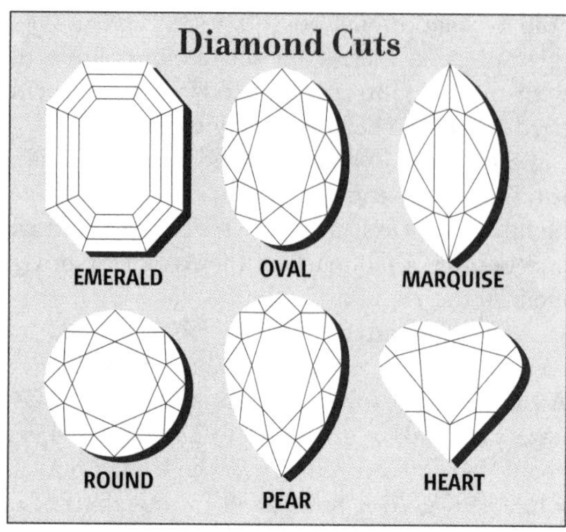

FIGURE 12.10
Traditional diamond cuts.

It has about 70 facets, and was originally developed to hide flaws.

Advanced technology in the new millennium has unleashed a new crop of innovative cuts. Among them is the square-shaped Context Cut, which is not cleaved, but based on the natural twelve sided rough diamond crystal. Other new cuts include the circular Spirit Sun cut and the triple-brilliant Gabrielle cut, which has 105 facets (compared to the traditional amount of 58) and is available in a wide range of classic shapes.[6]

A *solitaire* is the mounting of a single gemstone; a diamond solitaire is the traditional engagement ring. A *Tiffany setting* refers to a four- or six-prong setting that flares out from the base to the top, with long slender prongs that hold the stone. A *baguette* is a rectangular-shaped small stone used with a larger stone. A *pave setting* is one in which a number of small stones are set as closely together as possible, so that no metal shows between them, and they appear as an all-stone surface.

Real, or *oriental, pearls* are of animal origin, but are still considered precious stones. *Tahitian* and *South Sea pearls* are the most expensive real pearls. *Cultured pearls* are pearls formed by an oyster around an irritant placed in the oyster's body by man. They are not considered precious stones, although they can only be raised in limited parts of the world's oceans. *Freshwater pearls* are nugget-shaped pearls that grow in lakes or rivers; they are more abundant and less expensive than real or cultured pearls.

Pearls are measured in millimeters around and in length. Size contributes to the value of pearls; large pearls are hard for oysters to grow, and so are more expensive. Pearls cannot be cut or shaped like other gems. The more symmetrical the pearl, the more expensive it is. Pearls with irregular and asymmetrical shapes are called *baroque pearls*. The rarest—and most expensive pearls—are black; other natural tints are cream, a pinkish hue, or a bluish one.

The so-called semiprecious stones include a host of other natural stones that were once more costly and less rare than precious stones, but are still quite beautiful (see Table 12.1). The Jewelers of America Association holds that the division of gems into precious and semiprecious is invalid, because discoveries have added new varieties that are higher priced, because of their

TABLE 12.1 Fine Gemstones

Fine Gemstones
Alexandrite
Amber[a]
Amethyst
Aquamarine
Chrysoberyl
Citrine
Garnet
Iolite
Jade
Kunzite
Lapis lazuli
Moonstone
Opal
Peridot
Rubellite
Spinel
Tanzanite
Topaz
Tourmaline
Tsavorite
Turquoise
Zircon

[a]Really vegetable in origin, not mineral.

Source: Jewelers of America, Inc., *What You Should Know About Gems*. New York: Jewelers of America, Inc.

rarity, than the more well-known gems. For example, fine jade is more valuable than a lesser quality emerald. Tanzanite, first discovered near Mount Kilimanjaro in 1967, is a deep purple gemstone that Tiffany & Co. has popularized. Although it is considered a semiprecious stone, it is being used by fine-jewelry designers in very expensive pieces.

Chemists have succeeded in creating **synthetic stones** that are chemically identical to real stones. Synthetic stones are now used in combination with 14-carat gold and sterling silver. The most popular of the synthetics is zirconia, which offers the dazzle of diamonds at a fraction of the cost. Other synthetic stones include synthetic spinel, which looks like emeralds or aquamarines, and synthetic corumdum, which looks like amethysts.

Fine-jewelry production is still a handcraft industry. A **lapidary**, or stonecutter, transforms dull-looking stones in their natural states into gems by cutting, carving, and polishing them. Then the jeweler creates a setting for the stones to bring out their brilliance.

In the established fine-jewelry houses, as in haute couture houses, design, production, and retail sales typically take place under one roof—and one management. Many fine-jewelry firms sell only the jewelry they create, much of which is custom designed for them. Names such as Cartier and Tiffany have always been used to sell jewelry, but in the past, the designers, who were in the employ of these companies, were not well known. In the past few decades, though, individual designers have taken on new importance, and customers now look for jewelry designed by their favorite designers.

Paloma Picasso and Elsa Peretti designs are sold at Tiffany & Co. Other leading independent designers with large followings include Angela Cummings, Barry Kieselstein-Cord, Robert Lee Morris, David Yurman, and Steven Lagos. As another example, Bergdorf Goodman's fine-jewelry department carries the work of 46 designers, including the established designers listed above and newcomers Christopher Walling, Julie Baker, Stephen Dweck, Stephen Webster, and Angela Pintaldi of Italy.

Costume Jewelry

Costume or **fashion jewelry** is like mass-produced apparel. A wide range of materials—wood, glass, and base metals such as brass, aluminum, copper, tin, and lead—are used to make it. Base metals are sometimes coated with costlier precious metals such as gold, rhodium, or silver. The stones and simulated (fake) pearls used in costume jewelry are made from clay, glass, or plastic. While they are attractive and interesting in their surface appearance, they are less costly and lack the more desirable properties (durability for one) of natural stones.

Before the 1920s, costume jewelry as we know it did not exist. Most jewelry was made from gold or, more rarely, silver set with precious or semiprecious stones. Jewelry was worn for its sentimental or economic value and was never used to accessorize one's clothing.

The age of costume jewelry began with designer Coco Chanel. In the 1920s she introduced long, large, and obviously fake strands of pearls to be worn with her clothes. This new accessory was called costume jewelry since it was meant to coordinate with one's costume. The pearls were called *simulated* in English and *faux*, which means false, in French.

Chanel, it might be noted, not only helped to create an industry, but also continued to wear her trademark pearls for the rest of her life. Today, simulated pearls—indeed Chanel-style pearls—are a staple of the costume jewelry industry. Two first ladies also contributed to the popularity of pearls: Jackie Kennedy Onassis and Barbara Bush.

Costume jewelry has always gone through phases. At times, it is intended to look like fine jewelry; at other times, frankly fake-looking jewelry is in style. Beginning in the 1960s and continuing to today, Kenneth Jay Lane designed costume jewelry so real-looking that socialites and other fashion leaders favored it over their own authentic jewels.

There is always a market in costume jewelry for products that look like the real thing; most mass-produced jewelry, in fact, falls into this category. Large, popular-priced costume jewelry houses employ stylists who design seasonal lines or adapt styles from higher-priced lines. Mass-produced costume jewelry is made in Providence, Rhode Island, where small jewelry manufacturing firms are still located, though the industry there has shrunk considerably. Facilities are geared toward producing jewelry to the specifications of individual firms, much as apparel manufacturers contract out their work and use jobbers.

Mass-production methods are employed in contrast to the handwork that exemplifies the making of fine jewelry. While a fine jeweler pounds and hand shapes metal, manufacturers of costume jewelry cast metal by melting it and

FIGURE 12.11
When the estate of the late First Lady, Jacqueline Kennedy Onassis, auctioned the set of simulated pearls she wore in this widely-reproduced photograph, they fetched the amazing price $211,500! Copies were made by Carolee Jewelry; they sold for $300.
Courtesy, John. F. Kennedy Library.

then pouring it into molds to harden. Designs are applied to the hardened metal surface by painting it with colored enamel or embossing it by machine. **Electroplating** is the name of a process that coats inexpensive base materials with a thin coat of silver or gold.

Large firms dominate the industry. Examples are the Monet Group (Monet, Trifari, and Marvella) and Carolee. Victoria & Co Ltd. is a leading designer and marketer of branded and private label costume jewelry. Victoria manufactures and markets the licensed jewelry collection for Givnechy and Tommy Hilfiger and also creates jewelry under Napier and Richelieu, its own brands, as well as under the Nine West brand. While most large firms work with multiple price lines and many different materials, some companies do specialize. An example is Swarovski Jewelry U.S., which specializes in crystal jewelry, made under the company name and the Savvy label.

Still, more than 90 percent of U.S. jewelry producers are small, family-owned companies. Individuals with creative talent often open successful small retail or wholesale operations that cater to customers who are interested in individualized styling and trend-setting fashions. Such operations are an outgrowth of the handcraft movement of the 1960s and 1970s. Handmade jewelry had a major comeback at the beginning of the new millennium, which launched a rise of small, independent jewelry designers across the country.

Bridge Jewelry

Dramatic increases in the price of gold and silver in the early 1980s left jewelers seeking new ways to meet the public's demand for reasonably priced authentic jewelry. The solution was **bridge jewelry**, that is, jewelry that forms a bridge—in price, materials, and style—between fine and costume jewelry. Prices at retail range from about $100 to $2,500 for bridge jewelry. (Also see the discussion of bridge apparel in Chapter 7.)

The development of bridge jewelry led to increased use of sterling silver and its subsequent elevation to a precious metal. The boom in Native American jewelry in the early 1970s also helped to create interest in bridge jewelry. Many department stores and specialty stores created bridge departments to handle sterling silver and Native American jewelry, and when interest in it faded, they were open to other kinds of bridge jewelry that would help them keep the customer base they had developed.

Bridge jewelry departments at such stores as Marshall Field's, Neiman Marcus, and the May Company now carry gold-filled, vermeil, sterling silver, and some 14-carat fashion jewelry set with semiprecious stones. Sterling silver jewelry continues to grow rapidly in popularity. Bridge designers include Zina, Nancy & Rise, M. J. Savitt, and Bayanihan. Judith Jack specializes in *marcasite* (crystallized mineral) jewelry, which attracts both costume and fine jewelry customers.

Ethnic Jewelry

The category of **ethnic jewelry** includes pieces from all over the world at all price points, although some of these items are not made of intrinsically valuable materials, but rather of shells, stones, wood, or fabric. The artistry is so remarkable that these items can command a higher price than costume jewelry. As previously mentioned, Native American jewelry in silver and turquoise has been popular for decades (see Figure 12.12). Two famous styles of silver necklaces, the *squash blossom* necklace and the *liquid silver* necklace, continue to be reinterpreted by modern Native American designers.

Ralph Lauren popularized African jewelry with his 1997 collection that was inspired by

FIGURE 12.12
Native American jewelry has contributed to the widespread popularity of the turquoise stone, as seen in these pieces from Liz Palacios's semi precious collection.
Courtesy, Fairchild Publications, Inc.

the Masai of Kenya; it included arm cuffs, bead chokers, and hoop earrings. Similarly, traditional ethnic jewelry from India, made from 22K gold and decorated with ornate patterns and precious gemstones, became popular in the late 1990s after Nicole Kidman and Goldie Hawn began wearing these styles. Most people, however bought far less expensive designs in glass, brass, and silver. Chinese-inspired jewelry made of jade, coral, and mother-of-pearl is perennially popular, as is the yin-yang symbol. Moroccan beads, the Egyptian ankh, Guatemalan string figures, Greek worry beads, Caribbean shell necklaces, Peruvian hammered copper earrings—all have fans worldwide.

Another category of ethnic jewelry involves wearing religious or spiritual symbols in necklaces, earrings, rings, or pins, such as the Jewish Star of David, the Christian cross, the Buddhist lotus blossom, the Native American eagle feather, and the New Age crystal. The famous Indian "Navratan Haar" ring is made of nine gems with astrological significance: a diamond in the center, circled by eight rainbow-colored stones: ruby, emerald, cinnamon, coral, cat's eye, blue and yellow sapphires, and pearl.[7]

Designers must show sensitivity when adapting these powerful symbols into jewelry. A storm of protest arose when Madonna wore a cross as part of her on-stage costume during the early part of her career; it was interpreted by many as irreverent, even blasphemous.

Many people wear their so-called "birthstone," to which folklore attributes good luck, according to their sign of the zodiac. In fact, the concept of the birthstone was introduced in the United States in 1912 by the predecessor of the Jewelers of America association and is matched to calendar months rather than the Zodiac.

Another interesting development in ethnic jewelry is the growing number of firms making licensed copies or reproductions of museum pieces of jewelry. Museums around the world, from the State Historical Museum of Moscow, to the Vatican Library, to the Metropolitan Museum of Art in New York, are selling vast amounts of inexpensive reproductions of museum pieces in their stores and through catalogs. These pieces come from many different eras and many different cultures; what they have in common is that they have been preserved because of their beauty and power.

Watches

The useful, dependable wristwatch is a relative newcomer to the 500-year history of mechanical timepieces. Nineteenth-century craftsmen made the pocket watch efficient—and a thing of beauty. In 1904, Louis-Joseph Cartier introduced the first modern wristwatch, the Santos-Dumont, named for a Brazilian aviator. By 1997, Cartier was selling 40,000 Santos-Dumonts a year![8]

There are three basic types of watches made today: the mechanical, the self-winding, and the quartz movement. *Mechanical watches* are driven by a balance wheel and powered by a spring, which must be hand wound. *Automatic* or *self-winding watches* wind themselves as the wearer moves a wrist. The *quartz movement* invented in the 1970s offers very accurate timekeeping at a low cost. Most quartz watches have removable batteries that last about one year.

Analog watches have faces with hands that sweep around the numbers "clockwise" (see Figure 12.13). *Digital watches* display the time in numbers, generally using a liquid crystal display (LCD). Extra features available in some watches include night-light buttons, calendars, moon-phase indicators, stopwatch (or chronograph) features, alarms, and chimes. Some watches also give the time in other countries or

FIGURE 12.13
These analog watches each have unique designs to suit the needs of different customers.
Courtesy, Fairchild Publications, Inc.

time zones. But watches have always been a fashion statement as well as a useful device.

The inexpensive Timex watch of the 1960s, which "took a licking, but kept on ticking," broadened the market to include a huge number of people who could not afford even the mass market watches of previous decades.

During the 1980s, Swatch made a splash in the market with its casual watches, and has now spread its name and contemporary look into a number of other product categories such as sportswear, sunglasses, and other accessories. The Swatch lines have become so popular that some retailers have created Swatch boutiques. Other well-known companies include Movado, Fossil, and Armitron.

In the 1990s, many companies jumped onto the sports-watch bandwagon by adding resistance to water, wind, dust, shock, and magnetic fields. Chronograph watches that measure small fractions of a second were best-sellers; some are used to measure speeds, distances, and altitudes.

At the high-end of the watch market are the fabled Swiss watchmakers: the huge Rolex, with its famous "oyster case," and the smaller Audemars Piaget, Patek Philippe, and Vacheron Constantin. Their watches can cost from $2,000 to $2.7 million.[9]

At the other end of the market are children's watches. The Mickey Mouse watch for children was introduced in the 1930s. Today Timex makes watches for Disney, Joe Boxer, Nautica, and others. In 2001, Timex introduced TMXessories, a line aimed at tween and teen girls that included colorful, decorative watches disguised as bangle braclets, rings, and pendant necklaces. Armitron is another maker of cartoon-character watches, such as Tweety, Bugs Bunny, Garfield, and Scooby Doo. Mattel, the giant toy maker, has a line of Barbie watches.

Merchandising and Marketing

Jewelry manufacturers present their new styles and, in the case of costume jewelry manufacturers, their new lines at semiannual shows sponsored by the industry's trade association, the Jewelry Industry Council. A permanent showroom, the Worldwide Business Exchange (WBE), is also maintained in New York City. One of the largest trade shows is the Fashion Accessories Expo, held in New York in January, May, August, and November. Other major trade associations include the American Gem Society, the Diamond Council of America, the Fashion Jewelry Association of America, and the Jewelers of America.

Fine-jewelry manufacturers traditionally have concentrated on providing a wide range of basic pieces, most notably, diamond rings and watches. They support their lines with a variety of services offered to stores. Some advertising assistance is offered, but this has not been common in a business where brand names have been relatively unknown. However, with the emergence of designer jewelry names, this is changing.

For all types of jewelry, but especially diamond rings, the Christmas holidays and Valentine's Day are especially busy. Birthdays and anniversaries provide a steady year-round business, while watches show a sales spurt around graduation time. The renewed popularity of vintage clothing in the 1990s led to a renewed interest in "estate pieces," or fine jewelry of earlier eras, still in its original settings.

Costume jewelry firms offer seasonal lines designed to coordinate with what is currently fashionable in apparel. Most costume jewelry is produced on a contract basis, which offers the advantage of fast turnaround on individual items. When a particular item is suddenly in demand, costume jewelry manufacturers can switch gears and produce it quickly in a large quantity. One example is the colorful beaded or carved pendant necklaces that exploded on the market in the summer of 2002, after similar styles had been sported by famous actresses and models on the pages of *People* and *InStyle* magazines.[10]

The larger firms also market their goods under their nationally known brand names and advertise widely in national consumer publications. In addition, they offer cooperative advertising to retail outlets. Some manufacturers provide guidance and sales training to retailers.

Major jewelry store chains include the mall-oriented Zale's, Helzberg Diamond Shops, and the Fred Meyer chain. Tiffany's, Cartier, and Gumps occupy the high end of the market. Ross-Simons is a leading retailer-cataloger. Most department stores have extensive jewelry departments, carrying fine, bridge, and costume lines, with varying amounts of ethnic specialty items. Finlay Enterprises, Inc., operates over 1,000 leased shops, including those in Federated, Saks, and Dillard stores. Many thousands of small jewelry stores also exist across the country.

Industry research reveals that the largest segment of the jewelry market is women buying it for themselves. This has led the World Gold Council, among others, to advertise directly to women. Their strategy has paid off—women now buy 90 percent of all silver jewelry, 60 percent of all gold jewelry, and 30 percent of all platinum.[11] Retailers have also begun to focus their advertising on women. Zale's used the slogan "Just because they're solitaires, doesn't mean you have to be alone when you wear them." The romantic TV ads that promote diamond anniversary gifts that "tell her you'd marry her all over again" are directed to men—and subliminally to women.

All retailers report increasing problems with balancing the need for displaying jewelry with the need for keeping it secure. Shoplifting and armed robbery are real threats. Special locked display cases, drawers, and vaults have been used increasingly in major cities worldwide, as have a number of small antitheft tags attached to the merchandise.

Industry Trends

Today, all branches of the jewelry industry emphasize the production of designs that complement currently fashionable styles. For example, when turtlenecks are popular, jewelry companies make long chains and pendants that look graceful on high necklines. When sleeveless dresses are in fashion, bracelets become an important piece of jewelry. When french cuffs are in fashion, both men and women wear cufflinks. When prints are popular, jewelry styles become tailored; but when solid or somber colors are popular, jewelry often moves to center stage with more complex designs and bright colors.

Masculine and unisex designs in gold chains, earrings, rings, shirt studs, nose studs, and fashion/sports watches are popular. More men are also wearing colored gemstones.

To compete with costume jewelry, which has gained broad acceptance over the past few decades, fine-jewelry companies have begun to diversify. Some have broadened their lines by moving into bridge jewelry. Others have also diversified into complementary nonjewelry areas. Swank, for example, which for years has manufactured men's small jewelry items, now produces colognes, sunglasses, travel accessories, and a variety of men's gifts.

Designer jewelry is another major market force, especially in costume jewelry. Designers are thought to have been a major contributing factor to expanding sales. Chanel, Kenneth Cole, Anne Klein, Donna Karan, Yves Saint Laurent, Dior, Liz Claiborne, Givenchy, Pierre Cardin, and Ralph Lauren are some of the apparel designers who have been successful in licensing jewelry lines.

Celebrities, like Joan Rivers and Ivana Trump, have also launched successful jewelry lines that are sold on the TV home shopping networks. Television home shopping is the fastest-growing distribution channel for jewelry, because of its convenience and values, and because it lets the viewer see the item both up close and worn by a model, so the viewer gets a clear idea of its proportionate size.

Other Accessories

There are many categories of accessories—and much variation within categories—from dress shoes to jellies, from briefcases to lunch boxes, from hard hats to snoods, from anklets to ankhs. Other ornaments, like ribbons, bows, feathers, and fabric flowers, come and go in popularity. The accessory maker needs to move quickly in and out of these trends. Three other categories of accessories deserve mention; they are handkerchiefs, umbrellas, and hair ornaments (see Figure 12.14).

That most functional of accessories—the handkerchief—has had its main function usurped by paper tissues. Today most women's

FIGURE 12.14
From umbrellas to hats to hair ornaments, accessories are both functional and an important addition to the fashion industry.
Courtesy, Fairchild Publications, Inc.

handkerchiefs are produced in China or Japan, where they are a fashion item. Most men's handkerchiefs are packaged by the dozen (or baker's dozen—13) in all cotton or cotton-polyester blends. Some high-end stores will provide monogramming for an additional charge. Silk "show" handkerchiefs, called *pocket squares*, are produced for both men and women. They are puffed casually, not worn square, like standard cotton handkerchiefs. Children's handkerchiefs are a novelty item.

Umbrellas became unexpected fashion items in the 1990s, when museums began to license their famous paintings for use on the insides or outsides of umbrellas. Suddenly rainy days became easier to bear, when one gazed up at Michelangelo's ceiling of the Sistine Chapel or at Magritte's famous man floating in the clouds. Of course, many people continued to use plain black folding umbrellas, which remain at the top of the sales charts. Children continue to delight in Paddington Bear boots and matching umbrellas. The designer label craze that dominated the late 1990s and early 2000s also gave new life to the classically plaid Burberry umbrella, which became immensely popular among followers of fashion worldwide.

The popularity of hair ornaments waxes and wanes along with certain hair styles. Barrettes and clips of various kinds are always available in inexpensive materials. The hot new hair ornaments in the 1990s were used to hold long hair away from the face: the elasticized fabric "scrunchie," the hard plastic "banana clip," and the fabric headband all were available in a wide variety of colors.

Trends in the Fashion Accessories Industries

For accessory manufacturers, being supporters of apparel fashions does not necessarily mean being followers. In fact, accessory manufacturers must often be fashion leaders. In the fashion business, which always moves in the fast lane, accessory manufacturers must move in a faster lane than anyone else. They have to be able to adapt or change a style in mid-season if that is what is required to stay on top of current trends.

Market Weeks and Trade Shows

New accessory lines are shown during the five major fashion market weeks in New York so that merchants can buy a coordinated look. These include:

- Summer, January
- Transitional, March
- Fall, May
- Holiday, August
- Spring, November

In the United States, the Femme Show, held in New York's Javitz Center in January, May, and September, is the largest trade show for accessories. The Fashion Jewelry World Expo and Providence Expo both take place in Rhode Island.[12] Paris Premiere Classe, the Fashion Accessories Trade Show, is held in Paris in March and October. These shows are a reflection of the growing importance of accessories to retailers and consumers.

Retailing Accessories

Accessories are sold in every kind of store, ranging from the largest department stores to smaller boutiques to specialized stores carrying only one kind of accessory or a limited array of related accessories. Retailers have traditionally viewed accessories as **impulse items**—products that customers typically buy on the spur of the moment. A person who may not want to or is not able to update a wardrobe with the latest apparel styles each season can use accessories to look fashionable. As Denise Filchner, Accessories Coordinator at Macys, says:

Now, more than ever, accessories play a pivotal role in fashion. Today, accessories are accents on a background of ready-to-wear. They are meant to be noticed, not necessarily to match or even to blend, but to stand out for a more interesting look. Last year's little black dress is updated instantly with the latest patterns in textured hosiery. It's an easy and inexpensive way to take what you had and give it new life.[13]

Also, less expensive accessories are still purchased when there is price resistance to costlier items of apparel. Accessories are chosen because of their color, style, and newness or simply because one wants to give one's wardrobe—and spirits—a lift.

In recognition of this "impulse" buying pattern, most department stores position accessories on the main floor, or near the door or cash register in the case of small stores. More recently, they have experimented successfully with **outposts**, small accessory departments located next to apparel departments, and with movable kiosks, or large carts.

Some stores have begun to feature one-stop shopping with boutiques (often stocked exclusively by one designer) that allow customers to buy everything they need—apparel and accessories—in one department. One-stop shopping has proven especially successful with working women who have little time to shop. It also appeals to the women who are a little unsure of themselves and like the added help that one-stop shopping provides in coordinating their outfits. Designer signature stores featuring apparel have become a mainstay.

Some chains, like Accessories Place and Claire's, sell only accessories. Some chains sell only subspecialties, like The Knot Shops, which sell men's ties, or the Sunglass Hut. Many stores, of course, sell only shoes, or only jewelry. Catalogs are also increasingly popular places to sell accessories; every major apparel catalog also offers selected accessories. Specialty catalogers include Nature's Jewelry, Coldwater Creek, and Horchow. In addition, many catalogers selling accessories are on the Internet, like Ross-Simons, which has put its bridal registry on the Internet. Other general merchandisers also offer substantial selections of accessories over the Internet; from L. L. Bean to Spiegel to Talbots to the giant Service Merchandise.

Summary and Review

Specific accessories wax and wane in popularity, but some accessories are always popular as most people do not consider themselves fully dressed until they have accessorized an outfit. In recent years, the business overall has boomed. Many people feel the accessory business, like many other fashion categories, has been given a boost by its association with designer names.

And the benefits are mutual. At the haute couture shows of Paris and Milan, the clothing has become the designer's fashion statement, and accessories have generated the financial support—as well as supporting the look of the season—to allow designers to experiment. Made-to-order gowns and ensembles are individually produced by hand, whereas accessories can be machine-made in larger numbers and sold at higher margins.[14] Similarly, American ready-to-wear designers literally display their names or logos on licensed accessories such as belts, scarfs, caps, handbags, and sunglasses. For the purveyors of fashion as much as for the consumer, accessories support a complete, coordinated image. In addition, they are the source of a more attractive bottom line.

Trade Talk

Define or briefly explain each of the following terms:

alloyed
bridge jewelry
carat
costume or fashion jewelry
cut-up trade
electroplating
ethnic jewelry
outpost
millinery
minaudieres
personal goods
rack trade
readers
self belt
small leather goods
solid gold
sterling silver
synthetic stones
vermeil

For Review

1. Why have U.S. shoe producers moved their factories offshore? How has this trend affected the footwear industry?
2. How do changes in lifestyle and activities affect the shoe industry? Give examples.
3. Describe the merchandising and marketing of handbags in the United States today.
4. What are the current trends in the millinery industry?
5. What are the major types of neckties sold today?
6. Why are shoe and fine jewelry departments often leased?
7. What three metals are considered precious? What is the difference between solid gold and 14-karat gold?
8. What are the major gemstones used in the production of jewelry?
9. Give several examples of how women's apparel fashions influence jewelry fashions.
10. What categories of merchandise are to be found in fashion accessory departments today? In outposts?

For Discussion

1. How has the increasing informality of dress in the last decade affected the accessories industries?
2. List each of the current important fashion accessory items and discuss why they are important to the total fashion look. At which stage of the fashion cycle is each item positioned? Give reasons for your answers.

References

1. "About Our Company," www.payless.com, September 2002.
2. Bill Mongelluzzo, "China Connection: China Has Emerged as the Dominant Source of U.S. Footwear," *JoC Week*, April 2002, p. 18A.
3. "Top Sunglass Brands," *Daily News Record*, August 5, 2002, p. 24.
4. Ibid.
5. Carey Goldberg, "Where Style Is Made in the Shades," *New York Times*, September 15, 1996, p. 24.
6. "Revolutionary New Cuts Add Spice to Engagement Rings," Jewelry Information Center, www.jewlry.org, Summer 2001.
7. "Women's 1997 Accessory Census: Fashion Jewelry/Watches," *Accessories*, January 1998, p. 70.
8. Penny Proddow and Marion Fasel, "Signature Style: Passage to India," *In Style*, July 1, 1997, p. 91
9. Stacey Okun, "The Legend and The Legacy: The House of Cartier Celebrates 150 Years of History and Romance," *Town & Country Monthly*, March 1, 1997, p. 121.
10. "Charmed Circles," *People*, May 20, 2002, p. 73.
11. Nanz Aalund, "Women Who Buy Jewelry for Themselves," *Professional Jeweler Magazine*, March 2001.
12. Melanie Kletter, "As Boutique Bows Out, Buyers Upbeat," *Women's Wear Daily*, January 11, 2001.
13. Tara Parker-Pope, "All That Glitters Isn't Purchased by Men," *Wall Street Journal*, January 10, 1997, p. B1.

CHAPTER 13

Cosmetics and Fragrances

WHAT'S IN IT FOR YOU?

Everything you always wanted to know about cosmetics and fragrances.

Key Concepts:

- History and development of the cosmetics and fragrance industry
- Categories of cosmetics and fragrances
- Federal laws and environmental issues affecting cosmetics and fragrances
- Seven major market segments in the cosmetics and fragrance industry
- Distribution of mass and class cosmetics and fragrances
- Advertising and promotion of cosmetics and fragrances
- Trends in cosmetic and fragrance products

To be or not to be?—that is the question. Should we be bemused, bothered, and bewildered about our looks? Or should we revel in the beauty that is natural and nurtured? Whichever way you choose, the cosmetics and fragrance industries will meet your needs and wants with exciting new colors and potions, in both exotic test-tube creations or drawn from the world's natural fauna and flora. This quest for beauty is hardly new. For thousands of years people have smeared themselves with lotions and potions of every kind in the hope of making themselves as attractive as possible. As far back as 100 B.C., Cleopatra rubbed her face with lemon rinds, took milk baths, accentuated her eyes with kohl, and set her hair with mud. When Queen Elizabeth I of England died in 1603, her face was caked with a thick layer of chalk, the foundation of her day, which she wore to cover the pock marks of an early illness. Before modern hygiene dictated daily bathing, natural body odors were masked by perfumes. In the days of the Roman Empire, spices and scents were imported from Africa

and Asia. A popular Greek scent called Susinum is evidence of the existence of brands.[1] In the American colonial era, Caswell-Massey, predecessor of the modern drugstore, sold cologne to then-colonel George Washington.

Today, the cosmetics and fragrance industry is big business and getting bigger. It turns out hundreds of new products annually, each of which must compete for a share of the market. These days, the fashion-apparel business plays an important role in building the business of the cosmetics industry. Many designers have introduced their own cosmetic and fragrance lines, and they often work with the cosmetic manufacturers to help them design new products that will coordinate with each season's new styles. According to Annette Green, president of the Fragrance Foundation, a "signature scent" is a sure sign that a designer has arrived. "Until I do a fragrance, they [designers] tell her, I'm just another designer."[2]

Thanks to the new link to designers' new season's styles, cosmetics, like fashion, are now cyclical. For example, when sports clothes are popular, and a no-makeup look is in, the cosmetics industry, eager to maintain sales, has learned to respond with appropriately low-key cosmetics and fresh, country-like scents. When bright colors and elaborate clothes are in style, the industry touts more makeup, brighter palettes, and heavier scents.

FIGURE 13.1
Cosmetics have been used for millennia. This photo from the 1920s shows a woman powdering her knee, a part of the body newly exposed after centuries of long skirts.
UPI/Corbis-Bettmann.

History and Development of the Cosmetics and Fragrance Industry

For centuries, the pursuit of beauty was the prerogative of the rich. Special beauty aids concocted in temples, monasteries, alchemists' cells, and kitchens were available only to the privileged few. Makeup was called *maquillage*, and used only in court circles—and the demimonde. Only in the past 75 years has the pursuit of beauty found its way into modern laboratories and brought with it an ability to manufacture and distribute cosmetics on a widespread basis for ordinary people. Max Factor, the Hollywood makeup artist, is credited with popularizing the terms *lipstick*, *makeup*, and *eye shadow*. Before he made it respectable, nice girls just did not wear makeup.[3]

Although an elite segment of the market has survived, cosmetics and fragrances are now available to anyone who wants to use them. What were once luxuries are now viewed by many as necessities. This perception, in turn, has led to more innovation in mass production, advertising, and package design. The market has also become increasingly segmented as different kinds of cosmetics and scents are made available to customers based on their age, gender, ethnic group, lifestyles, and ability to pay.

Dreams Versus Science

With the move to the laboratory came a new emphasis on the scientific development of cosmetics. Whereas for decades the word "moisturize" alone was enough to sell a skin cream, new, improved creams were now promoted for their abilities to "nourish" and "renew" the skin.

Today, one takes a "daily dose" of skin care products, which are likely to be "pH-balanced." Cosmetics salespersons no longer help their customers select a makeup shade; they are trained technicians who can "diagnose" the customer's needs and prescribe the right "formula." Fragrances, too, are regarded with a more scientific approach despite the romantic allure that is attached to their use. One way of keeping down costs of mass-merchandised fragrances is the laboratory production of synthetic substitutes for expensive natural ingredients.

Until the 1960s, most women's use of colored makeup was limited. The development of easy to apply powders, gels, and glosses and the marketing of attractive packages brought about a change of buying habits. Estée Lauder's promotional brainstorm, offering a gift sample with a cosmetics purchase is still a popular way of luring customers to the cosmetics counter.

The 1970s saw the emergence of *natural* products made from such ingredients as aloe vera, honey, musk, almonds, and henna. Incense moved beyond the "head shop" into respectability. The trend toward natural cosmetics in the 1980s turned into a full-blown consumer preoccupation with health and self-image. The new emphasis was on the protective aspects of cosmetics. The buying public began to seek products that maintained and protected their skins rather than merely enhanced them cosmetically. Skin care products became the fastest-growing segment of the cosmetics industry. Although fashion and beauty have remained the driving force behind most cosmetics sales in the 1990s, more consumers than ever before are willing to spend money for products that enhance their overall health.

The yuppies of the 1980s matched their power suits with strong fragrances like Calvin Klein's Obsession, Poison by Dior, and Beverly Hills from Giorgio. With the waning display of opulence in the 1990s came lighter scents and comforting food-related scents, especially vanilla. "Share wear" or unisex fragrances, exemplified by Calvin Klein's cK One, also enjoyed a surge of popularity.

In the early 2000s, fragrance trends were a bit all over the place. While classic scents like Chanel No 5 and Estée Lauder's Beautiful were top sellers, a trend of innovative new fragrance concepts also started to emerge. For example, in September 2002, the smell of lipstick was incorporated in new fragrances from Chantal Thomass, Editions de Parfums de Frederic Malle, and L'Artisan Parfumeur.[4]

Legends Versus the New Entrepreneurs

The cosmetics and fragrance industry has always been dominated by personalities, a trait that shows little sign of abating. What has changed is the nature of the personalities and their purposes in their businesses.

An early worldwide celebrity associated with fragrance was Coco Chanel. More than 75 years ago, she introduced a perfume that, despite its unpretentious name, became associated with designer fashion: Chanel No. 5. Decades later, another French designer linked fragrance with designer fashion; he was Christian Dior. His Miss Dior accompanied his famous post-World War II New Look.

But the big names in cosmetics and fragrances were not all French. From the 1950s through the 1970s, a few flamboyant personalities in the United States, most notably, Elizabeth Arden, Helena Rubenstein, Charles Revson, Max Factor, and Estée Lauder, dominated the industry and virtually dictated its shape and scope. Less well known but equally innovative were Dorothy Gray, Hazel Bishop, and Harriet Hubbard Ayer. The drive, intuition, foresight, and promotional abilities of these pioneers are still felt in the industry, and have rarely been duplicated in other industries. By the mid-1980s, most of the companies founded by these individuals had become public corporations or part of multinational conglomerates.

Only Estée Lauder survived with her beauty empire still intact and run by her personally. This famous "nose" personally developed her fragrance lines while overseeing her cosmetics empire. Instead of being swallowed up by a larger organization, she built her own conglomerate with the Aramis, Clinique, and Prescriptives brands. Not until 1995, after she had turned management of the company over to her son, did it go public, and even then, the family retained control of 85 percent of the stock.

The cosmetics industry seems destined to be run by personalities, and a second generation, with names like Adrien Arpel, Madeleine Mono, Christine Valmy, Georgette Klinger, Merle Norman, Flori Roberts, Mary Kay Ash, and Don Bochner, soon emerged. Unlike the old stars, though, these new entrepreneurs relied less on personality and more on sound business strategies. In England, Anita Roddick opened her first Body Shop in 1976, making environmental protection the guiding force of her business decisions.

A

B

FIGURE 13.2
(a) Estée Lauder, Inc. was founded by one of the superstars of the first generation of the American cosmetics industry. (b) Chantal Thomass, although not a founder, is a popular leader in the cosmetic industry for today's generation.
Courtesy, Fairchild Publications, Inc.

A third generation of cosmetics personalities includes the late Frank Toskan of the Canadian firm MAC (Make-Up Art Cosmetics) and Bobbi Brown. Besides being makeup artists for the fashion industry who brought their expertise to the public, Brown and Toskan had in common their parent company, Estée Lauder.

Organization and Operation of the Industry

The cosmetics and fragrance industry has undergone significant changes in recent years in terms of its organization and operation. Once made up entirely of many small firms, none of which controlled a significant share of the market, it is now dominated by a few huge, global firms that command large market shares. Although the industry still supports 600 companies, many are now owned by conglomerates that also produce other consumer goods, such as processed foods, health care products, and household cleaners. The largest companies in the world with holdings in the cosmetics and fragrance industry are L'Oreal, in which Nestlé has a substantial interest; Procter & Gamble; Unilever; and Estée Lauder. Complicating the issues are licensing of designer brands and cosmetics, and the constant changes in mergers, sales, and acquisitions that take place according to changes in the market and the economy. For example, in 2000, Unilever entered a five-year-growth strategy that would reduce its brands from 1600 to 400.[5] In 2000, Unilever sold its Elizabeth Arden division to FFI Fragrances, and in 2002 announced that it was selling o ff its entire upmarket fragrance business (including Calvin Klein, Nautica, Vera Wang, Chloe, and Karl Lagerfeld) to concentrate on core high-yield brands. Following this strategy, Unilever unveiled plans in 2002 to enter the hair color market with a major new product launch, and compete with L'Oreal and Procter & Gamble, which had previously owned the bulk of the hair color market.[6]

A Global Business

The joining of cosmetics and fragrance firms in multinational conglomerates is part of the same trend that is manifested in the changing role of heads of companies from product development artists to master marketers. The giant parent companies can offer their cosmetics and fragrance industry subsidiaries clout and expertise in the consumer marketplace. As packaging, promotion, and distribution become as much a part of the product as the ingredients, the giant corporations develop global marketing strategies to get each product line into the hands of its targeted group of consumers.

Western Europe has a global cosmetics and fragrance industry of its own. Their marketing practices are similar to those in the United States, with subsidiaries and lines catering to various market segments. For example German-based Wella, known for its hair care products, has expanded by acquiring a fragrance company and developing new lines within the subsidiary's brands. In 2002, Wella boosted its Parfums Rochas subsidiary division by acquiring the Escada Beauty Group.[7]

Table 13.1 identifies the largest worldwide marketers of cosmetics and fragrances.

The Main Categories

All large, nationally advertised cosmetics firms produce hundreds of items. For sales and inventory purposes, products must thus be divided into broad categories. The typical order form of one large firm, for example, lists all the company's products, in the various sizes or colors available, under end-use categories such as:

- Fragrances
- Color cosmetics (facial makeup, including lip and cheek color; eye makeup; and liquid and powder foundations)
- Skin care

TABLE 13.1 The World's Largest Firms in the Cosmetics and Fragrance Industry

RANK	COMPANY/COUNTRY	EXAMPLES OF SUBSIDIARIES AND DIVISIONS
1	L'Oréal France	Marie Claire, Maybelline, Laura Ashley Perfumes, Redken, Lancôme, Helena Rubinstein, Parfums Ralph Lauren, Parfums Paloma Picasso, Parfums Giorgio Armani, Garnier
2	Procter & Gamble U.S.A.	Max Factor®, Giorgio Beverly Hills, Procter & Gamble Cosmetic and Fragrance Products including Cover Girl, Max Factor
3	Unilever Holland, England	Calvin Klein Cosmetics, Fabergé, Chesebrough Ponds, Helene Curtis, Elizabeth Taylor, Karl Lagerfeld, House of Cerruti, House of Valentino
4	Shiseido Japan	Shiseido, Carita
5	Estée Lauder U.S.A.	Estée Lauder, Clinique, Prescriptives, Aramis, Bobbi Brown, M.A.C., Kate Spade Beauty, Tommy Hilfiger
6	Avon Products U.S.A.	Avon
7	Johnson & Johnson U.S.A.	Johnson & Johnson, Neutrogena
8	Wella Group Germany	Parfums Pochas, René Garraud, Graham Webb, Nichi Claire
9	Sanofi France	Nina Ricci, Yves Saint Laurent, Oscar do la Renta Fragrances, Fendi Profumi
10	Beiersdorf Germany	Cosmed division (makers of Nivea), La Prairie
11	KAO Japan	Jergens, Goldwell, Sofina Cosmetics
12	Revlon U.S.A.	Revlon
13	Boots England	Boots the Chemist
14	LVMH (Louis Vuitton Moët Hennessy) France	Parfums Christain Dior, Poison, Parfums Givenchy, Parfums Shalimar, Parfums Kenzo, Guerlain, Donna Karan, Sephora
15	Kanebo, Ltd. Japan	Kanebo

Based on "A Who's Who of Cosmetics: The Beauty Top 75," *Women's Wear Daily*. Ranks are based on sales of cosmetics and fragrances and do not include the companies' other products.

- Sun care
- Nail care
- Hair care

If a firm produces men's as well as women's cosmetics, each of the two lines is given its own distinctive brand name, and, of course, separate sales and inventory records are kept for each brand line. We will discuss all but hair care in more detail.

Because of fashion and product obsolescence, as well as customer boredom, manufacturers are constantly updating and shipping new items to keep cosmetics customers buying new products, or new colors, or both. Manufacturers update formulas when they become aware of new technology and new ingredients to improve their products.

A system of product returns, unique to the cosmetics industry, aids the retailer in keeping the inventory current. The industry refers to this system as **rubber-banding**, which means that cosmetic products not sold within a specified period of time may be returned to the manufacturer to be replaced with others that will sell. This guarantees that the cosmetics retailer will never have to take a markdown on this merchandise. Only if a cosmetics company is discontinuing an item, does it permit markdowns by a store. (Other industries allow returns to vendors only for damages, over shipments, or wrong shipment.)

Fragrances

The term **fragrance** includes (in increasing order of strength, lasting power, and price) cologne, toilet water, eau de parfum, and perfume. Other forms of fragrances are spray perfume, after-shave lotion, and home fragrances. Scents are also added to other beauty products, such as soap, shampoo, bubble bath, and hand and body lotions, but the items in the fragrance category are designed specifically to enhance the smell of the person wearing them.

The scent of a fragrance is a combination of essential oils, often from plants, including a variety of trees, flowers, grasses, herbs and spices, and edible extracts—like the very popular vanilla. Other scents are concocted in the perfumer's laboratory. Each scent is called a **note**, and, like musical notes, they vary in strength and duration. The perfumer, like the composer, combines them in a harmonious whole. Alcohol carries the scent to the skin. The more alcohol, the less concentrated the fragrance.

Fragrances are affected by the body chemistry of the wearer; they may smell different on different people or even on the same person at different times. For example, diet may make one's skin more or less oily, and fragrance is more intense on oily skin. In addition, the scent of a single application of a fragrance changes over time. Virginia Bonofiglio, who teaches in the unique Fragrance Knowledge course at the Fashion Institute of Technology in New York describes "three major stages in the life of a perfume":

> *First, the top note—what you smell when you take a whiff from a bottle—usually a citrus or green smell, which lasts about fifteen minutes on the skin. Then the middle note, often a floral or wood, which lasts three to four hours. And finally the bottom note, usually a musk or vanilla, which lasts four to five hours.*[8]

Cosmetics manufacturers produce fragrances with their own brand names and, under licensing agreements, the names of designers and celebrities. Tommy and Tommy Girl, Tommy Hilfiger's fragrance lines, are manufactured by Estée Lauder, which also produces, under its own name, such scents as Beautiful, Knowing, and Youth Dew and, under the names of its subsidiaries, Aramis and Clinique's Aromatics, among others.

Continual innovation in fragrances is necessary to maintain growth in a fashion-conscious market. As many as 100 new fragrances may be launched in a season in various concentrations. In 2002, Coty Inc. released Jennifer Lopez's first perfume, Glow, and inked another fragrance deal with singer Celine Dion. Most fragrances are available as perfume and the lower-priced, less long-lasting toilet water and cologne. Many also come with accessory scents such as talcum powder and hand and body lotion. Fragrances are also bottled in a range of sizes, making even expensive perfumes available to a larger market.

Perfumes are worn predominantly by women 25 to 44 years old—a group that is both fashion-conscious and affluent enough to buy this luxury product. Toilet waters and colognes, also worn by the aforementioned group on informal occasions, have great appeal for younger women because they are lower-priced. They appeal to men because they are more subtle than most perfumes. These lower-priced products also are used to entice the male or female customer from any economic level to try a new product.

Top 5 Women's Scents in Department Stores

1. Estée Lauder's Beautiful
2. Clinique Happy
3. Estée Lauder's Pleasures
4. Ralph Lauren Romance
5. Chanel No. 5

A

Top 5 Men's Scents in Department Stores

1. Giorgio Armani's Acqua di Gió
2. Ralph Lauren's Polo Blue
3. Calvin Klein's Eternity for men
4. Tommy Hilfiger's Tommy
5. Liz Claiborne's Curve for men

B

FIGURE 13.3
(a) Top Five Women's Scents in Department Stores (b) Top Five Men's Scents in Department Stores
Source: NPD Biz, a Fairchild Publication.

Color Cosmetics

The term **color cosmetics** usually refers to facial makeup; nail color is categorized with other nail care products. Color is the primary feature of facial makeup, but the substance into which the pigment is mixed is also important. The oils, wax, and talc that are used in the bases of color cosmetics affect the wearer's skin and the finish of the makeup. The pigments also interact with the ingredients in the bases, so manufacturing products that are consistent from batch to batch requires a well-equipped factory staffed by experts.[9]

Lip coloring is produced in the form of lipstick and solid or gel-like glosses. It may be opaque or transparent, and the finish may be matte, glossy, or even glittery. This variety and the range of colors allows for mixing to achieve a look suitable to the occasion and the colors in one's outfit. A smash hit in 2002 were the triplet launches of "Outlast" from Revlon, "Lipfinity" from Max Factor, and "Endless" from L'Oreal. All three products were variations on lip color and gloss combinations that stayed on all day, even during lipstick-unfriendly activities such as eating or kissing.

Liquid, gel, and powder blushes, in addition to the more traditional rouge, provide similar variety in cheek color cosmetics. Liquid and powder foundations not only give the skin an even surface and color; the various formulations provide skin care for dry, oily, and normal skin.

Eye makeup, especially eye shadow, is available in a broad range of colors, not all of them natural, to set off this most expressive facial feature.

Estée Lauder, Lancôme, and Clinique are called "The Big Three" because they dominate color cosmetics. In addition to these prestige lines, mass-marketed color cosmetics manufacturers are influential in certain product categories, although most produce the full range. For example, Cover Girl, a division of Procter & Gamble, is noted for foundations, while Maybelline, a subsidiary of L'Oréal, is a big name in eye makeup. Figure 13.5 lists the top ten cosmetic companies.

FIGURE 13.4
The range-from eau de cologne to eau de toilette to eau do parfum to perfume-is now available in most well-known fragrances.
Courtesy, Estée Lauder, Inc.

Top 10 Cosmetic Companies	
Company	**Subsidiaries/Main Brands**
L'Oréal Group Clichy, France	Pléntitude, Féria, Elséve, Garnier, Maybelline, Club des Créateurs de Beauté, La Scad, Laboratoires Ylang, Lancôme, Biotherm, Parfums Armani, Cacharel, Ralph Lauren Paarfums, Paloma Picasso, Kiehl's, Guy Laroche, Vichy, Laroche-Possay, Technique Professionnelle, Kérastase, Redken, Inné, Matrix, Galderma, Soft Sheen Carson
Procter & Gamble Cincinnati, Ohio	Cover Girl, Max Factor, Olay, Hugo Boss, Pantene, Physique, VS Sassoon, SK II, Old Spice, Head & Shoulders, Herbal Essences, Noxzema, Pert Plus
Unilever PLC London/Rotterdam	Unilever HPC: Axe, Impulse, Rexona, Dove, Lux, Pond's, Vaseline, Sunsilk, Organics, Thermasilk. Unilever Cosmentcis International: Calvin Klein, Contradiction, CK One, CK Be, Escape, Obsession, Eternity, Truth, Calvin Klein Color, Cerruti, Lagerfeld, Chloé, Valentino, 1881, Cerruti Image, Vendetta, Nautica, BCBG Max Azria, Vera Wang
Shiseido Co. LTD Tokyo	Shiseido The Makeup, Shiseido The Skincare, Benefiance, Pureness, Vital Perfection, Shiseido Suncare, Shiseido Hair Care, BOP, Eudermine, Relaxing Fragance, Energizing Fragrance, ZEN, IPSA, Ettusais, 5S, FSP, Za, D'Icila
The Estée Lauder Cos. Inc. New York	Estée Lauder, Prescriptives, Stila, Clinique, Origins, Bobbi Brown, MAC Cosmetics, Jane, La Mer, Aramis, Jo Malone, Tommy Hilfiger, Aveda, Bumble and bumble, Donna Karan, Kate Spade Beauty, Doraphin, Michael Kers Fragrances
Avon Products Inc. New York	Anew, Avon Color, Skin-So-Soft, Advanced Tecniques Hair Care, beComing, Avon Wellness
Johnson & Johnson New Brunswick, New Jersey	Neutrogena, RoC, Clean & Clear, Johnson's (baby, skin and hair care), Renova, Retin-A
Kao Corp. Tokyo	Sofina Casmetics, Bioré, Jergens, Curél, Essential, Merit, Liese, Pur, Dofina, Aube, Raycious, Est, Very Very, Vital Roch, Braurié, Lavenus, Success
Beiersdorf AG Hamburg, Germany	Nivea, 8x4, Atrix, Basis ph, Juvenance, Personal Skin Collections, Rejuven Q10, Body Results, Sunsation, Discover, Color Cosmetics, La Prairie, Hidrofugal, Eucerin
Kanebo LTD. Tokyo	Kanebo, Faircrea, Dada, T'estimo, Revue, Fila, Naive, First Lady, Mild Coat, Paphelle, Blanchir, Chic Choc.

Figure 13.5
Adapted from: "The Beauty Top 100," *WWDBeauty Biz*, Septerber 2001, p. 38–39.

Skin Care

Soap, long the basis of skin care, is no longer the only product used for bathing. In a market that is constantly demanding new choices, alternatives to the familiar bar of soap are turning a bath or shower into a new experience. Bar soap is still the largest selling product for bathing, but the growth of sales is challenged by liquid soap, syndet bars (Dove, among others), and body washes and gels. The washes and gels are marketed as a way of avoiding the skin-drying effects of soap; they rely on mild detergents for cleansing, and net puffs packaged with the product help to make bathing an invigorating experience.

Perhaps because bathing is a routine daily activity rather than a luxury, mass merchandise products sold at low price point are at the forefront of the market. Some popular brands of washes are White Rain and Caress. Prestige products are also being marketed. Procter & Gamble, Gillette, Colgate Palmolive, Nivea, and Unilever all offer body washes (without puffs) targeted to men in Europe.

Of course, the skin care category is wider than just soap or soap substitutes. It includes hand, face, foot, and body lotions, as well as creams, scrubs, masks, moisturizers, and anti-cellulite treatments. The enormous impact of alpha hydroxy acids (AHAs) on these products cannot be overestimated. This emerging segment of skin care products is based on dermatology and promises to correct the visable signs of aging and promote new cell growth. (See the discussion under Federal Laws, later in this chapter.) The addition of antibacterial agents to skin care products is discussed later in this chapter under Trends, as is the antiallergenic versions of these products.

Sun Care

Sun care has become a major category of the cosmetics industry, as consumers have become increasingly aware of the health dangers—and aging effects—of the sun's rays. As a result, even the prestige manufacturers have rushed to produce a wide range of scientifically formulated sun products. An important feature of a sunscreen is its SPF, or sun protection factor. The SPF number, which indicates how long the screen will protect the wearer from burning, may go as high as 45, but most people are adequately protected by a sunscreen with an SPF of 15.

What once was category dominated by drug stores and mass merchants has now become a major business for department stores as well.

FIGURE 13.6
Estée Lauder's self tanner products allow you to get a tan without the harmful rays of the sun.
Courtesy, Fairchild Publications, Inc.

Some of the new products in this $400 million market combine protection from the sun with insect repellant. Waterproof lotions and non-sticky gels are also in demand. People who want to avoid exposure to the sun completely can tan artificially with "self tanners" (see Figure 13.6).

Nail Care

Nail care products really took off in the 1990s; according to industry experts, nail polish became a $350 million-a-year market. In addition to transparent nail enamels and colors echoing the range of lipstick colors, dramatic blues, greens, blacks, and yellows are now available for women—and men. The rapid growth of the 1990s flamboyant nail care trend launched a new slew of independent, style savvy nail care companies like Hard Candy and Urban Decay. These companies specialized in funky colors and provocative product names like "Libido" and "Pothole."

An equally flamboyant style of nail decoration is artificial nails, available in a selection of lengths, shapes, and colors. A popular brand is Flo Jo, named for the late Florence Griffith Joyner, the Olympic champion runner, who pioneered the decorated fingernail style. Independent nail salons, where manicures are not merely a service added on to hair care, have sprung up around the country. In these salons, one can acquire a set of nails painted in multicolor designs, including gold decorations.

Packaging

Packaging plays a vital role in marketing fragrances and cosmetics. Often it is the package rather than the contents that leads the customer to buy one product over another. Manufacturers have historically tried for unique packaging. In the early 1900s, when Coty perfume was the most expensive in France, Coty tried to get the exclusive rights to a newly invented—and enormously expensive packaging material—Cellophane.[10]

It often seems that the bottle and packaging take on incredible significance. In the next decade, according to the Fragrance Foundation, for every $100,000 in expected gross sales, a manufacturer should plan to spend $20,000 on the bottle (and the perfume in it) and $35,000 on advertising and promotion. An interesting example of a successful perfume marketing concept where the bottle played a vital role is Parfums Christian Dior's blockbuster scent J'Adore. Launches in 1999, at a time when best-selling fragrances were packaged in minimalist bottles like CK and CKOne, J'Adore set a new trend with a voluptuous amphora shaped bottle with a golden Masai-like "collar" around the neck. Patrick Choel, president of the Perfumes and Cosmetics Division at LVMH that released J'Adore, actually claims that the bottle is more important than the juice itself.[11]

Today, efforts to preserve natural resources by recycling packaging materials have had a mixed influence on the packaging of cosmetics and fragrances. (See Recyclable Packaging later in this chapter.)

Private Label Manufacturers

Although dominated by giant producers of nationally advertised brand lines, the industry has many **private label manufacturers**, producing merchandise to specification under the brand names of chain stores, mass merchants, department stores, small independent stores and hair salons, and direct-to-the-home marketers. Examples of private label fragrance lines are Volage sold by Neiman Marcus; Bloomies, sold by Bloomingdales; and Fireworks, sold by Bergdorf Goodman. The famous scent Giorgio was born in the Rodeo Drive Giorgio store. It was such a success that, although an original private label, it is now sold in fine stores from coast to coast. Competitors Avon Products and Mary Kay Cosmetics both sell products produced and packaged for them by the same private label manufacturer, Cosmetic Group USA of Sun Valley, California.

Some of the better-known private label manufacturers are Kolmar Laboratories of Port Jervis, New York; Quest International of Mount Olive, New Jersey; Parfumerie Douglas Cosmetics of Greenwich, Connecticut; and Private Label Cosmetics of Fair Lawn, New Jersey. Kolmar sells mass quantities to large users, but not all private label producers are big enough to meet large orders. Small private label manufacturers, such as Olin (a division of the House of Westmore), supply small distributors. A beauty salon owner can walk into a private label distributor's office, and in less than ten days and for about $500 have a complete private label line in his or her shop. Or a dermatologist may want a private label line of products to sell to patients. However, this line is based on what the private label house has already been manufacturing. Private label manufacturers do not develop new products for individual clients.

Retailers get little help from their private label suppliers. Private label firms do not share advertising costs, provide gift-with-purchase offers, or accept returns.

A serious threat to the private label industry is posed by federal ingredient-label requirements. Packing is usually kept to a minimum by private label firms in order to keep prices low. To get the government-required ingredient label on a small lipstick, however, an additional package is required. Through its lobbying group, the Independent Cosmetic Manufacturers and Distributors Association, the private label industry is fighting labeling requirements.

Copycat Scents

The conspicuous consumption of expensive designer fragrances in the 1980s gave rise to a new industry segment, producers of **copycat scents**. These products are unabashed imitations of the packaging as well as the aromas of popular designer fragrances. Comparison advertising highlights the price difference to assure customers who cannot afford the prestige brand that they are getting value for their dollar. In the more economically cautious 1990s, copycats have thrived in mass merchandise and off-price outlets, flea markets, and direct mail. Knockoff fragrances that appeal to young consumers, such as cK One and Tommy, have fared especially well.

The major players in this market are Fragrance Impressions, Tristar, Delagar, Jean Philippe, and Parfums de Coeur. They compete directly not only with the objects of their imitation but with each other as they go after the same scents. Rather than wait a year to gauge the success of a new launch, as they did in the past, the copycat manufacturers are producing their versions of a designer's latest line almost simultaneously with the prestige brand.[12]

Federal Laws

Because chemicals are the basis for most cosmetic products, the Food and Drug Administration (FDA) is the federal agency that polices and regulates the cosmetics industry. The Federal Trade Commission defines a **cosmetic** as any article other than soap that is intended to be "rubbed, poured, sprinkled, or sprayed on, introduced into, or otherwise applied to the human body for cleansing, beautifying, promoting attractiveness, or altering the appearance without affecting the body's structure or functions."[13]

Manufacturers are prevented by FDA regulations from using potentially harmful ingredients and from making exaggerated claims regarding the effects of their products. An example of the results of these regulations is the use of **alpha hydroxy acids (AHAs)**—which are extracted from fruits, vegetables, and sugar cane—in facial creams intended to prevent wrinkles. When they were introduced in 1994, AHAs came under federal scrutiny as the FDA considered whether to regulate their use as a drug. Drugs are subject to time-consuming independent tests of their potency and possible harmful side effects, which can delay approval to market a product. In manufacturers' tests, AHAs showed effectiveness, but while they awaited the FDA's decision, many producers limited the amount of AHAs in their product so that they could sell it as a cosmetic. Ultimately, the FDA decided not to regulate products with AHAs as drugs.[14]

The 1938 Federal Food, Drug, and Cosmetic Act was the first federal law controlling cosmetics. It prohibited the adulteration and misbranding of cosmetics. Amendments added to the law in 1952 made it more stringent. More amendments in 1960 required government review and approval of the safety of color additives used in cosmetics.

The Fair Packing and Labeling Act of 1966 prohibits unfair or deceptive methods of packaging and labeling. This act covers many consumer industries in addition to the cosmetics industry. All cosmetics labeled since April 15, 1977, must bear a list of their ingredients in descending order of weight. To help identify potentially dangerous ingredients for manufacturers, the Cosmetic Ingredient Review, an independent research group funded by the industry trade organization, the Cosmetic, Toiletry, and Fragrance Association (CTFA), was established in the early 1980s.

In any event, the major ingredients of most cosmetics in any price range do not vary much and mostly consist of fats, oils, waxes, talc, alcohol, glycerin, borax, coloring matter, and perfumes.

Constant surveillance by consumer and industry groups and advisory boards keeps the cosmetics industry sensitive to product liability. The FDA Modernization Act of 1997 focused on modernizing the regulation of medical products, food, and cosmetics. This act includes provisions for global harmonization of standards. Since the European Federation of Associations of Health Products Manufacturers (EHPM) has more stringent standards than the United States does, U.S. manufacturers expect to be required to register their products and formulas and to establish their safety before selling them to the European customer.

Although the Anticounterfeiting Consumer Protection Act increases the penalties for counterfeiting, federal courts have not made the problem a priority. Therefore, approximately 100 legitimate manufacturers, including producers of cosmetics and fragrances, have formed the International Anticounterfeiting Coalition, which has been lobbying state governments to impose stricter sentences on violators of state anticounterfeiting laws. These efforts have helped the manufacturers protect the reputations of their products and reduce losses of income.[15]

Environmental Concerns

Environmentalism, as a major issue of political and social concern, has had a strong effect on consumer buying habits and on industry practices to meet consumer's demands. Attention to health and fitness influences what people are willing to put on their skin and hair, so a demand for natural products and ingredients has arisen in the cosmetics and fragrances industry, just as it has in the food industry. Consumers are also becoming more educated about the effects of their behavior on natural resources.

FASHION FOCUS

A Look at Beauty – A Look at Jung

Wearing her signature choker pearls, Andrea Jung stands for the new look of leadership in the Beauty Biz. Although many women are famous for their signature beauty brands, Estée Lauder, Elizabeth Arden, Bobbi Brown, Helena Rubenstein among them, Jung was the first woman to crash the glass ceiling of the executive suites of a Fortune 500 Company.

In November 2001, Jung became part of America's corporate elite, appearing as the only woman on a *Fortune* magazine-sponsored panel alongside chairman and CEOs like Gordon Bethane of Continental Airlines and Jeffrey Immelt of General Electric. She also became the first female chairperson of the Cosmetic, Toiletry, and Fragrance Association in its 107-year history.

Jung works at achieving success—and admits that she has been working non-stop at it all her life. Education was very important to her family and she graduated high school in three years instead of four, then went to Princeton, where she earned a degree in English Literature magna laude.

So how did this Ivy League grad with a love and talent for classical music end up in a department store stocking shelves? She got signed up by a campus recruit for the management-training program at Bloomingdales. "There's a lot of gruel (in retail)," she acknowledges. "Whether you were a manager or not, you were always in the stock room, sometimes for six hours a day, doing things like changing hangers on Liz Claiborne pants. Many management trainees didn't stick it through. I (had) the ability to stick it out and persevere." She fell in love with the pace and constant change of the retail business. "But the real clincher," says Jung, "is being close to the consumers. I developed a passion for it."

In the early years of her career, she worked at Bloomingdales, I, Magnin, and Neiman Marcus, where she was executive vice-president. In the Jung/Avon timeline, you will see how she moved up the ladder at Avon until she became chairman in 2001.

Although her efforts to sell her customers at retail outlets such as J.C Penney, rather than directly to consumers was hailed as innovative thinking in 2001, by 2003 this alliance came to an end due to changing consumer spending patterns.

A pillow on the sofa of Jung's office reads, "The Best is yet to come" and looking at Jung's past movements in success – could she be the first U.S. female president? Why not?

Sources

Business.com – Company Web site – www.avon.com

Claudia H. Deutsch, "In a Kill Economy, Avon Finds a Hidden Gloss," *New York Times,* June 1, 2003, p. B04.

IGN Global Marketing, "Avon Innocence Peace to Append Into Retail Outlets," September 18, 2000.

Laura Klepacki, "Avon's First Lady," *Women's Wear Daily*, BeautiBiz, December 2001, pp. 48, 53, 58.

Laura Klepacki, "Avon Unveils Its BeComing Retail Brand," *Women's Wear Daily*, BeautiBiz, April 27, 2001, pp. 5, 8, 9.

Public Lines, "Spearheading a Marketing Makeover at Avon," *New York Times,* May 5, 2001, p. B2.

RR Newswire, "Superstar Venus Williams to Appear at the Avon National Representative Convention in New Orleans," August 8, 2001.

Reuters, "Avon, JC Penney End Retail Alliance," January 31, 2003.

Andrea Jung addresses a top level conference of cosmetic and fragrance experts.

FIGURE 13.7 *Jasmine Vanilla is a popular scent from the Bath and Body Works Aromatherapy Collection.* Courtesy, Fairchild Publications, Inc.

Natural or Botanical Products

Although everything on earth has a chemical composition, many people prefer products made from substances grown by nature to products produced by chemists in a laboratory. The cosmetic and therapeutic benefits of essential oils derived from plants prove that Mother Nature's recipes are effective, and many consumers do not believe that scientists can improve upon—or even equal—these ingredients (see Figure 13.7). Perhaps there is also a connection in some people's minds between the natural look in 1990s fashion and natural ingredients in the cosmetics that help them achieve that look.

Table 13.2 lists some oils that are harvested from nature for use in cosmetics. Some companies, notably The Body Shop, Aveda, and Origins, use only natural ingredients in their cosmetics. Adding to the appeal of the products themselves is the satisfaction consumers derive from knowing that their purchases benefit the populations of countries where the ingredients are found. Cosmetics and fragrance manufacturers, their suppliers, and ecological nonprofit agencies have helped set up locally run businesses in the Brazilian rain forests, near the Indonesian ecological preserves, and with African women's cooperatives.[16]

Animal Testing

The issue of testing cosmetic and fragrance formulas on animals to ensure that they were safe for human use reached the height of controversy in the late 1970s when animal rights activists protested the test of eye makeup on rabbits. Outraged that animals should be subjected to painful and blinding tests so that people could enjoy a luxury product, the protesters threatened boycotts of the offending manufacturers' products and picketing of their headquarters. The tests were eventually suspended when less controversial and equally reliable computerized analyses were developed to acquire the same kind of information.

Today, testing of cosmetics and fragrances on animals is much more limited, but producers who opposed these tests when they were more frequent continue to promote their products as not having been tested on animals. In 2002, the European Parliament called for an immediate ban on products under development that had been tested on animals and for which alternative testing procedures existed. The Parliament also ruled that starting in 2004, no cosmetics products that have been tested on animals could come to market.[17]

Recyclable Packaging

Packaging of cosmetics has been greatly influenced by interest in recycling. Refillable glass bottles at lower cost are available from The Body Shop, among others. But the elaborate glass bottles used for designer fragrances are not the object of serious recycling efforts because the product is a luxury item, which is often saved as an art object.

The cardboard outer packaging of many luxury cosmetics and fragrances are more of an issue. Many of the coatings used to give the packages an elegant appearance render the

TABLE 13.2 Some Popular Oils Used in Cosmetics

OIL	COSMETICS IN WHICH IT IS USED
Aloe leaf gel	Sun care products, shampoos, hair rinses
Apricot kernel oil	Hair preparations, bath oils
Avocado oil	Burn treatments, shaving cream
Babassu oil	Skin care products, suntan products
Black currant seed oil	Treatments for dry skin
Borage oil	Moisturizers
Castor oil	Lipstick
Cocoa butter	Sun care products
Coconut oil	Shampoo
Djarak isi oil	Products to treat skin diseases and wounds, products to promote hair growth
Groundnut oil	Skin cleansers
Japan wax	Makeup sticks, mascara
Jojoba oil	Sun care products
Keku nut oil	Treatments for dry skin, sunburn, and acne prevention; conditioning shampoos
Kiwi oil	Products to support cell growth
Macadamia nut oil	Baby oil
Mexican poppy oil	Treatments for dry skin
Sea buckthorn oil	Antiaging preparations
Wheat germ oil	Hair and skin care products

cardboard unsuitable for recycling. Producers who want to market their products globally have had to consider alternative packaging materials to comply with the recycling laws of the countries where their goods are sold.[18]

Mass-merchandised lines of such products as liquid soap, shampoo, and hand and body lotions are typically packaged in recyclable plastic containers.

Market Segments

The success of a perfume or cosmetic depends on accurate identification of the target customer and recognition of the product features, packaging, and promotional activities that will attract that customer's attention. Women have long been recognized as the primary market for cosmetics and fragrances, but six other major market segments have been identified. These segments overlap, but in defining the target for each product or line, the marketer focuses on particular characteristics. Currently, the most promising market segments are the male market, the teen market, the children's market, the ethnic market, the home market, and the export market.

The Male Market

The market for cosmetics and fragrances for men has expanded and is expected to experience above-average growth in the future. Changing male images are opening up new and larger markets in hair care, face and body care, and fragrances. Men are buying more diversified products, such as moisturizers, cleansers,

Then & Now

She is Beautiful! Can She Sell Beauty Products?

Instead of searching model agencies for new faces, beauty firms are now searching Hollywood. This is not a new phenomenon! Hollywood stars have been used for years to sell everything from fragrance to footwear, from cars to computers, from jewelry to jam. What better way to position a beauty product than to have the most glamorous, talented, beautiful women in the world tell you that you can look like a Hollywood star.

When one looks at Then and Now, there is one Hollywood star who still packs a marketing wallop – from the 1940 through 2003, Elizabeth Taylor still reigns.

Sources

Julie Naughton, with contributions from Jenny B. Fine, "Star Power?" *Women's Wear Daily*, BeautyBiz, April 2002, pp. 35-37.

Celebrities, Elizabeth Taylor and Halle Berry are featured in beauty ads.

and skin toners. Gillette, for one, is betting that the body wash market for men in the United States will grow dramatically as it has in Europe.[19]

Men, like women, are concerned about aging. Unlike women, they have done little about it until recently. Today, however, it has become socially acceptable for men to treat skin to retard the aging process. Many male baby boomers, concerned about keeping their jobs, are resorting to cosmetic surgery. For men seeking less drastic options, Aramis, the men's division of Estée Lauder offers Eye Time, designed to minimize dark circles under the eyes.[20]

A significant market is also being built for men's hair care products. Men's use of hair coloring products for their hair, mustaches, sideburns, and beards has skyrocketed since Grecian Formula 16 was introduced in 1961. Especially popular in the late 1990s were newly discovered treatments to help prevent or reverse hair loss. The availability of nonprescription Rogaine in the late 1990s gave a gigantic boost to the sales opportunities for hair loss products.

Premium by Phat Farm (launched in September 2001) was the first male fragrance from a clothing brand affiliated with the hip-hop industry. (Phat Farm is owned by Hip Hop mogul Russell Simmons.)[21] The target customer for this product was the typical consumer of men's cosmetics in general: an 18- to 24-year-old bachelor living in an urban area, quite likely to be Hispanic or African-American. An income suggestive of an early stage in this young man's career does not deter him from buying cosmetics. Marketing appeals to this customer also attract older men and the women who buy men's cosmetics and fragrances for the men in their lives—or for their own use.

In 2002, the male grooming industry was estimated to be worth $7.7 billion.[22] All indications are that men have accepted cosmetics and fragrances as an integral part of their lifestyle.

Most department stores and many specialty stores have installed complete men's cosmetic sections. Casual apparel businesses such as The Gap and Eddie Bauer are introducing unisex cosmetics and fragrance lines into their stores to outfit their customers completely.

The Teen Market

Buying a first tube of lipstick has been a rite of passage for teenage girls for generations, but the teenager of the 1990s has gone far beyond this initial plunge into cosmetic and fragrance purchases. The U.S. youth spending on cosmetics and toiletries is estimated to $8 billion annually.[23]

Furthermore, today's typical teen customer has her own tastes—literally. Bonne Bell, the pioneer in cosmetics lines for teens, features Lip Lix lipsticks in flavors as trendy as their color. Some of the new additions to the line, such as Manic Melon and Mad About Mocha, are available in both matte and shimmer finishes.

Bonne Bell's success has inspired other producers to offer cosmetics lines specifically for the teen market segment. Among them are M Professional, Fun Cosmetics, Jane, and Sel-Leb. They go after their target customer by following her into the mass merchandise store, the apparel specialty store, and the record store. They speak to her on MTV and on the Internet. Besides flavored lipstick, they offer her eye makeup and nail enamel in attention-getting colors. Jane, for example, added a nail enamel line called Hot Tips in 1997, shipping to 6,000 stores, or doors, to start. Thus Jane became the first manufacturer of teen-oriented products to offer a full nail program.[24] (Jane was subsequently bought by Estée Lauder to expand its offerings to teens and to give Lauder an entry to the mass market).[25]

Prestige cosmetics and fragrance producers appeal to the teenage customer with light and unisex scents. The ecologically oriented lines, such as The Body Shop, are also popular with this segment.

With over 31 million teenage girls spending an average of $2 per week, it is no surprise that the cosmetics and fragrance industry courts their business.[26] And the benefit is mutual: For a fraction of the price of a new dress or pair of jeans, a teen can express her style and indulge her shopping impulses.

Of course, both boys and girls spend heavily on acne treatments and concealers to help them deal with their teenage complexion problems. A success story was Bioré's wildly popular—and quickly imitated—dermal patch designed to remove blackheads.

The Children's Market

The children's market, which has existed since the 1950s, is now expanding.

Actually, this segment can be regarded as two markets: parents and the children themselves. Parents, particularly the parents of infants, want only the best to protect their children's sensitive skin. Dual wage-earner couples who have postponed parenthood have more income to spend on their children and a willingness to invest at least as much on their children's skin- and hair-care products as they spend on their own.

More than 200 personal care products for children have hit the market since 1994, many of them taking advantage of parental largesse. Examples of these upscale products are hair gel from Guess Kids, Crabtree & Evelyn's rice bran powder, and lip balm and diaper rash cream from Kiehl's.[27] California Baby and Aromatherapy for Kids even offer bath soaps and oils to soothe cranky babies' spirits. A proliferation of sunscreens is part of the fashion industry's response to consumers' concern about protection from ultraviolet rays. Summer hats and sunglasses for children as well as adults address the same concern.

Whatever influence the children have on their parents' purchases is directed toward products that are fun. For two- to eight-year-olds, fun means bubble bath, lip balm, printed bandages, candy-flavored toothpaste, and licensed products featuring their favorite cartoon characters. Mattel, Inc., manufacturer of the ever-popular Barbie, also markets through Avon's direct-to-the-home sales force a line of Barbie cosmetics, fragrances, and toiletry products for children.

The Ethnic Market

The complexion of the U.S. population is changing as the birth rates for people of color (a term referring collectively to African-Americans, Asian-Americans, Hispanics, and Native Americans) exceed that of Americans of European ancestry. Nearly one-third of the population of the United States is made up of African-Americans, Asian-Americans, and Hispanics, representing $1.2 trillion in joint purchasing power. By 2040 those groups will make up half the population. Thus, retail sales to people of color is one of the fastest growing segments of the cosmetics and fragrance industry. However, ethnic beauty products still don't have a strong market presence, compared to products geared toward Caucasians.[28]

Differences in skin shades and tones and hair texture among black women have stimulated the development of special products for this segment of the ethnic market. In the 1960s, companies such as Libra and Astarte pioneered in creating mass-market lines for black women. Another early pioneer, Flori Roberts, produced the first prestige cosmetic line for African Americans. Still a major force in the cosmetics industry, she also introduced the first fragrance within a black cosmetics line, initiated in-store seminars on careers for black women, and began in-store makeup demonstrations.

Today, specialized companies such as Flori Roberts, Fashion Fair, and BioCosmetic Research Labs continue to thrive by catering exclusively to the black market. Newer companies include AM Cosmetics, whose ethnic offerings include the Black Opal and Black Radiance brands. AM Cosmetics started in 1992 and is one of the leaders on the market. Another important start-up in the ethnic beauty business was supermodel Iman's launch of her own skin-care line Iman Cosmetics in 1994. In 2001, Iman expanded her business to include the makeup line I-Iman. In 2002, Colomer relaunched the packaging of its classic ethnic hair care lines African Pride and Crème of Nature so the products would appeal to a younger market. Other popular hair brands include Avlon, Joyce Williams, and Posner.

After Helena Rubenstein ran a makeup ad featuring black and white models in 1969, the major cosmetics companies began to pick up on the potential of the black market. Today, the major cosmetics companies such as Revlon and Avon produce foundation and lip products designed especially for black women. L'Oreal has had an increasingly important presence in the ethnic beauty market, since the company acquired Soft Sheen Products in 1998 and Carson Products, producers of the Dark and Lovely hair care range, in 2000. In 2001, L'Oreal also created its own institute for Ethnic Hair and Skin research.[29]

An American line for women of Asian background was launched in 1996 in Minneapolis. Zhen Cosmetics sells skin care products for face and body through its own catalog and at Nordstrom's.

Attention to the Hispanic market segment has mainly taken the form of promotion in ethnic media in Spanish rather than in the development of ethnic lines of cosmetics. With its high birth rate, the Hispanic population represents a young market segment, one that is ripe for its own cosmetics and fragrances. In 2001, AM Cosmetics reinvented its Tropez line, repositioning the brand from a multicultural consumer target to a strictly Hispanic consumer focus.[30] Several Florida companies that focus on the Hispanic customer are the Roberts Group of Boynton Beach, and Pharma-Nat and Palladio.

The Home Fragrances Market

Many industry experts feel that **home**, or environmental, **fragrances** will be the next major breakthrough in the perfume industry. The public's growing awareness of fragrance is not restricted to personal use but includes their homes as well. Many consumers are gaining satisfaction from enhancing their environment, and are taking in-home activities, such as gourmet cooking and home entertaining, more seriously.

Fashion designers were quick to pick up on the interest in environmental fragrances, and many have already produced scented candles, silk flowers, paperweights, and holiday gifts. The pioneer is Ralph Lauren, whose collection has been available since the late 1970s. Donna Karan and Oscar de la Renta also have designer home fragrance lines.

Two of the largest prestige cosmetics and fragrance manufactures, Estée Lauder and Charles of the Ritz, led the way in producing environmental fragrances. In 1981, Estée Lauder launched a line of environmental fragrances based on its Cinnabar, White Linen, and Youth Dew scents. In 1983, Charles of the Ritz introduced a high-tech gadget that played plastic "records" injected with fragrance oil.

Other companies have successfully specialized in more "low-tech" potpourris, sachets, incense, and air fresheners (see Figure 13.8). Lamp rings and wall plug-ins rely on heat to release their scents. The lamp ring contains fragrant oils; it is placed on a light bulb. Wall plug-ins are fitted into an electric outlet. Their cartridges are filled with fragrant gels.

The Export Market

The export market for U.S. cosmetics has grown in recent years partly because the "westernization" of much of the world has made the wearing of cosmetics acceptable. Until 1980, China had a law that banned the wearing of cosmetics, and in what was once the Soviet Union and its Eastern bloc satellites, American products were

FIGURE 13.8
Various types of potpourri, room fresheners, and candles are bought to make our homes and offices pleasing through fragrance.
Origins Natural Resources.

hardly known until recently. That has now changed. Japan, China, Western Europe, and South America have emerged as strong markets for U.S. cosmetics and fragrances.

Fortunately, American cosmetics and fragrances usually need little or no adjustment in formulas and packaging in order to succeed in the international market. An exception is Japan, where cosmetics are basically treated the same as pharmaceuticals, and require licensing for import and sale. The Japanese list of approved ingredients restricts some formulas, and specifies strict labeling requirements. But in the rest of the world, American products have enough variety for marketers to edit their offering to suit the demands of their customers abroad. Superior ingredients, promotion, and distribution work as well abroad as at home, and American companies have the expertise and money to ensure that their products continue to be best sellers the world over.

The U.S. Commerce Department has promoted efforts by small cosmetics companies to export to the more affluent third-world countries where per capita expenditures on cosmetics products are growing rapidly. Direct distribution, private label products produced for foreign firms, and licensing specialties for foreign production are considered the most productive prospects for this international market.

U.S. companies cashing in on the opening of the vast Chinese market to imported cosmetics include Revlon and direct sellers Avon and Amway. As the infrastructure improves and the Chinese become more familiar with these foreign products, demand is expected to increase.

A trade bloc of Asian–Pacific nations is emerging as another potential major market because of the standardization of import rules and the invitation to the United States to join the bloc. In contrast, India, despite its dense population and substantial middle class has placed itself off-limits with duty rates exceeding 100 percent.[31]

Merchandising and Marketing

The cosmetics and fragrance business is a highly visible one. Its products are used nearly every day by millions of people. In the prestige cosmetics market, competition for restricted distribution to quality department and specialty stores is keen. All of the prestige brand manufacturers want to sell their lines in the most prestigious store in each town. They offer these stores exclusives, specials, and cooperative advertising to guarantee that their products will receive prime locations. Limiting the doors where their products are available adds to the aura of exclusivity and uniqueness the manufacturer of each line wishes to convey to its target customers. Such merchandising techniques are used by most prestigious cosmetics brands, including Estée Lauder, Elizabeth Arden, Clinique, Orlane, Lancôme, Borghese, and Ultima II.

Distribution

The structure of distribution techniques in the cosmetics area is both distinctive and complex, involving such elements as class versus mass distribution, limited versus popular distribution, mass-market distribution, and distribution limited to in-store salons. The use of behind-the-counter brand-line representatives or direct selling techniques are also popular in the cosmetics and fragrance industry.

Class Versus Mass

Another name for "class" is "franchise," so when industry insiders talk about "class versus mass" they mean franchise versus mass. In **franchise distribution**, the manufacturer or exclusive distributor sells directly to the ultimate retailer. No wholesalers, jobbers, diverters, rack jobbers, or intermediaries of any kind are involved. Each vending retailer is on the books of the manufacturer or distributor as a direct-receivable account. A good example of this is Estée Lauder, which sells directly to stores such as Neiman Marcus and Saks Fifth Avenue. In contrast, third-party vendors, such as wholesalers, diverters, and jobbers, play a role in mass distribution. These third parties may sell to any one of a number of retailers of any type. No control is exercised over these intermediaries. Manufacturers may not know their retailers. Furthermore, territory or other definable exclusivity does not run from manufacturer to retailer in mass distribution as it does in the franchise or class relationship. A good example of this is Revlon's Natural Wonder line, which is sold in mass merchandise outlets such as variety stores, drugstores, and chain stores.

Limited Versus Popular

The franchise cosmetics business is described as being either limited or popular in its distribution pattern. In the industry, any line distributed to more than 5,000 doors is considered popular; any line distributed to fewer than 5,000 doors is limited.

Counter Brand-Line Representatives

Since a need exists to inform and educate cosmetics customers about the many products that are available to them, prestige cosmetics companies place their own **brand-line representatives** behind the counter as line salespeople. These line salespeople, also called beauty counselors, are well equipped to perform this important function. They are trained in the end-use of the hundreds of items carried in each specific line. In many instances, the salaries of these salespeople are paid by the cosmetic company directly. Sometimes, in an arrangement called **joint merchandising**, the store shares in the payment of their salaries. These salespeople are also responsible for stocking inventory. They keep detailed records that show what items are and are not selling. The cosmetics companies constantly keep their brand salespeople informed about new items, new colors, and new promotions through updated training and materials. As might be expected, the limited-door stores have the best-trained salespeople.

Mass Market Distribution

The **mass distribution** cosmetics market involves drugstores, discount stores, variety stores, and large national chains such as Sears and JCPenney. The volume of business done in these stores is growing. As they have become increasingly interested in distribution to these types of retail outlets, large cosmetics companies have planned and implemented new merchandising activities. Until a few years ago, the mass distribution outlets were limited to selling lines such as Cover Girl, Maybelline, or a store's own label line. Now large, nationally advertised brands such as Max Factor and Revlon have introduced their medium-priced lines into these outlets, enabling customers to select products more easily and thus increase sales. Mass market retailers are turning to open-access display systems and mass marketing displays.

In-Store Salons

In-store salons that provide a full range of hair, skin, and body services are another trend. Customers can now obtain specialized advice and beauty care right on the department store floor from such lines as Lancôme, Orlane, Payot, and Adrien Arpel. In-store salons have helped to introduce American women to the beauty regimens (routines) long favored by European women, and in turn, the products and regimens have been simplified to fit in with Americans' fast-paced lives. Regimens will become increasingly personalized as computers tailor them to individual customer's needs.

Direct Selling

A few companies sell their products to consumers only through individual or group presentations by their own salespeople. Three well-known examples are Avon, Mary Kay, and BeautiControl.

Advertising and Sales Promotion

National advertising budgets of cosmetics companies are immense, especially in comparison to sales. Fierce competition for retail shelf space forces companies to spend an average of $10 million annually to support a single fragrance line, even more if it is a new product.[32] And national advertising is not the only type of sales promotion in which a company must engage.

The expense of promotion and advertising is well worth the effort. A campaign combining direct mail, television, and print exposure often results in three times the usual amount of business generated by a particular product in any given week.

Television has become *the* medium for cosmetics that are sold by mail or phone order. Extended broadcast advertising is accomplished on QVC and the Home Shopping Network (HSN) and through "infomercials" on cable channels. Magazine ads continue to be the traditional way of reaching a targeted segment of the cosmetics market, while many retail store catalogs regularly push cosmetics and fragrances in their catalogs.

Premiums

An extensive publicity campaign is also mounted to introduce new products. These are often promoted by a celebrity, providing yet another basis for a publicity campaign. Many companies also promote their products with **premiums**, a gift-with-purchase or a purchase-with-purchase offer, a concept that originated with Estée Lauder. These premiums range from samples of products to cosmetic "paint boxes," umbrellas, tote bags, scarfs, and even small duffel bags.

Direct Mail

Because of the breadth and depth of its reach, many stores are finding direct mail one of the most successful forms of advertising for both promotions and regular-price cosmetics. Another advantage to the store is that direct mail campaigns are generally vendor-funded. The most common formats are order forms in four-color vendor mailers, bill insertion leaflets, and remittance envelope stubs. Estimates of sales volume from mail-order average about two to three percent of all cosmetics sales per year.

Scent and Color Strips

Another promotional tool that has gained a foothold in the cosmetics industry is the use of scent and color strips, sometimes as bill insertions, but more often as part of a company's advertisement in a magazine. A new method of sampling made possible by modern technology, scent and color strips allow consumers to experiment with new eyeshadow colors or try out new fragrances in the privacy of their own homes.

New technology has improved scent and color strips. Much to the relief to people who are ultra-sensitive to odors, scent samples can now be encapsulated so that they must be opened for the smell to be released. Liquids and creams can also be encapsulated in foil packets and distributed in magazines or bill inserts. Multiple-color samples can now be sealed under a plastic patch that peels away.

Computerized Displays

A number of cosmetics companies offer computerized assistance to help customers chose the products that are best suited to them. Computers create a virtual reality makeover in which the customer can see how various products will look on her. Less elaborate programs prepare a collection of cosmetics for a customer according to information about her coloring and skin type that she has typed into the computer.

The Internet

For mass-merchandised cosmetic lines, the Internet provides virtual counter space. Teens and young adults; who make up a large portion of the market for these lines, can go directly to the producer's Web page to find out about the latest colors or get other information about the company. Virtually every cosmetics and fragrance company now has their own Web site to promote and sell their products as well as provide chat rooms, information about company history, and locations of nearby retailers.

Trade Associations, Shows, and Publications

The Cosmetic, Toiletry, and Fragrance Association (CTFA) is the major cosmetics trade association. Its membership markets 90 percent of all cosmetics, toiletries, and fragrances sold in the United States. The CTFA coordinates the industry commitment to scientific and quality standards. It is the industry vehicle for information exchange about scientific developments among association members, consumers, and those who regulate the industry at federal, state, and local government levels. The CTFA also keeps members informed on government regulations and offers advice on interpretation and compliance. Through its home page on the Internet, CTFA offers members access to government agencies, product safety resources, international trade organizations, and the web sites of other members.

Another helpful organization is the Fragrance Foundation in New York. Founded in 1949, it has been under the direction of Annette Green since 1962. Manufacturers, suppliers, designers, packagers, retailers, and media and public relations personnel who are involved in the industry are members. The Fragrance Foundation maintains a library of print and video materials and a web page, and publishes industry reports and educational and sales training materials. It sponsors National Fragrance Week in June and honors an American and a European with "Fifi" awards. The Fragrance Foundation also sponsors a program at the Fashion Institute of Technology (FIT), in New York City, which offers a Bachelor of Science degree in cosmetics and fragrance marketing. The program includes mentoring, an internship, and placement assistance.

International trade shows bring together visitors and exhibitors from all facets of the cosmetics and fragrance industry—manufacturers, suppliers, packagers, retailers, and advertising and promotion specialists. The largest trade show in the United States is the HBA Global Expo, held in the Jacob K. Javits Center in New York. Bologna, Italy, is the site of the mammoth Cosmoprof, with around 130,000 visitors. Cosmoprof is the perfect occasion to launch a new line in front of the entire worldwide industry, and many producers do so.

Industry Trends

As noted earlier in this chapter, the cosmetics and fragrance industry is now a global one. This trend will accelerate in the coming decades. In the United States, sales of skin care products are expected to grow at a faster pace than color cosmetics, due to an older and more affluent population and the increasing popularity of men's products.

The market for fragrance will remain strong, in part because of the steadily increasing number of working women, who prefer a lighter fragrance when at work to the heavy perfumes they may wear in the evening. The concept of a **fragrance wardrobe** to suit the various roles a woman (or man) assumes is being promoted and has boosted demand. Men are also adapting (though more slowly) the idea of one fragrance for the office, another for sports, and another for evening.

Five other sectors predicted to continue solid growth include: (1) antiaging products, (2) antibacterial and antiallergenic products, (3) aromatherapy products, (4) spa products, and (5) individualized products.

Antiaging Products

Antiaging products are enjoying booming sales thanks to the baby boom generation. When the oldest members of this group turned 50 in 1996, they raced to the cosmetics counter for skin care products to ward off or lessen the appearance of wrinkles. About the same time, laboratory tests confirmed the effectiveness of alpha hydroxy acids (AHAs) for this purpose, and the FDA decided to regulate AHAs as cosmetics rather than as drugs.

Other products that appeal to this market segment include anticellulite creams and hair coloring and hair loss prevention products.

In the new millennium, the beauty industry seems to have picked up a trend for more "natural" anti-aging products, such as Shiseido's "Future Solution Total Revitalizing Cream." The product, which launched in 2002, is based on microscopic capsules of sea-algae, roots of the chai hu plant, and angelica.[33]

Antibacterial and Antiallergenic Products

Antibacterial and antiallergenic cleansing product have been available in both mass-merchandised and prestige lines for a long time. Almay and Clinique exemplify the two ends of the market. A novel entry into this line of products is being pursued by Ralph Lauren with Polo Sport and Polo Sport Woman. Fragrance ancillaries, that is, cleansing products with the scent of fragrance lines bearing the same name, are introduced first. Then fragrance-free scrubs and moisturizers are offered as part of the same line.[34]

Aromatherapy Products

Aromatherapy involves fragrant oils distilled from plants, herbs, and flowers; these oils have been used for centuries to stimulate or relax. So important has the study of the physiological effects of fragrance on humans become that Annette Green, executive director of the Fragrance Foundation, coined the term *aromachology* to describe the modern, research-based phenomenon. Dr. Alan Hirsch of the Smell and Taste Treatment and Research Foundation in Chicago explains that specific feelings can be transmitted through odor because the olfactory nerve of the nose attaches directly to the limbic system of the brain, which influences emotions, memory, hormone secretion, appetite, and sexuality.[35] This connection explains the association of smells with memories of people and places. Some scents that promote emotional responses and behaviors are listed in Table 13.3. Notice that food scents are especially influential.

The fragrance industry has this research to use in the development of home fragrances, and that segment of the market has consequently been thriving. The Association that actively promotes aromatherapy research is the Sense of Smell Institute.

Spa Products

The ultimate indulgence in personal care is a visit to a health spa. The word "spa" originally referred to a European institution built around a thermal spring, where doctors sent the chronically ill for treatments lasting weeks. Today, spas are springing up in health clubs, department stores, and beauty salons across the country; where they offer treatments lasting a day, or a few hours. Most modern **spas** offer a wide range of services, including massages, manicures, pedicures, waxings, and facials, which often are combined with aromatherapy. In addition, one can, for a price ranging from $20 to more than $200, be completely covered in a body wrap, which is thought to cleanse and heal the skin and relax the body. In a **body wrap**, herbs, seaweed, or mud is applied directly to the body, which is then wrapped like a mummy to allow the substances to penetrate

TABLE 13.3 The Effects of Scents

SCENT	EFFECT
Spiced apple	Lower blood pressure, ward off panic attacks, reduce stress
Plum, peach	Reduce pain
Jasmine, green apple	Lift depression
Geranium	Dispels anxiety
Peppermint, lemon	Restore energy
Camomile, rose, vanilla	Relax the spirit
Cloves, cinnamon, oriental spices	Increase sensuality
Seashore, cucumber	Combat claustrophobia
Floral scent	Promotes faster puzzle-solving
Lavender	Increase sensuality, promotes alertness

Source: Renee Covino Rouland, "The Bath and Shower Experience," *Discount Merchandiser* and Maxine Wilkie, "Scent of a Market," *American Demographics*.

the pores. In a similar procedure, the wrapping cloths are soaked in the substances and then wrapped around the body. Body wraps date back to Biblical times and came to America by way of Europe, where they have been popular for centuries. The muds and other substances used in spa products still have many of the same sources, like the famed Dead Sea salts. The experts who administer these therapies and the special equipment available at spas give them an aura of alternative medicine, providing a rationale for the consumer's investment. Spa products fit in with the trend in cosmetics toward products that promote the health of the skin.

Treatments with **fango**, a mud rich in minerals, are popular, as are **exfoliation treatments**, which remove dead cells, smooth the skin, and promote circulation. Anticellulite treatments are frequently available. Many spas also offer **thalassotherapy**, which involves sea water, seaweed, or sea algae, and is believed to hydrate and rejuvenate the skin.

Individualized Products

Another trend relies on modern technology, particularly on computers. Personalized toiletries, makeup, and fragrances are being developed at the cosmetics counter for—and sometimes by—the customer. For example, a computer at General Nutrition Company's Alive store in Altamonte Spring, Florida, allows the customer to program a set of products using a base—say, shampoo or liquid soap—and various additives. Sample scents are available at the counter, and the computer provides information about the benefits of various ingredients so that the customer can tailor the recipe to her needs and tastes. A machine mixes the product on the spot, and the computer's database stores the formula for easy reordering.

During Fragrance Fun Day, an event sponsored by the Fragrance Foundation, industry experts offer "fragrance makeovers." People fill out a fragrance profile chart and have a fragrance concocted just for them by prefumers and technicians.[36]

A more low-tech manifestation of product personalization is the promotional makeover by a brand-line representative at the department store counter. Like the do-it-yourself displays, the activity on the sales floor attracts the attention of passing shoppers and builds brand loyalty on the part of customers who acquire a customized cosmetics and fragrance collection.

Reflections of Trends

The focus of the cosmetics and fragrance industry in the 2000s echoes trends in other segments of the fashion industry. New and newly popular cosmetics products respond to the same trends as apparel and accessories, as the examples in Table 13.4 show.

TABLE 13.4 Fashion Trends in Apparel and Accessories to Cosmetics and Fragrances

TREND	APPAREL AND ACCESSORIES	COSMETICS AND FRAGRANCE
Health and fitness	Activewear, workout apparel, summer hats, and sunglasses to protect from sun's rays	Skin care products, spas and spa products, sun-protection products, hypoallergenic and antiaging products
Casual lifestyle	Dress-down Fridays and informal office dress codes	Light fragrances, light makeup for no-makeup look
Individuality	Easing of business dress codes, mix-and-match separates, size lines for different figure types, and custom-fit jeans	Customize cosmetics and fragrances, marketing in record stores and sporting goods stores
Internationalism	International corporations and conglomerates, global marketing, marketing on the Internet, breakdown of trade barriers, international sourcing	Same as apparel and accessories
Multiculturalism	Adaptation of ethnic themes by designers; textiles and patterns from around the world; Native American, Indian, and African jewelry and other accessories	Ethnic cosmetics lines, ethnic hair care products and hairstyles (hair extensions, dreadlocks), menhadi, shiatsu, reflexology, and thalassotherapy

SUMMARY AND REVIEW

Over the past ten years, cosmetics and fragrances have proliferated in the global marketplace, sparked by advances in science and technology. Today's consumer selects a cosmetic or fragrance not only for its ingredients, but also for its packaging, its promotion, and where it can be bought. Some stores are perceived as having higher status and therefore many product lines are only sold in these types of stores, through a manufacturer's own sales force, through direct mail, or the Internet.

The main categories in this industry are fragrance, color cosmetics, skin care, sun care, and nail care. While the U.S. cosmetics industry is regulated by a number of state and federal laws, it is currently less regulated than Europe or Japan. The increasingly global nature of the industry will doubtless mean increased regulation in the coming decades. Also, environmental concerns like animal testing, recyclable packaging, and "natural" or botanical ingredients are leading to higher industry standards worldwide.

As the industry continues to expand, new market segments beyond the traditional women's market, have attracted increased attention. These segments include the male market, the teen market, the children's market, the ethnic market, the home fragrances market, and the export market.

Trends in cosmetics and fragrances follow those in apparel and accessories, and bear close attention. The major trends include antiaging products, antibacterial and antiallergenic products, aromatherapy products, spa products, and individualized products.

Trade Talk

Define or briefly explain the following terms:

alpha hydroxy acids (AHAs)
aromatherapy
body wrap
brand-line representative
color cosmetics
copycat scent
cosmetic
exfoliation treatment
fango
fragrance
fragrance wardrobe
franchise distribution
home fragrances
joint merchandising
mass distribution
note

premiums
private label manufacturers
rubber-banding
spa
thalassotherapy

For Review

1. How do the heads of the major cosmetics and fragrance firms today differ from their predecessors in the first decades of the 20th century?
2. What distinguishes perfume from cologne and toilet water?
3. How does the cosmetics industry relate to the ready-to-wear industry?
4. Summarize the Food and Drug Administration's laws in regard to cosmetics.
5. Where are the international growth opportunities for cosmetics and fragrance producers?
6. Describe the products of the home fragrance market.
7. Outline the major distribution methods used by the cosmetics industry.
8. Describe the various advertising and promotion activities currently engaged in by the cosmetics industry.
9. Identify the major professional organizations of the cosmetics and fragrance industry and describe their activities.
10. Briefly discuss the most significant trends in cosmetics products today.

For Discussion

1. Discuss current trends in the cosmetics and fragrance industry as they relate to (a) mergers, (b) diversification of product lines, and (c) global marketing.
2. Discuss the recent growth in men's cosmetics and ethnic cosmetics lines.
3. Cosmetics salespersons, or brand-line representatives, exercise much more control over the products carried in their stock than do salespeople in other departments in a store. Discuss the system used, and its advantages and disadvantages.

References

1. Chris Tullett, "Global Goals," *Soap, Perfumery & Cosmetics*, October 1, 1995, p. 25.
2. Mary Tannen, "The Guest of Honor Sure Smells Good," *New York Times*, August 3, 1997, Styles, p. 37.
3. Dorothy Carey, "Max Factor," *Economist*, June 15, 1966, p. 82.
4. Ellen Tier, "Pulse," *New York Times*, September 17, 2002.
5. "Unilever Sells off Fragrance Brands," *Marketing*, August 15, 2002, p. 4.
6. Andrea M. Grossman, "Unilever Enters Hair Color Mix," *Women's Wear Daily*, June 2002, p. 2.
7. "Wella Group Acquires Escada Beauty Group," *European Report*, March 20, 2002, p. 600.
8. Vanessa Friedman, "What's in a Scent?" *Elle*, p. 86.
9. Jill Leovy, "Making a Name, Product for Itself; Cosmetic Group USA to Launch Hair-Care Line in Bid to Diversify," *Los Angeles Times*, January 3, 1995, p. 4.
10. Stephen Finichell as interviewed by Scott Simon on "Plastic—The Dominant Material of Our Time," *Weekend Edition—Saturday (National Public Radio)*, August 10, 1996.
11. Jennifer Weil, "Innovation is Perpetual Driver," *Women's Wear Daily*, July 19, 2002.
12. Faye Brookman, "Copycat Scents Looking Like the Real Deal," *Women's Wear Daily*, January 10, 1997, p. 6.
13. Definition, Federal Trade Commission.
14. Shari Roan, "Atop the Wrinkle-Cream Heap; Medicines: Renova Has the Backing no Competitor Does: the FDA's Blessing. It's no Wonder Drug, But It Does Reduce Facial Lines," *Los Angeles Times*, January 6, 1996, p. E-2.
15. Kyle Samperton, "Task Force: Stop Thief!" *Women's Wear Daily*, February 1997, p. 14.
16. Brian Alexander, "Eco-Wise Cosmetics," *Self*, June 1996, pp. 54–56.
17. "Top Notes," *Women's Wear Daily*, July 2002.

18. Hilary Schrafft, "Keeping Up Appearances," *Soap, Perfumery & Cosmetics*, October 1, 1995, p. 56.
19. Chantal Tode, "Gillette Cleans Up Men's Grooming," *Women's Wear Daily*, April 4, 1997, p. 10.
20. Pete Born. "Aramis Shines With Men's Skin," *Women's Wear Daily*, April 4, 1997, p. 8.
21. Kerry Diamond, "Premium by Phat Farm: Hip Hop in a Bottle," *Women's Wear Daily*, June 29, 2001.
22. Cosmetics International Products Report, June 2002, p. 7.
23. Regina Molano, "Teen Beat: Wondering What Makes Teens Tick?" *Global Cosmetic Industry*, July 2001, p. 20.
24. Fay Brookman, "Nail Color Is Jane's Latest Tip," *Women's Wear Daily*, April 4, 1997, p. 11.
25. "Sassaby Deal Opens Mass Market to Estee Lauder," *New York Times*, September 9, 1997, p. D-5.
26. Regina Molano, "Teen Beat: Wondering What Makes Teens Tick?" Global Cosmetics Industry, July 2001.
27. Emily Otani, "Upscale Scrub-a-Dub; Parents Sparing No Expense for Kids' Personal-Care Products," *Los Angeles Times*, January 30, 1997, p. D-1.
28. "Population Shifts Impact Retail," *MMR*, June 17, p. 74.
29. "Ethnic Research," *Soap & Cosmetics*, July 2001, p. 9.
30. Julie Naughton, "Shiseido's Future Solution," *Women's Wear Daily*, August 23, 2002, p. 7.
31. Jim Ostroff, "A New World Order," *Women's Wear Daily/CFTA Special Report*, February 1997, p. 28.
32. Phyllis Furman, "The Fjoul Scent in Fragrances," *Crain's New York Business*, December 21, 1997, p. 23.
33. Julie Naughton, "Shiseido's Future Solution."
34. Jenny B. Fine, "Ancillaries Shed Secondary Role," *Women's Wear Daily*, May 1996, p. 4.
35. Melinda Voss, "Aromatherapy—The Sweet Scent of Health," *Gannett News Service*, May 22, 1996, pp. arc.
36. Tip Gabriel, "That Aura of Masculinity, and Foliage," *New York Times*, June 8, 1997, Styles, p. 35.

CHAPTER 14

Home Fashions

WHAT'S IN IT FOR YOU?

Everything you always wanted to know about the home fashions industry.

Key Concepts:

- History of the home furnishings industries
- Organization, operation, and product categories of soft goods and tabletop goods industries
- Market segments of the home fashions industry
- Market centers and resources of the home fashions industry
- Fashion influences in the home fashions industry
- Influences of technology on the home fashions industry

It is said that a man or woman's home is his or her castle. Whether that home is a spacious, sprawling mansion or just one room that you can call your own, it is your castle. It is a place to relax, be solitary, entertain friends, and establish an environment that supports your lifestyle. Therefore, creating a sanctuary that you look forward to coming home to has become the dream of people in the 21st century.

As Americans spend more time at home, they are also spending more of their money on home decorating—and redecorating—and less on their personal wardrobes. This trend is especially apparent in the dominant markets segment for fashion goods—baby boom women. So fashion designers, textile manufacturers, and retailers are turning their attention to the home furnishings and home accessories business. **Home fashions** is the umbrella term used frequently today to describe the two fashion-driven industries that have long been called *home furnishings* and *home accessories*. In this text we use all three terms, since that is what you will see and hear in the field.

In this market, fashion exerts its greatest influence in the **soft goods** lines, including bed, bath, and table linens; curtains and draperies; upholstery fabric; and area rugs, and in the **tabletop** categories of dinnerware, glassware, flatware, hollowware, and giftware (see Figure 14.1). (Furniture, electronic equipment, home appliances, and wall-to-wall carpeting have slower fashion cycles; these items are typically one-time purchases or long-term investments. They are beyond the scope of our discussion.)

A serious problem for both manufacturers and retailers of home furnishings is the vast amount of product knowledge that is required to sell these products. The challenge of sales staff education is a great one; the most successful manufacturers share the burden with retailers by providing extensive sales aids.

History of the Home Furnishings Industries

The types of furnishings and household accessories in contemporary American homes are based primarily on models and ideas that the early European immigrants brought with them. Most of our beds and eating utensils, for example, are Western. But many of the fabrics and other material, the decorative patterns, and the objects themselves originated in the East and came to America *through* rather than *from* Europe. The rugs that covered the floors in medieval European castles were imported by the crusaders, and when later Europeans established their own rug factories, the designs evolved from patterns developed in Turkey, Persia, India, and China. China was also the source of the finest quality of clay for ceramic dinnerware. Before there were Wedgwood and Royal Doulton potteries in England, British nobles imported their custom designed dinnerware with the family crest from China through the British East India Company.

FIGURE 14.1
Even the most casual table settings can be stylish.
Courtesy, Fairchild Publications, Inc.

The Role of Linen

From ancient times, linen was used in the Middle East and Europe for clothing and bedding. When medieval Europeans began sitting at a table for meals rather than reclining, they wiped their hands on remnants of linen cloth covering the table. The association of linen with sheets, tablecloths, and towels was so strong that even today, when these household accessories are usually made of other textiles, we still refer to bed, table, and bath linens.

Today, linen household accessories are being revived by such designers as Ralph Lauren, Donna Karan, and Calvin Klein; sheer weaves are appearing as curtains; and Turkish rug producers are experimenting with the fiber.

The history of tabletop goods is more varied that that of linen and so will be discussed under each category.

The Evolution of Global Home Fashions

Travelers since Marco Polo have brought home examples of native crafts and handwork to beautify their homes and impress their friends. Today materials, designs, and finished goods move simultaneously in both directions between East and West and beyond. African kente cloth patterns appear on American bed linens; sisal from Brazil and Tanzania is imported into the United States for rugs; Japanese apartments feature Western rooms; and Americans buy their bedding from specialized futon shops. Home fashions retain their distinctive local character, but they are enjoyed in homes far from their point of origin.

Organization and Operation of the Industries

Manufacturers of soft goods and tabletop merchandise can be found all across the country. Their showrooms, however, are centered in

New York, like the showrooms for other categories of fashion merchandise. And as in other fashion businesses, the home fashions industry involves the widespread and growing use of licensing agreements.

Size and Location of Soft Goods Manufacturers

As the United States grew from an agricultural nation to a vast industrialized one, textile mills and manufacturers of textile home furnishing products were established in the cotton-growing South. The major American textile mills are also the largest manufacturers of goods produced from their fabrics. Some mills specialize in apparel textiles and products or in home furnishing textiles and products, and others manufacture both.

Because household linens are essentially flat sheets of cloth, they require little work beyond the manufacturing of the textiles, perhaps hemming or the addition of decorative trim. Bedspreads, comforters, blankets, and curtains are also manufactured by the same vertically integrated companies and may be coordinated with bed or bathroom linens. Similarly, area rugs are often manufactured by carpet mills.

Table 14.1 lists some of the major textile mills that also produce their own brands of home furnishings products. Acquisitions of companies or divisions by other firms has concentrated most of the business in a few giant corporations. According to the U.S. Department of Labor, more than two-thirds of the workforce in the industry work for firms with more than 100 employees, and these businesses account for nearly three-quarters of the wholesale value of the merchandise produced. Most of the low- to moderate-priced, standardized household linens come from the large mills. Typically, smaller companies specialize in high-end merchandise and purchase their textiles from carefully chosen domestic or overseas suppliers.[1]

Size and Location of Tabletop Manufacturers

The fashion influence on the marketing of household linens and other soft goods for the home is also apparent in the hard lines of home furnishings. Everything from furniture to kitchen appliances has a fashion cycle. Our discussion focuses on the categories of tabletop goods because the role of fashion is most apparent in these segments of the home furnishings industry. From the time the medieval Europeans began to use forks instead of fingers, the basic items in a table setting have not changed significantly in function. Design criteria drive the consumer's buying decision. Today, when home entertaining has become a widespread leisure time activity, the selection of fashionable tabletop goods is part of the fun.

Because the three categories of tabletop goods—dinnerware, glassware, and flatware—are used together, manufacturers in each category have grown through expansion into the other categories and through mergers and acquisitions. Some large firms also include companies or divisions that produce table linen and products outside of the home furnishings industry. For example, Lenox, the leading U.S. manufacturer of china dinnerware, also produces crystal and giftware; the company's parent corporation since 1983 is Brown-Forman, which also owns such other manufacturers of tabletop goods as Dansk Contemporary Tabletop, Gorham, and Kirk Stieff, as well as producers of wine and spirits (Jack Daniels, Southern Comfort, Bolla) and Hartmann, maker of upscale luggage and leather goods. There is no single geographic center in the United States or elsewhere for these companies that manufacture so many different products.

Other leading tabletop manufacturers include Fitz and Floyd, Syracuse China Company, Fiesta® by Homer Laughlin, Mikasa, Pfaltzgraff, Johnson Brothers, Villeroy & Boch, and Ralph Lauren.

Popular imports of tabletop products include Wedgwood, Franciscan (a division of Waterford Wedgwood USA Incorporated), Royal Doulton, Royal Albert, Royal Worcester, Portmeirion, and Spode from England. Limoges, Lalique, Baccarat, and Cristal d'Arques are famous French manufacturers. Orrefors crystal from Sweden is world famous as is Waterford crystal, which has been made in Ireland since 1731. In Italy, Silvestri and Bormioli Rocco E Figlio produce beautiful glassware. Versace and Armani, also from Italy, have a large collection of tabletop products, in addition to their world famous apparel collections. Rosenthal and Meissen china come from Germany, while Noritake, Sango, and Morimura are very popular lines from Japan.

Licensing

Designer names are not the only commodity licensed in the home furnishings industry. Colonial Williamsburg presents an example of

TABLE 14.1 Major Textile Manufacturers and Their Home Accessories Products

Name and Headquarters	Size ($ million in sales)	Selected Product Lines and Brands
Milliken & Company Spartansburg, SC	N.A.	Rugs
Mohawk Industries, Inc. Calhoun, GA	2,233	Rugs Aladdin, Bigelow, American Weavers, Karastan, Mohawk
Springs Industries, Inc. Fort Mill, SC	2,233	Bath linens, bed linens, bedspreads, window treatments Springmaid, Wamsutta bed and bath products, Bali, Graber window treatments Licensee of Walt Disney
WestPoint Stevens, Inc. West Point, GA	1,723.8	Bed and bath linens, bedspreads, blankets, comforters 5 Star Hotel bedding Lady Pepperell, Martex, Stevens, Utica bed and bath linens, Vellux blankets, Grand Potricion, Ralph Lauren, Disney, Joe Boxer
Pillowtex (bought Fieldcrest Cannon, Inc.) Dallas	1,055	Bath towels, bedding, blankets, throws, window treatments Cannon, Fieldcrest, Royal Velvet bed and bath products, Charisma
Crown Crafts, Inc. Berea, KY	219	Cotton throws, bedspreads, comforters, decorative pillows, draperies Licensee of Osh Gosh B'-Gosh, Disney's Winnie Classic Pooh, Sesame Street, Looney Tunes, Baby Guess, Royal Sateen, Churchill Weavers, Calvin Klein, Beatrix Potter
Thomaston Mills, Inc. Thomaston, GA	277.7	Bed linens, comforters, curtains Thomaston
Dan Rivers Roswell, Georgia	N.A.	Alexander Julian, Martha Stewart

Source: Compiled from a variety of sources, includiing Hoover's Company Profiles and Hoover's Company Capsules and the *New York Times*.

the stringent conditions of licensing by a cultural institution. Since 1981, Karastan has been producing its Colonial Williamsburg Collection of rugs in cooperation with the historic site. All designs in this collection are adaptations of actual 18th-century Indian and Persian imports that graced the homes of the Virginia gentry. All samples must be approved by Williamsburg curators and Karastan designers before the rug becomes part of the Colonial Williamsburg Collection.

Character licensing is the main form of licensing in the industries that manufacture tabletop goods, and most of the licensed characters appear on lines of dinnerware and glassware for children. Not surprisingly, Disney rules in the licensing of animated movie "stars" for glasses and dinnerware, as it does for sheets. The marketing campaigns for children's movies typically include a three to six month selling period for related merchandise, and the release of the movie in video form may add to the life of these products. In addition to sales through conventional retail channels, glassware featuring characters from movies and children's television shows is given away as promotional items by fast-food chains. Classic Disney characters—Mickey, Minnie, Donald, and friends—and classic literary characters like Winnie the Pooh have longer careers as licensed decorations.

Designing a Soft Goods Line

To meet and encourage the demand of cocooning consumers, manufacturers are designing coordinated lines of bedroom accessories. Sheets and pillowcases match or complement bed covers and window treatments; bath linen sets may also be coordinated with the bedroom lines (see Figure 14.2). These fashionable products generate replacement sales long before the replaced items wear out. However, the soft goods fashion cycle is slower than the apparel fashion cycle, lasting years rather than seasons. New colors and designs may be introduced annually or in two seasonal showings, but previous years' fashions are not totally replaced by new offerings. Some lines stop selling only when the producer discontinues them.

Even the need for color forecasting for home accessories is a 20th-century phenomenon. Earlier, bed linens were undyed, then they were bleached white, and finally colors and prints began to come on the market. For the past decade, the color cycle has been reduced from ten-year periods of recent decades to colors remaining fashionable for just a few years. Ironically, environmentalism has made the neutral hues of undyed textiles one of the hottest new color trends. Trends in color are monitored and predicted by organizations such as the Color Association of the United States (CAUS) and the International Color Authority (ICA) and by companies such as Color Box and the Color Marketing Group.

The success of a new line of household linens depends on accurate forecasting of fashions in prints, weaves, and fabrics, as well as color, and on production processes that ensure timely availability. With computers, textile designers can create decorative prints or translate their hand-drawn designs into repeated patterns. Computer-aided design (CAD) programs allow them to produce a print design in several color combinations, thereby expanding their lines at a minimal increase in cost. CAD programs even produce decorative stitching patterns for quilts and "instruct" computerized quilting machines in how to sew them more quickly and accurately than conventional equipment.

FIGURE 14.2 *Coordination of sheets and pillowcases encourages replacement purchases by making fashion a consideration in the buying decision.* Courtesy, Domestications, a division of Hanover Direct, Inc.

Other consumer demands that manufacturers must consider in designing a line include finishes that enhance the products for their intended purposes. For example, table linens may be treated for stain resistance, and wool carpeting may be treated for protection from mildew, molds, and moths. Filling for pillows and comforters can be treated with chemicals that protect allergy sufferers from bacteria and dust mites. Techniques for decorating linens with print patterns affect the feel—and price—of sheets and bath and kitchen towels.[2]

The demand by ecology-minded consumers for natural products has given rise to lines of 100 percent cotton bed and bath linens not treated with the bleaches that normally set dyes, or the formaldehyde in permanent-press finishes. These natural features create a fashion statement with their characteristic limited palette and wrinkles.

Importance of Name Designers

Whether the entry of apparel designers into the home furnishings industry made it a fashion business, or consumer interest in home decorating lured the designers into the home accessories market is a chicken-or-egg question. The important fact is that home fashions from name designers satisfy a consumer need. The designer's name on the label is assurance of a consistent look that the consumer recognizes from the designer's apparel lines. This is true even though the designer's involvement may be limited to providing—or merely approving—the print patterns and colors. Many licensing agreements leave textile selection and other production decisions, as well as the marketing plan, to the manufacturer.

Bill Blass was the first major American apparel designer to design a home fashions line in the 1960s. Laura Ashley followed in the 1970s, and Ralph Lauren in the 1980s. Since then Ralph Lauren has become the largest supplier of sheets, towels, and pillows to department stores, with annual sales exceeding $250 million. A number of designers have followed, among them Calvin Klein, Liz Claiborne, Ellen Tracy, Jessica McClintock, Donna Karan, Tommy Hilfiger, and Alexander Julian. Julian, who manages his home furnishings line rather than licensing his name, explains consumers' reliance on designer names this way:

Working on a wardrobe for their home is analogous to working on a wardrobe for their bodies. [If you are a designer,] your apparel and home furnishings lines are your means of facilitating people's understanding about you as well as pleasing yourself.[3]

Importance of Brand Names

If a designer's name conjures up a particular fashion image, brand names suggest other qualities that consumers also consider when they shop, such as textile selections and price points. The major textile mills that produce household linens are known to the public primarily by the brand names of their sheets and towels because consumers buy these end products more than they buy curtains, upholstery fabric, or bolts of fabric for home sewing.

Store brand names are also influential. When the Federated Department Stores conglomerate took over Macy's, one of the major attractions of the acquisition was Macy's expertise in marketing its private brands, such as the Charter Club brand of apparel and home accessories. By circumventing the middleman, retailers can sell their private brands for a lower price than comparable brand-name merchandise, even virtually identical goods manufactured by the same supplier. And the exclusivity of the private brand builds store loyalty. Charter Club is now carried by some other Federated stores, including The Bon Marché, Burdines, Goldsmith's, and Lazarus.

Some apparel specialty retailers who carry their own labels, such as The Gap, Banana Republic, Victoria's Secret, and catalog retailer Lands' End, have introduced home fashion lines.

Two high-end European manufacturers of bed linens are Porthault of France and Pratesi of Italy. Pratesi has seven "salons" in the United States, where a king-size sheet of Egyptian cotton sells for $3,000! In an arrangement that spans the Atlantic, famed Liberty of London has made a collection of its vast number of textile patterns available to Dan River of Virginia, for use in high quality bed linens.

Designing a Tabletop Line

Tabletop goods respond to the same trends that affect other segments of the home furnishings industry and other fashion industries. Producers rely on resources such as the Color Marketing Group for forecasts of color, design themes, and other changing consumer preferences. This information leads to the introduction of new patterns and sometimes the discontinuation of old ones. Waterford Wedgwood USA Incorporated, for example, addressing the trend toward an informal lifestyle in the 1990s, introduced updated designs in its Home and Embassy collections of casual china. Public interest in ecology, combined with the promotion of gardening by Martha Stewart and others, has given rise to the decoration of tabletop products with floral patterns and gardening themes. At the same time, plain white and white-on-white patterns have gained in popularity.

Producers also base technical production decisions and the allocation of resources to particular product categories on their analyses of trends in the marketplace. When consumers are cautious about investing in high-ticket purchases, manufacturers may promote giftware items and introduce more new pieces in that category rather than focusing on lines of formal china dinnerware or sterling flatware. Another strategy, exemplified in the manufacturing of dinnerware, is to improve productivity and reduce costs through technological advances. A new heat transfer processes for applying multicolor decorations to ceramic wares has enabled manufacturers to offer a more saleable product in moderately priced lines.

Importance of Brand Name

Although manufacturers of tabletop goods produce a variety of products, many of the larger firms are associated with the category that was their initial specialty. Indeed, some names conjure up a particular segment of a category or even the name of a pattern. The name Wedgwood is so closely identified with its most famous design that the background color is called Wedgwood blue.

Some manufacturers capitalize on their image in one home accessories category by developing coordinated or complementary lines in related categories. Waterford is using its reputation for fine lead crystal to gain entry into the market for table linens. It is having lines produced at different price point to attract different market segments. At the high end are lines for collectors of its glassware; and for newlyweds who want to own something with the Waterford name, the lower-priced lines are affordable. Hermés, the French luxury leather goods house, has expanded into table linens and accessories. The Hermés owned houses Lalique (glasswear and jewelry) and Puirforcat (handcrafted siverware) have also entered the dinnerwear market and offer glasswear, flatwear, and porcelain lines.

Product Categories of Selected Soft Goods

Textile fabrics and other materials, such as fur, leather, straw, cork, paper, and metal wire are used to decorate walls, floors, windows, and furniture. We will focus on the seven main categories of soft goods that bring fashion to home interior wardrobe (see Table 14.2).

Bed Linens

For several reasons, bed linens, especially sheets and pillowcases, are one of the most frequently purchased categories of home accessories. For a weekly change of freshly laundered sheets and pillowcases, a stock of three sets is recommended, "one set on the bed, one in the wash and one in the closet." Furthermore, a change of bedding is a relatively inexpensive way to achieve a dramatic change in the look of a room, especially if the colors and patterns of various items are mixed and matched. Buying a new bed often means buying new bed linens to fit, for example when a baby outgrows its crib or adults in the family opt for a larger bed. New mattresses, which may be as thick as 14 inches, may require new fitted sheets and mattress pads with more generous corner pockets than the bedding designed for older 8-inch-thick mattresses.

Although linen and even silk are used for luxury sheets, most sheets are made of cotton/polyester blends or cotton of a tight, smooth weave called **percale**. Two criteria are used to judge their quality, thread count and cotton content. **Thread count** refers to the number of threads per square inch. A higher count indicates a finer, softer sheet. Thread counts range from 180 to 350 or more; 200 is considered standard.

Cotton/polyester blends are common in mass-merchandised sheets and offer a no-iron finish and moderate price, but 100 percent cotton is preferred for its softness. **Pima** cotton sheets are woven with at least eight percent of a high-quality cotton fiber from Arizona. Supima sheets are made of 100 percent pima cotton. The finest cotton for sheets and pillowcases is imported Egyptian cotton. In harsh winter cli-

TABLE 14.2 Seven Major Categories of Soft Goods

CATEGORY	EXAMPLES
Bed linens	Sheets, pillowcases, bed covers, blankets, pillows
Bath linens	Towels, washcloths, floor coverings
Table linens	Tablecloths, napkins, placemats
Window treatments	Curtains, shades, blinds, valences
Upholstery fabric	Slipcovers, pillows
Miscellaneous	Throws, kitchen towels, appliance covers, etc.
Area rugs	Scatter rugs, runners

Then & Now

Betty Crocker Bakes . . . Martha Stewart Cooks!

Somewhere, possibly hidden in a drawer or in the attic, there is a copy of *The Betty Crocker Cookbook*, which was used by most American housewives in the 1920s, 1930s, 1940s, and 1950s. On the cover is an apple-cheeked, smiling woman who promises recipes for successful cakes and pies, stews and roasts. In those days, home cooking was considered "the way to a man's heart" and the guarantee of a happy marriage.

Today, the apple-cheeked woman whose face smiles out at you from books, magazines, and TV screens is more likely to be Martha Stewart. She can be found radiating confidence as she extols the virtues of the perfectly baked crust for chicken pot pie, or the best way to stack firewood, or how to use kitchen curtains as decorations for a birthday party.

Although both women are attractive and helpful, there are major differences between them. Betty Crocker is ficticious; her name is used by the giant General Mills Foods Company to persuade women to buy their products through the recipes in the cookbook. Martha Stewart is a living dynamo, who singlehandedly built a vast business empire that includes books, magazines, TV shows, bed and bath merchandise, designer paint, and, since May 1997, a Web site. In today's world of Calvin Klein, Ralph Lauren, and Tommy Hilfiger, Martha Stewart is now perhaps this country's preeminent female brand name, surpassing Donna Karan and Liz Claiborne.

In a 1945 poll, Betty Crocker was among the most recognized women in the country. By 1999, Martha Stewart could make the same claim. Then was Betty Crocker . . . now is Martha Stewart . . . except that there is also a Betty Crocker Web site today and her new cookbook is in its eighth edition. By 2003, Martha Stewart experienced international coverage, but not on her home products. Will Martha reign as long as Betty Crocker? Time will tell.

Sources

Betty Crocker Web Site. Available at http://www.bettycrocker.com.

Pogrebin, Robin. "Master of Her Own Destiny," *New York Times*, February 8, p. 31.

Martha Stewart Web Site. Available at http://www.marthastewart.com.

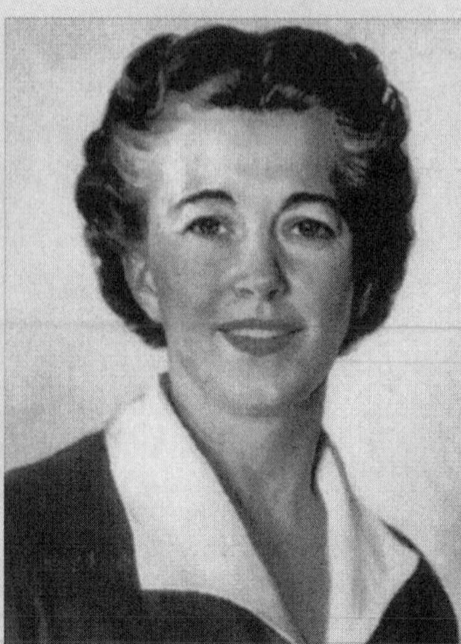

Betty Crocker, ca. 1955
Courtesy, General Mills.

Martha Stewart
Courtesy, Fairchild Publications, Inc.

mates, soft flannel (cotton brushed to raise the nap) sheets are often used for additional warmth.

There are many subcategories of bed linens, including sheets, pillowcases, bedcovers, blankets, and pillows. Some of the latest fashions involve the choice of bed covers. Replacing bedspreads with a cozier, less formal look are quilts, comforters, and duvets. The **duvet** (pronounced doo-VAY), a down-filled quilt in a cover, can serve as an all-in-one top sheet, comforter, blanket, and decorative covering. Some bedding sets include coordinated sheets and pillowcases, pillow **shams** (covers that go over the pillowcase when the bed is not in use), a duvet cover, and a dust ruffle or bed skirt (which tucks between the mattress and box spring and hangs to the floor). Sets of coordinated sheets, pillowcases, comforter, shams, and dust ruffle, called Bed-in-a-Bag, were introduced by Dan River; customers responded enthusiastically to the convenience of this product.

Sheets and pillowcases are sized to fit standard-sized mattresses and pillows. Note that a **California king** is an extra-long, extra-wide sheet, and that an extra-long twin sheet is the size usually found in dorm rooms.

FIGURE 14.3
This historic Hudson's Bay Point Blanket is carried by L .L Bean, Inc. Each short line or "point" represents one beaver pelt, used for trade by trappers two centuries ago. L .L Bean thought so highly of this blanket that he gave one as a wedding present to newly married employees-a practice that the company continues today.
Courtesy, L. L. Bean, Inc.

A version of traditional Japanese bedding has been adapted to Western use and sizing. In Japan, where people remove their shoes on entering a home, and floors are covered with thick *tatami* mats, bedding is placed on the *tatami* for sleeping and rolled up for storage during the day. A densely filled **futon** serves as a mattress, and a top futon, as a comforter. The Western version, the heavier bottom or mattress futon, is often sold with a hinged wooden frame. For sleeping, the futon is placed on the flat frame. The frame can be folded, and the futon draped over the back and seat to convert the bed into a couch.

Bath Linens

The most distinctive characteristic of bath linens is the cotton terry cloth that is used for virtually all towels. The loop construction of the threads creates a spongy fabric that holds water, thus enhancing the natural absorbency of cotton. The base from which the loops project may have a small amount of polyester woven with the cotton to prolong the life of the towel. The fabrication of textiles for other bathroom accessories, such as rugs and covers for toilet seat lids and toilet tanks, typically echoes the texture of terry cloth.

Because towels are a staple item produced in standardized sizes, they are a natural candidate for automated manufacturing. Machinery in some large mills can measure, cut, hem, and even fold towels. The plain-textured towels that make up the largest portion of the market are produced this way. The major manufacturers subcontract to smaller companies to produce towels with decorative features, such as embroidery.

Adding fashion to function are the rainbows of choices in single colors and patterns. Sculptured towels provide another design detail. Textures include waffle-weave, corduroy-like ribbing, chevrons, and other patterns. Along with the proliferation of soaps, body washes, shampoos, and lotions, giant fluffy bath sheets and other attractive bath linens add an element of luxury to personal hygiene (see Figure 14.4).

Table Linens

The informality of the contemporary American lifestyle has reduced the everyday use of table linens. Placemats and paper napkins are the

FIGURE 14.4
Today, bath towels are sometimes coordinated with other mechandise such as tumblers and soap dishes.
Courtesy, Coldwater Creek Bed and Bath Catalog, Coeur D'Alene, Idaho.

norm at many dinner tables. On the other hand, this informality has elevated the dinner party to the level of a state occasion, even when the guests are close friends and the atmosphere is casual. For the sizeable segment of the population who enjoy home entertaining as a leisure pastime, attractive table linens lend elegance to the meal.

Tablecloths are manufactured in a variety of sizes and shapes, and matching napkins are usually sold separately so that customers can buy as many as they need. The choices of textiles and weaves range from fine damask and cotton/linen blends, usually in white or off-white, for formal settings to more colorful synthetics for an informally decorated table. Stain-resistant and no-iron finishes are especially appealing to customers with small children. Several kinds of table coverings that may be placed over a tablecloth for protection from spills and crumbs (like vinyl cloths) also vary the table setting.

Window Treatments

As the link between a room and the outside world, windows are a focal point of interior design. There are so many ways of accenting a window with textiles—not to mention wooden shutters and plastic, metal, and wooden blinds—that labels like curtains or draperies are too limited. Interior decorators refer to this vast category as window treatments. There are many important subcategories and items. Each contributes to the character of the window and the room, creating an atmosphere of openness or privacy, casualness or formality, streamlined simplicity or ornateness.

The main distinction between curtains and draperies is in the weight of the fabric. Draperies are made of heavier, opaque material and are often lined. Typically, they are hung from rods by hooks and can be opened or closed by pulling a cord. Curtains are made of lighter weight, translucent fabric and are unlined. They may be hung from rods, like draperies, or they may frame the window. Some window treatments combine curtains and draperies. Either may have a matching **valance**, a horizontal strip across the top of the window, or a valance may be used alone.

Today, window treatments are often made of acrylic, polyester, nylon, and other synthetics that are more resistant than some natural fibers to the fading effects of sunlight. Curtains, especially, are easy to maintain; they may be laundered at home and changed to coordinate with bed linens. Draperies and Roman shades are more often selected to match fabric wall coverings or complement the fabrics of upholstered furniture, so these window treatments may be replaced less frequently than curtains.

Upholstery Fabric

Furniture is expensive, making the selection of upholstery fabric an infrequent decision, but an important one for fashion-conscious consumers. Whether they are purchasing a single piece or decorating an entire room, they shop for furniture that works well with other pieces and with the window treatments, floor coverings, and other home furnishings to achieve a coherent decor. In response to recent consumer demand for increased decorating options, **slipcovers** have reemerged as a home fashion item (see Figure 14.5). They can protect the permanent upholstery and give a chair or sofa a new look. They are also often machine washable. A wide range of plastic gadgets has been developed to improve the fit of slipcovers.

The choice of material also has a significant influence on the look of upholstery, as well as its durability and ease of maintenance. In the 1990s, polyester and other synthetics have gained the acceptance of interior designers, who, for many years, favored cotton, linen, and silk. Nontextiles, such as leather and vinyl are also available for upholstery. Some new nontextiles, such as metallic yarn and thinly sliced cork, are being used in combination with textiles for upholstery, window treatments, and other home decorating purposes.

Miscellaneous Soft Goods

A whole host of miscellaneous items are sold as accessories to the major categories of home furnishings. For example, the firms that manufacture bath linens and the stores and departments that sell them to consumers also produce and sell beach towels, even though they are not intended for use in the home. Other items may be associated with several major categories, such as decorative pillows, which are featured with both bed linens and upholstered furniture.

FIGURE 14.5
Slipcovers are enjoying renewed popularity as a quick and relatively inexpensive way to change the look of upholstered furniture.
Courtesy, Crate & Barrel.

Throws, small woven blankets about 50 by 60 inches, became "hot" during the "cocooning" 1990s. In the beginning of the 2000s, throws were often made of luxury fabrics that echoed ready-to-wear runway trends. Popular materials for throws included cashmere, pashmina, silk, velvet, and faux fur.[4] An earlier kind of throw, called an "afghan," was a knitted or crocheted item, often handmade, and frequently displayed over the back of a sofa. Probably the most famous afghan is the multicolored one on the sofa in the TV sitcom *Roseanne*, now in reruns.

Area Rugs

In the category of soft floor coverings, **area rugs**, which cover most of the floor of a room but are removable, offer greater flexibility in decorating than carpets, which are permanently tacked to the floor. The distinction between rugs and carpets is sometimes lost in the common reference to "oriental carpets," which are more accurately referred to as "oriental rugs" (see Figure 14.6). The first rugs were hand woven and hand dyed in Asia, and the craft is still practiced in China, India, Turkey, and Iran (formerly Persia). Antique rugs from these countries are highly valued home accessories. Each rug-making region has its own distinctive patterns and colors, but **oriental rugs** have in common a rectangular shape; an oblong central field; the use of repeated geometric and floral motifs; borders, often a main border and secondary borders; and nearly—but not entirely—symmetrical designs.

In colonial times, most rugs were made at home; hooked or braided styles were made of textile scraps. Rich families had hand-made needlepoint rugs and chair covers. Rug manufacturing developed in the United States after the Revolutionary War and with the invention of the power loom by Erastus Brigham Bigelow in 1839, it became a major industry, expanding its market from the wealthy to lower income levels.

Today, natural fiber rugs manufactured in the United States rely heavily on imported materials. The soft wool from domestically raised sheep is less suitable for rugs than the coarser, more durable wool from mountain-raised sheep from such widespread sources as New Zealand,

FIGURE 14.6
Hand-loomed oriental rugs are prized worldwide as works of art. Selling them requires extensive product knowledge.
Courtesy, ABC Carpet and Home.

Pakistan, and Argentina. **Sisal**, a fiber derived from the leaves of a plant cultivated in Brazil and Tanzania, is imported for casual, modern rugs, especially for summer use.

Product Categories of Selected Tabletop Goods

A well-appointed table sets the stage for fine dining and demonstrates the host's mastery of the art of gracious home entertaining. Today's consumers can choose from broad selections of dinnerware, glassware, and flatware to suit their needs, no matter what their taste or budget. Some of the most commonly used items in each category are listed in Table 14.3. Two other important categories—hollowware and giftware—are often combined at the retail level.

Dinnerware

The term **dinnerware** refers to the whole range of serving vessels for presenting food to diners and the cups, bowls, and plates for holding individual portions. These pieces are sometimes collectively called *dishes*, but that term also has the narrower meaning of plates. The generic term *china* also has a more limited meaning, labeling only one of the materials of which dinnerware may be made. We will use the industry term dinnerware to avoid confusion.

Categories of Dinnerware

Dinnerware is available in glass and, in response to consumer concerns about breakage and price, in melamine and other plastics. However, most dinnerware is ceramic, that is, made of baked—or *fired*—clay. The quality of the clay is a major factor in the quality of the product. In ascending order of quality, the major clay bodies used for dinnerware are peasant pottery, earthenware, ironstone, stoneware, china (or porcelain), and bone china. Peasant pottery is most often used only for serving pieces or decorative objects. Hand-decorated Delft pottery from Holland and Majolica from Italy are valued as craft objects for display. Stoneware is common for everyday dinnerware, and china and bone china, with more formal decorative patterns, for serving guests.

Glazes and other decorative features of dinnerware also affect their value and durability and raise safety issues. In formulating glazes, manufacturers must balance the desired colors against the resistance of the glaze to the chemicals in detergent. Decorative gold trim renders a piece unusable in a microwave, and other aspects of the chemical composition control

TABLE 14.3 Dinnerware, Glassware, and Flatware

DINNERWARE	GLASSWARE	FLATWARE
Place Setting	*Stemmed*	*Four-Piece Place Setting*
Dinner plate	Brandy snifter	Knife
Salad plate	Champagne flute	Dinner fork
Cup	Cocktail	Teaspoon
Saucer	Cordial	Salad fork
Bowl	Sherry	
	Water	*Five-Piece Place Setting*
Accessory Pieces	Wine	Soup spoon
Bread plate		
Soup bowl	*Tumblers*	*Accessory Pieces*
Rimmed soup bowl	Iced tea	Iced tea spoon
Mug	Beer mug	Steak knife
	Juice	Butter spreader
Serving Pieces	Double old-fashioned	
Vegetable dish (some covered)		*Serving Pieces*
Platter	*Serving Pieces*	Salad fork and spoon
Coffee pot	Decanters	Salad tongs
Tea pot	Pitchers	Serving spoons
Sugar bowl		Meat fork
Creamer		Pie server
Cake plate		Cake rack

whether a product is oven-proof, dishwasher-safe, and suitable for the refrigerator or freezer.

Sets of Dinnerware

Dinnerware is usually sold in sets of service for four, eight, or twelve, including serving pieces and basic place settings. Service for four is common in casual patterns for everyday family use. The number of serving pieces may be limited, and the place settings may include only a dinner plate and cup and saucer. Five-piece place settings add a salad plate and a bowl or bread and butter plate to the basic items.

Customers can expand their sets of dinnerware or replace broken pieces by purchasing additional place settings or individual items. Pieces sold individually are called **open stock.** The most elaborate sets of dinnerware include plates, bowls, and cups that vary in size and shape according to very specific use. For example, a coffee cup is larger than a tea cup and has straighter sides. Most modern patterns, however, include fewer types of items, and contemporary consumers, with their informal lifestyle, do not demand such fine distinctions. In fact, a common practice is to build a set of dinnerware from open stock, coordinating items in the same pattern but different colors.

Glassware

Glass has long been recognized as a versatile material with properties suitable for many uses. Essentially, glass is sand, melted in a furnace and molded or blown into the desired shape and allowed to harden. Because the main component is nonporous, glass is ideal for vessels for storing and serving food and beverages. Examples of beautifully colored opaque glass vessels from ancient Egypt, Syria, and Rome have survived for thousands of years.

The English colonists brought the manufacturing of glass to America. In the 19th century, Americans made several technical contributions to the industry. A pressing machine, introduced in 1825 allowed for the production of pressed-glass patterns. The production of the first electric light bulbs by Corning Glass Works in

1879 was an early example of this company's focus on innovations in industrial uses of glass. But later Corning also developed glass products for oven-to-table use, including Pyrex and Corning Ware.

At the end of the century, Michael J. Owens of the Libbey Company invented an automatic bottle machine that greatly improved production processes. Now the largest glassware manufacturer in the United States, Libbey makes more than two thousand products including its popularly priced lines of drinking glasses.

The top quality is leaded glass, which has a minimum of five percent lead oxide. Full lead crystal has at least 24 percent lead oxide. The softness of lead crystal makes it easy to hand cut, and it is the most brilliant crystal. Some questions have been raised, however, about the leaching of lead into wine decanters, because the wine usually remains in the decanter for long periods.

Place Settings

Three types of glassware categorized by shape are **tumblers**, cylindrical glasses; **footed tumblers**, tumblers with a heavy bottom; and **stemware**, bowl-shaped glasses on a stalk or, as the name suggests, stem. The various shapes are designed to hold specific beverages. Water may be served in any of the shapes. Milk, fruit and vegetable juices, and sodas are typically served in tumblers or footed tumblers, and cocktails, in footed tumblers.

Drinking wine from the correct glass enhances enjoyment because the shape captures the bouquet. At a formal table, appropriate stemware may be set out for red and white wine. But modern society is not strict about the rules. Although manufacturers of fine crystal offer sets in matched patterns, many customers prefer to buy glassware from open stock and to set their tables with just one or two glasses at each place.

Flatware

The use of flatware is a relatively recent phenomenon, and it is not as widespread as the use of dinnerware or glassware. Think of all the Asian countries where chopsticks are used and the not-so-primitive societies that have developed ways of eating neatly without utensils. In fact, hors d'oeuvres, sandwiches, and other finger foods are common in cultures that serve other foods with flatware.

In medieval Europe, a banquet invitation was a "bring your own flatware" occasion. People of high social status acquired a personal silver knife, fork, and spoon set at birth and used their own utensils—in addition to their hands—wherever they ate. The Italians of the 16th century were the first to eat their meat with a knife and fork, and the practice was not widely accepted elsewhere in Europe for a hundred years. But once the idea of having a variety of knives, forks, and spoons took hold, the choices became overwhelming. Different spoons were designed for coffee and tea and for cream soups and clear soups.

Today flatware contributes to the style of a table setting. It can be formal or casual, traditional or modern, elegant or utilitarian. Ideally it makes eating easier and more pleasant (see Figure 14.7).

Categories of Flatware

Like "china" that is actually stoneware, "linens" made of cotton, and plastic "glasses," not all "silverware" is silver. Only sterling silver can accurately wear that label. It must be 92.5 percent silver and only 7.5 percent alloy metal (copper, for example, which is added for strength). If the flatware is silver plate, the proportions of silver to alloy are more or less reversed: the silver is a coating over an alloy core. *Vermeil* (pronounced ver-MAY) silver flatware dipped in gold to prevent corrosion of the silver by the chemicals in certain foods, may be made up in whole sets of flatware, or a few pieces, likely to be exposed to damage, may be treated.

FIGURE 14.7
In addition to the typical place setting shown here, high-end flatware is made in a bewildering array of sizes and shapes.
Courtesy, Albert S. Smyth Company, Inc.

FASHION FOCUS

My Home Is My Castle

Williams Sonoma, Inc. is a home-centered business dedicated to developing an upscale everyday home life – good taste democratized! The company is comprised of Williams-Sonoma, Pottery Barn, Pottery Barn Kids, and Hold Everything.

Williams-Sonoma stores offer a wide selection of cooking and serving equipment, which include cookware, cookbooks, cutlery, informal dinnerware, glassware, table liners, specialty foods, and cooking ingredients. They certainly believe the eternal proverb – "The way to a man's heart is through his stomach" and vise versa.

Williams-Sonoma incorporated in 1956, during the first growth of young married homeowners who were looking for exciting, different and affordable home furnishings. In 1972, it introduced its direct-to-customer business with "A Catalog for Cooks," which marketed the Williams-Sonoma brand. In 1983 it developed the Hold Everything catalog that offered solutions for household storage made by providing organization solutions for every room in the house. In 1985, after the success of the catalog, it opened the first Hold Everything stores.

In 1986, the company acquired Pottery Barn, a retailer and direct-to-customer merchandiser that features large assortment of items in home furnishings, flatware, and table accessories. These are designed and developed internally and then produced worldwide to create a dynamic coordinated look in the home of the consumer.

In 1989, the company developed a mail-order catalog of high-quality linens, towels, robes, soaps, and accessories for the bed and bath called Chambers.

From 1999 to 2003, Williams-Sonoma entered the e-commerce world and launched the Williams-Sonoma Internet wedding Web site, Pottery Barn Kids Web site, and Pottery Barn online gift and bridal registry. During this same time, the company also launched the Pottery barn Kids catalog, which offers children's furnishings as will as Pottery Barn Kids stores across the United States. In addition, Williams-Sonoma, Pottery Barn, and Pottery Barn Kids retail stores were opened in Toronto, Canada.

A new catalog, called West Elm, that targets young, design-conscious consumers looking to furnish and accessorize their apartments, lofts, or first homes with quality products was launched in 2002. The categories include furniture, decorative accessories, tabletop items, and an extensive textile collection. The company plans to expand this concept at the retail level through the next decade.

Today there are 415 retail stores located in 41 states and Toronto, Canada. This represents 214 Williams-Sonoma, 145 Pottery Barn, 27 Pottery Barn Kids, 15 Hold Everything, and 14 outlet stores. The company plans to increase retail space by 14 to 15 percent over the next few years.

The direct-to-customer operations has six merchandising concepts and sells products through six-direct-mail catalog and four e-commerce Web sites. Of all the different concepts, the Pottery Barn brand has been the major source of sales growth for the past several years.

Producing over $2 billion in sales, the genius of Chuck Williams is seen in the success for good, functional items for the home. Make it simple, make it better, make it easy to buy . . . and they will come.

Sources

Profile – Williams-Sonoma, Inc. Available online at NYSE:WSM, http//www.big.yahoo.com, February 3, 2003.

http//www.potterybarn.com

http//www.potterybarnkids.com

http//www.wsweddings.com

http//www.Williams-sonoma.com

Stainless steel flatware is manufactured for everyday use, but some of it is of high enough quality to be used with fine china. The best-known American manufacturers of flatware—Oneida, Reed & Barton, Gorham, Towle, and Steiff among them—offer patterns in all four categories.

Place Settings and Serving Pieces

Like other tabletop goods, flatware is sold in sets for four, eight, and twelve as well as open stock. The typical place setting consists of a knife, dinner fork, salad fork, and teaspoon, and in some sets, a soup spoon. Serving utensils are designed to facilitate transfer of a portion from the serving dish to the individual's plate. Slotted vegetable spoons drain the vegetables; a pie server slides neatly under the slice; and so on.

Hollowware

The term **hollowware** covers a variety of metal service items such as trays, candlesticks, sugar bowls and creamers, coffee pots, and tea pots. Common materials for hollowware include sterling silver, silver plate, and pewter. Some items may be kept on display in the living room or dining room and used for buffet service.

Giftware

Giftware is a thriving segment of the home accessories industry because of recurring gift-giving occasions. Some gifts may be made from any of a number of materials. Picture frames in wood, ceramic materials, a variety of metals, and even leather and papier-mâché are all popular. Giftware can be displayed on coffee tables, desks, and shelves, adding decorative accents to a room. Table 14.4 lists some of the more frequently given gift items.

An interesting aspect of the gift market is the proliferation of museum reproductions now available from institutions worldwide. In the United States, reproductions have become available not only from the Museum of Fine Arts, Boston, the Art Institute of Chicago, the Smithsonian, and the Metropolitan Museum of Art of New York, but also from smaller institutions like the Winterthur Museum in Delaware, Carnagie Hall, Historic Natchez, and the Henry Ford Museum. Some of these museums also have set up free-standing stores outside the museum.

In France, the Reunion des Musées Nationaux, an association of more than 60 of France's world-renowned museums, including the Louvre and Versailles, have banded together to make reproductions of their *objets d'arte* available to the world. The British Museum, the Victoria & Albert Museum, and the Royal Academy of Arts have also entered this lucrative business, as have the Athens museum, the Vatican Museum, and the Historical Museum Beijing, among others. High-end retailers often stock a few of these products to add cachet to their store or catalog.

Market Segments

New homes, whether they are the first apartment of a newly married couple, the expanded home of a growing family, or the vacation home that is the prize of financial success, provide a dependable market for the home furnishings industry. Replacement purchases, spurred

TABLE 14.4 Giftware

ALL-OCCASIONS	BABY GIFTS	DESK SETS
Picture frames	Cups	Blotters
Mirrors	Spoons	Bookends
Vases	Rattles	Pencil holders
Flower pots	Teething rings	Note pad holders
Candlesticks	Porringer	Letter holders
Candles	Comb and brush set	Letter openers
Clocks		Pen holders
Figurines		

by the cocooning of baby boomers, add a direction for growth. Other huge market segments, beyond the scope of this text, are the institutional and military markets.

Bridal

Marriages are a source of celebration for the home furnishings industry as well as for the newlyweds because they generate spending disproportionate to the small percentage of households—less than three percent in the United States—they represent. According to a study by *Modern Bride* magazine and Roper Starch Worldwide in 2001, 78 percent of all engaged women say that even though they and their fiancés each have furniture, they plan to replace or add some more in the coming months.[5] Many couples experience a sudden surge of money as they combine their incomes and reduce the costs of separate housing. They spend their windfall on setting up their new home, and well-wishers among their friends and family buy them gifts. The fact that half of all purchases of sterling silver flatware and giftware are for the bridal market is a dramatic indicator of the impact of this segment.

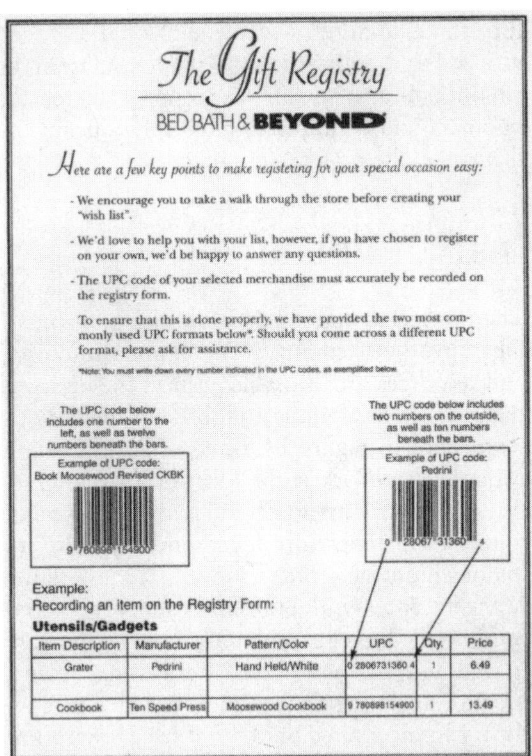

The Gift Registry

BED BATH & BEYOND

Here are a few key points to make registering for your special occasion easy:

- We encourage you to take a walk through the store before creating your "wish list".
- We'd love to help you with your list, however, if you have chosen to register on your own, we'd be happy to answer any questions.
- The UPC code of your selected merchandise must accurately be recorded on the registry form.

To ensure that this is done properly, we have provided the two most commonly used UPC formats below*. Should you come across a different UPC format, please ask for assistance.

*Note: You must write down every number indicated in the UPC codes, as exemplified below.

The UPC code below includes one number to the left, as well as twelve numbers beneath the bars.

Example of UPC code: Book Moosewood Revised CKBK

9 780898 154900

The UPC code below includes two numbers on the outside, as well as ten numbers beneath the bars.

Example of UPC code: Pedrini

0 28067 31360 4

Example:
Recording an item on the Registry Form:

Utensils/Gadgets

Item Description	Manufacturer	Pattern/Color	UPC	Qty.	Price
Grater	Pedrini	Hand Held/White	0 2806731360 4	1	6.49
Cookbook	Ten Speed Press	Moosewood Cookbook	9 780898154900	1	13.49

FIGURE 14.8
A gift registry scans the bar codes of the recipient's desired merchandise and the purchasers' selections onto computer for easy reference.
Courtesy, Bed Bath & Beyond.

Wedding or **bridal registries** in department stores and specialty stores give the retailer an opportunity to establish a good relationship with the customer by offering a service. They provide a record of the customer's taste and attract the business of gift-givers who want to be sure of making the right selection (see Figure 14.8). Today, most department stores and mass market retailers have added online registrations to compliment their computerized in-store registry programs. The store Target teamed up with NBC's *Today Show* to heighten the profile of its gift registration program Club Wedd. Club Wedd is the show's exclusive sponsor.[6] In 2002, the e-commerce giant Amazon.com launched a wedding registration service offering its customers wedding gifts in many categories, including electronics, tools, home entertainment systems, and DVDs.[7]

New Home/Vacation Home

When a family or individual moves into a new home, at whatever stage of the life cycle, possibilities open up for sellers of home furnishings. New housing starts tend to increase the demand for bedroom and bathroom products because the new homes typically have more bedrooms and bathrooms. Moves to accommodate the growth of a family feed the market for baby giftware as well as the market for bed linens. Going away to college involves buying bed and bath linens, perhaps even window treatments. Even a move into a retirement community involves home furnishing purchases; new window treatments, for example, when the old ones do not fit.

Vacation homes are often initially furnished with castoffs from the main residence. But the informal nature of life at the beach, in the mountains, or at a country retreat usually dictates a less formal style of decorating, with emphasis on easy upkeep. It is the rare vacation home that does not gradually get redecorated!

Replacement

The replacement market exists at many levels. Many young people begin their first apartments with hand-me-downs from relatives and friends. As their earnings grow, they replace the worst of the used items. Some households are seeking inexpensive replacements for broken or worn items. Many of these people will shop at garage sales, flea markets, thrift stores, or discounters. Others are trading up to slightly more expensive items. Thanks to cocooning baby boomers, redecorating has expanded the home furnishings market. This generational segment was a large proportion of the population in childhood, and as life expectancy increases, boomers will continue to have a significant influence on the replacement market.

Market Resources

The producers and marketers of home furnishings have both common and unique interests, and resources are available to meet the needs of the industry as a whole and those of the various segments (see Figure 14.9). As a world fashion capital, New York is the location of manufacturers' showrooms for home textiles and other home furnishings products and the site of major industry trade shows. The Atlanta Market Center, with 600 showrooms and proximity to the large textile mills, is also important in the international home furnishings scene. North Carolina is the center of the furniture industry in the United States and has showrooms that include upholstery, pillows, and other decorative objects. The vast Merchandise Mart in Chicago is devoted to furniture and various soft goods and tabletop merchandise.

Trade Associations

Organizations that promote all home furnishings industries include the Home Furnishings International Association in Washington, D.C., the International Home Furnishings Representatives Association in Chicago, and the International Housewares Association in Rosemont, Illinois, also maintain a broad overview.

The home textiles industry is served by trade associations that are also involved in apparel textiles. Cotton Incorporated and the Wool Council promote specific textiles, and the American Textile Manufacturers Institute has a more generalist mission. The Decorative Fabrics Association and the National Association of Decorative Fabrics Distributors focus on home textiles.

Because High Point, North Carolina, is the center of furniture manufacturing, it is also the home of the American Furniture Manufacturers Association and the Upholstered Furniture Action Council. Other associations that promote specific industry segments include the Carpet and Rug Institute in Dalton, Georgia; the National Association of Floor Covering Distributors in Chicago.

Trade Shows

New York, Chicago, and Atlanta, with their large numbers of permanent showrooms and vast convention facilities, host the biggest trade shows. The New York Home Textiles Show comes to the Javits Center each spring and fall. The New York Tabletop Market is also a major event.

The International Housewares Show in Chicago attracts thousands of buyers from around the world every January; the Chicago Merchandise Mart also draws buyers all year, because of the huge number of showrooms it contains. In Atlanta, the Atlanta International Area Rug Market features exhibitors and products from all over the world.[8]

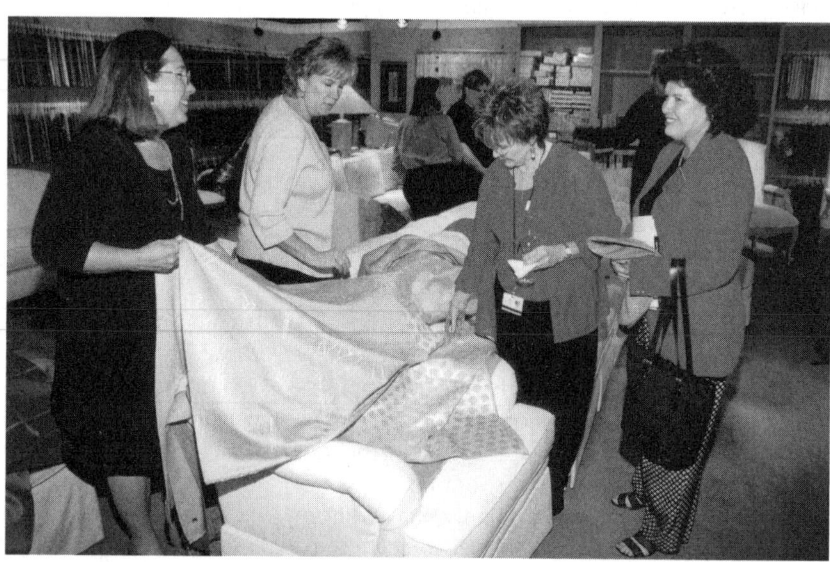

FIGURE 14.9
The International Gift and Home Accessories market in Dallas gives buyers the opportunity to see and feel the latest trends in home furnishings.
Courtesy, Dallas Market Center.

Another trade show is the Pacific Home Fashion Fair, which also provides opportunities for manufacturers, designers, jobbers, and retailers to meet.

Trade Publications

Weekly magazines for the home furnishings industry, such as *HFN—Home Furnishings News* and *Home Accents Today*, provide broad coverage. The following trade publications have a slightly narrower focus on home textiles: *Home Textiles Today*, and *LBD Interior Textiles*. Other trade publications, such as *Ceramic Industry* and *Upholstery Design & Manufacturing*, indicate by their name which segment of the market they serve. See Table 14.5 for more complete trade publications.

Merchandising and Marketing

Home furnishings can take many routes from manufacturer to consumer. Depending on the product, there may be a few or many stops along the way.

The distribution of textile products for the home is particularly complex and involves a number of professionals, each of whom adds service and expertise to the process. The major manufacturers display their household linens in their New York showrooms, and their sales representatives bring sample books with fabric swatches and photos of products to customers.

Retail Channels of Distribution

Consumers have a variety of resources to meet their home furnishings needs. For customized upholstered furniture and window treatments, as well as expert advice and access to goods not otherwise available, consumers can turn to professional interior designers. Some designers have their own firms and others are on staff at home furnishings and department stores.

Consumers who are making their own selections turn to different types of stores for different categories of goods. For example, mass merchandisers are the main source of household linens. The top sellers in this category are Wal-Mart, JCPenney, Kmart, and Target. Together they account for about 40 percent of the sales in this category.[9]

Some vendors see home centers as the fastest-growing channel. Many home center retailers are moving boldly into soft goods once thought incompatible with their hard lines and building products mix. One example is Home Depot's Right At Home decor program for its warehouse stores, which is growing rapidly.

For consumers who are bargain conscious but want more upscale merchandise than is available through the mass merchandisers, the category killer in home furnishings is the discount superstore. The leading chains are Bed, Bath & Beyond and Linens 'n Things. Overlapping their market is Williams-Sonoma, which are primarily retailers of housewares and appliances but also offer casual tabletop goods and other home fashion products. HomeGoods is the off-price chain of TJX Cos., which owns Marshalls and T. J. Maxx. Bath & Body Works

TABLE 14.5 Trade Publications for the Home Furnishings Industry

BROAD COVERAGE	SEGMENTS OF THE HOME FURNISHINGS INDUSTRY
FDM—Furniture Design and Manufacturing	*Ceramic Industry*
HFN—Home Furnishings News	*Floor Covering Weekly*
Home Accents Today	*Upholstery Design & Manufacturing*
Home Furnishings Executive	
Home Furnishings Review	
Homemarket Trends	
Interior Design	

At Home is the Limited's entry into this field. IKEA, a Swedish superstore chain, offers low-price furniture (some of which the customer assembles), home furnishings, and housewares. Manufacturers' factory outlets also appeal to this segment of the market.

The broad assortments in different product lines offered by the superstores have cut into the business of the traditional department stores. Some of the ways the department stores are holding onto their customers are by offering exclusive merchandise, including private brands; featuring designer lines in model room displays; and matching competitors' prices through periodic "white sales."

In categories in which the superstore discounters do not compete or where their offerings are limited, department stores continue as dominant players. They account for 40 percent of giftware purchases and about one-third of sterling silver flatware sales.

Specialty stores in this market segment compete by offering exclusive merchandise, often imported goods. Well-known examples are Pier 1, Crate & Barrel, Pottery Barn, The Bombay Company, and Domain. Specialty stores, with almost half the sales in the giftware segment, are the competitor to beat.

Nonstore retailing is another resource for consumers. Some stores, both specialist and general merchandise retailers, do a significant portion of their home furnishings business through catalog divisions. Bloomingdale's, Crate & Barrel, Eddie Bauer Home, Tiffany, and Gumps are a few examples that convey the range of retailers who have followed this route. Catalog retailers like Spiegel, Lands' End, and L. L. Bean have also added home furnishings to their lines. Specialty catalogs include Chambers (a high-end catalog from Williams-Sonoma/Pottery Barn), Ross-Simons Gift & Home Collection, the Horchow Collection, Domestications, Smith & Noble Windoware, and Country Curtains. All these companies also have their own Web sites that showcase and sell their products, as well as provide information about them.

Cable television retailers have entered this lucrative market. QVC has a special Linen Closet show on a regular basis. The latest development in home furnishings market is part of the larger trend to take advantage of the Internet. As the virtual neighborhood of the World Wide Web home pages grows, all segments of the market can play host or visitor to each other. The home page can be a store, an in-house public relations agency, and an advertising agency all rolled into one.

Advertising and Publicity

What could be more natural to cocooners and home decorating enthusiasts than to curl up with a magazine directed right at them? Home decorating magazines, known in the trade as **shelter magazines**, include *Architectural Digest*, *Better Homes and Gardens*, *House Beautiful*, *Metropolitan Homes*, *Colonial Homes*, *Country Living*, *Elle Decor*, and *Martha Stewart's Living*. They are a great medium for manufacturers to advertise to the public and build demand for their brands. Retailers, especially national chains, also advertise in these periodicals. Other magazines that feature ads for home furnishings include the bridal magazines like *Modern Bride*, women's magazines like *Woman's Day*, *The Ladies Home Journal*, and upscale magazines like *Town and Country* and *The New Yorker.* There are also a newer crop of magazines, including *Wallpaper*, *Surface*, and *City*, with content that focus on avant-garde trends in interior designs as well as fashion.

Magazines are perhaps even more beneficial as a source of publicity than as an advertising medium. They provide favorable mention by a presumably disinterested authority and show attractively photographed examples of a product or line in use.

Local newspapers are another advertising medium advantageous to both producers and retailers, who share the costs through cooperative advertising agreements. And local media can provide publicity to retailers for in-store events such as the opening of a new unit of a chain; a lecture by a home furnishings star; a home fashion show, perhaps featuring a designer; or a cooking demonstration that culminates in the presentation of a meal at a beautifully set table.

Store displays are also a vital component of home furnishings sales. As Dan Bonini of FSC Wallcoverings says:

> *Sales hinge on strong, coordinated merchandise displays that show customers how to create a complete room ensemble. I call it the mannequin effect. Customers want to buy what they see all put together for them.*[10]

Coordinated, mix-and-match choices are more popular than ever. Croscill Home Fashions, for example, offers a premerchandised display concept to both department stores and home centers.

Industry Trends

In the home furnishings industries, as in other aspects of daily life in the new millennium, fashion, technology, and environmentalism have been important influences. Responses at all levels to issues in these three areas affect each other and set the stage for the 21st century.

Growing Fashion Influence

We have already observed how baby boomers have turned their fashion interests toward their homes and how apparel designers, alert to the trend, have responded.

In some ways the cycle is speeding up. The collection of home furnishings designed by Martha Stewart, icon of gracious living, is now sold by Kmart. In 2003, with Kmart in bankruptcy, Martha Stewart began selling her products in other stores. Anyone, class or mass, who wants to know the latest news from designers, producers, or marketers of home fashions can find out on the Internet. The products themselves are available at affordable prices through discount superstores and factory outlets.

We have also seen how the life cycle of home fashion products has speeded up as consumers spend their money on replacement purchases that can give them a new look at relatively little expense. As producers use new technology to develop faster, more economical ways of manufacturing and delivering goods, their response has generated even greater demand.

Increased Automation in Design and Production

Computer-aided design (CAD) has arrived in both the hard and soft sides of the home furnishings industries. Hand-drawn designs can be scanned and patterns can be generated electronically. Manufacturing equipment can be programmed to reproduce these designs on dinnerware or upholstery fabrics. Employees are retrained to oversee automated production equipment rather than operate older machinery. American manufacturers have invested heavily in new automated equipment; for example, an automated hemming machine can hem all four sides of a flat sheet faster than manual sewing can (see Figure 14.11).

Automated production speeds up manufacturing and thereby enables producers to fill orders more quickly. Borrowing from the apparel industry, home furnishings manufacturers, especially textile producers, have instituted quick response procedures. Basically, quick response is a service that allows retailers to avoid the expense of excess inventory by placing orders on short notice. The retailer can keep enough stock to meet immediate demand but not be

FIGURE 14.10
Some companies offer both formal and informal tabletop products, to cover different lifestyles and different occasions.
Courtesy, Crate & Barrel.

FIGURE 14.11
This machine enables manufacturers to produce sheets using very wide fabric that is cut and hemmed by other computer-controlled machinery.
Courtesy, West Point Stevens

stuck with items that have passed their fashion peak. It is the computerized connection between retailer and supplier that enables both to analyze sales trends and adjust stock levels accordingly. Automation in the U.S. textile industry has had such a favorable impact on production costs that there is little impetus to reduce labor costs through offshore production.

Growth of Exports

One area in which the home furnishings industry is bucking a trend is international trade. Imports have focused on high-end merchandise, such as Egyptian cotton bed linens, Indian rugs, and fine china and crystal from famous European companies. Many of these products are valued for the tradition of artistry and craftsmanship they exemplify and for their distinctive designs. But the United States continues to lead the world in the design, manufacture, and export of mid-range bed and bath linens, rugs and carpets, and tabletop goods.

Increased Use of High-Tech Fabrics

New technology not only means faster and more highly automated production and delivery of products, but sometimes means changes in the very nature of the product. In the manufacturing of bedding, especially pillows, high-tech fibers now protect consumers from allergy-producing molds, mildews, fungi, and dust mites. **Antimicrobials**, compounds that are spun into acetate fibers, break down the cells of microbes that lurk in the moist atmosphere of bedding.

Other treatments of textiles include no-iron finishes on bed linens, antifungal finishes on drapery fabric, and pesticides in wool carpeting.

Increased Awareness of Ecological Issues

Countering the trend toward the use of high-tech fabrics is a demand for untreated natural materials. Manufacturers are responsive to this backlash, a manifestation of the growing concern about protecting the environment. Ecological issues affect both the processes of producing home furnishings and the resulting products.

For example, in the early 1990s, a chemical in the glue used on the back of carpeting was linked to a high incidence of leukemia among workers in a Georgia carpet factory. The chemical was also suspect in the sick feelings experienced by some consumers when their carpets were installed. Environmentalists called on the federal government to regulate the use of the glue or at least investigate its possible effects. The environmentalists also conducted tests of their own. They publicized recommendations that consumers replace carpets with area rugs made of untreated natural fibers.

This tale is one of many that demonstrate the interrelationship of fashion, technology, and ecology in shaping the home furnishings industries. With growing environmental awareness and a return to domesticity in the new millennium, there are an increasing number of companies that offer ecologically sound products and how-to tips for a healthy lifestyle. Gaiam (www.gaiam.com) is a Web site that offers eco-friendly products as well as editorial content on everything from non-toxic cleaning methods to yoga exercises.

Summary and Review

A trend toward spending more leisure time at home has prompted interest in home decorating and has speeded up the fashion life cycle of home furnishings in such categories as household linens, window treatments, upholstery fabrics, area rugs, and tabletop goods. Clothing designers have developed home fashions lines, often through licensing agreements with major textile manufacturers. National and store brands of household linens and tabletop goods have taken on distinctive fashion images. Computer-aided drafting has enabled designers and manufacturers to provide consumers with new patterns of soft goods and tabletop items to meet growing demand.

Major market segments for home accessories include the bridal market, the new home and vacation home segments, and a growing market for replacement merchandise. This last segment is propelled by home-centered leisure activity and the availability of relatively inexpensive purchases that can bring new looks to home decor.

The home furnishing industry is served by trade associations, trade shows, and trade publications that address both the collective interests of all segments and the specialized interests of the home textiles industry and other product line segments. New York is the main market center, and the Atlanta market is also important. Textile manufacturing and the production of household linens are centralized in the South. The production of tabletop goods is not centralized but is dominated by a few large producers.

Channels of distribution at the retail level include discount superstores, department stores, manufacturers' outlets, specialty retailers, and catalog retailers. Electronic shopping resources are becoming more important. Shelter magazines are a major medium for retail advertising and publicity.

The interplay of fashion, technology, and environmentalism dominates trends in the home furnishings industry. Some fashion trends are a casual lifestyle and a preference for natural fibers and other natural materials. Technological trends include computer-aided drafting, automated production, quick-response ordering systems, and the use of high-tech fabrics. Environmentalism is manifest in concern about the environmental impact of production processes and the effect of chemicals in home furnishing products on consumers and the environment.

Trade Talk

antimicrobials
area rug
California king
dinnerware
duvet
footed tumbler
futon
hollowware
home fashions
open stock
oriental rug
percale
pima
sham
shelter magazine
sisal
slipcover
soft goods
stemware
tabletop
thread count
throw
tumbler
valance
wedding or bridal registries

For Review

1. Why have apparel designers branched out into home furnishing lines?
2. Why are the names of textile mills important in the merchandising of household linens?
3. What benefits do natural fibers offer in household linens? What benefits do synthetics offer?
4. What do window treatments contribute to interior design?
5. Why have slipcovers become fashionable?
6. Name five shelter magazines.
7. What role do stages of the family life cycle play in defining market segments for home furnishings?

8. Name the major trade associations in the home furnishings industry. What services do they provide for their members?
9. Name five retail channels of distribution for home furnishings and describe the market of each of these types of retailer.
10. Identify three trends in the home furnishings industry.

For Discussion

1. Why is the home furnishings industry considered a fashion industry? Discuss the influence of fashion on the manufacturing, merchandising, and marketing of home furnishings.
2. Discuss the influence of computerized manufacturing on the home furnishings industry.
3. Discuss the influence of concern for environment on the fashion features of home furnishings. What role do ecological issues play in the selection of materials and treatment of textiles?

References

1. Robert Critchlow, "Productivity Growth Improves in Housefurnishings Industry," *Monthly Labor Review*, March 1, 1996, p. 25.
2. Deirdre McQuillan, "The Homecoming of Linen," *World & I*, March 1, 1996, p. 156.
3. Valerie J. Nelson, "You Snooze, You Lose; Getting the Best Linens for Your Money Means Knowing Your Egyptians From Your Pimas From Your Percales," *Los Angeles Times*, February 24, 1996, p. N-4.
4. Faye Musselman, "Throws: They're Everywhere You Are," *HFN*—The Weekly Newspaper for the Home Furnishing Network, January 17, 2000, p. 24.
5. "Here Comes the Bride's Checkbook," *American Demographics*, May 1, 2002, p. 12.
6. Andrea Lillo, "Registries Provide Retail Opportunity on Occasion," *Home Textiles Today*, May 21, 2001.
7. Michael Bartlett, "Amazon unveils Wedding Gifts Service on Valentine's Day," *Newsbytes*, February 14, 2002.
8. Crystal Honores, "Exhibitions Get Promotional with Pricing in Atlanta," *HFN-Home Furnishings News,* January, 28, 2002, p. 23.
9. Jennifer Negley, "Trading Places," *Home Textiles Today*, July 16, 2001, p. 40.
10. Carol Tice, "Making a Fuller Commitment to Home Décor," *National Home Center News*, November 1997, p. 19.

Exploring Careers at the Secondary Level: Other Producers

Each industry at the secondary level of the fashion business has its own fashion cycle and its own career opportunities in design, production, advertising and publicity, sales, and entrepreneurship. Although apparel sets the fashion trends, other secondary level businesses offer equally exciting job possibilities in meeting the fashion needs of consumers. This unit covers jobs in innerwear, bodywear, and legwear; accessories; cosmetics and fragrances; and home fashions.

Design

Designing fashion goods other than apparel requires the same basic skills as designing apparel. The difference is in the application of those skills. The function of a category dictates the materials used and the features sought in the materials and design, so designers in each category develop expertise in the properties of certain materials. Shoe and handbag designers, for example, need to be especially knowledgeable about leather, and jewelry designers must know about metals and gemstones. Designers of intimate apparel work with different kinds of fabrics from designers of household linens.

Formal training for designing these categories of fashion goods is available in specialized courses at fashion and art institutions. Courses in packaging design are helpful for careers in the cosmetics and fragrance industries, where packaging is an integral part of the product. Most major producers of fashion goods will expect new applicants to have training in the use of computer-aided design (CAD) programs.

The career ladder for a designer in any of these industries begins with positions such as assistant designer, junior designer, or sample maker. Where should you look for these jobs? Companies that specialize in a particular category are a good possibility; they may produce merchandise under their own brand name as well as lines licensed from major apparel design houses.

Production

Production jobs in many of the secondary level fashion industries—footwear is a striking example—involve coordination and monitoring of offshore contractors. However, other fashion goods, such as hosiery and household linens, continue to be manufactured mostly in domestic factories, and trained production supervisors and managers are needed at these plants.

Production Management

Coordinating production, whether at a manufacturing plant or through contractors, requires organizational, computational, and computer skills and attention to detail. Courses in operations management, as part of a degree in business administration, management, or engineering are good academic preparation. Entry-level jobs as production assistants may focus on one aspect of production, such as scheduling, inventory management, purchasing of materials, or quality control. With advancement comes increased responsibility, either for more lines or for more functions in the production of a single line.

Technical Jobs in Production

In each fashion industry, technical specialists contribute their expertise to the manufacturing process. For example, cosmetics companies rely on chemists to develop their products and on biologists to test the products for performance and safety. In the textile mills that produce household linens and fabrics, engineers program and maintain computer-aided manufacturing equipment.

Sourcing

Because production of fashion merchandise, especially nonapparel categories, is often licensed, and selected operations may be contracted to domestic or offshore facilities, specialists are employed to find and develop sources that will provide the best combination of quality, price, and scheduling to meet the producer's requirements. Much of the expertise and the all-important contacts needed to perform this work are acquired through on-the-job training. A degree from a fashion institution is helpful in securing an entry-level position on which to build a foundation of experience.

Advertising and Publicity

Producers of fashion goods typically aim their advertising and publicity at retailers and licensors, using trade publications and, increasingly, web sites. The major producers who advertise to consumers through the print and broadcast media usually rely on advertising agencies. The in-house staff is more likely to be involved in the management of promotional efforts than in the execution. However, there are opportunities for copywriters and artists in packaging, especially in the cosmetics and fragrance industries.

Sales

Entry-level jobs such as receptionist and sales assistant exist in showrooms for fashion goods, but many firms prefer—or even require—previous employment with a retailer for their sales managers and account executives. Sales professionals with retail experience have invaluable knowledge of retailers' needs, and they also bring to a fashion producer personal contacts that carry over into their new relationships with previous employers and colleagues.

Entrepreneurship

Specialization is often a good approach for entrepreneurial individuals who do not have easy access to large sums of money for start-up costs. A designer or craftsperson might consider launching a small vertically organized business selling hand-crafted or customized fashion goods directly to the consumer. In the jewelry industry, many businesses operate this way. Another route for small-scale entrepreneurs is to call on retail specialty stores that cater to a market for unique merchandise. Still another approach—one that may be used in combination with those mentioned above—is the craft fair circuit. This form of entrepreneurship minimizes the cost of retail selling space as craft fair organizers rent booths to vendors for either a flat fee or a percentage of revenues. Many of the responsibilities for publicity, security, and housekeeping services are borne by the organizers.

Assignments

1. Prepare Unit Four of your career journal by exploring the career opportunities in firms that are licensees of major fashion brands. Research trade publications, *The Licensing Newsletter*, and manufacturers' Web sites to prepare a list of manufacturers who license production of designer brands of innerwear, bodywear, legwear; accessories; cosmetics and fragrances; or home furnishings. Note the brands produced by each licensee. You can use your list as a reference when you evaluate manufacturers' job openings.
2. Environmental factors affect each secondary level industry of the fashion business. For each industry discussed in Unit Four—innerwear, bodywear, and legwear; accessories; cosmetics and fragrances; and home furnishings—give a current example of the effects of the natural, economic, social, and political/legal environment.

Carolina Herrera • Josie Natori • Mark Badgley • Bob Mackie • Helmut Lang • Calvin Klein • Isaac Mizrahi • Anna Sui

Design by Bob Mackie.

"I'd always thought I'd design a million movies, and it just didn't work out that way, and I always thought I'd work on the stage as a theater designer, but I stayed in L.A. But really, I don't mind being connected with glamour, because that's fun. I could have been connected with something much worse, like denim, and that's not nearly as interesting.

BOB MACKIE, 1999

"When I was 15, 16 years old, I wanted to be a vamp. Nowadays, women want to look like very young girls, but before, when we were young, we wanted to be grown-up and sophisticated."

CAROLINA HERRERA, 1991

"To be successful today in business you have to think globally. Women all over the world want to look feminine and sexy."

JOSIE NATORI, 1994

"I have no idea what the rest of the world wears for day, because our staff always look like they are going to a cocktail party."

MARK BADGLEY, 1998

"There's no reason why New York should not be the strongest fashion capital in the world. It is the capital in so many other fields. I believe it has that capacity. It is the most urban place."

HELMUT LANG, 1998

"I think some of the New York designers are crazy. I read that Donna said that the shows attract too much media. What does she think we do this for? Hello!"

CALVIN KLEIN, 1996

"No one can tell me what to do in a fitting. But when it comes to business, I'm not good at it. The only thing I can sell bold-facedly is my personality."

ISAAC MIZRAHI, CLOSING HIS BUSINESS IN 1998

"Our generation's got the power now. We're making things the way we want them to be. That's why we're indulging in the fashions we love."

ANNA SUI, 1993

Designer Bob Mackie.

The International Apparel Mart

GARDEN HOSTEL
3/FLOOR THIS BLDG.
60 HKS AIR CON.
CHINA VISA TOURS
HOTELS AIRFARES
TEL: 2723 2306
CITIZEN

WAL★MART

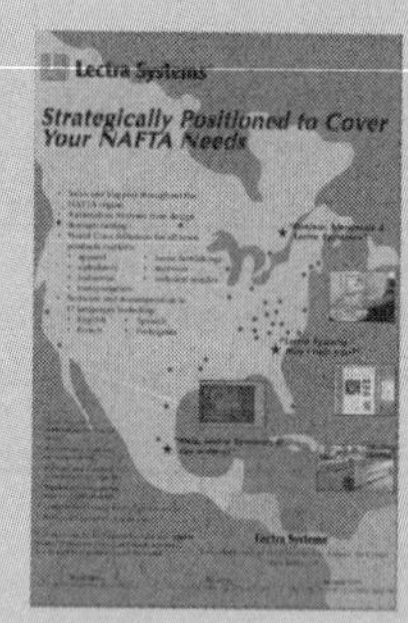
Lectra Systems
Strategically Positioned to Cover Your NAFTA Needs

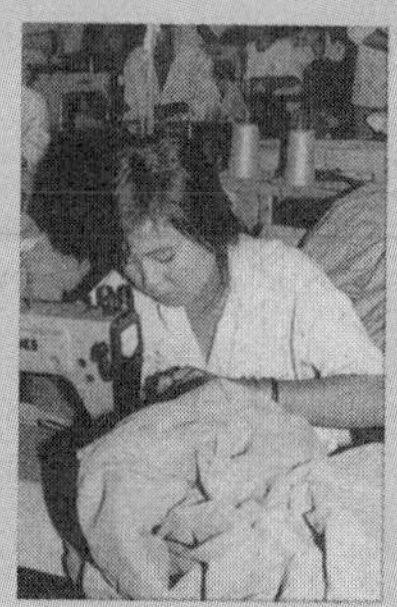

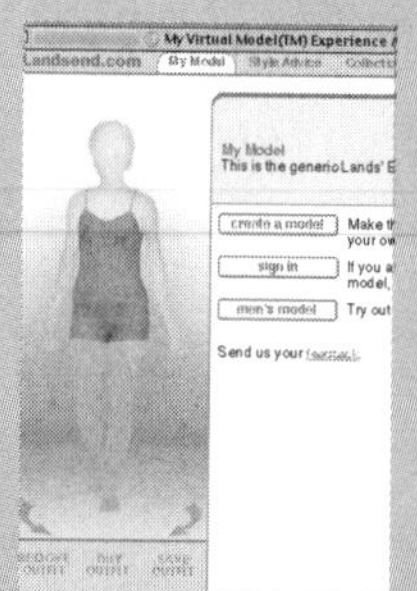
My Model
Style Advice
create a model
sign in
men's model

Cathy
by Cathy Guisewite
50% OFF
TOO MANY SALES. THAT'S THE PROBLEM WITH THIS COUNTRY, CATHY. NOBODY BELIEVES IN THEM ANYMORE.
WHEN WE GET THAT MESSAGE SMASHED INTO US 1000 TIMES A DAY THROUGH ADS AND STORE SIGNS, WE GET NUMB. WE GET HO-HUM, AND WORSE.

UNIT FIVE

THE RETAIL LEVEL: THE MARKETS FOR FASHION

The explosion of fashion markets and marts across America has been repeated not only in European markets, but also in Canada, South America, and several Asian countries including Japan, Hong Kong, and the rest of China. With the emergence of so many international markets, fashion has truly become global!

The most important market center for fashion in the United States is New York City. For many years, it was the only center, but today, Los Angeles, Miami, Dallas, Chicago, and Atlanta have captured large shares of the fashion business. Paris, which has reigned as the fashion capital of Europe for many years, now has competition from Italy, England, Belgium, Germany, and Spain. Global sourcing, the buying of foreign goods, is perhaps the most significant development in the fashion industry in many decades.

American manufacturers and retailers now routinely do direct importing and product development around the world. In addition to fashion fairs they hold in their countries, foreign sellers and producers are scheduling fashion fairs in the United States to showcase and sell their goods. Popular kinds of buying that are the most successful are specification buying, private label, and product development.

Unit Five focuses on the elements of fashion marketing and reveals how markets operate to help manufacturers sell their products. Chapter 15 is devoted to global fashion markets and their unique offerings and personalities. The expansion into foreign markets has not been without its difficulties for the American fashion business, and Chapter 16 takes a closer look at global sourcing, including its advantages and disadvantages for the American fashion industries. This chapter also discusses the single biggest problem confronting the American fashion industries today—the need to export American fashion around the world in order to reduce the trade deficit that has arisen from so many imports.

Chapter 17 outlines the history and development of fashion retailing in the United States. It explains the different types of retailers and changing retail patterns. Chapter 18 covers current policies and strategies in fashion retailing and how they affect merchandising, operations, and location. This chapter also details current trends and emerging retail strategies.

CHAPTER 15

Global Fashion Markets

WHAT'S IN IT FOR YOU?

Everything you always wanted to know about markets, market centers, marts, and trade shows.

Key Concepts:

- Meaning of the terms "market," "market center," "mart," and "trade show" and the function of each in bringing fashion from producers to consumers
- Locations and activities of markets, marts, and trade shows in the United States
- Locations and activities of foreign fashion markets
- Trends in U.S. and foreign fashion markets

As the popular children poem states, "To market, to market, to buy a fat pig; home again, home again, jiggety jig." Going to market can be an exciting and different experience, whether it is going to buy food, candy, sporting goods, or clothes. Most of us go to market with great expectations and plans—and once home from market, sometimes the purchase is perfect and other times it is just not right. Regardless of the outcome of the trip, it is your money and can be spent however you wish. However, this is not the case when you spend someone else's money, as is the case for store buyers. When buying for a store, you are using its money, which requires an exhausting amount of planning, organization, and hard work before you can even go to market.

Market Terminology

Markets . . . market centers . . . marts—what are they? You will hear these terms used frequently and even interchangeably, which makes them that much harder to sort out.

Market

The word "market" has several meanings. We have already spoken of the market, or demand, for a specific product, for instance, how much people want to buy athletic shoes, dress casual trousers, or coordinated bed linens. In this chapter, the word takes on yet another meaning. A **market** is the place where goods are produced and sold at wholesale prices to store buyers. It is an important step in the pipeline that takes clothes and other fashion items from manufacturer to customer. Buyers attend markets, in effect, to choose the styles we will all be wearing within a few months.

You may hear the term **domestic market**; it refers to the market in one's own country. For example, in the United States it refers to the places throughout the United States where goods are sold to retail buyers. The **foreign market** then refers to places outside the United States. If you live in Canada, Canada is your domestic market, and the United States is considered a foreign market. (Both domestic and foreign markets are discussed in detail later in this chapter.)

Market Center

Actually, there is no one giant shopping mall that serves as a market for the entire American fashion industry. Instead, several **market centers**, or geographic locations, exist throughout the country, and what are—to Americans—foreign market centers dot the globe. A market center is a city where fashion is produced and sold wholesale.

The first market center in the United States that comes to mind is New York City. For many people in and out of the fashion industry, New York City epitomizes the allure and excitement of the fashion world. Indeed, New York is the oldest market center in the United States and in many ways the most challenging to visit.

But in recent years, fashion has become regionalized, and while New York still produces much of America's fashion, it no longer produces all of it. In the past few decades, Los Angeles, Dallas, and Miami all have become flourishing market centers. Other cities that are not major apparel production centers, such as Chicago, Atlanta, and Denver, are considered markets rather than market centers, although the line between the two sometimes blurs. Chicago, for example, has always promoted itself as a market center.

Mart

A **mart** is a building or complex of buildings that houses a wholesale market, that is, an exhibition of fashions that are ready to be sold to retail stores (see Figure 15.1). Most marts are owned and operated by independent investors. Some marts are operated by the cities themselves, and at least one, the Carolina Mart in Charlotte, North Carolina, is operated by a trade association. A permanent, professional staff operates the mart, although a large number of temporary employees are hired for market weeks.

Like convention centers, marts consist almost entirely of exhibition space. Some space is rented out as full-time corporate showrooms, but in many marts, the space is rented only during market weeks. These marts often balance

FIGURE 15.1
The granddaddy of all the marts is the Chicago Merchandise Mart built in 1930. Its offspring, the Chicago Apparel Mart, to its left looks up-to-date.
Courtesy, Merchandise Mart Properties, Inc.

- still premiere market centre

their income by sponsoring other shows and conventions.

New York City, which, despite the rise of regional marts, in many ways still reigns as the country's premiere market center, is ironically the only market center without a mart. Part of the aura of a New York market week is the trek through the garment district from showroom to showroom.

The granddaddy of marts is The Merchandise Mart in Chicago, which opened its doors in the early 1930s, making Chicago New York's only rival for years. Because the Merchandise Mart was centrally located, buyers from across the country found it convenient to meet in this huge building on the Chicago River several times a year to do their wholesale buying. The Mart is still very much in use today for other goods, such as home furnishings, contract (office/institutional) furnishings, kitchen and bath, and gifts and decorative accessories.

Market Weeks

Buyers can and do travel to market centers and some marts at any time during the year to visit individual producers, but several times a year, they also gather for market week (see Table 15.1). Few buyers are willing to forego the glamour and excitement of **market week.** During market week, market centers and marts are filled to the rafters with producers and designers, all of whom exhibit their new lines with as much style and panache as possible. The atmosphere is electrifying, heady with new, innovative ideas and the latest trends.

As a purely physical convenience, it is immeasurably easier for buyers to take in new trends and make their buying decisions when they can see lots of clothes all at once. But beyond that, market week also gives everyone a chance to talk to each other and generally take in what is new in the industry.

Trade Shows

In this chapter, you will also learn about **trade shows,** periodic exhibits that are scheduled throughout the year in regional market centers and some marts. Smaller than market weeks, trade shows are typically attended by buyers from one region of the country. Exceptions are a few huge trade shows such as MAGIC, which attract buyers from all over the world.

History and Development of Market Centers in the United States

New York City was the first market center in the United States. When design and production clustered in New York, it followed that it would become a center for buying, too. The fact that New York was the most cosmopolitan and fashion-conscious of American cities also helped. Even when travel was a strenuous undertaking, buyers at major stores tried to travel to New York twice a year. To service them, manufacturers set up showrooms near their factories in the garment district.

But for many, twice-a-year buying trips were not enough to service a store properly. And many owners and buyers for small stores across the country could not afford to travel to New York. To handle accounts between New York buying trips and to help those who did not come to New York at all, manufacturers hired **sales representatives.**

The Role of Sales Representatives

Sales representatives played an important role in transforming other cities into market centers. For years, in addition to being the only

TABLE 15.1 A Basic Market Week Calendar

MONTH	MERCHANDISE SHOWN
January	Summer market
Late March–early April	Early fall market
Late May–early June	Late fall market
August–early September	Resort market
Late October–early November	Spring market

link between apparel manufacturers in New York and the rest of the country, these jobs were filled by men. Traveling at first by train, and later by car, sales reps, as they were familiarly called, mailed advance notices to key customers in each city to announce the date of their arrival. In the early days of the fashion business, sales reps carried only one line. Later, as the fashion business became more sophisticated, they carried several noncompeting lines so they could offer their clients more variety. Once a rep arrived in a city, he rented one or more hotel rooms which he used to exhibit his line of apparel.

For company more than anything else (the life of a sales rep was lonely), reps began to travel in groups. Soon, groups of sales reps were jointly renting clusters of adjoining rooms, so their customers could visit not just one but several exhibits at once. When they learned that this was good for business, the next step was to rent a large hotel ballroom or exhibition hall. This gradually led to the development of regional market centers, such as the Chicago Merchandise Mart, in 1930.

The Role of Marts

The Chicago Merchandise Mart had little competition until the 1960s, when other cities began to build their own marts, and regional markets took a giant step forward in their development. California had become a recognized center for selling sportswear by the 1940s, and it would soon become the second largest market center outside New York City. In 1964, the CaliforniaMart opened in Los Angeles, giving that city the capacity to sponsor a major market show rather than just sportswear shows. That same year, the dazzling Dallas Market Center opened and began servicing the western half of the country. The successes in Dallas and Los Angeles prompted other cities to open their own marts, and throughout the 1970s, Atlanta, Seattle, Miami, Denver, Pittsburgh, Minneapolis, and Charlotte, North Carolina, became important regional market centers.

Today, sales reps employed by large producers operate out of corporate showrooms in a fashion mart. If the rep can write up $1 million in orders, maintaining a permanent base at a mart is advantageous for the rep, the corporation, and their retail buyer customers. Apparel producers whose sales in a region do not warrant the investment in a corporate showroom often rely on multiline sales reps. These reps rent showroom space at the regional mart during market weeks.

Services of Market Centers and Marts

A market week is organized by manufacturers' associations, in cooperation with the market center or mart staff. It is the prime selling opportunity for market center or mart staffs, fashion producers, and sales reps, all of whom devote themselves to making the visit as easy and convenient as possible for the buyers (see Figure 15.2). Keeping buyers interested, com-

FIGURE 15.2
Sponsors for the Los Angeles mart prepare for their next event.
Courtesy, Fairchild Publications, Inc.

fortable, and happy encourages them to write orders.

Market weeks are scheduled several months before the clothes will be needed in the stores. Four or five market weeks are held each year for women's and children's wear, three to five for men's and boy's wear, and two to five for shoes. Separate market weeks are held in many market centers or marts for accessories, infants' and children's wear, lingerie, Western wear, sportswear, and bridal apparel. Table 15.1 lists the seasonal fashions shown at market weeks throughout the year. The chapters in Units Three and Four include more specific market week calendars for the various categories of fashion merchandise.

Physical Facilities

As will be discussed later in this chapter, the physical facilities vary between New York and the rest of the market centers and marts in the United States. The physical facilities of marts are designed for buyers' convenience. Exhibition space is arranged by fashion category; for example, handbags, small leather goods, and jewelry are typically located together; women's sportswear occupies another area, and lingerie still another.

Marts include an array of meeting rooms, ranging from auditoriums and theaters for fashion shows to smaller rooms for seminars and conferences. The newer marts even have office space where buyers can take a quiet moment to relax—and add up what they have spent.

Publicity

A market week is only as successful as the exhibitors it manages to attract, so most regional markets and marts mount an ongoing publicity program to draw interesting and exciting exhibitors. So the chemistry will be mutual, market centers and marts also do what they can to attract buyers. Flyers and brochures touting market weeks go out to stores and individual buyers several times a year. Buyers are also treated to buyers' breakfasts, luncheons, and cocktail parties throughout market week—all courtesy of the market center, mart, or a supporting organization.

The most popular form of publicity is the fashion shows that highlight every market week. The shows are hectic since they are so huge and so much is going on. They are also among the more extravagant and interesting fashion shows ever staged. Mostly this is because they are the work of many different designers, all of whom enter their most beautiful or interesting designs. In order to give some coherence to a market week fashion show, it is often organized around a theme, such as a particular color or, more often, an exciting new trend.

Special Services for Market Week

The market center or mart staff does everything in their power to make viewing and buying of seasonal lines easy for buyers who travel to market week. The endless rounds of exhibits are exhilarating but exhausting, and no one wants to lose buyers because they were not offered enough support.

Support services begin even before the buyer leaves home. Buyers are sent information on hotels with special rates, shuttle service to and from the fashion shows, and screening procedures. Only authorized manufacturers and buyers are admitted to market week, and security is high throughout the week.

Specialized support services are also planned. For example, models are hired to work in the showrooms in case a buyer wants to see someone wearing a particular garment. Beyond this, buyers are provided with an array of information, educational, and between-show services.

Information Services

Once the buyers arrive, they are given a buyer's directory and a calendar to help them find their way around and schedule events they want to see. A steady flow of daily publications—trade newspapers, flyers, brochures, and newsletters—continues throughout the week and keeps buyers abreast of breaking market week news.

Educational Services

An orientation program is typically scheduled for the first day, and consultants are on call throughout the week to discuss and deal with specific problems. Seminars and conferences are held to supply buyers with the latest information on fashion. Typical topics are new advances in fiber and fabrics, trends in fashion colors, the latest merchandising techniques, advertising and promotion ideas, and sales training hints.

General Services

The level of life and services between market weeks varies from place to place, but the trend is for both market centers and marts to stay open year-round. At the Miami International Merchandise Mart, for example, many tenants operate their showrooms year round.

The New York Market

As a market, New York belongs in a category by itself, not only because it is the city with the most resources to offer the fashion world, but also, as mentioned earlier, because it has no central mart building.

Trading Area and Economic Impact

The New York market is made up of literally thousands of showrooms, which line the streets of the garment district. Generally similar-quality apparel is grouped together. In the women's wholesale market, for example, the couture (pronounced koo-TUR) or higher-priced lines are situated primarily along Seventh Avenue in elegant showrooms. Moderate-priced lines and sportswear firms are housed around the corner on Broadway. Obviously, time and coordination are required to shop the New York market—as is a comfortable pair of shoes.

The lack of a central mart is a minor drawback compared to what many buyers consider the glory of shopping this *crème de la crème* of markets. New York, after all, is the fashion leader, the place where American fashion originates. Whatever is new will be seen here first. New York, most industry people agree, is the most dynamic and creative market center. Any buyers servicing stores of any size must come to New York to do so, regardless of the other markets they add to their schedule.

New York offers a wide-range of shopping. Every kind of fashion can be found here in every price range. Men's, women's, and children's wear, accessories, intimate apparel, and cosmetics are located within the garment district. Textile and fiber companies and home furnishings producers maintain showrooms in or near the garment district. Most local manufacturers feel that they must maintain a New York showroom, and many regional manufacturers sponsor one as well, if only during market weeks. Many foreign manufacturers participate in the New York market, and high fashion European designers like Helmut Lang, Alexander McQueen, and Nicolas Ghesquiere of Balenciaga have recently staged fashion shows here. Lang, who moved his business headquarter to New York at the end of the 1990s, has described it as "the most modern and urban place."[1]

A relatively new tradition, unique to New York, is the Mercedes-Benz Fashion Week, the American answer to the high fashion shows of Paris. Originally, New York Fashion Week was under the auspices of CFDA (Council of Fashion Designers of America), and organized by CFDA's off-shot "7th on Sixth." In September 2001, CFDA sold the 7th on Sixth trademark and operations to the sports management and marketing agency International Management Group (IMG). While 7th on Sixth still coordinates the event scheduling and registrations, they now operate under the auspices of IMG. You can look up fashion show schedules and general information on 7th on Sixth's Web site, www.mercedesbenzfashionweek.com.[2]

The New York market is open year-round, but specific times are still set aside for market weeks. (Chapters 5 through 14 contain specific listings of New York market weeks by industry.)

Advantages of the New York Market

Buyers who come to New York can shop not only the market but also the department stores and boutiques for which the city is known. New York is home to the flagship stores of Macy's, Bloomingdale's, Lord & Taylor, Barneys, Bergdorf Goodman, and Saks Fifth Avenue. There is also a high concentration of national and international flagship designer stores. Areas like the Upper East Side, Soho, and the Meat Market district are brimming with elegant flagship boutiques like Marc Jacobs, Donna Karan, and Ralph Lauren. As New York is one of the fashion capitals of the world, practically every important international fashion house has a flagship store here.

The city is also the hub of the fashion network. Many national organizations have headquarters here, and stand ready to provide assistance and support services to buyers. Even on a personal level, the networking possibilities are good. Local New York buyers attend market weeks as do buyers from all over the country. Buyers who can attend only a few market weeks each year generally head for New York.

Last but hardly least, part of the draw of New York is that it is the fashion capital of the

United States. The fashion publishing industry is located there. The Fashion Institute of Technology (FIT), founded in 1944 and located in the garment district, provides training in fashion design, production, and merchandising, and since the 1940s, its graduates have been making their mark on American design. The Metropolitan Museum of Art houses one of the world's largest archives of historic fashions. New York is also home to opera, theater, and ballet—all sources of inspiration to those in the fashion world. Here, too, are the restaurants and nightclubs where celebrities of the media and the international political scene present their own unofficial fashion shows.

Disadvantages of the New York Market

The city is also not without its disadvantages, particularly with regard to its ability to maintain its preeminence as a market center in the face of competition from regional markets. To retail merchants and buyers who have shopped at the newer marts, the lack of a central mart is sometimes considered a drawback. Many manufacturers, however, oppose the idea of a central mart, arguing that the garment district itself is the mart. They question whether the huge selection of merchandise—over 5,500 women's and children's lines alone—could ever fit into one building. The closest thing New York offers to such a site is the Jacob K. Javits Convention Center, and it does house a number of trade shows for various segments of the fashion industry (such as the men's wear shows, the National Shoe Fair, and the New York Home Textile Show). Bryant Park is the site of the women's wear shows and some men's shows.

Some fashion producers—mostly those who have moved their businesses out of the city—complain that many of the buildings that house showrooms are old and deteriorating. Moving stock through New York's crowded streets and nonstop rush hour is a major undertaking. The cost of doing business in New York is among the nation's highest. Rents are constantly spiral-

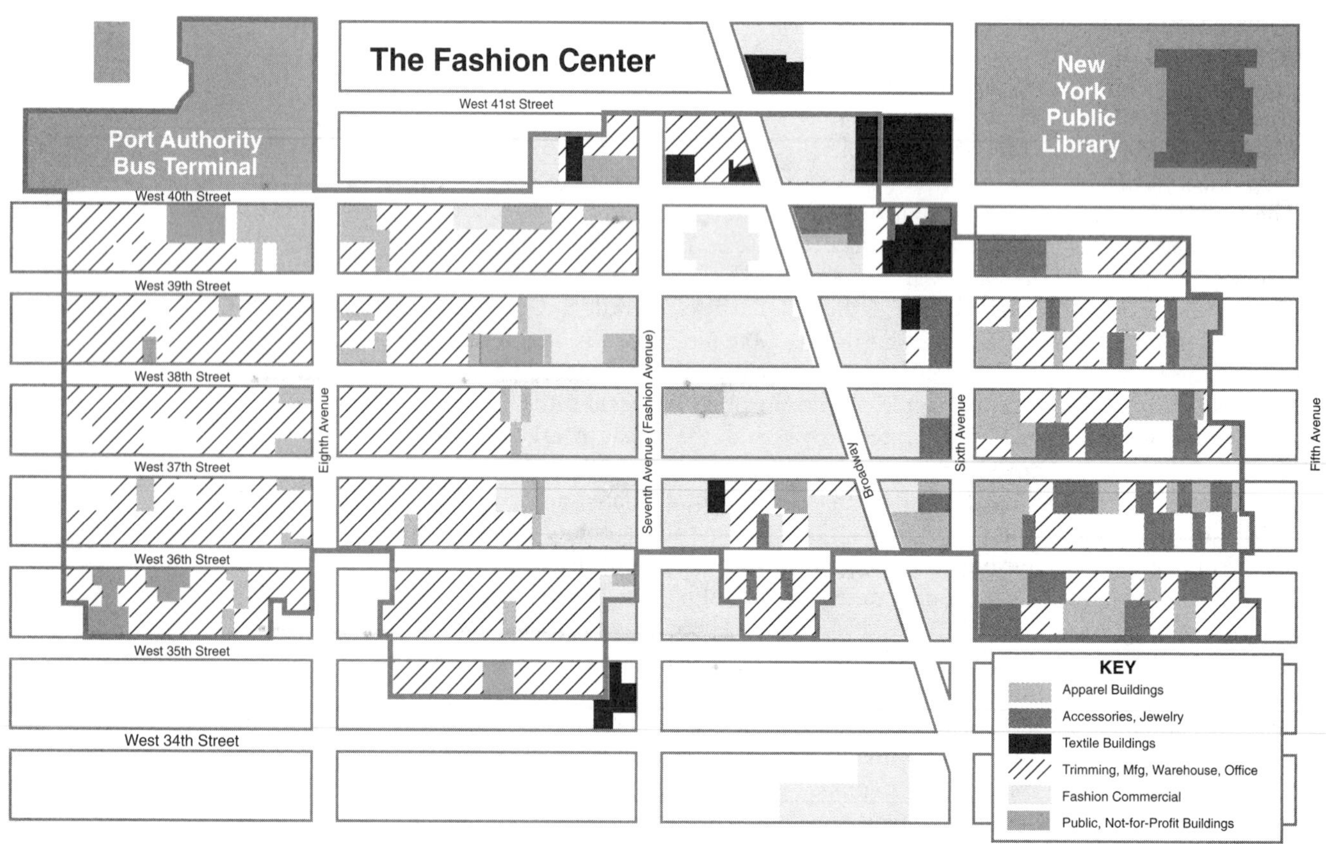

FIGURE 15.3

In New York, the design, production, and marketing of most fashion goods are done in an area known as the "Garment District" or the "Fashion Center."

ing, space shortages are a fact of life, and local taxes are high.

To counter these conditions, The Fashion Business Improvement District (BID) has been established to reenergize the garment district, which contains over 34 million square feet.

The Regional Market Centers

Each market center has its own unique flavor, as does each city, and buyers look forward to the varied experiences they will have at different markets. Many small retailers attend New York market weeks less often than they once did, relying instead on regional market centers closer to home. Travel costs are lower, less time is spent away from the stores, and for many, the atmosphere feels more personal. As regional markets become more sophisticated, thus drawing more exhibitors, New York loses even more of its allure. If regional markets can meet their needs, buyers ask, then why struggle through what many consider to be a grueling week in New York? Some retailers have cut out New York entirely, while others have reduced the number of trips they make and fill in with trips to regional markets in Los Angeles, Dallas, or Miami. They can visit them year-round or during special market weeks.

The Los Angeles Market

Much of the look and style of California's markets revolves around its casual lifestyle, which it seems to sell almost as much as it sells its clothing. California leads the nation in retail apparel sales, and Southern California is the nation's largest apparel manufacturing center. Los Angeles' fashion industry alone supports more than 130,000 jobs. The 82-block fashion district in downtown Los Angeles is responsible for 80 percent of California's apparel production.[3]

Since the 1930s, when California introduced pants for women, the West Coast has been the source of many important trends in sportswear. Today, Los Angeles is home to some of the country's largest sportswear manufacturers, GUESS?, Bugle Boy, BUM Equipment, L.A. Gear, and Speedo. Other recent Los Angeles successes are Bisou Bisou, Moschino, Laundry by Shelli Segal, Richard Tyler, St. John's Knits, and Rampage. Bob Mackie, who designs for Hollywood stars, and is frequently seen on television home shopping shows, is also based in Los Angeles.

Surf-fashion firms include companies such as Hurley, Billabong, and Blake Kuwahara's KATA Eyewear.

Apparel design, production, and distribution is spread out along the entire West Coast, but the heaviest concentrations are in Los Angeles, with more than 4,000 garment manufacturers, and San Francisco.[4] West Coast apparel producers have experienced phenomenal growth, in part because of the activities of the CaliforniaMart, the nation's largest apparel mart, located in downtown Los Angeles. With an expansion completed in 1996, the mart has permanent and temporary exhibition space not merely for California's lines, but for New York and Dallas lines as well, along with a growing number of foreign producers. The CaliforniaMart is open year-round and offers five market weeks and 20 specialty trade shows, such as ISAM (the International Swimwear & Activewear show), the Los Angeles International Textile Show, the Los Angeles Shoe Show, and the California Collections Preview.

San Francisco is also home to about 500 apparel companies, including Levi Strauss, Esprit, the Gap, Banana Republic, Old Navy, and Jessica McClintock.[5] Since the San Francisco Mart closed in the early 1990s, many of these companies now show in Los Angeles.

The Dallas Market

The mood at Dallas market weeks is strongly southwestern. Handcrafted clothes, or clothes that look handcrafted, with bright, vibrant colors are seen here. Once a center for budget garments, Dallas has become an important production and market center. Now the third-largest center in the country, it advertises itself as the "marketplace for the Southwest, the nation, and the world." Dallas-produced fashions are shown alongside fashions from New York, California, and around the world. Designers Anthony Marc Hankins and Victor Costa, the firms Jerrell and Poleci, and jewelry designers Elizabeth Showeres, Dian Malouf, and Joan & Co. are based in Dallas.

The Dallas Apparel Mart and the separate Menswear Mart are part of a multibuilding complex that offers more than two million square feet of exhibition space (see Figure 15.4). The Menswear Mart is the only mart in the world devoted exclusively to men's wear.

FIGURE 15.4
The International Apparel mart located at the Dallas Market Center.
Courtesy, the Dallas Market Center.

The Miami Market

The Miami market weeks have a highly international—mostly Hispanic and South American—flavor. Colors and styles are lively. The Miami market is also known for an outstanding selection of children's wear.

Greater Miami has become one of the most dynamic, cosmopolitan, and international fashion-producing centers in the country. Drawn by the temperate climate and quality labor force (many Cuban immigrants), many apparel designers and manufacturers now call South Florida home. Retailers find that Miami-produced clothing is well made, reasonably priced, and perfect for the semitropical weather that prevails in the Sun Belt. In Miami, three strong selling seasons—cruise wear, spring, and summer—are available year-round. In addition to cruise and resort wear, Miami design and production centers around budget and moderate-priced sportswear, swimwear, and children's clothing. Miami-based designers of better-priced daytime and evening wear are becoming known for their work.

The Miami International Merchandise Mart, opened in 1968, serves this area. Some exhibitors maintain permanent showrooms, but most show only during market week. Buyers from Latin America and the Caribbean account for much of the mart's business.

The Regional Marts

Although they are not major centers of fashion apparel production, several cities, such as Charlotte and Denver, have proven they can hold their own against larger marts. They do so primarily by emphasizing local design and production. Regional marts sponsor market weeks and in other ways operate much as the larger marts do.

Local marts have made inroads in servicing the stores in their trading area, and many department store buyers who regularly go to New York and Los Angeles feel they now must supplement these major buying trips with trips to their local regional market. Smaller store buyers often find the regional market is all they need to attend. In the early 1990s, both the San Francisco and Kansas City marts closed, victims of high-priced real estate and strong competition from the larger regional markets.

Trade Shows in the United States

Trade shows, which are held in market centers throughout the year, are sponsored by **trade associations**—professional organizations of manufacturers and sales representatives. A few of these events are major extravaganzas that attract buyers from across the country and even from abroad. MAGIC International, held twice a year at the Las Vegas Convention Center, has the atmosphere of an apparel mart market week minus the permanent facilities.

The typical U.S. trade show, however, is much smaller than a mart show and lasts two to four days. Regional trade shows are held in hotels and motels, civic centers, and small exhibition halls. Specialized trade shows cover areas of fashion that might otherwise get lost at major market weeks. B.A.T.M.A.N. show suits and outerwear for big and tall men, for example, and the Surf Expo Florida Show features surf equipment and surf-inspired sportswear.

These small trade shows show every sign of being able to hold their own against the proliferation of marts and market weeks. Trade shows are especially popular with small retailers and exhibitors because they are typically less expensive than market weeks for both groups of participants to attend. Small retailers like to deal with sales reps who are personally familiar with their needs and can cater to them at these smaller exhibits. Buyers from boutiques find that trade shows are their best outlet for the kind of unique and unusual merchandise they seek. Trade shows are known for displaying the work of unusual or small designers who do not ordinarily exhibit at the major marts.

The disadvantage of trade shows is that the exhibitors are limited in number. Buyers have difficulty doing across-the-board buying that is easily accomplished during market weeks at major marts. Trade shows also cannot feature the ongoing service that marts do as they are increasingly open year-round. See Figure 15.5 for a calendar of selected U.S. and foreign trade shows.

Foreign Fashion Markets

For several centuries, the foreign fashion market consisted entirely of French designers high fashions. In the 1960s, the ready-to-wear market emerged first in Italy and then in France. Today, cultural and economic changes and a renewed interest in nationalism and ethnicity have combined to encourage the development of fashion markets worldwide. American buyers no longer travel exclusively to France and Italy; they journey to fashion markets all over the globe.

At the opposite extreme from the fashion buyers who stick close to home are those who make a twice-yearly ritual of visiting the dazzling and often frenzied foreign fashion markets. As Americans have become increasingly fashion conscious, the foreign shows have taken on greater importance. Particularly for the retailers who cater to an upscale and fashion trend-setting clientele, even faithful attendance at the New York market weeks is not sufficient for staying in the forefront.

Foreign fashion markets are designed to show off the fashion industries around the world. In the leading foreign markets, clothing is typically designed and presented on two different levels. First in prestige and cost are the **haute couture** (pronounced "oat-koo-TUR") clothes. A French expression originally meaning "fine sewing," haute couture is today synonymous with high fashion. These original designs, which use luxury fabrics and are known for their exquisite detailing, are of necessity expensive and thus are made in very limited numbers. With prices that start in the thousands of dollars for a single garment, haute couture design is affordable to only a small group of wealthy women.

The next layer of fashion design is called **prêt-à-porter** (pronounced "pret-ah-por-TAY"). A French term meaning "ready-to-wear," prêt-à-porter is produced in far larger numbers than haute couture. Like haute couture, it is introduced in fashion foreign markets at semiannual shows where design collections are revealed to the fashion world. Haute couture and designer prêt-à-porter provide the inspiration for the inexpensive mass market designs that dominate the fashion market.

France

France first emerged as a fashion showcase during the reign of Louis XIV (1643–1715), often called the Sun King, partly because of his lavish lifestyle. The elaborate clothing worn by his court was widely copied by royalty and the wealthy throughout Europe. The splendor of his court at Versailles created a market for beautiful fabrics, tapestries, and lace. Textile production in Lyons and lace works in Alençon were established to meet these needs. Paris, already an important city and located only a few miles from Versailles, became the fashion capital.

Paris is still considered the cradle of the fashion world. New fashion is born there. After it is seen there, it is adopted and adapted by others around the world.

Paris Couture

France has been the center of haute couture since 1858, when the house of Charles Frederick Worth, generally regarded as the father of Paris couture, opened its doors. Beginning about 1907, Paul Poiret became the second great fashion legend of Paris. Poiret was the first to stage fashion shows and to branch out into the related

Global Trade Show Calendar

JANUARY

UNITED STATES	
RTW Markets (summer)	New York, L.A., Dallas, Chicago, Atlanta, Miami
New York Accessory Market Week	New York
New York Intimate Apparel Market Weeks	New York
NAMSB Show (men's)	New York
International Fashion Boutique Show	New York
International Kids Fashion Show	New York
Fashion Accessories Expo & Accessorie Circuit Show	New York
Los Angeles International Textile Show	L.A.
FOREIGN	
Haute Couture Collections (spring)	Paris
Designer Men's Collections	Paris
Mode Enfantine	Paris
Alta Moda Roma (couture) Collections (spring)	Rome
Milano Collegioni Uomo (men's)	Milan
Pitti Uomo and Uomo Italia (men's)	Florence
Hong Kong Fashion Week	Hong Kong
Tokyo Fashion Week	Tokyo

February

UNITED STATES	
New York RTW market (fall I)	New York
New York Premier Collections (fall I)	New York
FFANY (footwear)	New York
Fashion Coterie Show	New York
ENK Internations Women's Apparel	New York
ISAM (swimwear/activewear)	L.A.
The Active-Wear Show	Atlanta
Super Show (sportswear)	Atlanta
MAGIC International and WWD/MAGIC	Las Vegas
FOREIGN	
Prêt-à-Porter Féminin	Paris
SEHM (men's)	Paris
Take Off (Interstoff)	Frankfurt
CPD (glamour & wedding)	Düsseldorf
IMBX (men's & boys)	London
Pure Womens Wear	London
Disigner Collections (RTW)	Toronto
FACE (RTW)	Montreal
Cosmoprof (cosmetics)	Hong Kong
Hong Kong Fur and Fashion Fair	Hong Kong
Moda In (fabric)	Milan

MAY

UNITED STATES	
New York Accessory Market Week	New York
New York Intimate Apparel Market Weeks	New York
Fashion Accessories Expo	New York
Accessories Circuit	New York
Surtex	New York
Femme	New York
Moda Manhattan	New York
FOREIGN	
Chibie Cart and Chibimart	Milan
Intima Japan (intimate apparel)	Japan
Shanghai International Jewelry	Shanghai
Interselection (women's apparel/accessories)	France
Fatex (textiles)	France
Mercedes Australian Fashion	Australia

JUNE

UNITED STATES	
RTW Markets (fall II)	L.A., Dallas, Chicago, Atlanta, Miami
International Fashion Boutique Show	New York
Health and Beauty Aids Expo	New York
NAMSB Show (men's)	New York
Licensing Show	New York
FFANY (shoes)	New York
FOREIGN	
Uomo (menswear)	Milan
Moda Prima (knitwear)	Milan
Chibidue (jewelry)	Milan
Pitti Bimbo (children's)	Florence
Expofil (yarn)	Paris
Mode Accessories	Toronto
Hong Kong Jewelry and Accessories	Hong Kong
Shanghaitex (textiles)	China

SEPTEMBER

UNITED STATES	
MAGIC International	Las Vegas
Surf Expo	Orlando
New York Premier Collections	New York
Fashion Coterie	New York
The Bobbin show (sewn products)	Atlanta
FOREIGN	
Interstoff World (fabrics, fall/winter)	Frankfurt
Micam (footwear)	Bologna
Prêt-à-Porter (women's)	Paris
40 Degrees (men's and women's)	London
Moda In (fabric and accessories)	Milan
Mipel (accessories)	Milan
Ibermonda (men's)	Madrid

OCTOBER

UNITED STATES	
RTW markets (spring)	L.A., Dallas, Chicago, Atlanta, Miami
New York RTW market (spring)	New York
New York Accessory Market Week	New York
New York Intimate apparel Market Week	New York
ISAM (swimwear/activewear)	L.A.
Private Label Expo	New York
International Fashion Boutique Show	New York
International Kids Fashion Show	New York
International Fashion Fabric Exhibition (fall/winter)	New York
Los Angeles International Textile Show (fall/winter)	L.A.
B.A.T. Woman (plus and tall)	Las Vegas
Jeweler's International Showcase	Miami
IFN (lingerie)	Las Vegas
FOREIGN	
Premiere Vision (fabrics, fall/winter)	Paris
Moda Mont (supplies/trimmings)	Paris
Interstoff (fabrics, fall/winter)	Frankfurt
Interstoff Asia	Hong Kong
Ideacomo (fabrics, fall/winter)	Como
Premier Men's Wear	London

FIGURE 15.5

MARCH

UNITED STATES

RTW Markets (fall I)	L.A., Dallas, Chicago, Atlanta, Miami
New York RTW Market (fall I)	
New York Accessory Market Week	New York
New York Intimate Apparel Market Weeks	New York
NAMSB Show	New York
International Fashion Boutique Show	New York
International Kids Fashion Show	New York
International Fashion Fabrics Exhibition (spring/summer)	New York
International Jeanswear & Sportswear	Miami
Couture Bridal Show	New York

FOREIGN

Prêt-à-Porter	Paris
Premiere Visions (fabrics, spring/summer)	Paris
Poznan Fashion week	Poznan
British Fashion Wiie	London
Ideacomo (fabrics, spring/summer)	Como
Interstoff (fabrics)	Frankfurt
International Footwear Fair	Düsseldorf
Feris (costume jewelry)	Barcelona
Fenatec (textiles)	São Paulo
Semana Internacional de la Piel (leather)	Madrid
Micam (footwear)	Milan

APRIL

UNITED STATES

Bridal Market Wiids	New York, Chicago, Atlanta
Texitalia (fabrics, spring/summer)	New York
Los Angeles Textile Show (fabrics, spring/summer)	L.A.

FOREIGN

Interstoff Season (fabrics, spring/summer)	Frankfurt
Interstoff Asia (fabrics)	Hong Kong
Igedo (RTW)	Düsseldorf
Fenit (men's, women's, children's)	São Paulo
Bangkok int. Fashion Fair (RTW and textiles)	Bangkok
MIDO	Milan
Leather Fair	France
Asia-Pacific Leather Fair	Hong Kong

JULY

UNITED STATES

ISAM (swimwear/activewear)	L.A.

FOREIGN

Haute Couture Collections (fall/winter)	Paris
SEHM (men's disigner collections)	Paris
Mode Enfantine	Paris
Alta Moda Roma (couture) collections (fall/winter)	Rome
Tokyo Fashion Week	Tokyo
Hong Kong Fashion Week	Hong Kong
Asia Pacific Leather Fair	Hong Kong

AUGUST

RTW markets (resort)	L.A., Dallas, Chicago, Atlanta, Miami
New York RTW market (resort)	New York
New York Accessory Market Week	New York
New York Intimate apparel Market Week	New York
Accessorie Circuit show	New York
FFANY (footwear)	New York
Fashion Accessories Expo and Accessorie Circuit	New York
International Kids Fashion Show	New York
International Fashion Boutique Show	New York
WWD/MAGIC	Las Vegas
B.A.T.M.A.N. (big & tall men)	Denver
Chicago Men's Wear Collective	Chicago

FOREIGN

Idego (RTW)	Düsseldorf
CPD (glamour and wedding)	Düsseldorf
Istanbul Fashion Fair (men's, women's, children's)	Istanbul
columbia Moda (apparel and textiles)	Medellin
Mode Homme	Montreal
Festival of Canadian Fashion (women's)	Toronto

NOVEMBER

UNITED STATES

Texitalia (fabrics, fall/winter)	New York
Chicago Baby Faire	Chicago
International Gift and Accessories	Atlanta

FOREIGN

Garmetec Show (machinery)	Kuala Lumpur
Intertextile	Shanghai

DECEMBER

UNITED STATES

FFANY (footwear)	New York

FOREIGN

Moda Prima	Milan

*Note: months vary from year to year and shows are subject to change.

FASHION FOCUS

Fabulous Ford – A Great Design Engine

Tom Ford is riding high as the current poster boy for glamorous designers. Unlike many of his contemporaries, who sometimes appear eccentric and a bit over-the-top, Ford is the epitome of calm, cool and collected sophistication.

Ford was born in Austin, Texas, in 1962, but spent most of his childhood in Santa Fe, New Mexico, with his exotic grandmother, Mildred Ruth Ford, Ford 's version of "Auntie Mame." "She was a real Auntie Mame character," Tom says. "Whenever I used to complain as a child, whenever something wasn't right, she'd say there was one decision anyone had to make: you either have a great time and enjoy this, or you can have a bad time; you choose." In other words—Live! Live! Live!

In his teens, Ford moved to New York and studied art history at New York University as well as being trained as an actor. He later redirected his studies to concentrate on architecture at Parsons School of Design in New York and Paris.

In 1986, after returning from Paris, Tom joined the creative staff of American designer Cathy Hardwick. In 1988, he moved to Perry Ellis where he worked as Design Director. In 1990 Ford was hired by Gucci's then creative director Dawn Mello as chief women's ready-to-wear designer, and later appointed design director. When in 1994, Gucci was acquired by Investcorp, a Bahrain-based investment firm, Ford was promoted to Creative Director and moved to Milan with his partner, journalist Richard Buckley. It was talent and vision of fashion trends that got him appointed Creative Director after only two years.

In his first year at the helm, he was credited with putting the glamour back into fashion with velvet hipsters, skinny satin shirts, and car-finish metallic patent boots. He brought in French stylish Carie Roitfeld and photographer Mario Testino to create a series of new, modern ad campaigns for the company. By 1999, Gucci, which had been almost bankrupt when Ford joined, had become the success story of the fashion business.

In January 2000, following the acquisition of Yves Saint Laurent and YSL Beauté by Gucci Group, Tom assumed the position of Creative Director of Yves Saint Laurent, Rive Gauche and YSL Beauté. In addition to his existing duties at Gucci, Ford work with all creative teams at YSL to define the overall image and positioning of YSL brands and products as well as acting as Creative Director of Gucci Group. Not bad for a country boy from Texas!

His visionary look at the fashion industry had been the center of attraction as he has won many awards, among them three awards from the prestigious Council of Fashion Designers of America (CFDA) for International Designer of the Year for Gucci (1996), Womenswear Designer of the Year for Yves Saint Laurent Rive Gauche (2001), and Accessory Designer of the Year for Yves Saint Laurent Rive Gauche (2002); two awards from the Fashion Editor's Club of Japan (FEC) for International Designer of the Year for Gucci (1996) and best designer of the year for Gucci and Yves Saint Laurent Rive Gauche (1995), Menswear and Womenswear Designer of the year for Gucci (1995), Womenswear Designer of the Year for Gucci (1999), and most recently Designer of the Year for Yves Saint Laurent Rive Gauche Award (2002); the Style Icon Award in the 1999 Ellie Style Awards (UK); the British GQ International Man of the Year Award (2000); the Superstar Award at the Fashion Group International's Night of Stars (USA, 2000); Best Fashion Designer, *Time* Magazine (July 2001). In November of 2001, Ford was named Designer of the year by GQ America.

Ford is constantly working on new season designs, overseeing the design and concept of new retail stores opening worldwide and spreading into anything that is part of the business. "When I'm working one thing, it feeds everything else. One idea feeds other ideas for other collections. I'm much better under pressure. It's just the way I'm. I am much better when I have a lot to do."

"Work is my hobby," he says. "It's what I do the most because I like it that much. "People ask me, '"What are you doing when you're not working? Well, the answer is that I'm working," so says the fabulous Ford.

Sources

"FAB FORD," *Women's Wear Daily* (International Section), April 2001, pp. 130-132.

Elvis Mitchell, "American Beauty," *New York Times Fashion of the Times.*

Available: http://www.askmen.com. Man of the Week, Biography, January 31, 2003.

Available: http://www.vogue.co.uk/who_who Who's Who – Tom Ford.

Designer Tom Ford.
Courtesy, Fairchild Publications, Inc.

fields of perfume, accessories, fabric design, and interior decoration.

A **couture house** is an apparel firm for which a designer creates original designs and styles. The proprietor or designer of a couture house is known as a **couturier** (pronounced "koo-tour-ee-AY") if male, or **couturière** ("koo-tour-ee-AIR") if female. Most Paris couture houses are known by the names of their founders—Yves Saint Laurent, Givenchy, and Chanel, for example. The name may survive even after the original designer's retirement or death, but the signature style changes with his or her successor. In recent years, rapid changes of personnel and licensing of designer names has blurred the identity of the fashion houses and focused attention on individual designers. For example, Karl Lagerfeld designs for Chanel, Fendi, and Chloé, as well as for himself.

In 1868, an elite couture trade association, called the Chambre Syndicale de la Couture Parisienne, came into being. Membership in the Chambre Syndicale (pronounced "shahmbrah seen-dee-KAHL") was by invitation only and was restricted to couture houses that agreed to abide by its strict rules. In 1973, Federation Francaise de la Couture, du Prêt-à-Porter des Couturiers et des Createurs de Mode was established. La Federation is the executive organ of all the trade associations (or Chambre Syndicales) of each fashion division. Haute Couture, ready-to-wear, and men's wear each have their own Chambre Syndicale. You can look up fashion show schedules and general information on the federation's Web site www.modeaparis.com.[6]

The Chambre Syndicale is a strong force in the French fashion industry. From the foreign visitors' point of view, its most valuable contribution is the organization and scheduling of the twice-yearly market shows. It handles registration and issues the coveted (and limited) admission cards. It also registers and copyrights new fashion designs. It is illegal in France to copy a registered fashion design without making special arrangements and paying a fee. (In the United States, there is no copyright protection for clothing designs.) From its members' point of view, the Chambre Syndicale's most valuable contribution is that it represents its members in arbitration disputes and seeking regulation of wages and working hours.

Couture Shows. The Paris couture house trade shows are held twice yearly: The spring/summer collections are shown in late January, and the fall/winter ones in late July. These shows have evolved into a promotional outlet for the couturiers. Today they are an expense rather than a source of income, as in the past. All the clothes in an haute couture collection are made-to-measure. Customers select a sample from the runway show, then make an appointment with the fashion house's atelier to get the garment custom-made for them. This is, of course, outrageously expensive. The wealthy private customers in the audience, who order the clothes for their personal wardrobes, are too few in number for their purchases to exceed the costs of producing the samples and the show. The fashion press, who comprise the remainder of the audience, perform the mutually beneficial job of publicizing the exciting, glamorous news about the designers' creativity.

Other Couture Business Activities

The sales of haute couture clothing have steadily declined in recent years as prices have risen and customers have turned to the designer ready-to-wear lines. To survive, couture houses have expanded into other, more lucrative activities, such as the development of ready-to-wear collections and the establishment of boutiques and, the ever-present (and profitable), licensing arrangements.

Couturiers' Ready-to-Wear. Most couturiers' ready-to-wear clothes are sold to department and specialty stores, which often set aside special areas or departments to display these prestige items.

The exclusivity and cost of producing haute couture lines, in combination with declining craftsmanship skills among designers and atelier staff, have changed the Parisian fashion climate. The ready-to-wear business has completely eclipsed haute couture on the French prestige designer market. Ready-to-wear lines are not ordered directly by the customer, but are bought in bulk by buyers that select the styles that they like from the runway and then order them in various sizes and quantities. Although tomes houses still have a haute couture atelier, and participate in haute couture fashion shows, it's the ready-to-wear lines that are featured in their advertising, showrooms, and stores. Today, many famous fashion houses, like Balenciaga, Chloe, Louis Vuitton, and Yves Saint Laurent, only produce ready-to-wear lines.

Couture Boutiques. The French word for "shop," **boutique** (pronounced "boo-TEEK"), has come to mean, more specifically, a shop that carries exclusive merchandise. In the past, many couturiers installed boutiques on the first floor or a lower floor of their design houses. Most famous fashion labels also have their own flagship ready-to-wear stores in key cities around the world. Goods sold in these shops are usually designed by the couture house staff and are sometimes even made in the couture workrooms. All bear the famous label.

This was where the haute couture customers made their appointments. Some of these boutiques still exist, for example, Chanel's ready-to-wear flagship store on Rue Cambon in Paris, is still adjoined to the Chanel atelier. Today, most French fashion houses have several flagships boutiques that sell their ready-to-wear collections as well as accessories. These stores are designed to reflect the image of the house, and create an atmosphere that expresses the spirit of the label.

Licensing Agreements. The most lucrative business activities for couturiers are the numerous licensing arrangements they establish to sell their accessories and ready-to-wear lines and also a variety of goods produced by others on their behalf. The most popular prestige licenses include perfume, shoes, bags, sunglasses, and watches.

French Ready-to-Wear

The burgeoning French ready-to-wear (or prêt-à-porter) fashion has two distinct sources: designers and mass-market producers. Young, innovative ready-to-wear designers such as Dries van Noten, Olivier Theyskens, and Junya Watanabe have added much-needed excitement to the French fashion industry. These and other nonnative designers, like Alexander McQueen of the United Kingdon, are showing along with French designers. Thus they have changed the image of Paris as the center of French fashion to the French center of international fashion leadership.

To meet the needs of these ready-to-wear designers, the Chambre Syndicale created an autonomous section for designers who work exclusively in ready-to-wear, designating them **créateurs** (pronounced "kray-ah-TERS") to distinguish them from "couturiers." Among the créateurs are such important names as Karl Lagerfeld, Sonia Rykiel, Christian Lacroix, and Jean-Paul Gaultier.

Although their prestige is great, the couturiers and créateurs represent only a small part of the French fashion industry in terms of numbers and revenue. The remaining 1,200 companies are mass producers of ready-to-wear

Prêt-à-Porter Trade Shows. The French ready-to-wear producers present their collections at two market shows a year. The first, for the fall/winter collections, is held in March, and the second in October, for the spring/summer collections. Actually, two large trade shows take place simultaneously. The runway shows, sponsored by the Chambre Syndicale for the prêt-à-porter designers, take place at Carousel du Lourve. At

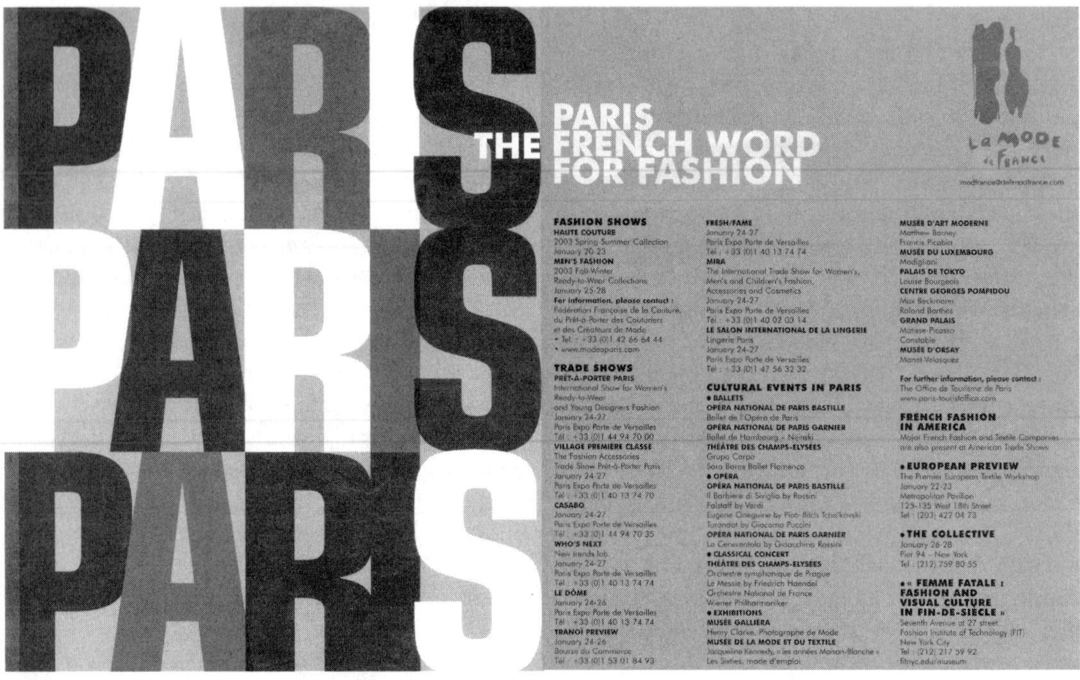

FIGURE 15.6
The French word for Fashion, Paris, is the rallying hall of La mode de France.

the other, sponsored by the Fédération, the mass market prêt-à-porter collections are exhibited at the Porte de Versailles Exhibition Center. This trade show, known as the *Salon du Prêt-à-Porter Féminin*, brings together more than 1,000 exhibitors from all over the world.

With each succeeding show, the press pays more attention and provides more coverage of this end of the French fashion business. About 40,000 buyers attend the prêt-à-porter shows, which are rivaled only by the ready-to-wear shows in Milan.[7]

A semiannual men's ready-to-wear show, *Prêt-à-Porter Mode Masculin*, traditionally held in January and July, is as important to the men's fashion industry as the women's ready-to-wear shows are to the women's fashion industry.

Italy

Italy is France's most serious rival in the fashion industry. In certain areas, such as knitwear and accessories, Italian design is considered superior to the French. Italy has long been recognized as a leader in men's apparel, knitwear, leather accessories, and textiles.

A centuries-old tradition of quality craftsmanship and a close relationship between designers and manufacturers are common features of Italy's otherwise disparate fashion houses. Ermenegildo Zegna, a firm which markets three lines of men's wear, also produces men's textiles. Rather than economize on labor costs through offshore manufacturing to the extent that designers in other developed countries do, Italian designers rely more on domestic factories. Consequently, much of their output is in the luxury price ranges. Italian manufacturers are also the sources for materials and production for many foreign designers, among them Hugo Boss, Calvin Klein, Helmut Lang, and Ralph Lauren.[8]

Italian Couture

Italy has long had couture houses named for the famous designers who head them—Valentino and Mila Schön. Its designers are members of Italy's couture trade group (a counterpart to the Chambre Syndicale) known as the Camera Nazionale della Moda Italiana. The Camera Moda organizes the bi-annual ready-to-wear fashion week runway shows that take place in Milan each year in March and September. You can look up schedule and general information at the association's Web site www.cameramoda.com.

Unlike French couture houses, however, Italian couture designers are not all located in a single city. Although Milan is the biggest fashion center, couture designers may be found in Rome, Florence, and other Italian cities.

Both Italian and French couture depend heavily on Italian fabric and yarn innovation and design. Most of the excitement today in print and woven textile design is created and produced in the fabric mills of Italy. Italian knits are also known for their avant-garde styles.

Only a handful of Italian houses have an haute couture business today. There are no haute couture runway shows in Italy. Valentino and Versace show their haute couture collections in Paris. They are scheduled one week prior to the Paris shows so that foreign buyers can cover both important fashion markets in a single trip.

Like their Paris counterparts, many Italian couture houses have set up boutiques for the sale of exclusive accessories and limited lines of apparel. The designs are usually those of the couture house staff, and the apparel and accessories are sometimes made in the couture workrooms. All items offered in boutiques bear the couture house label.

Italian couture designers also have established licensing agreements with foreign producers. Some design and produce uniforms for employees of business firms, most notably airlines and car rental agencies. Some accept commissions to create fashion products ranging from perfume to men's wear to home furnishings.

Italian Ready-to-Wear

Italy began to develop both its women's and men's ready-to-wear industries along with its couture fashions. As a result, it started exporting earlier than France, and today its economy relies heavily on its exporting program. The textile, apparel, footwear, and leather goods industries account for one-fifth of Italy's exports.[8] Much of this exported merchandise is in the medium- to high-price range, especially in knitwear and accessories.

Designers. Innovative Italian ready-to-wear designers make their shows as exciting as the Paris ready-to-wear shows have become. Giorgio Armani and Versace are considered the standard-bearers for two very different definitions of Italian design. Versace is noted for brightly colored prints, and Armani, for classic elegance combined with comfortable styling. Other well-known Italian ready-to-wear designers are equally protective of their reputations for distinctive, recognizable signature styles. Among the leading designers are Dolce & Gabbana, Gianfranco Ferré, Krizia, Missoni, and Miuccia Prada. Ferragamo and Gucci are major names in shoes and accessories, and Fendi in fur.

Trade Shows and Market Centers. Until the late 1960s, the most important Italian ready-to-wear shows were staged at the elegant Pitti and Strossi palaces in Florence. Milan grew as a fashion center in the 1970s, and many designers began to show there, in addition to or instead of Florence.

In addition to the ready-to-wear shows, Italy hosts a number of shows featuring the categories of apparel, accessories, and textiles for which Italian designers and manufacturers are internationally renowned. Leather shoes, handbags, gloves, and small leather goods are one major segment of Italy's fashion industry. Other accessories that are world famous are knitted hats, scarfs, and gloves; and silk scarfs and ties. There are 731 companies producing accessories in Italy. Como, the hub of Italy's silk industry, has 200 companies that finish raw silk imported from China. Together they produce 90 percent of Europe's silk export.

Trade shows are held in the regions where the respective industries are centralized. Figure 15.5 lists some of the shows that attract international attention.

Great Britain

For many years, London's Savile Row was for men's wear what Paris has been for women's apparel—the fountainhead of fashion inspiration. Savile Row is a wonderful place where each suit is handcrafted for its new owner, a process known as "bespoke tailoring." (*Bespoke*, an archaic word meaning to have reserved in advance, is applied in England to men's clothing that is made to measure, a process that takes six to ten weeks.)

In the 1980s, Italy became the main source of European-styled men's wear, and Britain's fashion reputation focused on the craftsmanship of its tailoring and the quality of its tweeds and woolens rather than on trend-setting designs. Then, in the late 1990s, the British fashion industry, harking back to its daring hippie, mod, and punk styles of the late 1960s and 1970s, began to revive its image as a place for cool, new designs. Today, London is a the place to look for innovative, although not always wearable, designs.

London Couture

Although Britain has never supported a couture industry the way that France and Italy have, it does offer famous design schools, such as the Royal College of Art, the London College of Fashion, and Central St. Martin's. St. Martin's alumni include internationally famous names John Galliano, Alexander McQueen, Hussein Chalayan, Julien MacDonald, Stella McCartney, and Clements-Ribeiro. In addition to their own lines, these designers have or have had designer posts at leading French fashion houses. Other recent graduates of these schools, both British and foreign, are bringing design back to London. Phillip Treacy is a four-time winner of the London Accessory Designer of the Year award for his striking hats.

British Ready-to-Wear

Ready-to-wear was a minor industry in Britain until after World War II. The fact that it entered a period of expansion after the war is largely due to the efforts of the government. According to one English fashion authority, the government became "the fairy godmother" responsible for "the survival of [British] couture and the rapid development of [Britain's] large and excellent ready-to-wear trade."[9]

Vivienne Westwood is a talent that has sparked and shocked the London fashion scene with her unorthodox clothes and lifestyle since the mid-1970s. Today, she continues to be an innovator and leader of the avant-garde pack.

Trade Shows

After a dormant period in the late 1980s and early 1990s, the British runway shows and trade shows are once again a required stop on the European fashion circuit. British and foreign designers are showing, and British and foreign audiences are looking. Some of the major events are listed in Figure 15.5.

Canada

The development of a group of new and innovative designers has given the Canadian fashion industry a growing sense of confidence that has paid off in real growth. The fashion industry is the fifth largest employer in Canada and gets bigger every year. It has two important centers: the largest is Montreal in Quebec; second is Toronto, in Ontario. Especially the Montreal fashion scene is gaining more and more international notoriety for its creativity and independ-

Then & Now

Is It Real . . . or Is It Fake?

It may look like a Versace, it may feel like a Versace, it may even have the word Versace printed on the label, but of course, if you look closely, you'll discover that the "Versace" shirt was made in Taipei and not Italy.

The business of knockoffs is huge, and people all over the world are reaping the benefits of ripping off designer names. You name it, and you can be sure a knockoff has been created on its behalf—bad for the designers, good for the counterfeiters worldwide.

Knockoffs are the affordable products that are inspired by the original items created by such big names as Louis Vuitton, Giorgio Armani, Christian Dior, Calvin Klein, and Ralph Lauren to name just a few. Besides the uncanny resemblance to the designer items, the products are in no way affiliated with the designers. So although you would like to believe that everything you bought on the street in New York, or in flea markets around the world is the real thing, chances are that you are wrong and it is a counterfeit.

Can you tell if this display of handbags is real or fake?
Courtesy, Fairchild Publications, Inc.

The view that fake designer goods are harmless fun is shared by many people who believe knockoffs have a minimal effect on the fashion designer or the fashion industry itself. But that view may soon change as fashion houses are battling against the counterfeit industry pitting customs officials, trading standards officers, private detectives, and police in an alliance against the counterfeiters.

The manufacture of fakes, ranging from T-shirts with designer logos to state-of-the-art watches, is spreading worldwide. Once focused in the Far East and countries such as Thailand, South Korea, and Taiwan, counterfeit activity is now reported growing in South America, North Africa, and Eastern Europe. The battle is increasingly being fought in Western Europe and the United States as production moves closer to the distribution source.

All-female parties in living rooms across the country are going back to the 1950s, but instead of Tupperware it is now "purses" that are being purchased. A posting on a popular online ad site www.Craigslist.com reads: "Host a purse party. All styles, Kate Spade...Tod's, Burberry," referring to counterfeits of the popular designer products. For a woman who desires a one-of-a-kind handmade bag or a designer purse that is bigger than her purse, fake Fendis and other imposters can be the life of a purse party!

The French luxury goods industry has worked hardest to fight counterfeiters. In 1994 French anti-counterfeiting legislation put counterfeiting in the same category as drugs and arms trafficking. Today, they are trying to make people understand that buying a counterfeit product is like buying drugs!

Sources:

Robert Galbraith, "Luxury Groups Battle a Wave of Counterfeit Goods," *International Herald Tribune*, September 29, 2001.

Kristina Henderson, "A Trendy Party is in the Bag," *The Washington Times*, January 30,2003.

Matheson, Ormsby, Prentice, "Combatting Counterfeiting: Recent Decisions", MOP Web site, March 2000.

Austin Silver, "The Big Business Of Knockoffs," www.AskMen.com, February 6,2003.

Roger Tredre, "As Fakes Flourish, Battle Heats Up to Save Profits and Name," *International Herald Tribune*, October 16, 1999.

ence. This is how emerging Montreal designer Yso describes the local sense of style:

"Montreal has its own look that's kind of Euro-American, derived from the cultural mix of people here as well as the trends from Europe and the U.S. People here, especially young people, take more fashion risks. They like to be noticed."[10]

Well-known Canadian designers from Montreal include Helene Barbeau, Marisa Minicucci, Marie Saint Pierre, Nadya Toto, and Simon Chang. Designers from Toronto include Brenda Beddone, Brian Bailey, Pat McDonagh and Alfred Sung. Internationally successful Toronto-based manufacturers and retailers include Club Monaco, M.A.C., and Roots. Roots made the uniforms for the Winter Olympics in 2002. It was the first time the Winter Olympics used a company outside sportswear giants like Nike and Adidas.

Most Canadian apparel manufacturing is located in Montreal but every province has a stake in the industry, and shows in each province bring local goods to the attention of other Canadians, buyers from the United States, and around the world. Montreal and Toronto each have their own fashion week twice a year, where local men's and women's wear designers showcase their new collections in runway shows. Other women's apparel and accessories shows include Western Apparel Market in Vancouver, the Alberta Fashion Market in Edmonton, the Prairie Apparel Markets in Winnipeg, the Saskatoon Apparel Market, and Toronto's Mode Accessories show. Children's Wear markets take place in Vancouver and Alberta, and the North American Fur and fashion exposition is featured at the Place Bonaventure in Montreal. Alberta, Montreal, Vancouver, and Toronto all host gift shows.

FIGURE 15.7
Igedo, in Düsseldorf, is the largest European fashion fair for women's ready-to-wear.
Courtesy, Igedo Düsseldorf.

Other European Countries

For leadership in Europe, the fashion industry definitely focuses on France, Italy, and Britain. Other countries do attract international interest, however. In the 1990s and the 2000s, the Belgian town Antwerp has become somewhat of a high fashion mecca. Antwerp natives, like Dries Van Noten, Ann Demeulemeester, Martin Margiela, Veronique Branquinho, AF Vandevorst, and Raf Simons, have achieved great success with their innovative and creative clothes. Although all these designers show and have their business head quarters in Paris, some of them still live in Antwerp. Other European countries that have a presence on the global fashion market are Ireland, with its traditional garments and fine linen, and Spain, with its swimwear, lingerie, and bridal fashion tradeshows. As the European Economic Community and other factors globalize the economy, however, national boundaries assume less significance than they once had.

Germany and Scandinavia

Until the mid-1980s, most American fashion buyers skipped Germany on their European buying trips. The country was still divided into East and West, and few West German designers were well known outside Europe. But a new wave of high-fashion women's designers is changing this. Two apparel firms, Escada and Mondi, are noteworthy successes with their high-fashion lines. Designers Hugo Boss and Wolfgang Joop have developed international followings.

Although Germany's fashion industry is relatively small, its international trade fairs have become a major source of fashion inspiration for new fabric and designs. The Igedo produces the CPD women's wear and men's wear fashion shows twice a year in Düsseldorf (see Figure 15.7). Interestingly, this company has exported the fashion trade show through joint ventures with exhibition producers in Hong Kong, London, and Beijing. For textiles, the major international show is Interstoff in Frankfurt, and Cologne hosts shows of men's wear, sportswear, children's wear, and apparel production machinery (see Figure 15.5).

Each of the four Scandinavian countries—Norway, Sweden, Denmark, and Finland—has its own fashion industries and specialties. However, even though each country has its roster of designers, the styles tend to be alike, with emphasis on simple silhouettes and sturdy materials like wool, leather, and linen.

Leather apparel, primarily in men's wear, is a popular Swedish product. Both Sweden and Norway are among the important suppliers of mink and other furs to countries around the world. Birger Christiansen and Saga are leading furriers.

Scandinavia also offers some interesting textile designs. The best known, internationally, are the work of Finland's Marimekko.

Excellent jewelry in all price ranges is available in Scandinavia. The area has long been known for its clean-cut designs in gold and silver. Some well-known Swedish-born, contemporary designers include expatriates Lars Nilsson and Richard Bengtsson.

Mexico and South America

For buyers and producers from the United States and Canada, the signing of the North American Free Trade Agreement (NAFTA) in 1994 brought new possibilities in the Mexican market. The rest of Central and South America and the Caribbean countries began to press for inclusion in this trading pact. (NAFTA will be discussed more in detail in Chapter 16.)

By the mid-1970s, the Central and South American market could be added to the growing list of international fashion markets. The fashion world began visiting market centers in Rio de Janeiro, Buenos Aires, São Paulo, and Bogotá.

Two factors contributed to this new presence in the fashion world. The first was the appeal to Americans and entrepreneurs from other developed countries of cheap sources of materials and labor. The second was the conveniently corresponding development of a fashion industry in Mexico and Central and South America. We will examine American outsourcing of production in this region in Chapter 16.

From the perspective of Mexico and the Central and South American governments, the fashion industry has come to be seen as a means of increasing their gross national product and their status in the world marketplace.

Fashion Products

The fashion industry in Mexico and South America offers fashion on three levels. First, several countries have developed their own high-fashion, or couture, industries, many of which are ripe for import to the United States and Europe. The second level revolves around the development of fashion products that reflect each country's national heritage of crafts. With a renewed interest in ethnicity throughout the world, such products are welcome. Third and finally, Central and South America and Mexico have become important "offshore" sources of products made to North American manufacturers' specifications.

Handbag buyers seek out the better-quality goods of Argentina and go to Brazil for moderate-quality goods. Uruguay is another important source of moderate- to high-quality handbags.

The most important shoe center is Brazil, where manufacturers concentrate on creating a stylish product made from lasts that fit North American feet. Belts and small leather goods are the specialty of Brazil, Argentina, and the Dominican Republic.

Costume jewelry is another important product from this region. Ecuador, Peru, and Mexico export silver and gold jewelry of native design.

Trade Shows in Mexico and South America

The single most important market center in South America is São Paulo, Brazil. At the turn of the millennium, the emergence of designer talents like Alexandre Herchovitch, Rosa Cha, and Icarius coincided with a major Brazilian boom in fashion in general. When superstar models like Gisele Bündchen appeared in these designers' shows, it attracted enough attention to put Sao Paolo fashion week on the map. Since then, Sao Paolo fashion week has been steadily growing in importance and it may become one of the most attended and publicized fashion events in the world.[11] Other important international fairs featuring textiles and textile products as well as fashion accessories are held in Bogotá, Colombia; Lima, Peru; San Salvador, El Salvador; and Santiago, Chile.

These shows offer not only an opportunity for buyers from North America and elsewhere, but also a place for U.S. textile producers to be seen by potential customers in the region. As the rampant inflation of the 1980s has been reduced in many Latin American countries, their fashion industries have become better able to satisfy the desire for textile products made in the United States. The efforts of the World Trade Organization to end textile and apparel quotas by 2005 and the possibility of the expansion of NAFTA into Central and South American countries suggest that trade among the countries of the Americas will grow in the coming years.

The Far East

The United States imports more apparel from the Far East than from any other area in the world. However, the major portion of these imports has been low-priced, high-volume merchandise, and hardly any of the apparel has qualified as "designer merchandise." There are definite signs that this situation is beginning to change, and now fashion buyers can find exciting, innovative styles offered by new design-oriented Asian stylists.

Buyers have used certain countries in the Far East as a market in which to have fashions they saw in the European fashion centers copied and adapted. A fashion buyer needs to know which areas in the Far East are best equipped to handle specific types of manufacturing. Japan and Hong Kong were once the two major contract or copyist countries. But Japan has upgraded its fashion image so that today it is a producer of outstanding high-styled, high-priced fashion apparel. Hong Kong is working to develop the apparel industry of China and promoting Chinese goods in its international trade fairs.

Japan

Japan, long known for its export of silks and pearls, has moved most apparel production out of Japan, to lower-cost countries like Thailand, China, and the Phillippines.

Many Japanese designer boutiques in Tokyo, Japan's fashion center, have their own design staffs who create exciting new looks. Because of their ability to produce fashion goods quickly, the Tokyo fashion scene is often six months to one year ahead of other fashion centers.

Japanese Ready-to-Wear. In the 1950s and 1960s the Japanese faithfully copied Western trends. Ironically, in the 1970s as Western dress had finally won acceptance in Japan, a group of highly original Japanese designers—Hanae Mori, Kenzo Takada, Issey Miyake, and Kansai Yamamoto—emerged. They first worked in Paris, where their lines were design sensations that rivaled the French prêt-à-porter designers. For over a decade, in fact, these daring, designers were thought of as French rather than Japanese. Some of them still show in Paris.

Japanese Designers. In the early 1980s, a mostly new wave of avant-garde designers—Rei Kawakubo of Comme des Garçons, Yohji Yamamoto, and Matsuhiro Matsuda—stormed the American fashion scene.

Although these Japanese designers continue to be a force in the American fashion world, and no one disputes their creative brilliance, their clothes never became commercially successful in America. U. S. retailers had trouble mass merchandising the designs, which appeal mostly to customers that are looking for strikingly unusual shapes and fabrics. Today, although their work is highly revered and regarded as a source of great inspiration for the fashion industry, they remain niche players on the market.[12]

In the 1990s, the latest generation of Japanese designers, catering to a domestic market, have, like their British contemporaries, focused on retro pop cultural influences such as hippie beads and T-shirts and 1970s punk. Today, young Japanese designers like Shinichiro Arakawa, Hiroake Ohya, Kosoke Tsumura, Masaki Matsushima, and Gomme, tend to create technically ingenious designs based on theme, a gimmick or a concept. For example, Oya produced a limited edition of dresses packaged in books that were sold in bookshops. To these designers, the concept is more important than commercial results. Which is why these talents often work for major design houses or commercial clients, (i.e. Arakawa collaborates with Kawasaki motorcycles) in order to finance their own label.[13]

China

The recent history of trade between China and the United States has been a story of steady but uncertain expansion. The issues of whether the United States should use the threat of cutting trade to pressure China to end human rights abuses was only one of the problems that complicated relations between the two countries. However, in 2000, the United States entered a trade agreement with China that gave China normal trader status. This paved the way for the country's entry into WTO (World Trade

Organization). Since then, China's growth in apparel industry has been clear – it's pulling ahead of Mexico as the number one supplier of imported garments to the United States and is expected to grow even more after quotas are lifted among WTO members in 2005.[14]

Among the products that China exports, one of the most sought after is silk. Although it is the world's largest silk producer, it is just beginning to acquire the modern technology need for quality weaving, printing, and dyeing. As the Chinese have been more proficient in these finishing processes, they have exported more finished silk fabrics and apparel products (see Figure 15.8). Cotton and polyester production, once big exports, now barely meets China's domestic needs. Inexpensive plastic shoes are another major export. Leather and fur are also important exports. Several trade shows in Beijing and Shanghai have been instituted by Western-owned exhibition producers to promote Chinese leather to the international market.

Hong Kong. In July 1997, Hong Kong rejoined mainland China after 156 years as a British Crown Colony. The world held its collective breath, waiting to see what would become of this quintessentially market-driven world trading center when it came under Communist rule. The agreement between Britain and China calls for the governing of Hong Kong as a Special Administrative Region for 50 years, and local businesses are reassuring their international customers that Hong Kong will continue to offer all the advantages they have enjoyed plus more. In addition to the political change, Hong Kong has experienced a move in its economy from manufacturing to trade and service industries, and its trade shows, once focused on promoting its own goods, now concentrate on serving as an international marketplace. Some of the advantages of participating in Hong Kong trade shows include the following:

- A duty-free port where exhibitors can bring in their samples and sell them from the exhibition.
- A newly expanded convention and exhibition center.
- A central location in Asia, easily reached by air.
- A thriving hospitality industry with a growing number of hotel rooms and world-class restaurants.

However, in recent years, the once thriving business climate in Hong Kong has been through some setbacks. Recession, high unemployment, and failing retail sales are some of the issues that affect the city. Another concern is China's growing importance as a center of apparel production. This may affect Hong Kong's status as the key gateway city to Asia.[15]

The Hong Kong Trade Development Council sponsors an international fashion week semiannually as well as several smaller shows. Miller Freeman Asia, a trade show producer based in Britain, produces the Asia Pacific Leather Fair, the premier event of its kind, and the Cosmoprof Asia beauty fair.[16]

FIGURE 15.8
Various fabrics are displayed at the intertextile show in Beijing.
Courtesy, Fairchild Publications, Inc.

Other Asian Countries

The other countries of Asia, being smaller and, in many cases, less industrialized than those discussed above, have less influence on the American apparel industry, but their roles as trading partners and sites of offshore production grow increasingly important.

Singapore has many of the advantages of Hong Kong—an easily accessible location, a multinational population, and expertise in international trade. It is Hong Kong's chief rival as a center for trade shows.

Korea, with a design history similar to Japan's, has some exciting young designers creating for the Korean fashion-conscious market. Much of the production of ready-to-wear in Korea is still contract work. But because of the fashion design movement among young Koreans, this is slowly beginning to change.

Indonesia, Thailand, Malaysia, Vietnam, and the Philippines are regarded by many Americans in the apparel industry as sites of offshore production, but that is only part of the story. As these developing countries become more industrialized and the standard of living improves, their own industries and markets are taking their place in the global economy. Thailand, for example, has for many years been a producer of fine printed silk and cotton.

India's centuries-old textile industry continues to make it a major force in the Asian textile market. India also has its own, rapidly expanding fashion industry. Homegrown designers are a relatively new phenomenon in India. Most set up their businesses at the end of the 1990s, in response to India's growing upper class and its appetite for global styles. New Delhi has had its own Lakme Indian Fashion Week since 1999, which draws tremendous attention and is produced by IMG, the same event marketing conglomerate that runs New York's Mercedes-Benz Fashion Week. Some emerging Indian designers are Bal, Ramani and Ranna Gill, and Raghavendra Rathore.[17]

India is also the home of the largest handloom industry in the world—over 13.5 million handlooms are in operation in India. Cotton and silk are the strongest growth areas of the Indian textile industry. India is the only country in the world that produces all four silk varieties: mulberry, tussah, eriand, and muga. Its textile industry employs more than ten million people, second only to the number who work in agriculture.

The Trade Development Council of India conducts promotions and fashion events with major retailers and assists American and European designers in developing sourcing contacts in India.[18]

Trends in Global Fashion Markets

The fashion industry survives through change. International fashion markets are working furiously to keep up with the five major changes that are necessary to remain viable in a highly competitive global market. Fashion is increasingly becoming a global business. At the present moment, there are international fashion weeks in Australia, Brazil, New Zealand, Canada, Columbia, Mexico, Iceland, Hong Kong, Thailand, Japan, and South Africa (see Figure 15.9). Most of these fashion weeks are geared toward promoting the local designer industry with the eventual goal of competing with the dominant world of fashion capitals of New York, Milan, and Paris. Many also receive government sponsorships because they help promote trade and taxes and boost the local economy with big business for hotels and airlines. But there are also other important industry changes.

First, mart managements and trade associations in the United States have responded to industry growth, shifts in population, and changes in buying habits. Marts have also of necessity become more competitive with one another. Elaborate promotions designed to lure buyers now routinely include offers of reduced airfare and hotel rooms. Seminars and cocktail receptions are further enticements. The move toward year-round service is another response to competition. Many facilities expanded their exhibition space and provided access to secretarial and clerical services.

Second, the expense of attending markets and trade shows has had an impact on buyers and exhibitors at home and abroad. For example, the haute couture showings in Paris have become promotional events; buyers attend them vicariously by reading the fashion press. Economic globalization has made fashion capitals like Paris, Milan, and New York showplaces for designers from all over the world, not just from the home country. Retail buying trips to the national and international market centers have become the province of senior staff, who must make decisions for more departments or store units. Designers and other ven-

FIGURE 15.9
The Australian trade shows are growing each year.
Courtesy, Fairchild Publications, Inc.

dors carefully weigh the costs and benefits of several less elaborate exhibitions against fewer, more lavish ones.

Third is another aspect of globalization: developing countries are now becoming major players in the fashion industries, primarily as sources of materials and production, but also as importers and exporters of finished goods.

Fourth is the increased worldwide use of computers and the Internet for buying, especially the basics. The Internet also provides buyers, press and consumers with instant information. For example, American Publisher Conde Nast's fashion Web site Style.com (www.style.com) publishes runway reviews and pictures of a collection only hours after it has been shown on the catwalks in Paris, New York, London, or Milan. Some people argue that all this product information has made the consumer's attention span for trends shorter. Pictures of collections are now shown so quickly, that the clothes look old by the time they hit the stores.

Fifth is the U.S. Commerce Department's International Buyer's Program, which does the research needed to find likely buyers for American products and bring them together with American companies at trade shows. This program has greatly increased the foreign attendance at shows like the International Fashion Boutique Show in New York and the Magic Shows in Las Vegas.

Summary and Review

A market is a meeting place of buyers and sellers. Retail buyers of fashion goods go to market several times a year during market weeks, at the market centers of New York, Los Angeles, and Miami, and regional marts in other cities, including Atlanta, Chicago, Dallas, and Denver. With the exception of New York, where an entire district serves as a marketplace, markets are located in large convention centers with exhibition halls called marts. In addition to visiting the manufacturers' sales representatives in their showrooms or multiline sales reps in temporary exhibition spaces, the buyers may attend trade shows and seminars sponsored by trade organizations.

In Europe, market weeks are semiannual. Designers' haute couture (custom designs) and ready-to-wear collections are shown in the market centers of Paris, Milan, and London. Numerous trade shows for apparel, accessories, and textiles are presented in other cities.

In Canada, market weeks and trade shows are more frequent. Quebec is the province with the largest fashion industry, but all the provinces have apparel manufacturers, and market weeks and trade shows are held in major cities across the country. Mexico and Central and South America are developing as centers for the production of wool and wool products, leather goods, and costume jewelry.

Japan's fashion designers and producers operate on an international scale with showings, boutiques, and manufacturing facilities at home and abroad. The biggest international market for fashion goods in Asia is Hong Kong. Apparel businesses there are using their manufacturing and marketing expertise to develop the silk, leather, and fur industries on the Chinese mainland. Singapore is also emerging as an important market center. The fashion industry is truly operating in a global economy.

Trade Talk

Define or briefly explain the following terms:

boutique	market
buyer's directory	market center
créateur	market week
couture house	mart
couturier/couturière	prêt-à-porter
domestic market	sales representative
foreign market	trade show
haute couture	trade association

For Review

1. What criteria must be met for an area to be considered a market center?
2. What support services for buyers are offered by the marts during and between market weeks?
3. What distinguishes New York City as the major fashion market center in the United States?
4. Describe the distinctive characteristics of the three regional market centers.
5. What are the advantages and disadvantages of trade shows?
6. What business activities have the Paris couture houses undertaken to offset the decline in sales of haute couture clothing?
7. Name the fashion products for which Italy and Britain, respectively, are considered leaders.
8. Name the fashion products for which Canada is considered a leader.
9. Name the fashion products for which Japan is considered a leader.
10. What role does Hong Kong play in the international fashion market?

For Discussion

1. Discuss the importance of the Far East to producers and retailers of fashion goods.
2. The reputation of Paris as a prime source of fashion inspiration began to develop several centuries ago as the result of many interrelating factors. Identify those factors and discuss their importance in the development of any major fashion design center.

References

1. Constance C. R. White, "Patterns," *New York Times*, June 3, 1997, p. 21.
2. Eric Wilson, "7th on Sixth, sold to IMG, Mallis to Resign as CFDA Director," *Women's Wear Daily,* February 5, 2001.
3. "Los Angeles [en] always in Fashion" LA Chamber of Commerce, www.lachamber.org, October 2002

4. Ibid.
5. Business & Industry," Fashion & Apparel manufacturers, San Francisco Chamber of Commerce, www.sfchamber.org, February 3 2002
6. "Federation Activities," www.modea-paris.com, September 2002
7. Press Release, www.pretparis.com, September 3, 2002
8. Charles P. Wallace, "Milan, Italy/Special Report: Good Looks Italian Design Carves a Niche in the Global Market and Creates an Industry That Sells at Face Value," *Time International*, April 21, 1997, p. 42.
9. Madge Garland, *The Changing Form of Fashion*. New York: Praeger Publishers, 1971, p. 73.
10. Susan Semenak, "Montreal's Distinctive Style," *International Herald Tribune*, March 13, 2001.
11. Michael Kepp, "Brazil chimes In on Date Debate," *Women's Wear Daily*, July 3, 2001.
12. Natalie Warady, "High Concepts, High Stakes," *Time Asia,* April 30, 2001.
13. Jose Teunissen, "Made In Japan," Utrecht Museum Press Release, January 2, 2001.
14. Scott Malone, "Getting Ready for 2005," *Women's Wear Daily*, September 24, 2002.
15. Constance Haisma-Kwok, "Shifting Trade Winds," *Women's Wear Daily*, September 24, 2002.
16. Josephine Bow, "Hong Kong Events on a Growth Track," *Women's Wear Daily*, May 28, 1997, pp. 32–33.
17. Eric Wilson, "Dehli Belly," *Women's Wear Daily*, September 3, 2002.
18. Ibid.

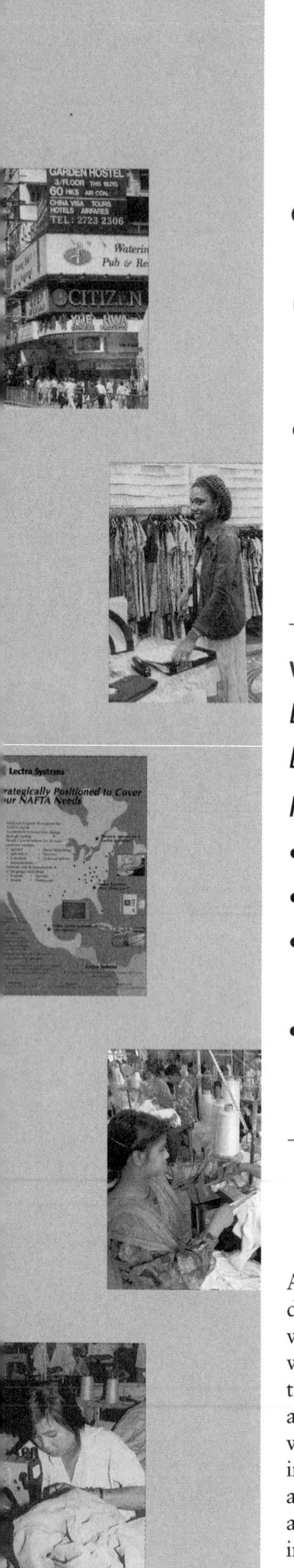

CHAPTER 16

Global Sourcing and Merchandising

WHAT'S IN IT FOR YOU?

Everything you always wanted to know about the international balance of trade.

Key Concepts:

- Means of importing for retailers and manufacturers
- The role of offshore production in product development
- The international balance of trade and its effects on the fashion industry
- International trading laws and agreements between the United States and its trading partners

As nations are no longer able or willing to produce all the goods and services they need and want, they rely on one another to supply them with what they cannot or choose not to produce themselves. In the process, the world's nations are becoming economically interdependent in ways they have never been before. The world is, in effect, becoming one huge global market. We are less a universe made up of individual nations and more one world in ways that were unimaginable even 20 years ago. Political scientists call this process—whereby the nations of the world become more interlinked with one another—globalization. The fashion industry is very much a part of the global economy, so much so that those who work in the business invented a term to describe the process of shopping for and purchasing imported goods: **global sourcing**. When a firm in a country, such as the United States, buys foreign goods, it **imports** them. The country that furnishes the goods, such as Italy, **exports** them. Most countries are both importers and exporters, although, as we shall see, they do not necessarily do each activity in equal amounts.

Fashion producers, retailers, and consumers in the United States have learned to expect the variety and sophistication that imports provide. The world of international trading is undeniably a fascinating one; this is its great appeal. Long gone are the days when foreign buying in the fashion industry consisted of buyers traveling to France a few times a year for the haute couture shows. Even then, very few U.S. retail store buyers actually bought haute couture. They bought ideas and patterns—and then came home to have them produced by American manufacturers. Eventually, as the world experienced a strong and growing post-World War II economy, other European countries—Italy at first, and then other Western European nations—developed their own fashion industries and began luring foreign—that is, American—buyers.

The rest of the world soon followed. Asia, long a source of import goods in home furnishings and a few other specialized areas, went after the U.S. fashion market. Mexico and the Central and South American countries have been the most recent to tap into the mother lode that many consider the American fashion consumer market to be. In sub-Saharan Africa, the manufacture of textiles presents a promising prospect for export; the establishment of this industry would help rebuild the economies of nations recovering from decades of political and military upheaval.

Today, American buyers have expanded their sources to cover, quite literally, the globe. There is no place in the world that American apparel buyers do not travel to in order to obtain goods. Where the Far Eastern circuit once meant shopping the markets in Hong Kong and Taiwan for raw materials, it now also means traveling to Japan for high fashion and places such as Sri Lanka, Indonesia, Malaysia, and the Philippines for their growing number of fashion specialties. American buyers have learned to use a global market to their advantage, molding it to current trends such as private label manufacturing and specification ordering. They have learned to work their way through the labyrinth of federal and international restrictions that regulate international trade.

Adding to the complexity of global sourcing is the increasing reliance of textile and apparel producers on **offshore production**, the use of foreign workers in one or more countries to complete the steps of manufacturing the goods that bear the producer's label. U.S.-owned firms, as well as companies based in Canada, Western Europe, and other industrialized nations, use a variety of arrangements to take advantage of the resources available in countries with developing textile and apparel industries. Company-owned factories abroad, contracts with factories owned by citizens of the foreign country, and joint ownership are all options. A garment may be made of fibers grown in one country, woven into fabric in another, cut in a third, and assembled in a fourth. Decisions of where and how such multinational goods will be made have implications for quality, production costs, and a host of legal issues involving import taxes and quotas. See Table 16.1 for a list of apparel worker wages in selected countries; the wide differences explain why so many manufacturers use offshore production, despite the confusing regulations and great distances often involved.

Importing by Retailers

Retailers are the primary importers of foreign goods in the fashion industry, although manufacturers also seek global sourcing. Retailers like imports for several reasons: their uniqueness, quality, cost, and the variety they add to their stock. They constantly seek merchandise that will make their stores stand out in special and unique ways that will set them apart from the competition. Foreign merchandise often fits that bill.

Global sourcing is a complex and often complicated business. What makes a foreign source attractive—its low cost and promise of higher profits—can be lost or diminished in a matter of minutes if something goes wrong. A shipment of dresses can languish in a warehouse in Sri Lanka, for example, if the importer has not paid attention to quotas. Merchandise deliberately mislabeled "Made in Hong Kong" to get around the quota for goods made on the Chinese mainland can be denied entry into the United States if the deception can be proved.[1]

Anyone who intends to buy goods from a foreign country needs to have a thorough knowledge of its local laws and regulations, particularly the laws that regulate exporting and importing, the efficiency of the transportation system, and the availability and skill of the

TABLE 16.1 Average Hourly Apparel Worker Wages for Selected Countries

COUNTRY	ACTUAL HOURLY WAGE ADJUSTED FOR PURCHASING POWER (U.S.$)	COMPARABLE U.S. HOURLY WAGE RATE (U.S.$)
Bangladesh	1.84	0.86
China	1.66	2.01
Dominican Republic	2.7	2.79
El Salvador	1.2	1.83
Honduras	1.01	1.28
Guatemala	2.52	2.6
India	0.87	0.86
Pakistan	1.8	1.48
Thailand	4.51	6.36
Turkey	1.63	3.38

Adapted from: http://www.sweatshops-retailers.org

labor force. The buyer must be well versed on the tax system and exchange rates. He or she must understand local and national customs and must be well informed about the current political and economic climate. Finally, the buyer must be up-to-date on U.S. import–export regulations, including any pending legislation and must know all this for any country in which he or she intends to do business. This is why importing is best done by someone with access to good suppliers and extensive experience in dealing with foreign manufacturers and import regulations.

To gain entry to foreign fashion markets, as well as to cover them extensively, U.S. buyers rely on the help and experience of intermediaries. These specialists help U.S. buyers shop in the international markets successfully. Foreign-made goods can be purchased:

- In foreign fashion markets
- By store-owned foreign buying offices

FIGURE 16.1
Traveling the globe is an everyday experience for today's buyers. Tsim Sha Shui, in Kowloon, is a neon-lit shopping district for expensive jewelry and clothing from around the world.
Courtesy, Fairchild Publications, Inc.

- By commissionaires or independent agents
- At import fairs held in the United States
- By importers

American Buyers' Visits to International Fashion Markets

Buyers like and need to travel to foreign fashion markets so they can observe new trends first-hand and buy goods suited to their customers. The international markets offer a variety of goods, but not all of them are suited to the American marketplace. By personally shopping in international markets, often during market weeks, American buyers can be sure that they are obtaining goods that will sell at home. They are also able to soak up the cultural and social climates of the countries to which they travel, which, in turn, helps them translate what is new and exciting to their customers.

Store-Owned Foreign Buying Offices

Some stores—those that are large enough to do so or whose image is very special—maintain company-owned foreign buying offices. Buyers who work in these offices support and advise store buyers by surveying the market for new trends, supervising purchases, and following up on delivery. Because they are an extension of the store, buyers in foreign buying offices are often authorized to make purchases just as store buyers are when they shop in foreign and domestic markets.

If the purchase is part of a new trend, stores need the goods when they are still new and customers are still eager to buy them. If it is part of a foreign theme promotion, goods must be delivered while the promotion is in progress. Delivery—especially timely delivery—has been a major problem with imported goods.

Stores generally locate their buying offices in major fashion capitals such as Paris, Rome, London, Hong Kong, and Tokyo, from which their buyers can travel to smaller markets around the world.

Saks Fifth Avenue, Neiman Marcus, and The May Company all maintain store-owned foreign buying offices, as do the big general-merchandise chains such as Sears, JCPenney, and Wal-Mart. Some stores that cannot afford their own foreign buying offices subscribe to the services of independently owned buying offices with foreign facilities, which shop exclusively for their member stores. Examples include Frederick Atkins, the Doneger Group, and the Associated Merchandising Corporation.

Foreign Commissionaires or Agents

In contrast to store-owned foreign buying offices are **commissionaires, or foreign-owned independent agents**. Commissionaires, whose offices are also located in key buying cities, tend to be smaller than store-owned offices. Commissionaires also represent both retailers and manufacturers.

Apart from these differences, though, they provide many of the same services as store-owned foreign buying offices. They often have specialized buyers, or market representatives, who work closely with clients, keeping them abreast of what is generally available and helping them locate specific goods. As is the case with store-owned buying offices, a substantial part of the staff's time is spent following up on purchases to make sure they are delivered when they are needed.

Unlike store buyers, who are authorized to purchase on the store's behalf, commissionaires do not purchase unless they have been authorized to do so.

Commissionaires are paid on a fee basis. Usually, they take a percentage of the **first cost**, or wholesale price, in the country of origin.

Foreign Import Fairs in the United States

Another way to buy foreign goods is to attend one or more of the foreign import fairs that are now regularly held in the United States. Many foreign countries participate in such shows or stage their own fashion fairs in the United States. The New York Prêt a semiannual event in New York City—is one of the largest and most prestigious of these U.S. based shows.

These shows perform two important functions. First, they give foreign manufacturers and designers the same chance to observe American culture that Americans get when they buy in foreign fashion markets. The result is usually closer collaboration between buyers and manufacturers to adapt styles and quality to American tastes. Second, they increase the size and depth of the import market by giving buyers of small- and intermediate-sized stores who would not ordinarily tap into the foreign market a chance to do so. To provide their customers with imported merchandise, these buy-

FASHION FOCUS

Going, Going, Gone–Global

Because it is a success in the United States, does not mean it will be a success worldwide. Knowing your customer's needs and wants is the rallying cry for successful companies, but we must realize that international customers differ from each other, and definitely differ from the United States.

Globalization involves a learning curve for most U.S. designers, manufacturers, and retailers. The most important factor is to learn from mistakes—concepts that are successful here might not work globally. Building a global business involves more than hiring an interpreter, contracting for manufacturing space, or building a store. It requires knowledge that what consumers abroad need and want may be different from what is successful in the domestic market.

Bringing fashion across borders is filled with promise, but also pitfalls, challenges, and surprises. Fashion is one of the strongest sectors in the world of global trade. Profits in consumer goods, which include textiles and apparel, keep increasing. The world today is truly one world!

However the U.S. International Trade Commission has a big question to answer regarding global trade: Who will win and lose when quotas are lifted on apparel and textile products in 2005? This year 2005 is designated by the World Trade Organization for when the 145 member countries will drop all quotas on textiles and apparel. Apparel and textile executives met to discuss the impact of quota-free world and reaching consensus on one point: China will dominate apparel and textile trade in 2005—and beyond.

Many industry and trade association executives look grimly on global trade dominated by China in the post-quota world. Many claim China will eliminate most of the current 125 countries that are suppliers of textiles and apparel, leaving only a handful to compete. American importers concede there will be a consolidation of suppliers, but insist companies will not place all of their production in one or two countries. They claim social responsibility, quality, proximity, and timely deliveries also factor into the equation.

It is not only the U.S. companies that are preparing for the end of quotas. Chinese companies are beginning to open U.S. offices in hopes of being positioned for strong growth in 2005. And, some U.S. manufacturers are taking an "if-you-can't-beat-'em-join-'em" approach to Chinese competition. In January 2003, The Greater Blouse, Skirt, and Undergarment Association, a group of contractors from Manhattan's Chinatown, sent an 11-member delegation to China to seek alliances. The idea is for contractors to serve as local offices for big Chinese factories. Chinatown companies could have closer contact with U.S. customers, while they could use their local factories for sampling and quick-response orders in season. There is little time left until the end of quotas and we have to get a head start! One good head start for students interested in global trade—learn a foreign language; start with Chinese!

Sources:

Kristi Ellis, "Ambitious Agenda for FTAA," *Women's Wear Daily* Section II, Sourcing Horizons, February 11, 2003, pp. 6–7.

Kristi Ellis, "Industry Discusses Quota Removal," *Women's Wear Daily*, January 23, 2003, p. 15.

Scott Malone, "2005: Awaiting China's Dawn," *Women's Wear Daily*, Section II, February 11, 2003, p. 9.

Scott Malone, "Africa's Opportunity," *Women's Wear Daily*, Section II, February 11, 2003, p. 10.

Johanna Ramey, "Central America's Push," *Women's Wear Daily*, Section II, February 11, 2003, p. 8.

Joanna Ramey, "NTA Voices U.S. Trade Policy Concerns," *Women's Wear Daily*, Section II, February 11, 2003, p. 23.

John Zarocostas, "WTO Talks Must Continue," *Women's Wear Daily*, Section II, February 11, 2003, p. 4.

FIGURE 16.2
For the small to mid-size retailer, foreign import fairs, such as this International Jeanswear trade show, bring merchandise to the U.S. buyers' doorstep.
Courtesy, Fairchild Publications, Inc.

ers need not maintain foreign representatives or shop in the foreign markets, neither of which would be cost-effective for their operations.

American Importers

Last but hardly least in a market that relies increasingly on foreign goods, American buyers purchase from American-owned importing firms. Import firms shop in the international markets to purchase their own "lines," which they put together and display to retailers. An example is Merchants Overseas of Providence, Rhode Island. This company imports Swarovski crystal, which it then resells to jewellers across the United States. Shopping these lines gives small retailers an opportunity to purchase foreign fashion merchandise that would not otherwise be available to them. The only drawback to this method is that it does not allow for the customized ordering that buyers from big stores and chains have come to expect.

Importing by Manufacturers

American manufacturers, initially upset about the growth of direct importing done by retailers, have increasingly turned to offshore sources for the same reasons that retailers do: price advantage, exclusivity, and workmanship. Like retailers, they often cite high domestic labor costs as a primary reason for resorting to imports. But labor costs must be viewed in the light of the other considerations if a manufacturer is to maintain control of its brands' images. For example, a sportswear manufacturer may combine fine quality knitwear produced overseas with domestically produced skirts or pants to create a line of separates. Peter Jacobi, president of Levi Strauss International, explained how offshore production fit in with his company's long-term strategy:

Private business has the responsibility to help emerging markets become global players. Before, we all did island-hopping. Now it's more an issue of sharing expertise [with a local partner]. The objectives are low cost, high quality, and dependability."[2]

Product Development: Specification and Private Label Buying

In addition to importing unique or distinctive goods, many retail operations use product development to set their assortment apart from those of their competitors. They may rely on domestic manufacturers or foreign sources for specification and private label buying.

As discussed in Chapter 7, these two terms may be used to describe the same items of merchandise, but the meanings are slightly different. If the retailer agrees, the manufacturer may design private label merchandise for the retailer. On the other hand, **specification buying** is a type of purchasing that is done to the store's rather than the manufacturer's standards. Retailers provide the standards and guidelines for the manufacture of clothes they order.

As they grow more successful with specification buying, stores are also using it for their private label lines. Initially intended as a way to keep production at home, a growing amount of private label stock is now purchased offshore. When stores began to pit their private label merchandise against national brands, they often found that foreign manufacture was one way to control the cost. Among the special concerns that arise when private label goods are manufactured offshore are the quality of the merchandise and the need to meet delivery schedules. Foreign producers are learning to meet American quality standards, but they are still likely to lose out to American manufacturers over delivery time.

A manufacturer can achieve economies of scale by sourcing both the national brand and the store label from the same offshore supplier.[3] Of course, products made to specification by foreign producers must also con-form to an array of industry and government standards.

International Balance of Trade

Just as there are two sides to every coin, there are also two sides to the global market. Throughout the early 1980s, the expanding international market seemed to work to everyone's advantage. The global market came about largely because the early 1980s were a period of prosperity at home and abroad. There was nothing wrong with a fashion market that was truly international so long as a balance was maintained between exports—what Americans sold abroad—and imports—what they bought abroad. For several decades, foreign countries were eager to import American-made goods, which were much sought-after for their high quality.

Unfortunately, by the mid-1980s, the downside of a global market—what happened when the trade balance shifted—revealed itself. The U.S. dollar grew weak, which meant that American goods became expensive, often too expensive to be of interest for export. The American reputation for producing quality goods suffered by comparison as other nations learned how to turn out quality products. The Japanese were soon beating Americans at their own game—cars and electronics. And the clothing industry proved itself woefully inept at competing at all. At first, Americans bought foreign clothes because they were so much cheaper than domestically produced goods. Eventually, though, they began to buy them because of their excellent workmanship and distinctive design.

When the dollar weakened, foreign countries only increased their exports to the United States. The resulting tidal wave of imports caused severe trauma to American industry generally and to the U.S. apparel manufacturing industry specifically. As foreign producers gained ground, domestic producers lost out. The American economy improved in the 1990s, and increases in apparel exports were part of that improvement; between March 1995 and March 1996, the increase was 17.6 percent for a record $6.38 billion. In 2001, due to a sharp decline in overall merchandise trade growth, and a downturn in the economy, caused U.S. textile and apparel exports to drop by almost three percent.[4] However, overall apparel and textile imports continue to exceed exports by significant amounts and are expected to continue to do so (see Table 16.2).

These few cold statistics seem to paint a discouraging picture for the U.S. fashion industry, but a closer examination of the situation from several perspectives shows that the outlook is far from uniformly bleak. In order to understand the present state of the import–export market, it is important to know something about the **balance of trade**. This is the difference between the value of exports and the value of imports. When the value of goods that a country imports exceeds the value of its exports, it experiences a **trade deficit**. When a country's exports exceed its imports, it has a **trade surplus**. Since the mid-1980s, the United States has imported more from the Japanese than it has sold to them. Thus, the United States has suffered from a trade deficit with Japan, while Japan has experienced a trade surplus with the United States. A trade surplus is advantageous; a trade deficit hurts a country's economy (see Figure 16.3).

TABLE 16.2 Textile and Apparel Trade Balances–U.S. and World (in millions of dollars)

TYPE OF PRODUCT	1999	2000	2001	2002	% CHANGES
Yarn	-16	-90	-81	-230	187.74
Fabric	386	954	943	777	-17.63
Made-Up	-6,260	-6,492	-5,023	-6,403	6.29
Apparel	-51,920	-52,874	-49,496	-49,672	0.35
Total	-57,810	-58,502	-54,658	-55,527	1.59

Adapted from: U.S. Department of Commerce, trade and Data Division, Office of Textiles and Apparel, January 17, 2003.

The deficit problems of the United States are not limited to Japan. In recent years, the United States has become the world's largest clothing importer, buying nearly one-third of all the imported clothing in the world. In contrast, for many of the world's developing countries, the manufacturing of clothing and textiles for export is the first step toward a sound national economy. The so-called "Four Tigers" of Asia—Hong Kong, Singapore, South Korea, and Taiwan—illustrated the success of this industrial development strategy, until a banking crisis led to troubled economies for these countries in the late 1990s.

The United States is not the only country with trade deficit problems. Around the world, trade statistics show that the industrial countries are relying more and more on imports while the developing countries are becoming the exporters. Although indications are that the growth in the U.S. trade deficit has slowed, the United States remains the single largest contributor to the world trade imbalance.

The conditions that traditionally encouraged consumers to purchase domestic goods—a devalued dollar and heightened tariffs—seem to have done little to turn the American public away from foreign merchandise. While the promotion "Crafted with Pride in the U.S.A.," which urges Americans to buy American, has created a sentimental support for domestic goods, at the point of purchase, consumers seem less interested in the origin of the goods than in getting the best value at a given price point. Furthermore, the distinction between domestic and foreign goods is clouded by the widespread practice of offshore production. The name of a U.S.-owned company on a label does not indicate anything at all about the nationality of the workers who made the product or the origin of the materials they used.

Some people believe that sterner measures—higher tariffs and stricter import quotas among them—are necessary to protect American industry from imports. Others oppose such measures. They argue that the real problem is the

FIGURE 16.3
The dilemmas of foreign trade policy affect every consumer.
Signe Wilkinson for the Philadelphia Daily News, Philadelphia USA/ Cartoonists & Writers Syndicate.

inefficiency of American industry, which will not be made stronger by import restrictions. These two groups support two opposing ideologies regarding the conduct of American business.

Protectionism is the name given to an economic and political doctrine that seeks to exclude or limit foreign goods. The opposing doctrine, **free trade**, supports the free exchange of goods among nations. Since the balance of trade affects the nation's economic health, and the federal government is constantly passing and revising legislation about importing and exporting, advocates of both doctrines are well represented in Washington, D.C., by lobbyists who seek to promote legislation supporting their views.

FIGURE 16.4
Merchandise bears a hang-tag or label with this logo, to remind consumers to "buy American."

Protectionism

The first import restrictions on goods brought into the country date back to 1789, when the United States, a newly founded republic which was still mostly rural, feared that it would not be able to compete with the world's industrial powers. To reduce its considerable reliance on imported goods, it slapped a 50 percent tariff, or import tax, on 70 different articles imported from France and England. Tariffs have come and gone, but the debate over whether protectionism is good—or necessary—has persisted for more than 200 years.

In the fashion industry, the leading supporters of protectionist legislation are manufacturers, who are most hurt when Americans buy imported rather than domestic goods. Industry trade associations and UNITE, the apparel and textile workers' union, offer the most organized support for protectionism. Most consumers recognize their work through their campaigns, "Crafted with Pride in the U.S.A." and "Made in the U.S.A." which encourage people to buy American (see Figure 16.4). But the manufacturers have also mounted a behind-the-scenes campaign designed to inform retailers about the advantages of buying domestically produced goods.

The industry has also changed its attitude in recent years, moving from a "Here's what we can do for you" stance to a "What can we do for you?" posture. Among the advantages of domestic buying promoted by the industry are quality, Quick Response, and flexibility.

Free Trade

Free traders believe that restrictions on trade will threaten the nation's ability to grow and compete in the global marketplace. Retailers and most consumers are among those who support free trade. They believe the buying public should be free to buy imported as well as domestic goods.

Except for those times when protectionists are active, free traders do not do much to promote their cause. In many respects, they already have the support of the federal government. The history of the United States as the model of a capitalistic economy, the financial interests of powerful U.S. businesses in multinational conglomerates, and the interrelationship of the nation's role in international politics with its position as an economic power all favor a free trade stance.

The struggle over free trade versus protectionism is played out in several arenas, such as international trading laws, U.S. regulations, and preferential programs sponsored by various trading nations.

International Trading Laws

In the global economy, trade is truly international, not merely a set of bilateral agreements among pairs of nations. (A "bilateral agreement" is one in which two countries reach a separate agreement.) The trade relationship between any two nations affect the relationship of each party with its other trading partners as well. International trade laws have therefore developed out of need.

General Agreement on Tariffs and Trade (GATT) and World Trade Organization (WTO)

In 1947, the United States and 23 other nations met in Geneva, Switzerland, to write an agreement known as the **General Agreement on Tariffs and Trade** (GATT). This agreement played a major role in reducing trade barriers and unifying trading practices among member nations. Membership grew to 92, and representatives met every few years to negotiate new trade arrangements among member nations. In 1995, GATT was succeeded by the **World Trade Organization** (**WTO**), which has continued to adjust member agreements to meet the changing needs of the global economy. Some of the agreements apply specifically to the textile and apparel industries.

However, the free trade agreements have come under a lot of criticism. One of the arguments is that the interest of powerful nations and corporations are shaping the terms of world trade. This could mean that the interest of the people would be compromised, while a decreasing number of people would prosper. It could also threaten the domestic industries of industrialized countries, whose production costs can't compete with those of developing nations. There are also special agreements made between large companies and leaders of poor countries that are eager to attract foreign businesses. For example, billions of dollars in imports from poor countries enter the United States duty free through preferential trade agreements and free trade pacts.[5]

Free trade agreements have caused a lot of friction worldwide. China's entry to the World Trade Organization in 2001 was seen as a huge threat to the domestic industries in many nations. China's seemingly unlimited supply of low-cost labor makes it a very attractive place for foreign corporations, and many textile and industry workers in countries with higher wages fear that this will cause them to lose their jobs. In 1999, there were large demonstrations and protests in conjunction with the World Trade Organization Summit in Seattle. The demonstrators were protesting for different reasons. Some were concerned with the future of domestic industries, some focused on environmental issues, and others rallied against the exploitation of workers in third world "sweat shops." The demonstrators clashed repeatedly with the police and hundreds of people were arrested.[6]

Multi-Fiber and Textile Agreement (MFA)

In 1973, the United States and 53 other nations signed the first multinational agreement specifically regulating the flow of textile products. A primary purpose of the **Multi-Fiber and Textile Agreement** (**MFA**) was to establish ground rules for bilateral agreements and unilateral actions designed to restrict the free flow of these products. The United States, Canada, and some of the industrialized nations of Western Europe wanted to protect their textile industries from cheaper imports from less developed countries.

The MFA was renewed twice without any essential changes in its stated purpose or goals. It was also renewed in 1986, but this time not without controversy. The 1986 renewal attempted to deal with two changes in the status of textile trade:

1. Growing pressure in the United States to enact tighter quotas on textile imports
2. The United States' insistence that the Big Three textile-exporting nations—Hong Kong, Korea, and Taiwan—revise their bilateral agreements with the United States.

Despite the substantial revision, many American producers felt it did not give them the measure of relief they sought. They pointed out, for example, that the MFA limits the number of units that can be brought into the country rather than the cost value of merchandise. Faced with quantity limits, many foreign producers have merely shifted to higher-priced merchandise, a move that hurts the domestic market even more than limiting cheap imports does.

The textile exporters were dissatisfied for the opposite reason. They did not want their fledgling textile export industries to be singled out for quotas at all. Particularly galling to these less developed nations was the imposition of protectionist policies by an organization that was supposedly formed to promote free trade. Like David battling Goliath, the exporters won, and the MFA is being phased out in three stages over the period between 1995 and 2005 (see Figure 16.6).

U.S. Regulation of Textile and Apparel Imports

Some of the specific measures the United States—or any other country—is liable to undertake or has undertaken to promote its own trade interests are quotas, tariffs and duties, and preferential programs.

Import Quotas

Under the provisions of the MFA, the United States has negotiated bilateral agreements to impose quotas on textile imports from certain

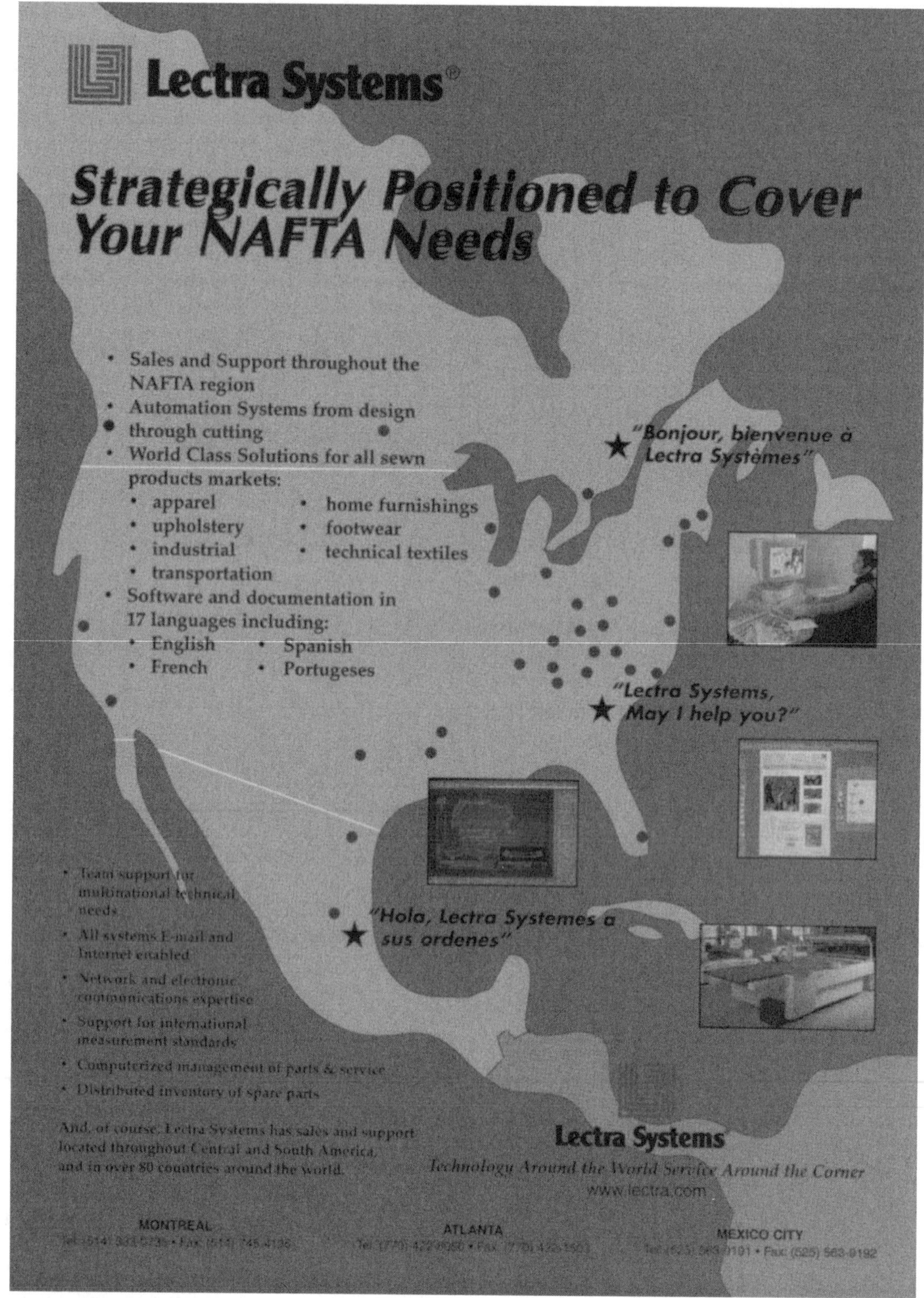

FIGURE 16.5

As this trade ad for Lectra Systems points out, NAFTA requires facility in at least three languages.

Courtesy, Lectra Systems®.

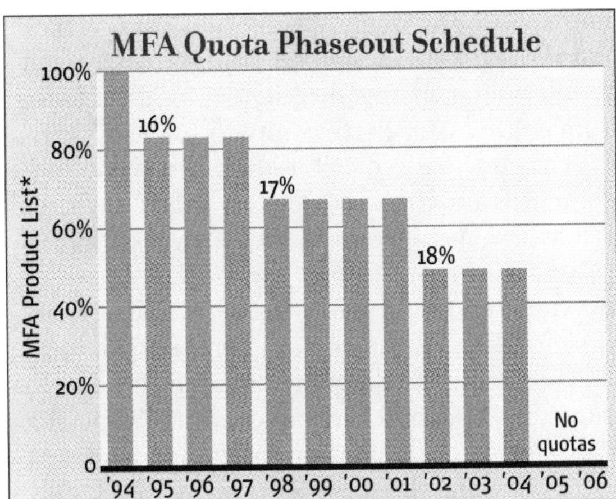

*Percentages are based on the assumption all products are covered by quotas, which is not the case.

FIGURE 16.6

The MFA calls for a 3-stage phasing out of quotas between 1995 and 2005.

Source: The U.S. manufactured fiber market under NAFTA and the WTO (p. 10) by P. O'Day. Presented to the 33rd International Man-Made Fibres Congress, Dornbirn, Austria.
Reprinted by permission by Paul O'Day and the American Fiber Manufacturers Association.

countries. In determining where quotas are needed to protect domestic textile production, the United States considers the price of textile imports from each potential trading partner.

Part of the analysis is an assessment of the stage of development of the country's economy. **Developed countries** (**DCs**), such as Canada, Japan, and members of the European Union and **less developed countries** (**LDCs**), including, among others, Haiti, Bangladesh, and many sub-Saharan African nations, are usually not targeted for quotas; the DCs, with their high standards of living and well-paid labor forces are unlikely to undersell domestic producers, and the LDCs, if they have an export market, do not have a large enough one to compete seriously. It is the **newly industrialized countries** (**NICs**) that are typically subject to quotas by the United States and other DCs. Examples of NICs include Malaysia and the Phillippines.

The United States has negotiated bilateral trade treaties over the past few years with its five major Asian suppliers—Hong Kong, Taiwan, China, South Korea, and Japan. (Although Japan is a DC, its protectionist policies have influenced its trade agreements with the United States.) These treaties have been successful in reducing the general level of imports to the United States from these countries, but at the same time, other countries such as Indonesia, Malaysia, and the Philippines have taken up the slack as they grew from LDCs to NICs, so there have been no overall reductions in imports from these areas.

Import quotas are limits set to restrict the number of specific goods that may be brought into the country for a specific period of time. Quotas, which are established either by presidential proclamation or legislation, are either absolute or tariff-rate.

Absolute Quotas

Absolute quotas limit the quantity of goods that may enter the United States. When the limit is reached, no more goods of that kind may be imported until the quota period ends. Absolute quotas may be global or directed to specific countries. Imports in excess of a quota may be exported or detained for entry during the next quota period. To keep accurate and consistent records of apparel and other textile imports, these items are counted in terms of **square meter equivalents** (**SMEs**).

Tariff-Rate Quotas

Tariff-rate quotas set a limit after which a higher duty is charged on goods entering the country. When a certain number of goods have entered at the lower rate, customs raises the duty on any additional goods, which, in effect, also raises their price in the market.

Transshipment

Although quotas are scheduled to be phased out, some exporters seem unable to wait until they can import their goods into the United States without these limitations. They have resorted to **transshipment**, an illegal means of circumventing the quota system. For example, Chinese goods are sent from the mainland to Hong Kong, where "Made in Hong Kong" labels are sewn in. Although Hong Kong is now part of China, for trade purposes, it is treated differently and is not subject to China's quota for imports into the United States. When mislabeled goods defy trade quotas in this way and enter the United States, U.S. manufacturers lose the protection that the quota system was intended to provide, The Chinese exporters and their confederates in Hong Kong lose the trust of U.S. importers and cast doubt on the fair trading practices of their countrymen.[7]

Taxes: Tariffs and Duties

Most fashion merchandise is subject to an import tax, called a **duty** or **tariff**. This is a fee assessed by the government on certain goods that it wishes to restrict or limit. Tariffs and duties are imposed on imported goods that the government wishes to make more competitive in price with domestically produced goods. The tax varies depending upon the category of merchandise, but it is usually a percentage of the first cost.

Antisweatshop Commitments

The downside of relying on offshore production for cheap labor became apparent to American fashion producers when sweatshop conditions in third-world countries—and even in some domestic factories employing illegal aliens—came to light in the mid-1990s. Horror stories of workers held in virtual captivity, required to work long hours for less than subsistence wages, and subject to corporal punishment for the slightest infraction of inhumane work rules made front page news. Realizing the threat to their reputations as good corporate citizens, many apparel manufacturers were quick to recognize the need for self-regulation. Television personality Kathie Lee Gifford expressed shock when it was revealed that a line of clothing bearing her name and sold at Wal-Mart was being produced by Honduran children working for less than a dollar a day. She promised to pay for immediate correction and monitoring of the situation. Nike became the subject of negative publicity when the incomes of owner Ray Knight and his advertising spokesperson, basketball star Michael Jordan, were contrasted to the paltry wages and mistreatment of the laborers who manufactured the athletic shoes in Asian sweatshops. Even Nike's appointment of a commission headed by former United Nations ambassador and civil rights activist Andrew Young to investigate the company's adherence to new, humane policy was not enough to convince the public that the problem had been rectified.

The Gap has also been accused of using sweatshop labor. In February 2002, the protestors surrounding the World Economic Forum in Manhattan singled out the Gap as a symbol of globalism gone bad. The demonstrators charged that one of the factories that produces the Gap's apparel in Guatemala underpays and abuses its workers.[8]

The American Apparel Manufacturers Association of Arlington, Virginia, formed a 12-member labor task force to address the sweatshop problem, and in August 1996, representatives of 18 organizations, including human rights advocacy groups and labor unions, as well as apparel manufacturers and retailers, joined together in the White House Apparel Industry Partnership.

This advisory panel established voluntary standards for the working conditions in factories where members of the U.S. apparel industry do business. Among the provisions are a maximum 60-hour work week, including overtime; one day off from work per week; and pay meeting or exceeding the minimum wage in countries where the firms operate. Balancing the reliance of families in developing countries on their children's contributions to the family income against the protection of the children, the standards set the minimum age for hiring at 15 years, reduced to 14 only in countries that allow the employment of factory workers younger than age 15. Prison labor and other forced labor may not be employed. Workers are protected from abuse or harassment, and they have the right to form unions and bargain collectively. To ensure compliance, monitoring by the apparel companies and independent observers from labor, human rights, and religious groups are part of the agreement.[9]

These standards are called the WRAP (Worldwide Responsible Apparel Production) principles. Global support for WRAP continues to grow monthly. So far manufacturers' organizations in Guatemala, Sri Lanka, Turkey, and 12 other countries that have been known to have factories with sub-standard worker conditions, have endorsed WRAP.[10]

In 2000, The American Apparel Manufacturers Association merged with the Footwear Industries of America and The Fashion Association to become the American Apparel and Footwear Association (AAFA). The AAFA continues to demonstrate its commitment to responsible business practices.[11]

Another problem that both large and small apparel businesses face is political turmoil in a particular region. British designer Sophia Swire, who regularly goes to Nepal to have her silk accessories hand-embroidered and beaded, says:

"If you're working in the developing world, you have to be aware of the political situation. You must not be too reliant on any one region, because you don't want to be a victim of world circumstances. On the other hand, you don't want to pull out of a certain region, and deprive people of jobs, if there's no immediate threat."[12]

Then & Now

Sweatshops

Sweatshops were with us *then*—and sadly they are with us *now*. Sweatshops were spawned by the Industrial Revolution in England in the 19th century. Their truly horrendous conditions were documented by Charles Dickens in his novels *Hard Times* and *David Copperfield*. Sweatshops soon spread around the world.

In New York, on March 25, 1911, a fire broke out in a sweatshop run by the Triangle Shirtwaist Company. As a result of this fire, 146 people, mostly young immigrant women, died. Company officials had locked the doors to prevent theft. Escape was impossible. This disaster touched off a national movement for safer working conditions and led to the creation of health and safety legislation, including factory fire codes. The Triangle Shirtwaist Company fire also helped shape future labor laws, including child labor laws.

That was *then*. What has happened since? Why are we *now*, at the start of the 21st century, facing many of the problems we thought we had eradicated at the beginning of the 20th century? Fighting sweatshops is difficult in a world where (1) manufacturers depend on such shops for fast delivery, (2) large groups of illegal immigrants are so eager for work that they accept extremely low wages and are too afraid to complain, and (3) we, the customers, always look for the lowest prices.

The worst sweatshops are in third world countries, but sweatshops still exist in the United States. Again, it took a catastrophe to highlight the recurring problem of sweatshops in the United States. In El Monte, California, in August 1995, the abuse of garment workers came to the attention of the nation. It was revealed that 72 Thai immigrant workers were being held in what amounted to slave labor conditions. They worked 17 hours a day, lived in squalid conditions, and earned as little as 70 cents an hour. It was a wake-up call for the American public: the sweatshop was back!

The U.S. General Accounting Office investigated New York City's garment industry and estimated at least one third of the 6,000 factories are sweatshops that routinely violate federal labor laws. A U.S. congressman went undercover to garment factories in the city's Chinatown, and found filthy, dilapidated factories with barred windows and doors. Many of the workers were illegal immigrants who had been smuggled into the country. They were forced to work 16 to 18 hours a day and paid as little as $1.30 to $3.00 an hour.

In 1997, U.S. Labor Secretary Alexis Herman started a new youth-oriented campaign called "Getta Clue." This campaign was designed to educate young Americans about the sweatshop issue. Young people have always proven to be willing workers for various human rights groups and have been very forceful in their support of better working conditions for apparel workers.

In April 1998, the Smithsonian Institution mounted a sweatshop exhibit that created great controversy. It was titled "Between a Rock and a Hard Place: American Sweatshops 1820–Present." Some people felt it raised questions about the integrity of today's U.S. apparel industry. Peter Leibhold, one of the exhibit's curators, said "We recognize that no one has the right answer about why there are sweatshops and what to do about them."

One of the worst abuses in sweatshops in third world countries is the use and abuse of child workers. About 250 million of the world's children under 14 years of age are working, most of them full time. If no change is made, they will remain forever locked into misery and poverty because they cannot go to school to better themselves and upgrade their skills. In 1998, a Global March Against Child Labor moved from country to country through Asia, Africa, and the Americas. More than 7,000 non-profit organizations around the world supported the March, which endorsed an international treaty calling for the immediate abolition of the three most exploitative forms of child labor: (1) slavery; (2) the use of children for illegal activities, such as drug dealing and pornography; and (3) hazardous work.

As in 1911, these shocking news stories outraged the American public and were the sparks that ignited the movement toward safer working conditions and guarantee of a living wage.

In 1998, the White House anti-sweatshop task force, formally known as the Apparel Industry Partnership, wrote a global factory monitoring plan and urged companies to sign up.

Let this be a lesson. We must always be aware that without vigilance, sweatshops will rise again. As National Retail Federation president Tracy Mullin said: "vigilance and cooperation by all parties involved—manufacturers, enforcement agencies, and retailers—are essential if these conditions are to end for good."

Courtesy, Fairchild Publications, Inc.

Sources

Kristi Ellis, "Fewer Sweatshops in 2001," *Women's Wear Daily*, March 29, 2002, pp. 2-14.

Leslie Kaufman and David Gonzales, "Labor Standards Clash with Global Reality," *New York Times*, International Section, April 24, 2001, pp. 1–A10.

Scott Malone, "Anti-Globalization Targets: Why Gap is Number One," *Women's Wear Daily*, February 27, 2002, pp. 2–8.

"UNITE! Stop Sweatshop Campaign," available online at http://www.uniteunion.org/sweatshops/action, June 25, 2001.

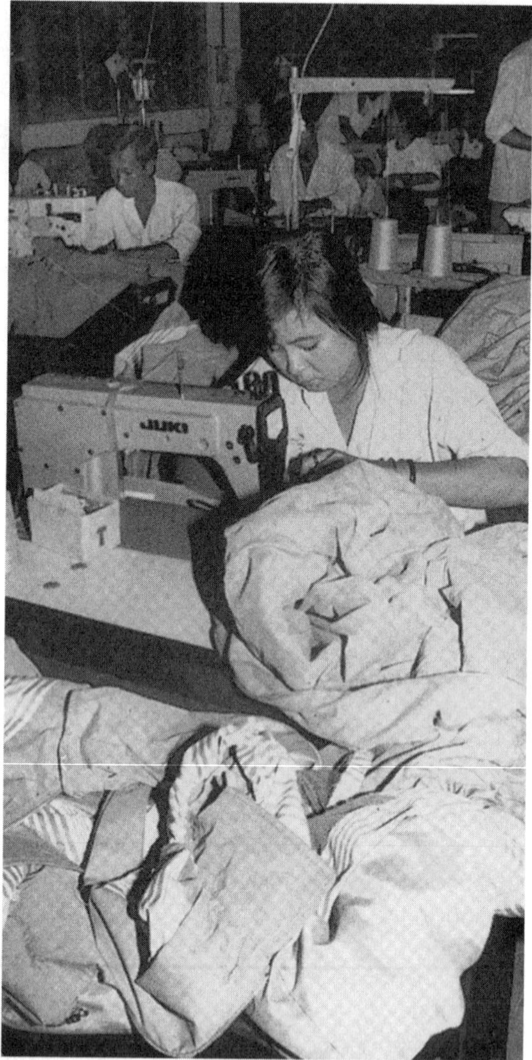

FIGURE 16.7
Sewing is a major cost for most garments; this has led to global sourcing for the sewing function to cut costs.
Courtesy, Fairchild Publications, Inc.

Counterfeit, Black Market, and Gray Market Goods

Three illegal practices that plague both importers and exporters are the importing of counterfeit, black market, and gray market goods. Counterfeit goods, like counterfeit currency, are inferior imitations passed off as the genuine article. Luxury goods and designer brands are the chief objects of counterfeiters. An example is a horde of silk baseball jackets found by a detective working for *Fortune* magazine. They had the famous Louis Vuitton logo, but at that time, Vuitton did not make clothes!

Another famous black market story took place in 1999 when a truck containing 1,300 pieces of Nicole Miller merchandise (worth at least $132,000 wholesale) was stolen. Most of the clothes were later recovered, thanks to a woman who bought a dress on the street and then called the Miller showroom to try to exchange it for another color.

The sale of counterfeit goods at "bargain" prices devalues the real brand and deprives legitimate businesses of their fairly earned profits. U.S. Customs officials are authorized to seize imported counterfeit goods.

Another problem for manufacturers are **bootleg** goods. Many of these goods are not cheap rip-offs, rather they cannot be distinguished from the real ones. They are being made by the same manufacturers that make the real ones, but who are selling some goods to the black market. An example is a Prada shoulder bag sold in the Prada store in Manhattan for $390; the bootleg copy sold on the streets of Rome for $117.[13]

Gray market goods are those that were not intended for sale in the country in which they are being sold; for example, an expensive Swiss watch is sold at a remarkably low price in the United States, but it does not have a warranty valid in the United States. The unfortunate customer usually does not realize this until repairs are needed.

These practices are often referred to as *industrial piracy*. In the late 1990s, the United States rated the worst industrial pirates as Turkey, China, Thailand, Italy, and Columbia.[14]

Preferential Programs

Over the years, the United States has been a proponent of aid to developing countries. Among the incentives offered in its many preferential programs are arrangements that permit the imports from certain nations to enter the country quota- and duty-free and that allow other countries low tariffs or generous quotas.

Most-Favored Nations

The term *most-favored nations* may seem almost self-contradictory because it is applied to trading partners that are not necessarily regarded with favor by the United States. In the era when the Soviet Union dominated Eastern Europe, "favored" status in trade relationships was part of the political and diplomatic efforts to win countries over to a market economy. Since the breakup of the Soviet Union, the term is heard mostly with reference to trade negotiations between the United States and China. The debate within the federal government focuses on whether to tie granting of most-favored nation status to correction of China's human rights abuses. So far, trade has continued to expand, and there is no clear evidence to indicate whether the ongoing negotiations have any influence on China's treatment of its political prisoners.

Tariff Schedules 807 (9802) and 807A

These two tariff schedules provide for preferential access of goods that originate or are partly manufactured in the United States and are also partially made abroad. These schedules favor American manufacturers. Item 807 of the United States tariff schedule (renumbered 9802 in 1989 but still referred to by its old number within the apparel industry) allows cut piece goods and trim items to be exported from the United States, assembled or sewn abroad, and then returned to United States with duties owed only on the value that was added abroad. In other words, duty is paid only on the labor that was done abroad.

A revision, 807A, requires that the piece goods taken out of the country be of U.S. origin. Approximately 80 percent of the value of 807A exports comes from the United States. Item 807A is also referred to as Super 807, because it provides special access for goods that are domestically cut and made of U.S. fabrics.

Caribbean nations have taken advantage of these arrangements to increase their share of U.S. apparel imports from 6 percent in 1985 to 22 percent 10 years later. In 1999, the Dominican Republic exported the highest percentage (by value) of goods into the United States under the 807 and 807A. They were followed by El Salvador, Honduras, Mexico, and Guatemala.[15]

Items produced under 807 and 807A must bear a special label indicating the country of origin, which is considered to be the country where the garment is assembled. "Assembled in _______ of U.S. components" is the most common form of the label.

Caribbean Basin Initiative (CBI)

Latin American imports have been an area of growing concern to Americans. While U.S. manufacturers worry that a flood of imports from Latin America will hurt domestic industry, Americans also see these countries as customers for U.S.-made goods and have a special interest in promoting their neighbors' economic development. The Caribbean Basin Initiative (CBI) was designed to do two things: offer trade protection to U.S. manufacturers at the same time as it encourages the growth of an import industry in Latin America. One major feature of the CBI—duty-free entry of goods into the United States—was not applied to apparel and textile products, but, as noted above, 807 and 807A production favors the CBI countries in these industries.

However, since the North American Free Trade Agreement (NAFTA) passage in 1994, these countries have found themselves at disadvantage with Mexico (see discussion on NAFTA in the following section). While continuing to lobby for NAFTA-like treatment, Central American countries like the Dominican Republic, Honduras, and Costa Rica looked for new ways to compete with Mexico, such as developing full package capabilities and higher quality production facilities. In 2000, the Caribbean Basin Trade Partnership Act (CBTPA) granted NAFTA-type duty treatment to U.S. imports of footwear from eligible Caribbean and Central American countries. U.S. industries believe that the CBTPA will facilitate U.S. investments in the region.[16]

North American Free Trade Agreement (NAFTA)

The **North American Free Trade Agreement (NAFTA)**, which went into effect in January, 1994 eliminated quotas and tariffs for goods shipped between the United States and Canada and Mexico. Its effects have been hotly debated. Canada, long the United States's largest trading partner, is still the largest. Since the NAFTA entered into force the Canadian economy has grown by an annual average of 3.8 percent. This has translated into close to 2.1 million jobs. Canada's merchandise trade with the United States reached $588.7 billion in 2000.[17]

The impact of the agreement on trade with Mexico has been a subject of great controversy. Some U.S. manufacturers have seen Mexican factories as a threat to their own plants, and others have considered opening facilities there. U.S. textile and apparel workers fear losing their jobs to lower-paid Mexican laborers. In California alone, some 12,200 apparel jobs have been lost since the implementation of the

NAFTA in 1994.[18] The total number of jobs lost in the United States because of free trade is close to 400.000.[19] On the other hand, Mexico's NAFTA membership has helped the Mexican economy grow at an annualized rate of 2.3 percent.[20]

One example that points up these complex issues is that of Pendleton Woolen Mills, which moved its Sellwood, Oregon, plant to Mexico in 1996. The cost was 119 U.S. jobs. Even before NAFTA, Pendleton had begun buying fabric and some finished shirts from Hong Kong because of global competition. As Gary Bensen of Pendleton said:

It wasn't so much the lure of NAFTA, as the pressures we were under to cut prices and Mexico's proximity, which promised a quick turnaround on orders. NAFTA just happened to be there.[21]

Free trade agreements with China have complicated the issue further. In April 2001, 400 people in New England lost their jobs when California manufacturer Power-One moved their Allston facilities to less costly plants in Mexico and China.[22] It is likely that this will continue to occur. In 2005, quotas will be lifted on all apparel and textile imports for the 144 countries in the World Trade Organization. Charles Bremer, director of international trade at the American Textile Manufactures Institute, predicts more job losses:

"I expect more textile plant closures and there will be no apparel industry in the U.S. to speak of. The only way the textile industry will survive, at least in the apparel fabric sector, is to export to the CBI and other countries with which the U.S. has preferential trade agreements."[23]

United States and Mexico trade has increased dramatically since NAFTA. In 1993, the year before NAFTA took effect, U.S. exports to Mexico totaled $41.6 billion and U.S. imports from Mexico totaled $40.7 billion. By the end of 1999, U.S. exports had risen to $87 billion and imports from Mexico were $110 billion. From 1994– 2000, according to U.S. data, two-way trade increased from $82.3 billion to $261.7 billion.[24]

One unexpected result of NAFTA was the rapid movement of production facilities from the Caribbean to Mexico—especially of underwear—which resulted in many job losses in the Dominican Republic and Jamaica. Mexico rejects this conclusion.

Economist Nora Lustig, a fellow at the Brookings Institute reports that:

A majority of the nearly $450 billion in North American cross-border trade is intrafirm, meaning companies are shifting semifinished products across frontiers during different stages of manufacturing to seek maximum efficiency. Moreover, a high percentage of Mexican exports are produced by a small number of very large companies, meaning that free trade has an uneven impact.[25]

The United States is seeking to expand NAFTA to include South America and Africa.

Penetration of the U.S. Market by Foreign Investors

Direct investment in U.S. properties and businesses is extremely attractive to foreigners. Since so many textiles and apparel items are imported into the United States, foreign investors have long been interested in buying into American textile and apparel manufacturing companies. Only recently have they succeeded in doing so. Foreign investors, mostly from Europe and the Far East, have taken three routes to ownership: joint ventures, total ownership, and licensing.

For example, L'Oréal of France purchased three important U.S. cosmetic labels: Maybelline, Redken, and Helena Rubenstein. While the purchasing of manufacturers is a relatively new form of foreign investment, many retail operations have been foreign-owned for some time, and there is even more activity in this sector than in manufacturing. Two other foreign retailing successes are Laura Ashley, which is British-owned, and Benetton, which is Italian-owned.

New York's Madison Avenue, Chicago's Michigan Avenue, and Los Angeles' Rodeo Drive are lined with the boutiques of such Italian designers as Valentino, Armani, Ungaro, Dolce & Gabbana, Missoni, and Prada.[26] Their presence in the United States is just a part of their global retailing strategy.

Licensing

Actually, investment by foreign manufacturers in the fashion industry is not entirely new. Licensing arrangements, which often involve ownership of domestic companies, were initiated over 25 years ago by companies such as Christian Dior, Pierre Cardin, and Hubert Givenchy. Today, the European presence is widespread. For example, Donna Karan's and

Marc Jacobs' collections are financed by the French LVMH-Louis Vuitton Moet Hennessy family.[27]

Penetration of Foreign Markets by U.S. Companies

In order to counterbalance foreign investment, American businesses have been interested in investing in foreign countries, where U.S. management is often welcomed because American know-how and standards for high quality are much-respected commodities. U.S. investment in foreign countries also helps the balance of trade.

Licensing

Just as foreign manufacturers first penetrated the U.S. retail market with licensed products, so too have American companies been able to license products abroad. American character licenses such as Mickey Mouse, Kermit the Frog, Superman, and Miss Piggy have been great successes abroad, as have sports licenses and brand names, such as Nike, and designer names, such as Calvin Klein, Donna Karan, and Ralph Lauren.

Today, many companies are switching from licensing to importing strategies in order to establish and strengthen brand identity. As international distribution continues to develop, particularly in Asia, U.S. manufacturers are finding that a mix of locally licensed product and U.S.-manufactured apparel is the most effective way to sell locally.[28]

Joint Ownership

While the United States permits total ownership by foreign investors, most other countries only allow foreign investors to be partners or joint owners. Among the American companies that are joint owners in foreign manufacturing firms is Blue Bell, producer of Wrangler jeans in Asia, Italy, and Spain.

U.S. Exporting

Because the "Made in the U.S.A." label is desirable all over the world, the United States can export its fashion products around the globe. Increased U.S. exports, in fact, are seen by many industry experts as the solution to the U.S. trade deficit. The United States does not need to keep out foreign competitors as much as it needs to sell and promote its products abroad.

By the mid-1990s, U.S. fashion producers had begun to see exporting as a solution to another challenge as well. With the domestic market saturated with their goods, they turned to other countries as a source of growth. The U.S. industry's reputation for quality and trendsetting styles brought about a 17.6 percent increase in apparel exports from 1995 to 1996. The numbers continued to grow, and in 2000, U.S. exports of textile and apparel increased to record levels of $10.5 billion. But in 2001, the economy turned and textile and apparel exports fell almost three percent.[29]

Individual American designers have their followings abroad, not only as representative of U.S. fashion but because of their unique styles. Calvin Klein, for example, began his business in Japan in 1995. Within 2 years, his ready-to-wear and accessories business generated $214 million and his jeans line $25 million. Isaac Lagnado, a New York retailing consultant, points out that:

> *Fashion worldwide is increasingly becoming homogenized. American designers and names are increasingly institutions [in other countries] as foreign shoppers visiting the United States are taking back armloads of goods.*[30]

Although U.S. designer fashions are available in upscale department stores around the globe, a common strategy is to establish a presence in a new foreign market with a freestanding "signature store," or boutique. The ability to monitor consumer reaction to the designer's merchandise allows for rapid adjustment to local tastes and preferences, just as is true at home. Bud Kohnheim, chief executive officer of Nicole Miller, predicts that: "By the end of the century, the term 'going global' will have lost its meaning. Foreign sales will just be another part of every firm's account list."[31]

Meanwhile, as U.S. exporters await the easing of trade barriers, their goods are often subjected to the same kinds of trade restrictions that the United States imposes on other countries. U.S. manufacturers seeking to export their products must work their way through a maze of foreign country quota, duty, and tariff regulations.

Because the United States is a major industrial giant, it is not the beneficiary of foreign-sponsored preferential programs such as it frequently sponsors for other nations. But recently, many domestic programs have been developed to help U.S. manufacturers become more successful exporters. The new programs are usually sponsored by the federal and state departments of commerce.

One active program is the Textile and Apparel Export Expansion Program, sponsored by the U.S. Department of Commerce. At the Fashion Institute of Technology, the Export Advisory Service Extension (EASE) maintains an active program for fashion industry exporters. EASE counsels individual manufacturers on the advisability of exporting their products and through conferences, workshops, and seminars, works closely with members of the fashion industry to encourage exporting.

SUMMARY AND REVIEW

Through imports, offshore production, and exports, the U.S. textile and apparel industry is a major player in the global economy. Importing is a major source of merchandise for retailers, who rely on visits to foreign markets, store-owned foreign buying offices, commissionaires, import fairs, and U.S. import firms. Apparel manufacturers are also purchasers of foreign products, especially fabrics and other materials and trimming. Retailers may develop products bearing their private label by having their designs produced by foreign manufacturers.

U.S. apparel manufacturers have turned to offshore sources for all or part of the production of their goods. To improve the unfavorable balance of trade that has resulted from this extensive import activity, the government has imposed quotas and tariffs on selected goods from countries whose products have a competitive advantage. The United States participates in multinational agreements such as those of the World Trade Organization and in separate trade agreements with individual countries or groups of countries.

U.S. and foreign businesses mutually penetrate each other's markets through licensing arrangements, investments in manufacturing, and establishment of retail outlets. Export of U.S.-made fashion goods is a growing aspect of the country's role in the global economy.

Trade Talk

Define or briefly explain the following terms:

absolute quota
balance of trade
bootleg
commissionaire
developed countries (DCs)
duty
export
first cost
free trade
General Agreement on Tariffs and Trade (GATT)
global sourcing
gray market goods
import
import quota
less developed countries (LDCs)
Multi-Fiber and Textile Agreement (MFA)
newly industrialized countries (NICs)
North American Free Trade Agreement (NAFTA)
offshore production
protectionism
specification buying
square meter equivalents (SMEs)
tariff
tariff-rate quota
trade deficit

For Review

1. What advantages do imports give retailers?
2. Name the five ways foreign-made fashion merchandise can be purchased.
3. What are the two important functions of foreign import shows in the United States?
4. What are the concerns that arise when retailers do specification buying of private label merchandise?
5. Who are the advocates of protectionism in the fashion industry? Why?
6. Who are the advocates of free trade in the fashion industry? Why?
7. What is the purpose of WTO? MFA? NAFTA?
8. What are the provisions of Tariff Schedules 807 and 807A?
9. What rules has the Apparel Industry Partnership established for U.S. apparel manufacturers who do business with offshore factories in order to eliminate sweatshops?
10. What forms do American investing in foreign countries fashion industries take?

For Discussion

1. As a fashion consumer, do you advocate protectionism or free trade? What major items of your current wardrobe would you have been unable to purchase if broad protective legislation prohibiting imports had been in place?
2. What are the advantages of using a store-owned foreign buying office? A commissionaire?

References

1. Raymond Bonner, "Altering Labels, Not Clothes, China Sidesteps Trade Limits," *New York Times*, April 12, 1997, p. A4.
2. Katherine Weisman, "Making Global Connections," *Women's Wear Daily*, May 24, 1996, p. 12.
3. Anne D'Innocenzio, "The Private Label Push," *Women's Wear Daily*, January 8, 1997, p. 18.
4. "Textile Industry Year-End Trade & Economic Report," American Textile Manufacturers Institute, www.atmi.org
5. Kristi Ellis, "Feeling The aftershocks – A World trade Organization Report Registers the Toll Sept 11 Has Taken on Overseas Trade," *Women's Wear Daily*, November 28, 2001.
6. "In Pictures: Day Two of Seattle Clashes," *BBC News*, www.sbb.co.uk, December 2, 1999.
7. Bonner, "Altering Labels, Not Clothes," p. A1.
8. Scott Malone, "Anti-Globalization targets: Why Gap is Number One," *Women's Wear Daily*, February 2, 2002. p.2.
9. "No Sweat? Sweatshop Code Is Just First Step to End Worker Abuse," *Solidarity*, June/July, 1997, p. 9.
10. "WRAP principles", www.wrapapparel.org, October 2002
11. Ibid.
12. Samantha Conn, "Europe Soldiers On," *Women's Wear Daily,* Sourcing Horizons, February 2002.
13. John Tagliabue, "Fakes Blot A Nation's Good Names," *New York Times*, July 3, 1997, p. D1.
14. Jim Ostroff, "Without Parity, 807 Keys CBI Growth," *Women's Wear Daily*, July 23, 1996, p. 19.
15. Jordan K Spear, "CBI Splashdown," *Bobbin Magazine*, November 2000.
16. "Developments in the Trade and Customs Arena," *Footwear Industries America Newsletter*, May 2000.
17. "Overview" Canadian Departent of Foreign Affairs and International trade, www.dfait-maeci.gc.ca, February 2002.
18. Katherine Bowers/Kristin Young, "California Wage-Hike: can Industry Afford to Produce In-State?" *Women's Wear Daily*, January 16 2002.
19. Edward Mason, "Will More New England Companies Seek NAFTA Aid?" *Boston Business Journal*, November 23, 2001, p. 12.
20. "The North American Trade Agreement – Mexico Background", http://environment.about.com, February 2002.
21. Art Pine, "Jobs Issues Hide NAFTA's Real Intent," *Los Angeles Times*, July 9, 1997, p. A1.
22. Ibid.
23. Kristi Ellis, "US Mills Threatened as Quotas are Lifted," *Women's Wear Daily*, January 29, 2002.
24. "Textile Industry Year-End Trade and Economic Report"
25. William J. Holstein, Linda Robinson, and Lucy Conger, "NAFTA Thoughts," *U.S. News & World Report*, July 7, 1997, p. 59.
26. Mervyn Rothstein, "The Invisible but Sought-After Parameters of Chic," *New York Times*, July 2, 1997, p. B5.
27. Holstein et al., "NAFTA Thoughts."
28. Eric Wilson and Kiji Hirano, "International Licensing: A Two-Pronged Strategy," *Women's Wear Daily*, April 16, 1997, p. 8.
29. Jules Abend, "Exporters Tout Western Europe," *Bobbin*, September 1996, p.38.
30. Jules Abend, "Exporters Tout Western Europe," *Bobbin*, September 1996, p. 38.
31. "Exports Hit Their Stride," *Women's Wear Daily*, August 7, 1996, p. 28.

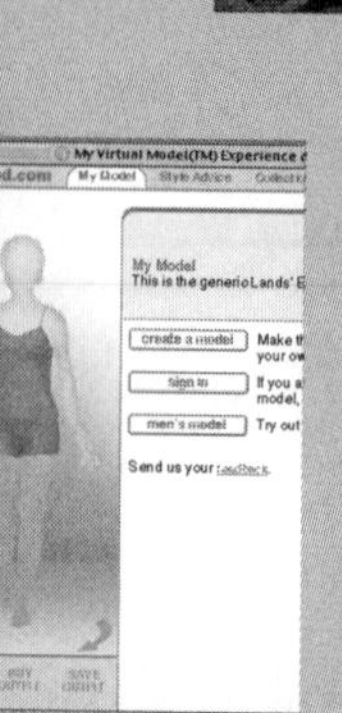

CHAPTER 17

Fashion Retailing

WHAT'S IN IT FOR YOU?

Everything you always wanted to know about the organization, operation, differences, and new trends in various types of retail organizations.

Key Concepts:

- History and development of fashion retailing in the United States
- Organization for buying and merchandising in department stores, specialty stores, and discount stores
- Organization for buying and merchandising in chains, leased departments, and franchises
- Operation of off-price retailers, factory outlet stores, category killers, boutiques, and showcase stores
- Operation of nonstore retailers, including direct sellers, catalog stores, TV home shopping, and Internet sites.
- Trends in retail patterns.

The business of everybody in fashion business is store business, whether one designs, manufactures, buys, sells, promotes, displays, reports, or photographs clothes, shoes, accessories, or beauty products. Eventually, the goods must be where the people are, and the people must come to where the goods are, and what is in the stores must be desired and bought by people—people continuously "shopping"; seeing, desiring, paying, and possessing. That is store business, and, in one way or another, it is the business of everybody in the fashion business.

—Estelle Hamburger, "*Fashion Business—It's All Yours,*" Harper & Row, 1976.

Retailing is the business of buying and selling goods to those who will use them, the ultimate consumers. Retailing is a vital industry in the United States today. With over two million retailers, the nation generates about $3 trillion in sales annually in 2000.[1] **Fashion retailing** involves the business of buying and selling—or merchandising—apparel and accessories and home fashions. It is the way fashion products are moved from the designer or manufacturer to the customer.

Retailing is in many ways the heart of the fashion industry. It is the most challenging end of the fashion business, existing as it does in a constant state of change. Retailers must, for example, be among the first to spot and act on new trends. They must be attuned to their customers' needs and desires to a degree that is required in few other businesses. Retailers must react to a constantly changing and often unsettled economic climate.[2]

An extraordinary amount of planning and effort goes into the merchandising of fashion products. For people who are not in the fashion business, the processing of merchandising fashion products can look very easy. Fashion moves from concept to customer; that is, from designer to manufacturer to retailer to you—the customer! The most intricate part lies in the merchandising and retailing of the goods. As mentioned previously, an old adage among fashion retailers, called the five R's, stands for choosing:

- The Right merchandise
- At the Right price
- In the Right place
- At the Right time
- In the Right quantities

If any one of these R's is incorrect, it will collapse all the R's. Think of it as smoothly juggling five balls at once. You must keep them all in the air at the same time; constantly moving, never touching. Your timing must be flawless. If you let one ball slip, they will all fall. And you must keep smiling and make it look effortless. That is like fashion merchandising—it looks easy but is hard to do!

History and Development of Fashion Retailing

People have been swapping, trading, or selling each other various goods for thousands of years. In the Orient and eastern Mediterranean, bazaars and marketplaces still operate on the sites they have occupied for centuries. Not until the mid-1800s and the opening of the first department store—the Bon Marché in Paris—did modern merchandising as we know it begin to develop. Even then, it developed differently in the United States than in Europe. In this chapter, we shall explore the development of retailing in the United States.

Retailing in the United States grew directly out of the frontier. It was an attempt to meet the needs of countless numbers of settlers who were moving west to populate a huge country. The first settlements in the United States were situated along its eastern coast. There, settlers built cities and towns that resembled what they had left behind in Europe. Philadelphia, New York, and Boston were soon populous centers of commerce and culture. Their shops were patterned after those in London and Paris. No one is sure who should be credited with the founding of the first department store in the United States. Most authorities claim it was R. H. Macy in about 1860. Others claim it was The Fair in Chicago in 1874, or Wanamaker's in Philadelphia in 1876. On the frontier, however, such sophistication was not possible, nor would it have served the needs of western buyers. Instead, three elements—general stores, peddlers, and mail-order sellers—each uniquely geared to life on the frontier, combined to give birth to modern retailing in the United States.

General Stores

When the West was in the very early stages of settlement, there were no stores—and very few women to buy anything in them anyway. Apart from the settled areas along the East Coast, most of North America was populated by Indians, fur traders, and explorers. Groups of Indians had long traded goods among themselves, and the Europeans who traveled west soon learned to follow suit. They began by trading with Indians, but soon European traders opened trading posts. There, fur traders swapped furs for basic supplies.

Gradually, as the West became more settled, and pioneer men and women moved across the country, trading posts evolved into **general stores.** Where trading posts had carried only such basics as guns, gun parts, and food supplies, general stores sought to expand their stock by adding such goods as saddles, salt pork, lamp oil, and even ladies' bonnets. Money was a scarce commodity on the frontier, so general stores were still willing to take goods as well as cash for payment. A farmer's wife might make bonnets or lace collars to exchange for the few supplies she needed from the general store. As people became more settled, they became interested in buying more than basic supplies, and general stores were soon stocking a greater variety of items such as dress fabric, sewing notions, and fancier bonnets.

Not surprisingly, in a place where life was spartan and store-bought goods were one of life's few pleasures, people liked to linger over their purchases. As a result, general stores also functioned as community social centers as well as gathering places for political debate. To this day, general stores still serve many small communities in rural areas of the United States.

Gradually, as settlers became more prosperous, the general stores stopped bartering and began to operate on a cash-only basis. The new influx of capital could be used for expansion. Over time, some general stores—such as Meier & Frank in Portland, Oregon, and Filene's in Boston—grew into full-fledged department stores.

Peddlers

Even with general stores located in communities and trading posts scattered along well-traveled trails, many homesteads were too isolated to make regular use of them. Itinerant peddlers began to service these remote customers. A peddler visited some areas only once a year, so he was accorded a warm welcome.

In many ways, peddlers were the first marketing experts. In addition to their wares, which typically consisted of pots and pans, shoes and boots, sewing notions, and a few luxury items such as lace, combs, and ribbons, they carried news of the latest fashions being worn in the cities back east. The reverse was also true, and they carried word back east about specific items that pleased or displeased customers in the Midwest or West.

Mail-Order Sellers

The final element in the development of modern retailing was the mail-order seller. Mail-order companies, which began in the late 1800s, serviced the rural areas of the United States. At that time, the United States was largely rural, so this meant almost everyone was a mail-order customer. Montgomery Ward, which mailed its first catalog in 1872, was the first company to do the bulk of its business by mail. By 1886, it had a competitor, Sears Roebuck, and the mail-order business was in full swing. Such companies were only able to operate after the establishment of rural free delivery (RFD), a system of free mail delivery to rural areas, and later, parcel post, a system of low-cost mail delivery that replaced RFD.

The mail-order catalog brought a new and expansive world to the lives of rural Americans. Hundreds of fashion items, furnishings for the home, and tools for the farm were offered in the catalogs. The illustrations were clear, goods were described in detail, and best of all, from a farm woman's point of view, prices were reasonable. The catalogs did not offer high fashion, but to rural women their variety and prices were still enough to delight. Women who had been limited to the scant provisions that a peddler was able to carry on his wagon or the barely filled shelves of general stores now felt as if the world was at their fingertips.

By 1895, a mere nine years after its first issue was mailed, the Sears catalog had expanded to fill 532 pages. The fledgling company posted astonishing sales of $750,000 that year.[3]

FIGURE 17.1

In the latter part of the 19th century, the Sears, Roebuck catalogs opened a whole new world of fashion to rural Americans who lived far away from shops.

Despite the growth of towns and cities, which brought far more cosmopolitan shops to the entire country, the appeal of mail-order shopping never completely lost its luster, and today, mail-order remains a major segment of retail business.

Traditional Types of Fashion Retailers

As the frontier turned into towns and cities, peddlers became sales representatives and general stores and mail-order businesses evolved into something entirely different from their ancestors. Today, hundreds of thousands of retail stores exist to serve the over 285 million consumers in the United States.[4]

Today retailers usually can be classified into one of two broad categories—general and specialized—depending on the kinds of merchandise they carry. In each of these categories are many different kinds of retail operations: department stores, specialty stores, chain operations, discount stores, and leased departments, to name a few. Almost all retail stores offer some form of mail-order or telephone or fax buying service, and there are also retailers that deal exclusively in mail order. Many retailers are setting up Internet sites. Some stores have grown into giant operations, but many others are still small independently owned and operated business.

The retail scene is dominated by **general merchandise retailers**, such as JCPenney, Sears, and Target. These retailers typically sell many kinds of merchandise in addition to clothing. They try to appeal to a broad range of customers. Most general merchandisers very broadly target their merchandise to several price ranges, and only a few limit themselves to narrow price ranges.

Specialty retailers, in contrast, offer limited lines of related merchandise targeted to a more specific customer. They define their customers by age, size, or shared tastes. Their customers are more homogeneous than those of general merchandisers. Examples are Crate & Barrel, Tiffany's, and Talbots.

Today, the differences between types of retailers are not as clearly defined as they used to be. It has, for example, become increasingly difficult to distinguish a department store from a chain operation, a discounter from an off-pricer, a franchiser from a chain. In this section, we will look at three traditional types of fashion retailers: department stores, specialty stores, and discount stores.

Department Stores

The **department store** is the type of general retailer most familiar to the buying public. Many are even tourist landmarks. Few people, for example, visit New York without seeing Macy's or Bloomingdale's. People also make special trips to see Marshall Field's in Chicago and Rich's in Atlanta. In London, Harrods is a big tourist attraction, as is Le Printemps in Paris.

Department stores are in a state of flux that makes them difficult to define. The Census Bureau defines a department store as a retail store carrying a general line of apparel, home furnishings, and housewares, and employing more than 50 people. Despite this official definition, however, many department stores have eliminated their appliances and furniture departments. And at least one major trade magazine, *Stores*, published by the National Retail Federation, includes "multidepartment soft goods stores (or specialized department stores) with a fashion orientation [and] full markup policy" on its list of traditional department stores.[5] Both the government's lapse and the magazine's eagerness to revamp the definition of a department store are indicative of the changing image of department stores, and for that matter, other stores today.

Department stores reigned as kings of retailers well into the 1960s, when there was only about 4 square feet of retail space per person in the United States. They had long dominated downtowns with main stores called "flagships." In the 1960s and 1970s, department stores anchored malls. But in the turbulent 1980s, department stores failed all across the country; victims of overexpansion, mergers and acquisitions, and increased competition. By 2000, there was 20 square feet of retail space per person, much of it occupied by chain specialty stores and category killers.[6]

Department stores strengthened in the mid-1990s. As Arnold Aronson of Kurt Salmon Associates, a management consulting firm, put it: "Department stores have been the main targets of new formats, because they basically have it all. Everybody has targeted a piece of the department store, but nobody has been able to target the entire package. In the end, department stores are the dominant concept under one roof."[7] Table 17.1 list the survivors and Table 17.2 lists the fallen among the retail industry.

TABLE 17.1 The Top 10 Department Stores in the United States

RANK	CHAIN (HEADQUARTERS)	SALES ($)
1.	Sears (Hoffman Estates, IL)*	35,843,000
2.	JCPenny (Plano, TX)	18,157,000
3.	Federated Department Stores (Cincinnati, OH)	15,651,000
4.	May (St. Louis, MO)	14,175,000
5.	Dillard's (Little Rock,AR)	8,155,000
6.	Kohl's (Menomonee Falls, WI)	7,488,654
7.	Saks Fifth Avenue (New York, NY)	6,070,568
8.	Nordstrom (Seattle, WA)	5,634,130
9.	Mervyn's (Hayward, CA)	4,038,000
10.	Neiman Marcus (Chestnut Hill, MA)	3,015,534

*Includes specialty stores
Adapted from: http://www.stores.org/archives/2002department.html

TABLE 17.2 Gone But Not Forgotten

Do you remember these once-powerful retailers? Can you categorize them as department stores, chains, specialty, or discount stores? How many names can you add to the list?	
Abraham & Straus	Jordan Marsh
Alexander's	Korvette's
Arnold Constable	Maas Brothers
B. Altman's	McCory
Best & Co.	Merry-Go-Round
Bonwit Teller	Mill Rhoades
Bulloch's	Neisner
Cignal	Ohrbach's
Dejaiz	Oppenheim Collins
5-7-9	Peck & Peck
Foxmoor	Robert Hall
G. Fox	S.S. Kresge
Garfinkel's	Sterns
Gertz	Susie's
Gimbel's	Thalheimer's
Goldblatt's	Ups 'N Downs
Herman's Sporting Goods	W.T. Grant
Horne's	Weibolts
I. Magnin	Woolworth's

Before getting into the ways in which stores are changing, let us look at how various kinds of traditional retailers operate and merchandise themselves. As general merchandisers, department stores typically serve a larger portion of the community than other stores and often offer a variety of quality and price ranges. A department store usually offers a category of apparel at several price points, each in a different part of the store. Figure 17.2 shows that a typical department store offers dresses on many floors, in many departments, with varying rates of return.

Department stores have also traditionally enjoyed a certain prestige that often extends even beyond the communities they serve. They are usually actively involved in their communities. A department store, for example, will eagerly stage a fashion show for a local charity, knowing that such activities create goodwill and enhance the store's overall reputation.

Organization for Buying and Merchandising

Department stores are organized into special areas, or departments, such as sportswear, dresses, men's clothing, and furniture. Generally, buyers purchase for their departments, although in very large department stores, even the departments may be departmentalized, with individual buyers purchasing only part of the stock for a department (see Figure 17.3). In some sportswear departments, for example, one buyer may purchase tops, while another buys bottoms.

Most department stores have a parent store, and many also operate branch stores. Buyers may buy for the branches as well as for the main store, or if the branches are located in another town or very far from the parent stores, they may have their own buyers.

Entertainment Values

The weaving of entertainment into modern retailing is reshaping the shopping experience. Entertainment values in retailing are defined in a number of ways. The most traditional way is by "simply having a compelling, often changing, merchandise assortment." Many retailers think of their stores as theaters that provide entertainment. The walls are the stage, the fixtures are the sets, and the merchandise is the star.

Other popular entertainment strategies include providing video walls, interactive Internet sites, store visits by celebrities, designer trunk shows, sponsoring charity fund raisers, and on and on.

Contrary to the rumors that the department store is a dinosaur, many department stores are fighting back by adding entertainment value. One way that department stores have built relationships with their customers is through award and loyalty programs. These programs reward high-spending customers with bonuses, and make members feel like they are part of a VIP club. The stores will arrange events that range from meet-the-designer product launches to luncheons and cocktail parties. Neiman Marcus, for example, hosts lunches for its In-Circle program that has featured guests like

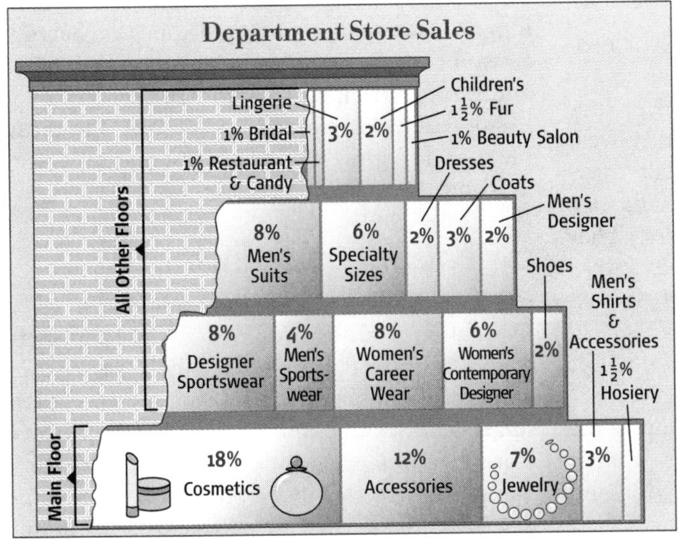

FIGURE 17.2
This diagram of a typical flagship store for a department store chain shows the percent of business it gets from each department.

FIGURE 17.3 *The traditional department store "look" features separate, departmentalized classifications, as in this distinctively styled men's wear department.* Courtesy, Harry Grethel, Watertower, Chicago, Illinois

Robin Leach and Larry King. Jeff Henry, Vice President of San Francisco-based retail design firm Gensler, offers his vision of what successful contemporary retail should look like:

"Retailing in the new millennium will have a 'deliberate calmness' about it. The heavy emphasis on entertainment during the previous decade will give way to experiences that are simple, direct and authentic. Artifice will not be welcomed. Service and caring for customers will be the rule."[8]

Specialty Stores

A **specialty store** carries a limited line of merchandise, whether it is clothing, accessories, or furniture. Examples of specialty stores include shoe stores, jewelry stores, maternity-wear stores, and boutiques. As noted, specialty merchandisers tend to target a more specific customer than do general merchandisers. They may offer a single line; just shoes, for example. Or they may offer related limited lines, for example, children's apparel, shoes, and other accessories. Or they may offer a subspecialty, like just athletic shoes, or just socks!

Another variation of the specialty store is the private label retailer, which sells only what it manufacturers itself. The Gap, Ann Taylor, and Brooks Brothers are leading examples.

Most of us are familiar with specialty stores but do not realize how varied they are. A specialty store can be one tiny hat shop, or it can be a chain of large, multidepartment stores such as Saks Fifth Avenue, which specializes in apparel. The latter is the type that *Stores* magazine reclassified as full-fledged department stores.

The majority of specialty stores in the United States are individually owned and have no branches. The composite sales of these single-unit specialty stores, however, represent only somewhat less than half of the total sales volume of all specialty stores. These stores are having an increasingly difficult time as harried consumers have less time to spend on shopping, and want convenience and low prices.

Specialty stores attract customers all across the world; Asprey's Jewellers in London, Gucci in Rome, Hermès in Paris.

Organization for Buying and Merchandising

In small specialty stores, the buying and merchandising are done by the owner or a store manager, sometimes with the assistance of a small staff. Large multidepartment specialty stores are organized along the lines of department stores, with buyers purchasing merchandise for their own departments. Multiunit specialty stores belonging to chain organizations are set up in a unique way that is described under chain organizations, later in this chapter.

Entertainment Values

Entertainment is a natural activity for specialty stores. In addition to exciting visual merchandising, many specialty stores now offer related entertainment. NikeTown began the trend with its video wall, and then expanded to a Town Square with a staffed counter, banks of video monitors, and information about local and national sports teams. Gaylan's Trading Company, the sports division of The Limited, offers indoor and outdoor climbing walls, and an in-line skating area. Contempo Casuals Girl's Room is an in-store boutique that features magazines, incense, black lights, and photo booths. A small chain of specialty stores called Hot Topics feature a so-called Rock Wall, a 30-foot-long display of T-shirts of alternative musicians such as Nine Inch Nails, and computer stations that allow customers to surf the Internet.[9]

Discount Stores

The discount business got its start after World War II, when servicemen and servicewomen came home with a well-thought-out agenda for their lives: get married, establish a home, and start a family. Within a few years, with the help of the G.I. bill, which funded both education and mortgages, they had managed to achieve at least one of their wishes. Millions of new houses had been built in "new" suburban towns. The next step was to furnish them.

Discounters saw a need and began to fill it. The first discounters sold household goods. They ran weekend operations, usually setting up shop in an empty warehouse, barn, or lot just out side the city limits. Their stock varied from week to week, but they managed to have what people needed. One weekend toasters were featured; on another bath and bed linens were on sale. The selection was not particularly good, but the prices were right, so people came to buy. Through word-of-mouth, discount businesses began to grow. Some even expanded into permanent stores.

The discounters sold name-brand merchandise at less than retail prices. They did it by keeping their overhead low and offering minimal services—two facets of discount selling that prevail to this day. Cash-and-carry was the rule.

Fair trade laws made the sale of goods at more than retail or "list" price illegal. Discounters discovered, however, that the fair trade laws did not apply to selling lower than list price. Soon they were doing exactly that. In a sense, the fair trade laws, designed to prevent gouging by retailers, made the discounter's low price more recognizable and reputable.

Today a **discount store** is any retail operation that sell goods at less than full retail prices. Discounters are called "discount stores," "mass merchandisers," "promotional department stores," and "off-pricers." Discounters, who may be either general or specialty merchandisers, sell everything from cosmetics, accessories, and apparel, to health and beauty aids, to major appliances (See Table 17.3).

As noted, discounters make a profit by keeping their overhead low and service minimal. Most discount stores have centralized checkout counters and rely on self-service. Volume and size are used to compensate for low markups. Discount stores typically aim to do a minimum annual sales volume of $500,000 and maintain stores with at least 10,000 square feet. Often they occupy the so-called **big boxes**. As Cynthia Turk of Marketplace 2000 noted:

> *It is important to note that a big box is NOT a separate category of store, but rather a concept for a store that presents a large selection of goods in a selling space typically oversize for its merchandise category. For example, Jared's Jewelry at 8,000 square feet is big box. A wedding dress superstore at 12,000 square feet is big box.*[10]

Discount stores may be independently owned or part of a chain operation such as Wal-Mart (see Figure 17.4). Even department stores have gotten into the act, opening wholly owned divisions of the parent firm. Target Stores, for example, is a discount operation of the Dayton Hudson department store group.

The first fashion discounters established themselves in New England. They rented warehouses and factories that had once been textile mills. Today, fashion discount operations have begun to resemble other retailers. Credit cards are often accepted. Self-service and centralized checkouts are still the rule, but there is a trend toward more personalized service on the floor.

Organization for Buying and Merchandising

Early discounters searched the marketplace for closeout and special-price promotions. Their inventories consisted almost entirely of this type of goods. Today, discounters specialize in low-end open-market goods or special lines

TABLE 17.3 The Top 10 Discount Stores in the United States

RANK	CHAIN (HEADQUARTERS)	SALES ($)
1.	Wal-Mart (Bentonville, AR)	139,131,000
2.	Kmart (Troy, MI)	37,000,000
3.	Costco (Issaquah, WA)	34,797,037
4.	Target (Minneapolis, MN)	32,588,000
5.	Sam's Club (Bentonville, AR)	29,395,000
6.	Meijer (Grand Rapids, MI)	11,450,000
7.	Dollar General (Nashville, TN)	5,322,895
8.	BJ's Wholesale (Natick, MA)	5,161,164
9.	Fred Meyer (Portland, OR)	3,724,839
10.	Consolidated (Columbus, OH)	2,647,500

Source: http://www.stores.org.

made exclusively for them. Most conventional retail operations do not want their buyers to purchase goods that will be sold to discounters, but this has not stopped manufacturers from making special lines for discounters. Some designers and manufacturers use discount outlets to sell their overstocks or slow-moving items.

Independently owned and nonchain discounters follow the same buying and merchandising practices as other retailers of similar volume and size. Chain discounters follow the usual practices of their business, with one exception. In chain discount buying, buyers are usually responsible for several departments rather than a single category of merchandise.

Experts estimate that 30 percent of all retail and 19 percent of all apparel sales in the country take place in discount stores.[11] Ninety million people—or approximately 1/3 of the U.S. Population—walk into a Wal-mart every week. The large and widespread customer base is one reason analysts and economic observers look to the retail giants as an indicator of the economic condition.[12] Discounters have a tremendous stake in the future of fashion retailing.

FIGURE 17.4
Discounters make a profit by keeping their overhead low; most rely on self-service, with simple signage and large parking lots.
Courtesy, Fairchild Publications, Inc.

Entertainment Values

Discounters added "greeters" early on to welcome people to their vast stores and direct them to the correct spot within the store. Some early discounters also used "blue light" specials to stimulate customer interest. Discounters in malls usually rely on the mall to draw and entertain customers, while they focus on keeping prices low. As people tire of plain stores with rows of fluorescent lights, and hundreds of counters in rigid rows, some discounters are upgrading their visual merchandising and looking for related entertainment values.

Forms of Ownership

There are four types of ownership commonly found in U.S. retailing today: sole proprietors, chains, leased departments, and franchises. Partnerships, once a very popular form of retail ownership (Sears and Roebuck, Abraham and Straus, etc.), are seldom found today because of liability issues and tax considerations.

Owners use many different formats, including the traditional department store, specialty store, or discount store, or the newer off-price, factory outlet, or category killer formats.

Sole Proprietors

Sole proprietors, or owners, are the entrepreneurs that shaped American retailing. Many of the retailing greats, JCPenney, John Wanamaker, Adam Gimbel, and Isaac and Mary Ann Magnin, began as sole proprietors with a great idea and went on from there to found great retailing empires.

Today, over 90 percent of all U.S. retailers own and operate a single store. Sole proprietors usually have small stores, because of the huge amount of capital required to support an adequate inventory for a large business. These so-called **mom-and-pop stores** are usually single stores, managed by the owner with a few assistants. They are most frequently specialty stores, because department stores require more space and more inventory. If the owner prospers and expands to more than four stores, he or she is said to have a "chain."

Chain Organizations

A **chain organization** is a group of centrally owned stores, four or more according to the Bureau of the Census definition, each of which handles similar goods and merchandise. A chain organization may be local, regional, or national, although it is the national chains that have had the largest impact on retailing. They also may be general or specialty merchandisers, and depending upon the kind of stores they are, they will target their customer broadly or narrowly. A chain organization can be a mass merchandiser known for its low prices, a department store known for high quality mid-priced goods, or a specialty merchandiser selling exclusive designs at high prices. Apparel chains may focus on a special size, age, or income group.

The oldest and best-known chain organizations are JCPenney and Sears, Roebuck, which *Stores* magazine categorizes as department stores. Newer chains include Kmart and Wal-Mart, which are categorized as discount stores. Prestigious specialty chains are Talbots and Eddie Bauer. Wet Seal is a juniors' specialty chain. The Limited is an example of a women's apparel specialty chain. Lane Bryant is a chain within The Limited chain; it caters to large-sized women. See Table 17.4 for a list of major retail chains.

Organization for Buying and Merchandising

Most chain stores are departmentalized, but not in the same way as department stores. Chain-store buyers are typically assigned to buy a specific category or classification of apparel within a department instead of buying all categories for a department the way a department store buyer does. This practice is referred to as **category buying** or **classification buying**. Buyers in department stores, in contrast, are said to be responsible for **departmental buying**.

A departmental buyer in a sportswear department, for example, would buy swimwear, tops, jeans, sweaters, and slacks. A chain-store buyer who bought in the sportswear department might buy only swimsuits or only swimwear accessories. Category buying is necessary because huge quantities of goods are needed to stock the individual stores of a chain operation. Some chain operations have merchandise units numbering in the hundreds of thousands.

In addition to centralized buying and merchandising, most chains also have a system of central distribution. Merchandise is distributed to the units from a central warehouse or from regional distribution centers. Computer systems keep track of stock so that it can be re-

TABLE 17.4 Selected Major Retail Chains

BFC	Baby Depot Burlington Coat Factory Cohoes	Decelle Luxury Linens
FEDERATED DEPARTMENT STORES, INC.	Bloomingdale's The Bon Marché Burdines Lazarus	Macy's (East) Macy's (West) Rich's Goldsmith's
DAYTON HUDSON CORPORATION	*Department Stores* Dayton's Minneapolis Hudson's Michigan Marshall Field's	Mervyn's *Discount Stores* Target
THE GAP, INC.	Gap Banana Republic babyGap	GapKids Old Navy Gap Body
THE LIMITED, INC.	*Specialty Stores* The White Barn Candle Company Bath & Body Works Bath & Body Works at Home Express Henri Bendel Lerner New York Mast Industries New York & Co The Limited	 Structure Victoria's Secret Victoria's Secret Bath Shops *Direct Mail* Lane Bryant Direct Lerner Direct Victoria's Secret Catalog
THE MAY DEPARTMENT STORES COMPANY	*Department Stores* David's Bridal Famous-Barr Filene's Foley's Hecht's Kaufman's Lord & Taylor L.S. Ayres	May California May Co. Ohio Robinsons-May Strawbridge's The Jones Store *Specialty Store* Payless Shoe Priscilla of Boston
THE TJX COMPANIES, INC.	T.J. Maxx T.K. Maxx Winners	Marshall's Homegoods A.J. Wright
CASUAL CORNER GROUP	August Max Casual Corner	Casual Corner Annex Petite Sophisticate

ordered as needed; they also keep buyers informed of what is selling.

Like department and discount stores, specialty stores are searching for ways to set themselves apart by adding entertainment value. Wet Seal was one of the first stores to add video walls to its stores to entertain both its female customers and the boyfriends that accompany them. The company's latest innovation is the Limbo Lounge concept, a store that offers both men's and junior's apparel and accessories, along with several virtual reality stations, and a juice bar. Both teenage and older couples are drawn to these stores. Old Navy is trying to win customers by "putting the fun back into shopping."

Leased Departments

Leased departments, which were first discussed in Chapter 4, are sections of a retail store that are owned and operated by outside organizations. The outside organization usually owns the department's stock, merchandises and staffs the department, and pays for its own advertising. It is, in turn, required to abide by the host store's policies and regulations. In return for the leasing arrangement, the outside organization pays the store a percentage of its sales as rent.

Leased departments work best where some specialized knowledge is required. Jewelry, fur, and shoe departments are often leased, as are beauty salons. Glemby Company and Seligman and Latz, for example, lease many of the beauty salons in stores. Footstar leases athletic shoe departments in Macy's and Bloomingdale's.[13]

Department stores, chains, and discount organizations will lease both service and merchandise departments, while specialty stores usually restrict leased operations to services, such as jewelry or shoe repair or leather and suede cleaning.

Organization for Buying and Merchandising

Leased operations vary from the independent who operates in only one store to major chain organizations that operate in many stores. In chain organizations, centralized buying and merchandising prevail. Supervisors regularly visit each location to consult with local sales staff and department store managers. At such meetings, they assess current sales, deal with any problems, and plan for the future.

As the buying and selling functions have become increasingly separate from one another, operators of leased departments enjoy a unique—and at this point, rather old-fashioned—position within the fashion industry. Most operate in a variety of stores. They are furthermore buyers who maintain daily contact with their markets and their suppliers, which allows them to make excellent projections about future trends as well as giving outstanding fashion guidance to their customers.

Franchises

Franchises established themselves as a viable form of retailing when shops featuring fast food, bath linens, cookware, fabrics, unfinished furniture, electronics, and computers were successfully franchised. In a **franchise** agreement, the franchisee (owner-operator) pays a fee plus a royalty on all sales for the right to operate a store with an established name in an exclusive trading area. The franchiser (parent company) provides merchandise, and assistance in organizing and merchandising, plus training (see Figure 17.5). Customers often think that franchises are chains because they look alike.

With the exception of one or two bridal wear franchises and the maternity shop Lady Madonna, the fashion industry was not part of the initial franchise boom. It seems to have made up lost time, however, in the second wave of franchising that proliferated during the 1980s. Firms as diverse as Benetton and Gymboree have adopted this form of ownership. Athletic footwear, tennis apparel, and men's sportswear have all produced lucrative and popular franchises. Athlete's Foot, for example, which sells athletic footwear and activewear, has750 locations in 45 countries.[14]

The latest trend is for designers to get in the act. Examples of successful worldwide franchises by designers are Ralph Lauren's Polo Shops, Calvin Klein shops, and Yves Saint Laurent's Rive Gauche shops.

FIGURE 17.5
To encourage growth, licensors make the purchase of a franchise as "user-friendly" as they can.
Courtesy, Uniforms of America.

Then & Now

50 Years of Store Design

1950s

The 1950s were the beginning of consumerism, and retailers scrambled to cash in on shoppers' growing appetite for goods and services. In their rush to stock the shelves with desired items, the stores lacked individuality. Only a handful of merchants used store design to convey a fashion statement. For most, store design consisted of organizing the merchandise on the floor and creating an environment for customers to shop with ease and comfort.

1960s

With the emergence of alternative lifestyles and the burgeoning of youth culture, store design took on new importance in the 1960s. Retailers, anxious to capture a targeted consumer, began cultivating a unique identity via store design. Super-graphics became a popular visual element and merchandisers favored designs and art different from the store's competitors.

Store escalators of the 1950s.
Courtesy, C & J Partners, Inc. Pasedena, California.

1970s

Store design was elevated to a higher profile in the 1970s, as the look and feel of retail environments captured the fashion flair of their shoppers. Junior departments, reflecting the psychedelic movement of the decade, are a good example of the trend. Space planning enmeshed with store set-up became an integral component of store design.

1980s

Store design evolved into visual merchandising in the 1980s. As shoppers relied on fashion to reflect their status, retailers followed suit; glitz became the operative word as merchants dramatically upscaled their store environments. Visual merchandising put a whole new spin on the concept of "show and sell."

1990s

Visual merchandising packs a subliminal punch in the 1990s as retailers toy with experiential store design and entertainment retailing. Brighter, easier-to-shop stores are the trend as store design becomes a polished art. However, such sophistication has begun to create problems in the area of cost management and store operation.

2000 and beyond

Sophisticated visual merchandising with cost efficiency will be the challenge of designers and architects in the future. A continued emphasis on ease-of-shopping and time-saving techniques is likely to continue, as is the need for fixturing and for POP material that educates shoppers about increasingly complex products.

The streamlines 1990s.
Courtesy, C & J Partners, Inc. Pasedena, California.

Reprinted with permission from an article by C & J Partners, Inc. of Pasedena, California.

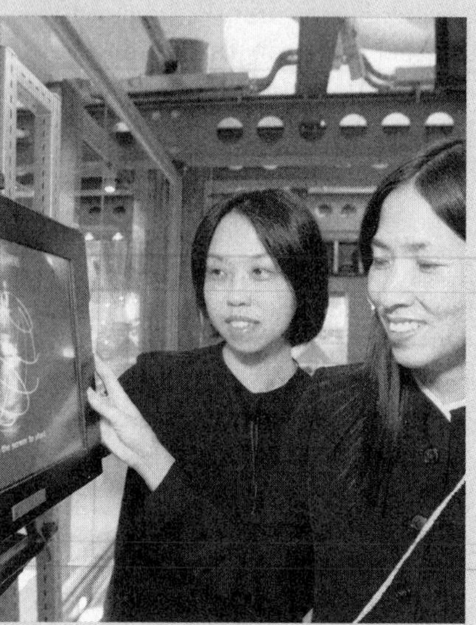

Today, more technology is being used to provide information for customers.
Courtesy, Fairchild Publications, Inc.

Industry experts see no signs that franchising will slow its pace and many feel that this form of retailing will continue to grow.

Other Types of Fashion Retailers Today

In addition to the traditional retail formats discussed above, a new group of businesses have evolved over the past 30 years that adapt some of the attributes of the traditional retailers with some new ideas, as retail formats continue to evolve. Talbots vice president Ron Ramseyer noted:

We've focused on being a single brand rather than one separate channel versus any other. Any direct marketing strategy to support stores includes anything that supports catalogs and vice versa.[15]

Types of retail formats popular today include off-price retailers, factory outlet stores, convenience stores, category killers, catalog showrooms, and boutiques or showcase stores, among others. Many overlap with existing traditional formats. Many are chains. We will focus on those that are most important to apparel, accessories, and home furnishings.

Off-Price Retailers

One area that is experiencing strong growth is **off-price retailing**, the selling of brand-name and designer merchandise at lower-than-normal retail prices when they are at the late rise or early peak in the fashion cycle. In contrast, regular discounters sell merchandise in the late peak and decline stages of the fashion cycle.

Off-price retailers attribute part of their success to the fact that they provide an invaluable service to manufacturers and price-conscious customers. Because manufacturers must commit to fabric houses so far in advance (up to 18 months before garments will be in the stores), they risk not having enough orders to use the fabric they have ordered. For many years, manufacturers took a loss when this happened. Then in the 1980s, when they had fewer orders than anticipated, they turned to off-pricers, who often pay full price for the fabric if the manufacturers will make it into garments at a lower cost. The manufacturers can more easily afford to cut their production costs than the cost of material they have already paid for. Off-pricers have in effect helped to smooth out the cyclical and often financially disastrous course of apparel manufacturing. Customers, in turn, benefit from being able to buy garments very similar to those that are being sold in exclusive stores for less than they would pay in those stores.

The first major off-price retailer in the United States was Loehmann's, which set up shop in Brooklyn in 1920 to sell "better" women's wear. Until then, high-quality women's garments had been available only through exclusive department stores. The regular-priced stores, for their part, did not fail to notice the arrival of Loehmann's on the retail scene. Department stores demanded that the discounter remove the labels so customers would not know what they were buying. That convention held for decades, but labels are rarely removed today.

The growth of off-price retailing in the 1980s drew other retailers into the market. The Zayre Corporation started two off-price chains, T. J. Maxx (Figure 17.6) and Hit or Miss. Today TJX, which now owns T. J. Maxx and Marshalls, is the second-largest apparel chain in the United States. Dress Barn is another off-price chain that has enjoyed great success, offering moderately conservative fashion for customers with limited incomes. Even small off-pricers, such as Syms, experienced phenomenal growth in the 1980s and 1990s.

Off-pricers managed to capture an important share of the brand-name market. The success of brand names such as Donna Karan, Bill Blass, and Calvin Klein meant that designers no longer had to give department stores exclusives, and they were soon selling their products to off-pricers. More recently, however, many designers have begun to prefer selling their overstocks in their own stores. This has put severe pressure on off-pricers like Loehmann's and Syms to get enough inventory.

One other disadvantage seems to be built into off-price retailing: Off-price retailers get the goods later than regular-priced retailers. While a department store puts designer spring and summer clothing on the selling floor during the winter, the off-pricer does not get the same merchandise until several months later. As a result, the off-pricer has a shorter selling season than the regular-price retailer.

Industry experts worry that off-pricers will overextend themselves, as retailers did during the mid- to late 1980s, in the rush to cash in on a strong market. Other signs indicate that off-

FIGURE 17.6
T.J. Maxx stores successfully fill the consumer's appetite for brand-name and designer clothes at discounted prices.
Courtesy, Fairchild Publications, Inc.

price retailing has still more muscle to flex. Burlington Coat factory turned in $2 billion in sales in 1999, a remarkable demonstration of the consumer's appetite for brand-name and designer garments at reduced prices.

Factory Outlet Stores

Factory outlet stores, a discount operation run by a manufacturer, or increasingly these days, by a designer, are another booming area of discount retailing (see Figure 17.7). Industry figures indicate that factory outlets have grown at a furious pace—while there were fewer than 100 outlet centers nationwide in 1988, today there are almost 360 outlet centers across the United States.

Factory outlet stores began in the 1920s in New England. For many years, they experienced little or no growth. A manufacturer would open a little store in one corner of a plant to sell company products—slightly defective goods and overstocks—at reduced rates to company employees. Kayser-Roth and William Carter Co. were among the first to sponsor factory outlet stores. Other manufacturers followed suit, usually opening their outlets on the premises, which also always meant in the Northeast where the apparel factories were located. Over time, manufacturers opened their stores to the buying public—that is, those who drove by their often obscure locations.

The proliferation of factory outlet stores can be traced to a recession in the early 1980s, which created a market for stores that could meet the demand for bargain-hungry shoppers. Not only did the already-established factory outlets, such as Warnaco, Inc., Manhattan Industries, and Blue Bell continue to operate, but big-name designers such as Calvin Klein, Anne Klein, and Harvé Bernard and brand-name organizations like Adidas, Bass Shoes, and Van Heusen men's wear opened factory outlet stores.

Factory stores also left the factory, often to band together with one another in malls. The latest development is the emergence of entire communities, such as Freeport, Maine; Manchester, Vermont; and Secaucus, New Jersey, devoted almost exclusively to the selling of factory outlet goods. (The draw in Freeport was the presence of L. L. Bean, an established force in mail-order retailing that expanded its factory store outlet throughout the 1980s from a small outpost to a huge multibuilding operation.) See Chapter 18 for a discussion of retail locations.

Like off-price discounters, factory outlets offer certain advantages to manufacturers and customers. Most important is the fact that they provide manufacturers and designers with a backup channel of distribution, which improves inventory control. Canceled orders and overstocks can be funneled into discount stores, which, if run correctly, also can be enormous image enhancers. Not to be underestimated is the possibility of strong profits. An outlet buys merchandise from the parent company for 30 percent off the regular wholesale prices and sells it for the same markup percentage as regular-priced retailers.

Designers and brand-name manufacturers use their outlets for overstocks and canceled orders. Some better sportswear manufacturers have 100 to 150 outlet stores, but they do not publicize them to avoid offending the department stores. Large manufacturers, such as

FIGURE 17.7
Belgium's first designer outlet mall in Maasmechlen Village is increasingly popular among shoppers.
Courtesy, Fairchild Publications, Inc.

Kayser-Roth and Carter, are careful to use their outlets only for closeouts and seconds. The latter are unwilling to risk offending department stores and other major customers with more direct competition. But now even the department stores have opened outlet stores: Saks Fifth Avenue has Saks Off Fifth, while Nordstrom has the Rack.

Originally, most outlet stores were pipe rack operations in dingy surroundings. Many looked like the factories out of which they had originally operated. Today, factory outlets resemble regular-priced retailers more and more, offering attractive merchandise displays and customer service that compares to that offered by full-priced retailers.

Experts speculate on how well factory outlets will do when the market cools off, as it inevitably will, and as already appears to be happening. In the late 1990s, for example, customers' expectations regarding factory outlets were raised by the proliferation of attractive, full-service, professionally run designer shops. Yet, ironically, factory outlet customers are not people who must look for bargains. Instead, they are people with incomes far above average. Their motto is "NPR" or "Never Pay Retail." For these customers, bargain hunting is a leisure pastime, one that could easily be given up if factory outlet stores had to raise prices or cut services.

Another potential trouble area for factory outlet stores is the same kind of overexpansion that derailed regular-priced retailers in the mid-1980s. These fears are minimal, however, and most industry experts expect continued growth for factory outlet stores. They believe this new store format has carved out a permanent niche.

Category Killers

Superstores or category specialists carry one type of goods that they are able to offer in great depth at low prices because of volume buying. They so dominate a market that they drive out or "kill" smaller specialty stores, and so are known as **category killers**. They offer a narrow but deep assortment of goods in stores over 8,000 square feet. Because of their buying power they can get not only rock-bottom prices, but also excellent terms, and an assured supply of scarce goods.

The first category killer was Toys 'R Us, in the 1970s, which wiped out thousands of mom-and-pop toy stores. It then went on to affect the toy departments of major department stores, to the point where few survived the 1980s. By 1995, it accounted for over 40 percent of all toys and games sold in the United States.[16]

Examples of category killers include Bed, Bath and Beyond; Home Depot; Barnes & Noble; and Baby Superstore. Typically these are huge freestanding stores, often called "big boxes." They are rarely located in malls. They carry thousands of related products, at low prices, which they think offset no-frills service and decor.

Barnes & Noble is famous for adding entertainment value to its stores through its kids' theaters, coffee bars, poetry readings, and book signings.

We Do, a wedding superstore in Columbus, Ohio, provides one-stop shopping for apparel for the bride, groom, and wedding party, as well as gifts, thus cutting across traditional product categories to merchandise based on related needs.

A huge Viacom Entertainment Store in Chicago, while not a traditional category killer, is an interactive entertainment concept, combining its "brands" like, MTV, Star Trek, VH-1, Nickelodeon, and Paramount. It sells interactive entertainment as well as T-shirts, caps, mugs, and accessories bearing these logos.

Boutiques/Showcase Stores

Although boutiques originated as small shops with French couture houses, they really came to life as small, individually owned shops in the antiestablishment 1960s. The first freestanding boutiques opened in London and quickly spread to the United States. Their appeal lies in their potential for individuality. These stores are often owned and operated by highly creative persons who are eager to promote their own fashion enthusiasms (see Figure 17.8a and b). Their target customers are like-minded souls who share their unique attitudes about dressing.

Some boutique owners design their own merchandise; others buy and sell other people's designs. Boutiques are one of the few outlets for avant-garde merchandise that is too risky for department and specialty stores to carry.

Department stores have not, however, been above capitalizing on the success of boutiques. Bloomingdale's and Henri Bendel in New York City revolutionized merchandising display in the 1960s when they created special shops-within-shops on their selling floors. Frequently organized around the collections of a single designer, in-store boutiques offered customers a more complete fashion look. They were a fad that did not pass, and many department stores are now organized along boutique lines.

The newest trend in boutiques has been for designers to open their own shops. The French designers were the first to experiment with freestanding boutiques in the United States, but American designers soon followed suit. Among the French who have opened successful boutiques in the United States are Cardin, Valentino, Yves Saint Laurent, and Givenchy. Italian designers and manufacturers such as Armani, Gucci, and Ferragamo were quick to follow. Successful British firms that pioneered in boutique selling on both sides of the Atlantic were Laura Ashley and Liberty of London.

Many American designers are expanding by opening showcase stores. A **showcase store** is a manufacturer's or designer's store that sells merchandise at the introductory and early rise stages of the fashion cycle. In addition to generating income, showcase stores are testing grounds for new products. Ralph Lauren, Donna Karan, Calvin Klein, Tommy Hilfiger, Anna Sui, and Esprit operate showcase stores in addition to factory outlets. As less well-known designers rush to open showcase stores, there is little doubt that this form of retailing will continue to grow.

Entertainment values abound in boutiques and showcase stores. Some customers see the Ralph Lauren flagship store on Madison Avenue in New York as the "ultimate fantasy residence-cum-store. Some visit just to take in the lush environment, which includes dark wood paneling and fireplaces, all designed to enhance Lauren's identity and the mood of the clothes."[17]

Another trend in boutiques is the "vintage boutique" that features clothes and accessories from the 1930s to the 1980s—and even earlier decades, if the owners can find them. These small stores, long popular in major cities, have caught on in smaller communities across the country. The retro wave in fashion has also benefited many charities that sell used clothing, like the Goodwill Industries.[18]

Nonstore Retailers

Nonstore retailing today is composed of four major formats: direct selling, catalog retailers, TV home shopping, and Internet shopping

FIGURE 17.8A AND B
Beautiful inside and out French-inspired specialty boutique, Luna, has unique hand-painted floors by artist Chris Meihls.
Courtesy, Luna, Inc.

sites. The lines between these types are already starting to blur, as are those between nonstore retailers and traditional retailers. Store-based retailers are looking to expand their customer base through catalogs and electronic options. For example, not only have leading catalogers such as Lillian Vernon and Spiegel established major presences on the Internet, but retailers like JCPenney and The Gap have giant online virtual storefronts.

Direct Selling

Direct selling, which used to be known as direct-to-the-home selling, is still a major force in the United States. In 2000, direct selling sales totaled $25 billion. Almost all the 5.5 million people who work in direct sales in the United States are independent part-time salespeople, who buy merchandise from a large firm and distribute it by selling it to customers in their territories.

Although Avon entered a partnership with JC Penney in 2001, and launched the company's first ever retail line, which was not successful, it is still one of the largest direct selling companies in the world.[19] Many other fashion companies also sell in this way, mainly cosmetics, fragrances, and jewelry. Entertainment value is provided in the "party plan" format used by Sara Coventry for jewelry and Doncaster for women's apparel.

Catalog Retailers

Catalog retailing, or mail-order retailing as it was traditionally called, has been popular in the United States since the 1880s. But by 1982, the explosive growth of mail-order retailers had reached such proportions that *Time* magazine ran a cover story on it. Mail-order retailing has expanded every year since then; in 2000 it chalked up sales totaling $110 billion.[20]

Clearly, this is not your great-grandma's mail order! She got a catalog once a year, mailed in her order with a check or money order, and waited 2 to 3 weeks for the package to be delivered by the mail carrier. Today, you can get a catalog from the same company mailed to you 22 times a year. You can fax in your order and have it delivered by Federal Express or UPS within 2 days.

The evolution of air delivery and computerized distribution have played a vital role in increasing direct-mail and catalog sales. With computers, companies were able to target their customers in very specific ways, by age, income, geographic region, lifestyle, and interests. As a result, almost 90 percent of all catalog sales are now from specialized catalogs. Other boosts to mail-order selling are the toll-free 800 telephone number, the fax order capacity, and the ability to use national credit cards to pay for merchandise.

Mail-order houses have benefited from the growing numbers of women who now work

Who? What? Where? Why?—Kohl's

You've read the headlines: "The fastest-growing retailer in the nation." In this world of retail consolidation and bankruptcies, it is heartening to learn about a successful, growing retail success where career opportunities abound.

WHO? Kohl's is a department store with vision. Kohl's was founded by the Kohl family in Milwaukee, Wisconsin, in 1962, and has grown over the years to become the Kohl Corporation, owner of 485 store locations nationwide.

WHAT? Kohl's believes in satisfying their target customer! They have a commitment to family, value, and national brands. The brands featured are today's premier names in apparel, footwear, and home goods, such as Dockers, Lee, Levi's, Haggar, Champion, Carter's, Jockey, Healthtex, Vanity Fair, Reebok, Columbia Sportswear Company, Pfaltzgraff, Krups, KitchenAid, and more. They also provide value in their private label brands, like Genuine Sionoma Jeans Company, Bodysource, and Croft & Barrow.

WHERE? Kohl's department stores are conveniently located in suburban areas and always feature easy access and ample parking. Averaging 86,500 square feet in size, the stores are designed to ensure a satisfying, hassle-free shopping experience. Presently, Kohl's has stores in over 40 states and is aggressively expanding on those states, as well as planning growth into other states. Today, you can shop Kohl's online, 24 hours a day, 7 days a week.

WHY? As one of the fastest growing retailers in America, Kohl's is always looking for energetic, committed people to join their team. The career opportunities abound and there is probably a Kohl's right in your neighborhood. Their expansion means unlimited opportunity for you. As they build new stores, you build your career. Kohl's is committed to performance-based advancement, and believes in challenging their employees to take on responsibility—empowering you on your career path.

Timeline

1962

Kohl's founded by Kohl family in Milwaukee, Wisconsin.

1978

Kohl's Corporation becomes wholly owned by the BATUS Retail Groups. Expands from 10 to 39 stores throughout Wisconsin, Illinois, and Indiana.

1986

Kohl's is purchased by a group of investors led by Kohl's senior management. The company opens its 40th store.

1988

Kohl's acquires 26 Main Street Stores, expanding to 66 stores.

1992

Kohl's offers 11.1 million shares of the company's stock to the public in one of the largest public stock offerings ever made by a Wisconsin company.

1993-1996

Kohl's continues its expansion. In 1993, it opens 11 new stores; in 1994, addes another 18 locations. In both 1995 and 1996 Kohl's adds 22 stores.

1997

Kohl's enters Washington, D.C., Philadelphia, and Pittsburgh, expanding with 32 new stores.

1998

Kohl's is listed on the Standard & Poors 500. It continues expansion with 32 additional stores including locations in Winston-Salem/Greensboro, Richmond, and Knoxville. Kohl's stock splits two for one.

1999

The company unveils new stores in St. Louis and the Dallas/Fort Worth and Denver markets. Kohl's expands its headquarter facilities in Menomonee Falls, Wisconsin.

2000

Kohl's opens 60 stores operating 320 stores in 26 states by year-end. New market entries include Connecticut, New York, New Jersey, Long Island, and Oklahoma. Market expansion opening include Illinois, Indiana, Kentucky, Michigan, Minnesota, Missouri, Nebraska, and Pennsylvania.

Kohl's stock splits two for one on March 6th. The company adds a fourth distribution center in Blue Springs, Missouri, and a fifth distribution center for its e-commerce initiative in Monroe, Ohio.

2001

Kohl's expands into the Southeast region of the United States with brand-new stores in Atlanta, Georgia. Plus, the company extends its expansion into the South Central United States with stores in Oklahoma City, Austin, Fayetteville, and El Paso. Kohl's fifth distribution center opens in Corsicana, Texas.

2002

Kohl's expands into Southern California, Arizona, and Nevada. A new distribution in San Bernardino, California opens. It also enters Houston with 12 stores and Boston with 13 stores.

2003

Doubled the number of stores in California and expanded into the burgeoning Florida market. Kohl's is now reporting revenues of over $110 billion.

Beyond?

The sky seems to be the only limit.

Sources:

www.kohlscorporation.com

_______, "What to Watch—on Kohl's Western Trail," *Women's Wear Daily*, December 31, 2002, p. 3.

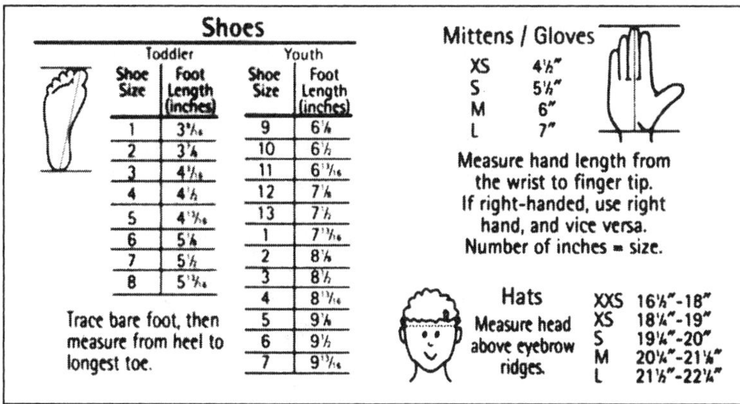

FIGURE 17.9
Note the easy sizing instructions from this Lands' End Kids' Catalog.
Permission granted by Lands' End, Inc.

and no longer have much leisure time to shop. In 2000, 67 percent of all the primary catalog shoppers were women.[21]

Not willing to rest on its laurels, catalogers have also sought new ways to develop their business. One way is marketing to Japan, where mail order has long been popular. U.S. catalogers like Lands' End, Eddie Bauer, Patagonia, J. Crew, Coldwater Creek, and Williams-Sonoma have experienced remarkable sales, despite the language problem. L. L. Bean's sales in Japan increased from $5 million to $50 million in just 2 years! In 2001, L.L. Bean and J. Crew broadened their appeal to Japanese consumers by adopting a new multichannel strategy involving stores, catalogs, and the Internet. However, the Japanese economy was too weak for the catalog companies to achieve sales akin to those in the mid-1990s.[22] Not all the success stories involved large firms; After The Stork has been successful with its children's products catalog.

Another way to grow the catalog business is to improve the repeat-purchase rate, by using customer-appreciation programs. Old Pueblo Traders, based in Tucson, Arizona, offers gift certificates to regular customers. Other catalogers offer free delivery during slow periods or on purchases over a specified dollar amount.

Direct-mail selling has become so lucrative that other retailers have established their own programs, and department store bills now arrive stuffed with offers to purchase through direct mail. More than half of the top 50 department stores also sell through catalogs. The Neiman Marcus catalog, long famous for its his-and-her Christmas gifts, added a new twist in 1996 by adding editorial content to its catalog, dubbed a "magalog."

In an ironic twist, many catalog retailers eventually open stores, using their mailings as a marketing device. As Peter Sapienza of the trendy activewear company Patagonia said: "We have a strong suspicion that people use our catalog as a shopping guide to our stores." Cataloger/retailers also use their catalogs to test products. "We have found that catalog customers buy seasonal merchandise earlier than store customers, and this gives us a preview of which will be the hot items," says Ron Ramsayer of Talbots.[23]

Two big problems are plaguing catalog retailers. One is the steadily increasing cost of paper—and mail. Another is that the average U.S. household receives about 140 catalogs a year—a deluge that is prompting more and more negative customer response.

Still, many customers still respond enthusiastically to catalogs as providing great entertainment value, as well as shopping venues. Think of the romantic travelogue copy, the informative product information, or the provocative photos featured in your favorite catalog.

TV Home Shopping

One of the most talked about developments in retailing has been the growth of home TV shopping, a form of retailing that takes the catalog sales techniques one step further. The potential of television as a direct-mail sales tool has long been recognized; witness the late-night gadget demonstrations and the ubiquitous storm window advertisements. Not until the advent of cable television, however, with its lower production standards and lower costs, was it feasible to produce infomercials and to set up home shopping services that sell an array of goods.

The cable TV infomercial with its enthusiastic host and wildly appreciative audience has been used to sell a large variety of goods, from Suzanne Somers' "thighmaster" to Cher's cosmetics.

The pioneer in the TV home shopping business was Home Shopping Network (HSN), of Clearwater, Florida (see Figure 17.10). On the air 24 hours a day, 7 days a week, HSN is the world's most widely distributed TV shopping network. In 2001, HSN had grown into a global multi-channel retailer with sales of almost $2 billion and a customer base of over five million. Soap opera actress Susan Lucci sells an exclusive line of "head-to-toe-fashion" products (accessories, skincare, clothing) on HSN. Orders are entered directly into a computer, which keeps track of inventory, and if all goes well, are sent out within a day.[24]

The second largest television shopping service is QVC of West Chester, Pennsylvania, with 79 million viewers, but substantially higher revenue than HSN. QVC offers on-screen demonstrations of merchandise that ranges from simple cookware to sophisticated electronics. QVC sells enormous amounts of apparel and accessories, especially jewelry, and a wide array of home furnishings, tabletop goods, and gift items. QVC has separate weekly shows for gold jewelry, silver jewelry, simulated-diamond jewelry, men's jewelry, and watches. Los Angeles designer Bob Mackie has made many appearances on QVC, selling out their stock of his scarves and tops. Similarly, comedian Joan Rivers, promotes her line of costume jewelry, effectively combining selling and entertainment. Besides its TV shopping network, QVC also operates sales from its Web site www.qvc.com and a retail operation in Mall of America in Bloomington called QVC@themall. In 2001, QVC also made significant investments in Japan and Germany.[25]

The third big TV home shopping company is Shop At Home of Knoxville, Tennessee, which has 20 million viewers. As with the other TV home shopping companies, Shop At Home buys products at wholesale and marks them up to "everyday-low" levels close to a discount store price.

ValueVision of Eden Prairie, Minnesota, is the fourth largest TV home shopping service, with 13.5 million viewers, on cable only. It too offers an extensive array of products, including The Hollywood Collection, jewelry reproductions of the jewels worn by movie stars, produced in Thailand by designer Charlene Lake.

The advent of high definition television is expected to improve the quality of the TV picture before the end of the century. There are a num-

FIGURE 17.10 *Television home-shopping adds to the excitement and visual appeal of merchandise.* Courtesy, HSN.

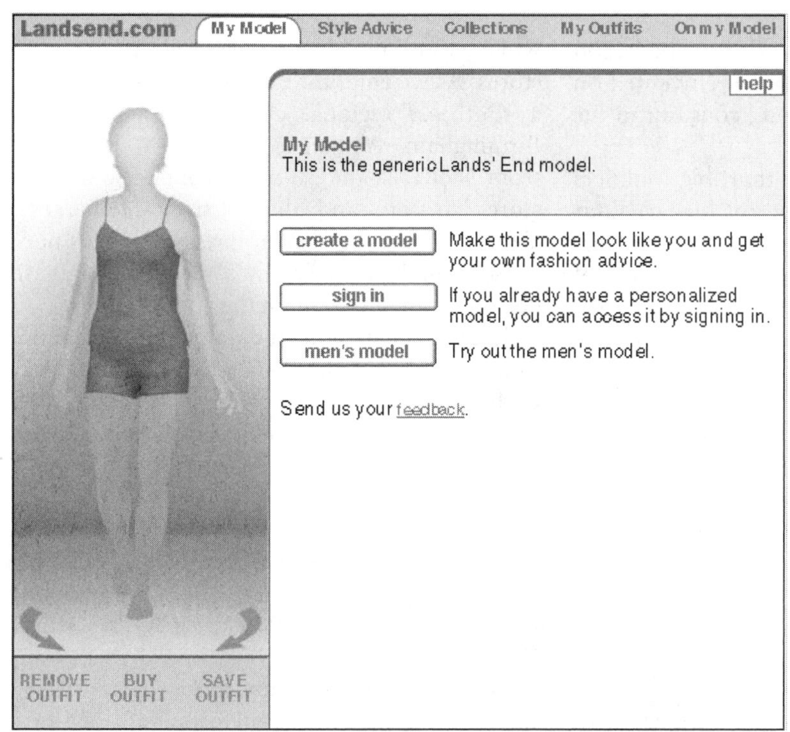

FIGURE 17.11
This Lands' End virtual model allows Internet shoppers to try on merchandise from their home computer! This feature can be accessed by visiting www.landsend.com.
© 2003 Lands' End, Inc. Used with permission.

ber of experiments underway to bring interactive technologies into customers' homes—more cheaply than the computer/modem capability required by the Internet.

Internet Shopping Sites

At the end of the 1990s, the expectations of e-commerce were sky-high. At the same time as large retail companies rushed to build a presence online, many new independent e-commerce fashion sites were launched. These sites were conceived to be the virtual version of specialty stores, with a selection of apparel, beauty, or accessory merchandise targeted to a specific type of customers. Moreover, these sites would also provide editorial content and enticing visual effects to make the most out of the e-commerce shopping experience. However, many of these costly ventures collapsed very quickly. In February 2001 alone, 58 e-commerce companies folded.[26] The interest in online retail cooled off considerably, and currently, very few new e-tail companies are being launched. But that doesn't mean that all e-commerce business has failed.

While online sales are growing slower than what was predicted during the heady dot.com years of 1998-1999, they are still growing. Improved customer service, timely deliveries, and a growing sense of security about the submission of their personal data online, have boosted Americans' spending in cyberspace. Holiday spending in 2002 were estimated to be up 23 percent compared to the figures of 2001. A 2002 Yahoo/AC Nielsen survey revealed that the biggest online spenders have broadband access, are college educated, and between the ages of 25 to 34.[27]

The e-tail players that have been the most successful so far, are the online channels of apparel retail and catalog giants like JCPenney.com, Landsend.com, jcrew.com, and LLBean.com.[28]

Mergers and Acquisitions

Until the 1930s, most department stores in the United States were independently owned. Most, in fact, were owned by the families whose names they bore, names such as Marshall Field, John Wanamaker, Gimbel Bros., and J. L. Hudson. By the 1980s, most of these long-established stores had changed hands, and with these changes in ownership came new images and sometimes even new names.

So much change has occurred in the retail business recently that you need a scorecard to track the remaining players. Consolidations, changes in distribution channels, bankruptcies, altered buying organizations, and foreign investments have all caused the retail scene as we knew it to change. (See Chapters 4 and 16.) As Arnold Arenson of Kurt Salmon Associates, a management consulting firm, said: "The lesson is that every business needs to be reinvented on a periodic basis. The only thing constant in the retail business is change."[29]

Just when you thought that big retailers were really big enough, they got bigger! Four companies—Federated Department Stores, the May Company, and Kohl's—now own most of the big city department stores.

Although mergers have taken their toll on the department stores, causing some old, established stores to close their doors, some good has been served. Without mergers, many of the established department stores would not have survived the onslaught of competition from chains and discounters. In fact, mergers generally occur for one of two reasons: a need to reorganize for greater efficiency and a need to expand.

Merging for Efficiency

In the early 1980s, chain organizations, with their centralized buying, had developed a competitive edge over department stores even though department stores had tried to keep up by expanding the number of branch stores. The department stores soon realized that the real way to meet the competition was to develop more streamlined, efficient internal organizations. This was often achieved by merging one or more internal divisions in order to create a parent organization large enough to sponsor centralized buying, shipping, and merchandising.

Macy's, after years of operating the New Jersey department store, Bamberger's, streamlined both organizations by merging the merchandising and operational functions; Bamberger's lost its name in the process. Then Macy's, after a complex series of acquisitions and buyouts, became part of Federated Department Stores, but retained its name.

Merging for Expansion

Faced with the rapid expansion throughout the 1980s of huge national chains, retail department stores began to merge with one another and with parent organizations so they, too, could join the expansion boom. It is obviously easier and less expensive to expand by acquiring an established retail outlet than it is to build an entire new store from scratch. For example, the Arkansas-based Dillard's vaulted itself into the position of the country's fifth ranked department store in the mid-1990s through a series of acquisitions of other department stores—all of which were immediately converted to Dillard's stores. As we enter the new millenium, Proffitt's, a southeast regional chain headquartered in Birmingham, Alabama, has bought 29 stores from McRea's, the 50-store Younkers, the 41-store Parisian, and the 40-store Herberger's chain the 32-store Carson Pirie Scott. This purchase would make Proffitt's the fourth largest department store chain in the United States.[30]

In 2002, Sears bought catalog retailer Lands' End and apparel line Covington, and launched both labels in Sears' stores in September 2002.The merger and acquisition story is not over yet—stay tuned in.

Trends: Changing Retail Patterns

Retail operations not only must constantly respond to change in their environments, but they themselves must change if they are to survive. One theory, suggested by Malcolm P. McNair, retailing authority and professor emeritus at the Harvard Business School, describes the way in which retail organizations naturally change or evolve.

According to McNair's theory, called the Wheel of Retailing, most retail organizations begin life as lower-priced distributors. They offer strictly functional facilities, limited assortments, and minimal customer services. As time elapses, the successful businesses need to grow in order to survive, so they begin to trade up in an effort to broaden their customer profile. Facilities are modernized. Store decor becomes more attractive. Assortments become more varied and of higher quality. Promotional efforts are initiated or increased, and some customer services are introduced.

The process of trading up, however, involves considerable capital investment in the physical plant, equipment, and stock. Operating expenses spiral. As a result, retailers are forced to charge higher prices to cover the increased cost of doing business. To justify the higher prices, they also begin to stock more expensive merchandise.

According to McNair's theory, as retailers move out of the low-priced end of the market into the moderate-to-high-priced field, they create a vacuum at the bottom of the retailing structure. The vacuum does not exist for long, though. Enterprising new retailers move quickly to fill the vacated and temporarily uncompetitive low-priced area to meet the demands of customers who either need or prefer to patronize low-priced retailers. This pattern keeps repeating itself as successful retailers trade up and new ones move into the vacuum. This theory also applies to catalog companies—Spiegel is one example of a firm that moved upscale.

Even those who move up must still constantly cope with the ever-changing nature of the fashion business. In Chapter 18, the most important challenges and trends confronting today's retailers will be discussed, along with strategies to overcome them.

SUMMARY AND REVIEW

The history of fashion retailing in the United States is an interesting one. From general stores and peddlers to the earliest mail-order sellers, all early retailers sought customer satisfaction. Today's retailers seek the same goals through a variety of formats.

Three traditional retailing formats were the department store, the specialty store, and the discount store. Newer formats include off-price retailers, factory outlet stores, category killers, and boutiques and showcase stores. All of these formats can be owned in one of four ways: sole proprietors, chains, leased departments, or franchises.

Four types of nonstore retailing are popular today: direct selling, catalog or mail-order selling (the largest), TV home shopping, and Internet sites.

Mergers and acquisitions have changed the face of retailing as we knew it, and will probably continue to do so. Malcom McNair's theory of how retailers evolve and change proposes that most retailers begin as lower-priced distributors and then move upscale. This creates an opportunity for new retailers to fill the lower-priced niche. McNair calls this the Wheel of Retailing.

Trade Talk

Define or briefly explain the following terms:

big boxes
category buying or classification buying
category killer
chain organization
department store
departmental buying
discount store
factory outlet store
fashion retailing
franchise
general merchandise retailer
general store

For Review

1. Name and briefly explain the characteristics and importance of three early forms of retail distribution in the United States.
2. How is the buying function handled by a department store?
3. What is a specialty store? How are buying and merchandising handled in a specialty store?
4. What is a chain organization? How are buying and merchandising handled in chain operations?
5. How do successful discounters make a profit?
6. What is a leased department and how does it operate? Name the departments in a retail store that are frequently leased.
7. What is a category killer?
8. What stage or stages of the fashion cycle would most likely be emphasized by (a) a specialty store, (b) a department store, and (c) a discount store?
9. What is the difference between home TV shopping and shopping on the Internet?
10. According to Malcolm P. McNair, how do retail organizations typically evolve?

For Discussion

1. Compare and contrast the organization for buying and merchandising among (a) prestigious chain organizations, department stores, and large specialty stores; (b) discounters and off-price mass merchandisers; and (c) franchises and leased departments. Give examples of different types of retailers in your community.
2. What examples in your community can you cite that support McNair's theory of trading up by retailers?

References

1. "Retail Industry Trends," Plunkett Research, Ltd., www.plunkettresearch.org, February 2002.

2. "Retailers in America," *American Business Index*, February 12, 2002.
3. "Sears History" available at http://www.sears.com/our company.
4. Laura K. Yax," Population Estimates," U.S. Census Bureau, eire.gov.org, January 28, 2002.
5. "Top Stores," *Stores*, July 1997, p. S-16.
6. Melissa Preddy, "Department Stores Struggling to Adjust In Volatile Industry," *Detroit News, Gannett News Service*, January 14, 1997, p. S-12.
7. "The Major Chains: Dominance Through More Doors," *Women's Wear Daily Infotrac*, June 1997, p. 18.
8. Jeff Henry, "Truth not artifice," *Visual Merchandising and Store Design*, February 2000.
9. Jennifer Pendleton, "Melrose Place: Hot Topic Brings Urban Hip to Suburban Malls," *Los Angeles Times*, April 12, 1997, p. B-1.
10. Vilma Barr, "Attention Shoppers: Big Box Stores Now Available in New Shapes and Sizes," *Retail Store Image*, April 1997, p. 44.
11. "Industry Environment," *U.S. Business Reporter*, February 5, 2002.
12. Deborah Weinswig, *Women's Wear Weekly*, February 21, 2001, pp. 2-12.
13. "Footstar to Operate Federated Department Stores Shoe Departments," *Memphis Business Journal*, January 3, 2002.
14. "Company Capsule-the Athlete's Foot Inc," *Hoover's Online*, www.hoovers.com, February 2002.
15. Marsha Doeblin, "The New Retail Landscape," *Hermes*, Fall 1996, p. 15.
16. Michael Levy and Barton A. Weitz, *Essentials of Retailing*. Irwin/McGraw-Hill, New York: 1996, p. 31.
17. Patricia Sellers, "Giants of the Fortune 500: Sears: The Turnaround is Ending; The Revolution Has Begun," *Fortune*, April 28, 1997, p. 106.
18. Sharon Edelson, "Entertainment Value: Does All That Glitter Turn to Gold," *Women's Wear Daily*, August 6, 1996, p. 1.
19. Laura Klepacki, "Avon Breaks Into Retailing," *Women's Wear Daily*, December 10, 2001.
20. "Catalog Sales Growth Continues to Outpace Overall Retail Growth," Direct Marketing Association, http://retailindustry.about.com, June 4, 2001.
21. Giada Bresaola, ABACUS Spring 2001 Catalog Industry Trend Report, www.abacus-direct.com, June 5, 2001.
22. Masahiro Nawata, "L. L. Bean, J. Crew Test Strategies in Japan," Siam Future Development, Co Ltd. www.siamfuture.com/asian news, June 16, 2001.
23. Holly Haber, "Deep in the Heart of Texans," *Women's Wear Daily*, July 21, 1997, p. 8.
24. www.hsn.com, Company information.
25. "QVC Bucks Trend, Shows Gains," *Women's Wear Daily*, February 7, 2002.
26. Valerie Seckler, "Survival of the Fittest Online," *Women's Wear Daily*, May 9, 2001.
27. Valerie Seckler, "Yule Outlook Rosy for 'Net Sales," *Women's Wear Daily,* October 1, 2002
28. Valerie Seckler, "Apparel Starring in Cyberspace," *Women's Wear Daily*, August 27, 2001.
29. Heather Green, Gail DeGeorge, and Amy Barrett, "The Virtual Mall Gets Real," *Business Week*, January 26, 1998, p. 90.

CHAPTER 18

Policies and Strategies in Fashion Retailing

WHAT'S IN IT FOR YOU?

Everything you always wanted to know about the major merchandising, operational, and location policies of retailers.

Key Concepts:

- The six major merchandising policies that must be set by each retailer
- The five operational policies that must be set by each retail store
- The major strategies retailers are using to respond to customer concerns
- The major trends in merchandising and operational policies

Retailing is ruled by imitation. A successful new retailing format or concept will soon be duplicated. Yet, certain retail innovators continue to flourish despite the intensifying competition. One reason is the innovator's knowledge that is difficult to imitate. Competitors can duplicate Wal-Mart's large stores, cross-selling of food and general merchandise, even its use of "people-greeter's," but few, if any, can match the productivity of its core competencies: inventory management and distribution. The former are visible to the eye, the latter are knowledge-based and invisible.

—*Chain Store Age*

Stores use their merchandising, operating, and location policies to differentiate themselves from the competition and to attract different kinds of customers. Successful retailers realize

that "you cannot be all things to all people," as the old saying has it. So they carefully craft a unique mix of merchandise, policies, and store locations to attract a loyal customer following. At the same time, they must respond to changing trends—a challenging balancing act.

Merchandising Policies

Regardless of whether a retailer is a chain or a mom-and-pop operation, a general or specialty merchandiser, it seeks to maximize its profits by going after a target group of customers. In order to better target their customers, retailers establish **merchandising policies**. These are general and specific guidelines and goals established by store management and adjusted according to current trends and marketplace needs to keep the store on target.

Of the many elements that go into a store's merchandising policies, the six most important are the store's overall general goals regarding:

1. Stage of the fashion cycle that will be emphasized
2. Level of quality that will be maintained
3. Price range or ranges that will be offered
4. Depth and breadth of merchandise assortments
5. Brand policies
6. Exclusivity

Fashion Cycle Emphasis

As a means of establishing its image, every retailer decides to emphasize one phase of the fashion cycle over others. It then chooses its merchandise to fit that phase. Most stores want to ride the tide of new fashion. Few knowingly highlight styles once they have reached the decline stage, but stores still must choose whether to emphasize styles in their introductory, rise, culmination, or peak stages.

A retailer who chooses to buy styles in the introductory phase is opting to be a fashion leader, while a store that waits for the styles to become slightly established, that is, to enter the rise stage, has decided to aim for being a close second to the fashion leader. Finally, a retailer may buy clothes in the culmination or peak stages, thus making itself a follower of fashion trends—as indeed most women are. The majority of stores across the country probably fall into this category.

Naturally, a store's choice about fashion emphasis must accord with its targeted customers' needs and wants. Henri Bendel's in New York, which for many years had a reputation for extreme trendiness, knew that its target customers were a small, elite group of young and very stylish women who wanted to be the first to wear whatever was new. When The Limited bought Bendel's, management changed Bendel's target customer and shifted the store's emphasis, moving from a position of fashion leadership to one of pursuing a broader market. In the late 1990s, it changed back to the narrower, less competitive niche of the fashion leader customer. Today, Bendel's has reestablished its reputation for featuring and nurturing young, fashion forward talent, with exclusive in-store boutiques and "designer-in-residence" programs.

Quality

Retailers can choose from three general levels of quality:

1. The top level, which involves the finest materials and workmanship
2. The intermediate level, which exhibits concern for quality and workmanship but always with an eye to maintaining certain price levels
3. The serviceable level, which involves materials and workmanship of a fairly low level, consistent with equally low prices

Just as retailers are known for their chosen emphasis within the fashion cycle, they are also known for their decisions regarding quality. Quality and high fashion, however, do not always go hand in hand. Although most introductory styles are high-priced, this is not always the case. Some stores that assert themselves as fashion leaders do not bother with high quality, preferring merely to push what is new and exciting. In contrast, retailers that emphasize the rise or culmination stage also often stake their reputations on the high quality of their merchandise. They are thus able to emphasize their apparel's lasting qualities in ways that fashion leaders often cannot and do not want to. One example is Sears' boy's wear, which stresses sturdy workmanship.

Once a store has set its quality policies, it must make more specific decisions, such as whether it will accept nothing less than perfect goods or whether it will permit irregulars and second-quality goods to be offered.

Price Ranges

What people earn affects what they can spend, especially for clothing, where a variety of choices regarding quality and price are available. As a result, pricing policies are an important merchandising decision. A store's pricing policies play a major role in determining the kinds of customers it will attract.

There is actually no direct correlation between price and quality. Items of relatively low quality may carry a high price tag if there is a reason for them to do so, such as the presence of a designer's name or the fact that they are in the introductory phase of the fashion cycle. Despite the lack of a correlation, however, most retailers do attempt to tie their price ranges to quality standards. A store policy of buying only top quality also permits high price ranges, whereas a store that features intermediate quality usually sets some bottom limits that it will not go below. Stores that emphasize serviceable quality usually tend to also emphasize their low prices.

Ineffective pricing can drain a retailer's profits, muddle its image, and undermine customer trust. Many stores now stress a "value pricing" policy. For example, JCPenney launched a line of value-priced jeans called the Arizona Jean Company. By contracting with its own manufacturers, JCPenney could buy cheap, set quality standards, and underprice Levis. The result was overwhelming sales, and imitation of this strategy by Sears' Canyon River Blues jeans.

Depth and Breadth of Assortments

An **assortment** refers to the range of stock a retailer features. A store can feature a **narrow and deep assortment**, in which it stocks relatively few styles but has them in many sizes and colors. Or it can stock a **broad and shallow assortment** in which it offers many different styles in limited sizes and colors.

The two are mutually exclusive since space and cost are limiting factors in retail operations. A policy of stocking a broad assortment usually limits the depth to which those items can be stocked, and conversely, if depth is desired, variety must usually be limited. Prestige stores tend to stock broad and shallow assortments, offering small stocks of many styles in limited sizes and colors.

In stores that cater to mid-range fashion and quality, assortments are broad and shallow

A

B

FIGURE 18.1
Judging from these ads, at which stage is the fashion cycle emphasis at Filene's Basement? At the department stores mentioned in the Jantzen ad?
(a) Ad provided by Filene's Basement (b) ©Janzten Inc.

early in a season when new styles are being tested. Once the demand for a style has become clear, the store begins concentrating on narrow and deep assortments of proven styles.

Mass merchandisers focus on narrow and deep assortments of styles in the culmination stage. Target, for example, has built an enviable reputation for fashionableness and fresh selection, yet its selections are not particularly deep. But its meticulous attention to housekeeping ensures that its counters and shelves give the impression of being well-stocked. Its apparel assortment is largely basics. But a handful of items in cutting-edge styles and colors give it an upscale look.[1]

Brand Policies

Stores also must establish policies regarding the brands they will carry. A brand is a name, trademark, or logo that is used to identify the products of a specific manufacturer or seller. Brands help to differentiate products from their competition. Some brands, those associated with designers like Ralph Lauren, for example, acquire a special status that permits them to be sold at higher prices. Status and price, however, are not the only things that help a brand sell well. National brands and private labels have also become important.

A national brand, which identifies the manufacturer of a product, is widely distributed in many stores across the country. National brands, which hold out the promise of consistent quality, have become the backbone of many retailers' stocks. Today the names of some designers, such as Tommy Hilfiger and Eileen Fisher, to name but two, have become so well known to consumers that their labels are considered national brands. These name brands have acquired a value in the consumers' mind that is distinct from any intrinsic value in the products themselves. To minimize competition over national brands, some major retailers insist on buying exclusive, or **confined styles** from national brand manufacturers. Also, some manufacturers limit the number of stores that can carry their products. Nike, for example, allows only The Lockeroom and Belk's to sell its products in Newton County, Georgia, while the Russell Corporation allows only a few stores in the same county to sell its baseball and basketball uniforms.

Retailers are also riding the wave of popularity of brand names by promoting their own private labels or store brands. Store brands have proven to be an excellent way to meet price competition and achieve exclusivity. JCPenney's, for example, has seen its private label, Arizona Jeans Company, become a blockbuster success.

Prestige specialty stores tend to feature their own store labels and designer names, a strategy Bergdorf Goodman pursued with a private label collection of classic but luxurious sportswear. Many department stores have adopted private labels with great success. Federated Department Stores with its I.N.C., Charter Club, M.T. Studio, and Arnold Palmer collections is a prime example. Mass merchandisers have always offered their own private labels, typically sold alongside unbranded merchandise, as a means of keeping prices low. Kmart, for example, sells "celebrity" lines, including apparel by Jaclyn Smith and Martha Stewart's linens and home fashions. Home Depot's spokesperson, Lynette Jennings, is a well-known interior designer with a highly rated TV show. Target has established a slew of both clothing and beauty licenses through exclusive agreements and designer partnerships with Michael Graves, Stephen Sprouse, Mossimo, Sonia Kashuk, and Cherokee.[2] Wal-Mart sells a line by Kathie Lee Gifford. Even mass merchandisers, however, have been swept into the tidal wave of national brand names and now carry them.

Exclusivity

Exclusivity is something many stores strive for but few are able to achieve. Several store policies can help retailers establish a reputation for exclusivity.

- They may prevail upon vendors to confine one or more styles to their store for a period of time and/or within their trading area.
- They can buy from producers who will manufacture goods to their specifications.
- They can become the sole agent within their trading area for new, young designers.
- They can seek out and buy from domestic or foreign sources of supply that no one else has discovered.

However, the first two policies (confined lines and specification buying) are options only when a store can place a large enough initial order to make production profitable for the manufacturer. Neiman Marcus, Bergdorf Goodman, and Holt Renfrew, for example, are featuring a private label called Dei Tre, de-

FIGURE 18.2
Too many sales undermine customers' trust.
CATHY © Cathy Guisewite. Reprinted with permission of UNIVERSAL PRESS SYNDICATE. All Rights Reserved.

signed exclusively for them by Louis Dell'Olio, the longtime Anne Klein designer. By joining forces, they can more easily meet the initial order quantity.

The last two policies do not necessarily demand high volume. They are thus invaluable to prestige stores who need exclusivity as part of their images but cannot hope to compete in volume with mass merchandisers or even big department stores.

Operational Store Policies

After a retailer has defined its target customers and set its merchandise policies in a manner designed to attract them, it must next establish **operational policies**. Often more specific in nature than merchandising policies, these are primarily designed to keep the customers once they are attracted enough to come into the store. What merchandising policies do to establish a retailer's image, operational policies do to build a store's reputation. Operational policies also serve to enhance merchandising policies. They establish such things as the store's ambiance, its customer services, its selling services, its promotional activities, and last but hardly least, its frequent shopper plans.

Ambiance

Ambiance, the atmosphere you encounter when you enter a store, does much to create the image of a store. Prestige department and specialty stores work hard to provide pleasant and even luxurious surroundings. Decor matters, and usually consists of carpeted or wood floors, wood counters and display cases, chandeliers and other expensive lighting. Dressing rooms are numerous, large, and private. The store is pleasing to the eye. Merchandise is attractively displayed on a variety of fixtures. Just think of the strong link between the store design of a Crate & Barrel and its displays and merchandise (see Figure 18.3). Its use of textured woods, colorful textiles, and bright pottery has made its merchandise the stars of an exciting show. (Store design and display are discussed in more detail in Chapter 19.)

Len Berry coined the term **sensory retailing**, which means in-store stimulation of all the customers' senses. Sensory retailing is becoming a more significant competitive weapon in retailing. Think of the sensuous aroma, mood music, and dramatic lighting of merchandise displays in a Victoria's Secret. In fact, the music played in Victoria's Secret stores has become a successful business in itself. In the history of classical music, 11 compact disks have sold over a million copies. The label that released five of them—Victoria's Secret! This success has led to other retailers selling their own albums; among them are The Limited, Express, Lane Bryant, Polo, the Gap, and Pottery Barn.

The success of Victoria's Secret with its signature scent has not been as easily duplicated. Frederick's of Hollywood, which sells racier lingerie, tried a similarly sweet floral scent in its stores—and sales dropped. The scent was discontinued. Experts believe that Frederick's customers—mainly men—were turned off by the scent. The Knot Shop, which sells men's ties, had better results with its signature scent, a mix of oak, leather, and tobacco, that it keeps at a very low, almost subconscious level.

In contrast, at low-range and discount stores, ambiance may count for little. The intention is to send the customer a clear message: Shop here in less than luxurious surroundings, and we will give you the lowest possible price. Fixtures are usually plain, garments crowded on racks or "rounders," with supermarket style signage. Fitting room space may be limited or may consist only of a large, shared dressing room, commonly referred to as a "snake pit" by customers.

FIGURE 18.3
The ambiance of Crate & Barrel store sends a message of good taste and good visual merchandising, which customers can see immediately as they approach one of their glass-fronted stores.
Courtesy, Crate & Barrel.

Customer Services

Department stores pioneered in offering customer services. They were the first retailers to offer their customers store charge privileges and generous return policies. Their willingness to accept merchandise returns, in fact, originated with John Wanamaker and his Philadelphia store of the same name. His first store, opened in 1876 in an old railroad freight station, was a men's clothing store. A year later, he added departments for ladies' goods, household linens, upholstery, and shoes, for a then unheard of total of 16 departments. Wanamaker further shocked the retail world by advertising that if anything did not please "the folks at home" or was unsatisfactory for any other reason, it could be returned for a cash refund within ten days.

Today, it is commonplace for department and specialty stores to offer their customers an array of services designed to increase their edge over the competition. The more familiar customer services include several credit plans, liberal merchandise return policies, telephone ordering, free or inexpensive delivery, in-store

FIGURE 18.4
The brand policies of this small specialty chain are prominently featured in its advertising.
Etoile's Inc. Reprinted with permission.

restaurants, free parking, and a variety of services such as alterations and jewelry repair. As competition, particularly from chains and discounters, has increased, general merchandisers have met it by offering still more services, such as fax order facilities, on-line ordering, and extended shopping hours. As Dennis Toffolo, president of Hudson's Detroit, said: "We used to be a business that was all-day-long. Then, more people entered the work force. Retailing went to noon and evening, and now it's evening and weekend."[3]

Discount stores, especially small ones, offer a more limited range of services than do department and specialty stores. Discounters took a lead in establishing extended hours. At small discount stores, transactions are usually on a cash-and-carry basis, although most accept major credit cards. Most large discounters offer their own credit plans, with greater emphasis on installment buying. Refund policies are less liberal than those of department stores; however, most discounters will accept unused goods (often for credit rather than cash) if they are returned in a specified period of time, usually seven to ten days. Delivery service, if available, is restricted to bulky items and usually costs extra.

Large discount chains like Target, proving Malcolm MacNair's theory discussed in Chapter 17, have raised their level of services. They have "guest amenity kiosks" with phones that shoppers can use to summon a salesperson or get a question answered. Target also has pint-sized shopping carts to help keep shoppers' children amused (see Figure 18.5). The Swedish discount chain IKEA offers baby-sitting services.

FIGURE 18.5
A child with a mini-size shopping cart at Target demonstrates this chain's strong customer service policies. They realize that a contented child enables Mom to shop longer!
Photograph: © David Corio.

Selling Services

In all but the higher-priced specialty stores these days, self-service is the rule. In discount stores and low- to moderate-priced chain stores, clerks are present on the selling floor to direct customers to merchandise and ring up sales. In most department and specialty stores, salespersons are available on the sales floor to answer some questions and complete sales transactions.

The old service of catering exclusively to one client at a time, bringing clothes into the dressing room, and offering fit and style advice is gone in most department stores, probably forever. An exception to this rule is Nordstrom, which has maintained a high degree of selling services. In fact, it is the success of its sales help that has made Nordstrom one of the most successful specialty stores in America. Other very high-end specialty stores, like Bergdorf Goodman and Lord & Taylor also offer highly personalized selling techniques, which include recording what individual customers have purchased in the past and alerting them by phone or mail to new merchandise that may interest them. Very often, these high-level salespeople work on commission, so they have a real incentive to offer personalized service.

Promotional Activities

All retailers engage in some promotional activities, whether it is advertising or publicity. Advertising and publicity are a store's two chief means of communicating with its customers. How much a retail organization promotes itself, however, varies depending upon the type of retail operation.

Discount stores are the heaviest promoters, and they rely heavily on advertising as opposed to publicity or public relations. All kinds of advertising—newspaper, television, radio, and direct mail—are employed to get their message across. Their advertising emphasizes low prices and in many instances invites customers to comparison shop. Discount operations tend to run frequent sales or special promotions. In a very popular promotion, IKEA, the Swedish home furnishings retailer, cooperated with public health officials in Houston to offer a day of free vaccinations and dental checkups for children of shoppers.[4]

Compared to the discounters, department and chain stores and specialty stores engage in a more moderate amount of promotional activity, although, of course, large budgets are allotted for this purpose. Department stores rely most heavily on newspaper advertising, although some prestigious department and specialty stores also advertise in the major fashion magazines, or local magazines, or local cable television. Specialty chains like the Gap, Esprit, and Pier 1 have begun to use general magazines as much as fashion magazines or shelter magazines to reach their target customers. Internet sites are being used more and more by both large and small retailers as a new way to reach affluent customers interested in convenience.

The more prestigious stores use direct mail. Monthly bills, stuffed with advertising and special catalogs, are mailed regularly to charge customers. These retailers also do a moderate number of "special sale" and "special purchase" advertising campaigns. Sales are usually tied to special events, such as a holiday (the Columbus Day coat sales are one example), an anniversary, or an end-of-the-month clearance. Department stores were the leaders in pioneering traditional seasonal sales: white sales in January and August, back-to-school promotions in late summer and early fall.

The content of advertising varies with the type of retailer. Discount and mass merchandisers' ads are heavily product-oriented, displaying the product and its price in a direct manner. The prestige stores run some advertisements for individual items, but their advertisements are more likely to feature a designer or a new design collection. Advertisements may emphasize a new fashion look or trend at the expense of promoting the apparel in the ad.

Frequent Shopper Plans

A policy that the airlines have used to great advantage—frequent flier plans—have been adopted by many other businesses. Also referred to as "loyalty marketing," or "customer retention programs," this policy is also widely used by hotels, who reward frequent guests with special rates, their favorite newspaper, special easy checkout, and other "perks." In today's "overstored" environment, retailers are searching for ways to stand out. Some retailers are adapting this policy by rewarding frequent shoppers with special sales, special discounts, newsletters, and clubs. This trend is spreading as retailers see the advantages of keeping existing customers and encouraging them to shop more often. Since the bank credit card has assumed near-universal acceptance, retailers own charge card programs have suffered. The frequent shopper club, such as Club Macy's, is a method retailers are using to promote customer loyalty.

Duane Reade's Dollar Rewards frequent-shopper program features in-store delivery vehicles that give customers tailored offers. The devices allow consumers to access individualized point-of-sale offers while they shop. When customers scan their Dollar Rewards card (see Figure 18.6) at terminals in different parts of a store they get a reading on discounts or product

FIGURE 18.6
The Duane Reade's Dollar Rewards program provides benefits for frequent shoppers.
Courtesy, Duane Read, Inc.

FASHION FOCUS

Allen Questrom: An All American Retailng Star

From management trainee to Chairman and Chief Executive Officer, Allen Questrom is the poster boy of retail career advancement and success. Questrom began his retailing career at Abraham & Strauss, part of Federated Department Stores, in 1964 as a management trainee. He worked his way through the levels of management positions and became chairman and chief executive officer of the Rich's Division in 1980 and of the former Bullocks Division in 1984, all part of Federated Department Stores.

He was promoted to Executive Vice President of Federated Department Stores prior to the takeover by Campau Corporation in 1988, after which he left the company. From 1988 to 1990, he was President and Chief Executive Officer of Neiman Marcus. Then a call from Federated Department Stores called him back to the company where he started his retailing career.

Federated was in trouble and had just declared bankruptcy. Here was one of the leading department store corporations in dire need of leadership and vision in order to remain a force in the business economy of the country. Riding to the rescue was Allen Questrom, with his knowledge of retailing and his fantastic people skills, becoming Chairman and Chief Executive Officer of Federated Department Stores.

From 1990 to 1997, he led the company out of bankruptcy, and acquired R. H. Macy & Company, Inc. and the Broadway Stores who became part of the stellar lineup of Federated Department Stores. It was a time of great success and growth, and under his leadership, many new and talented merchants were added to the ranks of Federated Department Stores. Federated was doing well, Questrom trained executives, and merchants were now ready to take over the reins of leadership at Federated, and Questrom decided to retire in 1997!

Questrom then toured the world, not for merchandise or new production sources, but to bike and ski and study during many global trips. Two years into his retirement, he was approached by the top management of Barney's and asked to return to the world of retailing to again lead a troubled retailer to new success—and that he did! As Simon Doonan, creative director for Barney's said, "There are not too many fabulous people in retail. We are lucky that we got one."

In a move that surprised many of the retail pundits, Questrom left Barney's, and in September 2000, with his background mostly in high-end, upscale retailing, was appointed Chairman of the Board and Chief Executive Officer of the J. C. Penney Company, one of America's largest department store, drugstore, catalog, and e-commerce retailers. What a change for Questrom!

By 2003, Questrom had directed a turnaround in the business of J. C. Penney and was leading the company back to profitability and customer loyalty. J. C. Penney operates 1,061 department stores and owns 3,656 Eckerd drugstores, and employs over 250,000 people. It also owns a catalog and Internet business and Questrom has instituted changes that have helped them become more profitable. "The turnaround of department stores is well underway, and our direct to consumer business is strengthened, uniquely positioning J. C. Penney as a three-channel retailer," said Questrom.

Questrom is just one example of the success that can be attained in the world of retailing. If you have a feel for the business, are not afraid of hard work, have good people skills, and want to succeed—retailing is for you!

Allen Questrom.
Courtesy, Fairchild Publications, Inc.

Sources:

Maura Egan, "Questrom Authority," *New York Magazine*, December 6, 1999.

"J. C. Penney Chairman and CEO" to Deliver 'Melvin Jacobs Retail Leadership Lecture,'" The Pennsylvania State University, January 31, 2003, press release.

"J. C. Penney," *American City Business Journals*, January 6, 2003.

www.jcpenney.net (company Web site)

offers based on their purchase histories within four seconds. More than 2 million Dollar Rewards cards are currently in circulation, and about 55 percent of all purchases at the chain are made with the cards, according to Duane Reade.[5]

Location Policies

In addition to the ever-present neighborhood shopping center, retailers are exploring a wide range of locations, including larger malls, airports and train stations, downtowns, and resort areas. They are using carts and kiosks, and even setting up traveling, temporary shops. Experts classify shopping centers in many ways; for our purposes, we will use the following simplified system.

Shopping Centers and Malls

A **shopping center** is a coordinated group of retail stores, plus a parking area. By 2001 there were 45,115 shopping centers in the United States.[6] Those shopping centers that are enclosed and climate-controlled are known as **malls.** While most malls have one floor, two or three floor malls are becoming more common. In central business districts, more **vertical malls,** multistory buildings taller than they are wide, have been built to conserve valuable land. Water Tower Place in Chicago was the first vertical mall; it has seven levels of prestige stores, and is next door to a Ritz-Carlton hotel.

Customers are increasingly seen as bored with cookie-cutter malls and stores. Too many malls look the same, contain the same stores, and lack any regional flavor. If dropped into the average mall, a customer would not know if he or she were in Alaska, Iowa, or Texas. Consequently, the number of Americans who shop frequently at malls is only 34 percent of the shopping public.[7] As Allen Questrom, former CEO of Federated Department Stores, said:

> *There's too much retail space out there. The world needs another mall like it needs a hole in the head. We have 19 square feet of retail space for every person in this country. It's bad for us and bad for most communities to oversaturate them with retail. It's not good for the retailers or the owners of these malls. Developers have to be very guarded. A lot of these new malls will not pay a dividend.*[8]

The competition for customers is so great that existing malls feel that they must continually renovate and expand, just to keep larger, newer centers from moving into their territory. The Taubman Cos., a developer of malls, is turning the common areas in its malls into lounges that resemble plush hotel lobbies. "It's all part of entertainment," said Barbara Ashley of Taubman.[9] Other entertainment-driven strategies include play zones for children and how-to classes for adults. (See Chapter 17 for other examples of entertainment values in retailing.)

Power centers or **power strips** are outdoor shopping centers that offer three or four category killers together, so a range of merchandise is available at highly discounted prices. They may be built close to existing regional malls, and contain off-price apparel retailers or category killers like Filene's Basement, Mervyn's, the Cosmetic Center, Toys 'R Us, or Burlington Coat Factory. In the 1990s, these centers cannibalized market shares so fast that the traditional malls had to reinvent themselves to keep up with the competition. Some of the strategies that malls are using to attracting shoppers are featuring new, innovative retailers for shoppers that are looking for something other than the usual national chains, and an interior, maze-like lay-out that guides shoppers throughout different departments of a store and connects to other shops on the property.[10]

Larger Malls

As older, small malls are ailing, larger and larger malls continue to be built. **Regional malls,** for example, usually contain at least two "anchor" department stores, as well as many specialty stores and a food court or restaurants. Their trading area is at least a 5-mile radius. Prestige regional malls like North-brook Court near Chicago offer services like weekend valet parking, free strollers, and free newspapers.

Superregional malls are, as their name implies, even larger than regional malls, often containing up to one million square feet. They contain at least three department stores or major chain stores, with 100 to 300 specialty stores and services. Their trading area is up to an hour's driving time. An example is Oak Park Mall in Overland Park, Kansas, which recently added a new concourse and a new anchor, Nordstrom, as well as another Dillard's and an expanded JCPenney.

Another type of huge shopping center (four to five million square feet) has emerged in the last decade—the **megamall.** The first megamall was built in West Edmonton in Alberta, Canada; it is still the world's largest, with over

800 stores. The world's second megamall is in the United States; it is The Mall of America, in Bloomington, Minnesota. With over 525 specialty stores stores, it is 10 times the size of an average regional mall. It combines shopping with entertainment in a major way: with 50 restaurants, 7 nightclubs, 14 movies, and Camp Snoopy, an amusement park! To draw customers one weekend the mall hired Ringo Starr and the Beach Boys to play at a "Jam Against Hunger" in its vast parking lot. These two megamalls draw people from all over Canada and the United States.[11]

Outlet malls, like the various "Mills" developed by the Mills Corporation—Gurnee Mills, outside of Chicago; Ontario Mills, in suburban Los Angeles; and Potomac Mills, outside of Washington D.C.—are increasingly popular. Entertainment, like Sega Game Works and IMAX 3-D theaters, plays a key role in these developments. As Mills Corp. chairman Laurance Siegel says:

"Increasingly, we have built on our realization that people do not just go out for the function of shopping [en] they want to be entertained. We think like show business: bring in people by being creative, different and unique. Value is still part of our success, and it is a buffer if any economic weakness makes consumers even more value-conscious."[12]

Air Malls

Airport retailing as a whole is certainly nothing new. Food concessions have been in airports for decades. What is new is the number of well-known retailers, from The Disney Store to Gap to Victoria's Secret, that are opening in what are being called **air malls**. With plane traffic booming, and delays more frequent, airports have become the busiest street corners in America. The length of time that an average person stays in an airport is 61 minutes; just 3 minutes shorter than the time spent in a typical shopping mall. Further, the typical air passenger is a high-end shopper. So average sales per square foot are more than $1,000 versus $225 for the typical suburban mall.

Downtown Sites

Faced with dwindling traffic in malls, some national chains are moving to downtown sites in search of growth. Besides pedestrian traffic, retailers are attracted to revitalized downtowns because the price of doing business there can be lower than at a mall; $40 to $50 a square foot rather than the $60 to $70 a square foot at the average middle American mall.

Some malls are actually rebuilding their centers to create a "street-like" shopping experience. At Meydenbauer Place in Bellevue, Washington, for example, a two-million-square-foot development includes a convention center, movie complex, and a made-to-order Main Street, containing a Banana Republic, among other national chains. Ken Himmel, the developer of this project, is a pioneer of upscale urban development. "Our projects in urban areas or suburban areas are about creating a downtown theme," he says. "We formed the company in answer to the public's outcry to return to street retailing. We're trying to reinvent retail presentations that are not dependent on the mall model."[13]

Another downtown variation on the shopping center is called a **mixed-use center**. A shopping mall is attached to office buildings, a hotel, or apartment houses. An example is Crystal City, Virginia, near Washington, D.C., which offers a place for people to live, work, play, and shop—all within the center.

Resort Retailing

Progressive retailers are positioning themselves where their customers are when they are relaxed. For many, this has meant catalogs. For some others, however, it means putting stores in resort areas. In the ski resort town of Aspen, Colorado, for example, major retailers like Banana Republic and the Chanel Boutique have opened stores. Some resort towns have established themselves as unique shopping destinations. Seaside, a planned resort community in the Florida panhandle, is one such place. It has an open-air bazaar called Per-spi-cas-ity, which features the work of local craftspeople and retailers, in intriguing displays of casual clothes and accessories.

Carts and Kiosks

Carts and kiosks are selling spaces in common mall areas and airports and train stations. Smaller and often on wheels, thus more flexible than even the smallest shop, **carts** are increasingly popular for selling accessories, T-shirts, and caps. Kiosks, on the other hand, are larger than carts, and more stationary. Like a newsstand, a **kiosk** offers movable shelves or racks for merchandise. It is very popular for sunglasses, jewelry, and legwear.

Then & Now

What the World Needs Now . . . Are New Retail Stars

In the fast-paced world of fashion dynamics, retailers are constantly seeking new recruits who will be able to learn and grow, and eventually join the top ranks of management. For some retail companies, one of the best sources of new talent is the college campus.

Putting together the many and varied attributes needed for success in the multifaceted fashion business, we begin to build an ideal closely resembling a "Wonder Woman" or "Superman." Retailing, with its direct contact with the customer, is one of the most interesting, exciting, and well-paid of all career paths in the fashion business. However, for the past decade, retail careers did not convey the excitement and glamour of industries such as Wall Street, entertainment, e-commerce, design, public relations, and media.

Too bad! Now is the time for all good men and women to come to the aid of the industry that impacts the life of everyone everywhere—retailing! Here is the career path that is made for success. There is a shortage of young people starting up the career ladder now and this is the time for bright, energetic, and interested college students to enter these ranks and rise to the top of the ladder—sooner rather than later.

Over the past two or three years, there has been much conversation about what attributes and skills are needed to become a successful retail merchant. In the past, top-down dictatorships were the model that made companies great. Today a spirit of cooperation in the way a business is run better achieves a successful company. From heads of executive search firms, corporate offices of major store chains, and professional research papers on what makes for success in retailing, the following traits and attributes rank among the most desired in CEO's:

- Leadership—An ability to articulate a vision that is easily understood by others
- Motivation—An ability to make people want to work on this vision together
- Charisma—An ability to attract and appeal to a diverse team of executives

Always necessary are traits and skills that are the cornerstone of every successful manager and top executive along the career path. They are: dedication, enthusiasm, awareness, honesty, and stamina, mixed with decision-making, communication, and negotiation skills. As one of the top headhunters of retail talent said, "Retailers today must put together a vision of what the business should be and be able to execute that plan. That's a tough road to hoe. Few retailers out there today really have vision, are great leaders and motivators." So the search for new up-and-coming retail stars is on! Are you one of them?

Sources:

David Moin, "Execs in the Wings: The Ones to Watch Amid a Narrow Field," *Women's Wear Daily*, August 6, 2001, pp. 1, 30.

David Moin, "Female Store Execs Awaiting Last Great Leap to CEO Title," *Women's Wear Daily*, July 3, 2001. pp. 1, 4–5.

David Moin, "Searching for Saviors: Can Retailers Truly Find the Perfect Chief Exec?" *Women's Wear Daily*, February 20, 2003, pp. 1, 3.

Vicki M. Young, "Building Better Management," *Women's Wear Daily*, October 1, 2001, pp. 25–26.

Temporary Sites

Temporary retailers, who typically set up shop in empty storefronts or kiosks or carts in malls, are a booming business. Temporary holiday shops became commonplace in the 1990s. And specialty leasing retailers are not temporary anymore. This market segment has grown to a $10 billion, year-round business that can add millions of dollars to a developer's bottom line.[14]

Emerging Retail Strategies

Customers are demanding more convenient shopping, more varied products, and lower prices at the same time that they are shifting their loyalty from retailer to retailer, shopping at Kmart one week and Macy's the next. Retailers have developed a number of strategies to respond to them. Perhaps the strongest response is to more clearly define the store's fashion image, "no longer trying to succeed through broad appeal, but by narrowing [the] product assortments to present a very distinct point of view."[15]

Let us examine retailer's responses in more detail.

Responding to the Customers' Desire for Convenience

As life grows ever faster-paced, customers continue to look for easier ways to shop. The consumer has less time, is smarter, and more demanding. There are more products. There is less sales help. As retail consultant Walter Loeb said "The slogan of the 1980s was 'Shop till you drop,' now it's 'Find it, buy it, and get out.'"[16] With this axiom in mind retailers are investing heavily in new technology, and in more sales help.

Surveys have found that a large number of shoppers will walk out of a store if the checkout lines are too long, the store is too crowded, or a salesperson is surly. Over 22 percent of shoppers report leaving a store for lack of sales help.

The four dimensions of customer convenience that retailers must consider are:

- *Locational*—where customers have to go to make purchases
- *Time-of-day*—when customers can make purchases
- *Process*—ease and speed of shopping and returns
- *Assortment*—what can they buy here and where else will they have to go.

Responding to the Decline of Customer Loyalty

Remember that retailing is all about people, anticipating their needs, knowing their lifestyles, their preferences, their expectations, and taking the time to observe what they do and how they do it—to try to understand them, and then, when they come to your store, to give them just a little bit more than what they expected—that's the secret of success in retailing.[17]

—*Allen Questrom*

Many types of retailers are experimenting with lifestyle and lifestage strategies to attract loyal customers. Pier 1, for example, frequently crosses categories to present a lifestyle concept. One summer backyard poolside display featured wicker furniture, plastic glasses and plates with color-coordinated placemats and napkins, candles in windproof holders, and bags of lemonade mix. Simply Southwest By Mail is a cataloger that focuses on apparel, accessories, and decorative items, all with a southwestern flavor.

Lifestage marketing has long been the specialty of catalog retailers. Newport News, Spiegel's catalog aimed at younger customers, hired Jasmine Bleeth of *Baywatch* to promote its line of swimwear. The junior apparel chains like Wet Seal/Contempo and Rampage are well-known examples of lifestage retailers.

Responding to Customers' Complaints About Sameness

Differentiation and customer loyalty can be achieved through proper positioning and image creation. With the glut of brands, it's imperative to create a distinctive image and niche in the consumer's mind. This provides an emotional benefit as well as the real benefits of credible value, quality, and reduced shopping time.[18]

Private label merchandise is growing at an astronomical rate, as retailers try to differentiate themselves and their merchandise in response to customers' complaints about the sameness of merchandise everywhere. Private labels are discussed in Chapter 17.

Responding to the High Cost of Product Development by Forging Strategic Alliances

A **strategic alliance** is a form of business combination in which retailers and manufacturers join forces to operate more efficiently, thus improving both companies' profits, while enabling them to give the customer a better product at a lower price. Although strategic alliances between retailers and manufacturers are difficult to form and to maintain, they are perceived as increasingly critical for success in today's highly competitive marketplace.

"Essentially, it now takes the entire supply chain working as a team to serve the consumers' mounting demands," says Robin Lewis, executive editor of *Women's Wear Daily's Infotracs on Strategic Alliances*.[19] He cites as an example of a highly profitable alliance, the agreement between Sara Lee Intimates and Wal-Mart, which has led from an initial $134 million account to a $1 billion partnership in 8 years. Both Wal-Mart and Sara Lee have teams of merchandise, operations, management information services, and marketing executives, who are devoted to this alliance. They meet regularly to iron out problems and plan joint market share goals.

The characteristics of strategic alliances as opposed to traditional retailer/manufacturer relationships are outlined in Table 18.1.

In 2001, Wal-Mart set up a strategic alliance with America Online, through which it launched an Internet service called Wal-Mart Connect. The partnership between the world's largest retailer and the world's largest Internet service provider brought Wal-Mart Connect users Internet access for less than $10 a month, as well as instant-messaging service. The AOL deal was designed to bring Wal-Mart's Web site, www.walmart.com, greater visibility, more customers, and, of course, more sales dollars, while creating a new revenue stream for AOL through the low access fee.[20]

TABLE 18.1 Characteristics of Traditional Relationships and Strategic Alliances

TRADITIONAL APPROACH	ALLIANCE APPROACH
Individual goals	Shared common goals
Independent performance	Joint performance
Independently defined goals	Supply chain definitions
Sequential processes and activities	Simultaneous processes
Activities performed by individual companies	Partner with greatest competency performs the activity
Rewards competed for	Rewards shared
Penalties absorbed by supplier	Penalties or losses shared
Many suppliers	Few select suppliers
Sequential improvements	Continuous improvements
Information is kept secret	Information is shared

Adapted from Robin Lewis, "Partner or Perish," *WWD Infotracs: Strategic Alliances.*

Trends in Retail Policies

Merchandising and operational policies continue to change at a dizzying rate. As the economy cycles through periods of boom and bust, retailers scramble to interpret and respond to changing customer needs and preferences. Of the many trends discussed in this chapter, two seem dominant: (1) using new technology, and (2) creating new job opportunities. Let us look at each of these trends in more detail.

Using New Technology

Retailers' use of new technology varies widely in sophistication and cost. It can be as simple as the Gap providing sales associates with wireless headsets, so that they can get inventory information for a customer immediately. Or it may be equipping salespeople with beepers, so that a customer can summon them to a dressing room with the touch of a button. Or the technology may be as complex as establishing a multibillion-dollar data warehouse of customer information, as Sears has done.

Four ways that retailers are using new technology are in faster shipping, in videoconferencing, in starting data warehouses, and in using the Internet.

Faster Shipping

To get the right product to the customer at the right time, manufacturers, shippers, and retailers are employing a variety of new technological developments. The widespread use of scanners and universal product codes (UPC) and electronic data interchange (EDI) was covered in Chapter 7. Some retailers have already moved beyond these technologies. For example, some apparel and cosmetics are already being shipped internationally and domestically using an extended EAN-128 code, which carries more information about the product's source and destination than the conventional UPC code. This code was developed at the request of shippers, who are looking to cut transportation time by reducing manual shipping documents.

Videoconferencing

PictureTel, Microsoft, and 3Com are bringing videoconferences to desktop computers, which will vastly increase the market and lower the cost. Meanwhile, large companies such as JCPenney are already using videoconferencing for a variety of purposes, including staff training, vendor conferences, and product development. Since several sites can participate in a videoconference, videoconferencing is an effective, low-cost way of doing staff training for very large businesses (Penney's has 1,230 stores), because it cuts down on staff travel time and expenses. JCPenney uses videoconferencing in the design and production of its private label lines by linking its in-house designers in Plano, Texas, with mills overseas. Also, videoconferencing is used for dealing with vendors about problems. As Ron Fazio, manager of communications for Penney's, said:

If we have a problem with a garment, for example, and we want to improve a collar or its fabrication, we can show it directly to the supplier without hav-

ing to mail samples. We solve a lot of problems simply by setting a 3-way conference between ourselves, a supplier, and his manufacturer in the Far East.[21]

Data Warehousing

To squeeze more profit out of each store, retailers are increasingly turning to a new technique called data warehousing. A **data warehouse** is a group of superpowerful computers hooked together and filled with information about customers, transactions, and finances. Its role is to make this mass of data easily accessible, by organizing it into categories like purchase history, vendors, sales promotions, and so forth. The data warehouse is typically separate from existing operational systems.

Retailers with the largest data warehouses include Wal-Mart, Sears, and Target. Target was one of the first companies to set up a data warehouse; the company is using it to try to tailor 30 percent of the merchandise mix to each individual store. Lands' End uses its data warehouse to track items that customers order that are out of stock. Burlington Coat Factory uses its system to target big and tall customers for special promotions.

At the North County Fair Mall in Escondito, California, mall managers can generate reports that show which stores mall patrons are shopping in, what they buy, and how much they spend. This information is then shared with the retailers in the mall.

Data warehousing can also be used as a powerful marketing tool. Customer profiling can help the retail staff target people that look like they fit the best-customer profile. Best-customer profiling also helps identify narrow targets within the highest revenue-generating customer base. With these tools, a store can identify clusters of customers and/or prospects that can be addressed with relevant messages and offers via email or e-cards.[22]

The Internet

The Internet is hastening the blurring of the line between store and nonstore retailing, which began decades ago when catalog companies opened stores and stores began sending catalogs. Now both catalogers, like Lillian Vernon and Spiegel, and stores, like Macy's and JCPenney's, have Web sites. The customer information they gather on the Internet is then fed into the customer portion of their data warehouse. This information then enables them to customize further approaches to this customer.

Stores and catalogers are already tailoring their Internet sites to fit their needs. The Lands' End Web site, for example, has an overstock area that is very popular among net-surfers, and that is moving excess inventory quickly (see Figure18.7). JCPenney offers special online discounts to attract customers to its photography services.

Retailers are also using the Internet to communicate with suppliers all over the world. "The clock runs much faster in apparel retail than in most any other kind of business, so being able to have information and react on a global basis will be crucial," said Mark Smith, a retail industry expert.[23]

The specialty retailer/cataloger Talbots is using a groupware computer program combined with the Internet to share critical information among members of its product development team: the product manager, who is responsible for developing new clothing lines; a source, who is responsible for getting an item manufactured once it has been designed; and a buyer, who decides on quantity and price. As Annie Stobbs, project manager at Talbots, said: "All these people need to collaborate on product development, and we need to be able to track the progress." Since Talbots' designs and manufactures 90 percent of all the merchandise it sells, this tracking is especially crucial.[24]

Creating New Job Opportunities

The human element remains a critical component of successful retailing. To develop a business that is truly customer-focused requires a greater investment in workers than most retail-

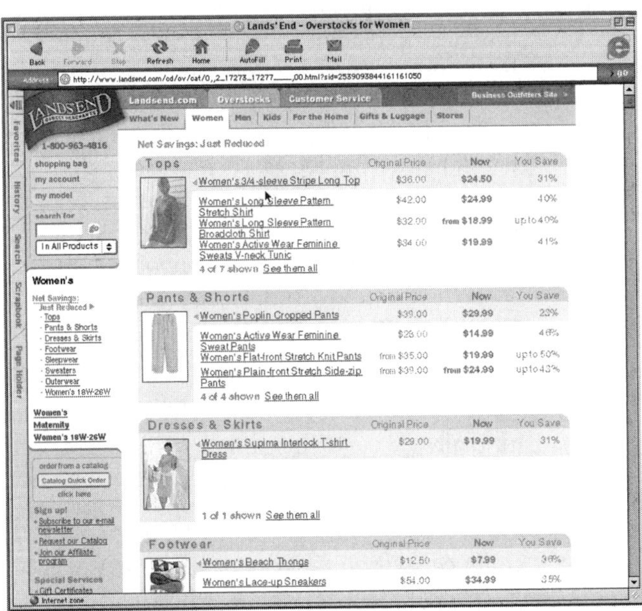

FIGURE 18.7
This overstock section of the Lands' End Web site sells both excess inventory and the store's image.
Courtesy, © 2003 Lands' End, Inc. Used with permission.

ers were willing to make in the 1980s and 1990s, when many retailers found themselves in a low-wage/high-turnover trap.

Since experts assume that technology will play a greater role in the sales clerk function, funds will be freed up to allow companies to hire more full-time sales associates, who can establish relationships with valued customers. These associates require more advanced training in product knowledge, suggestion selling, and conflict resolution so that they can act as "product advisors." Personal shoppers are becoming more prevalent, both in stores and on the Internet.

The role of the buyer is also changing, especially in situations where retailers have strategic alliances with suppliers. Freed from record-keeping functions by computers, buyers can become trend analysts, trendsetters, and product developers.

Additional employment opportunities exist for visual merchandisers and store designers, as chain stores try to customize each location. Even category killers are placing less emphasis on mass presentations of products. Also, experts predict that fashion retailers in particular will frequently change their total store environment to keep customers' interest.

Retailers are beginning to place more emphasis on developing employee loyalty through higher incentives, and real career paths. Nordstrom's has been joined by a growing number of other retailers in pursuing this goal.

Summary and Review

There are six merchandising policies that every retailer must establish; they are (1) fashion cycle emphasis, (2) quality, (3) price ranges, (4) depth and breadth of assortments, (5) brand policies, and (6) exclusivity. Five major operational policies must also be determined: (1) ambiance, (2) customer services, (3) selling services, (4) promotional activities, and (5) frequent shopper plans.

Retail location policies include sites such as shopping centers, malls, air malls, downtown sites, resorts, carts and kiosks, and temporary sites.

Emerging retail strategies include responding to: (1) the customer's desire for convenience, (2) the decline of customer loyalty, (3) customer's complaints about sameness, and (4) the high cost of product development by forging strategic alliances.

Trends in retail policies include using a number of new technologies, such as faster shipping, videoconferencing, data warehousing, and the Internet. Along with these new technologies come corresponding new job opportunities.

Trade Talk

Define or briefly explain the following terms:

air mall	megamall
ambiance	merchandising policies
assortment	mixed-use center
confined style	narrow and deep assortment
data warehouse	operational policies
kiosk	outlet mall
mall	power center or strip
regional mall	superregional mall
sensory retailing	vertical mall
shopping center	videoconferencing
strategic alliance	

For Review

1. What are the six major merchandising policies that a retailer must establish?
2. What stage or stages of the fashion cycle would most likely be emphasized by (a) a specialty store, (b) a department store, and (c) a discount store?
3. What are the five types of operational policies that a retail store owner must establish?
4. What are the major kinds of shopping centers in the United States today?
5. What is the difference between a cart and a kiosk? Where can they usually be found?
6. What strategies are retailers using to respond to the customer's desire for more convenient shopping?
7. How are retailers responding to the decline of customer loyalty?
8. What are strategic alliances? What are their goals? Give some examples of these agreements.
9. Explain how new technological developments in shipping, data warehousing, and videoconferencing are being used in the fashion industries.
10. Name some new job opportunities that are being created in retailing today as a result of the emerging trends mentioned in this chapter.

For Discussion

1. Compare and contrast the selling and fashion services of (a) department stores, (b) specialty stores, and (c) discount stores. Give examples of selling and fashion services offered by different types of retailers in your community.
2. Explain and discuss the following statement by Laurance Siegel, citing current examples to illustrate how it does or does not apply to your community:

   Traditional malls are all the same. They all have three or four anchors, a bunch of specialty stores in between, and maybe a multi-screen movie theater. There's little reason to drive past one to get to another...[25]

References

1. Jennifer Negley, "There's More Than Mirrors Behind Target's Mystique," *Discount Store News*, April 1, 1997.
2. Evan Clark, "Discounters Dominate Fundamentally," *Women's Wear Daily*, June 17, 2002.
3. Melissa Preddy, "Department Stores Struggling to Adjust in Volatile Industry," *Detroit News, Gannett News Service*, January 14, 1997, p. S-12.
4. Hage and Koshel, "Driving a Hard Bargain."
5. "Dollar Rewards Program Yields Multiple Benefits," *Chain Drug Review,* September 2, 2002, p. 36.
6. "15 Year Trends," NRB Census Shopping Center Database, www.icsc.org, July 2001.
7. Lydia Saad, "Men Enjoy Shopping as Much as Women Do." Gallup Poll News Service, August 9, 2001.
8. "Mall Mania: At Whose Expense?" *Women's Wear Daily*, January 22, 1997, p. 1.
9. Sharon Edelson, "Stores Breaking the Design Mold," *Women's Wear Daily*, January 16, 1997, p. 29.
10. "Doldrums Don't Scare Creative Retailers," *Pacific Business News*, August 3, 2001.
11. "Mall of America", Bloomington and the Twin Cities, www.bloomington.org, February 2002.
12. John Lucas, "Can Mills Duplicate Theme Store Success?" *Business*, February 19, 2002.
13. Sharon Edelson, "Re-Storing Downtown U.S.A.," *Women's Wear Daily/Global*, July 1997, p. 68.
14. Debra Hazel, "Temporary Tenants: Specialty Leasing's Big Challenge," *International Council of Shopping Centers*, February 2001.
15. "Apparel Stores: Narrower Strategies Lead to Upward Growth," *Chain Store Age*, August 1997, p. 12A.
16. Bill Bottege, "What's Happening," *Shoe Retailing Today*, http://www.com/NSRA/PUBS/What's Happening.
17. "Interactive Retailing" *Chain Store Age*, January 1997.
18. Robin Lewis, "Partner or Perish," *Women's Wear Daily Infotracs: Strategic Alliances*, February 24, 1997, p. 7.
19. Lewis, "Partner or Perish," *Women's Wear Daily,* p. 4.
20. Don Yaeger, "Wal-Mart To Spend $9 Billion," *Women's Wear Daily*, June 4 2001.
21. Jeanette Hye, "Penney's Designing By Video Conference," *Women's Wear Daily*, July 9, 1997, p. 18.
22. John M. Coe, "A Road Map for B-to-B – Database Marketing," *Target Marketing*, June 2001, p. 65.
23. Kim Ann Zimmermann, "Internet: The Vital Link in Global Supply Management," *Women's Wear Daily/Global*, July 1997, p. 78.
24. Kim Ann Zimmermann, "Talbots' Groupware Strategy," *Women's Wear Daily,* July 7, 1997, p. 18.
25. Reda, "Mills Find Cure for Outlet Doldrums by Focusing on Entertainment Theme," *Stores*, April 1997, p. 106.

Exploring Careers at the Retail Level

One of the best ways to begin a career in fashion is as a salesperson in a retail organization. Experience in selling to customers is a must for all people interested in any career in the fashion field. For it is the salesperson who has direct contact with the customer, and in the fashion field it is the customer who is always right.

Executive training programs in the major retail chains provide both a classroom and on-the-job education that is an excellent first step on a career path in retailing. Macy's has perhaps the best known and certainly among the most selective of these valuable programs. Competing for a position in such a training class is, in itself, an excellent introduction to a career in fashion retailing.

Merchandising Careers

The starting place for most merchandising careers is in selling. Here you experience face-to-face encounters with customers and the problem of anticipating what they will want.

Traditionally, the merchandising career ladder has moved from a sales position up through the ranks to the buyer's position. However, in recent years many large firms with many branches have provided a choice: an aspiring fashion merchant may choose either the traditional sales-to-buyer route or a strictly management route.

The Buying Route

A person who chooses the buying route can go from head of stock to assistant buyer to buyer to divisional merchandise manager and finally to general merchandise manager. The responsibilities of each position are given below.

Executive Trainee

This is a position in which one may do some selling, but it mainly involves replenishing stock in the selling area from the stockroom, reporting "outs," noticing and reporting slow sellers, and advising the buyer on unfilled customer wants.

Assistant Buyer

The assistant buyer's job is the next step upward. As an understudy to the buyer, the assistant buyer may be called in to view the line of a visiting sales representative and may be taken occasionally to the market on a buying trip. Usually, however, the assistant buyer relieves the buyer of floor supervision, helps to train and supervise salespeople, processes branch questions and requests, and writes up reorders for basic stocks, subject to the buyer's approval.

Buyer

Buyers are virtually in business for themselves, in the sense that they have to budget and plan their expenditures, select the actual merchandise for resale, and decide what is to be advertised or displayed and why. The job usually involves from two to a dozen or more market trips a year. As computer technology automates the record keeping and calculating aspects of the position, buyers are able to focus more on the buying and developing merchandise that will appeal to their stores' customers.

Divisional Merchandise Manager

In large stores, buyers of departments handling related merchandise are supervised by a divisional merchandise manager. Examples of related departments are infants' and children's wear, women's ready-to-wear, men's wear, boys' wear, and home furnishings.

The merchandise manager coordinates the efforts of a group of departments, with or without the aid of a fashion director, so that the fashion picture each department presents to the public is related in theme, timing, and emphasis to those presented by the others.

General Merchandise Manager

The final rung on the merchandising career ladder is general merchandise manager, a top management position that demands, in addition to fashion and merchandising know-how, an understanding of every phase of store operation, from housekeeping to finances.

The Management Route

A person who chooses the management route can go from assistant group sales manager to group sales manager to divisional sales manager and finally to store manager. The responsibilities of each position follow:

Assistant Group Sales Manager

The assistant group sales manager works closely with the group sales manager in directing the activities of several related departments in a branch store.

Group Sales Manager

The group sales manager (GSM) coordinates the personnel, merchandising, and operations aspects of several departments in a branch store. The person employed in this position must be both a merchant and a manager of people, learning to delegate responsibility in increasingly larger areas with a growing staff. A very large chain of stores might have several levels of group sales manager positions, with top-level GSMs managing the activities of two or three other executives.

Divisional Sales Manager

The divisional sales manager is responsible for a large segment of a store. It is the responsibility of the divisional sales manager to develop the skills of the group sales managers so that they can better manage, control, and direct the efforts of their areas to maximize profitable retail sales volume.

Store Manager

Store manager positions are near the top of the career ladder in management, second only to the chief executive officer and board of directors of the organization. The store manager is responsible for the total store operation in a single location.

Sales Promotion Careers

Career opportunities in sales promotion include jobs on the advertising staff, the publicity and public relations staff, and the visual merchandising staff. In addition to the "creative" jobs within the promotional departments, there are positions for managers, who coordinate the promotional campaigns in collaboration with executives from merchandising and other store divisions. Managing budgets and schedules is a major responsibility. These executives also decide when and how to use outside resources, such as advertising agencies, and they must constantly evaluate the results of their efforts in terms of sales and refine their short- and long-term promotional plans accordingly.

Copywriters

Copywriters who begin in retailing usually enjoy a tremendous advantage ever afterward. If they leave the field and go into advertising agencies or consumer or trade publications, or go to work for producers, they carry with them an understanding of consumer reaction that can be learned in no better school than the retail store.

Artists

Layout artists and illustrators who work for the in-house advertising departments of large retail chains can have a long and full career in this environment. As stores expand into nonstore selling through catalogs and Web sites, artists have many outlets for their artistic talents and fashion knowledge. Fashion artists can also transport their skills and knowledge into positions with trade and consumer publications and advertising agencies.

Public Relations

Publicity assignments usually grow out of copywriting jobs, although outsiders, particularly those with experience in the entertainment industry, are sometimes hired for this work. Retailing has often been compared to theatrical production, and this analogy is especially apt for the people who plan the special events that attract an "audience" to a store. Involved are such diverse activities as alerting the local press to newsworthy happenings, arranging for television interviews of visiting celebrities, and working up elaborate events—whether in the name of fashion, community, or charity—that will brighten the store image.

Visual Merchandising and Display

Visual merchandising and display executives usually start as assistants with a willingness to work hard. They advance in position if they demonstrate artistic sense, a knowledge of fashion and fashion merchandising, the ability to speak in visual terms to the store's customers, and the ability to pick up important selling points about merchandise. A large store may divide responsibilities between a window manager and interior manager, both reporting to a visual merchandising director. In some regional or national chains, visual merchandising executives prepare plans for the individual store units to provide a consistent message and image for the company's entire market.

Fashion Coordination and Fashion Direction

Partly merchandising and partly promotion, the jobs of fashion coordinator and fashion director are ideal for people who are extremely interested in fashion, know how to work with others, and have an unlimited supply of energy! These jobs involve working with a great many people, from merchandise or fashion information resources to store staff to customers, and their goals are accomplished largely through recommendations and advice rather than direct order.

In a large chain, the fashion director is often one of the key store executives who travel with buyers and merchandise managers to overseas markets as well as domestic markets. He or she may also be a member of a buying committee that travels to Asia to contract for large orders to be produced exclusively for the chain according to store specifications.

As exciting as these jobs are, there are actually very few full-time fashion directors or coordinators employed, even in large cities.

Sales-Supporting Careers

Retail stores have openings in fields not directly related to the buying, selling, and promoting of merchandise. These activities, which may involve more than half the employees of a store, include personnel employment and training, accounting, customer services, and adjustments, among many others. Even in the rapidly growing area of data processing jobs, fashion knowledge can be a valuable asset. For instance, add a knowledge of fashion merchandising to an understanding of computer programming, and the result is the kind of background that can lead to a career in computer program design for fashion-oriented companies.

Professional Fashion Sales Careers

Surprisingly enough, many commissioned salespeople in top fashion stores earn more than the buyers or store managers! Individuals who truly enjoy working one-on-one with a customer, who take a personal interest in the customer's lifestyle and clothing needs, and who derive a great deal of pleasure from completing a sale and seeing a satisfied customer walk out of the store should consider professional sales as a career.

One position growing out of the professional salesperson's role as consultant to customers—rather than mere order-taker—is that of personal shopper. Busy executives have long relied on the advice of these sales professionals, but more and more, stores are promoting this service to middle-class customers.

Chain and Mail-Order Careers

Chain and catalog firms offer careers that are similar to those offered by independent stores, with this important exception: Buying, merchandising, publicity, and fashion coordination are handled by the headquarters staff rather than by the individual stores.

Career advancement up the retail management ladder, if one starts in a unit of a chain or in a catalog organization, begins with selling and moves to department manager, merchandise manager, store manager, and finally to district, regional, or central management. Those interested in such fields as buying, fashion coordination, promotion, catalog preparation, merchandising, and quality control start as assistants in regional or central headquarters, where central buyers and merchandise managers are located.

Many highly specialized jobs in the chain and catalog companies call for intimate knowledge of the fashion business. For instance, the quality control department of one chain was called upon by the merchandising division to devise a size range for girls who fell between two size ranges currently offered by the children's market. The chain then made its new size range measurements available to any producers who wished to adopt them, whether or not they were resources of that chain.

Whatever special assets the beginner presents—apparel production techniques, laboratory know-how, or experience in copywriting, art, selling, buying, or coordination—the chain and the catalog companies can use them. If chain store or catalog retailing appeals to you, you should seriously consider moving to a new city or region if that is where the openings are.

Entrepreneurship in Fashion Retailing

If you are a generalist within the fashion industry, with interests and talents in management, sales, and marketing and a flair for fashions that appeal to a particular market segment, you may aspire to open your own store. Being a successful entrepreneur requires true dedication, especially in a field as competitive and fast-moving as fashion retailing. The risks are great, the hours are long, and the tasks range from the menial to those most demanding of professional expertise.

You need not be an expert in every facet of the business, but you must have a clear sense of what expertise is required and be able to find the human resources whose skills and talents complement your own. These people may be consultants and vendors, partners, or employees. Being the final decision maker does not mean working alone, and ultimately, your customers will be your boss.

If owning a store is your career goal, your best preparation is experience working for a successful retailer. Acceptance into an executive training program will jump-start your career, but you can also plan your own training by carefully mapping out a career path in different facets of the industry. With talent, training, determination, and an element of good luck, if you give it your all, you can have it all.

Assignments

1. Prepare Unit Five of your career journal by finding help wanted advertisements for positions within the retail level of the fashion industry. These openings may be found in general circulation newspapers, trade publications, online resources, or notices in your school's career development office. For each position, list the positive and negative aspects for you personally. Consider your interests, career goals, training, and experience. If you do not yet meet the job requirements, what further training or experience would you need in order to qualify?
2. Environmental factors affect all businesses at the retail level of the fashion business. Considering both store and nonstore retailers and both local and national companies, give a current example of the effects of the natural, economic, social, and political/legal environment.

UNIT FIVE: 2000s

Pauline Trigère • Ralph Lauren • Oscar de la Renta • Bill Blass • Eleanor Lambert • Miguel Adrover • Tommy Hilfiger • Marc Jacobs • Nicole Miller

"I live very close to the theater, and when I go out and see older people with canes, coming and going, I say, 'My God, they are not very pretty...' When I saw those walking sticks, I said to myself, 'Why not an elegant cane with a gold handle that would go with her jewelry?'"

PAULINE TRIGÈRE, 2000, LAUNCHING A LINE OF ACCESSORIES FOR OLDER WOMEN

"I do a collection for myself and my stores. It's not about salable or nonsalable. It's about what I do and what I believe. I have a strong vision of the women and men who buy my clothes...Whether it's a suit or a beat-up leather jacket, it's aimed at my customer."

RALPH LAUREN, 2001

"We're dealing with a very, very different consumer. Fashion today comes from the streets. We're dealing with a working woman. It's the workforce that makes fashion today. We create clothes for the masses, this is what brought our name into fame."

OSCAR DE LA RENTA, 2001

"One thing I certainly do not regret is not being active in the business in this day and age, but it's hard to remove yourself from a business that you've been in for 50 years. It never really gets out of your system...[Fashion today] belongs to a much younger person. No matter what they tell you, it's still a business for the young."

BILL BLASS, 2002

"All I did was start it [the CFDA]. I've always said that getting people together as a community helps further their identity as a whole. We were a group of people of equal qualifications and equal thoughts about moving forward."

ELEANOR LAMBERT IN 2000, RECALLING THE FORMATION OF THE CFDA

"It's really easy to shock people. You could find a girl who would walk out on the runway and shoot herself. Fashion is not about fun lately, but if I don't have fun, I'm not going to do it anymore. It's not just about shocking people, it's also about having a laugh."

MIGUEL ADROVER, 2000

"The American preppy heritage we started with is so important to so many of our businesses. We don't want to lose sight of it. I feel it gets us back to where we belong as a brand. This is the beginning of my strong emphasis on American classics."

TOMMY HILFIGER, 2000

"I'm not interested in designing with a calculator. Success scares me. Business people don't understand that fashion is still just a whim."

MARC JACOBS, 2001

Designer Bill Blass.

"People here are certainly as creative, but what we don't have are the same resources. Paris and Milan have amazing factories and capabilities, as well as the whole haute couture industry. There are a lot of young designers out there who are very innovative, but we don't get as complex in the detailing because you can't produce it."

NICOLE MILLER, 2001

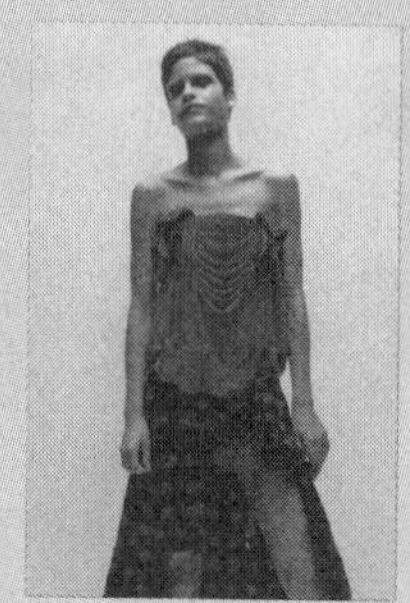

Climara
Electrasol
Tabs
DeVries

take
me
out

UNIT SIX

The Auxiliary Level: Supporting Services

Just as customers coordinate their fashion looks, including all the fashion products seen or not seen, the fashion industry also coordinates all auxiliary services, seen or not seen, to the successful selling of the latest fashion products to the customer. The auxiliary services that support and enhance all the other levels of the fashion industries have an interconnecting role in the big fashion picture.

What would the fashion world be without these services? Think of a new fashion season without fashion shows, magazines, fashion stylists, trade shows, visual merchandisers, TV, advertising agencies, public relations agencies, and the myriad of other services that support and grow this phenomenon known as the FASHION BUSINESS.

Understanding the role these varied services play is important to an understanding of how and why the fashion business goes from design to consumer, and the individual and specific services that play a part in completing the whole.

In this unit, the roles of magazines, newspapers, broadcast and TV media, fashion consultants, and visual merchandisers are explained, as well as trade associations and product development offices. These services may be auxiliary, but—just like the Oscar awarded to supporting roles—they deserve a place of honor in the fashion business.

CHAPTER 19

Fashion Auxiliary Services

WHAT'S IN IT FOR YOU?

Everything you always wanted to know about the services and information provided to producers and retailers.

Key Concepts:

- Differences among advertising, publicity, and public relations
- Services provided to fashion merchandisers by such media as trade and consumer publications and broadcast media
- Role of store designers and visual merchandisers
- Information provided to fashion producers and retailers by fashion consultants and research agencies, trade associations and trade shows, and buying, merchandising, and product development offices

As consumers we expect to find what we want, when we want it, and where we want it every day of the year. In the fall, back-to-school merchandise better be in stores, and the colors must be new and up-to-date. During the holiday months, gift merchandise and new items for holiday parties are expected. During spring and summer months we expect new colors, silhouettes, and fabrics to brighten up our wardrobes and take us through spring days to the hot, muggy days of summer. How do the stores see into the future and anticipate our needs and wants? How do they keep stocks peaked when we want them and marked down when we are tired of them? They do not have crystal balls, or fortune tellers leading the way; what they do have are the fashion auxiliary services.

As a professional in the fashion industry, you know that this marvelous spectacle did not occur by magic. In fact, it required elaborate planning and execution of plans for months in advance. As you enjoy the offerings for the upcoming season, you are well aware that preparations are already underway for the next season and for the seasons beyond.

Bringing you and your fellow consumers the styles you want to wear is so huge and all-encompassing a task that the fashion industry requires many support, or auxiliary, services. Some services—computer, bookkeeping, legal—are typical of those needed by any business, and may not be particularly tailored to the fashion business. Others, though, are specific to the fashion industry. They have either been created specifically to serve it, as in the case of buying, merchandising, and product development organizations, or their function has been tailored to the fashion industry's specific needs, as in the case of advertising and public relations agencies; fashion magazines, and the variety of consultants and marketing groups. In this chapter you will learn about the most important auxiliary services such as trade and consumer fashion publications; the broadcast media; advertising and public relations agencies, store design and visual merchandising services; consulting and market research groups; trade associations; and buying, merchandising, and product development organizations.

Fashion Auxiliary Services Offered by the Media

The media offer three broad categories of fashion auxiliary services: advertising, publicity, and public relations. **Advertising**, which appears in everything from magazines and newspapers to radio and television, is space and time that is paid for. **Publicity** is the free and voluntary mention of a firm, product, or person in the media. Its purpose is to inform or enhance public interest about something specific. **Public relations**, a broader term than publicity, is also free and voluntary mention, but it is designed to enhance a long-term goal, such as the shaping of a company's public image. All three efforts are important elements of the remaining auxiliary services.

One difference between advertising and publicity/public relations is the amount of control a manufacturer or retailer can exercise over each. Since advertising is purchased, a great deal of control can be exercised over its execution. Public relations and publicity can be carefully developed and well presented to the media, but there is no guarantee that the material and information supplied will be used well—or used at all.

Some people think that the newer broadcast media—like cable TV and the Internet—will replace the more traditional media, like newspapers and magazines. Others strongly disagree. Edwin Diamond, author of an online media column for the *Times-Mirror*, said: "New media find a place at the table, but nobody gets displaced. Cable didn't replace TV; TV didn't replace radio; radio didn't replace newspapers."[1]

Some other low-tech print media have recently received a high-tech boost (see Figure 19.1). Billboards carrying a retailer's phone number receive calls from drivers using their cell phones; Golden Creations of Murrysville, Pennsylvania reported increased jewelry sales from this kind of billboard.

FIGURE 19.1 *Billboards are an effective way to advertise fashion goods to a wide range of people. For example, this Jockey advertisement appeared in Times Square in New York.* Courtesy, Jockey.

Fashion Magazines

Fashion magazines, which combine advertising, publicity, and public relations, came into existence about 150 years ago in the form of a single publication called *Godey's Lady's Book.* Prior to that, women discussed the newest fashions with one another but had no authoritative source from which they could learn what was new and exciting. The magazine's first editor, Sara Joseph Hale, is now best remembered for her early feminism, especially her struggle to help women win acceptance in professions, but her influence on fashion was equally important. *Godey's Lady's Book* reported on the latest styles and was the forerunner of today's fashion magazines, such as *Vogue*, *Harper's Bazaar*, *Glamour*, and *Seventeen* for young women.

For years, these magazines held sway and while they competed with one another, they were not subject to new competition. In recent years, though, fashion has become so important that *Women's Wear Daily* has spun off a successful monthly publication called *W* geared to general consumers. Several other magazines have also established themselves as fashion arbiters, most notably, *Elle*, which competes with *Glamour* and *Marie Claire*, and *Nylon*, which specializes in avant garde fashion. In the mid- to late 1990s, two new important lifestyle magazines appeared on the scene. The first was *In Style*, a monthly glossy that married celebrity and style editorial by covering fashion trends among celebrities and rigorously reporting on red carpet ceremony dressing. *In Style* was launched in 1994, and quickly became hugely successful. In 2002, the magazine had a monthly circulation of 1.6 million copies. Another important newcomer was *Lucky*, a publication that called itself "The magazine about shopping." The concept behind *Lucky* was very close to that of a catalog. It is almost exclusively based on still life pictures of clothing and brief descriptions on what a garment is and where it is retailed. Lucky reached a rate base with 750,000 readers in 2002.[2] Magazines that appeal to specific ethnic markets include: *Essence*, *Ebony*, and *Today's Black Woman* for African-Americans; and the bilingual *Latina* for Hispanics. Even more specialized are such magazines as *Modern Bride* and *Bride's*, which report on wedding fashions, and *Mode*, which caters to full-figured women.

Gentlemen's Quarterly (*GQ*) is the largest circulating men's fashion magazine. *Esquire*, which covers topics beyond fashion, is still widely regarded as an authority on the latest trends in men's wear. Other men's magazines that cover fashion in addition to other topics like health and sports include *Details*, *Men's Fitness*, *Men's Health*, *Playboy*, *Men's Journal*, *Outside*, *FHM*, and *Maxim*. Some men's magazines, like *Maxim* and *FHM*, also have their own bi-annual men's fashion magazine editions, which tend to be considerably more upscale than their parent magazines.

The "shelter magazines" are devoted to home fashions. Among the better known are *Elle Decor*, *Metropolitan Life*, *Architectural Digest*, *House and Garden*, *House Beautiful*, *Martha Stewart Living*, *Wallpaper*, and *Surface*.

Fashion magazines' pages are filled with advertisements for apparel, cosmetics, and accessories. The business of reporting and interpreting the fashion news, however, is their primary function. Fashion editors visit manufacturers' showrooms to choose the latest fashions as subjects for articles and photographs in the editorial pages of their magazines. These visits provide opportunities for useful exchanges of information about trends in markets that the manufacturers and publications share. In addition, most magazines prepare reports of their market research for the manufacturers and retailers that are both the subject of their editorial copy and their advertising accounts. These reports include reader surveys, such as those conducted by *Glamour*, and fashion forecasts of colors and styles for upcoming seasons. Like the fashion producers and retailers, the magazines must plan well in advance of offering their product to the public, so their reports can be relied upon for timely information.

Fashions that appear in magazine articles are accompanied by an **editorial credit**, a unique form of publicity that names the manufacturer and lists retail stores where the clothes may be purchased (see Figure 19.2). Editorial credit benefits even stores that are not listed, for if they have seen a magazine in advance, they can often stock the fashions. For advertisers whose merchandise is featured and credited in the editorial pages of a magazine, this publicity reinforces the paid advertising message.

General Consumer Publications

General interest consumer publications also play a role in disseminating fashion news to the public. Practically every newspaper reports on fashion, and some, such as the *New York Times*, *The Los Angeles Times*, *Chicago Tribune*, and *Washington Post*, devote regular weekly sec-

FIGURE 19.2
Editorial credits, such as these on a page from Jane, provide priceless promotion for designers and manufacturers, rather than targeting the consumer.

tions to apparel and home fashion design. Their fashion editors cover fashion openings, press weeks, and trade shows around the world. Twice a year, the *New York Times Magazine* has a second section for each of three fashion markets, *Fashions of The Times* for women's fashions, *Men's Fashions of The Times*, and *Home Design*. In *Paper*, *Time Out*, *City*, and other magazines that deal with pop culture, fashion gets extensive coverage. *Time*, *Newsweek*, and *People* provide occasional but important fashion coverage, as do the traditional women's magazines such as *Good Housekeeping* and *Ladies' Home Journal*. *Cosmopolitan*, whose primary market is young singles, has a circulation of 2.6 million. Other women's magazines that are geared to women who are not full-time homemakers also carry fashion news for their market segments. Among the most influential are *Oprah*, *Ms.*, and *Working Woman*, which cover career fashions; *Jane*, which is aimed at women 18 to 34; and *Cosmo Girl*, *YM*, *Seventeen*, *Teen Vogue*, and *Elle Girl*, which are designed for young teenagers. Women's sports magazines, such as *Self*, *Shape*, *Fitness*, and *Sports Illustrated Women/Sport*, include articles that cater to the fashion interests of female athletes and sports fans. *Playboy* and *Men's Health* are among the men's magazines that cover men's fashions.

The New Yorker, *Vanity Fair*, *Harper's*, and *Atlantic Monthly* occasionally bring fashion news to their urbane, sophisticated audiences.

Spanish language versions of *People*, *Playboy*, *Cosmopolitan*, *Harper's Bazaar*, *Elle*, and *Marie Claire* are also in the market. The Spanish version of *Reader's Digest*, called *Selecciones*, is widely circulated. The publicity departments of most stores across America usually have no difficulty getting their messages across in local newspapers since apparel stores are a major source of advertising revenue for newspapers.

Trade Publications

One of the most important aids to the merchandising of fashion is the **trade publication.** Unlike the fashion magazines, trade newspapers and magazines are published just for the industry. Many discourage subscriptions from people outside their field; few are available at newsstands, except in fashion markets and marts.

Just as general publications like city newspapers and national news magazines keep the public informed about what is going on in the world, trade publications keep their special readers informed about what is going on in the fashion world—from the acquisition of raw materials to reports on retail sales. These publications announce new technical developments, analyze fashion trends, report on current business conditions, and generally help all who work in the fashion industry keep up-to-date on a staggering number of new products, techniques, and markets. Even government regulations are covered, as are personnel changes and classified ads for jobs.

The best-known fashion trade publication is *Women's Wear Daily*, often referred to as the bible of the industry. It is one of the oldest publications of its kind, having first been published in 1910. Beginning as a page in the *Daily Trade Record*, this newspaper quickly became a separate six-day-a-week publication. Since its inception, it has played a prominent role in the fashion business. *Women's Wear Daily*, called

WWD by those who read it, is now published five days a week. It covers every aspect of the fashion industry from fiber and fabric to apparel, from day-to-day developments to new directions and trends. In the past 20 years, *WWD* has even covered the social scene, reporting on fashions worn by trendsetters at social events and parties. In addition, it is an advertising vehicle, and business notices, employment opportunities, and arrivals of buyers in the New York market are also reported. The Monday, Thursday, and Friday issues highlight children's wear, innerwear, legwear, and fashion accessories, respectively. In addition, *Infotracs*, or special supplements devoted entirely to examining a critical issue in depth, are published from time to time, as a joint venture by *WWD* and the *Daily News Record* (*DNR*). Special *WWD/Global* issues are published, providing an overview of the major international markets that prepares readers for the upcoming spring and fall fashion weeks.

Numerous trade publications serve the needs of specialized segments of the fashion industry. The *Daily News Record*, known as *DNR*, published every Monday, specializes in textiles and menswear. *DNR*, the counterpart to *WWD*, is actually the older publication, beginning in 1892 as the *Daily Trade Record*, a mimeographed report distributed at the Chicago World's Fair.

Footwear News and *Accessories* cover their specialties as intensely as *WWD* covers the women's market and *DNR* covers the men's market (see Figure 19.3). The youth market is covered in *Children's Business* and *Earnshaw's Infants', Girls' and Boys' Wear Review*. Department store and specialty store management and merchandising executives read *Stores* and *Chain Store Age*. The fiber and fabric professionals read *Bobbin Magazine* and *Textile World*.

The Broadcast Media

Fashion merchandisers have a choice of standard broadcast mediums: television, cable television, and radio. Or they may choose the newest medium—the Internet. Unlike the print media, the broadcast media are time-rather than space-oriented. Radio and television stations sell three levels of commercials, in descending order of cost: network, spot, and local.

Broadcast media focused on children have received a good deal of critical attention in recent years, as advertising in children-specific

FIGURE 19.3
Footwear News, Women's Wear Daily, and The Daily News Record are leading trade publications in the fashion industry.

media grew more than 50 percent, to $1.5 billion from 1993 to 1996 alone. Many new children's channels were launched and the kid's market seemed like a place of golden opportunity for advertisers. However, the climate slowed down at the turn of the millennium and the children channels that turned a profit were the already established and relatively inexpensive giants like Cartoon Network and Nickelodeon.[3] Other children's channels include Fox Kids, Kids'WB, and ABC/Disney.

Television

One cannot turn on the television today without learning something about current apparel fashions. The fashion industry obtains invaluable publicity from the simple fact that everyone who acts in a show or hosts or appears on a newscast or talk show wants to—and usually does—wear the latest fashions.

In addition to this general across-the-board exposure, short segments on fashion are generally presented in many news and talk shows. News of the fashion world is reported, as are the latest styles. Occasionally manufacturers and designers get a chance to exhibit their work.

Network television advertising is expensive enough to be prohibitive to all but a few fashion giants. Until the early 1980s, only huge companies such as Sears Roebuck and J.C.Penney or fiber firms like DuPont and Monsanto could afford to advertise on television. Increasingly, though, retailers and manufacturers have built television advertising into their budgets because they have seen that this is the best way to reach a generation reared on television. Manufacturers of sportswear—specifically, makers of jeans—were among the first to use television, but now designers such as Calvin Klein use television to transmit their fashion message. Sometimes designers or manufacturers offer retailers cooperative advertising with time for a "voice over" for store advertising of their brand. The manufacturer can thus get a local advertising rate for the brand while the retailer gets the professionally produced commercial.

Because of the technical expertise and high level of quality required for network television, outside advertising agencies are usually hired to produce television advertising. Agencies develop an idea, present it in storyboard form to their client, photograph the advertisement, obtain or create the music, and provide tapes to individual stations for on-air viewing. Television commercials for national brands of apparel, such as Levi's jeans, are now being shown in movie theaters as well.

Some experts are predicting a brighter future for television advertising with the coming of interactive capability. They envision a customer watching an episode of *Friends*, noticing an attractive shirt, and then ordering it right from the TV set!

Cable Television

Cable television has become an increasingly attractive option for fashion advertisers, largely because it costs so much less than network television. Many more outlets also exist for cable television, which reduces the competition to buy space. Cable television is also the home of the **infomercial**, the extended commercial in which a sponsor presents information about its product in a program format. Several celebrity-owned or -franchised cosmetics lines have relied on this advertising medium. The 1982 debut of the Home Shopping Network (HSN) marked the beginning of a new outlet for sales as well as advertising. By 2000, HSN and the other major shopping cable channel, QVC, were reaching more than 270 million homes.[4]

Cable television has also made possible the launching of channels with programming devoted to the interests of niche markets. Thus, fashion advertisers can target commercials for Spanish-language channels, for example. Fashion is also receiving more attention in programming. CNN was the first news channel to endorse the newsworthiness of fashion by launching *Style With Elsa Klensch* in 1980. It was the first show to feature runways and top international designers. Klensch has since retired from CNN and moved on to produce the series *Trio World Fashion Tour* for WNBC. This show was so successful it spawned a host of imitators at a lower price point.[5] In 1998, the New York cable channel Metro TV launched *Full Frontal Fashion* in conjunction with the New York Mercedes-Benz Fashion Week. *Full Frontal Fashion* offers round-the-clock coverage of the runway shows as well as behind-the-scenes reportages, industry commentary and designer interviews. E! Entertainment television offers the Style network, a 24-hour channel devoted to fashion and beauty. Among the shows on Style are: *Fashion Emergency*, which features makeovers; *Model! Model TV*, *Fashion File*, and *Video Fashion*.

Of special importance to the fashion industry are the channels that appeal to the youth market, namely MTV and VH-1 (see Figure 19.4). As part of their lifestyle programming,

FIGURE 19.4 *Gwen Stefani performed on the MTV award show in a unique design from her own clothing line.* Courtesy, Fairchild Publications, Inc.

these channels air, respectively *House of Style* and *All Access*. The annual VH-1-*Vogue* fashion awards are enormously popular.[6]

Radio

While television is unsurpassed as a fashion advertising medium because of its visual qualities, radio is popular because it is inexpensive and can reach large but targeted audiences. Stations exist that serve only the youth market; others, such as classical radio stations, are geared to an older market. Others broadcast news and can deliver a virtual captive audience during the morning and evening commutes, the so-called "drive time."

The use of radio to sell fashion was tied to the rise of rock music in the 1950s and the youth-oriented market it created. The youth market has remained strong, but radio advertising, if chosen carefully, also reaches adults and families.

In terms of cost per customer reached, spot commercials on local radio stations are economical; most of the store's customers live and work within the range of the station's signal. Commercials announcing sales and other storewide events can use radio effectively because they do not depend on visual appeals. To attract advertisers, stations provide assistance with the preparation of copy, which may be delivered by disk jockeys and other announcers.

Radio is also a source of publicity as products and fashion news are discussed on regular shows.

As with television, most retailers and manufacturers rely on outside agencies to write and produce radio commercials, although some use their in-house talent to prepare commercials and then hire time-buying groups to place them.

The Internet

Look at a fashion magazine ad for a designer or fashion retailer, and more often than not, you will see, in addition to location, a Web site address. As the Internet has expanded from a communication system for scholars and researchers to include the commercial world, fashion merchandisers have reached out to their markets with home pages on the World Wide Web (see Figure 19.5). The chief advantage of the Internet as a promotional medium is that a company can address its audience directly. Furthermore, through Web pages accessible from the home page, the company can reach selected market segments and respond to their specific needs at any given moment. For example, retail customers can locate the nearest outlet of a favorite chain store, job applicants can find out about available positions and can submit their résumés, and employees can communicate with each other, as well as with customers and vendors.

In the fashion industry, even more than in businesses that do not market image, a well-designed Web page is a reflection of a firm's identity. Professionals, sometimes on the staff of the in-house advertising and promotion department, sometimes freelance Web site designers design the Web site and keep it up-to-date.

Most of the leading fashion and general interest magazines now have Internet sites, as do hundreds of retailers. The *Elle* site, for example, now gets about four million page views a month.[7] Many of these sites are linked to each other, so it is possible to spend hours online, just surfing from one fashion site to another.

An interesting fact is that magazines and catalog companies are not just putting their existing products on the Web. They are using Internet traits that distinguish electronic content from print; namely, interactive quizzes,

FIGURE 19.5
Jockey uses their home page for advertising both products and special offers to their target market.
Courtesy, Jockey.

games, chat rooms, and lists of FAQ (frequently asked questions). As the technology improves, industry experts predict that more and more shopping will be done online.

Advertising, Publicity, and Public Relations Agencies

Advertising, publicity, and public relations agencies do far more for the fashion industry than prepare and sell advertising. An agency in any of these three areas may be deeply involved in creating a multimedia campaign designed to shape the public's image of a client company. These campaigns are used for ongoing maintenance of a company's image as well as for an image change.

Advertising Agencies

Advertising agencies provide many services, all of which are tied to the selling of commercial advertising space and/or time. Some agencies are specialized and deal only with one medium or one type of client, while others are general, offering a full range of services for many different types of clients. Agencies vary from a one-person shop to a giant agency that employs hundreds of people around the world. Small agencies claim to offer personal attention, but even large agencies divide their staff into creative teams so they, too, promise and often deliver a specialized service.

Small manufacturers and retailers and even fairly large department stores tend to rely on in-house advertising departments for all advertising except television and radio. Only the very large fiber and apparel companies regularly use advertising agencies, but those that can afford to do so find the investment worthwhile. For example, in an effort to expand their male market, Lee jeans began a new marketing campaign with advertising agency Fallon targeted at teenage boys. The campaign used the Internet as its main tool. In July 2000, Fallon released unbranded homepages of fictional, ironic, pop culture stereotypes, like the audaciously white-trash racecar driver Curry (see Figure 19.6). At the same time the company also began circulating unbranded video clips starring the same characters on the Web, as well as plastering "wild postings" of them throughout college towns like Austin, Texas. By the time the commercials that connected these characters to Lee jeans arrived on television, Curry and his friends had already gained underground notoriety among video game-playing young men. The campaign continued to work at an interactive media level. The Web sites featured video games that could be further enhanced by using codes that could only be found on the tag on a pair of Lee dungarees. The campaign paid off.

FIGURE 19.6
Lee jeans partnered with Fallon advertising agency to create this successful ad that sent profits skyrocketing!
Courtesy, Fallon Worldwide, LLC./Lee jeans. Reprinted with permission.

Eighteen months later, Lee sales had doubled, and Lee's junior's carpenter pants became the top-selling blue jeans in the stores where they were carried.[8]

Public Relations Agencies

Public relations firms are involved in the creation of publicity as well as in public relations. Publicity and public relations require that the agency work closely with its client, keeping abreast of what is new and newsworthy and announcing it to the world, either through press releases, often accompanied by photographs, or with story ideas presented to trade and consumer magazines and newspapers. As noted, public relations also involves, on a much deeper level, the shaping of a company's image. To this end, a public relations agency may suggest or help to plan and coordinate an event or activity, such as the rendering of a public service or gift to a charity or community or the presentation of a scholarship or endowment to an institution or foundation. Examples include Piaget sponsorship of the opening night at Carnegie Hall's 106th season, and Miuccia Prada's Fondazione Prada supports exhibition projects by contemporary artists. Many of these events are produced and concepted by the New York Public Relations and Creative Services agency KCD. Fashion organizations also produce events with the backing of other glamour industries. For example, the presentation of the Cutty Sark Fashion Award, given annually to a designer, is an industry-wide public relations activity. Similarly, Dom Pérignon has underwritten the awards ceremony of the Council of Fashion Designers of America.

The larger the company, the more likely it is to depend on an outside public relations firm. For example, KCD manages the public relations for Victoria's Secret's fashion show, a yearly event that is broadcast live on the Internet and on TV channels worldwide. Retailers, however, largely tend to have their own in-house publicity departments that work with top management to present the company's best face to the public. Among the well-known public relations agencies that specialize in the fashion industry are the huge Edelman PR Worldwide, headquartered in Chicago, Cone Communications in Boston, the Hart Agency in Dallas, and DeVries in New York (see Figure 19.7).

Other Advertising and Public Relations Services

Maintaining the corporate image of a fashion producer or retailer requires the services of a number of "creative" specialists, who may be company employees, agency employees, or freelancers. For example, **fashion stylists** may select

FIGURE 19.7
Public relations agencies advertise their clients to attract still more clients.
Courtesy, DeVries Public Relations.

and coordinate the apparel and accessories for store catalogs and print ads, for magazine articles, or for commercials. The job of the stylist involves juggling many tasks in one day, often including charming celebrities into posing in outfits they dislike. Many stylists work in either Los Angeles or New York, but more job opportunities are growing across the country. Hollywood's top stylists include Phillip Bloch, Jeannine Braden, Deborah Waknin, Lisa Michelle, and Stacy Young. Stylists must work cooperatively with the rest of the team; the photographers, the makeup artist, the hairdresser, the magazine editor, and the celebrity's agent or publicist.

Fashion illustrators' and photographers' work appears in advertising and in the editorial pages of consumer and trade publications. Skilled fashion photographers command creative control of a shoot as well as high pay.

Independent fashion show production companies offer their services to producers, retailers, and trade organizations.

Store Design and Visual Merchandising Services

Two important on-site promotional activities that support the selling of fashion merchandise are store design and visual merchandising. The layout and design of any retail business have an impact on sales. Even catalog retailers and others who do not come face-to-face with their customers have to consider how much room

Then & Now

Reserved for The VIP'S—Now Open to The Public

The Showings! Fashion Week! Seventh on Sixth! VIP Parties! Elegant Gift Bags!— all usually reserved for the "in crowd," the professionals who design, make, and market the latest fashions, and some of their friends. That was THEN.

NOW this has changed! No longer does your chance of getting a ticket to these extravagant showings depend upon your social standing or who you know, you too can see the latest shows, share the fashion gossip and fashion trends with the so-called "in crowd." Style.com, a Web site run by *Vogue* and *W* magazines, has come to the rescue.

In 2003 the editors, retailers, designers, and other impresarios of the runways broadcast their insider briefings on the Web, in stores, and in other public spaces, as part of an effort to market Fashion Week directly to consumers, those who will ultimately buy the clothes. Continuous runway video displayed in store windows and in other gathering places like Grand Central Station garnered the attention of mobs of young and old fashionistas alike.

Ralph Lauren marketed a piece of the frenzy under the tents in Bryant Park, and on Style.com, which offered an Internet link to Polo.com, his company's Web site. His Web site also displays fresh film from the runways and offers visitors the chance to play fashion editor by voting online for their favorite outfit.

Style.com, not to be outdone, offers consumers insider tips on new designers and models, and on the season's most sought-after events. More than 700,000 visitors, most of them ordinary shoppers, visited the Web site. The success of the site attests to a "tremendous appetite by ordinary people to know what's going to be in stores for the next season," said Janet Ozzard, the executive editor for Style.com. "They want a sense of being at the shows."

SOURCES:

Ruth La Ferla, "Opening the Tent to Woo More Fans," *New York Times*, February 9, 2003, p. 11.

Greg Lindsay and Jacob Bernstein, "Look Who's Talking," *Women's Wear Daily* Section II, February 7, 2002, pp. 26–27.

Eric Wilson, "Who Can Save New York Fashion?" *Women's Wear Daily*, Section II WWDINSIDE/NEW YORK, February 7, 2002, pp. 8–9.

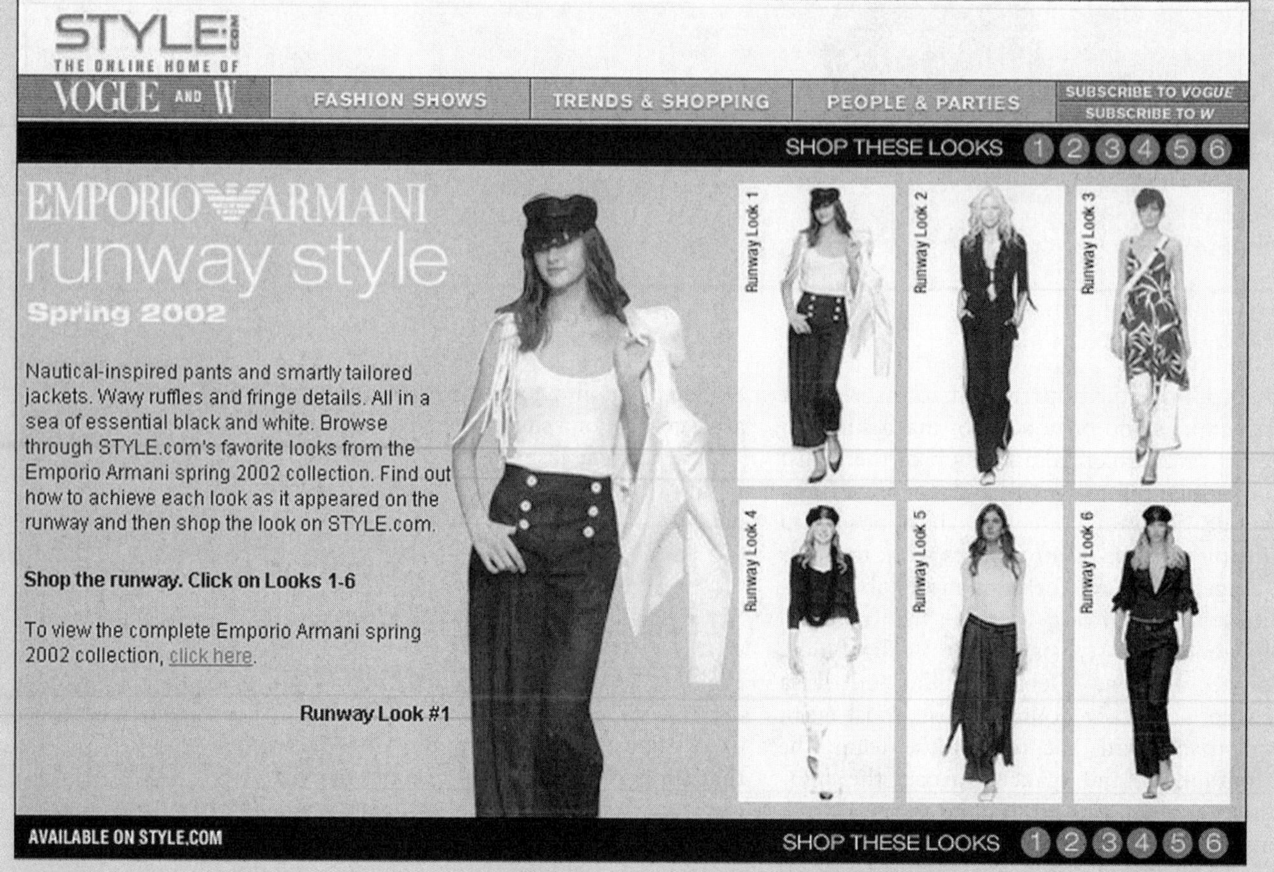

Fashionable looks found on style.com.

they have for inventory and how stock should be arranged to expedite finding items and filling orders. For the traditional retailer operating in a store, the selling floor serves the critical purpose of presenting the merchandise to the customer, a function that is essential in selling fashion goods, for which appearance is a primary feature. Manufacturers' and designers' showrooms are their selling floors and thus require the same attention to interior design and visual merchandising.

Store Design

Planning the layout for a store or department is even more daunting than designing the interior of one's own home. Some of the objectives are the same—visual appeal, ease of movement, and comfort, all within budget—but a space for the sale of merchandise must fulfill additional needs (see Figure 19.8a and b). The designer must be attuned to the tastes of the target customer, and the environment must not only be pleasant but must encourage shopping and buying. Shoppers may regard their visit as a recreational activity, but for the store, it is a business trip, and everything possible must be done to gain the customers' business. Placement of fixtures must take into account security considerations and easy access to exits in case of fire. Local building codes for commercial buildings must be met, and, to comply with the Americans with Disabilities Act, certain feature, such as ramps to ensure wheelchair access and braille on the elevator buttons, may be required. Meeting all of these demands calls for the services of a professional, not just an architect or interior designer, but one who specializes in store design.

Fortunately, a retailer who moves into a mall or a manufacturer with a showroom at an apparel mart may be renting space that has already passed inspection. Still, planning a selling area to maximize sales is not easy. Selecting fixtures that are suitable for the merchandise and the store image, choosing a color scheme, planning the lighting so that it will show off the merchandise in a flattering but accurate way—all these tasks and more must be considered. Major fashion designers, such as Ralph Lauren, have been known to supervise personally the furnishing and interior design of their boutiques within department stores as well as their freestanding outlets. As apparel designers have extended their business into home furnishings and even furniture lines, the connection between store design and fashion image has become even more pronounced (see Figure 19.9). With the need for professional help as great as it is, the existence of trade shows and periodicals for store designers is not surprising.

Visual Merchandising

The term **visual merchandising** includes the arrangement and presentation of merchandise in store windows and on the selling floor. It covers the arrangement of items that are for sale as well as the display of sample items on mannequins and other props. The term is broader than the older term "display," reflecting not only the *showing* of merchandise but the *reason* for showing it, namely to sell it.

Like all other successful promotional activities, a store's visual merchandising supports and exemplifies the retailer's image. For example, a designer boutique, though it may be small, is not cluttered. There is room for cus-

FIGURE 19.8A AND B *Ideally, a store's layout is attuned to the tastes of its target customer.* Courtesy, Fairchild Publications, Inc.

FIGURE 19.9
This store has a relaxing lounge setting including computers where customers can access their e-mail accounts or check out the store's Web site.
Courtesy, Fairchild Publications, Inc.

tomers to step back and admire the exclusive merchandise. Coordinated and accessorized outfits are displayed to help customers assemble their own wardrobes. In the windows, no expense is spared to create an attention-getting environment for the featured merchandise. One or two outfits might be shown in a setting in which they could be worn, or they may be set off in an empty space with dramatic lighting and a few well-chosen props. Perhaps the price is indicated on a small, discreetly placed sign.

In contrast, the mass merchandiser's windows and selling floor send a message of availability and affordability. Windows are crowded with mannequins wearing a variety of outfits. Brightly colored banners announce bargain prices. Inside, closely packed racks house a full range of sizes and colors for each style. No exclusivity is offered here, and none is desired.

What these two examples have in common is that each reveals an image carefully planned to appeal to the target customer. For retailers from single-unit specialty shops to giant department store chains, visual merchandising is an essential promotional service. In larger stores, the work is typically carried out by a staff under the leadership of a visual merchandising director. At the corporate, regional, or store level, window and interior managers may help to coordinate the visual merchandising plan with the merchandising and advertising plans. The staff who execute the plan must include employees who are skilled in carpentry, lighting, sign-making, collection of props, and dressing of mannequins—to name just some of their responsibilities. Small businesses, depending on their resources, may hire an independent visual merchandising firm or an individual freelancer. For self-help in deciding where to put merchandise on the selling floor, **planograms** are available. These computer-generated floor plans massage information about the sales of selected items or categories and factor those numbers in with other information about such items as the physical dimensions of the merchandise and the selling space. Feed that information to the computer, and it responds with a picture of the selling floor with merchandise in the best place.

Fixtures

Display fixtures serve the dual purpose of showing and storing merchandise on the selling floor. Typically, they are purchased when the store is designed, but their use becomes part of the visual merchandising plan for each new selling season. The material and style of the fixtures should be selected to support the store image and the type of merchandise. See examples of fixtures in Figure 19.10a and b. Three types of racks are typically used for hanging apparel: straight racks, rounders, and four-way fixtures.

- *Straight racks* may be installed in a recessed area against the wall, or they may be freestanding. Wall racks are ubiquitous for hanging dresses and other long garments, but freestanding straight racks tend not to be used for this purpose in upscale stores because the rack must be positioned high enough to keep the garments from dragging on the floor. Such racks take up considerable space and block the view of other merchandise. For a mass merchandise or factory outlet store, however, freestanding straight racks are appropriate for hanging all types of apparel. Rows of racks hold large amounts of merchandise, making it available for self-service selection. However, straight racks do not show a frontal view of the garments.
- *Rounders* are circular racks mounted on pedestals. Like straight racks, they hold a large amount of merchandise but do not provide a full view of it. Low rounders are suitable for tops, skirts, and folded trousers; they take up a fair amount of floor space, but because they do not obstruct the shopper's view, they do not make the selling floor look crowded.
- *Four-way fixtures* have two bars crossing at right angles. The customer can walk around the fixture for frontal views of four garments, and more apparel can be hung behind the item in front. An effective way of displaying merchandise on a four-way is to assemble an outfit on the outside hanger, for example, a shirt and jacket with the jacket buttoned to hide the shirt-tail. With pants or a skirt hanging below the jacket hem, the arrangement presents an indication of how the clothing will look when worn.

An important factor in using racks effectively is housekeeping. Usually salespeople are responsible for arranging the merchandise by size, style, and color and hanging clothing neatly and in its proper place when it is returned from the fitting room. Maintaining order and neatness is important for the store's image and for the convenience of shoppers and salespeople who want to locate a garment in a particular size or color.

Another common fixture for apparel is the *gondola*, a freestanding island with a flat surface or bin on top and often with shelves or storage drawers below. It can be used to show stacks of folded tops or, if a bargain image is desired, a jumble of small items, such as socks, scarfs, or underwear.

Built-in cubicles have been used by the Gap and Benetton to show jeans and tops, decoratively sorted by style, size, and color. These fixtures are also suitable for displaying household linens. The stacks of merchandise create an attractive pattern, and it is easy to see the assortment and find the desired item.

Signs and Graphics

Signs and graphics enhance merchandise presentations both in windows and on the selling floor. Temporary signs to announce a sale or special event or inform shoppers of a price can be produced easily with computer software. More permanent signage, such as directional

A

B

FIGURE 19.10A AND B *Fixtures serve two purposes: They display the merchandise and make stock available to customers. Each retailer must select the best fixtures for the merchandise offered.*
(a) Courtesy, Esprit, London. (b) Courtesy, Crate & Barrel.

signs for elevators, escalators, and rest rooms and signs identifying departments are more typically prepared by professionals. Like other aspects of visual merchandising, signs should be in keeping with the store's image.

Information Resources

The fashion business is so huge and complex that no one individual or company can keep abreast of everything that is happening in it. It is a business made up in large part of trends and news in addition to its products. As a result, the auxiliary service provided by fashion consultants and research agencies, whose role is to supply information, is vital to the industry.

Fashion Consultants and Information Services

Fashion consultants are individuals and groups who provide information and services to producers and retailers. The most famous pioneer in fashion consulting was Tobé Coller Davis, who founded her agency, Tobé Associates, in 1927. It has continued to be an important source of information for the industry for decades (see Figure 19.11). Other well-known consultants today are Kurt Barnard and Walter F. Loeb. Other firms working in the fashion and retailing consulting area today include Kurt Salmon Associates in Atlanta, Greenhouse Inc., in Chicago, State Street Research in Boston, Retail Management Consultants in San Marcos, California; and WSL Strategic Retail in New York.

The Fashion Group International, Inc.

Another vital source of industry information is The Fashion Group, Inc., a nonprofit global association of professional women who work in the industry and the associated beauty and home fashions industries. It was founded in 1930 to create executive jobs for women. Over the ensuing decades, however, it has become an important consulting and research agency. Its services are offered to members and, in some instances, nonmembers. Originally a group of 17 fashion leaders in New York, it now has over 6,000 members in chapters in fashion centers across the world.

The Fashion Group is known for its exciting and prophetic fashion presentations. Through lavish fashion shows and fiber displays, it offers the fashion industry its expert and insightful analysis of upcoming trends. It covers the American, European, and Far Eastern fashion scene. The Fashion Group also publishes monthly news bulletins and maintains a valuable Web site (at www.fgi.org), an online information service featuring directories of industry executives and professional services, calendars of events, trend reports and forecasts, classified job listings, and email, public announcements, conferences, and Internet access.

FIGURE 19.11
These are covers of Tobé Reports, which contain information and resources for their retail customers.
Courtesy, Tobé Report.

FASHION FOCUS

The Fashion Group International–Global Fashion Forum

The Fashion Group International is a global nonprofit association of over 6,000 professionals of achievement and influence representing all areas of the fashion, apparel, accessories, beauty, and home industries.

It all began in 1928 when 17 women, gathered by Edna Woolman Chase, Editor-in-Chief of *Vogue*, met for a luncheon in a modest midtown New York restaurant. They had three things in common: each held a job of consequence in the business of fashion, each held all the others in high regard, and together they held a belief that fashion needed a forum, a stage, or a force to express and enhance a widening awareness of the American fashion business and of women's roles in that business. The Fashion Group became an organization in 1930, with a place, a purpose, by-laws, officers, and women eager to be members.

Famous names among the founding members were; Elizabeth Arden, Helena Rubinstein, Eleanor Roosevelt, Lilly Dache, Edith Head, Claire McCardell, Dorothy Shaver, and Carmel Snow. Their first office space was donated by Louis Fairchild in his *Women's Wear Daily* Building on East 12th Street. The second office was at 572 Madison Avenue, donated by *Harper's Bazaar*. In 1934 the Fashion Group moved into 30 Rockefeller Center where they remained until 1992 when they relocated to 597 Fifth Avenue.

The goals of the organization are: advance professionalism in fashion; provide a public forum for examination of important contemporary issues in fashion and the business of fashion; present timely information regarding national and global trends; attain greater recognition of women's achievement in business; promote career opportunities; provide activities and programs that enhance networking skills to further professional, social and personal development of members.

Since 1983, The Fashion Group International has held the "Night of Stars Gala" to pay tribute to individuals who are significant creative forces in their field, those who leave an indelible mark on the way we live and look. Honorees have included such design luminaries as Tom Ford, George Lucas, Audrey Hepburn, Badgley Michka, Karl Largerfeld, Jill Sander, Angela Bassett, Elizabeth Tilberis, Nino Cerruti, and many more. Revenue from the "Night of the Stars Gala" is used to support public service activities, and to promote educational programs devoted to fashion and the related businesses through the creation and awarding of scholarships, establishment of internship programs, and the provision of career counseling services. All these activities are administered through The Fashion Group Foundation.

Developed in 1997, The Fashion Group introduced the "Rising Star Awards" that honors seven individuals who are up-and-coming style-makers of the future. The awards recognize the extraordinary talent and drive of those who can capture imaginations and flourish in the ever-more complex fashion world. The categories include beauty, women's apparel, men's apparel, accessories, interior design, communications, and retail.

Good luck to all of you and may you be the recipient of both the "Rising Star Award" and later in your career, an honoree of the "Night of the Stars Gala." Happy career!

Sources:

www.fgi.org/about us

George Lucas and Sophia Coppola enjoy an evening at the "Night of the Stars Gala," coordinated by the Fashion Group International.

Specialized Information Services

A number of services disseminate reports on various segments of the fashion industry. For example, Nigel French, a British company, issues reports on fabrics, knitwear, and color. The *International Colour Authority*, a British publication, and the Color Association of the United States (CAUS) specialize in reporting on color trends in women's and men's wear.

Market Research Agencies

Because knowing what is new and what is now at the very heart of fashion, businesses in all segments of the industry avidly consume the raw data and trend analyses published by market research agencies. The services of these professional prophets are expensive, but many of their findings are made public in time to be useful to a larger following. Among the better-known agencies is Kurt Salmon Associates (KSA), known for its extensive work with textile and apparel manufacturers and softgoods retailers.

The major accounting firms also have special divisions devoted to the fashion industries. Ernst & Young, Deloite & Touche, and Management Horizons (a division of Price Waterhouse) all offer respected management consulting services on a global basis.

A new breed of researchers and forecasters who rely on a variety of resources—including their own anecdotal observations and gut instincts as well as polls and surveys—is epitomized by Faith Popcorn (who identified and labeled the cocooning trend discussed in Chapter 14). BrainReserve, the company she founded in 1974, has a staff of 28, but it also retains its "TalentBank" of 5,000 authorities in a variety of businesses whom it consults regularly. BrainReserve's public opinion surveying technique involves hour-long face-to-face interviews. Popcorn boasts a 95 percent accuracy rate in her predictions.

Exemplifying a trend themselves, a number of trend-forecasting agencies specialize, and the youth culture is a well-studied specialty. Manhattan-based Sputnik and Cheskin in Southern California are typical of the fashion forecasters who follow their subjects to their natural habitats: night clubs, rock concerts, health food stores, and so on. Much of their information is collected by insiders, under-30 interviewers and observers, some armed with video cameras to document the trends they see. As consumers become more aware of trends, they become more aware that they are trendsetters, and the fashion industry, instead of attempting to dictate what will be worn next season, is actively seeking out the influential consumers and taking a cue from them.

Trade Associations and Trade Shows

Associations of manufacturers and retailers assist fashion buyers in many ways. The nature and frequency of assistance available, though, are not uniform throughout the industry, and buyers soon learn how much assistance will be forthcoming from their particular trade. (See Units Two, Three, and Four for the names and activities of trade associations and trade shows for the major segments of the fashion industry.)

Retailers Group

The National Retail Federation (NRF) is the largest retail trade association in the United States, counting among its members all the major department and specialty stores. It disseminates information and advice through its monthly magazine, *Stores*, and other periodicals and through regional and national meetings. An annual general convention is sponsored by the National Retail Federation in New York City in January. Vendors of products and services as diverse as market research, management software, and shopping bags exhibit at this meeting. Members gather at seminars and workshops to learn from retailing authorities and from each other. A special feature at this convention is a session devoted to outstanding fashion promotions during the previous year.

Buyers Groups

Specialized associations or buying clubs provide an opportunity for an exchange of opinions and ideas among members. Retail buyers' groups also transmit the preferences of their members on matters as varied as the dates when lines should be opened and the appropriate sizes of stock boxes for specific products. Trade associations are often subsidized by outside sources, either the industry itself or a trade publication. Again, these associations are covered in Units Two, Three, and Four.

Trade Shows

Retail and manufacturing groups, as well as independent organizations, sometimes sponsor trade shows, at which many exhibitors gather to show their products and lines in one place, usually a hotel or convention center. Trade shows save time that would otherwise be spent trudging from showroom to showroom and also provide buyers with a chance to meet and exchange ideas with one another. They are especially helpful in fashion areas made up of many small firms. Exhibitors also find them a place to meet their counterparts from other regions or countries.

The shoe, notions, piece goods, and men's sportswear industries regularly sponsor trade shows. (See Chapter 15 for a discussion of trade shows and market weeks at U.S. and foreign markets and marts.)

Buying, Merchandising, and Product Development Organizations

Another type of auxiliary service—one developed especially for the fashion industry—is the **buying, merchandising**, and **product development organization.** This type of organization evolved from a service called a *resident buying office (RBO)*, and to understand the function of a buying, merchandising, and product development organization, one must first know something about RBOs. The buying offices came into being to serve the ongoing needs of a store or group of stores for a steady supply of new merchandise. Because a store's buyers worked out of the store and made only occasional market trips, they came to rely on a service located at the market centers for ongoing, daily attention to the store's needs. Originally, RBOs existed only to place orders for out-of-town retailers. Today, their functions and their clients have become so diverse that the term "resident buying office" is no longer complete or accurate.

Although their main job remains buying and coordinating orders, buying offices provide many support services—not just to retailer buyers, but also, in some instances, to wholesalers and apparel manufacturers. They watch and report on fashion trends, help with strategic planning, make vendor recommendations, coordinate imports, and assist in product development. They help to organize fashion weeks and ensure that they go smoothly for their client stores' buyers. A good buying office continually adds to its list of services, and many have even expanded into areas such as sales promotion and advertising, personnel operations, and computer processing.

Location

Most American buying offices, including the largest firms—The Doneger Group, Associated Merchandising Corporation (AMC), and Federated (both Federated Merchandising and Federated Product Development)—are headquartered in New York's garment center. But a number of buying offices are located in Los Angeles or have West Coast offices there. The four organizations mentioned above all have Los Angeles offices. Marshall Kline Buying Service is an example of a Los Angeles-based buying office; it serves department stores and women's, men's, and children's apparel and home furnishings specialty stores. Some retail fashion chains, such as Ross Stores (a California off-price specialty chain), which maintain their own buying offices, have West Coast offices in Los Angeles.

The large buying, merchandising, and product development organizations also maintain branches abroad, and smaller companies have affiliates in the major foreign market centers.

Specialization

Some organizations that began as buying offices have built their business by specializing in serving particular segments of the fashion industry. Atlas Buying Corporation, for example, has carved out its own niche by specializing in discount stores owned by department store chains. Other offices work only with stores selling off-price merchandise. Another type of specialization is by product category: Carol Hoffman, a division of the Doneger Group, specializes in contemporary and bridge sportswear. Pam Roth is an example of a specialist in bridal and formal wear for women, and Peter Nathan, Inc., deals in furs. A number of firms have followed the broader industry trend toward niche selling and specialize in large-, half-, and petite-sized fashions. Alper International's specialties are buying fabric and trimmings for garment manufacturers and women's wear for retailers worldwide; its clients are as near as Canada and Mexico and as far as South Africa, Australia, Saudi Arabia, and Jordan.

Types of Ownership

Buying offices are either independent or store-owned. An independent office works for non-competing clients that it seeks out, while a store-owned office is owned by a group of stores, or—less often—one store, for whom it works exclusively.

Independent Offices

Independent offices are more numerous than store-owned offices simply because there are relatively few retailing giants that can afford to own and manage such a resource. The number of buying offices has declined in recent years because of mergers and acquisitions among their retailer clients and among buying offices themselves.

Independent offices typically represent non-competing moderate-priced department and specialty stores in mid-sized and secondary markets. To avoid conflicts, most independents restrict themselves to one client in each trading area, although they may have clients who serve different market segments within a single area. For example, a resident office's clients within a trading area may include a department store; a bridal shop; a shoe store; stores specializing in activewear, men's sportswear, and children's wear; and stores catering to customers at different price points.

The staff familiarizes themselves with each client's needs and attempt to meet those needs with as wide a range of services as possible. One aspect of service that buying offices are promoting to attract new clients is personal attention. Small operations, which offer exclusivity to their customers, claim that in a business consumed by "mergermania," they are better able to service their clients, who may themselves be expanding, by continuing to provide personalized and individual service.

Larger firms have responded by forming divisions that cater to the needs of different groups of clients. The largest independent resident buying office—in fact the largest resident buying office of any type—in the United States is The Doneger Group. Its ten divisions include specialized buying offices for retailers in such markets as apparel for large women, apparel for tall women, children's wear, men's wear, home furnishings, and off-price retailing. Other divisions provide research and forecasting services and assistance in import and export.

Typically an independent office charges each client store an annual, stipulated fee, which is based on the store's sales volume.

Store-Owned Offices

Store-owned offices are either associated or corporate-owned. An **associated** or **cooperative office** is cooperatively owned and operated by a group of privately owned stores for their mutual use. It never takes outside private clients; membership is by invitation only. It is considerably more expensive than if the store were a client of an independent office since members buy shares in the cooperative when they join. The amount of shares that must be purchased is keyed to member stores' sales volume.

One advantage of belonging to an associated office is that it provides members with an important exchange of information, often including financial information and merchandising experience. The best-known and largest associated buying offices is AMC.

The **corporate-owned** or **syndicated office** as it is sometimes called, is maintained by a parent organization exclusively for the stores it owns. One advantage of this type of organization is that it can be given more authority than an independent office, although some corporate-owned offices still require authorization from store buyers for major purchases. The Federated corporate office, which serves Bloomingdale's, The Bon Marché, Burdines, Goldsmith's, Lazarus, and Macy's, department stores and a number of smaller specialty shops, is an example of this type of office.

Functions of the Buying, Merchandising, and Product Development Organization

Even with instant communication by electronic mail and faxes, the buying function benefits from the services of a representative and advisor who is actually at the market. Some of the functions that buying offices perform on behalf of their clients are purchasing, preparing for market weeks, importing, and developing products.

Purchasing

Buying offices offer store buyers advice and support in various buying situations. For example, an office can place an order large enough to qualify for a manufacturer's quantity discount and then divide the goods among several small clients. The organization's staff can visit manufacturers' showrooms and make recommendations to their clients about specials, trends, and hot items (see Figure 19.12). Size and location give the buying office clout with vendors when it comes to reordering in midseason or making sure that the right goods are delivered on schedule.

Preparing for Market Weeks

As noted in Chapter 15, market weeks are hectic times for fashion buyers, with many showrooms visits and other information-gathering

FIGURE 19.12
The buying, merchandising, and product development organization helps its clients prepare for their buying trips by presenting a preview of the vendors' offerings.
The Fashion Institute of Technology, New York/Photograph: John Senzer.

events. A buying office can provide services similar to those of a tour guide to make the buying trip smooth and efficient. Staff members visit the showrooms in advance and assess each manufacturer's lines on behalf of their various clients. When the store buyers arrive, the buying office may give presentations to let them know what to expect. Sometimes personnel from a buying office accompany visiting buyers to vendors' showrooms and offer on-the-spot advice about orders.

Importing

In response to the increasingly global nature of the fashion business, many buying offices maintain divisions in key foreign cities or affiliate with a *commissionaires* overseas. (A commissionaire is an agent that represents stores in foreign markets. See Chapter 14 for further discussion.) Overseas divisions and commissionaires work closely with the merchandising division and with client stores. In addition to performing the buying functions of a domestic buying office, these services deal with the unique challenges of importing, such as quotas, tariffs, long lead times for delivery, and interpretation of the buyer's orders for vendors who speak a different language. Having an advisor and consultant overseas is especially beneficial for buyers who are attending a market week or trade show or having private label goods produced in a foreign country.

Developing Products

Buying offices have played an important role in the development of private labels. Most corporate-owned buying offices have a private label program for their member stores.

Associated Merchandising Corporation has established a particularly strong retail presence developing private labels for their member stores. AMC is known for its Preswick & Moore label, aimed at the high-end, traditional customer, and Architect, geared toward the young, career-oriented customer.

Corporate offices have also aggressively pursued private label business. When the Federated conglomerate acquired Macy's, it expanded on the store's well-established product development program, placing the Charter Club apparel and home furnishing lines in its other mid-range department stores. Federated's product development program employs 400 people in 18 countries to design, develop, and identify manufacturers for its private brands, which include its brands of cookware and other household goods as well as its fashion labels.

SUMMARY AND REVIEW

Fashion producers and retailers depend on a variety of auxiliary services to support the merchandising function. Depending on the size and resources of a company, it may rely on its own staff for these service or hire outside firms to perform them.

The media regard fashion businesses as clients and offer assistance in preparing and placing advertising (print ads in newspapers and consumer and trade magazines and commercials on television and radio). To attract advertisers, the media offer fashion businesses color and style forecasts and other trend information. Advertising and public relations agencies also provide auxiliary services in placing paid advertisements and free publicity in the media. Store design and visual merchandising are other promotional services that may be performed by staff members or independent suppliers.

For information about industry trends and fashion forecasts, retailers and producers can take advantage of the services offered by fashion consulting firms, market research agencies, trade associations, and trade shows.

A source of information unique to the fashion industry is the buying, merchandising, and product development organization. This type of business began as resident buying offices, representing out-of-town retailers in the major markets. Some firms were independent, selling their services to non-competing retailers. Others were corporate-owned, either as cooperatives owned by several retailers or as divisions of large retail chains. Resident buying offices have evolved into businesses that include wholesalers and producers among their clients and that provide a full range of services, including liaisons with vendors; advice and assistance in buying, merchandising; and forecasting and other information services.

Trade Talk

Define or briefly explain the following:

advertising
associated or cooperative office
buying, merchandising, and product development organization
corporate-owned or syndicated office
editorial credit
fashion stylist
infomercial
planogram
public relations
publicity
trade publication
visual merchandising

For Review

1. What is the difference between advertising and publicity/public relations?
2. Describe the contents of *Women's Wear Daily*.
3. What are the advantages of television and radio for fashion exposure?
4. What tasks do public relations firms undertake for their clients?
5. What advantages does a web site offer as a promotional medium?
6. How does a store design contribute to the store's image?
7. What resources are available to a small specialty store for effective visual merchandising?
8. Describe the research methods that trend forecasters use.
9. What is the major function of buying, merchandising, and product development organizations? What additional services do they perform?
10. What are the similarities and differences between independent and corporate buying, merchandising, and product development offices?

For Discussion

1. As a consumer, where do you get your information about fashion? How does each medium influence your buying decisions?
2. You own a small boutique that caters to upscale young women. What services of a buying, merchandising, and product development organization would be most useful to you? Why?

References

1. Lisa Lockwood, "What Will You Read in 2006?" *Women's Wear Daily*, May 24, 1996, p. 10.

2. David Carr, "In Style's World of Fashion," *New York Times*, February 25, 2001, p.C7.
3. Megan Larson, "Kids Anticlimax: Upfront Is A Dud," *Mediaweek*, August 13, 2001.
4. Carole Nicksin, "HSN vs. QVC," *Home Furnishing Network*, March 12, 2001.
5. "Klensch Is Back," In Brief, *Women's Wear Daily*, February 7, 2002, p. 2.
6. Metro TV," New York Metro, www.newyorkmetro.com, September 2002
7. PR Newswire, February 4, 2002
8. Kayte VanScoy, "Can't Bust 'Em [en] For Its Ambitious Ad Campaign, Lee Jeans Took to the Web," Smart Business For The New Economy, July 2001.

Exploring Careers at the Auxiliary Level

A wide variety of job opportunities are available in the service organizations that aid and assist the wholesale and retail fashion industries. These service organizations, such as advertising and publicity agencies, consumer and trade publications, trade associations, and consulting firms, perform functions that have a show-business quality about them. Work in these fields is hectic and, for those suited to it, fun. Each area has its own requirements, but in all of them there are important jobs in which an understanding of fashion is vital.

Advertising Agencies

Beginners, even those with special skills, often have a hard time entering the agency field. College graduates complain that they go to dozens of agencies and are offered nothing more exciting than a mail room or receptionist job. A solution to the beginner's problem may be to avoid the biggest and best-known agencies and seek a starting job in an agency of modest or small size. There the pay is likely to be small, the office tiny, and the future problematic, but the opportunities to work and learn are good and provide the experience necessary to qualify later for a good job in a major agency. Another starting place is the in-house advertising department of a major retail chain or catalog retailer.

The careers in advertising agencies in which a fashion background can be useful include account executive, copywriter, illustrator, layout artist, and fashion consultant.

Consumer Publications

Nearly all consumer publications carry some sort of fashion material, and some are devoted exclusively to fashion. Career opportunities with such publications are immensely varied, ranging from editorial work to those numerous, behind-the-scenes activities that go into the publishing of a magazine or newspaper.

Most of the magazines with a nationwide readership are headquartered in New York City or its metropolitan area, but if you are interested in working on the business side of a publication, you may also find a position in a regional business office. A bachelor's degree is required for most jobs with potential for advancement. The appropriate academic background depends on the duties within a specific department, whether they involve writing, art direction, or business and financial decision making.

Fashion Editor

When fashion is presented in a publication, that publication's fashion judgment must be authoritative. Whether the publication is devoted entirely to fashion or simply runs a fashion section, the editor's job is to discover what the reader responds to, locate those fashions in the market, and illustrate examples of them at the right time. Timing must accommodate publishing schedules as well as the seasonal showings of new lines. The editorial job can be all the more complicated because of pressures from publicity hungry producers. An editor may cover the entire fashion market or just one segment of it, depending on the type of publication and the size of the publication's staff.

Merchandising Editor

Behind the scenes, the merchandising editors of national publications and their staffs work to make sure that readers anywhere in the country can buy the merchandise that is featured editorially. They do this by reporting to retailers in advance of publication the details of what is to run, why it is important, and from what resources it is available. With their formidable knowledge of markets, merchandise, and retailing, these editors are also well equipped to offer retailers practical suggestions about how to promote merchandise successfully and how to display the items featured in their publications.

Stylist

A fashion shoot is a team effort, and the stylist's role is critical to its success. The stylist is responsible for assembling the apparel and accessories to be worn by each model. This duty involves decision making about how various items of apparel are to be combined and accessorized to show each off to its best advantage. The stylist must also attend to the details of ensuring that the right sizes and colors are available for the right model. If the model is a celebrity, the appropriateness of the ensemble to his or her image becomes an additional factor. The stylist must be a diplomat to win the cooperation of everyone involved in the shoot.

In addition to magazine work, stylists may find employment with advertising agencies, working on print ads or TV commercials.

Advertising Sale's Representative

Selling advertising space is the major source of revenue for a publication. The many aspects of selling accommodate various talents. Those who like selling deal with producers and their advertising agencies. People with a flair for research help the sales representatives to sell advertising space in the publication by supplying facts that indicate the publication's ability to enlist retail cooperation or that measure the buying power of the publication's readers. Those with a flair for persuasive writing may find a place on the advertising promotion staff, where presentations are developed to help the sales representatives conduct meetings with prospective advertisers.

Trade Publications

Some trade publications are very narrowly specialized, such as Accessories and *Upholstery Design & Manufacturing* and are likely to be published monthly. Some are less specialized, such as *Retail Week*, and tend to be published weekly or semimonthly. *Women's Wear Daily* (covering the women's apparel field) provides in-depth coverage and is published 5 days a week, Monday through Friday, except holidays. Similarly, the *Daily News Record* is published three times a week for the men's wear and textiles fields. All trade publications may offer opportunities for beginners with an interest in fashion.

Consulting Services

Change is at the heart of the fashion industry, and keeping up with new trends is essential to the success of any fashion business from textile manufacturers to producers to retailers. Even individual consumers whose fashion image is important to their careers rely on a variety of fashion consulting services.

Consultants to the Fashion Industry

The most glamorous of the consulting services involved in the fashion field is of course, the fashion consultant. Of these, the oldest and best-known is the Tobé service, founded in 1927 by the late Tobé Coller Davis. Fashion consulting services cover and interpret fashion news in such a way that buying, merchandising, and coordination executives can be guided by the views of skilled observers in every important fashion center. Reports, bulletins, clinics, videotapes, and individual advice are the subscribers' diet.

Buying/Merchandising/Product Development Careers

Fashion careers in buying offices center around market work. Market representatives "live" in their markets, see every line that is important (and many that are not), and know supply and delivery conditions in those markets as well as they know the fashion aspects of the merchandise. Market representatives also learn to work with any number of bosses: their own superiors, the heads of the client stores, and the buyers in the stores they serve. As the resident buying office has evolved into a buying/merchandising/product development office, the career opportunities have expanded. The personnel in these offices still serve as their buyer clients' representatives to the manufacturers, arranging and tracking merchandise orders. But the relationship with manufacturers has expanded into a collaborative effort to produce private label lines. Product development has resulted in the development of new jobs and responsibilities for employees in the manufacturing and retailing firms as well as the buying office. There are also positions in buying offices for fashion forecasters.

Entry into the market representative's job is through the position of apprentice. Beginners work as assistants, literally running errands in the market daily. The major job of an assistant is follow up on details, to check with sources on deliveries and other questions that may arise, and to save the time of the market representative. In the process, the beginner gets to know the markets, the buying office routines, and the needs of the client stores. If the work is done against a background of fashion training, it is more easily mastered and promotion is apt to be more rapid. This career path is worth considering if you thrive on the excitement of the major market centers and want to relocate to a large city, possibly even abroad.

Trade Associations

One of the more interesting areas of employment in the fashion field is trade association work. Industries, retailers, and professionals of all types form associations and hire executive staffs to do research, publicity, and public relations work. These associations also handle legislative contacts, run conventions, publish periodicals, and run trade shows. The associations often perform any other services members may require. Trade associations serve every segment of the fashion industry, from producers of textiles and other materials to designers and manufacturers of fashion products to retailers. Some, like the Mohair Council of America or the National Women's Neckwear and Scarf Association, are narrowly focused, while others, such as the American Textile Manufacturers Institute, the American Apparel Manufacturers Association, and The Fashion Group International, Inc. have a broader membership.

Small or large, a trade association provides a great variety of work to its staff. Versatility is thus a paramount requirement. An assistant entering trade association work will find a background in the specific field served helpful, but the ability to communicate well is just as important.

Consulting Services for Consumers

In recent years, fashion consumer consulting services have grown in popularity. Consulting services may be offered by fashion-trained entrepreneurs who wish to begin their own business on a part-time basis; these services can often grow to a full-time, profitable business. Such businesses can be started with relatively little capital but, to succeed, need a considerable amount of promotion from self-starting individuals with previous experience in the field of fashion.

Image and Wardrobe Consultant

Wardrobe or image consultants act as wardrobe counselors to individuals who wish to look fashionable and project an individual image. Such consumers may lack confidence in their own ability to plan a wardrobe or may simply lack the time and knowledge necessary to choose the fashions that are most flattering and suitable for their lifestyle.

Color Consultant

Another type of consumer consultant that has become popular is the color consultant or specialist. The extent of services offered varies widely, as do the background and training of these individuals. Many color specialists offer only one service, that of developing a color chart for the individual client illustrating the client's best colors. This color chart is then used for all clothing purchases so that the individual can closely coordinate his or her wardrobe, thus avoiding costly mistakes in purchasing items that do not match other garments in the wardrobe. Other color specialists also offer services such as recommending the client's best fashion "type" or look, whether it be sophisticated, ingenue, or country.

Many color specialists develop workshops each season to present fashion looks to their clients, drawing from the selections offered in many stores in their shopping area. Workshops are also presented to corporate groups who want to improve the personal image of their employees.

The Association of Image Consultants has been seeking to professionalize both the wardrobe/image consultant's job and the color consultant's job. Certification courses are available in schools throughout the country, as well as through workshops offered by the organization.

Cosmetics Consultant or Makeup Artist

More and more beauty salons and spas are adding cosmetics consultants or makeup artists to their staffs. Formerly limited to Hollywood or New York, or to a few high-end department stores, makeup artists around the country today also have private clients.

Interior Designer or Decorator

The terms "interior designer" and "interior decorator" seem similar, but in the trade they have very different meanings. In an increasing number of states, the term "interior designer" can be used only by those who have been certified by the National Council for Interior Design Qualification (NCIDQ). This certification requires education, experience, and passing of an examination. Both jobs involve designing interiors of homes and businesses and providing suggestions for layout, furniture, and materials, all within a specified budget. Some designers also actually purchase the furniture and materials for their clients, and oversee their installation.

Television and Internet Productions

Fashion-oriented specialists are beginning to find exciting careers in television. Many advertising agencies today engage outside companies to create fashion commercials for client producers or retailers. The high cost of television time and production limits its appeal to retailers, but some make good use of television to present fashion. National advertising by major manufacturers and retailers—for example, Calvin Klein and Sears—is most common. The growth of cable television, with local access channels, has provided fashion advertisers with a less costly outlet than network television, and production costs are lower than ever. Cable shopping networks have opened up a whole new form of retailing, including fashion retailing. Cable has also brought fashion to the program content of television, especially on MTV and VH-1, with their fashion-conscious young adult audiences.

The Internet also offers many job opportunities for people with fashion flair and some technical expertise. Most leading designers and manufacturers have web sites that must be updated and expanded regularly. Internet shopping is poised on the brink of worldwide expansion; when security issues are resolved, you can expect to see many job opportunities in this communications medium.

Teaching

Opportunities to teach fashion-related courses are varied. Individuals with extensive experience in the industry can often teach in private schools offering one- or two-year training programs, without the necessity of a college degree. Teachers in secondary schools with specialized fashion merchandising and design programs generally are required to have a four-year degree, often with additional college hours in teaching methods. To teach on the junior college or baccalaureate level, a master's degree is usually required. In any case, credibility is greatly enhanced by a solid background of direct experience in the fashion business.

Other opportunities for teaching occur in nonacademic settings. These include working in the training department of a large store or chain, and providing freelance seminars on fashion-related topics. As stores compete not only with each other but with catalog, television, and Internet retailers, the need for a well trained staff, especially the sales staff, has created a demand for people who can provide a practical education in terms of product knowledge and the essential skills of fashion retailing.

Teaching and training are natural careers for people who work in the fashion industry, where the exchange of information and the need to keep up with fast breaking news and new trends are part of everyone's business. If you think about it, virtually every fashion industry job involves elements of both teaching and learning. The opportunities for fulfilling careers in which you can put your talents and interests to work are virtually limitless.

Assignments

1. Prepare the last unit of your career journal by rewriting your résumé to give it a slant toward the career of your choice.
2. Environmental factors affect all auxiliary services of the fashion business. Considering services within businesses at all levels of the fashion industry as well as external resources, such as print and broadcast media, advertising agencies, and information services, give a current example of the effects of the natural, economic, social, and political/legal environment.

Zac Posen • Lazaro Hernandez & Jack McCollough • Tara Subkoff & Matt Damhave • Alice Roi• William Reid • Nicole Noselli & Daphne Gutierrez

"It is really important for us to make clothes that look beautiful, feminine and intelligent. I'm passionate about women looking great in the clothes, strong and powerful and modern and sexy."

ZAC POSEN, 2003

"There are designers who have a certain 'thing' that they do. Gucci does sex and Channel does classicism. Those are things that you can build a career on, because they last forever. But some people do collections based on something that is of the moment, and when that moment passes, so does your company. We're trying to base it on something that will last the test of time...like excellence."

LAZARO HERNANDEZ & JACK MCCOLLOUGH
FOR PROENZA SCHOULER, 2003

"We're against the mass reproduction of thrift store clothing. It's like no one's thinking for themselves."

TARA SUBKOFF & MATT DAMHAVE
FOR IMITATION OF CHRIST, 2001

"On vacations I'm usually faxing and calling and then measuring my traveling companion with a tape measure for specs."

ALICE ROI, 2001

"I was designing to see what worked, and that Southern quality is something that feels right for us. For the last couple of seasons, we have tried to ground ourselves and it takes a while to evolve into what you think your collection is about."

WILLIAM REID, 2001

" The nomination for the Perry Ellis Award will help with business, but we are continuing to take small steps to reaching our goals. We want to continue to be designers and not deal too much with the retail side. We will never tell anyone what the real meaning of 'Bruce' is, it's much more interesting to see what people think it means."

NICOLE NOSELLI & DAPHNE GUTIERREZ
FOR BRUCE, 2001

Designer Zac Posen.

My 100 Top Apparel Designers

This is my personal list—you and your instructor may have many different candidates. That's what makes top 100 lists so much fun: the intense debate, evaluation, and reevaluation they inspire. It's also what makes them such a valuable learning experience.

Some of the people included are famous figures in the history of design, others are more recent designers whom I have known personally or through their clothes. Others are included because their work strikes a chord with the times they designed in—and others captivated the young! My list does not include any accessory designers, because I found so many favorites that they would fill another list! Perhaps in the next edition. . . .

So, enjoy my list. Then add your own favorites and subtract those names you don't agree with. And, of course, state the reasons for your choices.

	Name	Decades of Influence	Defining Characteristics
1	Adolfo	60s–80s	Chanel-inspired knit suits . . . has a devoted following of "status" dressers
2	Adrian, Gilbert	30s–40s	Movie marvel . . . MGM's top designer in the 30s and 40s . . . dressed Joan Crawford, Garbo, and Harlow
3	Armani, Giorgio	80s–2000s	Impacted both men's and women's fashions . . . fluid tailoring, luxurious light fabrics, self-assured style
4	Ashley, Laura	70s–80s	Romantic Victorian looks in fabrics and fashion . . . built a London-based empire in clothes and home furnishings
5	Balenciaga, Cristobal	40s–60s	One of the 20th century's greatest . . . his influence inspired the later work of Hubert de Givenchy, Emanuel Ungaro, and André Courrèges
6	Balmain, Pierre	40s–50s	Classic daytime looks and extravagant evening gowns . . . opened Paris house in 1945
7	Beene, Geoffrey	60s–80s	Relaxed, elegant look, superb cut, and beautiful fabrics
8	Blass, Bill	70s–90s	Mr. Sophisication . . . great taste, refined cut, and innovative use of fabrics
9	Bohan, Marc	60s–80s	Started in early 60s with Dior and was the lead designer there until 1989
10	Boss, Hugo	80s–2000s	First name in men's wear

	Name	Decades of Influence	Defining Characteristics
11	Burrows, Stephen	70s–80s	Draped matte jerseys-to die for! . . . body-conscious clothes in vibrant colors
12	Cardin, Pierre	50s–60s	King of the licensing game . . . first designer to show his line in China
13	Carnegie, Hattie	30s–40s	Influential in the 30s and 40s . . . her designs influenced Norell, Trigère, and McCardell
14	Cashin, Bonnie	40s–50s	Mother of the American Sportswear Look . . . championed separates and the "layered look" . . . stretch ski pants, pedal pushers, capri pants
15	Cassini, Oleg	60s–80s	Official designer for Jacqueline Kennedy in her White House years . . . now king of the licensed suit
16	Chanel, "Coco"	20s–40s	Her innovations have become timeless classics: sweaters, sailor looks, tweed suits
17	Claiborne, Liz	80s–2000s	The "Executive Lady" . . . innovator of career apparel
18	Courrèges, André	60s–70s	First couturier to raise hemlines to mid-thigh . . . white boots, tough chic
19	Connolly, Sybil	60s–70s	Ireland's most prestigious designer . . . famous for fine wools and tweeds
20	de la Renta, Oscar	60s–2000s	Luxury designer . . . opulent eveningwear, sophisticated daywear
21	Demeulemeester, Ann	90s–2000s	Precision tailored suits . . . clever cutting of jersey fabrics . . . monochrome color palette
22	Dior, Christian	40s–50s	The "New Look" in 1947 . . . cinched waist, pushed up bosom, short jacket emphasized hips, full long skirts
23	Dolce, Domenico and Gabbana, Stefano	90s–2000s	Inspired the young to dress up . . . sexy lingerie looks are their signature . . . glorification of female physique is the message of their designs
24	Ellis, Perry	70s–80s	Added high-fashion pizzazz to classic looks . . . young in spirit . . . natural fibers, hand-knitted sweaters
25	Fath, Jacques	40s–50s	Sexy clothes . . . hourglass shapes . . . plunging necklines
26	Ferré, Gianfranco	80s–90s	Architectural look to his designs . . . was educated as an architect and he shows well-defined construction in his clothes
27	Fisher, Eileen	90s–2000s	The empress of understatement . . . easy fitting clothes for an imperfect figure
28	Fogarty, Anne	50s–60s	Introduced fashion innovations to the junior-size world
29	Ford, Tom	90s–2000s	New design voice of Gucci
30	Fortuny, Mariano	20s–30s	Pleated artistry . . . his clothes are now collector's items
31	Galanos, James	40s–50s	First American couturier . . . elegant haute couture designs
32	Galliano, John	90s –2000s	Theatrical design . . . knitted lace dresses
33	Gaultier, Jean-Paul	80s–2000s	Trendy and controversial . . . advocate of the "punk look" . . . daring and avant garde

	Name	Decades of Influence	Defining Characteristics
34	Gernreich, Rudi	60s–70s	Topless swimsuit . . . the "no-bra" . . . see-through blouses
35	Givenchy, Hubert	50s–80s	His fashion muse was Audrey Hepburn . . . introduced chemise or sack dress
36	Grès, Alix	30s–50s	The duchess of draping . . . her Grecian column dresses are draped to perfection
37	Halston	70s–80s	Unconstructed separates, lush cashmeres . . . Studio 54
38	Hartnell, Norman	30s–40s	Biggest couture house in London in 30s . . . designed coronation gown for Queen Elizabeth II
39	Head, Edith	30s–50s	One of Hollywood's best-known designers . . . dressed Liz Taylor, Lana Turner
40	Herman, Stan	60s–90s	President of the Council of Fashion Designers of America . . . leading uniform designer of the world . . . think airlines, McDonald's
41	Herrera, Carolina	80s–2000s	Caters to high-society clientele . . . dressy eveningwear . . . luxurious fabrics
42	Hilfiger, Tommy	80s–2000s	"Brand image" designer
43	Jacobs, Marc	90s–2000s	Designed for the Perry Ellis label . . . exceptional in leather and fur design
44	James, Charles	40s–50s	The Dali of Design
45	Johnson, Betsey	60s–70s	The Betsey of "Betsey, Bunky, and Nini" . . . designed for "Paraphernalia" stores
46	Joop, Wolfgang	90s	Leading 90s designer from Germany
47	Kamali, Norma	80s–90s	Sweatshirt clothes made high fashion news . . . appeals to the young
48	Karan, Donna	80s–2000s	High-fashion elegant sportswear . . . simple silhouettes, sarong skirts, easy-fitting dresses
49	Kawabuko, Rei	80s–90s	Avant garde clothes challenged classic idea of femininity
50	Kenzo	70s–80s	Attentive to the quality of fabrics . . . uses splashes of irreverent color . . . now into home fashions
51	Khanh, Emmanuelle	60s–70s	One of the first major ready-to-wear designers in Paris . . . kicky, young clothes
52	Klein, Anne	50s–60s	Classic American sportswear designer . . . "Junior Sophisticates" was her company
53	Klein, Calvin	70s–2000s	King of the minimalism look . . . designer jeans . . . sexually-charged advertising
54	Kors, Michael	90s–2000s	Strong on shape and line, devoid of ornamentation
55	Lacroix, Christian	80s–90s	Introduced the "pouf" silhouette . . . fanciful apparel and elaborate wedding gowns
56	Lagerfeld, Karl	80s–2000s	Produces 16 collections a year! . . . perfect technique and witty design resurrected the Chanel name
57	Lanvin, Jeanne	20s–30s	One of the earliest Paris couturiers

	Name	Decades of Influence	Defining Characteristics
58	Lauren, Ralph	80s–2000s	Western look for men and women . . . creates upper-crust lifestyle looks . . . classic silhouettes
59	Mackie, Bob	60s–70s–80s	Dresses TV and movie stars . . . lots of glitz
60	McCardell, Claire	40s–50s	Introduced dirndl skirt as a high fashion icon . . . leading proponent of American sportswear look
61	McFadden, Mary	70s–80s	Fortuny successor . . . used pleats to emphasize her enticing looks
62	McQueen, Alexander	90s . . .	Started as a Saville Row tailor in London . . . now designs couture for Givenchy
63	Mainbocher	30s–40s	An American in Paris . . . introduced strapless evening gowns . . . designed the wedding dress of Wallis Simpson, the Duchess of Windsor
64	Miller, Nicole	80s–2000s	Innovative prints . . . pure, simple designs for the 90s
65	Missoni, Rosita and Ottavio	50s–90s	Bold, multiple-color combinations in knitwear . . . simple but sophisticated knitwear designs
66	Miyake, Issey	80s–90s	Developer of new fabrics and design techniques . . . produces innovations like oilcloth clothes
67	Mizrahi, Isaac	80s–90s	Flashed on fashion scene under Chanel backing . . . moved on to theatrical and movie works
68	Montana, Claude	80s–90s	Wedge-shaped silhouette . . . architectural shapes in original designs
69	Moschino, Franco	90s . . .	Fashion spoofs made him famous
70	Mori, Hanae	80s	Mines the gap between East and West . . . Chanel inspired her designs
71	Mugler, Thierry	70s–90s	Extravagant and innovative . . . spans from lots of ornamentation to rigorous minimalism
72	Muir, Jean	60s–70s	Elegantly, intricately detailed classic clothes
73	Natori, Josie	80s–2000s	Banished the borders between inner and outerwear . . . success based on mix of comfort, practicality, and style
74	Norell, Norman	40s–60s	Winner of first Coty award in 1943 . . . his shimmering sequined dresses are worn and treasured forever
75	Oldham, Todd	90s . . .	Whimsical mix of commercial and offbeat . . . designs sophisticated and youthful clothes with a sense of humor
76	Patou, Jean	20s–30s	Elegant, ladylike couture clothes . . . successful businessman and showman
77	Piquet, Robert	30s–40s	Influenced Givenchy and Dior, both of whom worked for him
78	Poiret, Paul	20s–30s	First Paris couturier of 20th century to become a trend- setter . . . liberated women from corsets
79	Prada, Miuccia	90s–2000s	Clothing and accessories global trendsetters . . . secondary line Miu Miu a rage with the young
80	Pucci, Emilio	50s–60s	His colorful graphic prints on jersey revolutionized Italian fashion at that time

	Name	Decades of Influence	Defining Characteristics
81	Quant, Mary	60s–70s	Swinging sixties London scene . . . popularized miniskirts, colored tights, and football sweaters
82	Rabanne, Paco	70s–80s	Produced clothes of plastic, chain metal, fiber-optic wire, and doorknobs . . . fashion's heavy metal guru . . . a revolution in fashion
83	Rhodes, Zandra	70s–80s	Glamorized print designs . . . soft fabrics, handscreened prints . . . started as a textile designer
84	Rodriguez, Narciso	90s–2000s	Designs for Loewe, a Spanish design company
85	Rykiel, Sonia	70s–80s	Knitwear her forté . . . sense of fashion humor, mixing the outrageous with the feminine
86	Saint Laurent, Yves	60s–90s	Exploded on scene in 60s . . . "Infant Terrible" . . . famous for pantsuits, pea jackets, "le smoking," safari suits . . . Rive Gauche
87	Sander, Jil	90s–2000s	Highest quality in materials and craftsmanship . . . expert tailoring in suits and coats
88	Simpson, Adele	50s–60s	A durable of Seventh Avenue . . . known for conservative good taste in design
89	Schiaparelli, Elsa	30s–40s	Avant garde designer in Paris . . . famous for introducing "shocking pink"
90	Sui, Anna	90s–2000s	Free-spirited approach to design . . . mix of hip and haute couture
91	Trigère, Pauline	40s–80s	Pioneer American designer . . . her coat silhouettes are famous . . . attention to detail
92	Tyler, Richard	90s	Custom tailoring, graceful cut . . . sophisticated styling and expert cut . . . appeals to the 90s Hollywood crowd
93	Ungaro, Emanuel	70s–80s	Space-age inspired . . . bold colors . . . sharp edged
94	Valentino	60s–90s	His famous V-shaped emblems crown his collection . . . simple, subtle design
95	Versace, Gianni	80s–90s	Kinetic, kaleidoscope prints . . . metallic mesh garments . . . king of fashion for the rock and roll set
96	Wang, Vera	90s–2000s	Wonder of the wedding dress . . . besides bridal parties, has expanded to evening clothes
97	Weitz, John	60s–90s	Women's sportswear with a menswear look . . . designs in all fields (once "designed" a cigar!)
98	Westwood, Vivienne	80s–90s	Punk rock fashion . . . T-shirts with outragious messages . . . named her boutique "Sex"
99	Worth, Charles Frederick	The originator of fashion	He created the "designer name" as we know it . . . established the pattern of regular seasoned fashion shows
100	Yamamoto, Yohji	80s–90s	Sparse, understated fashions . . . dark, strong designs . . . asymmetrical cuts

Adapted from a variety of sources, including *WWD: 75 Years in Fashion 1910–1985, WWD Century,* September 1998.

Glossary of Key Terms

Absolute quota A limit to the quantity of goods entering United States. *Ch 16*

Activewear The sector of sportswear that includes casual attire worn for sports such as running, jogging, tennis, and racquetball. Sometimes called "active sportswear." *Ch 9*

Adaptations Designs that have all the dominant features of the style that inspired them but do not claim to be exact copies. *Ch 1*

Advertising The paid use of space or time in any medium. This includes newspapers, magazines, direct-mail pieces, shopping news bulletins, theater programs, catalogs, bus cards, billboards, radio, TV, and the Internet. *Ch 19*

Ambiance The atmosphere encountered when entering a store. *Ch 18*

Anchor A design from a previous season reworked in a different color or fabric. *Ch 7*

Apparel contractor A firm whose sole function is to supply sewing services to the apparel industry. *Ch 7*

Apparel jobber (manufacturing) A firm that handles the designing, planning and purchasing of materials, and usually the cutting, selling, and shipping of apparel, but does not handle the actual garment sewing. *Ch 7*

Apparel manufacturer A firm that performs all the operations required to produce a garment. *Ch 7*

Aromatherapy Fragrant oils are extracted from plants, herbs, and flowers, and used to stimulate or relax people. *Ch 13*

Assortment The range of stock a retailer features. See also *merchandise assortment*. *Ch 18*

Auxiliary level Composed of all the support services that are working with primary producers, secondary manufacturers, and retailers to keep consumers aware of the fashion merchandise produced for ultimate consumption. *Ch 4*

Baby-boom generation People born in the United States between 1946 and 1954; the largest generation group ever recorded. *Ch 2*

Balance of trade The difference between the value of exports and the value of imports. *Ch 16*

Big boxes A concept for a store that presents a large selection of goods in a selling space oversized for its merchandise category. *Ch 17*

Bodywear Coordinated leotards, tights, and wrap skirts. *Ch 11*

Body wrap Herbs, seaweed, or mud is applied directly to the body, which is then wrapped like a mummy to allow the substances to penetrate the pores. *Ch 13*

Bootleg goods Quality products made by the same manufacturer that produces the genuine branded products; these are sold to the black market. *Ch 16*

Boutique A shop associated with few-of-a-kind merchandise, generally of very new or extreme styling, with an imaginative presentation of goods. French word for "shop." *Ch 15*

Brand A name, trademark, or logo that is used to identify the products of a specific maker or seller and to differentiate the products from those of the competition. Also called "brand name." *Ch 5*

Brand-line representative (cosmetics) A trained cosmetician who advises customers in the selection and use of a specific brand of cosmetics, and handles the sales of that brand in a retail store. *Ch 13*

Bridal registry See *wedding registry. Ch 14*

Bridge (apparel—women's and men's wear) A price zone that bridges the gap between designer and better prices. *Chs 8 and 9*

Bridge jewelry Merchandise ranging from costume to fine jewelry in price, materials, and newness of styling. *Ch 11*

Bundling Assembling the cut pieces of each pattern—sleeves, collars, fronts, and backs—into bundles according to their sizes. Usually done by hand. *Ch 7*

Buyer's directory A list (and often a map) of the manufacturers' showrooms in a particular market or mart; it is furnished to retail buyers to assist them in "working the market." *Ch 15*

Buying, merchandising, and product development office *Associated/Cooperative:* One that is jointly owned and operated by a group of independently-owned stores. *Private*: One that is owned and operated by a single, out-of-town store organization, and which performs market work exclusively for that store organization. *Salaried, Fee or Paid*: One that is independently owned and operated, and which charges the stores it represents for the work it does. *Syndicate/Corporate*: One that is maintained by a parent organization that owns a group of stores, and which performs market work exclusively for those stores. *Ch 19*

Carat A measure of weight of precious stones; equal to 200 milligrams or 1/142 of an ounce. See also *karat. Ch 12*

Career A profession for which one trains and which is undertaken as a permanent calling. *Career Project 1*

Career path or ladder The order of occupations in a person's life. *Career Project 2*

Category or classification buying A practice whereby a chain store buyer located in a central buying office is usually assigned to purchase only a specific category or classification of merchandise instead of buying all categories carried in a single department. See also *departmental buying. Ch 17*

Category killer Superstores or category specialists who so dominate a market that they drive out or "kill" smaller specialty stores. *Ch 17*

Chain organization A group of 12 or more centrally owned stores, each handling somewhat similar goods, which are merchandised and controlled from a central headquarters office (as defined by the Bureau of the Census.) *Ch 17*

Chargebacks Financial penalties imposed on manufacturers by retailers. *Ch 7*

Classic A style or design that satisfies a basic need and remains in general fashion acceptance for an extended period of time. *Ch 1*

Collection A term used in the United States and Europe for an expensive line. *Ch 7*

Commissionaire (pronounced "ko-mee-see-oh-NAIR") An independent retailers' service organization usually located in the major city of a foreign market area. It is roughly the foreign equivalent of an American resident buying office. *Ch 16*

Computer-Aided Design (CAD) A computer program that allows designers to manipulate their designs easily. *Ch 7*

Computer-Aided Manufacturing (CAM) Stand-alone computerized manufacturing equipment, including computerized sewing, pattern-making, and cutting machines. *Ch 7*

Computer-Integrated Manufacturing (CIM) Many computers within a manufacturing company are linked from the design through the production stages. *Ch 7*

Confined style(s) Styles that a vendor agrees to sell to only one store in a given trading area. See also *exclusivity. Ch 18*

Consignment selling A manufacturer places merchandise in a retail store for resale but permits any unsold portion to be returned to the wholesale source by a specific date. *Ch 6*

Contemporary A type of styling and a price zone that is often also referred to as "updated," "better," or "young." Applies to all categories of apparel and furnishings. *Chs 8 and 9*

Contract buying See *specification buying.*

Contract tanneries Business firms that process hides and skins to the specifications of converters but are not involved in the sale of the finished product. *Ch 6*

Contractors See *apparel contractor. Ch 7*

Converter, leather Firms that buy hides and skins, farm out their processing to contract tanneries, and sell the finished product. *Ch 6*

Converter, textiles A producer who buys fabrics in the greige, contracts to have them finished (dyed, bleached, printed, or subjected to other treatments) in plants specializing in each operation, and sells the finished goods. *Ch 5*

Copycat scents Imitations of the aromas (and sometimes the packaging) of popular designer fragrances; sold at much lower prices. *Ch 13*

Corporation A company established by a legal charter that defines its scope and activity. *Ch 4*

Corporate licensing The use of a company's name on (sometimes) related merchandise. *Ch 7*

Corporate-owned or syndicated office See *buying, merchandising, and product development office. Ch 19*

Cosmetics Articles other than soap that are intended to be rubbed, poured, sprinkled, or sprayed on the person for purposes of cleansing, beautifying, promoting attractiveness, or altering the appearance (as defined by the Federal Trade Commission). *Ch 13*

Costume jewelry Mass-produced jewelry made of brass or other base metals, plastic, wood, or glass, and set with simulated or non-precious stones. Also called "fashion jewelry." *Ch 12*

Couture house (pronounced "koo-TOUR") An apparel firm for which the designer creates original styles. *Ch 15*

Couturier (male) or ***couturière*** (female) (pronounced "koo-tour-ee-AY" and "koo-tour-ee-AIR") The proprietor or designer of a French couture house. *Ch 15*

Créateurs (pronounced "kray-ah-TOURS") French ready-to-wear designers. *Ch 15*

Culmination (stage) See *fashion cycle. Ch 1*

Custom-made Clothing fitted specifically to the wearer. *Ch 7*

Cut-up trade Manufacturers of belts that are sold as part of a dress, skirt, or pants. *Ch 12*

Data warehouse A group of super-powerful computers hooked together and filled with easily accessible information about customers, transactions, and finances. *Ch 18*

Decline (stage) See *fashion cycle. Ch 1*

Demographics Studies that divide broad groups of consumers into smaller, more homogeneous target segments; the variables include population distribution, age, sex, family life cycle, race, religion, nationality, education, occupation, and income. *Ch 2*

Departmental buying A practice whereby a department buyer is responsible for buying all the various categories of merchandise carried in that department. See also *category buying. Ch 17*

Department store As defined by the Bureau of the Census, a store that employs 25 or more people and sells general lines of merchandise in each of three categories: (1) home furnishings, (2) household linens and dry goods (an old trade term meaning piece goods and sewing notions), and (3) apparel and accessories for the entire family. *Ch 17*

Design A specific version or variation of a style. In everyday usage, however, fashion producers and retailers refer to a design as a "style," a "style number," or simply a "number." *Ch 1*

Designer signature collection (price zone) The highest price zone. *Ch 8*

Details The individual elements that give a silhouette its form or shape. These include trimmings; skirt and pant length and width; and shoulder, waist, and sleeve treatment. *Ch 1*

Developed countries (DCs) Countries in the stage of economic development marked by a well-paid labor force and a high standard of living. *Ch 16*

Direct mail A form of sales promotion aimed at an individual customer and sent through the mail. Includes letters, catalogs, and credit statement inserts. See also *catalog retailing. Ch 17*

Discount store A departmentalized retail store using many self-service techniques to sell its goods. It operates usually at low profit margins, has a minimum annual volume of $500,000 and is at least 10,000 sq. ft. in size. *Ch 17*

Discretionary income The money that an individual or family has to spend or save after buying such necessities as food, clothing, shelter, and basic transportation. *Ch 2*

Disposable personal income The amount of money a person has left to spend or save after paying taxes. It is roughly equivalent to what an employee calls "take-home pay" and provides an approximation of the purchasing power of each consumer during any given year. *Ch 2*

Diversification The addition of various lines, products, or services to serve different markets. *Ch 4*

Divestiture Sale of part of a company for economic gain or debt management. *Ch 4*

Domestic market A fashion market center located in one's own country; for example, the United States. *Ch 15*

Downward-flow theory The theory of fashion adoption which maintains that to be identified as a true fashion, a style must first be adopted by people at the top of the social pyramid. The style then gradually wins acceptance at progressively lower social levels. Also called the "trickle-down" theory. *Ch 3*

Drop (men's wear) Refers to the difference between the waist and chest measurements of a man's jacket. Designer suits are sized on a seven-inch drop; traditional suits are styled with a six-inch drop. *Ch 9*

Dual distribution A manufacturer's policy of selling goods at both wholesale and retail. *Ch 9*

Duty See *tariff.*

Editorial credit The mention, in a magazine or newspaper, of a store name as a retail source for merchandise that is being editorially featured by the publication. *Ch 19*

Electronic Data Interchange (EDI) The electronic exchange of machine-readable data in standard formats between one company's computers and another company's computers. *Ch 7*

Entrepreneurs People who start new business ventures. *Career Project 1*

Entry-level job One requiring little or no specific training and experience. *Career Project 1*

Environment The conditions under which we live that affect our lives and influence our actions. *Ch 2*

Erogenous Sexually stimulating. *Ch 3*

European styling (men's wear) Features more fitted jackets that hug the body and have extremely square shoulders. *Ch 9*

Exclusivity Allowing sole use within a given trading area of a style or styles. An important competitive retail weapon. *Ch 18*

Export When a country provides goods to another country. *Ch 16*

Fabrics Materials formed from knitted, woven, or bonded yarns. *Ch 5*

Factor Financial institution that specializes in buying accounts receivable at a discount. *Ch 7*

Factory outlet store Manufacturer-owned store that sells company products at reduced prices in austere surroundings with minimum services. *Ch 17*

Fad A short-lived fashion. *Ch 1*

Fashion A style that is accepted and used by the majority of group at any one time. *Ch 1*

Fashion business Any business concerned with goods or services in which fashion is an element—including fiber, fabric, and apparel manufacturing, distribution, advertising, publishing, and consulting. *Ch 4*

Fashion cycle The rise, widespread popularity, and then decline in acceptance of a style. *Rise*: The acceptance of either a newly introduced design or its adaptations by an increasing number of consumers. *Culmination*: That period when a fashion is at the height of its popularity and use. The fashion then is in such demand that it can be mass-produced, mass-distributed, and sold at prices within the reach of most consumers. *Decline*: The decrease in consumer demand because of boredom resulting from widespread use of a fashion. *Obsolescence*: When disinterest occurs and a style can no longer be sold at any price. *Ch 1*

Fashion industries Those engaged in producing the materials used in the production of apparel and accessories for men, women, and children. *Ch 1*

Fashion influential A person whose advice is sought by associates. A fashion influential's adoption of a new style gives it prestige among a group. *Ch 3*

Fashion innovator A person first to try out a new style. *Ch 3*

Fashion jewelry See *costume jewelry*. *Ch 12*

Fashion trend The direction in which fashion is moving. *Ch 1*

Fiber A threadlike unit of raw material from which yarn and, eventually, textile fabric is made. *Ch 5*

First cost The wholesale price of merchandise in the country of origin. *Ch 16*

Floor ready Merchandise that has been ticketed with bar-coded price, and packed in labeled cartons with all shipping documents attached. If the merchandise is a garment, it has been pressed, and folded or hung on a hanger with a plastic bag over it. *Ch 7*

Foreign market Markets outside the domestic market; for example, to businesses in the United States, France is a foreign market. See also *market* and *domestic market*. *Ch 15*

Foundations The trade term for such women's undergarments as brassieres, girdles, panty girdles, garter belts, and shapers. *Ch 11*

Fragrance Includes cologne, toilet water, perfume, spray perfume, aftershave lotion, and environmental scents. *Ch 13*

Franchise A contractual agreement in which a firm or individual buys the exclusive right to conduct a retail business within a specified trading area under a franchiser's registered or trademarked name. *Ch 4*

Franchise distribution (cosmetics) The manufacturer or exclusive distributor sells directly to the ultimate retailer. *Ch 13*

Free trade The unrestricted exchange of goods between nations. *Ch 16*

Freelancing Working independently on an individual job or on a contractual basis for a variety of clients. *Career Project 2*

Fur farming The breeding and raising of fur-bearing animals under controlled conditions. *Ch 6*

General Agreement on Tariffs and Trade (GATT) A 1947 agreement, between many countries, to reduce trade barriers and unify trading practices. It was replaced by the World Trade Organization (WTO) in 1995. *Ch 16*

Generation X The "baby boomlet" group, born from 1966 to 1976. *Ch 2*

Generation Y The second "baby bust" group, born from 1977 to 1987. *Ch 2*

General merchandise retailer Retail stores which sell a number of lines of merchandise—for example, apparel and accessories; furniture and home furnishings; household lines and drygoods; hardware, appliances, and smallwares—under one roof. Stores included in this group are commonly known as mass-merchandisers, department stores, variety stores, general merchandise stores, or general stores. *Ch 17*

General store An early form of retail store which carried a wide variety of mainly utilitarian consumer goods. *Ch 17*

Generic name Non-trademarked names assigned by the Federal Trade Commission to 23 manufactured fibers. *Ch 5*

Geographics Population studies that focus on where people live. *Ch 2*

Geotextiles Manufactured, permeable textiles currently used in reinforcing or stabilizing civil engineering projects. *Ch 5*

Global sourcing Term used to describe the process of shopping for and purchasing imported goods. *Ch 16*

Grading Adjustment of a style's sample pattern to meet the dimensional requirements of each size in which the style is to be made. Also referred to as "sloping." *Ch 7*

Gray market goods Goods not intended for sale in the country in which they are being sold, often with an invalid warranty. *Ch 16*

Greige goods (pronounced "grayzh goods") Fabric that has received no preparation, dyeing, or finishing treatment after having been produced by any textile process. *Ch 5*

Group A subdivision of a line, linked by a common theme such as color, fabric, or style. *Ch 7*

Haute couture (pronounced "oat-koo-TOUR") The French term literally meaning "fine sewing" but actually having much the same sense as our own term "high fashion." *Ch 15*

Hides Animals skins that weigh over 25 pounds when shipped to a tannery. *Ch 6*

High fashion Those styles or designs accepted by a limited group of fashion leaders—the elite among consumers—who are first to accept fashion change. *Ch 7*

High fashion, or name, designer A person who creates designs, chooses the fabric, texture, and color for each design. Often, this person is involved with the development of the production model as well as with plans for the promotion of the line. Name designers may work for fashion houses, own his/her own firm, or work for a publicly owned firm. *Ch 7*

High-tech fabrics A fabric that has been constructed, finished, or processed in a way that gives it certain innovative, unusual, or hard-to-achieve qualities not normally available. *Ch 5*

Home fragrances Fragrances used to scent a place rather than a person; also called environmental fragrances. *Ch 13*

Horizontal growth A company expands on the level on which it has been performing. See also *vertical growth*. *Ch 4*

Horizontal-flow theory The theory of fashion adoption that holds that fashions move horizontally between groups on similar social levels rather than vertically from one level to another. Also called the "mass-market theory." *Ch 3*

Import When a country buys goods from a foreign country. *Ch 16*

Import quota Limits set to restrict the number of specific goods entering the country. *Ch 16*

Impulse items Items a customer buys on an impulse rather than as a result of planning. *Ch 12*

Inflation A substantial and continuing rise in the general price level. *Ch 2*

Innerwear The trade term for women's underwear; usually divided into foundations, lingerie, and loungewear. *Ch 11*

Inside shops Garment factories owned and operated by men's wear manufacturers who perform all the operations required to produce finished garments. *Ch 9*

Intimate apparel The trade term for women's foundations, lingerie, and loungewear. Also called inner fashions, body fashions, and innerwear. *Ch 11*

Item house Contractors that specialize in the production of one product. *Ch 7*

Job A specific position within an industry. *Career Project 1*

Jobber A middleman who buys from manufacturers and sells to retailers. See also *apparel jobber*. *Ch 7*

Joint merchandising An arrangement in which a retail store pays part of the salary of the cosmetic/fragrance salespeople who represent one manufacturer's line. *Ch 13*

Karat A measure of the weight of the gold content of jewelry; abbreviated as "K." *Ch 12*

Kiosk A stand that offers shelves or racks for merchandise. *Ch 18*

Kips Animal skins weighing from 15 to 25 pounds when shipped to a tannery. *Ch 6*

Knockoffs A trade term referring to the copying, at a lower price, of an item that has had good acceptance at higher prices. *Ch 1*

Layette A collection of crib and bath linens, sleepwear, and underwear for newborns. *Ch 10*

Leased department A department ostensibly operated by the store in which it is found but actually run by an outsider who pays a percentage of sales to the store as rent. *Ch 6*

Less developed countries (LDCs) Countries in the early stages of economic development; they have a low standard of living and lack a well-paid labor force. *Ch 16*

Let-out (furs) A cutting and re-sewing operation to make short skins into longer-length skins adequate for garment purposes. *Ch 6*

Leverage Use of borrowed funds to finance a portion of an investment. *Ch 4*

Licensed trademark (fibers) A fiber's registered trademark used under a licensing agreement whereby use of the trademark is permitted only to those manufacturers whose end products pass established tests for their specific end use or application. *Ch 5*

Licensing An arrangement whereby firms are given permission to produce and market merchandise in the name of the licensor, who is paid a percentage of sales for permitting his or her name to be used. *Ch 4*

Line An assortment of new designs offered by manufacturers to their customers, usually on a seasonal basis. *Ch 4*

Line-for-line copies These are exactly like the original designs except that they have been mass-produced in less expensive fabrics to standard size measurements. *Ch 7*

Lingerie A general undergarment category that includes slips, petticoats, camisoles, bras, panties, nightgowns, and pajamas. Underclothing is considered "daywear," while nightgowns and pajamas are classified as "sleepwear." *Ch 11*

Long-run fashion A fashion that takes more seasons to complete its cycle than what might be considered its average life expectancy. *Ch 1*

Loungewear The trade term for the intimate apparel category that includes robes, bed jackets, and housecoats. *Ch 11*

Mall An enclosed, climate-controlled shopping center. *Ch 18*

Management position A responsible position requiring specific training, experience, and leadership. *Career Project 1*

Manufactured fiber A fiber invented in a laboratory; also called "man-made" or "synthetic." *Ch 5*

Manufacturer See *apparel manufacturer.*

Marker (apparel manufacturing) A long piece of paper upon which the pieces of the pattern of a garment in all its sizes are outlined and which is placed on top of many layers of material for cutting purposes. *Ch 7*

Market (1) A group of potential customers. (2) The place or area in which buyers and sellers meet for the purpose of trading ownership of goods at wholesale prices. *Ch 15*

Market center A geographic center for the creation and production of fashion merchandise, as well as for exchanging ownership. *Ch 15*

Market segmentation The separating of the total consumer market into smaller groups known as "market segments." *Ch 2*

Market weeks Scheduled periods throughout the year during which producers and their sales representatives introduce new lines for the upcoming season to retail buyers. *Ch 15*

Marketing A total system of business activities designed to plan, price, promote, and place (distribute) products and services to present and potential customers. *Ch 1*

Mart A building or building complex housing both permanent and transient showrooms of producers and their sales representatives. *Ch 15*

Mass distribution (cosmetics) Third-party vendors, such as wholesalers, diverters, and jobbers, often interposed between the manufacturer and the retailer. *Ch 13*

Mass or volume fashion Those styles or designs that are widely accepted. *Ch 1*

Megamall Larger than a superregional mall, it contains four to five million square feet. *Ch 18*

Merchandise assortment A collection of varied types of related merchandise, essentially intended for the same general end-use and usually grouped together in one selling area of a retail store. *Broad*: A merchandise assortment that includes many styles. *Deep*: A merchandise assortment that includes a comprehensive range of colors and sizes in each style. *Narrow*: A merchandise assortment that includes relatively few styles. *Shallow*: A merchandise assortment that contains only a few sizes and colors in each style. *Ch 18*

Merchandising The planning required on the part of retailers to have, for a specific consumer target group, the right merchandise at the right time, in the right place, in the right quantities, at the right price, and with the right promotion. *Ch 1*

Merchandising policies Guidelines established by store management for merchandising executives to follow in order that the store organization may win the patronage of the specific target group(s) of customers it has chosen to serve. *Ch 18*

Merger A sale of one company to another with the result that only one company exists. *Ch 4*

Microfiber A fiber two or three times thinner than a human hair, and thinner than wool, cotton, flax, or silk fibers. It has a touch and texture similar to silk or cashmere, but is wrinkle-resistant. *Ch 5*

Mid-management position One requiring some experience and training as a manager, and involving a higher degree of responsibility than an entry-level management position. *Career Project 2*

Millinery The women's hat industry. *Ch 12*

Minimum order The quantity, number of styles, and/or dollar amount required by the manufacturer in order to accept the retail store buyer's order. *Ch 7*

Mixed-use center A shopping mall attached to an office building, hotel, or apartment house. *Ch 18*

Mom-and-Pop store A small store run by the proprietor with few or no hired assistants. *Ch 17*

Multi-Fiber and Textile Agreement (MFA) The first multinational agreement specifically regulating the flow of textile products; it is being phased out. *Ch 16*

Narrow and deep assortment One in which there are relatively few styles, but these styles are stocked in all available sizes and colors. *Ch 18*

Newly industrialized countries (NICs) Countries in the first stage of economic development; they have small to no export markets. *Ch 16*

North American Free Trade Agreement (NAFTA) An agreement that eliminated quotas and tariffs for goods shipped between Canada, the United States, and Mexico. *Ch 16*

Note (fragrances) Each scent that make up a fragrance; notes vary in strength and duration. *Ch 13*

Obsolescence (stage) See *fashion cycle.*

Off-shore production The importation of goods by domestic apparel producers, either from their own plants operating in cheap, labor-rich foreign areas, or through their long-term supply arrangements with foreign producers. *Ch 7*

Operational policies Policies designed to keep customers once they are attracted to come into a store; by establishing the store's ambiance, customer services, promotions, and frequent shopper plans. See also *merchandising policies. Ch 18*

Outlet mall A shopping center containing outlet stores and often, entertainment facilities. *Ch 18*

Outpost Small accessory departments located next to apparel departments or near store entrances, sometimes with moveable kiosks, carts, or racks. *Ch 12*

Outside shops See *apparel contractor.* Ch 7

Pelt The skin of a fur-bearing animal. *Ch 6*

Per capita personal income The wages, salaries, interest, dividends and all other income received by the population as a whole, divided by the number of people in the population. *Ch 2*

PETA People for the Ethical Treatment of Animals, a nonprofit organization devoted to animal rights. *Ch 6*

Personal income The total or gross amount of income received from all sources by the population as a whole. It consists of wages, salaries, interest, dividends, and all other income for everyone in the country. See also *disposable personal income* and *discretionary income. Ch 2*

Piece-dyed The process of dyeing fabrics after they are knitted or woven; it gives the manufacturer maximum flexibility. See also *yarn-dyed. Ch 5*

Piece-work A production method in which an operator sews only a section of the garment to speed the production process. See *section work. Ch 7*

Planogram A computer-generated floor plan that shows the selling floor with merchandise in the best position. *Ch 19*

Power center or strip An outdoor shopping center that offers three or four category killers together. *Ch 18*

Precious stones These include the diamond, emerald, ruby, sapphire, and real (or oriental) pearl. *Ch 12*

Premiums A gift-with-purchase offered by a manufacturer to promote a product. *Ch 13*

Prêt-à-porter (pronounced "preht-ah-por-TAY") A French term meaning ready-to-wear. *Ch 15*

Price zone A series of somewhat contiguous price lines that appeal to specific target groups of customers. *Ch 8*

Primary level Composed of the growers and producers of the raw materials of fashion—the fiber, fabric, leather, and fur producers who function in the raw materials market. *Ch 4*

Primary suppliers Producers of fibers, textile fabrics, finished leathers, and furs. *Ch 5*

Private label or store brand Merchandise that meets standards specified by a retail firm and that belongs to it exclusively. Primarily used to insure consistent quality of product as well as to meet price competition. *Ch 7*

Product development team A small group within a large apparel manufacturing firm that is responsible for one particular product line or brand. Usually consists of at least a merchandiser, designer, and product manager. *Ch 7*

Product manager See *specification manager.*

Profit The amount of money a business earns in excess of its expenses; net income. *Ch 4*

Prophetic styles Particularly interesting new styles that are still in the introductory phase of their fashion cycles. *Ch 3*

Protectionism An economic and political doctrine that seeks to exclude or limit foreign goods. *Ch 16*

Psychographics Studies that develop fuller, more personal portraits of potential customers, including personality, attitude, interest, personal opinions, and actual product benefits desired. *Ch 2*

Public relations Works to improve a client's public image and may develop long-range plans and directions for this purpose. *Ch 19*

Publicity The mention of a firm, brand, product, or person in some form of media. *Ch 19*

Purchasing power The value of the dollar as it relates to the amount of goods or services it will buy. A decline in purchasing power is caused by inflation. *Ch 2*

Quality Assurance (QA) Inspection of each component of a garment to ensure that it meets the standards established for it. *Ch 7*

Quick Response (QR) A strategy used by manufacturers to shorten the ordering cycle to compete with foreign imports. *Ch 7*

Rack trade Refers to manufacturers of belts sold as separate fashion accessory items. *Ch12*

Ramie A minor natural fiber from a woody-leafed Asian plant grown mostly in China. *Ch 5*

Readers Nonprescription reading glasses. *Ch12*

Ready-to-wear (RTW) Apparel made in factories to standard size measurements. *Ch 8*

Recession A low point in a business cycle, when money and credit become scarce and unemployment is high. *Ch 2*

Regional mall An indoor shopping center with a trading area of at least a five-mile radius. It usually contains at least two anchor department stores, as well as many specialty stores and a food court or restaurants. *Ch 18*

Regular tanneries Those companies that purchase and process hides and skins to the specifications of converters but are not involved in the sales of the finished products. *Ch 6*

Resident buying office An old term used to describe a service organization located in a major market area that provides market information and representation to its non-competing client stores. See *buying, merchandising, and product development office. Ch 19*

Retail level The ultimate distribution-level outlets for fashion goods directly to the consumer. *Ch 4*

Rise (stage) See *fashion cycle. Ch 1*

Royalty fee Percentage of licensee sales paid to the licensor. See also *licensing. Ch 4*

Rubber-banding Cosmetic products that can be returned to the manufacturer and replaced with other products, if not sold within a specified period of time. *Ch 13*

Sales representatives Company representatives who exhibit merchandise to potential customers. *Ch 15*

Sample hand The designer's assistant who sews the sample garment. *Ch 7*

Secondary level Composed of industries—manufacturers and contractors—that produce the semifinished or finished fashion goods from the materials supplied by the primary level. *Ch 4*

Section work The division of labor in apparel manufacturing whereby each sewing-machine operator sews only a certain section of the garment, such as a sleeve or hem. *Ch 7*

Sensory retailing In-store stimulation of all the customer's senses, using pleasant aromas, mood music, dramatic lighting. *Ch 18*

Shelter magazines Home-decorating magazines. *Ch 14*

Shopping center A coordinated group of retail stores, plus a parking area. *Ch 18*

Short-run fashion A fashion that takes fewer seasons to complete its cycle than what might be considered its average life expectancy. *Ch 1*

Silhouette The overall outline or contour of a costume. Also frequently referred to as "shape" or "form." *Ch 1*

Skins Animals skins that weigh 15 pounds or less when shipped to a tannery. *Ch 6*

Sloping See *grading.*

Slop shops A name associated with the first shops offering men's ready-to-wear in this country. Garments lacked careful fit and detail work found in custom-tailored clothing of the period. *Ch 9*

Small leather goods A category that includes wallets, key cases and chains, jewelry cases, briefcases, and carrying cases for cell phones and laptop computers. *Ch 12*

Source (of supply) See *vendor.*

Spa Formerly "health spa," now a service business offering a wide variety of beauty treatments, including massages, manicures, pedicures, waxings, facials, aromatherapy, and thalassotherapy. *Ch 13*

Specification buying A type of purchasing that is done to the store's rather than to the manufacturer's standards. See also *private label. Ch 7*

Specification manager Manager who oversees the purchasing and manufacturing process for a private label. Also called "product manager." *Ch 7*

Spinnerette A mechanical device through which a thick liquid base is forced to produce fibers of varying lengths. *Ch 5*

Spreader A laying up machine that carries material along a guide on either side of a cutting table, spreading the material evenly, layer upon layer. *Ch 7*

Sterling silver A term used for jewelry and flatware with at least 92.5 parts of silver; the remaining 7.5 parts are usually copper. *Ch 12*

Strategic alliance A form of business combination in which a retailer and a manufacturer join forces to operate more efficiently, thus improving profits for both companies, while offering customers a better product at a lower price. *Ch 18*

Style A characteristic or distinctive mode of presentation or conceptualization in a particular field. In apparel, style is the characteristic or distinctive appearance of a garment, the combination of features that makes it different from other garments. *Ch 1*

Style number The number manufacturers and retailers assigned to a design. The number identifies the product for manufacturing, ordering, and selling. *Ch 1*

Stylist-designer A person who adapts or changes the successful designs of others. *Ch 7*

Suit separates (men's wear) Sports jacket and trousers worn much as the tailored suit used to be. *Ch 9*

Sumptuary laws Laws regulating consumer purchases, for example, dress, on religious or moral grounds. *Ch 3*

Superregional mall Even larger than a regional mall, they often contain up to one million square feet, with at least three department or major chain stores, and 100 to 300 specialty stores. Their trading area is a distance up to one-hour's driving time away. *Ch 18*

Sustainable use An environmental program that encourages land owners to preserve animal young and habitats in return for the right to use a percentage of the grown animals. *Ch 6*

Sweatshop A garment manufacturing plant employing workers under unfair, unsanitary, and sometimes dangerous conditions. *Ch 8*

Tabletop (goods) Categories of merchandise commonly found on tabletops, including dinnerware, glassware, flatware, hollowware, and giftware. *Ch 14*

Tailored clothing firms Those mens' wear firms that produce structured or semistructured suits, overcoats, topcoats, sportcoats, and or separate trousers in which a specific number of hand-tailoring operations are required. *Ch 9*

Tanning The process of transforming animal skins into leather. *Ch 6*

Target market A specific group of potential customers that manufacturers and retailers are attempting to turn into regular customers. *Ch 2*

Tariff A fee assessed by government on certain goods that it wishes to restrict or limit. *Ch 16*

Tariff-rate quota A set limit after which a higher duty is charged on goods entering the country. *Ch 16*

Taste The recognition of what is and is not attractive and appropriate. Good taste in fashion means sensitivity not only to what is artistic but to these considerations as well. *Ch 1*

Textile fabric Cloth or material made from fibers by weaving, knitting, braiding, felting, crocheting, knotting, laminating, or bonding. *Ch 5*

Textile converter See *converter*. *Ch 5*

Texture The look and feel of material, woven or unwoven. *Ch 1*

Thalassotherapy A skin treatment involving sea water, seaweed, or sea algae. *Ch 13*

Trade association Professional organizations for manufacturers or sales representatives. *Ch 15*

Trade deficit When the value of goods that a country imports exceeds the value of its exports. *Ch 16*

Trade publications Newspapers or magazines published specifically for professionals in a special field, such as fashion. *Ch 19*

Trade shows Periodic merchandise exhibits stages in various regional trading areas around the country by groups of producers and their sales representatives for the specific purpose of making sales of their products to retailers in that area. *Ch 15*

Trade surplus When a country's exports exceed its imports. *Ch 16*

Transshipment An illegal method of avoiding the quota system by mislabeling goods as to country of origin and sending them through another country. *Ch 16*

Trend A general direction or movement. See also *fashion trend*. *Ch 1*

Trimmings All the materials—excluding the fabric—used in the construction of a garment; including braid, bows, buckles, buttons, elastic, interfacing, padding, self-belts, thread, zippers, etc. *Ch 5*

Trunk show A form of pre-testing that involves a designer or manufacturer sending a representative to a store with samples of the current line, and exhibiting those samples to customers at scheduled, announced showings. *Ch 8*

Uniform Product Code (UPC) The most widely accepted of a number of bar codes used for automatic identification of items scanned at retail cash registers. *Ch 7*

Upward-flow theory The theory of fashion adoption that holds that the young—particularly those of low-income families as well as those of higher income who adopt low-income lifestyles—are quicker than any other social group to create or adopt new and different fashions. *Ch 3*

Vendor One who sells goods to others; a source of supply. *Ch 12*

Vermeil (pronounced "vur-MAY") A composite of gold over sterling silver. *Ch 12*

Vertical growth A company expands on a different level than its original one. *Ch 4*

Vertical mall An indoor, multistory shopping center, taller than it is wide. *Ch 18*

Videoconferencing A system that combines the telephone with a television image of a meeting. *Ch 18*

Visual merchandising Everything visual that is done to, with, or for a product and its surroundings to encourage its sale. This includes display, store layout, and store decor. *Ch 19*

Wedding or bridal registry A store's list of a bridal couple's desired merchandise, upon which gift-givers' selections are recorded as they are purchased. Today it is often called merely a "gift registry" and is computerized. *Ch 14*

Wicking The ability of a fabric to carry the moisture of perspiration away from the skin. *Ch 11*

Yarn A continuous thread formed by spinning or twisting fibers together. *Ch 5*

Yarn-dyed Refers to dyeing yarns before they are woven or knitted; this process results in deep, rich colors. See also *piece-dyed*. *Ch 5*

Internet Resources

Following is a selection of Internet addresses relating to the fashion industry. Readers may wish to use a search engine such as AltaVista, or a directory like Yahoo! or Go to find additional sites related to the glossary terms, designers, manufacturers, retailers, and professional organizations mentioned in this book. Be aware that new sites are launched constantly while others disappear just as quickly. You may also contact Elaine Stone directly at: **elaine_stone@fitny.edu.**

General Information and Fashion Links

http://members.aol.com/nebula5/costume.html *(Costuming Resources Online)* Frequently-updated compilation of over 2,000 costume-related links, created and managed by a subscriber to America Online.

http://members.tripod.com/~cjlutz *(Fashion Index with Hearts* SM) Historic and current fashion, cosmetics, jewelry, fashion photography and illustration, software, newsgroups, sources, and chat room.

http://www.canapple.org/english/Page_Contents *(The Consulate General of Canada)*

http://www.costumes.org/pages/victlinks.htm *(The Consumer Manifesto—Victorian Fashion Links)*

http://www.fgi.org *(The Fashion Group)* International industry news, trend reports and forecasts, directories of professional services, job listings, and events calendar.

http://www.ivillage.com *(iVillage)* Links to fashion and beauty news, plus a chat site.

http://www.infomat.com *(Infomat)* Features over 75,000 international links to sites concerning women's, men's, and children's wear, accessories, manufacturers, marts, retailers, showrooms, and associations.

http://www.insidefashion.com *(Inside Fashion)* Useful links, plus information about courses and careers, fashion terminology, and organizations.

http://www.made-in-italy.com *(Made*In*Italy*On*Line)* Italian clothing and accessories manufacturers, fashion publications, model agencies, and show schedules.

http://www.tafensw.edu.au *(TAFE Fashion Studylinks)* Includes international fashion links compiled by Australia's largest educational institution.

http://www.thealexanderreport.com *(The Alexander Report)*

http://www.virtualrags.com/links.htm *(Virtual Rags)* Links to international apparel industry sites.

http://www.wto.org *(World Trade Organization)* Trade new and government policies about every industry including fashion.

Fibers, Fabrics, and Furs

http://www.aatcc.org *(American Association of Textile Chemists and Colorists)* Under construction at press time; worth checking out.

http://www.atexinc.com/great_links.htm *(Apparel & Textile Education Xchange)*

http://www.atmi.org *(American Textile Manufacturers Institute)* Textile news, publications, products, and manufacturers'directory.

http://www.cashmere.org *(Camel Hair and Cashmere Institute)* Facts about these fibers and products manufactured from them.

http://www.cottonincorp.com *(Cotton Incorporated)* All about cotton, from crop economics to consumers; includes the CottonWorks Fabric Library of mills, knitters, and converters relating to woven fabrics, knits, home furnishings, and trimmings.

http://www.fabriclink.com *(Fabric Link)* Technology, terminology, history, and care of fabrics and textiles.

http://www.fabrics.com/links.htm *(Fabric Stock Exchange)* Links to many apparel and fabric sites.

http://www.fibersource.com *(Fiber Source)* All about man-made synthetic and cellulosic fibers: fiber facts and history, economic statistics, industry news, and careers, plus the events calendar for American Fiber Manufacturers Association.

http://www.fur.ca *(The Fur Institute of Canada)* Bilingual, covers the Canadian fur industry from trappers and farmers through retail products.

http://www.fur.org *(The Fur Industry in America)* Fur fashions and care, animal welfare issues, and fur facts.

http://www.hfnmag.com *(Home Furnishings News)* Leading weekly of the home products industry.

http://www.itaa.org *(ITAA)* Textiles links, educational and career information, and industry/organization news from the International Textile and Apparel Association.

http://www.nzpossumproducts.co.nz/industry/fur-fashiohnindustry.htm

http://www.scelastic.com *(South Carolina Elastic)* History and use of "narrow fabrics" in apparel and home fashions.

http://www.textileweb.com *(Textile Web)* News and global links regarding yarn and fiber, fabrics and textiles, and textile manufacturing and sales.

http://www.texnet.it *(Textile Net)* Month-by-month listings of textile exhibitions worldwide.

http://www.woolmark.com *(The Wool Bureau)* Beautifully designed site about wool, from yarn through apparel.

http://www.wwd.com *(Women's Wear Daily)* Fashion industry's daily news source.

Manufacturing, Merchandising, and Retailing

http://www.mfinfo.com *(Manufacturers Information Net)* Directory of suppliers, jobbers, software and CAD/CAM, and new and used industrial equipment for all areas of manufacturing including fashion.

http://nrf.com *(National Retail Federation)* Site of the world's largest retail trade association, offering news, events, survey results, and *Stores* magazine.

http://www.apparel.net *(Apparel Net)* Apparel-related products, services, and companies.

http://www.dailynewsrecord.com *(DNR)* Premier news magazine of men's fashion and retail.

http://www.fashiondex.com *(Fashiondex)* Apparel industry sourcing site for over 60 categories and more than 2,600 suppliers of everything from buttons to yarn.

http://www.footwearnews.com *(Footwear News)* Leading publication in the international shoe industry.

http://www.garment.com *(The Virtual Garment Center)* Database of manufacturers, retailers, textile companies, suppliers, jobbers/ brokers, contractors, buying offices, and service providers.

http://www.garmentonline.com *(Garment of NYC)* Directory of women's apparel manufacturers and wholesalers, searchable by category, name, and locale.

http://www.gerbertechnology.com *(Gerber Technology)* Information about the automated equipment used in the sewn goods industries, from one of the world's largest manufacturers and suppliers of such machinery.

http://www.gidc.com *(Garment Industry Development Corporation)* Information about the training of apparel workers, domestic sourcing, global marketing, and product improvement.

http://www.hfnmag.com *(Home Furnishings News)* Leading weekly of the home products industry.

http://www.lectra.com *(Lectra Systèmes)* Information about computer-aided design and manufacturing in the apparel, footwear, upholstery, and leather industries, from a major manufacturer and supplier of CAD/CAM equipment.

http://www.techexchange.com *(Techexchange.com)* Articles bank, education information, career opportunities, and news about technological advances relating to computer technology in the apparel, textile, and home furnishings industries.

http://www.wwd.com *(Women's Wear Daily)* Fashion industry's daily news source.

Contemporary Apparel Design

http://www.apparelnews.net

http://www.bizrate.com *(Bizrate)* Consumer collection of ecommerce sites with a strong section on apparel.

http://www.dailynewsrecord.com *(DNR)* Premier news magazine of men's fashion and retail.

http://www.fashionshowroom.com *(Fashion Showroom)* Designers' catalogs online.

http://www.firstview.com *(firstVIEW Collections Online)* Photos of every garment in over 175 fashion collections—men's, women's, shoes, and accessories—searchable by category, season, and designer.

http://www.magiconline.com*(International Kids Fashion Show)* Colorful site for trade news, photos, links, and trend reports about children's wear.

http://www.mercedesbenzfashionweek.com*(7th on Sixth)* Photos from the New York collections of men's and women's apparel.

http://www.fashionlive.fr/fashion*(Fashion Live)* French fashion site (available in English) with designer database, "trendwatch," and international catwalk coverage.

http://www.wwd.com *(Women's Wear Daily)* Fashion industry's daily news source.

*Many designers have their own sites, easily accessible by typing the designer's name followed by "**.com.**" **http://www.ralphlauren.com** is a good example of such sites.*

Accessories and Intimate Apparel

http://www.ags.org *(American Gem Society)* Good overview of the jewelry industry, facts about specific gemstones, and care of jewelry.

http://corsethome.eu.org/dictionary *(Corset Home Dictionary)* Developing, photo-illustrated dictionary of lingerie and lingerie materials, from historical garments through the present.

http://www.diamondcouncil.org *(Diamond Council of America)* Everything you need to know about diamonds.

http://www.ffany.org *(Fashion Footwear Association of NY)* Runway news, New York Shoe Expo information; membership of over 800 international brand names.

http://www.fia.org *(Footwear Industries of America)* Educational programs, trade shoe calendar, suppliers directory for materials and products through computer technology.

http://www.jewelers.org *(Jewelers of America)* Information and news about fine jewelry, and educational programs.

http://www.nahm.com *(National Association of Hosiery Manufacturers)* Hosiery news, international trade and shows, and statistics.

*Manufacturers and retailers of accessories and intimate apparel may have their own sites, which you may visit by typing their name plus a "**.com.**" **http://www .victoriassecret.com** is a very popular site featuring every kind of lingerie from terry robes to silk underwear.*

Cosmetics and Fragrance

http://www.cctfa.org *(Cosmetic, Toiletry, and Fragrance Association)* Leading U.S. trade association for personal care products industry, with a membership of over 500 member companies.

http://www.fragrance.org *(Fragrance Foundation)* History, tips, trends, "Fifi Award," and Q&As.

http://fragrancecounter.com *(Fragrance Counter)* Comprehensive online perfume store.

http://www.salonnews.com *(Salon News)* Professional monthly publication of the salon business.

*Many individual cosmetics firms and designer fragrance discounters have sites accessible by typing their name followed by "**.com.**" **http://www.clinique.com** is one of the major sites of this kind.*

Home Fashions

http://www.carpetcity.com *(Carpet City)* Informative site about carpet tufting, padding, fiber content, care, and selection, as well as manufacturers.

http://www.hfnmag.com *(Home Furnishings News)* Leading weekly of the home products industry.

http://www.islamicart.com *(Oriental Rugs)* Excellent source for the history, weaving and dyeing, and classification of oriental rugs.

http://www.iida.com *(International Interior Design Association)* Job opportunities, education, and trade shows.

http://www.thehome.com *(Home Fashion Information Network)* How to choose floor coverings, upholstery, bed and bath, and window products; information about manufacturers.

*Designers, manufacturers, retailers, and style gurus of home fashion products often maintain Web sites, usually consisting of their name followed by ".com." One of the most popular home fashions sites is **http://www .martha stewart.com.***

Domestic and International Marts and Shows

http://www.bobbin.com *(The Bobbin Show Daily News)* Information about Bobbin World (the International Sewn Products Expo).

http://www.dallasmarketcenter.com *(Dallas Market Center)* News and exhibition dates for over 50 annual markets held at the world's first and largest wholesale and merchandise mart.

http://www.igedo.com *(Igedo)* Fashion fair calendars for Düsseldorf, London, Miami, Hong Kong, and Shanghai.

http://www.magiconline.com *(MAGIC International)* Event information for the world's largest market of women's, men's, and kids' apparel.

http://www.montrealfashionmart.com *(Montreal Fashion Mart)* Canada's most expansive listing of fashion resources.

http://www.pretaporter.com *(Prêt-à-Porter)* Parisian "ready-to-wear" show site featuring trend news and show schedules covering 15 different sectors of fashion.

http://www.textileshow.com *(Textile Show)* Online trade show focusing upon 17 key areas within the textile industry, with free membership registration.

http://www.tsnn.com *(Trade Show News Network)* Leading Internet site for the trade show industry.

Style News and Online Shopping

http://www.aol.com/shopping *(America Online Shopping)* AOL's online shopping site for apparel, accessories, cosmetics, and home products, searchable by category or store name.

http://www.babystyle.com *(Babystyle)*

http://www.bluefly.com *(Bluefly)* Discount department store selling designer men's, women's, and children's apparel, accessories, and home products.

http://cnn.com/STYLE *(CNN Style)* Interactive Web site for news about fashion and home décor.

http://www.designeroutlet.com *(Designer Outlet)* Discount outlet for overstock apparel from over 150 designers and manufacturers.

http://www.fashion.net *(Fashion Net)* Online shopping, chat site, fashion-specific search engine, fashion news (with optional signup for daily fashion news via email).

http://www.fashionangel.com *(Angel of Fashion)* Shopping, zines, alternative trends, links.

http://www.fashioncenter.com *(The Fashion Center)* Industry links within New York City, including a map of the Garment District.

http://www.fashion-icon.com *(Fashion-Icon)* Fun site of fashion news from street style through leading designers.

http://www.fashionmall.com *(Fashionmall .com)* First and largest online fashion shopping site, featuring an assortment of designer shops plus links to several fashion magazines.

http://www.fashion-planet.com/shopping/shop_dir.html

http://www.fashionshoppingoutlet.com/women/index/htm *(Fashion Shopping Outlet)*

http://www.fashiontripnet.com *(The Fashion Directory)* Amazon.com-sponsored site about models, advertising, magazine covers, fashion TV, and fashion books.

http://www.girlshop.com *(Girlshop.com)* Mini-boutiques of apparel and accessories for "stylish urban girls ages 18 to 35."

http://www.guppy22.com *(Guppy 22)* Fastest-growing teen clothing site.

http://www.home.netscape.com/shopping *(Netscape Shopping)*

http://www.hsn.com *(Home Shopping Network)* HSN's online shopping site, including their own company news and job openings.

http://www.janemag.com *(Jane)* Lifestyle magazine for confident, media-savvy, 18-34 year old women.

http://www.kfn.com *(Kids Fashion Network)* Directory of manufacturers and full color catalogs of children's wear, by category.

http://www.nygard.net *(Nygård)* Canadian prêt-à-porter manufacturer and retailer's site, featuring fashion news, shopping mall, and *N* magazine online.

http://www.nystyle.com *(NYStyle)* Shopping network for fashion, sportswear, and accessory designers.

http://www.nytimes.com/pages/fashion *(New York Times)*

http://www.papermag.com/stylin/fashion

(Papermag) "Fashion Schmashion" zine-style coverage of shows, designers, and models.

http://qvc.com *(iQVC Shop)* QVC's online shopping site, indexed by such categories as fashion, jewelry, and home fashion.

http://www.outletmall.com *(Outletmall.com)* Name-brand designer merchandise offered at deep discount in a shopping-list format.

http://www.stylexperts.com *(Stylexperts)* Top names in the business provide advice and information on design, modeling, cosmetics, home fashions, and other topics.

More and more retail stores and manufacturers have Web sites that extensively catalog their products. Often adding ".com" to their name is sufficient to bring up their site, e.g., ***http://www.gap.com and http://www.landsend.com.***

Advertising and Promotion

http://www.adage.com *(Advertising Age)* Web site for preeminent publisher of marketing, advertising, and media news.

http://advweb.cocom.utexas.edu *(Marketing Communications)* Directory of advertising design and design awards, books about advertising, ad agencies, market research and demographics, and many other related topics.

http://www.fashion.tripnet.se *(The Fashion Directory)* Amazon.com-sponsored site about models, advertising, magazine covers, fashion TV, and fashion books.

http://fmi.csoft.net *(Fashion Model Index)* Interactive international models' biographies and photos.

http://www.headbooks.com *(Headbooks Online)* Model agencies' headsheets and services for fashion and other industries.

http://www.usadata.com *(USADATA)* Provider of reports and data maps on consumer demographics, expenditure, and behavior; and company advertising and expenditures.

Fashion Books and Related Media

http://www.aimagazine.com *(Apparel Industry Magazine)* Magazine Web site providing news, career opportunities, and virtual trade show for the apparel industry.

http://www.amazon.com *(Amazon.com)* Bookstore site for fashion-related titles.

http://barnesandnoble.com *(Barnes & Noble)* Bookstore site featuring new and used books about the fashion industry.

http://www.bookstore.com/fash1.html *(A Clean Well-Lighted Place for Books)* Bookstore database of costume books that may be ordered online, organized chronologically by topic from ancient times to the present.

http://www.fabricad.com *(Fabricad)* Online version of a publication about CAD/CAM developments in fabrics and textiles.

http://www.fairchildbooks.com *(Fairchild Books)* Online catalog for Fairchild Publications' books and visual media.

http://www.fashion-planet.com *(Fashion Planet)* Award-winning magazine-style Web site about the businesses and personalities of the New York fashion industry.

http://www.fashionshowroom.com/books/fashion.htm *(Fashion)* Amazon.com-sponsored alphabetical database of 100,000 fashion-related books that may be ordered online.

http://www.lookonline.com/htdocs/b.htm *(Look On-Line)* Another fashion-industry specific book database sponsored by Amazon.com.

http://ares.redsword.com/dduperault/hist.htm *(Historical Costuming)* Privately-written extensive bibliography (by author only, not subject) of books about the history of costume and fashion.

http://www.treschicmag.com *(Tres Chic Magazine)*

Major newspapers, such as the New York Times *and* Washington Post, *regularly feature apparel and home fashion reports in their online editions; and most fashion and lifestyle magazines now have a Web site of their own.*

Costume History

http://costumesocietyamerica.com *(Costume Society of America)* Membership organization hosting over 400 Web pages and providing free links to costume collections and other such organizations.

http://www.erte.com *(Erté Museum)* The illustrations and designs of Art Deco-era Erté by category, plus museum links, and poster and museum shopping.

Also check individual museum sites for news about fashion collections and special exhibits.

Trade and Industry-Related Organizations

http://www.amcricanapparel.org *(American Apparel Manufacturers Association)*

http://www.aatcc.org *(American Association of Textile Chemists and Colorists)*

http://www.ansi.org *(American National Standards Institute)*

http://www.astm.org *(American Society of Testing and Materials)*

http://www.bttg.co.uk *(British Textile Technology Group)*

http://www.apparel.ca *(Canadian Apparel Federation)*

http://www.citda.org *(Computer Integrated Textile Design Association)*

http://www.dama.tc2.com *(Demand Activated Manufacturing Architecture)*

http://www.fgi.org *(Fashion Group International)*

http://www.gidc.org *(Garment Industry Development Corporation)*

http://www.iafnet.org *(International Apparel Federation)*

http://www.ifi.org *(International Fabricare Institute)*

http://www.itaaonline.org *(International Textiles and Apparel Association)*

http://www.kta-usa.org *(Knitted Textiles Association)*

http://www.nrf.com *(National Retail Federation)*

http://www.ota.com *(Organic Trade Association)*

http://www.sdahq.org *(Soap and Detergent Association)*

http://www.sweatshopwatch.org *(Sweatshop Watch)*

http://www.tc2.com *(Textile/Clothing Technology Corporation)*

http://www.texi.org *(Textile Institute)*

http://www.uc-council.org *(Uniform Code Council)*

http://www.uniteunion.org *(Union of Needletrades, Industrial and Textile Employees)*

http://wto.org *(World Trade Organization)*

Index

f denotes figures

B

F

G

N

T